S0-CFA-224

Religion and Politics in India
During the Thirteenth Century

Professor Khaliq Ahmad Nizami, 1925-97

BL
2003
.N52
2002

110702-308048

To
Dr Zakir Husain
as a token of
respect for the man
and
admiration for the educationist

To
Dr Zakir Husain,
as a token of
respect for the man
and
admiration for the educationist

FOREWORD

The most important of recent trends in the writing of Indian history is the ever-increasing output by Indians. This is a natural, healthy, commendable tendency, the inevitable result of emancipation from foreign rule and of a desire to draw attention to their ancient heritage. Unfortunately, the British public is not familiar with the results of historical research by Indian scholars, many of whose 'finds' have been printed in comparatively obscure Indian journals. In the past, English and European scholars have sometimes, so far as ancient and medieval India is concerned, been given more credit than was their due because they developed ideas first adumbrated in some little-known Indian journal, or because the Indian historian wrote his monograph in Urdu, Hindi, or Bengali. I am glad therefore that Mr Nizami has done me the honour of asking me to write a foreword to his book as this gives me an opportunity of drawing attention to his publications which form a solid contribution to the history of the Sultanate of Delhi, a period of vital importance in India's long history.

In this important book Mr Nizami first deals with the political expansion and ideological integration of Islam down to the Ghurid conquest of northern India. The second part of the book discusses the establishment of Muslim power and the nature of Muslim rule in northern India during the thirteenth century. Mr Nizami fully realizes the impossibility of writing the history of India before the intrusion of the European nations by sea without a detailed examination of what was happening in the Central Asian background. In assessing the reasons for the rapid expansion of Islam in this century, due attention is paid to the work of Muslim missionaries, a factor usually neglected by historians. A close study of the strategy and tactics of the Muslim invaders also shows how speed, mobility, and shock tactics have played an important part in Muslim military history, from the swiftly moving forces of Chengiz Khan to Shaibani Khan's adoption of the *tulghma* and Babur's victory at Panipat. Mr Nizami's purpose has been to reveal the personality of Iltutmish and Balban rather than to provide the reader with a rehash of the facts unearthed by previous writers. Other topics discussed are the position of the *'ulama* in thirteenth-century India; the part played

by Muslim mystics, especially the Chishti and Suhrawardi orders; the status
and treatment of Hindus; and the foreign policy of the Delhi Sultanate. The
chapters dealing with Muslim religious life and thought break fresh ground.
The whole book is based on a careful examination of contemporary sources,
both in manuscript and in print. This well-documented study should find a
place on the bookshelves of every Islamic scholar and student of Muslim
rule in India.

Balliol College
Oxford   Dr C.C. Davies

PREFACE

Professor K.A. Nizami (1925–97) was a pre-eminent historian of medieval India. He was a pioneer in the study of the social, religious, cultural, and political history of Islam in South Asia. In a career spanning nearly half a century, Professor Nizami wrote nearly fifty scholarly books and hundreds of articles in English and Urdu, covering different facets of Indo-Muslim history: Sufi orders and religious thinkers, the medieval state and political dynasties, social and cultural trends, the Aligarh movement, and the contribution of Muslims to the Indian freedom struggle. It would be difficult to write on any of these themes without referring to one or another of his many works.

The publication of *Religion and Politics in India During the Thirteenth Century* both initiated and served to mark an important shift in Indian historical writing from an exclusively political to a more comprehensive social, cultural, and political analysis. During the four decades since it was published in 1961, the book has held its place as one of the most authoritative introductions to the history of the period. It places the early Delhi Sultanate within the context of its Central Asian neighbourhood and the wider Islamic world. It discusses the impact of Islamic notions of brotherhood and equality on Indian society and explains the influence of medieval Persian ideas of kingship on the Turkish political institutions of the time. Following an account of pre-Ghurid Indian society, Professor Nizami goes on to discuss the nature of Muslim settlements, the methods of warfare, the social implications of the interaction between Indian and Turkish legal and political systems, the Turkish theory of kingship and its racial connotations, the composition of the nobility and its economic underpinning in the *iqta'* system, the role of the *'ulama* and the Sufis, the attitude of the sultans towards the non-Muslims, and their relations with the outside world. Professor Nizami's comprehensive analysis facilitates a fuller and better understanding of the nature of the Delhi Sultanate and, more generally, of the Muslim presence in India.

Religion and Politics in India During the Thirteenth Century was a pioneering work in two important respects. First, through its critical and adroit use of a new range of primary sources, including literary, poetical, scientific, legal, religious and, most particularly, mystical (*malfuz*) texts, it demonstrated ways of breaking through the constraints of political chronicles in reconstructing the medieval world of both the rulers and the ruled. Professor Nizami was a vigilant as well as a diligent scholar, willing to subject these new sources to critical scrutiny before either discarding them or using them to tell a far richer, truer, and more inclusive story. Second, in its sustained effort to present Indo-Muslim society both 'from the foot of the throne as well as the hut of the ordinary man' this book helped to widen the historical gaze. Besides being a necessary corrective to the political accounts that preceded it, *Religion and Politics in India During the Thirteenth Century* has had a sobering influence on a later historiographical trend in which the role of ideas has been almost entirely ignored, to be replaced by a fixation with the role of the economic forces in history. The book has been widely acclaimed for its comprehensiveness and balanced approach, and it is to these qualities in particular that it owes its continued reputation and success.

I am pleased that Oxford University Press, India is bringing out a new edition of this book. I should like to thank the editors at OUP for the efficient and courteous manner in which they have carried out this task.

Magdalen College
Oxford
November 2001   F.A. Nizami

OXFORD
UNIVERSITY PRESS

YMCA Library Building, Jai Singh Road, New Delhi 110 001

Oxford University Press is a department of the University of Oxford. It furthers the
University's objective of excellence in research, scholarship, and education
by publishing worldwide in

Oxford   New York

Auckland   Bangkok   Buenos Aires   Cape Town   Chennai
Dar es Salaam   Delhi   Hong Kong   Istanbul   Karachi   Kolkata
Kuala Lumpur   Madrid   Melbourne   Mexico City   Mumbai   Nairobi
São Paulo   Shanghai   Singapore   Taipei   Tokyo   Toronto

with an associated company in Berlin

Oxford is a registered trade mark of Oxford University Press
in the UK and in certain other countries

Published in India
By Oxford University Press, New Delhi

© Oxford University Press 2002

The moral rights of the author have been asserted
Database right Oxford University Press (maker)
First published 1961
By Idarah-i Adabiyat-i Delli
New edition 2002
By Oxford University Press, New Delhi

All rights reserved. No part of this publication may be reproduced,
stored in a retrieval system, or transmitted, in any form or by any means,
without the prior permission in writing of Oxford University Press,
or as expressly permitted by law, or under terms agreed with the appropriate
reprographics rights organization. Enquiries concerning reproduction
outside the scope of the above should be sent to the Rights Department,
Oxford University Press, at the address above

You must not circulate this book in any other binding or cover
and you must impose this same condition on any acquirer

ISBN 019 565500 1

Printed in India at Rashtriya Printers, Delhi 110 032
and published by Manzar Khan, Oxford University Press
YMCA Library Building, Jai Singh Road, New Delhi 110 001

Religion and Politics in India
During the Thirteenth Century

Khaliq Ahmad Nizami

OXFORD

UNIVERSITY PRESS

CONTENTS

Tomb of Iltutmish

The Qutb Minar

سمع جميع هذا الكتاب وهو مشارق الأنوار النبوية من صحاح الأخبار
المصطفوية على مصنفه الشيخ الإمام العالم الأوحد رئيس أصحاب القدر
الكبير المميز ... قدوة الأئمة وعمدة الأئمة النبي ... الله تعالى رضي الدين
... الصغاني رحمة ... بن الحسن الصغاني رضي الله عنه يقرأه ...
... الجامع المتقن حال الأمير ... بكر محمد بن أحمد بن محمد الذكرى الترمذي ...
... السادة الفقهاء ... الأمير ... أسد دعاه المكناسي وسعد ...
سعد بن أحمد بن أحمد بن عبد الله الحدادي البنا ... الجبر على نرع ترى
النيسابوري التغزنا ... وحي الدين سلمى ... يوسف بن محمد بن ... عثمان الملبا ... سنان
الدمياطي ... عبد الله محمد ... بكر السبتي المالكي ... سنين الأمراني عبد الله محمد ...
بن على النحوي وعبد الله بن محمد بن أبي بكر الغساني الأندلسي المالكي عفا الله عنه
في مجالس آخرها يوم الثلاثاء ثامن العشرون من جمادى الآخر سنة سبع
ولاية وتمامه وصح ذلك وكتب محضر الشيخ المصنف من باب الأنج
وكتب عبد الله بن محمد بن أبي بكر الغساني والحمد لله وحده وصلواته
على محمد وآله وسلم ...

صحيح ذلك وكتب للملق الى حرم الله تعالى
الحسن بن محمد بن الحسن الله ... الغاني أحمد أعلم الله الأعلى
مجالا اولى الفضل والهجوى وجعله علما في الأفاضل
كما ينجم فى الدجى شاهدا او مطلبا؟

Autograph of Saghani, the most outstanding Indian 'alim of the 13th century

INTRODUCTION

My colleague, Mr Khaliq Ahmad Nizami, has after years of study produced the best work we have on all aspects (including the political) of Indo-Muslim life in India during the thirteenth century. All Persian printed works have been utilized for the purpose, as well as all manuscripts that have yet been discovered. His attitude is critical and scientific, and he has avoided both polemics and propaganda.

I

The Muslim settlement in India is very often misrepresented as a military venture—an act of force. It is true that Shihab-u'd-din Ghuri won the second battle of Tarain in 1192 and that within fourteen years his general, Bakhtiyar Khalji, had reached the bank of the Brahmaputra. This rapid conquest of northern India—even if it be partial and of the main cities only—established a centralized political structure that was destined to stay; and, on the face of it, the military achievement seems great. But there is another side of the picture which cannot be ignored. Judged by Central Asian standards, the Turkish leaders of the day were woefully behind the times in strategy and courage, as well as the enforcement of discipline among their soldiers. In 1205 Sultan Shihab-u'd-din was signally defeated by the non-Muslim Qara-Khitai Turks at the battle of Andkhud; his officers and soldiers deserted him and he fled for refuge to the fort with about a hundred men. In 1218 Chengiz Khan, the greatest killer in world history (if we exclude the statesmen responsible for the last two world wars), started his famous march for the conquest of Muslim Asia and, within forty years, the Mongols had brought all lands up to the frontiers of Poland and Syria under their sway and had conquered India up to Lahore. To ensure the permanence of their power, the Mongol conquerors massacred the population of the more important cities. "Where there had been a hundred thousand people," 'Ala-u'd-din Ata Malik Juwaini, the Secretary of Halaku Khan, writes, "there remained without exaggeration not a hundred souls alive."[1] The inhabitants of the great centres of Muslim civilization—Samarqand, Bukhara, Tirmiz, Khwarazm,

1. *Tarikh-i-Jahan Gusha*, Vol. II, p. 17.

Naishapur, Merv, and others which I have not space to enumerate—were so carefully slaughtered that only a few beggars were left. At Merv, every Mongol soldier was ordered to execute three to four hundred men and women, and one Maulana 'Imad-u'd-din, who had managed to escape with a few friends, finding himself unable to bury the corpses, spent thirteen days and nights in counting them; they were one million and three hundred thousand in number. In the flourishing and historic city of Naishapur, every living creature was killed, including cats and dogs, and no one was left to count the dead. In the city of Herat, according to the *Tarikh-i-Herat,* only the Khatib Maulana Sharf-u'd-din and fifteen other persons (whom it names) escaped the massacre, but after the Mongols had withdrawn, they were joined by fifteen men who had escaped the massacre in the suburbs. "For fifteen years there was no one in the city of Herat except these forty men; they lived in the mausoleum of Malik Ghiyas-u'd-din." The number of men and women massacred is given as one million and six hundred thousand for Herat and the surrounding towns.[2] When Chengiz Khan marched from Samarqand to the bank of the Indus, no one along the route of his march was allowed to survive.

Even according to the most modest estimate, the Mongols during this period (1228–60) must have killed at least eight million Muslim men and women in cold blood for the establishment of their political authority. The return of prosperity was not easy. Juwaini, writing in 1259–60, says that the districts of Mawaraun Nahr, which had been subjected to plunder only once, had in some cases attained to their pre-Mongol prosperity or closely approached it. "It is otherwise with Khorasan and Iraq which countries are afflicted with a hectic fever and a chronic ague. Every town and every village has been several times subjected to pillage and massacre and has suffered confusion for years, so that even though there be generation and increase until the Resurrection, the population will not attain to a tenth of what it was before. The history thereof may be ascertained from the record of ruins and mudden-heaps declaring how fate has painted here deeds upon palace walls."[3] Hamdullah, the *Mustaufi* (Auditor-General) of Iran, writing about a century after Chengiz's invasion, declares in his *Nuzhatul Qulub* that the country had not attained to even a third of its pre-Mongol prosperity. Nevertheless, by the year 1300 AD almost all the Mongols in Muslim lands had been converted to the Muslim faith. Apart from the destruction wrought, the sole result of Chengiz's work was to replace one Turkish governing class

2. *Rauzat-u's-Safa*, Vol. V, pp. 38–9.
3. *Tarikh-i-Jahan Gusha*, Vol. I, p. 15, Boyle's trans.

by another. Outer Mongolia is the only country where the Mongols now survive. It may be said with confidence that no Mussalman bears them any ill-will. Past wrongs, however great, must be forgotten. That is a precondition of world prosperity and peace.

I have referred to the Mongol conquest of Muslim Asia and southwestern Europe because it is the basic fact of world history in the thirteenth century and deeply influenced the fortunes of all Asian states and of the Empire of Delhi. The Mongols took good care to prevent the inhabitants of the cities which they had determined to slaughter from escaping their doom. Still, according to the best authority available, the *Yuan-Chao-Pi-Shi* (*Secret History of the Mongol Dynasty*), the army of Chengiz Khan did not exceed 90,000 as against the Khwarazmian army of 4 to 5 lacs. It was impossible for the conquerors to seal up the whole of Central Asia. India was the only country where the refugees could find both security and livelihood. A large number of refugees, who belonged to distinguished families and who were capable of taking part in the administration, got employment under Iltutmish but were later on liquidated by "the Forty". The names of a few scholars, who migrated, have been recorded. We have also references to ordinary Mussalmans—men of no account either in their own country or here—but their advent made no difference to the political and military structure of the country.

II

Mr Nizami has prefaced his work by an excellent analysis of the Islamic Revolution and its consequences, up to the thirteenth century. It is impossible for me to add to what he says, but perhaps the following reflections will enable the reader to coordinate the Islamic Revolution with the general trend of world history.

(a) All revolutions, whether claiming to be religious or secular, attempt to resolve conflicts, contradictions, or discriminations. But if the revolution succeeds in resolving these conflicts at a lower level, they reappear at a higher level and often in a more acute form. The distinctive character of Islam as a religion is its uncompromising monotheism, and the application of this principle to social life, as Mr Nizami makes clear, meant the elimination of discrimination to the utmost extent possible under the circumstances. The Prophet was not an Arab nationalist, but in the ten years during which he was in charge of the government of Medina, he eliminated all Arab tribal conflicts and organized a fairly egalitarian and classless society. But after various non-Arab peoples had been brought within the fold of Islam, national conflicts appeared and there was no Prophet or even a statesman of the calibre of the second Caliph to resolve these conflicts. As a result, the unified Caliphate broke up into national and semi-national groups, which are still with us. The Shuabia Movement declares all Mussalmans to be equal but it has not been in practice possible to enforce this principle in the sphere of politics and economics, though all Mussalmans admit it in the sphere of religious rites.

(b) The Muslim *Shari'at* in the earlier centuries was the best civil law available; under happier circumstances it could have helped in the establishment of a proper social order for the whole world. But it was, unfortunately, afflicted by two misfortunes which led to an inner paralysis. First, the attempt was made to follow mechanically the injunctions of the Quran and the precepts of the Prophet, while the objectives—the end, aim, or purpose—of these injunctions was completely ignored. To take one example only: the Prophet did not ask for taxes but alms for the purposes defined in the Quran—the help of the orphan, the wayfarer, persons out of employment (*miskin*), persons incapable of earning their livelihood (*fuqara*), persons with too much self-respect to ask for the help they needed, and the wages of those employed by the state—but 2½ per cent was the utmost he could demand as *zakat* under the economic conditions of Arabia. But for countries with great differences between the rich and the poor, *zakat* should have been made a progressive and not merely a proportionate tax, if it was to achieve its aim. Instead of this, the lower type of legists attempted to find ways by which *zakat* might be avoided altogether, while mechanically adhering to the conditions for *zakat* which the Prophet had laid down. This criticism applies to a very large part of the *Shari'at*; the rules were remembered on the basis of authority, while the social objectives for which these rules had been formulated were completely ignored and no reference to them was considered valid. Second, it was accepted as a basic principle that *ijtihad*—the adaptation of the law to suit new circumstances—was no longer possible and that the *Shari'at* must stand unchanged for all time. For the Sunnis (as Molvi Amir Ali Sahib points out in his Introduction to the *Fatawa-i-Alamgiri*), the *Shari'at* meant the commentaries on the works of Imam Muhammad and the textbooks (*fatawa*) of enormous size collecting the opinions expressed in these commentaries, without any attempt at reconciling them. As a result, Mr Nizami rightly remarks, "the law of Islam has remained in a petrified state and has not marched with the times." But since mankind cannot live without laws suited to the circumstances of the age, the laws (*zawabit, a'in, torah*) that were needed were made and amended by the state.

(c) Mr Nizami gives an excellent account of the conflict of Muslim theologians and of the enormous labour put in by the compilers of the Prophet's precepts, who began their work a century or more after his death. But so far as the Sunnis are concerned, the scholastic theology of al-Ash'ari (ob. 930 AD) prevailed and all other schools of thought (with the exception of the mystics) were suppressed. "This new principle," Mr Nizami declares, "served as a damper on free thought and research." Among other things it killed science, which had reached a fairly advanced stage with Alberuni and Avicenna; and it was left to the Europeans to march from pure to applied science and lay the foundations of the modern industrial system with the immense benefits it has brought to the European communities and the great future it holds out to all mankind.

(d) The Prophet left the organization of political and administrative affairs to the secular good sense (*ijma'*) of his community. Amir Mu'awiya changed the Caliphate into a *mulk* or monarchy, though he continued the name. With the rise of the Ghaznavid power the first Sultanate in Islamic history was established. "The Sultanate," Mr Nizami declares, "had no sanction in the *Shari'at*; it was not a legal institution. Its laws were the result of the legislative activity of the rulers and the governing class."

Still the chief features of the monarchy as it developed among the Mussalmans have to be noted as it was radically different from the monarchy of the Hindus and the Europeans. "A Hindu king," according to the statement of a scholar of the status of my revered friend, Mr K.M. Munshi, "instead of being the only source of power, was no more than the first among equals, the head of inter-related overlordship, never in the position to overrule the wishes of his feudal lords."[4] The European rulers of the Middle Ages were bound by feudal customs and none of them, judged by oriental standards, had much power for good or evil. The Church also restricted his authority.

Among the Mussalmans, on the other hand, the king claimed a singularity of both 'status and power'. He was expected to respect the rights of private property—of the citizen to his house, of the farmer to his land and, if tradition so demanded, even of the *zamindar*, *dahqan*, or *marzuban* to his ancestral rights to a part of the land revenue. Nevertheless, the whole of the administration was under his personal control; he appointed and dismissed all the higher and even ordinary military, civil, ecclesiastical, and semi-ecclesiastical officers, if he so desired. Even the appointment of minor officers was made subject to his sanction. There were no definite limits to his legislative authority except that he had to leave the laws appertaining to marriage and inheritance untouched. There was only one 'governing

4. *The Struggle for Empire*, Foreword.

class' among the Muslim communities—the officers of the state appointed and dismissed by the king. Feudalism in all its forms was quite unknown. The king could appoint his successors from among his sons and brothers, but his nomination was subject to the assent of the nobles, which was given after his death. If no agreement could be arrived at, there would be a war of succession—an unfortunate and recurrent affair in the history of Islam.

The essence of monarchy among the Mussalmans was its extraordinary concentration of power in the hands of one man and his advisers for the maintenance of internal peace and external expansion. The glory or the sin of laying the foundation of such an institution goes to Amir Mu'awiya and his successors. "At the end of the first century of the Hijra," says Gibbon, "the Caliphs were the most potent and absolute monarchs of the globe. Their prerogatives were not prescribed, either in right or in fact, by the power of the nobles, the freedom of the commons, the privileges of the church, the votes of the senate, or the memory of a free constitution. The authority of the Companions of Mohammad expired with their lives and the chiefs of the Arabian tribes left behind in the desert their spirit of equality and independence. The regal and sacerdotal characters were united in the successors of Mohammad, and if the Quran was the rule of their actions, they were the supreme interpreters of that divine book. They reigned by the right of conquest over the nations of the East, to whom the name of liberty was unknown, and who were accustomed to applaud in their tyrants the acts of violence and severity that were exercised at their own expense. Under the last of the Omayyads the Arabian Empire extended two hundred days' journey from the confines of Tartary and India to the shores of the Atlantic Ocean."[5]

The absolute monarchy here described lasted as long as hereditary rulers were tolerated among the Mussalmans—in India right till the death of Aurangzeb; and one of the elements that contributed to its maintenance— fear of anarchy—still expresses itself in the present-day Muslim preference of autocratic to democratic regimes. Nevertheless, Gibbon's sweeping judgement requires substantial modification. (i) "The larger the state, the less the liberty", Rousseau has rightly said. The Mussalmans of medieval 'Ajam preferred states of enormous size, many of their regions produced only a limited number of commodities, and they could only provide all the requisites of their lives by trade and commerce backed up by a culture and law common to all regions. So they preferred a big empire to a set of smaller kingdoms. Representative institutions were, of course, unknown, and could not have worked under the circumstances. (ii) It is obvious, secondly, that

5. *Decline and Fall of the Roman Empire*, LI.

absolute power over extensive countries could only be exercised by men of extraordinary ability and powerful diligence; worthless, pleasure-seeking rulers were soon liquidated. (iii) Public opinion was always a force to be reckoned with, specially when it was supported by the government officers; in many regions, the tribes and their chiefs also limited the power of the central government. (iv) Lastly, the ablest of emperors could only establish and maintain his power by organizing a proper administrative system run by officers whom he had appointed, a stable land revenue and a commendable body of state laws. The permanence of his dynasty (apart from the fact that his successors might be unworthy) depended upon the value of this administrative system. Generally speaking, the best administrative system that could be evolved in the Middle Ages degenerated or became out of date in a century, more or less.

The power of the monarch among the Mussalmans was closely related to that of the officers of the state. These officers could be appointed and dismissed by the ruler; on the other hand, they had a hand in the selection of a new ruler, who also depended upon them for the maintenance of his authority. The chief problem for a Muslim monarch was to manage his officers, most of whom were appointed by his predecessor and all of whom resented central control. This fact is so well illustrated by the history of India during the thirteenth century that further discussion of it is unnecessary.

It is obvious that the ruler had to draw his officers from a single culture group. (In the case of the Mughal Empire, which is rather singular, they were drawn from various culture groups on the basis of mutual tolerance.) Amir Mu'awiya and the Omayyads chose their high officers from the noble Arab clans, the Abbasids preferred to rely on highly Arabicized Persians as well as some noble-born Arabs, but in the period of the minor Abbasids after Mu'tasim, the Turks who had been brought in as the Caliph's bodyguard proved stronger than any other group. Meanwhile, the Samanid rulers, who were Persian in origin but who governed a predominantly Turkish population, carefully organized the Turkish slaves for the service of the state. As a result of these two movements, the higher as well as the second-rate offices came into the hands of various Turkish groups in all Muslim countries. For a non-Turk to occupy a high office was exceptional, though if we take the Muslim lands as a whole, there were plenty of exceptions. But Muslim social consciousness seemed to accept the fact that there was no alternative to a Turkish governing-class, whether good or bad. The Turkish communities may be defined as the people living north of a line joining the Gulf of Alexandretta to southern Badakhshan, though several Turkish groups such as the Ghurians and Gharjistanis lived south of this line. Turkish rule in Iran was overthrown after six centuries by Shah Isma'il Safavi, a contemporary of Babur, but in many Muslim countries it lasted till the rise of modern European imperialism. Concerning the social composition of Akbar's *mansabdars*, Mr Moreland states: "Omitting a small number of officers whose origin is not on record, I find that just under 70 per cent of the remainder belonged to families which had either come to India with Humayun or had arrived at Court after the accession of Akbar. The remaining 30 per cent of the appointments were held by Indians, rather more than half by (Indian) Muslims, and rather less than half by Hindus."[6] During the thirteenth century, as Mr Nizami's narrative makes clear, many of the Indian Muslims, who aspired to high office, were put to death.

(e) No living scholar has studied Indo-Muslim mysticism (*tasawwuf*) with more care than Mr Nizami. Since something of mysticism is found in all religions, non-Muslim writers have tried to find the origin of Muslim mysticism in Christianity, Hellenism, Manicheism, Buddhism, Hinduism, and Parseeism. "But Muslim mystics," says Mr Nizami, "have always combated such theories and have claimed that mysticism is based on the Quran and the traditions of the Prophet. That *tasawwuf* (mysticism) is essentially Islamic in *origin* is as true as the fact that as the mystic movement spread to various regions it assimilated and imbibed elements from cultures and religions that were different from its own." This is correct. Within my limited study I have only come across one reference to a non-Muslim authority; the *Misbahu-l-Hidayah* in discussing the doctrine of repentance bases it on a saying of Christ: "You shall not enter the kingdom of heaven unless you are born again." On the other hand, many mystic conceptions among the Mussalmans have a purely non-Muslim origin. The foundation of the *silsilah*, which Mr Nizami has explained with such clarity, is the authority of the spiritual teacher or *guru*. But the Quran, and in fact Arabic classical literature, has no term for such a conception; so the word, *shaikh*, which means a leader, a distinguished man, or a tribal chief, was used to indicate a mystic spiritual guide. How far the higher grades of mystic saints—*Qutbu-l-Aqtab* (Axis of the Axes), *Qutb* (Axis), etc.—were suggested by theories about the Boddhisatvas then current in Central Asia is a matter of speculation. The same may be said about the territories (*wilayats*) of the saints.

I have nothing to add to what Mr Nizami says about the Chishti and the Suhrawardi *silsilahs* in India. But the story is left unfinished. Many Companions of the Prophet kept away from the empire which Amir Muʻawiya had formed because it was a thing of sin, an organization of the governing class based on the exploitation of the governed, while they were not in a

6. *India at the Death of Akbar*, pp. 69–70.

position to oppose it. Most religious leaders, mystic and non-mystic, of the Middle Ages adopted the same attitude. The great Chishti shaikhs up to the successors of Shaikh Nizam-u'd-din Auliya (*circa* 1350 AD) followed this principle. After that, mystics of repute began to seek for their disciples among high officers or the kings of minor dynasties, who could afford to maintain them; at the same time, they appointed their sons as their chief successors in order to maintain the prosperity of their families. Since these mystics lived under administrative protection, they lost touch with the public. Muslim mystic thought, properly so called, ceased to advance. A new type of Indian teachers appeared, who are best represented by Kabir. Dr Tara Chand in his classic work enumerates some seventeen sects which substantially taught the same doctrines as Kabir: "All the men and women that are created are Thy form; Kabir is the son of *Allah* and Rama. He is Kabir's *Guru* and *Pir*. The Hindus and the Turks have one path which the True Teacher has pointed out... The religion of those who understand is one, whether they are *Pandits* or Shaikhs."[7] All these teachers affirmed faith in one God, by whatever name He be called; they rejected caste, affirmed the equality of man, considered Hinduism and Islam to be equally true, and were completely free from all bias against Islam. They were pacific and non-violent and asked both Hindus and Mussalmans to discard their exclusiveness, to respect all living creatures, and to abstain from bloodshed. Like the Chishti mystics before them, they appealed to their fellow countrymen, mostly of the lower orders, and did not seek the patronage of any sultan, raja, amir or wazir. The members of these sects were either cultivators or traders with small capital. The absence of any anti-Muslim feeling among these sects is certainly a proof that they had not suffered from any Muslim religious persecution. Dr R.C. Majumdar is correct in saying that the number of persons belonging to these sects was very small. But what mattered really was the deep influence of their attitude both towards the Hindus and the Mussalmans, and owing to that influence a new India was born.

III

The main part of Mr Nizami's work is concerned with various aspects of Muslim life in the thirteenth century; there is much in it that is new, based on manuscripts the author has discovered or studied for the first time, and little that can be a matter for controversy.

But as to the "Advent of the Turks", Mr Nizami remarks: "The Turkish invasions were not inspired by any religious or proselytizing fervour. Shihab-u'd-din's first conflict on the Indian soil took place not with a Hindu raja

---

7. *Influence of Islam on Indian Culture*, p. 165.

but with a Muslim co-religionist and he faced them with the same determination and spirit in which he carried his arms into Aryavarta. The Ghurid successes were not followed by any retaliatory action inspired by religious zeal or fanaticism. They handled the situation in the light of expediency and entered into a series of compromises without any partiality or prejudice.'

No correct comprehension of the political events of the thirteenth century and, in fact, of the Middle Ages is possible unless a clear distinction is drawn between the Turkish governing-class group and the ordinary Indian-born Mussalmans. Hinduism is a tolerant creed and, as the accounts of the Arab travellers definitely prove, the Hindu rajas allowed Mussalmans to settle in the suburbs of their capitals and gave them lands for their houses, mosques, and graves. The works of the Arab travellers also show that in spite of the caste system the Muslims had the free run of the land. Small cultural Muslim colonies seem to have been gradually established in many parts of India. These Mussalmans and the Hindu converts who joined them had no say in the policy of the government of medieval India.

The Turks, on the other hand, were a definite governing-class group, who insisted on maintaining their identity and monopolizing most, if not all, high offices. The whole responsibility of the policy of the government rested upon these Turks or Turanis. During the Mughul Empire they formed a closed group of *mansabdars*, called *khanazadas*. But what has happened to these Turks? It is impossible to find a Turk anywhere in India today. Our census ignores them. You can only after prolonged search find a Turkish village in India. Even Indo-Muslim families tracing their origin to Mughal *mansabdars* are limited in number. The Rajput families have kept some memory of their ancestors, correct or legendary. It is strange that the descendants of the great Turkish officers of the Sultanate period did nothing of the kind. We only know of the Turks from the historical works of the Middle Ages, from the buildings and mausoleums they have left, and the temples they are alleged to have destroyed. No living memory of them remains. The Turks or Turushkas have shared the fate of the Yavanas, the Hunas, the Sakas, and other conquering settlers in India, and are not to be found anywhere. Also nobody knows for certain how they vanished.

The Mussalmans of India, on the other hand, have not for centuries been conscious of any foreign affiliations. It has to be added that neither in Persia nor in India has modern research been able to find any authentic contemporary literature to show how Islam spread in either country. But even a cursory glance at the homelands of the Delhi Empire, where the Mussalmans number only about ten per cent, will show that there were no conversions in the countryside and the conversions in the *qasba*s and cities were confined to the lower non-caste groups, such as weavers, elephant-drivers, butchers, fishermen, and the like, whom the *Manusmriti* classified as non-caste groups and who were denied the privilege of living within the cities and walled towns.[8] These conversions probably took place on the basis of the decision of the local caste guilds. But once the decision was taken, it was impossible to go back upon it. The Mussalmans of India, as an organized community, are not responsible for the policy of the medieval state. But they are responsible for organizing an internal *social life* of their own quite different from that of their Hindu neighbours with whom they have otherwise mixed freely in all the common affairs of life. But so long as Hindu society was organized on the basis of caste, they really had no alternative. The doctrine of contamination, which is the basis of caste, is alien to their whole outlook. "The mouths of all men are clean, regardless of their religion," says the *Shari'at* textbook, the *Kanz-u d-Daqa'iq*, "and the mouths of all animals are clean, except of the dog and the pig." Had the reformers of the sixteenth and seventeenth centuries succeeded in abolishing the caste system, the pace of the unifying forces would have been accelerated.

But to return to our theme. The invasions of Sultan Mahmud only brought disgrace to the creed he professed. It must be remembered, however, that Mas'ud brought back to India a good part of the treasures his father had taken away and that Hindu constructive capacity soon rebuilt Somnath and whatever other temples he had destroyed. Also if the Ghaznavid historians and their successors had not been there to tell us of the havoc Sultan Mahmud wrought, Hinduism would have no living memory about him and no records either.

The army which Shihab-u'd-din Ghuri led to defeat at the first battle of Tarain consisted entirely of Ghurian Turks (now called Hazaras) and the Khaljis, who lived on the banks of the river Helmund. The Mussalmans of India, whose number then was small but not insignificant, took no part in this enterprise and reaped none of its fruits.

What was the cause of the Ghurian success? Mr Nizami's answer is the caste system! Is that a correct answer? It has been an established convention since the eighth century that educated Mussalmans have the privilege of associating with the upper-class Hindus (so far as caste rules allow) on an equal basis. As a result they have known neither the privileges and happiness that come to the Brahmans and the Kshattriyas as the consequence of their birth nor the degradation and miseries that the *sudras* and the *chandalas* have to face from the cradle to the grave. Muslim descriptions of the caste system have been purely formal and are devoid of depth and critical

---

8. *Manusmriti*, Buhler's trans., I, 93, 99, 100, 105; III, 119; X, 25–45, 51–62.

appreciation. The caste system can only be understood by those who have been born into it, who have lived surrounded by it but who have succeeded in transcending it. We must be guided about it by the opinion of our Hindu historians, who have a first-hand knowledge of this institution both from books and personal experience.

(i) The most important authority is Sir Jadunath Sarkar, 'the doyen of modern medieval historians'. In his volume on *Shivaji* (Chapter XVI) he remarks:

> Caste grows by fission! It is antagonistic to national union. In proportion as Shivaji's ideal of a Hindu *swaraj* was based on orthodoxy, it contained within itself the seed of its own decay.
>
> As Rabindranath Tagore remarks: 'A temporary enthusiasm sweeps over the country and we imagine that it has been united; but the rents and holes in our body social do their work secretly; we cannot retain any noble idea long.'
>
> Shivaji aimed at preserving the rents; he wished to save from Mughal attack a Hindu society to which ceremonial distinctions and isolation of castes are the very breath of life. He wanted to make this heterogeneous society triumphant over *all* India. He wove ropes of sand; he attempted the impossible. It is beyond the power of any man, it is opposed to the divine law of the universe, to establish the *swaraj* of such a caste-ridden, isolated, internally-torn sect over a vast continent like India.
>
> Shivaji and his father-in-law, Gaikwar, were *Marathas*, i.e. members of a despised caste. Before the rise of the national movement in the Deccan in the closing years of the nineteenth century, a Brahman of Maharashtra used to be insulted if he was called a Maratha. "No", he would reply with warmth, "I am a *Dakshina* Brahman." Shivaji keenly felt his humiliation at the hands of the Brahman to whose defence and prosperity he had devoted his life. Their insistence on treating him as a Shudra drove him into the arms of Balaji Avji, the leader of the Kaysthas, and another victim of Brahmanic pride.

At the end of his classical work on *Aurangzeb*, the great historian gives his final and very correct verdict:

> The rigidity of Islam has enabled its followers in all lands to succeed up to a certain point. But there they have stopped, while progress is the law of life in the living world. While Europe has been steadily advancing, the stationary East has been relatively falling back, and every year that passes increases the distance between Europe and Asia in knowledge, organisation, accumulated resources and acquired capacity and makes it increasingly difficult for the Asiatics to compete with the Europeans...which is only another way of saying that the enterprising families are constantly replacing sleepy self-satisfied ones in the leadership of our own society...If India is to be the home of a nation able to keep peace within and guard the frontier, develop the economic resources and promote art and

science, then both Hinduism and Islam must die and be born again. Each of these creeds must pass through a rigorous vigil and penance, each must be purified and rejuvenated under the sway of reason and science. That such a rebirth for Islam is not impossible has been demonstrated in our own days by the conqueror of Smyrna. Ghazi Mustafa Kamal Pasha has proved that the greatest Muslim State of the age can secularise its constitution, abolish polygamy and the servile seclusion of women, grant equality to all creeds, and yet not cease to be a land of Islam.

(ii) Harshavardhana, the last ruler of the whole of northern India died in 647 AD—just fifteen years after the Prophet of Islam. In the five and a half centuries that followed, Hinduism, which had been an expanding culture, developed the psychology of territorial retreat from foreign lands, leaving its great achievements in architecture and sculpture behind it. At home no advance was made on the science of the Gupta Age, which the Mussalmans studied with such sedulous care and handed on to Europe. The mental attitude of the age is best illustrated by the fact that the place of honour is occupied by the commentaries on the *Smritis*, which are mostly repetitive. The Sanskrit scholars, who have contributed to volume V of the Vidyabhavan Series (*Struggle for Empire*), are all united in declaring that, compared with the history of Hindu culture and Sanskrit literature as a whole, this period was singularly unproductive. Meanwhile, the Kshattriya rajas (the term Rajput did not come into use till the Mughal period) fought with each other year after year not for self-defence or profit but apparently from habit and a sense of duty; the obligation of killing and being killed is a sacred duty imposed by the *Manusmriti* and similar scriptures on all Kshattriyas. As a result (a) northern India was split up into a number of dynasties constantly at war. (b) These wars were probably confined to the rajas and their retainers, who had land grants on the condition of fighting for their rajas; still they could not but create intense hatred at the dynastic level between the Kshattriya groups, and this made any union in the face of the Ghurian invaders quite impossible.

Mr K.M. Munshi, for whom I have the most profound respect, is a great lawyer well acquainted with Muslim ways of life, a profound scholar, and a far-sighted statesman. Nevertheless, his review of this period is full of contradictions. It is impossible to reconcile the contradiction of the following statements (Foreword, *Struggle for Empire*).

(a) "The Indian kings, all of whom accepted, at any rate in theory, the law of *Dharmasastras* as inalienable, waged wars according to certain humane rules. Whatever the provocation, the shrine, the Brahmana and the cow were sacrosanct to them. War being a special privilege of the martial classes, harassment of the civil population during military operation was considered a serious lapse from the code of honour. Still war means killing and being killed—a process which is bound to evoke not love but hatred; and if fighting is made 'the special privilege of the martial classes' and groups of the martial classes are always at war, the collapse of the country is inevitable.

(b) "The 'Aryavarta-consciousness' was mainly religio-cultural in content.... This consciousness in its political aspect had all but disappeared during the few decades which preceded AD 1000 on account of the recurrent upheavals in Northern India... At the turn of the tenth century, therefore, there was no generally accepted national focus in the country, as Kannauj had once been, and no military power in North India strong enough to keep the warring kings in check or to coordinate their activities against the foreign invader."

(c) But to complete the set of amusing contradictions, it has to be added that Mr Munshi does not live according to the caste system and, as his name indicates, he comes from a highly-respected family of Hindus who have been eminent as Persian scholars, and the Persian work of one of his ancestors is being edited by my friend, Professor Sa'id Hasan of Allahabad. Nevertheless, it pleases him to stand forth as an advocate of the caste system:

> *Chaturvarnya*, the divinely ordained four-fold order of society embraced all social groups... Century after century, the system, first formulated by the *Manuṣmriti*, was accepted throughout the country, never by force of arms, less by royal fiats than by the sanction implied in the belief that 'God gave it and the ancestors obeyed it'... Its fundamental aim was to produce a synthetic urge towards human betterment, which treated economic, social, material, and ethical and spiritual well-being as indivisible; an aim which has yet to be improved upon by any other system.

Now if God Himself is responsible for dividing His chosen people in India into four groups with a view to their improvement, while He has left the rest of mankind free to organize its affairs on other lines, the student of history, who knows nothing about 'the ways of God', is perforce silenced. Also the Hindu community has the exclusive right of interpreting its own scriptures. But modern Hindu leaders from Raja Ram Mohan Roy to Mahatmaji have rejected the caste system.

(iii) Dr Parmatama Saran, the only contributor to the *Struggle for Empire*, who is a distinguished scholar of both Sanskrit and Persian, and who is also well acquainted with the working of the caste system at all levels, has attempted to solve the problem, and his verdict deserves a careful consideration:

> The astounding rapidity of the Turkish conquest constitutes an important problem for the students of Indian history. It is puzzling, nay almost baffling, to explain the almost complete collapse of Northern India, within an incredibly short time, before the onslaught of invaders whose powers and resources were hardly equal to some of the bigger Hindu states, not to speak of a combination of them....History would be meaningless if facts of such outstanding importance cannot be viewed in their true perspective against a proper background....Apart from a few incidental notices or brief allusions, the Hindu sources are silent about the great episode. It is equally unwarranted to attribute it (the Ghurian success) solely to the social and religious peculiarities of the Hindus, for our ideas about them are also vague and indistinct and based on no sure knowledge of facts.

The version of the defenders is unknown and there cannot, therefore, be any finality in our judgement. But subject to these 'natural limitations', Dr Saran proceeds to enumerate the probable causes of the Ghurian success:

> The foremost among these seems to be the iniquitous system of caste and the absence of contact with the outside world. The first resulted in a fragmentation of Indian society into mutually exclusive classes, among whom the privileged minority kept their vested interests by depriving the masses of many civic rights, specially of education and of free intercourse and association on equal terms with their fellow-men, and further, by imposing on them the most irritating disabilities on the one hand, and a tremendous weight of innumerable duties and obligations towards the privileged classes on the other. And this evil led to another. It bred among the leaders of the Indian people a vain pride in isolationism and insularity and that attitude of arrogance which has been noticed by Alberuni...
>
> This spirit of exclusive superiority was created and maintained by a process of intellectual fraud, inasmuch as the entire literature of the period was utilised for this purpose and the masses were asked to follow it blindly in the name of the Holy Writ, to question whose authority was an unpardonable sin. It thus became a part of the Hindu *dharma* not to cross the seas or even the territorial limits of certain hallowed areas!...
>
> The degraded level to which the majority were pushed down made them indifferent to the country-wide dangers and kindred problems. This alone made possible the woeful situation that while the invaders swept across the country, the masses mostly remained inert. The people of the land, with few exceptions, were indifferent to what was happening around them. Their voice had been hushed in silence by a religio-social tyranny. No public upheaval greets the foreigner, nor are any organised efforts made to stop him. Like a paralysed body,

the Indian people helplessly look on while the conqueror marches over their corpse. They look staggered, for a moment, only to sink back into an acquiescence to the inevitable to which they have been taught to submit...

History had no meaning for the Hindu kings who presided over the destinies of this woe-stricken land. The repeated warnings of the past went unheeded... One thing seems to be reasonably certain. The utter and precipitate prostration of such a vast and ancient land, endowed with resources far superior and greater [than] her invaders, can be the result mainly of internal decay and not merely of external attacks, which were its effect rather than its cause.

(iv) One of the most balanced of our modern authorities, Dr Tara Chand, comments as follows:

India on the eve of the Muslim conquest resembled Greece before the rise of the Macedonian into power. There was the same incapacity in both regions to create a political union, and there was the same keenness in the pursuit of science, literature and art. The analogy went further, for if the Macedonian was the semi-hellenised Greek, the Turk that swept over India was a non-Hinduised Rajput... The Muslim conquest had a tremendous effect upon the evolution of Indian culture. Superficially, it upset everything... Fundamentally, it had a different effect.

When Qutb-u'd-din Aibek decided to stay in Hindustan, he had no other choice but to retain the Hindu staff which was familiar with the civil administration, for without it all government, including the collection of revenue, would have fallen into chaos...The Muslims who came into India made it their home. They lived surrounded by the Hindu people and a state of perennial hostility with them was impossible. Mutual intercourse led to mutual understanding. Many who had changed their faith differed little from those whom they had left. Thus after the first shock of conquest was over, the Hindus and Muslims preferred to find a *via media* whereby to live as neighbours. The efforts to seek a new life led to the development of a new culture which was neither exclusively Hindu not purely Muslim. It was indeed Muslim-Hindu culture. Not only did Hindu religion, Hindu art, Hindu literature and Hindu science absorb Muslim elements, but the very spirit of Hindu culture and the very stuff of Hindu mind were altered, and the Muslim reciprocated by responding to the change in every department of life.

IV

In view of the extracts given above, the reader will be safe in accepting the opinions expressed in Mr Nizami's chapters on the "Advent of the Turks" and the "Character of the Empire" as fundamentally correct. He sums up the authorities quoted above in a single sentence: "Had the Hindu *masses* resisted the Turkish rule in India, the Ghurids would not have been able to retain even an inch of Indian territory."

Since Mr Nizami is only concerned with the social and cultural life of the Mussalmans, I will venture to offer a few considerations that will enable the reader to coordinate Mr Nizami's ideas with the well-known works of Indian history.

(i) The cultural unification of India was an Aryan achievement. Without that common culture India could never have been unified. By the tenth century the caste system was out of date in India and everywhere else. But in ancient times there was no alternative to it. The Hindu teachers could only teach people what they could understand—the sacred scriptures, such as the Vedas to the elect and the stories of the Ramayana and the Mahabharata to the multitude. Mr Nizami says that Islam is designed as a city creed; he should also have added that Hinduism, with its songs, dances, and popular festivals in which all can share, is suited more to the countryside. But the administrative unification of India was a Turkish achievement and they were driven to it by circumstances rather than by conscious planning. Shihab-u'd-din Ghuri apparently wanted several governments in India to replace the governments of the Hindu rulers, and had had established at least three centres in India—Aiybek at Lahore, Baha-u'd-din Tughril at Bayana, and Qubacha in Sind. Tughril was apparently expected to conquer regions further east; but the Rai of Gwalior preferred to submit to Aiybek, Tughril died before he could wage a war with Aiybek, and Shihab-u'd-din accepted the accomplished fact. Qubacha's power was weakened by the Mongol invasions, and Iltutmish, the real founder of the Delhi Sultanate, succeeded in crushing Qubacha in the east and 'Auz Khalji in the west. So the state of Delhi, which (with two interregna of a century and a century and a half) still stands, appeared in history for the first time. All the slaves of Shihab-u'd-din and Iltutmish—"the Forty"—desired independence, but they were not prepared to liquidate the central authority completely. After a struggle between the centrifugal and the centripetal powers, the centripetal power prevailed, for the average Turkish governor realized that without a centralized authority, he would be crushed between the Hindu rulers and the Mongols.

(ii) Mr Munshi says that in three-fourths of the country India followed its unbroken way of life, where the *Dharmasastra* were honoured and obeyed and Hinduism flourished unobstructed. Now if Hinduism means 'Aryavarta-consciousness'—i.e. religious freedom—then it was alive in the whole of India. The best *vaid*s and Hindu astrologers were to be found in Delhi and the best Hindu teachers at Banaras. The great centres of Hindu culture in northern India, such as Mathura, Hardwar, Kara, etc. were within the Empire of Delhi. All authorities, including fanatics such as Barani and

Badauni, are united in declaring that Delhi throughout had a majority Hindu population and that the upper-class Hindus were more prosperous than the upper-class Mussalmans. The great officers of the Empire, who were given a fair percentage of the revenues of prosperous Indian provinces, never succeeded in balancing their budget and were constantly in debt to the *saha*s (bankers) of Delhi.

But more concretely the position during the thirteenth century may be described as follows:

(a) From the Indus to the Brahmaputra there is a flat plain studded with cities. It was easy for the Turks to conquer these cities, the Turks allowed the non-caste groups or the *chandala*s to settle within the cities, and the cities, as Mr Nizami explains, grew in size, productive capacity, and prosperity.

(b) But the Turks were unable to conquer at one sweep the great hill-forts, the hill tracts, and the desert plains. Here the independent and semi-independent rajas held sway; and with reference to them the ruler of Delhi had to embark on 'the labours of Sisyphus'. Forts and principalities were conquered and lost again and again. It was not till Akbar promulgated his theory of *Watan-jagir* that the problem was partly solved. A Turk was only appointed to his *mansab* for life, subject to demotion, promotion, and dismissal. A Rajpat raja, if he joined the *mansabdari* system, was guaranteed his hereditary lands on a hereditary basis as his *watan*, in addition to it he was granted a *mansab*, the income of which was considerably greater than the income of his *watan*; which the leaders of his class insisted on sharing with him.

(c) The Turkish rulers were unable to establish their power in the rural areas. Here there were Hindu chiefs, who can be divided into two groups—first, the *rai*s, *rana*s, and *rawat*s, who had armies of their own and were, for example, able to join Malik Chajju in his rebellion against Sultan Jalal-u'd-din. Secondly, the village headmen (*chaudhari*s, *muqaddam*s, *khot*s) who, according to 'Ala-u'd-din Khalji, imitated their betters, kept small armies, and imprisoned the agents of the imperial revenue department. It appears that the Turkish government made written agreements (*khat*) with local Hindu chiefs about the sums they were to pay while leaving them free to tax the cultivator (*bilahir*) in whatever way they wanted. But the Turkish rulers could only be certain of the revenues of their cities, including taxes on the commodities brought into them from the countryside. The revenue from the rural areas could often only be realized at the point of the sword. On a rough calculation I am inclined to conclude that the revenue realized by the Delhi government did not exceed in amount the military expenditure it incurred on these revenue-collecting campaigns.

(d) "The Hindus," says Mr Munshi, "remained in the sphere of trade, commerce and banking. The Muslims, however intolerant, had to treat the Hindu mercantile community with consideration, though it was inspired by self-interest and often grudging." According to the contemporary evidence of the fanatical Barani, they not only remained but flourished. The Mussalmans of northern India, when educated, were given small clerical jobs or they became teachers or got junior posts as muezzins and prayer leaders of the mosques. The Turks considered business below their dignity. Add to it, business is not possible without loans and interest, and since Islam prohibits interest, it inevitably makes business loans impossible. Small shopkeepers, whom Barani hates, may have been both Hindus and Mussalmans. But the great merchants, whom he accuses of cornering and regrating, were Hindus—Hindu traders (*Saudagar-i-Karawani*) and Hindu wholesale dealers (*Saudagar-i-bazari*). Behind them were the *saha*s (merchants) who financed both. The establishment of the Empire of Delhi—the growth of the towns and their industries, the security of roads, the elimination of internal taxes—greatly contributed to the growth of the Hindu mercantile community. Under the old regime the Hindu merchants—a non-warlike community—was not a part of the governing class. It got no government jobs under the new governments either. But it got the government contracts it wanted and could undertake. 'Ala-u'd-din Khalji, when organizing his economic reforms, had to depend upon the Hindu *nayak*s for grain and the Hindu merchants of Multan for cloth. And these are the two basic commodities of the market.

I cannot close this discussion without quoting the fanatical paragraph (*Fatawa-i-Jahandari*, Advice XI) in which Zia-u'd-din Barani describes the position of the Hindus after Firoz Shah Tughluq had reigned for about ten years:

> In the capital (Delhi) and in the cities of the Mussalmans the customs of infidelity are openly practised, idols are publicly worshipped, and the traditions of infidelity are adhered to with greater insistence than before.....Openly and without fear, the infidels continue their rejoicings during their festivals with the beat of drums and dhols and with singing and dancing. By paying merely a few tankas and the jizya, they are able to continue the traditions of infidelity by giving lessons in the books of their false faith and enforcing the orders of these books.
>
> The desire for overthrowing infidels and knocking down idolaters does not fill the hearts of the Muslim kings (of India). On the other hand, out of consideration for the fact that infidels and polytheists are payers of taxes and protected persons, these infidels are honoured, distinguished, favoured and made eminent; the kings bestow drums, banners, ornaments, cloaks of brocade and caparisoned horses upon them and appoint them to governorships, high posts and offices. And in their capital (Delhi), owing to the status of which the status of all other

Muslim cities is raised, Muslim kings not only allow but are pleased with the fact that infidels, polytheists, idol-worshippers and cow-dung worshippers build houses like palaces, wear clothes of brocade and ride Arab horses caparisoned with gold and silver ornaments. They are equipped with a hundred thousand sources of strength. They live in delights and comfort. They take Mussalmans into their service and make them run before their horses, poor Mussalmans beg of them at their doors; and in the capital of Islam owing to which the edifice of Islam is elevated, they are called *rais* (great rulers), *ranas* (minor rulers), *thakurs* (warriors), *sahas* (bankers), *mehtas* (clerks, officers), and *pandits* (priests).

Professor Mohammad Habib

Political Expansion and Ideological Integration
of Islam till the Thirteenth Century

RISE OF ISLAM AND SIGNIFICANCE OF THE ISLAMIC REVOLUTION IN WORLD HISTORY

The rise and expansion of Islam is one of the most significant events of world history. In 610 AD the Prophet Muhammad began to preach a new faith in Arabia, a country then sunk in barbarism and superstition. Within a century of the Prophet's death, the banner of Islam was floating on the confines of India, on the one side, and the shores of the Atlantic, on the other. Two of the greatest empires of the Middle Ages—the Byzantine and the Sassanid—were shaken to their foundations. To attribute this phenomenal success of the new faith to the might of Arab arms alone would be to over-emphasize the function of force in human achievements. An explanation of this success should be sought, not so much in the strength of the Muslim armies, but in the revolutionary import of the principles of the new social order which Islam preached and strove to establish. People hail a new order not out of mere curiosity, but under the compulsion of despair and frustration born of suffering. Once a social idea appears at such a stage of human suffering 'it grips the masses and becomes a material force'.

The Prophet Muhammad began his teachings with two revolutionary concepts—unity of God[1] and unity of human origin.[2] These principles had

1. Monotheism, it may be pointed out, was not something new to be preached by the Prophet of Islam. All preceding prophets had preached it but, as Le Bon very aptly says, no religion had ever preached monotheism in such clear and unequivocal terms as Islam did (*Tamaddun-i-'Arab*, p. 120). The *differentia* of Islam in this respect, according to Shah Wali-ullah, is not merely the affirmation of the unity of Godhead but also the rejection of all other gods except God. See *Hujjat-ullah al-Balighah*, Chapter XXXVII on *Tauhid*, pp. 58–59.

2. In the Middle Ages we very often find the rulers and the nobility tracing their ancestry to the sun and the moon or to some supernatural power. This was done in order to make their position unassailable and impress on the mind of the common people their superior status on account of their birth. Islam smashed this idea by declaring:

O mankind! We created
You from a single (pair)

a very deep and far-reaching effect on the social and economic institutions of the Middle Ages.

Apart from its theological and metaphysical significance, faith in the unity of God is of supreme social value. "The essence of *Tauhid*," observes Dr Muhammad Iqbal, "as a working idea is equality, solidarity and freedom".[3] The principle of unity in cosmic order which naturally follows from it acts as a great integrating and cohesive force in human society. The place of local, tribal, and family gods is taken by one Supreme God. It is a change from heterogeneity to homogeneity, from confusion to order, and from diversity to unity. All people, high and low, approach Him in the same manner; He listens to everyone and is directly approachable by everyone. There is no need of an intermediary to invoke His help. In fact, the very idea of direct communion with God—the All-Powerful, the Almighty—revolutionizes the whole life of man. It broadens his outlook and enables him to adjust his relations and loyalties with worldly authorities on a human and equitable level. "Islam as a polity," says Iqbal, "is only a practical means of making this principle [of *Tauhid*] a living factor in the intellectual and emotional life of mankind. *It demands loyalty to God not to thrones. And since God is the ultimate spiritual basis of all life, loyalty to God virtually amounts to man's loyalty to his own ideal nature.*"[4] This monotheistic conception of God united the Arab tribes and enabled them to found an international community. It exercised the same stabilizing and sobering effect on the religious life of the people of Persia, Mesopotamia, Syria, Palestine, and Egypt where the conflicts of Magian mysticism, Jewish conservativism, and Christian bigotry had hopelessly confused the religious outlook of man and had prevented the growth of a coherent and integrated view of life. Islam emerged into the civilized world "as a moral

---

Of a male and a female,
And made you into
Nations and tribes, that
Ye may know each other
Not that ye may despise
Each other. Verily
The most honoured of you
In the sight of God
Is (he who is) the most
Righteous of you.
—S. XLIX: 13. See also S. XXII: 5; S. IV: I; S. VI: 98.

3. Muhammad Iqbal, *The Reconstruction of Religious Thought in Islam* (Lahore, 1944), p. 154.

4. Ibid, p. 147.

force that commanded respect and a coherent doctrine that could challenge on their own ground the Christianity of East Rome and the Zoroastrianism of Persia".[5] Islamic monotheism tended to introduce unity and homogeneity in social, religious, and civic spheres.

The principle of human equality, which naturally follows from the principle of the unity of human origin, revolutionized social relations. It contrasted sharply with the laws governing the class-ridden societies of the Roman, Byzantine, Persian, and, later, of the Indian, empires. Islam took the most effective step towards the elimination of all discriminations in human society and pronounced in unambiguous terms the equality of men before the law.

In his last speech at Mecca the Prophet thus explained the principles on which the socio-political organization of Islam was to rest:

> Hearken to my words, O men, for I know not whether I shall see you here another year.
> All customs of paganism have been abolished under my feet.
> The Arab is not superior to the non-Arab; the non-Arab is not superior to the Arab. You are all sons of Adam and Adam was made of earth. Verily all Muslims are brothers.
> Your slaves! Feed them as you feed yourselves and dress them as you dress yourselves.
> The blood feuds of the Time of Ignorance are prohibited.
> Remember Allah [in your dealings] with respect to women. You have rights over them and they have rights over you.
> Verily, you should consider each other's blood, property and reputation inviolable unto the Day of Judgement.
> Verily, a man is responsible only for his own acts. A son is not responsible for the crimes of his father, nor is a father responsible for the crimes of his son. If a deformed Abyssinian slave holds authority over you and leads you according to the Book of Allah, obey him.[6]

The main features of medieval social and political life were the (1) divinity of kings or the divine right of kings, (2) racial discrimination, (3) social distinctions and social disabilities, (4) slavery, (5) economic exploitation of the worker, (6) subjection of women, (7) disregard of an individual's life or right of property, and (8) indiscriminate punishments. The Prophet made clear the attitude of Islam with reference to these problems. "All the fundamental principles of the Muslim State," remarks Professor Habib, "are here. Racial differences are to count for naught; all

---

5. H.A.R. Gibb, *Mohammadanism* (London, 1951), p. 4.

6. This speech has been quoted by Ibn-i-Hisham, Ibn-i-Khaldun, Waqidi, and others in their works. See also Maulana Shibli, *Sirat-un-Nabi* (Azamgarh, 1369 AH), Vol. I, Part 2, pp. 153–68.

are equals; all are brothers; neither law nor social opinion must make any differences between the high-born and the low. A man's right to his person, to the produce of his labour and to the reputation his character has earned for him, is as sacred and inviolable as the holiest of places; no alleged state-necessity, no fanatical prejudices or party interests, can be allowed to infringe them. Civil war is to be abhorred. No monopoly of offices or power; no kings; no oligarchy; no priesthood—the humblest of slaves has as much right to be at the head of the State as the noblest of Quraish. A righteous government alone is entitled to the allegiance of its subjects; all else is usurpation and must be swept aside. There are to be no 'pariah' or low castes: the slave is entitled to the same food and drink as his master and has the same political privileges as a freeman. The customs of paganism—blood-feuds, usury, the subjection of women—are abolished once for all."[7]

To appreciate the role of Islam in the medieval world one has to make a comparative study of the Islamic *Shari'at* with reference to the legal and social set-up of the two great empires of the Middle Ages—the Roman and the Sassanid. When we refer to the Roman Law we do not mean the law of any particular community or any particular area. "It was," rightly observes Dr H.J. Roby, "with more or less modifications from local customs and ecclesiastical authority, the only system of law throughout the Middle Age."[8] A comparison of the Muslim *Shari'at* with the Roman Law, therefore, means a comparative study of Muslim *Shari'at* with reference to the law of the Middle Ages as a whole. A comparison with the Sassanid legal system will reveal the causes of the success of Islam in Persia and Central Asia—lands where most of the social and political institutions of medieval India originated and developed.

STRATIFICATION OF SOCIETY

According to the legal system of Rome, people were grouped into a number of classes, each distinguished from the other by the status assigned to it by law. On the one hand, there were the free born (*ingenuous*) citizens (*civis*) of full age and complete capacity, who enjoyed the widest rights; on the other hand, there were the slaves who were deprived of all claims to the enjoyment of legal rights in the society. Between these two extremes there were a number of intermediate classes of persons, each with their distinguishing characteristics.[9]

---

7. 'The Arab Conquest of Sind' (*Islamic Culture*, October, 1929), pp. 592–94.
8. *Cambridge Medieval History*, Vol. II, p. 53.
9. R.W. Leage, *Roman Private Law*, p. 49.

The Sassanids divided the entire society into the following classes:[10]

1. *Azarvan* (theologians),
2. *Artaishtaran* (warriors),
3. *Dabiran* (government officers),
4. Common people—including peasants (*vastarushan*), artisans, and traders (*hutkhashan*).

This division of society was permanent and rigid. No one could cross over from one class to the other. The law was made to perpetuate this distinction in society and the privileges of the first three classes were jealously protected and guaranteed by the State. It was not possible for a person born into a low family—however gifted he might be—to get employment in any of the departments of the government.[11] No one could follow a profession except that of his ancestors,[12] and no one could aspire to a rank higher than that in which he was born.[13]

The law of Islam did away with all these discriminations and rendered all distinctions between man and man invalid.[14] It proclaimed that there was no virtue except in good deeds, and no nobility except in piety (*ittiqa*). This occasioned, as Sayed Qutb remarks, "a revolution in human thinking".[15]

DISCRIMINATIONS IN THE LEGAL SYSTEMS OF THE MIDDLE AGES

The Roman and the Sassanid laws were essentially laws of discriminations. Both in the civil and the criminal spheres, distinctions were made between different sections of the population on various grounds.

A man's legal personality in Roman Law was determined with reference to (a) birth, (b) age, (c) health, (d) sex, (e) reputation, (f) religion, and (g) domicile.[16] The legal position of women was inferior to that of men. Women could not adopt, could not exercise the calling of a banker, and were explicitly excluded from all civil or public functions.[17] If a woman

10. A. Christensen, *L'Iran sous les Sassanides* (Urdu trans. by Dr Muhammad Iqbal; Anjuman Tarraqi-i-Urdu, Delhi, 1941), p. 126.

11. Ibid, p. 422.

12. Ibid, p. 22.

13. Ibid, pp. 418–19.

14. Quran, S. XLIX: 13.

15. *Al-'Adalah al-Ijtima 'iyah fi al-Islam*, by Sayed Qutb, Eng. trans. by John B. Hardie: *Social Justice in Islam* (Washington, 1953), p. 46, et seq.

16. Sheldon Amos, *The History and Principles of the Civil Law of Rome*, p. 106.

17. Ibid, p. 110.

stood as security for another person, even for her husband or son or father, so as to make her liable for them, the obligation was invalid.[18] Religious orthodoxy was the test of personality. Only Catholic Christians were in full possession of civil rights. Pagans were not considered capable of owning things movable or immovable, which consequently lapsed to the public treasury.[19] Intermarriages between Jews and Christians were not only forbidden but were punishable as adulterous.[20] The testimony of Jews and of heretics was equally excluded as against orthodox Christians.[21] Heretics and Jews were not considered good witnesses.[22] Jews were disqualified to hold any office or honour.[23] With respect to Donatists and Manichaeans it was laid down that "this sort of men have neither by law nor custom anything in common with others".[24] They could acquire property neither by gift nor succession. They could make no will and their children could enter into their inheritance only if they abandoned their fathers' heresy.[25]

A few institutions peculiar to Roman Law—the *Patria Potestas* and the *Manus*—further curtailed individual liberty. The *Patria Potestas* gave absolute power to fathers over their children. "This fatherly power endured irrespectively of the age or social or political position of his sons and daughters."[26] The father could expose the child to perish of cold and hunger.[27] A son, even though of full age, married and with children, could not own any property unless emancipated by his father. He could sue and be sued only in his father's name.[28] In the same way, a woman, when married, passed into the *manus* of her husband and occupied the position of a daughter.[29]

Apart from these discriminations in the civil and personal laws of the Romans, there were grave and serious discriminations in the criminal law as well. Punishments were not uniform for all persons. Justinian's *Digest* recognized three classes of persons—*honestiores*, *humiliores*, and *servi*. The *honestiores* class, which comprised Senators, their descendants, knights,

---

18. *Cambridge Medieval History*, Vol. II, p. 94.
19. *History and Principles of the Civil Law of Rome*, p. 114.
20. Ibid. p. 115.
21. Ibid.
22. *Cambridge Medieval History*, Vol. II, p. 108.
23. *History and Principles of the Civil of Law of Rome*, p. 115.
24. Ibid.
25. Ibid.
26. *Cambridge Medieval History*, Vol. II, p. 66.
27. *Roman Private Law*, p. 90.
28. *Cambridge Medieval History*, Vol. II, p. 66.
29. Ibid. p. 71.

soldiers, etc., was not ordinarily liable to the penalty of death, nor could it be condemned to the mines or compulsory labour. The *humiliores* were punished for grave offences by death, but more frequently the punishment given to them was condemnation to the mines and public beating. The third class comprised slaves who were punished for crimes of a serious nature by beheading, burning, or exposure to wild beasts; for lesser crimes they were flogged and compelled to work in the mines. The laws of Constantine and Arcadius, retained by Justinian, directed that any servant (*familiaris*) or slave bringing an accusation against his master should at once be put to death without any inquiry into the case or production of witnesses.[30]

The Sassanid law made discriminations on grounds of (a) birth, (b) property, (c) religion, and (d) sex. Christensen very correctly observes that the entire Sassanid legal system was designed to protect and maintain the distinctions in society based on considerations of birth and property.[31]

There were seven old families in Iran and all important government offices were distributed among them on a hereditary basis. One family controlled the finances, another the army, another home affairs, and so on.[32] No low-born person, however gifted, could be entrusted with any government work.[33] The property of the high-born people was protected by law.[34] No low-born person could purchase the property of a high-born person. The names of the distinguished families were recorded in government registers and it was the duty of the government to safeguard their rights and distinctive positions in society.[35]

The peasants had no protection whatsoever in the Sassanid law.[36] The State did not take any notice of their misery. They were subjected to forced labour. The landlords considered themselves masters of their lives.[37]

Punishments were severe and indiscriminate under the Sassanid law. Sometimes a whole family was executed for one man's crime.[38]

Women had no status in Sassanid law.[39] Men could, however, invest them with legal status.[40] A man's wife and his slave were treated as equal

30. Ibid. p. 103.
31. *L'Iran sous les Sassanides*, p. 444.
32. Ibid. p. 137.
33. Ibid, p. 422.
34. Ibid, p. 419.
35. Ibid. p. 420.
36. Ibid. p. 424.
37. Ibid. p. 424.
38. Ibid. p. 402.
39. Ibid, p. 437.
40. Ibid. p. 434.

in the eyes of the law,[41] and the wife could be transferred to another person.[42] Women could not be adopted in more than one family,[43] while men could be adopted in many.[44] Wives were classified into two categories: (1) *zan-i-pazshaheha*, and (2) *zan-i-chigariha*.[45] The *zan-i-pazshaheha* enjoyed more rights and privileges than those belonging to the second category.

They and their sons got equal shares in the property. An unmarried daughter got only one half. Women belonging to the second category as well as their children got nothing at all.[46]

THE DIFFERENTIA OF ISLAM

In a world thus torn by almost insuperable barriers of caste, colour, birth, and creed, the *Shari'at* of Islam sought to create a classless society. All those discriminations which had been the bane of the Roman and the Sassanid societies were brushed aside. The Prophet declared: "I have been sent to perfect the morality of mankind" (بعث لأتمم مكارم الأخلاق), and the basis of the new morality was the concept of human equality.

The *Shari'at* recognizes no distinction artificially created by birth, status, education, wealth, race, nationality, or even religion for that matter. All free-born men are declared equal in the eyes of the law. Even the rights of slaves are recognized and enforced by law. Only four discriminations are, however, permitted on grounds of sex: (1) A daughter gets half the share to which her brother is entitled. (2) The evidence of two women is treated as equal to the evidence of one man. (3) While the husband can divorce his wife by a unilateral act, the wife has to go to the law court for the dissolution of her marriage tie. (4) A woman is allowed no share in *vila* (heritage of a freed slave).

Some of these discriminations, however, cease to be so, when the family law of Islam is clearly understood. Marriage, according to Islamic Law, is a civil contract. The wife, at the time of her marriage, is at liberty to get the husband's right to divorce delegated to her on stated conditions, and thus secure equality of divorce with her husband. From the inequality of shares in the property it should not be inferred that the rule assumes the superiority of males over females. The Quran clearly declares:

41. Ibid, p. 437.
42. Ibid.
43. Ibid, p. 440.
44. Ibid.
45. Ibid, p. 427.
46. Ibid, p. 441.

Men shall have a portion of what their parents and their near relatives leave; and women shall have a portion of what their parents and their near relatives leave.[47]

The share of the daughter is lesser not on account of any inferiority inherent in her, but in view of her better economic position (the dower money; the husband's responsibility to maintain his wife, and her consequent economic freedom).

In criminal law also—unlike the Romans—no distinction of any sort was made between one man and another, not even on grounds of religion. The Caliph 'Ali is reported to have declared: "The blood of the *zimmi* is like the blood of the Muslim."[48]

SLAVERY

Slavery is one of the most important institutions of the Middle Ages and the attitude of the different legal systems towards it deserves to be noted.

According to the Roman Law, a slave was a *res* or chattel without legal or property rights.[49] He could be killed or tortured at his master's caprice; he could own no property, nor could he be regarded as capable of entering into any contract.[50] He had no *locus standi* in a court of law. His master was responsible for him as he was for any domestic animal he kept.[51] Manumitted slaves retained traces of their former servile condition. A long and complicated procedure was prescribed for manumission. The property of an informally emancipated slave passed to his former master as a slave's *peculium*.[52] The freed man continued to be under the limited control of his former master or his children. "A patron could claim respect (*obsequim*), services and succession to some or all of his property at death if he had no children as heirs."[53] If guilty of insolence or ingratitude he was remanded to his patron's power.

The serfs, though free in some respects, were no better than slaves. They and their descendants were inseparably attached to the soil. They were part of its permanent stock. If a serf left the estate, he could be reclaimed by

---

47. Quran, S. IV: 7.
48. Amir Ali, *The Spirit of Islam* (London, 1931), p. 268.

'Umar, the Great, instructed his governors: "Treat all men justly and on equal footing when they appear before you in the court.' Shibli, *al-Faruq* (Kanpur, 1889), II, p. 49.

49. *Cambridge Medieval History*, Vol. II, p. 62. *Roman Private Law*, p. 60.
50. *Roman Private Law*, p. 60.
51. *Cambridge Medieval History*, Vol. II, p. 63.
52. Ibid. Vol. II, p. 63.
53. Ibid, p. 64.

his master as if he was a runaway slave. If he married a free-woman he was liable by statute to be kept in chains and flogged on that score. He could sell the surplus produce of his farm, and his savings, called his *peculium,* were in a way his property and inalienable for all practical purposes. If he died childless, his property passed to his lord. A serf could not sue his lord in the law court except when the lord attempted to increase the rent.[54] Thus it was difficult for a serf to improve his status.[55]

Slavery was tolerated by Islam because it was so interwoven with the economic system of the Middle Ages that it was not possible to dispense with it completely. Nevertheless, its character was changed and the ground was prepared for its eventual abolition from human society. The Prophet told his followers that there was no act more commendable in the eyes of God than liberating a slave. He prescribed the manumission of slaves as an act of atonement for certain acts of omission and commission. He ordered that slaves be allowed to purchase their liberty by the wages earned by them. In case that was not possible, money could be advanced to the slaves from the public treasury to purchase their liberty. Of the eight recognized items of expenditure of *zakat* money, one is, therefore, set apart for getting slaves freed. In Islam, slavery was an accident and not a constitution of nature.[56]

CONTEMPORARY RELIGIONS

From the point of view of strict theological dogma, Christianity had lost its earlier vitality. Disquisitions about the Trinity and the Incarnation had not only destroyed the purity of the faith but had also rendered it grossly incomprehensible.[57] Richard Bell says: "In place of the abstruse speculations as to the nature of God and the relation of the Divine to the human with which the attention of the Church had been so largely taken up in its Trinitarian and Christological controversies, Islam harked back to the idea of a God of power and of moral will."[58]

Dogmas apart, the organization of the Church had seriously suffered on account of its abject compromise with the ruling classes. It had, in fact,

54. Ibid, p. 65.
55. Ibid. p. 66.
56. *Spirit of Islam*, p. 264.
57. From the beginning of the fourth century the Church was disturbed by doctrinal disputes. The relation of the divine and the human in Jesus had become the subject of great controversies. "In the mazes of these intellectual and philosophical problems the Eastern Church lost itself": Richard Bell, *The Origin of Islam in its Christian Atmosphere* (London, 1926), p. 2.
58. Ibid, p. 183.

become an instrument for the exploitation of the weak. The 'Kingdom of Heaven' was promised to those who tamely submitted to the tyranny of the State. Oertel rightly observes that the support of the Church gave to the Empire "a religious veneer and stamped subjection as resignation to the will of God."[59]

The growth of the monastic institution, which was essentially parasitic in character, further led to disastrous social and economic consequences.[60] "From one point of view," remarks Bell, "the triumph of Islam in the East in the 7th century AD may be regarded as the judgement of history upon a degenerate Christianity."[61]

Zoroastrianism suffered from equally grave abuses. It was the State religion of Sassanid Persia. The Zoroastrian priests controlled and regulated the life of the individual from cradle to grave and played a very vital role in politics.[62] They controlled not only the educational system but also the judicial administration.[63] The priests helped the State in maintaining social distinctions. Barthold remarks, "The obsolete social hierarchy was sanctified by the religion. Only three classes, the clergy, the military aristocracy and the landowners were taken into consideration: the fourth class of merchants and manufacturers had no privileges, such as were accorded exclusively to the above mentioned classes. The incompatibility of such an organization with the claims of real life was one of the reasons of such frequent rebellions against the imperial power and of so many cases of apostasy from the State-religion."[64]

ECONOMIC CONDITION

The Romans had pursued with great zeal, both in the East and the West, a policy of developing city life. This process of urbanization divided society into two groups—the rulers and the ruled, the privileged bourgeoisie and the working classes, the landowners and the peasants, the businessmen and

---

59. *Cambridge Ancient History*, Vol. XII, p. 270.

60. The priesthood joined with the State in the exploitation of the weaker people by impressing upon them the fact that obedience to the State was a religious duty and that reward awaited the patient sufferers. Movements which appeared as a revolt against this exploitation by the Church and the State—like the movement of the Monophysites—were crushed ruthlessly. J.B. Bury, *History of the Later Roman Empire* (London, 1923), Vol. II, Chapter XXII, pp. 361–72.

61. *Origin of Islam in its Christian Atmosphere*, p. 1.

62. *L'Iran sous les Sassanides*, p. 151.

63. Ibid, p. 157.

64. Barthold, *Iran* (Eng. trans., G.K. Nariman; Bombay), p. 38.

the slaves. As the number of cities increased, the gulf between the two classes became wider. Every increase in the number of the privileged classes meant heavier work for the unprivileged. This division of the population into two classes, which in course of time crystallized into two castes, was not felt so long as the empire was expanding. But when the process of expansion came to an end, "the existence of two castes, one ever more oppressed, the other ever more idle and indulging in the easy life of men of means, lay like an incubus on the Empire and arrested economic progress."[65] Discontent naturally grew apace. At the time of the advent of Islam, the unprivileged classes were resentful of the position to which they had been reduced. Forced labour and involuntary servitude weighed heavily on them.

Equally distressing were the conditions in Sassanid Persia. The peasants were subjected to forced labour[66] and the artisans and craftsmen were hated on religious grounds.[67]

ECONOMIC ASPECT OF THE ISLAMIC REVOLUTION

Islam revolutionized the lives of the people in the Middle Ages by discouraging involuntary and slave labour and substituting it by free labour. The Prophet firmly opposed the practice of putting a labourer to work without settling beforehand his wages or the terms of his labour.[68] He exhorted his people to "pay the labourer's wages before his sweat has dried."[69]

Now, slave labour means a restricted internal market, lack of incentive for the worker, stagnation of economic relations, and technological retardation. By substituting free labour for slave labour, Islam opened up enormous possibilities for the development of technology and progress in art and industry.

The position of workers underwent a great change in Islamic lands. In the Roman world as well as in all other lands of ancient civilization, the ruling classes hated all productive labour and looked upon industry and trade as highly undignified. Plato pictures a Utopian community in his *Republic* and divides it into three sharply differentiated classes, endowing

65. M. Rostovtzeff, *The Social and Economic History of the Roman Empire* Oxford, 1957, vol. 1, p. 380.

66. *L'Iran sous les Sassanides*, p. 424.

67. As the Zoroastrians worshipped the elements of nature, they did not like anybody to mix dirt in water and prepare pots. They did not even like to wash hands and feet with it. Ibid, p. 189.

68–69. Baihaqi, *Sunan al-Kubra*, Chapter on *Ijara*, pp. 12–73. See also Bukhari's Chapter on *Ijara*.

each with some imaginary "metallic" quality—such as Guardians with a golden cast of mind to govern; auxiliaries with an admixture of silver to fight; and finally, workers sharing in the base metals to do the work of society and obey. Aristotle writes: "The best form of State will not admit them (the artisans) to citizenship."[70] He, therefore, advises people: "certainly the good man ... and the good citizen ought not to learn the crafts of the inferiors except for their own occasional use; if they habitually practise them, there will cease to be distinction between master and slave."[71]

The Prophet of Islam declared that those who earned their bread with the sweat of their brow were loved by God (الكاسب حبيب الله) and unequivocally condemned the parasites. Medina, under him, became a working class republic in which the enslaved and the much despised worker were enfranchised and elevated. It provided a unique incentive to the workers and the artisans set out to improve the techniques of their trades and develop their industries. Production increased and the need for larger and better markets was felt. The entire Islamic world was now one huge market for the merchants. The taxes were lighter and there was more security of life and property in Islamic lands than in the Roman or the Sassanid realms.

The northern routes of trade with China, which passed through Constantinople to Italy and other countries of western Europe, had become extremely risky and unsafe owing to the Scythian inroads and the ruinous fiscal policy of the Byzantine Empire. After their conquest of Syria, Mesopotamia, Persia, and the territories across the Oxus, the Arabs captured the Chinese trade and diverted it to pass through their territories in North Africa and Spain, which connected it with the markets of western Europe.

Between the eighth and the eleventh centuries the entire trade between India and China, on the one hand, and Europe, on the other, was in the hands of the Arabs. The enfranchisement of the workers and the artisans was ultimately responsible for this feverish economic activity all over the Islamic world.

URBAN CHARACTER OF THE ISLAMIC REVOLUTION

The fact also deserves to be noted that the Islamic revolution was essentially urban in character. To say that Islam was planned exclusively as a

---

70. *Politics*, III, p. 31278 as quoted by F.W. Walbank, *The Decline of the Roman Empire in the West*, p. 24.

71. As cited in Ibid, p. 25.

Cicero considered trading and manual work as *base, menial, contemptible, degrading.*

city creed would be incorrect. Nevertheless, there is no denying the fact that it unfolded itself in urban environments. It was only in the cities that institutions such as the Friday mosque, the school, and the *khanqah*—by which the faith gained solidarity and oneness—could flourish. The Quranic laws about family, inheritance, etc., could only be enforced in the cities. There is much truth in Von Grunebaum's remark: "The legislation of the Quran envisages city life."[72] The nomad Bedouins could not possibly be the woof and warp of Islamic society.[73]

A stable social life was possible in the cities alone and it is not for nothing that in Arabic the same root word is used for 'city' and 'civilization' (*tamaddun madanivat*).[74] Besides, Muslim historians have named, and probably not unconsciously, most of the states after their capitals—e.g. the Caliphate of Baghdad, the Sultanate of Delhi, etc.

72. Von Grunebaum, *Medieval Islam* (Chicago, 1946), p. 173.

73. The Quran views the nomad Bedouins with distrust and says of them that they are '*strong in unbelief and in hypocrisy and more apt not to know the limits of what Allah hath sent down to his Messenger*'. (9: 98)

Ibn-i Khaldun praises the military virtues of the Bedouins, but declares that no state can achieve continuity on desert life. The lack of restraint and discipline that go with nomadism are hostile to progress of any sort. The Bedouin will oppress the settled people to such a degree as to ruin them economically, break up their social order, and bring about the fall of civilization. Ibn-i Khaldun therefore says that stable political forces must centre on cities. See *Muqaddimah* (Urdu trans., Lahore, 1904), Vol. I, pp. 178–97.

74. *Introduction* to Elliot and Dowson's *History of India* (revised edn, Aligarh, 1952), Vol. II, pp. 4–5.

THE POLITICAL STRUCTURE OF ISLAM

The Battle of Badr (624 AD) marks the turning point in the history of Islam. "Hitherto it had been a religion within a state; in al-Madinah, after Badr, it passed into something more than a state-religion—it itself became the state."[1] The history of the political structure of Islam, its system of government, laws, and institutions virtually starts from that date.

The Prophet's political task was by no means easy. The Arabian society was at a primitive communistic level. The tribes were held together externally by the need for self-defence and internally by the blood tie of descent. They were obliged to work in common if they preferred not to die of starvation or fall victim to beasts of prey. Labour in common thus led to their joint ownership of the means of production as also the fruits of their productive efforts.

Out of this crude society the Prophet evolved the political structure of Islam and established a working class republic in Medina based on the two revolutionary concepts already explained in the preceding section. Dr Muhammad Iqbal writes: "The essence of Tauhid as a working idea, is equality, solidarity and freedom. The state, from the Islamic standpoint, is an endeavour to transform these principles into space-time forces, an aspiration to realize them in definite human organization."[2] The republic of Medina translated those principles into practice. All matters were decided after open deliberations and free consultations in which everyone, irrespective of his status, could participate. In these councils the Prophet's word had no decisive power, except when he spoke on Divine Authority. There was no governing class then and no subject people. All kinds of discriminations were eliminated. Faith replaced blood as the social bond and the tribe—the dominating feature of Arab heathenism—gave way to the newly born sense of religious unity. On being asked about his family, Salman al-Farisi, a companion of the Prophet, replied: "*Salman bin*

---

1. P.K. Hitti, *History of the Arabs* (London, 1951), p. 117. See also W.M. Watt, *Muhammad at Medina* (Oxford, 1956), Chapter VII, pp. 221–60.

2. *Reconstruction of Religious Thought in Islam*, p. 154.

Islam."[3] Nothing illustrates better the spirit of the new republic than this reply of Salman.

Jointly with his band of devoted followers, the Prophet built up, during the last ten years of his life, a state with its own system of government, laws, and institutions, centred in Medina and firmly controlling the Hejaz, parts of the Nejd, and exercising loose authority over other parts of Arabia.

When the Prophet died (632 AD), the Mussalmans found themselves face to face with a difficult problem. The Prophet had given no directions about the choice of his successor. The Quran was silent about this beyond making two broad observations—"Decide your matters by consultation"[4] and "Obey God, obey the Prophet and obey those with authority amongst you."[5] Acting upon these broad directions and guided, of course, by the tribal traditions, the Quresh of Medina elected Abu Bakr as their Khalifah.[6] Abu Bakr (ob. 634 AD) nominated 'Umar, as his successor, while 'Umar, in his turn, entrusted the task to a tribunal of six and 'Usman was selected by them. A tendency towards narrowing down the number of electors was, thus, gradually taking shape. This was, to a large extent, due to the circumstances. Abu Bakr had to face many centrifugal tendencies in the religious as well as the political sphere. Soon after the death of the Prophet, a number of Arabian tribes shook off their allegiance to Islam and went back to their ancestral beliefs; some of them refused to pay the *zakat* and very soon false prophets appeared. In order to preserve the structure of Islam from dissolution at the hands of these fissiparous tendencies, it was necessary to nominate a successor and avoid a contest for the *khilafat*. During the time of 'Umar, the realms of Islam consisted of various linguistic areas divided into racial groups with conflicting traditions. How was the vast multitude of people, inside and outside Arabia, to elect a Khalifah? The early traditions could work well in a city-state, but they could not be applied to a territorial state where medieval conditions of transport and communication rendered it impossible to hold an election on a large scale. 'Umar therefore entrusted the task of nominating his successor to an electoral college. This was a device to harmonize the spirit of Islam with the exigencies of the time, and the requirements of the age. Whatever the

3. Maulana Abul Kalam Azad, *Tazkirah*, p. 25.

For Salman, see G. Levi Della Vida's article in the *Encyclopaedia of Islam*, Vol. IV, pp. 116–17.

4. Quran, S. III: 159.

5. Quran, S. IV: 59.

6. For a detailed study of the circumstances in which the institution of *Khilafat* was born and its role in the political life of the Mussalmans in subsequent centuries, see *Izalat-u'l-Khifa* by Shah Waliullah of Delhi. Among modern works Arnold's *Caliphate* (Oxford, 1914) and Maulana Abul Kalam Azad's *Masa'la-i-Khilafat-aur-Jazirah-i-'Arab* supply valuable information on the subject. See also

difficulties, the semblance of election was retained all through, and after selecting a Khalifah, the people were required to endorse the selection by making *bay'a* at his hands or that of governors appointed by him.

The Caliph 'Umar was, rightly observes Amir Ali, the practical founder of the political administration of Islam.[7] He was anxious to see the city-state of Medina develop into a universal state on purely Islamic lines. But as soon as a city-state develops into a universal state, the rise of an aristocracy becomes rather inevitable. 'Umar adopted some very bold measures to prevent it. It was, no doubt, a revolutionary task in the context of the tendencies rife in the Middle Ages. His political wisdom soon discovered that such an aristocracy could arise either from the Quresh tribe (the Hashimites and the Umayyads) or from the military leaders or from the governors of various provinces. His attitude towards them was determined by his desire to prevent them from developing into a permanent governing class. He did not allow the Arabs to occupy the conquered lands,[8] for it might lead to the rise of a feudal aristocracy.[9] He excluded the Hashimites from appointment to government offices, for it would have made them immensely rich and powerful.[10] He kept strict control over provincial governors and never allowed them to amass wealth. Every governor had to submit a list of his property before taking charge of his office, and his property was checked against this list on his retirement.[11] The governors were called to Mecca every year at the time of Hajj and complaints were heard against them.[12] No governor was allowed to remain at one place for a long period.[13] His dealings with Amir Mu'awiyah, 'Amr bin al-'As, and Mughira bin Shu'ba—the three talented persons about whom he thought they would consolidate their power and develop aristocratic ways—illustrate his attitude to such high-placed officers. He used their talent but never allowed them any opportunity to grow powerful.[14] Khalid, the talented general whose exploits

---

S.M. Yusuf's article: 'The Choice of a Caliph in Islam—A Study in Early Conventions', (*Islamic Culture*, October, 1943, pp. 378–96).

7. *Short History of the Saracens* (London, 1927), p. 60.

8. *Al-Faruq*, Vol. II, pp. 41, et seq.

9. The annulment of this order during the *khilafat* of 'Usman was, therefore, naturally followed by the rise of a feudal aristocracy.

10. *Al-Faruq*, Vol. II, p. 194.

11. Ibid, p. 31.

12. Ibid, pp. 32–37.

13. Ibid, p. 186. The activities of the governors were closely watched and reported by Muhammad b. Maslama al-Ansari, who was a man of great honesty and integrity of character. (Ibid, p. 34.)

14. Ibid, p. 186.

were universally applauded, was dismissed by him when at the height of his glory, and 'Umar wrote to all districts:

> I have not dismissed Khalid on account of any displeasure or any charge of malversation; he has been removed because people are getting attracted towards him; lest they place confidence in him.[15]

Besides, 'Umar placed an interdict on Arabs being made slaves. This step also went a long way in checking the growth of a ruling class.

"It is doubtful," observes Von Kremer, "whether 'Umar could have long kept this system of government intact. Had all the Arabs been as unselfish as he, had all been fired by the same religious fervour as he, he might possibly have succeeded. But he did not reckon with one of the most powerful springs of human action—personal interest."[16]

Caliph 'Usman who succeeded 'Umar was a weak and mild man. He belonged to the Umayyad branch of the Quresh tribe—a group that hungered after power. During his *khilafat* the rise of an aristocracy could not be long prevented. The Umayyads migrated to the provinces, consolidated their power there, and carved out estates for themselves. Mu'awiyah, the governor of Syria, wrote to the Caliph to grant him unappropriated lands in Syria and the Caliph consented. Thus the seed for the rise of a feudal aristocracy was sown.[17]

With the murder of 'Usman, a civil war became unavoidable. 'Usman's mildness had excited the cupidity of all factions and groups and every one was anxious to establish his own hegemony. The issue as to which tribe would constitute the ruling class in future had to be decided and a civil war alone could decide it. Three persons swore to kill at one time 'Ali at Kufa, Mu'awiyah at Damascus, and Amr bin al-'As at the old Cairo. Of them only 'Ali was fatally wounded.

The 'Alids were defeated in the struggle. Finding the outer world in the hands of their rivals, with whom they could never compromise on account of their firm faith in 'legitimacy', and failing to establish in the external, tangible world their political supremacy, they elaborated an inner order of spiritual succession and developed quaint theories about *Imamat*, the spiritual authority of the Imam, his secret succession, and finally the emergence of a Mehdi who would deliver and set all things aright. Though the Fatimids and the Imams of Alamut appeared long afterwards, intellectually the ground was prepared for the same in the first century of Islam.

15. Tabari, as cited in ibid, Vol. II, p. 187.

16. *Politics in Islam* (2nd edn, Lahore, 1948), p. 26.

17. Talha had purchased the estate of Nashtasag in Kufa during the time of 'Umar. 'Umar annulled the transaction, but 'Usman sanctioned it.

The Mussalmans accepted the Umayyad rule. For what else could they do? Some sort of government was essential to preserve the new community. The civil wars had already sapped the solidarity of the Muslims and further dissensions would have spelled ruin to the Muslim social and political life.

With the rise of the Umayyads, the political spirit of Islam underwent a radical change. Amir Mu'awiyah changed the *khilafat* into a monarchy.[18] He nominated his son, Yazid, as his successor. It then became a convention among the caliphs, as amongst the sultans later, to nominate their successor and have his nomination accepted by the leading officers of the state.

Amir Mu'awiyah organized the Umayyads into a governing class. 'Umar's life work was undone. But with the developments that were taking place in the political life of the Mussalmans, it had become almost inevitable. An empire without an aristocracy or a governing class was an anomaly in the medieval context of things.

During the time of Walid (705–15 AD) this Arab aristocracy fully benefited from the wars that were being continuously waged. The Umayyads appropriated big estates and converted them from *kharaji* to *'ushri* lands. This meant great loss to the exchequer. In the interest of the governing class the practice had to be continued and the financial requirements met by further exploiting the non-Arabs. Taxes not sanctioned by Islam were imposed upon the people.[19] The fact that many complaints of forceful possession by the strong were brought before 'Umar bin 'Abdul 'Aziz shows that the process of acquiring land was not fair in all cases. 'Umar II himself declared that more than half the wealth was in the hands of Banu Marwan and that most of it was acquired through means not permitted by the *Shari'at*.

When these lands were exhausted, Abdul Malik and Walid permitted the Mussalmans to purchase lands from the subject races. The purchase money went into the treasury in payment of the arrears of the land tax. The land tax henceforward disappeared and in its place *'ushr* was substituted. The Umayyad aristocracy was now a full-fledged exploiting class. The vast non-Arab population deeply resented this state of affairs.

The discontent against this attitude of the Umayyads was expressed in the Qadarite metaphysics, in the Kharajite[20] revolts, and in the Mawali

---

18. Sai'id ibn Mus'ayab said: "May God retaliate upon Mu'awiyah for he was the first who converted this thing (the rule over the faithful) into a *mulk*." Khuda Bakhsh, *Essays: Indian and Islamic* (London, 1912), p. 29.

19. For details about the taxation system at this time, see *Islamic Taxation in the Classic Period* by Frede Lokkegard (Copenhagen, 1950).

20. For Qadarites and Kharajites, see *infra*, Section IV.

agitation. Discussing the significance of the Kharajite revolts, Hurgronje observes: "Their anarchistic revolutions, which during more than a century occasionally gave much trouble to the *khilafat* caused Islam to accentuate the aristocratic character of its monarchy."[21]

The Umayyad Empire fell when it had exhausted all possibilities of further exploitation. Racial discriminations, class interests, aristocratic ways, and luxurious tastes weakened the moral basis of the Umayyad dynasty which disappeared in the terrible blood-bath of 750 AD.

With the advent of the Abbasids, the era of expansion came to an end and the age of the consolidation of realms and the integration of ideas began. While the Umayyad Empire was essentially an Arab empire, the Abbasid Caliphate was an empire of the non-Arabs in which the Arabs were only one of the many component races. This was the source of their strength as well as their weakness. So long as these elements worked harmoniously everything went on well. The moment tribal instincts, racial considerations, or local jealousies gained an upper hand, the Abbasid polity began to disintegrate and decompose. It was the Persianized Arab culture which had held these elements together but once that cultural hold was weakened, the parts fell apart.

Under the early Abbasids, the Persians—of whom the Barmakids are a typical illustration—constituted the governing class. With changes in political conditions this governing class was later replaced by the Turks who monopolized all political power and laid the foundations of the Turko-Persian empires, which played a very important part in the history of medieval 'Ajam.

The Abbasid Caliphs ruled over a vast empire extending from the shores of the eastern Mediterranean to the frontiers of China, but the Caliphate was not coterminous with Islam. Political unity, which was the deepest longing of Muslim political consciousness, was utterly destroyed.[22] Spain, North Africa, Uman, and Sind did not acknowledge the Abbasid Caliphs.

21. *Mohammedanism* (Lectures on its origin, its religious and political growth and its present state) by G. Snouckc Hurgronje (London, 1916), p. 99.

22. In 755–56 AD a member of the Umayyad dynasty made himself independent master of Spain. In 788–89 a descendant of 'Ali, named Idris, established a dynasty in Morocco which lasted till 975. About the same time Ibrahim b. Aghlab became independent in Tunis. Egypt was lost to the empire in 868 when Ahmad b. Tulun, the governor, cast off the yoke of the Abbasids. The Tulunids were supplanted about 935 by the Ikhshids and the Ikhshids were succeeded in 969 by the Fatimids, who had established their power in North Africa in the middle of the third century AH.

Within the Abbasid Caliphate, however, the provinces formed a more or less loose confederation. The central authority dealt with them not through departmental ministries, but every province had its own board (*diwan*) in Baghdad which managed its affairs.

The great Abbasid Caliphs from Mansur to Mutawakkil (754–861 AD) were endowed with great administrative capacity. They ruled over an extensive empire with great tact, courage, and firmness. After them disintegration set in. The tribes which had constituted the Muslim soldiery settled in the luxurious estates, and city life developed rapidly. The army became indifferent to active life. The military spirit of the Arabs (both in town and country) almost disappeared. Foreign mercenaries were consequently recruited in large numbers. At the beginning of the tenth century, a general considered troops coming from Baghdad as unfit for a strenuous campaign on the ground that "they were accustomed to houses on the Tigris, to wine, to ice, to wet felt and female musicians."[23]

With the decay of the Arab national life, the forces of social and moral disintegration gathered momentum. Exploitation and overtaxation became rampant.[24] Heavy taxation drove the merchants out of Baghdad.[25] Discontent grew apace. Baghdad was reduced to such a position that in 942 AD Ibn Hamdi, the chief of a robber band, plundered the town under the protection of Ibn Shirzad, who, as secretary to the Turkish commander-in-chief, stood at the head of the government.[26] The government itself, in its eagerness to remove discontent, resorted to methods that were strange and incredible. In 972 AD a large conflagration—caused by the connivance of the government itself—reduced 300 shops and 33 mosques to ashes and played havoc with 17,000 lives. Insecurity increased to such an extent that robbers climbed into the house of a *qadi* in broad daylight. The result was that during the tenth century many minor dynasties rose in 'Ajam. These states formally acknowledged the Caliph, but were, for all practical purposes, independent in their own kingdoms and carried on government without any reference to the Caliph.

The most important of these dynasties were the following:

1. The Tahirids (820–872)
2. The Saffarids (863–903)
3. The Samanids (874–999)
4. The Buwayhids (945–1055)

23. Adam Mez, *The Renaissance of Islam* (London, 1937), pp. 380–81.
24. Hitti, *History of the Arabs*, p. 484.
25. *Renaissance of Islam*, pp. 6–7.
26. Ibid.

These minor dynasties developed their own political institutions and ideas and gave to 'Ajam what it needed most, a stable government which could guarantee peace and encourage trade and industries. Then appeared the Turko-Persian empires—the Ghaznavid Empire (999–1040), the Seljuq Empire (1037–1157), and the Khwarizmian Empire (1157–1231). The role of these dynasties can be appreciated only if the general economic condition of 'Ajam is borne in mind.

Apart from Fars[27] and the South Caspian provinces, the vast area of 'Ajam is useless for agriculture. There is no rainfall and agriculture depends on artificial irrigation.[28] So far as the Turkish lands were concerned, there were a number of rivers—Marwarud, Oxus, Jaxartes, Zarafshan, etc. These rivers were the source of an extensive canal system.[29] Where water was available, soil being fertile, agriculture flourished, but where there was no water, the Turkish tribes wandered over the steppe, grazing their flocks of sheep and goats on the sparse vegetation. A large part of 'Ajam's population lived by cattle-breeding. Agriculture as an art was unknown.[30]

The minor dynasties as well as the Turko-Persian empires made extensive trade possible by enfranchising the city labourer and establishing security of the roads. The Seljuqian Empire's great achievement in the eyes of Ibn-i-Khallikan was: "all the roads were safe—safe for travellers and caravans—from Transoxiana to Syria."[31] These peaceful conditions led to amazing economic development. Trade reacted on industries and the great cities of 'Ajam once again thrived and prospered. These new states had the full support of the working classes. The trader wanted peace and security and in return for it he placed the surplus value at the disposal of the builders of these states.

The Tahirid dynasty was founded by Tahir bin Husain of Khurasan, a trusted general of Ma'mun (813–33), and a descendant of a Persian slave. The Tahirids remained, on the whole, loyal supporters of the Abbasid Caliphate.[32] They enjoyed peacefully the government of the richest province of the Caliphate and regularly paid tribute to the central government. The Tahirids were anxious to act according to the Islamic laws.[33] 'Abdullah

27. *Hudud al-'Alam*, p. 126.

28. Barthold, *Iran*, p. 51.

29. Barthold has made a masterly study of this aspect of Turkish history in his Russian work: *Notes on the History of Irrigation in Turkistan*.

30. See Professor Habib's *Introduction* to Elliot and Dowson's *History of India*, Vol. II, pp. 16–17.

31. *Ibn-i-Khallikan*, Vol. II, p. 587.

32. Amir Hasan, *Caliphate and Kingship in Medieval Persia*, p. 22.

33. 'Abdullah asked the jurists of Khurasan to work out, in collaboration with some *faqihs* from Iraq, the legal principles regarding the use of water. The 'Book

bin Tahir protected the interests of the peasants[34] and introduced free universal education.[35] Barthold rightly calls the epoch of the Tahirids the epoch of "enlightened absolutism".[36] In 872 AD the Tahirids were superseded by the Saffarids.

The Saffarid dynasty, which reigned in Persia for 41 years, was founded by Ya'qub bin Lais al-Saffar, a coppersmith by profession. He based his rights on the sword alone and consolidated his power and prestige with the help of a strong army. But he remained throughout his life a soldier of simple tastes and decided all matters personally. The Saffarids were the first in Persia to challenge the political supremacy of the Abbasids and reduce their temporal power to the minimum. Their names were included in the *Khutbah* and inscribed on the coins, while they did not pay regular tribute to Baghdad. The Samanids fell heir to a large portion of the Saffarid state.

The Samanid dynasty, founded by Nasr bin Ahmad, great-grandson of Saman, a Zoroastrian noble of Balkh, effected the final subjugation of Transoxiana to Muslim rule. It is considered "one of the most enlightened of the Iranian dynasties."[37] As most of the institutions of the Samanids were borrowed by the Ghaznavids and from them by the Ghurids and the Sultans of Delhi, their history deserves to be noticed in some detail.

The Samanids formed a powerful state in Transoxiana and carried on a determined struggle against the nomad tribes which continued to attack the fertile oases and towns of Central Asia. The establishment of peace led to considerable economic development. Maqdisi has given us a list of the exports of Transoxiana which shows that under the Samanids, Tirmiz, Bukhara, Karminiya, Rabinjan, Khorezmia, Bulghar, Samarqand, Dizak, Banakath, Shash, Farghana, and Isfijab were important centres of trade. Soap, saddles, tents, hides, coloured fabrics, etc. were exported from these places. Silk and cotton fabrics of the valley of Zarafshan and the metal articles of Farghana were reputed throughout the Muslim world. Paper manufactured in Samarqand replaced papyrus and parchment in Muslim

---

of Canals' (*Kitab al-Quniy*) was the result of his efforts in that direction (Barthold, *Turkistan down to the Mongol Invasion* (trans., H.A.R. Gibb, London, 1928), p. 213.

34. He wrote to the officers: 'God feeds us by their hands, welcomes us through their mouths and forbids their ill treatment.' Ibid, p. 213.

35. He said: 'Knowledge must be accessible to the worthy and unworthy; knowledge will look after itself and not remain with the unworthy.' Ibid.

36. Barthold, *Four Studies on the History of Central Asia* (trans., S.V. and T. Minovsky, Vol. I, Leyden, 1956), p. 70.

37. Hitti, *History of the Arabs*, p. 463.

countries.[38] There were no burdensome taxes, a fact which greatly encouraged industry.[39] Favourable economic conditions enhanced the cultural glory of the Samanids and Bukhara and Samarqand soon eclipsed Baghdad as centres of learning and art.

The Samanid administrative system was highly efficient and extremely well organized. The Samanid ruler was an enlightened despot, but he was answerable to God alone. In the eyes of the Baghdad government he was an Amir or client of the Khalifah, but, actually, he was free of all control. The Samanids, however, remained loyal to the authority of the Caliphate and did not oppose it even when their own rights were infringed.[40]

What strengthened the hand and the position of the Samanid kings was their slave household. It served as the "most effective social and military instrument for the maintenance of their authority".[41] The Turkish slaves of the Samanids were put through a long and minutely graded probation. Nizam-ul Mulk thus describes the career of a Turkish slave at the Samanid court:

> They advanced slaves gradually, taking account of their services, their courage and their merit. Thus a slave who had just been purchased served one year on foot. Clothed in a cotton tunic he walked beside the stirrup of his chief; they did not have him mount on horseback either in public or in private and he would be punished if it were learnt that he had done so. When his first year of service was ended the head of the Chamber informed the Chamberlain and the latter gave the slave a Turkish horse which had only a rope in its mouth, a bridle and a halter in one. When he had served one year on horseback, whip in hand he was given a leather girth to put about the horse. The fifth year they gave him a better saddle, a bridle ornamented with stars, a tunic of cotton mixed with silk and a mace which he suspended by a ring from his saddle bow. In the sixth year he received a garment of a more splendid colour and in his seventh year they gave him a tent held up by a pole and fixed by sixteen pegs; he had three slaves in his suite and he was honoured with the title of a head of the Chamber; he wore on his head a hat of black felt embroidered with silver and he was clothed with a silk robe. Every year he was advanced in place and dignity, his retinue and escort were increased until the time when he reached the rank of chief of squadron and finally that of a Chamberlain. Though his capacity and merit might be recognised, though he had done some noteworthy deed and acquired universal esteem and

38. *Turkestan*, p. 237.
39. Ibid, p. 238.
40. *Caliphate and Kingship in Medieval Persia*, p. 45.
41. S.A. Rashid, "The Imperial Slave Household" (*Islamic Literature*, February, 1950).

the affection of his sovereign, he was obliged nevertheless to wait until the age of thirty-five years before obtaining the title of Amir and a government.[42]

At the head of the whole court establishment was the *Hajib-i-Buzurg*. The second office of importance was that of the *Amir-i-Haras* (captain of the watch). All the offices of the *dargah* (palace) were assigned to the Turkish slaves. Sometimes even governorships were conferred upon Turkish slaves as a reward for meritorious services.

The following were the ten principal government offices at Bukhara:

1. Diwan of the Wazir
2. Diwan of the Mustaufi
3. Diwan-i-'Amid-ul Mulk
4. Diwan-i-Sahibri Shurat
5. Diwan-i-Mushrif
6. Diwan-i-Sahib-i Barid
7. Diwan of the private domains of the ruler
8. Diwan of the Muhtasib
9. Diwan of the Awqaf
10. Diwan of the *Qazi*

The wazir, called the *Khwajah-i-Buzurg*, stood at the head of the whole bureaucratic machinery. Nizam-ul-Mulk considered it desirable to have a hereditary wazir. During the Samanid period we come across dynasties of wazirs, such as the *Jayhani*, *Bal'ami*, and *'Utbi*, though there is no evidence that the son ever succeeded his father in this office of distinction. The chief *qazi* headed the judicial administration. In the provinces we find the same offices and departments as obtained in the capital. Under the Samanids and the Ghaznavids provincial officers were appointed by the sovereign himself. But later, as the power of the bureaucracy increased, the heads of the several departments came to appoint their substitutes in the provincial towns themselves.

Nizam-ul-Mulk informs us that the Samanids and the Ghaznavids paid their officials in cash and did not usually distribute *iqta's* to the army.[43]

---

42. *Siyasat Namah*, pp. 74–75.
43. Ibn-i Khallikan and Gardizi have preserved for us an account of the distribution of pay to the army under the Saffarid ruler, Amr. The *'Ariz* who distributed the pay took his seat in a place appointed for the ceremony, and on hearing the sound of large drums the whole army assembled there. In front of the *'Ariz* lay sacks of money; the *'Ariz*'s assistant had before him a list of the soldiers and read over the names. The first called was Amr himself; the *'Ariz* made a close inspection of his horse and equipment, then expressed his approval and gave him

This system "gave a better guarantee against illegal requisitions than did the system of military fiefs subsequently established".[44]

Disgruntled educated proletariat (i.e., the representatives of the numerous official class who had failed to gain a position in the service of the state) and the turbulent military aristocracy paved the way for the disruption of the Samanid state. The place of the Samanids was taken by the Ghaznavids.

A new epoch begins in the history of Islam with the advent of Sultan Mahmud of Ghaznin (999–1030), who is reckoned as the first *Sultan* of 'Ajam. Thereafter the Empire (or *Sultanate*) became the administrative authority of 'Ajam, while the Abbasid Caliphate continued as a formal symbol till it was extinguished by Hulagu Khan in 1258 AD. "The concept of the State," rightly observes Barthold, "was brought to its extreme expression under the Ghaznavids, and especially under Mahmud."[45]

Throwing off the yoke of his Samanid overlords, Mahmud approached the Caliph with the request to grant him the patent of sovereignty and thus accord sanction to the rise of a new dynasty. The grant of *manshur* by the Caliph in 999 AD confirmed Mahmud in his newly acquired territories and re-established, though nominally, the religious and the political supremacy of the Caliphate, which had broken down at the end of the Samanid period. Still, Mahmud never cared for the Caliph's wishes when his own interests were involved. In 1012–13 he compelled the Caliph, Al-Qadir Billah, to hand over to him some districts of Khurasan and when the latter refused, Mahmud threatened the Caliph's ambassador in these words: "Do you wish me to come to the capital of the Caliphate with a thousand elephants in order to lay it waste and bring its earth on the backs of my elephants to Ghaznin?" On another occasion, when the Caliph demanded the execution of Hasnak, he assumed a definitely defiant attitude. But Mahmud fully realized the magnitude of the Caliph's moral prestige and, in spite of his quarrels, continued to humour and placate him. In law Mahmud was the lieutenant of the Caliph.

---

300 *dirhams*. Amr placed the money in the leg of his boot and said: 'God be praised, that He Hath permitted me to serve faithfully the Commander of the Faithful, and hath made me worthy of his favours.' After this Amr took his seat on an eminence and watched horsemen and infantry in turns present themselves before the *'Ariz*, undergo the scrutiny and receive their money. Ibn-i Khallikan rightly points out the resemblance between the custom of Amr and the picture of the review of the armies of Sassanid Persia, under Khusrau Anushirvan. *Turkestan down to the Mongol Invasion*, p. 221.

44. Ibid, p. 239.

45. *Four Studies on the History of Central Asia*, p. 70.

Like his former overlords, the Samanids, Mahmud also strutted as an absolute autocrat. He was 'the Shadow of God on earth'. He had the supreme legislative, judicial, and executive authority. Though the Wazir was officially responsible for the smooth running of the government machinery, the Sultan, nevertheless, personally supervised every department of government. He kept a vigilant eye on the military commanders of his empire, and personally directed foreign policy and supervised all correspondence. High appointments were all made by him and he was not bound to consult his ministers in state affairs. When confronted with a serious problem, he sometimes summoned a council which was at best a deliberative body.

The kingdom of Ghazna, being a dependency of Bukhara in its earlier days, was administered as a part of the Samanid Empire. Sultan Mahmud continued the system of the Samanids and did not introduce any appreciable alterations. There were five *Diwans*:

1. *Diwan-i-Wazarat* (Finance Department)
2. *Diwan-i-'Arz* (War Department)
3. *Diwan-i-Risalat* (Correspondence Department)
4. *Diwan-i-Shughl-i Ishraf-i-Mamlukat* (Secret Service Department)
5. *Diwan-i-Wikalat* (Household Department)

Every appointment in the state was just a matter of *contract*.[46] Before assuming charge every officer had to enter into a covenant with his royal master.[47] The important offices in the state were not the monopoly of any particular class, but, actually, the Persians were in complete control of the civil administration of the empire. Thus a regular hierarchy of officials was established and one entering the service as a clerk could, in course of time, aspire to rise to the position of a wazir.[48]

The wazir was directly in charge of the finance department. He appointed the *'amils* for different provinces who collected the state revenue. The *Mustaufi-i-Mamalik* (Accountant General) was responsible to the wazir and kept an account of all items of income and expenditure. He exercised a general supervision over all the departments of government.

The *Wazarat* under the early Ghaznavid rulers had some significant features. The nobles and the officials suggested a panel from which the Sultan selected one. The reasons for selection and rejection were, however,

46. Muhammad Nazim, *Sultan Mahmud of Ghazna*, p. 130.
47. Ibid, p. 130, citing Baihaqi, *Tarikh-i-'Al-i-Subuktigin*, p. 326.
48. Ibid, p. 131, citing Baihaqi, *Tarikh-i-'Al-i-Subuktigin*, p. 166.

indicated.[49] "In the constitution where there was no organized public body this method of selection was probably the best one."[50] Besides, great importance was attached to the office of the wazir. Khwaja Ahmad did not accept office until the Sultan had given him in writing a letter of appointment indicating the extent of his powers and the nature of the functions he was expected to perform.[51]

The next important minister was the *'Ariz*, the head of the military department. The *'Ariz* reviewed the army, looked after the welfare of the soldiers, and kept their muster-roll.[52] In times of war he acted as the quarter-master general of the army.

The military service under the Sultan was highly organized. The Sultan was his own commander-in-chief. The next highest office under him was that of the commander of the troops of Khurasan. Besides this, every province had a commander of the local troops, who was usually a Turkoman.[53]

Every provincial army had its own *'Ariz*. Services in the army were carefully graded. The lowest officer was the *Khail-tash* (commander of ten horses). Then came *Qaid, Sarhang, Hajib*, etc. Every soldier was required to make his own commissariat arrangements.

The *Diwan-i-Risalat* was placed under the charge of a tried and trusted servant of advanced age and ripe experience. Baihaqi was considered too young for this post at the age of forty-five.[54] The *Sahib-i-Diwan-i-Risalat* wrote letters to the Caliph and the princes on behalf of the Sultan. Confidential reports were also submitted by him. The *Diwan-i-Risalat* had a numerous staff of *Dabir*s. Here also services followed gradations.

If the institutions of the Ghaznavids are studied as a whole, it would appear that they had been greatly influenced by the traditions of Baghdad and Bukhara. Almost all their chief officials, e.g., the *Mustaufi*, the

---

49. Twice the opposition of the nobles led Mahmud to dismiss his ministers. The Sultan, therefore, asked them to propose the name of a person competent to be appointed a wazir. The nobles submitted a panel of four, out of which the Sultan might select one: Abul Qasim, Abul Hasan, Ahmad, and Hasnak. Mahmud told them that the services of Abul Qasim were too valuable in the military department; Abul Hasan lacked polished manners; Ahmad was indispensable in Khwarizm; and Hasnak was too young. (See *Baihaqi*, pp. 453–54, and R.P. Tripathi, *Some Aspects of the Muslim Administration* [Allahabad, 1936], pp. 166–67.)

50. Tripathi, *Some Aspects of Muslim Administration*, p. 171.

51. *Asar-ul-'Wuzara*, as quoted in Ibid, p. 172.

52. *Baihaqi*, p. 532.

53. *Sultan Mahmud of Ghazna*, p. 141.

54. *Baihaqi*, pp. 629–808.

Mushrif, and their principal departments, such as the *Diwan-i-Mumlakat-i-Khas, Diwan-i-Muhtasib, Diwan-i-Auqaf*, and *Diwan-i-'Arz*, were borrowed from the Samanids. In the days of the early Ghaznavids these institutions and officers came to the Punjab, then a part of the Ghaznavid Empire.

Mahmud's dominions included, besides northern India in the east and the Persian Iraq in the west, all Khurasan, Tukharistan with its centre Balkh, part of Transoxiana in the north, and Sijistan in the south. But this vast empire was loosely held by mere force of arms, and as soon as the powerful hand of Sultan Mahmud was removed, the component parts began to fall away. The Khans of Turkestan, the Great Seljuqs of Persia, and the Ghurids of Afghanistan knocked this vast empire to pieces. In 1186 Shihab-u'd-din of Ghur overthrew Khusrau Malik, the last of the Ghaznavid rulers of the Punjab.

The Seljuqs, who supplanted the Ghaznavids, established an empire which extended from Kashghar to Jerusalem and from Constantinople to the Caspian Sea. This empire was built on a tribal basis. The Persian conception of the monarch as the sole ruler of the state was foreign to the early Seljuqs, who looked upon the empire as the property of the whole family.[55] Nothing illustrates better their attitude in this respect than the fact that in some cities of Khurasan the *Khutbah* was read in the name of Tughril and in others in the name of his brother, Da'ud.[56] The same attitude towards kingship was probably responsible for the abolition of the espionage system and the reduction in the position and powers of the *sahib-i-haras*.[57]

The system of military fiefs established in 1087 by Nizam-ul-Mulk, according to which grants for the first time came to be hereditary, led to the immediate establishment of semi-independent states and destroyed the compactness and solidarity of the Seljuq Empire. The separate sub-divisions attained virtual independence in different parts of the wide kingdom, while the main line—the Great Seljuqs of Persia—maintained only a nominal suzerainty down to 1157.

The Seljuq Empire at last succumbed to the attack of the Khwarizmian state. Sanjar (ob. 1157) was the last of the great Seljuqs. His early successes over Ghaznin, Samarqand, and Ghur were followed by disastrous defeats which paralysed the entire structure of the Seljuq Empire. In 1137 the Qara-Khitai Turks invaded Samarqand and obtained a decisive victory over Sanjar's vassal. Five years later Sanjar himself suffered the greatest

55. Barthold, *Turkestan*, pp. 306–07.
56. *Ibn-i Asir*, IX, pp. 327–28 as cited in ibid, p. 307.
57. Ibid, p. 306.

defeat of his life and escaped only with a few followers. The final disaster to his empire was the eruption of the Ghuzz Turks,[58] who captured him in 1153. He secured his release in 1157 but died soon after.[59]

The Khwarizmian dynasty was founded by Qutb-ud-din Muhammad, to whom the administration of the country was entrusted by Sultan Sanjar. His son and successor, Atsiz, was the real founder of Khwarizm's greatness. He was "cultured, learned, a poet and a fighter".[60] He rebelled against his overlord Sanjar, who marched to Khwarizm and put his son, Altigh, to death. Atsiz fled but submitted later. But, whenever he got an opportunity, he took to arms. His successor, Il-Arsalan (1156–72), did not like to approach the Caliph for the grant of any deed of investiture, but immediately secured it from Sultan Sanjar.[61] The last Seljuq ruler of Persia, Tughril, fell in battle against Takash (the successor of Il-Arsalan) in 1194. The Khwarizm Shah could now regard himself as the successor of the Seljuq sultans in their dominions over western Asia. The capital of Khwarizm was, in those days, one of the most splendid cities of the East. Barthold holds that the rise of Khwarizm to a first-class power was due to the development of its wide trading connections.[62] Muhammad Khwarizm Shah's (1200–20) attempt to utilize these commercial connections for his political advantage led to a war between him and Chengiz Khan, and ultimately to the fall of his empire.

Khwarizm Shah's struggle with the Ghuzz and the Qara-Khitai Turks provided an opportunity to the rulers of a small principality—Ghur—to extend their power.

The province of Ghur was bounded on its northern side by the hills of Gharjistans,[63] by the province of Herat in the west, by Garmsir and Nimruz in the south, and by Kabul and Qandhar in the east. Minhaj speaks of its five big mountain chains which the people of Ghur thought to be the loftiest in the world.[64] The roads were usually blocked by snow in the winter season.[65] These geographical features were responsible for her political and cultural isolation from the rest of the world.

---

58. The Arabic name for the Oghuz branch of the Turkish people. Their migration to Muslim territory began towards the end of the tenth century. See also W. Barthold's article on 'Ghuzz' in the *Encyclopaedia of Islam*, Vol. II, pp. 168–69.

59. For details see Barthold, *Turkestan*, p. 329, et seq.

60. *Tarikh-i Jahan Gusha*, p. 3.

61. Amir Hasan, *Caliphate and Kingship in Medieval Persia*, p. 152.

62. *Encyclopaedia of Islam*, Vol. III, p. 909, Barthold's article on *Khwarizm*.

63. 'A province amid mountains and rugged country.' *Hudud al-'Alam*, p. 110.

64. *Tabaqat-i-Nasiri*, p. 39.

65. Ibid, p. 113.

Ghur was conquered by the Arabs in the first century of Islam.[66] But it could not be retained by the Arab conquerors. Taking advantage of its geographical position, the rulers of this place often rebelled[67] and never permanently submitted to the Muslim political power. As late as the tenth century and even afterwards when all the surrounding regions were Muslim, Ghur continued to be "for the most part heathen".[68] 'Utbi says that Mahmud waged war against the Ghurids because their infidelity and insolence in levying heavy imposts on caravans and traders required chastisement.[69] Later on, when Sultan Mas'ud marched against Ghur he also met with non-Muslims.[70] It is certain, therefore, that by the middle of the eleventh century the people of Ghur were for the most part non-Muslims. In the twelfth century, when Ghiyas-u'd-din and Shihab-u'd-din appear on the stage of Ghur, the roots of Muslim culture do not seem to have gone down very deep.[71]

The early history of the Shansabaniah dynasty, to which Ghiyas-u'd-din and Shihab-u'd-din belonged, is lost in myth and romance. The first ancestor of this dynasty was Zuhak, an Arab tyrant who was imprisoned by Faridun, the hero of the Persian national revolution. The descendants of Zuhak settled in an inaccessible valley, appropriately named *Zu-Mayandash* (don't be afraid). Shansab, after whom the dynasty is named, was a descendant of Zuhak. Minhaj says that Zuhak accepted Islam at the hands of the Caliph 'Ali.[72] The author of *Rauzat-us-Safa* says that Shansab

---

66. Tabari (838–923 AD) writes in his account of the 47th year of *Hijra* that Hakam bin 'Amr waged war in the hilly regions of Ghur and conquered it by force of arms (Vol. II, part I, p. 65. Urdu trans., Hyderabad). Ibn-i Asir's (1160–1234 AD) account shows that the campaign of the year 47 AH was due to the fact that the Ghurids had become *refractory* (Vol. III, p. 55, Hyderabad). Mirhaj says that it was during the Caliphate of 'Ali that Ghur was conquered and converted to Islam (*Tabaqat-i Nasiri*, p. 29). Ferishtah says that it was in 31 AH that Ghur was conquered by 'Abdullah bin Amir during the Caliphate of 'Usman. It is, however, certain that Ghur was attacked and conquered in the first century of Islam but, due to its geographical position, it did not remain under Muslim control.

67. In 10 AH again armies had to be sent to Ghur to reconquer the region. Tabari, Vol. II, part III, p. 127.

68. *Turkestan down to the Mongol Invasion*, p. 338.

69. *Tarikh-Yamini*, p. 364–65; *Baihaqi*, p. 127.

70. *Baihaqi*, pp. 134–35.

71. Professor Habib, "Sultan Shahabuddin of Ghur" (*Aligarh Muslim University Journal*, 1930).

72. *Tabaqat-i-Nasiri*, p. 29.

had obtained a written order from Hazrat 'Ali to occupy Ghur and that order was preserved by the dynasty till the time of Bahram Shah of Ghaznin[73] (ob. 1152 AD).

The Shansabaniahs came into prominence during the reign of Bahram Shah of Ghaznin who treacherously murdered Malik Qutb-u'd-din Hasan, a Ghurid prince who had taken refuge in his court and had been married to one of his daughters.[74] The Ghurids at once took to arms and a brother of the deceased, Saif-u'd-din Suri, led an attack against Ghaznin and captured the city in September 1148 and assumed the title of Sultan—the first Ghurid to assume such a title.[75] Bahram fled but returned soon afterwards and occupied Ghaznin. Suri was subjected to all possible insults and was brutally murdered. Suri's younger brother, 'Ala-u'd-din Husain, swore to wreak vengeance upon the House of Ghaznin. He marched at the head of a large army and set the city on fire. Later on 'Ala-u'd-din suffered a defeat at the hands of Sanjar who threw him into prison. But the personal qualities of 'Ala-u'd-din elicited admiration from his captor and he set him free. On his release 'Ala-u'd-din again embarked on his schemes of conquest. He conquered Bamian, Tukharistan, the districts of Jarum and Bust, Gharjistan, and Tulak near Herat. There were a number of reversals in his life but the policy of advance into Khurasan which he had initiated was consistently followed by his successors—Saif-u'd-din and Ghiyas-u'd-din. The Ghurid attempt at penetration in Khurasan made a conflict with Khwarizm Shah almost inevitable. Sultan Shah, son of Il-Arsalan, entered into an alliance with the Qara-Khitai, and with their help wrested Merv, Sarakhs, Tus, and Nishapur, and, in 1187, he raided the territories of Ghur also. The Ghurids defeated him and his ally, Tughril of Herat. But Ghiyas-u'd-din could not extend his dominions because Sultan Shah's brother, Takash, who controlled the whole of Khurasan, stoutly resisted his progress. On Takash's death in 1200 the Ghurid troops entered Khurasan[76] and captured Nishapur, Merv, Sarakhs, Tus, and other places. Within a short time the whole of Khurasan was overrun by them. The period of Ghurid ascendancy had reached its highest watermark. A turn in the tide was imminent.

'Ala-u'd-din, who succeeded Takash, husbanded his resources carefully and turned to reclaim the lost territories. 'He jumped up like a ferocious

73. *Rauzat-us-Safa* (1915), Vol. IV, p. 36.

74. For details about Bahram's life, see Ghulam Mustafa Khan, *A History of Bahram Shah of Ghaznin* (Lahore, 1955).

75. Ibid, p. 46.

76. For details see *Tarikh-i-Jahan Gusha*, 'Ata Malik Juwaini (trans. J.A. Boyle: *The History of the World Conqueror*), Vol. I, p. 315, et seq.

tiger and advanced with the rapidity of lightening.' He recovered Nishapur, Herat, and other places. In retaliation Shihab-u'd-din now planned an attack on Gurganj, the capital of 'Ala-u'd-din. The latter sought the help of the Qara-Khitai. The Ghurids foresaw the defeat and disgrace that awaited them. Shihab-u'd-din beat a hasty retreat, but the Qara-Khitais pursued him and inflicted on him a signal defeat at Andkhud.[77] A large part of Afghanistan passed into the hands of 'Ala-u'd-din Khwarizmshah. The dissolution of the Central Asian empire of Ghur was complete when Shihab-u'd-din's viceroy, Yalduz, was driven out in 1215 and Ghaznin was attached by Jalal-u'd-din, the crown prince of Khwarizm.

Discussing the nature of the Ghurid political organization, Professor Mohammad Habib remarks: "Behind the Ghorian Empire there was no imperial idea, no conception of kingdom, state or even government of any sort. Historical parallels are dangerous, but if we ignore mere difference in size, the institution that approaches the Shansabaniah kingdom most closely is the joint family system of the Hindus."[78] What had led him to this conclusion is the fact that both the brothers—Ghiyas-u'd-din and Shihab-u'd-din—used the title of the 'Sultan' simultaneously and there was no superior title to distinguish the one from the other, and yet in their relations with foreign powers they were regarded as one. But this was not a peculiar feature of Ghurid political life, for the early Seljuqs and the Mongols had almost similar traditions.

Shihab-u'd-din had no son and on being asked by a bold courtier as to who would succeed him, replied: "Other kings have only a few sons, but I have several thousand sons, namely my Turkish slaves, who will rule my kingdom in my name after I am dead and gone."[79] The bureaucracy of slaves thus created consolidated one of the greatest empires of the Middle Ages—the Sultanate of Delhi.

77. The present-day Andkhui in northern Afghanistan.
78. "Sultan Shahabuddin of Ghur" (*Aligarh Muslim University Journal*, 1930), p. 34.
79. *Tabaqat-i-Nasiri*, pp. 131–32.

THE LEGAL STRUCTURE OF ISLAM

"Islamic Law," remarks Sir Hamilton Gibb, "was the most far-reaching and effective agent in moulding the social order and the community life of the Muslim peoples ... [It] gave practical expression to the characteristic Muslim quest for unity. In all essentials it was uniform, although the various schools differed in points of detail. To its operation was due the striking convergence of social ideals and ways of life throughout the medieval Muslim world. It went deeper than Roman Law; by reason of its religious bases and its theocractic sanctions it was the spiritual regulator, the conscience of the Muslim community in all its parts and activities."[1]

The Prophet's decision to leave Mecca and settle in Medina was very significant. He had delivered the message and enunciated the broad principles of religion and morality.[2] Now it was necessary to translate those ideal principles into space-time forces and build up, on their basis, a socio-political structure. The foundations of the legal structure of Islam were thus laid in Medina, where the Prophet's time was taken up by the stupendous task of integrating, moulding, and shaping an Islamic socio-political organization out of the crude, rough-hewn, and lawless tribes of Arabia. In this task he was guided by divine revelations and his own intuitive intelligence which had a keen awareness of the requirements of the time.

The Quran gives certain laws, foundational and basic in nature, on which the Islamic society should be organized. The laws relate specially to the family—the ultimate basis of social life (marriage, divorce, inheritance, will, etc.); but incidentally many other matters have been referred to. With regard to political organization only two broad observations are made; the rest is left to the secular instincts and legislative activity of

---

1. *Mohammedanism*, p. 10.
2. The Medinan revelations are radically different from the Meccan revelations. In the Meccan revelations the entire humanity (يا بنی آدم' يا ايـها الـنـاس) is addressed; in the Medinan revelations only those who embraced Islam (يا ايـها الذينَ آمـنوا) have been addressed. The former contain general ethical and religious principles, while the Medinan revelations deal with the foundational and basic laws according to which the Islamic society had to be integrated and organized.

mankind. Acting on these broad principles the Prophet gave shape to the institutions of Islam.

How did the Prophet develop these institutions? The prophetic method of teaching, according to Shah Walliullah, is that, generally speaking, the law revealed by a prophet takes special notice of the habits, ways, and peculiarities of the people to whom he is specially sent. The prophet who aims at all-embracing principles, however, can neither reveal different principles for different peoples, nor leave them to work out their own rules of conduct. His method is to train one particular people, and to use them as a nucleus for the building up of a universal *Shari'at*. In doing so he accentuates the principles underlying the social life of all mankind, and applies them to concrete cases in the light of the specific habits of the people immediately before him. The *Shari'at* values (*ahkam*) resulting from this application (e.g., relating to penalties for crimes) are, in a sense, specific to that people and since their observance is not an end in itself they cannot be strictly enforced in the case of future generations.[3]

With the Prophet's death the situation completely changed. The Quranic revelations which used to direct the actions of the Mussalmans, whenever necessary, had now ceased for ever. Whatever the Prophet had left—the Quran and the Sunnah—had to be carefully studied and applied with intelligence.

The Pious Caliphs adhered to the Quran and the Sunnah of the Prophet. If the Quran gave explicit instructions on a particular matter, it was final. If not, recourse was had to the traditions of the Prophet. If the Prophet's tradition did not contain anything to guide, then the caliphs exercised their own common sense and equity. It would, however, be incorrect to think that the attitude of the first four caliphs was one of rigid conservatism. There were occasions when, with the spirit of the Quran in view, they adopted measures, in some cases, radically different from those of the Prophet. Their outlook was essentially dynamic and they were always prepared to solve a problem in the light of what the circumstances demanded. But, during this period, no matters of such vital importance cropped up as to constitute a challenge to Muslim thought.

In the century that followed, the wave of Muslim conquest reached upto Samarqand, beyond the Oxus, and to Tours in central France. With the extension of Muslim territory there cropped up a number of new legal problems neither contained in the Quran nor anticipated by the Prophet. Consequently, in the great cities of the conquered lands—Basra, Kufa,

3. As quoted by Iqbal in *Reconstruction of Religious Thought in Islam*, pp. 171–72.

Fustat, etc.—speculations in jurisprudence became rife and moulded the Muslim system of laws.[4] Hundreds of schools of Jurisprudence appeared but few could crystallize into definite systems. "Some five hundred schools of Jurisprudence," writes Mez, "are said to have disappeared at or about the beginning of the 3rd/9th century."[5]

Four schools of law, however, stand out prominently in the history of Islam: the Hanafite, the Malikite, the Shafi'ite, and the Hanbalite.

The founder of the *Hanafite school* was Imam Abu Hanifah (699–766 AD). A Persian by birth, he was fully alive to the new demands on religion as a consequence of the expansion of Muslim political power. His chief instruments in establishing his system were *opinion* and *analogy*. He started with the Quranic text and developed from it further details. He also insisted upon the right of preference (*Istihsan*), which necessitated a careful study of actual conditions in legal thinking.

Imam Abu Hanifah did not utilize *ahadis* (traditions of the Prophet) in constructing his legal system. Some writers say that this was due to the fact that no regular collections of traditions were available then. But this is not correct. Thirty years before his death, Abdul Malik and Zahiri had made collections of *ahadis*. If these collections did not reach him or did not contain traditions of a legal import, could he not, like Imam Malik and Imam Hanbal, make his own collections? Why did he then refrain from using *ahadis*? Probably this attitude was born of a conviction that the *ahadis* related to particular conditions of time and space and could not be indiscriminately applied to the new conditions.

Imam Abu Hanifah believed in careful study of the actual conditions and an intelligent application of the Quranic spirit to solve new problems. Consequently, his school is considered "as the most tolerant school of Islam,"[6] and "it possesses greater power of creative adaptation than any other school of Mohammadan Law."[7] As a system of religio-judicial thought, Von Kremer considers it to be the "highest and the loftiest achievement of which Islam was capable."[8]

---

4. Some writers have laid too much emphasis on the influence of Romano-Byzantine law on these systems. A discussion of that aspect does not fall within the scope of this dissertation. Maulana Shibli has criticized these exaggerated notions in his *Sirat Al-Nu'man*. Von Grunebaum writes: "In spite of extensive borrowings from the laws of the countries they conquered, the *fiqh* as a system is *profoundly original*." (*Medieval Islam*, p. 153.)

5. *The Renaissance of Islam* (London, 1937), p. 212.

6. Hitti, *History of the Arabs*, pp. 397–98.

7. *Reconstruction of Religious Thought in Islam*, p. 177.

8. As cited in *History of the Arabs*, p. 398.

The founder of the *Malikite* school, Imam Malik b. Anas (715–95 AD) was born and brought up in Medina, "the mother-city of Muslim law".[9] He was a judge and was in practical touch with actual life but his outlook was narrowed by his instinctive partiality towards the legal tradition of the Hejaz.

Imam Malik did not place much reliance on *qiyas*. He was chiefly guided by the Sunnah and the *Ijma'* of Medina. His *Muwatta*, which is usually taken primarily as a book of tradition, is really a *corpus iurius*, not a *corpus traditionum*.[10] It forms a connecting link between the *fiqh* literature of earlier days and the *hadis* collections of later times.[11]

The Medinan School of Jurisprudence criticized the Iraqian School. The conflict between them was "essentially the controversy between the deductive and inductive methods in legal research."[12]

Between the liberal Iraq and the conservative Medina, many schools arose. Imam Muhammad bin Idris Shafi'i (767–820 AD), a pupil of Imam Malik and Imam Muhammad, acted as an intermediary between independent legal investigation and the traditionism of his time. He founded the science of *Usul* and perfected the doctrine of *Ijma'*. In his *Risalah* he investigated the principles and methods of jurisprudence.

Imam Hanbal (780–855 AD), the founder of the fourth important school, was originally the pupil of Imam Shafi'i. He strictly adhered to *hadis* and rejected the attitude of *ahl-ur rai* and opposed the extension of *Ijma'* and *qiyas*. His school represents the attitude of extreme orthodox intransigence. Tabari refused to recognize him as a jurist (*faqih*), for he considered him to be nothing more than a mere traditionist (*muhaddis*).

The sources utilized by these jurists for building up the legal structure of Islam were—the Quran, the *ahadis*, the *Ijma'*, and the *qiyas*.[13] In the beginning there was great disagreement amongst the various schools about the comparative value of the '*four roots*' and the Shafi'ites fought bloody battles with the Hanbalites in the streets of Baghdad and the Hanafites slaughtered the Shafi'ites at Isfahan, but at last the period of active recrimination came to an end and the believers in these schools succeeded in determining the respective roles of these principles of Muslim law.

The Quran is the primary basis of Islamic law. Next come the *ahadis*. An intricate science has been built up to distinguish between the genuine

9. D.B. MacDonald, *Development of Muslim Theology* (London, 1903), p. 99.

10. Ibid, p. 78.

11. *Encyclopaedia of Islam*, III, p. 205; Fyzee, p. 23.

12. *Reconstruction of Religious Thought in Islam*, p. 177.

13. For a detailed study, see J. Schacht, *Origins of Muhammadan Jurisprudence*, (Oxford, 1950).

and the spurious *ahadis*. The genuine *ahadis* have again been classified into categories of '*good*', '*less good*', and '*weak*'. On these two pillars is erected the legal structure of Islam.

Ijma',[14] the third source is "the most important legal notion in Islam".[15] According to Professor Gibb: "*Vox populi*, the expressed will of the community—not as measured by the counting of votes or the decisions of councils at any given moment, but as demonstrated by the slowly accumulating pressure of opinion over a long period of time—is recognized in orthodox Islam next after *Vox Dei* and *Vox Prophetae* as a third infallible source of religious truth."[16] Though the principle of *Ijma'* remained effective, it never assumed the form of a permanent legislative institution,[17] probably because it went against the political interests of the Umayyads and the Abbasids.

The fourth basis is *qiyas*, analogical reasoning in legislation. The legitimacy of this method was strongly contested at first. In fact, it was the last of the four principles to gain explicit recognition. Imam Abu Hanifah came in for criticism by Imam Malik and Imam Shafi'i for introducing this principle. In practice *qiyas* is only another name for *Ijtihad*.[18]

Some authorities were inclined to admit custom ('*urf* or '*ada*) among the principles of *fiqh*. The *Shari'at* refers to custom only for settling details, which in the nature of things differ from place to place (e.g., the amount of dowry payable by the husband); but temporal authorities sought to justify on its score their secular enactments. Mawardi says that '*urf* was at least as well recognized amongst Muslims as the *Shari'at* itself.

After the formation of these schools, the later scholars confined themselves to the methods of interpretation and application laid down by the founders of these schools. No attempt was made to go to the main sources. Instead, the doctrine of *Taqlid* (adherence) was emphasized and it was maintained that the "Gate of *Ijtihad* was closed after the death of Imam Hanbal".[19] This was contrary even to the attitude of the founders of the schools.[20] None of them ever claimed the finality which the later generations assigned to them.

14. See D.B. MacDonald's article on *Idjma* in the *Encyclopaedia of Islam*. III. p. 448.

15. *Reconstruction of Religious Thought in Islam*. p. 173.

16. *Modern Trends in Islam* (Chicago, 1946), p. 11.

17. *Reconstruction of Religious Thought in Islam*. p. 173.

18. See D.B. MacDonald's article on *Idjtihad* in the *Encyclopaedia of Islam*. Vol. II, pp. 448–49.

19. R. Levy. *The Social Structure of Islam* (Cambridge. 1957), p. 182.

20. Harun-ur Rashid wanted the *Muwatta* of Imam Malik to be nailed to the walls of the *Ka'ba* and everyone forced to act upon it. The Imam objected to it and said that his was not the final word. There was room for further interpretation.

The tenth century marks the close of all efforts at the interpretation of the Quran and the *ahadis* by the aid of individual insight. Textbooks were profusely written on the different aspects of Muslim jurisprudence, but no attempt was made to go to the roots of Islamic law. The decisions of the old masters were classified under special rubrics and neatly collected in manuals. The *Hedayah* of Imam Abul Hasan Burhan ud-din 'Ali Abu Bakr of Marghinan, and the *Kanz-u'd-Daqaiq* of Maulana 'Abdullah bin Ahmad bin Mahmud Nasafi are the two most outstanding works of this kind.

Why was this attitude of *Taqlid*[21] developed by the *'Ulama* of Islam and why was the *Shari'at* reduced to a static state? This attitude was, in part, due to a fear of rationalism and analytic thought. Free thought was muzzled lest it may endanger the solidarity of Islamic society. From the thirteenth century there is a tendency amongst the legists of Islam for over-organisation by a false reverence for the past. Professor Gibb observes: "Its very lack of flexibility contributed to those results (unifying force in Islamic culture) by preventing divergences and disintegration into purely *local* systems."[22]

The law of Islam has since then remained in a petrified state and has not marched with the times. There were, however, men like Imam Ibn-i Taimiyya (ob. 1328), Ibn Daqiqil-Id (ob. 1302), Suyuti (ob. 1505), Juwaini (ob. 1085), and others who rebelled against the finality claimed by the schools and insisted upon the freedom of *Ijtihad*. Their thought, no doubt, exercised tremendous influence in their respective areas of activity but it could not give a new orientation and a forward pull to the Muslim juristic activity and could not crystallize into a movement.

What was then the law administered by the *qazis* in the law courts? The law courts enforced just the law contained in these manuals. No *qazi* could think of going back to the primary sources of law—the Quran and the Sunnah. If the *qazis* or the *muftis* anywhere exercised their individual judgement it was only in regard to secondary points where the editors of the school compendiums did not agree and even in that case an attempt at reconciliation was all that they made. The decisions of the *muftis* (i.e., *fatwas*) based on earlier authorities were often collected together and thus a large number of books of *fatwas* came into being.

So far as the attitude of Muslim governments towards the *qazis* was concerned, they gave them perfect freedom in civil and personal matters

21. Professor J. Schacht, however, holds that "the *taklid*... is not to be held responsible for the deadening of the stimulus to the development of *fiqh* in later times." *Encyclopaedia of Islam*, Vol. III, article on *Taklid* I, p. 630.

22. *Mohammedanism*, p. 106.

concerning marriage, inheritance, *waqf*, etc., but in regard to administrative matters they sought to restrict the jurisdiction of the *qazis*.[23] If the *fatwa* collections of the Middle Ages are scrutinized as a whole, it would appear that while innumerable problems relating to civil, personal, and religious matters have been discussed in detail, there is hardly any reference to political or administrative problems. The reason is not far to discover. In administrative matters the Muslim governments were guided, not by the *Shari'at* laws, but by what Barani calls the *zawabit*,[24] i.e., the secular regulations framed by the rulers in the light of the exigencies of the time. It is, however, interesting to note that while Imam Ghazzali admitted that the acts of the secular administration were valid in view of the circumstances of the time,[25] Ibn-i Khaldun rejected the validity of this secular legislation, declaring it to be concerned only with this world, fleeting and vain, whereas the laws of the *Shari'at* are designed to secure man's welfare both here and hereafter.[26]

23. In the tenth century AH a Jewish rabbi wrote about Egypt: 'They have two kinds of justice, the one *shar'i* and the other *'urfi*. The *shar'i* justice is in the hands of the chief *qazi*, who decides what is the religious law, the princes being charged to carry out his decisions, while the *'urf* justice is entrusted to the prince of the country who may put a man to death by *'urfi* law even if it be contrary to the religious law and without the knowledge of the chief *qazi*.' (*The Social Structure of Islam*, p. 262. For the reference see Goldziher, *Zahiriten*, p. 205.)

24. *Fatawa-i-Jahandari* (Rotograph). Maqrizi writes: "People are in our day, and have been ever since the beginning of the Turkish [*Mamluk*] regime in Egypt and Syria, under the impression that laws are of two kinds, the first that of the *Shari'at* and the second that of *siyasa* [i.e., the State]." *Khitat* (Bulaq. 1270 AH). Vol. II, p. 220.

25. *Iqtisad fi'l-i'tiqad* (Cairo, 1327 AH), pp. 98, et seq.

26. *Prolegomènes* ed. Quatremere I, p. 342, as cited by Levy in *The Social Structure of Islam*, p. 259.

THE THEOLOGICAL STRUCTURE OF ISLAM

The basis of all theological studies in Islam is the Quran. All efforts of the Mussalmans in the theological sphere have clustered round it. When the Mussalmans tried to explain the verses of the Quran, they developed *'Ilm-i Tafsir* (Science of Exegesis); when they turned to the acts and deeds of the messenger of the Quran, they founded *'Ilm-i Hadis* (Science of Traditions); when they discussed doctrinal details of the Quran, they developed *'Ilm-i Kalam*; when the legal maxims of the Quran were discussed, the science of *fiqh* (Jurisprudence) was born. The attempt to recite the Quran properly led to the development of the science of *tajwid* and *qirat* (Recitation and Punctuation). The study of its grammar led to the growth of *sarf* and *nahv* (Grammar and Syntax). Thus almost every literary endeavour of the Mussalmans started from the Quran.

The contribution of 'Ajam to the development of theological sciences was very great. The majority of the commentators of the Quran belonged to the Persian lands; of the great compilers of *ahadis* too, only Imam Malik belonged to the Arab race. In other branches of theological studies also, 'Ajam played a leading role.

If the history of the development of the theological sciences is surveyed as a whole, it would appear that from the third to the eighth century AH a remarkably original contribution was made in all spheres. The creative genius of the Mussalmans was at its best during this period but in the centuries that followed all progress virtually stopped and the scholars were satisfied with merely restating, summarizing, and annotating what the old masters had said.[1]

'Ilm-i Tafsir (Quranic Exegesis): The *'Ilm-i Tafsir* sets out to resolve all the problems of hermeneutics. Though oral glosses on points of language

---

1. An illustration will make the point more clear. In 417/1026. Shaikh 'Abdul Qadir Jurjani wrote two books: *Dala'il-ul-Ai'jaz* and *Asrar ul-Balaghah*. Imam Razi (ob. 606/1290) summarized them in *al-Ejaz fi-dala'il al Aijaz*. Sikaki (ob. 626/1228) summarized *Al-Ejaz* in the third volume of his *Miftah ul'Ulum*. Khatib Qazwini (ob. 793/1338) summarized *Miftah* in his *Talkhis-ul Miftah* and Sa'd-u'd-din Taftazani (ob. 793/1390) wrote two commentaries on it.

or interpretation were preserved from the very beginning, the first critical study of these materials was made by Tabari[2] (838–922 AD), whose *Jami'al-Bayan fi Tafsir al-Quran* sums up in thirty volumes[3] the whole Quranic learning of the three centuries of the *Hijrah*. Besides being an outstanding philologist, Tabari was well versed in the historical, religious, and juridic literature of Islam. Professor Gibb rightly remarks that his work "laid the foundations upon which later scholars built their more specialized commentaries."[4] Then appeared the *Kashshaf*[5] of Abul Qasim Mahmud bin 'Umar al-Zamakhshari[6] (1075–1143 AD). Zamakhshari belonged to the Mu'tazilite school and so he tried to excise from the Quran all traces of material favourable to determinism, anthropomorphism, and other theories to which Mu'tazilism is opposed.[7] But Zamakhshari was a scholar of penetrating intelligence, a moralist of delicate sensibilities, and a philologist of consummate skill. In spite of his Mu'tazilite leanings, his work has remained the standard work on exegesis and later commentators have mainly drawn from him.

Then appeared the *Tafsir-i Kabir* of Imam Fakhr-u'd-din Razi (ob. 1209 AD). It was characterized by an anti-Mu'tazilite and anti-Zahirite approach. In the next century 'Abdullah b. 'Umar al-Baizawi (ob. 1316 AD) produced his *Anwar-ul-Tanzil wa Asrar-ul-Tawil*, which is largely based on the *Kashshaf* of Zamakhshari. Baizawi has fixed the beliefs of the pious Muslims as regards the interpretation of the sacred Book.[8] Gibb correctly remarks that "modern orthodox interpretation stands on his (Baizawi's) shoulders."[9]

Essentially and basically, therefore, it is *Kashshaf* which has fixed Muslim beliefs as regards exegesis. A fourteenth-century mystic of India thus estimates the importance of Zamakhshari's work: "Whatever is given in other works is from this book; whatever the people have liked, they have copied from it and have compiled a separate work in their own name."[10]

2. For Tabari, see R. Paret's article in the *Encyclopaedia of Islam*, Vol. IV, pp. 578–79.

3. Printed at Bulaq in 1323–29 and at Cairo in 1331 AH.

4. *Mohammedanism*, p. 51.

5. *al-Kashshaf 'an Haqa'iq al-Tanzil*, edited by W. Nassau Leess Khadim Hussain, and 'Abdul Hai (Calcutta, 1856).

6. For his life, see C. Brockelmann's article in the *Encyclopaedia of Islam*, Vol. IV, pp. 1205–07.

7. H. Lammens, *Islam: Beliefs and Institutions* (London, 1929), p. 44.

8. See B. Carra De Vaux's article on *Tafsir* in the *Encyclopaedia of Islam*, Vol. IV, p. 604.

9. *Mohammedanism*, p. 52.

10. *Sarur-u's-Sudur* (MS), p. 44.

The fact, however, remains that after Zamakhshari no original work on *Tafsir* appeared. In India the *'Ulama* were content with repeating and restating what the great Zamakhshari had written.

Next to the Quran rank the traditions of the Prophet (*ahadis*). MacDonald has thus traced the origin and growth of the *hadis* literature:

> What he (the Prophet) said, and what he did; what he refrained from doing; what he gave his quasi-approval to by silence; all was passed on in rapidly increasing, pregnant little narratives. First, his immediate companions would note, either by committal to memory or to a written record, his utterances and table talks generally.... Above all, a record was being gathered of all the cases judged by him, and his decisions; of all the answers which he gave to formal questions on religious life and faith. All this was jotted down by the Companions on *sahifas*—odd sheets.... At first each man had his own collection in memory or in writing. Then after the death of the Prophet and when his first Companions were dropping off, these collections were passed on to others of the second generation. And so the chain ran on and in time a tradition came to consist formally of two things—the text or matter (*matn*) so handed on, and the succession (*isnad*) over whose lips it had passed.[11]

No books of *hadis*, however, appeared during the Umayyad period. The first book of *hadis* is the *Muwatta* of Imam Malik (ob. 794 AD). To Imam Malik the *matn* or text of a tradition was the only thing of importance. To the *isnad* he paid little attention. Then appeared the *Musnad* of Imam Ahmad b. Hanbal (ob. 855 AD). The third century of the *Hijrah* saw the compilation of the following works on *hadis*: (1) *Al Jami' al-Sahih*[12] by Muhammad bin Isma'il Bukhari. In this work 7275 traditions of the Prophet have been classified according to subject matter. Imam Bukhari wanted to furnish the jurists and theologians with authentic traditions on all matters for ready reference. His classification served the purpose he had in view. (2) *Al-Sahih* by Imam Abul Hasan Muslim Nishapuri[13] (ob. 874 AD). It differs from other collections of *ahadis* on two points: firstly, it is not divided into chapters and, secondly, peculiar attention has been paid here to the *isnad*. (3) *Kitab-ul Sunan* by Abu Da'ud Sulaiman[14] of Basra

11. *Development of Muslim Theology*, p. 75.

12. Edited by L. Krehl (Leyden) 1862–68; Vol. IV, edited by T.W. Juynboll (Leyden), 1907–08.

13. For Imam Muslim, see A.J. Wensinck's article in the *Encyclopaedia of Islam*, Vol. III, p. 756. The *Sahih Muslim* was printed at Cairo (1283 AH) in 5 volumes.

14. For Abu Da'ud, see W. Marcais's article in the *Encyclopaedia of Islam*, Vol. I, pp. 82–83. His *Sunan* was printed at Cairo (1292 AH) in 2 volumes.

(ob. 888 AD). It differs from other works in that it does not concern itself with historical, ethical, or dogmatical enquiries. Its contents are almost exclusively juridical. (4) *Jami*[15] by Abu 'Isa Muhammad Tirmizi (ob. 892 AD). Tirmizi has pointed out differences between the *mazahib* and from this point of view his work is the oldest. (5) *Sunan*[16] of Abu 'Abdullah Muhammad b. Maja of Qazwin (824–86 AD). (6) *Sunan* of Abu 'Abdul Rahman Ahmad al-Nasa'i (830–915 AD).[17]

These collections are considered authentic (*Siha Sitta*). Shah Walliullah, who has classified the entire *hadis* literature under five categories in order to determine the relative importance and authenticity of the various collections, places the *Muwatta, Sahih al-Bukhari*, and the *Sahih al-Muslim* in the first category, with the *Muwatta* given the pride of place. He approvingly quotes Imam Shafi'i who is reported to have said: "The truest book after the Book of God is the *Muwatta* of Imam Malik."

To the second category belong *Sunan-i Abu Da'ud, Jami'-i Tirmizi, Nasa'i*, and *Musnad-i Imam Ahmad*. Under the third category Shah Walliullah has placed the following works: *Musnand-i Abu 'Ali, 'Abdur Razzaq: Abu Bakr b. Abi Shiba, Musnand-i 'Abd bin Hamid, Tiyalsi, Baihaqi, Tahavi*, and *Tabrani*. To the fourth category belong the following: *Ibn-i Haban, Kamil ibn-i 'Adi, Abu Naim, Jauzqani, Ibn-i Asakir, Ibn-i Najar, Daylami*, and *Musnad-i Khwarazmi*. Under the fifth and last category he includes the traditions current among the jurists and the mystics.

The process of collecting *hadis* could not go on indefinitely. It had to come to an end. With the discontinuance of this process the energies of the *'Ulama* turned towards developing the science of testing the nature and value of recorded traditions and making a critical study of *isnad*. The *usul-i Hadis* and *Isma-ur-Rijal* were the result of this critical study. About the *usul-i-isnad*, Hitti says that it "meets the most essential requirements of modern historiography."[18]

Later scholars summarized and rearranged from different points of view the works of the six great compilers of *ahadis*. Maulana Razi-u'd-din Hasati of Bada'un selected *ahadis* from the works of Muslim and Bukhari in a compilation known as *Mashariq-ul-Anwar*.

'Ilm-i-Kalam (Muslim theological ideas): The development of Muslim theology began after the death of the Prophet. "So long as he (the Prophet) lived and received infallible revelations in solution of all questions of faith or usage that might come up, it is obvious that no system of theology could

15. Cairo, 1292 AH in 2 volumes.
16. Cairo, 1313 AH in 2 volumes.
17. Cairo, 1312 AH in 2 volumes.
18. *The Origins of the Islamic State* (New York, 1916), *Introduction*, p. 3.

be formed or even thought of."[19] After his death, whenever anybody differed from his practice or committed a mistake in the performance of any religious duty the question of right or wrong at once cropped up. In the beginning these differences remained on a purely private basis.[20]

Later, when the political frontiers of Islam expanded and people belonging to different mental climates joined the fold of Islam, theological controversies started because everyone interpreted Islam in terms of his own peculiar national instincts and racial inclinations. Broadly speaking, there were three different attitudes towards theological controversies. Some tackled the problems in a traditional way (naql), others through reason ('aql); others still through mystic intuition (kashf).

Definite theories, however, arose out of the question of practical politics.[21] The murder of the Caliph 'Usman, and the civil war that followed it, raised the question: What makes the Imam the head of the community? Two answers were given to this question. One group said that the choice of the community was the deciding factor; the other said that the relationship with the Prophet was the main thing. Divergent views became the basis of two parties—the Sunnites and the Shi'ites.[22]

After the Battle of Siffin this question entered a second stage when a group deserted 'Ali and became known as the Kharijites.[23] They claimed to be the only true believers. Thus the Kharijites for the first time raised the question of *faith* and *heresy*. In opposition to the Kharijites there appeared the Murji'ites.

The Kharijites rejected the idea of Imam and declared that an Imam was unnecessary when men knew how to order their social life by the Book of God. Neither reason nor revelation demands an Imam.[23] The Kharijite

---

19. *Development of Muslim Theology*, p. 12; Shibli, *Sirat Al-Nu'man*, pp. 193–94.

20. Shah Walliullah of Delhi has made a very careful and critical study of the circumstances in which early theological controversies led to the formation of schools in his *Insaf fi Biyan-i-Sabab-al Ikhtilaf* (Delhi, 1308 AH).

21. Shibli, *'Ilm ul-Kalam*, p. 17.

22. 'Abdullah bin Saba was the founder and organizer of the Shi'a sect. His doctrines gave a theological system to Shi'ism (Nicholson, *Literary History of the Arabs*, p. 217). According to him, the Imamate belonged to 'Ali by right. He emphasized the supernatural character of the Imam, the return of the dead to this world, and the messianic idea. Later on, belief in the survival of the Shi'a Imam, in his reappearance, in metempsychosis, and in the total or partial incarnation of the Divinity in the person of the 'Alids became common among most of the Shi'as. See Tritton, *Muslim Theology*, p. 21, et seq.

23. Ibid, p. 38.

attitude was, in fact, the result of extreme disgust and distrust of the aristocratic party of Mecca and the hierarchical clique of Medina. That this dissatisfaction expressed itself in a religious form was, in fact, inevitable in the medieval context of things.

A Kharijite thought that his sect alone was right; all others were damned. The Murji'ites held that there was hope for all. 'Judgement on what is doubtful must be postponed. All who call themselves Muslims are Muslims'—such was their attitude. They held that faith was the one thing needed. If faith is present, sins do not harm; if not, virtuous acts do no good.

Out of these controversies there arose the problem of predestination and free will.[24] The Murji'ite view helped to strengthen the hands of the Umayyad aristocracy which wanted the people to believe in predestination and tamely submit to the Umayyad rule. Ma'bad Juhami declared that man possessed *qadar* or power over his actions. He had to pay the penalty for this view, but his doctrines assumed a revolutionary character.[25] Under the protection of the Qadarite doctrines the foundations of the Umayyad power were shattered. It relieved the people from the political as well as the ideological domination of the Umayyads.

The rationalist movement in Islam became very powerful during the early Abbasid period, particularly during the reign of Ma'mun (813–33 AD). The study of Greek philosophy released new intellectual forces and broadened mental horizons in all spheres of thought and action. "The fresh intellectual vigour imparted by the assimilation of Greek philosophy, which was studied with great avidity, led immediately to a critical examination of Islamic monotheism."[26]

The *Mu'tazilite* conception of God and their theory of matter deserve to be noted. They deny the separate reality of divine attributes, and declare their absolute identity with the absolute Divine Principle. "God," says Abdul Huzail, "is knowing, all-powerful, living: and His knowledge, power and life constitute His very essence (*zat*)."

The Abbasid support to the Mu'tazilite doctrine had some political reasons also. The Mu'tazilites rejected the theory of *Sifat* (Attributes) and *Tashbih* (Resemblance) and *Halul* (Fusion). Once 'attributes' are denied, the whole structure on which the Shi'a ideology of the Divine attributes of the Imam is based falls to the ground.

24. See W.M. Watt, *Free Will and Predestination in Early Islam* (London, 1948).

25. When Yazid b. Walid raised the standard of revolt he declared himself a Qadarite and thousands of people joined his banner.

26. Muhammad Iqbal, *The Development of Metaphysics in Persia*, p. 46.

The Mu'tazilite doctrines were challenged and refuted by Abul Hasan 'Ali al-Ash'ari of Baghdad (ob. 936 AD). He became the founder of the scholastic theology (*Kalam*) in Islam. To al-Ash'ari is also attributed the introduction of the formula *bila kayf* (without modality), according to which one is expected to accept the anthropomorphic expressions in the Quran without any explanation demanded or given. This new principle served as a damper on free thought and research. With a view to propagating the Ash'arite system the famous *Madrasa-i Nizamiyah* was established by the Seljuq Wazir, Nizam-ul-Mulk.

Al-Ash'ari was followed by Imam Ghazzali, whose clear, lucid, and intelligent exposition of the principles of Islam ushered in the dawn of a new era in the realm of Muslim theological ideas. His works were read avidly and were prescribed in the various courses of studies in India.

Side by side with the development of Mu'tazilism we see many other movements expressive of new tendencies and religious moods, e.g. *Sufism*[27] and *Isma'ilism*.

A claim for 'Alid legitimism produced Shi'ism which later on became divided into two groups: the Sab'iyya and the *Asnai Ash'ariyya*. The main point of difference was the actual number and succession of the Imams. The Sab'iyyas believed in seven Imams, and regarded Isma'il Ja'far's eldest son as the seventh and the last of them. The latter recognized Isma'il's younger son, Musa, and his successors down to the twelfth Imam. The believers of the seven Imams are known as the *Isma'ilis*. The Isma'ili movement expressed itself in a number of forms: the Carmathians, the Fatimid Caliphs of Cairo, the *Ikhwan-us Safa*, the *Assassins*—all being different facets of the same movement.[28] The Isma'ili movement became a force to reckon with under the influence of 'Abdullah al-Maimun al-Qaddah. Iqbal writes about him: "...he made an attempt under the pious cloak of the doctrine of *Imamat* (Authority) to synthesise all the dominating ideas of the time. Greek Philosophy, Christianity, Rationalism, Sufism, Manichaeanism, Persian heresies, and above all the idea of reincarnation, all came forward to contribute their respective shares to the boldly conceived Ismailian whole, the various aspects of which were to be gradually revealed to the initiated, by the 'Leader'—ever the ever-incarnating Universal Reason—according to the intellectual development of the age in which he incarnated himself."[29]

The organization of the Isma'ilis and the Carmathians was secret, but their methods of propaganda were highly effective. They succeeded in

27. A discussion of the mystic movement occurs in the following chapter.
28. Lewis, *The Origins of Ismailism* (Cambridge, 1940), p. 1.
29. *The Development of Metaphysics in Persia*, pp. 58–59.

winning over the lower section of the population and the uneducated people to their fold. Tabari says that the Carmathians consisted mainly of peasants and tillers. Imam Ghazzali also clearly realized the special appeal of the movement to the *'awam*[30] and said that the chief danger of the heresy lay in the attraction it had for the labouring and the artisan classes.

Of the numerous sects, that appeared at this time, the Karramiyan sect deserves special notice on account of the influence it exercised on the religious thought of the early Ghurids.[31] The founder of this sect was Abu 'Abdullah Muhammad b. Karram, son of a vintner of Nishapur.[32] Though he was persecuted in the earlier stages of his religious propaganda, his sect spread rapidly in Ghur, Gharjistan, Bamiyan, and other adjoining regions. Baghdadi says that the 'weavers' and the 'distressed ones' of the villages of Nishapur particularly felt attracted towards this sect.[33] 'Utbi quotes verses from a poet of the period, according to which the only true creed (*din*) was that of Muhammad b. Karram, just as the only genuine system of law was that of Abu Hanifah.[34] Even Sultan Mahmud of Ghaznin extended his patronage to this sect. Abu Mansur 'Abdul Qahir Baghdadi (ob. 1037) gives the following account of the doctrines of the Karramiya sect:

> Ibn Karram urged his followers to ascribe corporeality to the object of his worship. He held that He is a body, possessing an end and limit below, where He comes in contact with His throne... In one of his books Ibn Karram has described the object of his worship as a substance... In this vein·he wrote in the preface to his book, which is entitled *The Tortures in the Grave*, that God is a Unit of essence and a Unit of substance...Ibn Karram writes in his work that God touches His throne and that the throne is a place for Him...Ibn Karram and his adherents hold that the Object of their Worship is a subject in which created entities exist. They believe that His utterances, His will, His visual and auditory perceptions, His contiguity to the uppermost surface of the Universe, are all accidents originated in Him and He is the place for these

30. *The Origins of Ismailism*, p. 93.

31. Sultan Shihab-u'd-din and his brother, Ghiyas-u'd-din, originally belonged to this sect. *Tabaqat-i-Nasiri*, p. 77.

32. For details about the life and teachings of the founder, see Ibn-i Asir, *Tarikh al-Kamil* (Egypt edition, 1290 AH), Vol. VII, p. 77; Shahrastani, *Kitab-ul-Milal wan-Nihal* (London, 1946), pp. 85–96; *Mizan al-I'tidal*, Vol. III, p. 149. See also Margoliouth's article on *Karramiya* in the *Encyclopaedia of Islam*, III, pp. 773–74.

33. Abu Mansur 'Abd at Qahirat Baghdadi, *Al-Farq bain al-Firaq* (*Moslem Schism and Sects*; English trans. by A.S. Halkin), II, pp. 18–19.

34. *Turkestan Down to the Mongol Invasion*, p. 290.

creations which originated in Him... The Karramiya also attacked the problem of faith. They hold that it consists only of a single confession made at the beginning of time. Its repetition is not regarded as an act of faith except from an apostate who confesses it after his apostasy...it is sufficient for the traveller to say the *Allah Akbar* twice without kneeling, bowing, standing, sitting or reciting the *Shahada* or the salutation...He also ruled out the washing of the dead and prayer after them as customs not ordained by law. What is obligatory consists merely in shrouding and burying them. He also recognized the validity of prayer, fasting, or the pilgrimage unaccompanied by concentration.[35]

Many people who were brought up in the traditions of Mahayana Buddhism found something akin to their own religious beliefs in the anthropomorphism of the Karramiyans and so they accepted it without hesitation.

35. *Al-Farq bain al-Firaq*, pp. 18–30.

THE MYSTIC STRUCTURE OF ISLAM

Few aspects of Muslim religious life during the Middle Ages are of such absorbing interest as the origin and growth of the mystic ideology and institutions. A mystical sense, it may be noted, is not "the sole prerogative of any race, language or nation".[1] All people, at one stage or the other, usually after having passed through the meridian of their glory, develop mystic tendencies and *Weltanschaung*. But the mystic movement in Islam has certain peculiar features of its own which make its study a necessary adjunct to a proper understanding of the history of medieval 'Ajam, including India. It is all the more so because the movement of popular religion in Islam is very closely connected with the history of Islamic mysticism.[2] And further because it has been through the mystic channels alone that dynamic and progressive elements have entered the social structure of Islam. The orthodox theologians, often conservative and reactionary, rarely appreciated the change in the moods of the time and seldom tried to reconstruct their religious thought accordingly. The mystic thought has proved, in this sense, the *protecting glacis* of the Muslim society and has given it new vitality by removing the contradictions between static theology and the rapidly changing conditions of life. "Through the course of Islamic history," writes Professor Gibb, "Islam's culture was challenged, but never overpowered, for the *sufi* and other mystical thought always came to the rescue of its most dogmatic preaching and always gave it that strength and power which no challenge could destroy."[3] Besides, unlike mystics of most other creeds, the *sufi*s (specially after the rise of the *silsilah*s) did not aim at merely personal salvation, but worked for the spiritual culture of humanity as a whole.

RISE OF THE MYSTIC MOVEMENT

Various theories have been advanced about the origin of mystic ideas in Islam. Christianity, Hellenism, Manicheism, Buddhism, Hinduism, and

---

1. Louis Massignon, as quoted by Lammens in *Islam: Belief and Institutions* (London, 1929), p. 11.
2. Gibb, *Mohammedanism*, p. 128.
3. As quoted in *Islamic Culture*, July 1942, p. 264.

Parseeism have all been suggested as its main sources. But Muslim mystics have always firmly combated such theories and have claimed that mysticism is based on the Quran and the traditions of the Prophet. That *Tasawwuf* is essentially Islamic in its *origin* is as true as the fact that as the mystic movement spread to various regions it assimilated and imbibed elements from cultures and religions that were different from its own. The Quran is often allegorical with a mystical touch. It defines a Muslim in these words: "Those who believe in the Unseen, establish daily prayers and spend out of what we have given them."[4] Further, as to the Unseen, it says that it is your own soul. "We are nigher to him (man) than his own jugular vein."[5] Again, the essential nature of the Unseen is pure light: "God is the light of the heavens and earth."[6] Out of these verses the *sufis* have developed their pantheistic views about the Reality behind all creation.

The *sufis* say that the Prophet had an esoteric teaching as distinguished from the teaching contained in the Book and cite the following verse in their support: "As we have sent a Prophet to you from among yourselves who reads our verses to you, purifies you, teaches you the Book and the Wisdom, and teaches you what you did not know before."[7]

If by mysticism we mean 'interiorization' in the rites of worship and a deep and restless devotion to God, to the exclusion of all earthly ties, the germination of the mystic spirit may be traced back to the days of the Prophet who himself used to retire to the cave of Hira to meditate for a certain period of time every year. Some seventy persons—known as *Ahle Suffa*—lived in the mosque of the Prophet and prayed day and night during his lifetime. They had no earthly attachments and no worldly engagements. Besides, two companions of the Prophet—Abu Zar Ghiffari (ob. 652 AD) and Huzaifa (ob. 657 AD)—who were known for their piety and other-worldly outlook, set the traditions of the mystic attitude in Islam.

The circumstances that led to the birth and growth of the mystic ideal of life call for some explanation. The causes were psychological, social, and personal.

Firstly, its basis may be sought in the human aspiration to a personal, direct approach to, and a more intense experience of, the Supreme Being and the religious truth. The Prophet himself had direct consciousness of the Divine presence. Mystics were eager to tread the same path. Besides, a strong religious emotion could not be satisfied by any orthodox or formal

4. S. II: 2.
5. S. L: 15.
6. S. XXIV: 35.
7. S. II: 146.

approach to the Ultimate Reality. The 'Ulama had reduced Islam to a set of lifeless rituals and ceremonies. Intensely religious spirits, hungering after a deeper communion, naturally turned to mystic speculation and experience as the real source of religious progress and spiritual development. A consciousness of contradiction in the metaphysical and ethical aspects of popular theology further encouraged the mystic attitude, which is essentially an attempt to transcend discord and reduce all contradictions into an absolute unity.

Secondly, mysticism represents a reaction against over-intellectualism, formalism, and hair-splitting theology. It was under the influence of Greek thought that the Muslim scholars had adopted a sophisticated approach towards religion. Their attitude was characterized by artificialism (wazi 'at) and they tried to represent the simple facts of faith in terms derived mainly from Greek logic and metaphysics. Hair-splitting controversies which started in theology—particularly amongst the Ash'arites and the Mu'tazilites—froze the heat of spiritual life. Naturally, people who yearned for a direct and natural approach towards religion turned towards the spiritual aspects of religion. They developed cosmic emotions as an antidote to over-intellectualism. Iqbal very significantly remarks: "The germs of scepticism latent in Rationalism ultimately necessitated an appeal to a super-intellectual source of knowledge which asserted itself in the Risala of Al-Qushairi (ob. 968 AD)."[8]

Besides, the rigidity and formalism of the various schools of fiqh found its reaction in the development of mystic thought. The Hanbalites were the bitterest enemies of independent thought. Mysticism is at its higher level a form of free-thinking. The following couplet very neatly expresses the mystic challenge to the jurists:

در کنز و هدایه نتوان دید خدارا

آئینه دل بین که کتابے به ازیں نیست

(You cannot see God in Kanz or Hidayah,
Look into the mirror of the heart; for there is no book better than this.)

Lastly, the mystic call in Islam was the result of an inner rebellion of conscience against the social injustices of the age. The rise of the Umayyads gave a rude shock to the religious sentiments of those Mussalmans who thought that Islam had not come simply to establish empires. They looked with dismay at the spectacle of the Mussalmans drifting away from the ideals of Islam and wallowing in sordid materialism. The impious ways of the Muslim governing classes provoked great disgust in sensitive minds.

8. *The Development of Metaphysics in Persia*, p. 100.

If in the field of politics the Umayyad imperialism gave birth to the *Mawali* movement, it gave rise to the *Shu'ubiyyah*[9] movement in the cultural sphere and the mystic ideology in the religious sphere.

It is significant that the main centres of mysticism during the early years of its development were Kufa and Basra, the two cantonment towns of Iraq, which had witnessed horrible scenes of Umayyad atrocities. Sensitive souls could not help being driven inwards and looked elsewhere for spiritual solace.

In the latter half of the eighth century we find persecution of the Zindiqs,[10] and the revolts of Persian heretics (Sindbah 755–56; Ustadhis 766–68; the Veiled Prophet of Khorasan 777–80) who cloaked political and economic dissatisfaction under the guise of religion. The movement of the Mazdakite Babak (816–38 AD) and the Shu'ubiyyah controversy created an atmosphere which drove away the "spirits of devotional character from the scenes of continual unrest to the blissful peace of an ever-deepening contemplative life".[11]

GROWTH OF THE MYSTIC MOVEMENT

Broadly speaking there were three distinct stages in the development and growth of the mystic movement in Islam: (1) the period of the Quietists, (2) the period of the mystic philosophers, and (3) the period of the *silsilah*s. During the period of the Quietists which roughly extends from 661 AD to 850 AD, the mystic movement had an individual basis. Persons dissatisfied with the conditions of the external world retired into seclusion and cut themselves off from worldly attachments. The lives of these Quietists were cases of repentance (*tauba*). The mystical element of love and adoration, if not entirely absent, was secondary and unstressed.[12] They laboured under a deep and disturbing consciousness of sin. To them this world was transitory and deceitful. They were terribly afraid of the world to come. Imam Hasan Basri (ob. 728 AD), Ibrahim b. Adham (ob.

9. For details about the *Shu'ubiyyah* movement see Khuda Bakhsh, *Essays Indian and Islamic*. pp. 56–126.

10. "The polemics of the conservatives describe as a *zindiq* or free thinker any one whose external profession of Islam seems to them not sufficiently sincere." (Massignon). The word was used for the first time in 742 AD in connection with the execution of Ja'd b. Dirham. The *Sufis* were also persecuted as *Zindiqs*. See Louis Massignon's article on *Zindiq* in the *Encyclopaedia of Islam*, Vol. IV, pp. 1228–29.

11. Iqbal, *Development of Metaphysics in Persia*, p. 99.

12. Gibb, *Mohammedanism*, p. 133.

777 AD), Abu Hashim (ob. 777), and Rabia Basri (ob. 776) belong to this Quietist school of mysticism.

In the last half of the ninth century mystic sects (*garoh, mazhab*) appeared. They were concerned with the problem of mystic metaphysics. The founders of these sects were men of great learning and produced extensive literature on mystic subjects. They specialized in *risalah*s or short treatises on special topics. Though these *risalah*s, written in Arabic, contained valuable discussions yet a consistent mystic philosophy had not developed. Ma'ruf Karkhi introduced the doctrine of *total forgetfulness*, while Sari Saqti (ob. 870 AD) that of *Tauhid* (Oneness). Zunnun Misri (ob. 859 AD) formulated the doctrines of *hal* (state) and *maqam* (stage). Mansur Hallaj (ob. 921 AD) introduced the pantheistic element in Islam. He mixed up un-Islamic doctrines with Sufism, such as *hulul* (fusion), *ittihad* (union), *tanasukh* (transmigration), *rijat* (return), etc. These doctrines formed the subjects of large Arabic manuals that appeared in the succeeding centuries.

Shaikh 'Ali Hajweri (ob. 1072) enumerates twelve schools, or rather tendencies, among the mystics of his day. "The whole body of aspirants to Sufism," he writes in his *Kashf-ul-Mahjub*, "is composed of twelve sects or schools (*garoh, mazhab*), two of which are condemned (*mardud*) while the remaining ten are approved (*maqbul*)."

(1) *Hululi*s	(Transmigrationists or reincarnationists).
(2) *Hallaji*s	followers of Mansur Hallaj.
(3) *Taifuri*s	followers of Shaikh Abu Yazid Taifur Bustami. They considered *rapture* superior to *sobriety*.
(4) *Qussari*s	followers of Abu Saleh Hamdun bin Ahmad al-Qussar. They put forward the *doctrine of blame*. Later they came to be known as *Malamati*s.
(5) *Kharrazi*s	followers of Abu Sa'id Kharraz. They propounded the doctrine of *fana* (annihilation) and *baqa* (subsistence).
(6) *Khufaifi*s	followers of Abu 'Abdullah Mohammad bin Khafif Shirazi. They introduced the doctrine of *huzur* (presence) and *ghaib* (absence).
(7) *Sayyari*s	followers of Abul 'Abbas Sayyar, the Imam of Merv. They enunciated the doctrine of *shauq* (joy) and *alam* (gloom).
(8) *Muhasibi*s	followers of Abu 'Ubeid-ullah Hariz bin Asadul Muhasibi. They laid down precepts for taking stock of one's self, and understanding one's *maqam* and *hal* (permanent and temporary states).

(9) *Tustari*s	followers of Sahl bin 'Abdullah Tuster. They drew attention to the necessity of controlling, punishing, or satisfying the lower soul (*nafs*).
(10) *Hakimi*s	followers of Abu 'Abdullah Muhammad bin Hakim al-Tirmizi. They affirmed the doctrine of saintship (*wilayat*) and marked out territories within a mystic's jurisdiction as *wilayat*. Hakim Tirmizi graded and classified the mystics and their jurisdictions.
(11) *Nuri*s	followers of Abul Hasan Nuri. They protested that the real object of *tasawwuf* was superior to *faqr* which was only a means to an end. He preferred *suhbat* (society) to *'uzlat* (solitude).
(12) *Junaidi*s	followers of Shaikh Junaid of Baghdad.[13] They believed in sobriety (*sahv*) and kept aloof from rapture (*sukr*). They claimed to be absolutely orthodox in matters of religion.[14]

After these sects, appeared mystic philosophers who consolidated the doctrines of the above-mentioned schools along with other religious and mystic ideas into a consistent mystic philosophy. Imam Ghazzali (ob. 1111 AD) was the second great scholar after Imam Qushairi (ob. 1074 AD) to write a systematic account of mysticism. According to Ibn Khaldun, it was he who systematized *tasawwuf* into a science.[15] He defined a number of mystic terms and fixed their connotations more correctly and exhaustively than Imam Qushairi had done. He distinguished between *'ulama-i zahir* (externalist scholars) and *'ulama-i batin* (saints, mystics) and said that while the former proceed from *knowledge* to *action*, the latter proceed from *action* to *knowledge*.[16] Ghazzali taught that the intellect should be used to destroy trust in itself and that the only trustworthy knowledge was that gained through *experience*. The theological doctrines could not be proved by speculative methods, but only by the direct knowledge with which God floods the heart of the believer.[17]

In the thirteenth century there appeared three great figures—Shaikh Muhi-u'd-din Ibn-i 'Arabi (ob. 1248 AD), Shaikh Shihab-u'd-din

---

13. For brief biographical notices of the saints referred to here, see the *Nafahat-ul Uns* of Maulāna 'Abdur Rahman, Jami.

14. *Kashf al-Mahjub* (English trans. by Nicholson), p. 150, et seq.

15. Cited by Shibli in *Al-Ghazzali*, p. 187.

16. Ibid.

17. MacDonald's article on Ghazzali in the *Encyclopaedia of Islam*, Vol. II. p. 146.

Suhrawardi (ob. 1234 AD), and Maulana Jalal u'd-din Rumi (ob. 1273 AD) who consolidated the thought of their predecessors and gave to mysticism a consistent philosophy, a discipline, and a warm fund of emotions. All three had met each other.

Shaikh Muhi-u'd-din Ibn-i 'Arabi propounded in his two famous works, *Futuhat-i Makkiya*[18] and *Fusus-ul Hikam*,[19] the philosophy of *Wahdat-ul-Wujud* (Unity of the phenomenal and the noumenal world). He held that all being is essentially one, as it is a manifestation of divine substance. There were mystics[20] before Ibn-i-'Arabi who had uttered phrases purporting to pantheism, but Ibn-i-'Arabi "was the first to interpret his own experience of *Tauhid* or Unity in such a way as to be intelligible to others."[21] His works exercised enormous influence on mystic thought in Islam.[22]

Ibn-i 'Arabi's works reached India very early. They came through 'Iraqi (ob. 1289 AD), a mystic poet, but it appears that the first reception was not very warm. However, soon afterwards commentaries on his works began to pour in and people began to take a keen interest in his works.[23] Ibn-i Taimiyya's disciples reached India at a time when the country was in the grip of pantheistic doctrines. The policies of Sultan Muhammad bin Tughlaq and Firuz Shah seem to have been very greatly influenced by these tendencies of the age.

Maulana Jalal-u'd-din Rumi, the famous author of the *Masnavi*, popularized pantheistic ideas through his warm and breathing verses. What people had refused to accept in prose they readily accepted in verse. Rumi's *masnavi* came to be regarded as the Persian recension of the Quran. We find his verses being recited in the mystic circles of Delhi in the fourteenth century.[24]

Shaikh Shihab-u'd-din Suhrawardi wrote his *'Awarif-ul Ma'arif* which is a book of moderate or centrist mysticism and was, therefore, readily accepted by the mystics of all schools. *'Awarif* contained exact explanations

---

18. Printed in Bulaq in 1274 AH, Cairo, 1329 AH.

19. Printed with 'Abdur Razzaq Kashani's commentary in Cairo, 1309, 1321 AH.

20. Bayazid Bustami (ob. 261/874) exclaimed: 'Holy am I, how great is my glory'. Mansur (ob. 309/921) declared: 'I am Truth'.

21. Burhan Ahmad Faruqi, *The Mujaddid's Conception of Tauhid*, p. 80.

22. For details about his life and works, see *Muhy-u'd-din Ibn al-'Arabi*, Afifi.

23. For details about his influence on India, see my article "Shaikh Muhi-u'd-din Ibn-i-Arabi aur Hindustan," published in the journal *Burhan* of Delhi (January, 1950), pp. 9–25.

24. *Khair-u'l-Majalis* (ed. K.A. Nizami, Aligarh, n.d.), p. 163.

of the mystic terms and dealt with the principles of *khanqah* organization and discipline. It had a practical bias and a practical value. The book was brought to India very early, probably by the disciples of the Shaikh himself. The Chishtis also prized it very greatly. Shaikh Farid-u'd-din Mas'ud Ganj-i Shakar used to teach it to his elder disciples and a later mystic *tazkirah* attributes a summary of this work to him.[25]

RISE OF THE *SILSILAH*S

By the middle of the thirteenth century mystic thought, both in prose and verse, had reached its finale. Since this development in mystic thought had taken place in Muslim lands in the same generation which saw the establishment of the Delhi Sultanate, mystic ideology was imported into India bodily in its developed form. The principles of the earlier mystics were explained, illustrated, re-stated, and summarized, but no original contribution to mystic thought was made.[26] But, so far as the practical application is concerned, India had much to contribute by developing the mystic *silsilah*s to a degree probably unknown in other lands. Here the abstract mystic principles were applied to concrete conditions of society and transformed into space-time forces.

The last and the most important phase in the development of Islamic mysticism was, of course, the rise of the *silsilah*s in the twelfth century. The utter ruin of Muslim social life and the degeneration of Muslim morals during the period preceding and following the sack of Baghdad by Hulagu came as a challenge to mystic thought. Would Muslim mysticism remain merely a cult for the interiorization of religious rites and lose its social value or would it organize a world-wide movement for the spiritual culture of humanity and thus save Muslim society from moral and spiritual inertia? The mystics chose the second alternative and concentrated all their energies on the regeneration of Muslim society. At a time when Muslim political power was at its lowest ebb and anarchy and indiscipline reigned supreme,[27] they divided the universe into spiritual territories

25. *Gulzar-i-Abrar* (MS).

26. Shaikh Ahmad Sirhindi's (ob. 1624 AD) theory of *Wahdat-u'sh-Shuhud* (unity of the phenomenal world) as opposed to the theory of *Wahdat-u'l-Wujud* (unity of the phenomenal and the noumenal world), and Khwaja Mir Dard's (ob. 1776 AD) theory of *'Ilm-i-Ilahi Muhammadi* (knowledge of God based on the teachings of Muhammad) and his concept of *nur*, were, in fact, a contribution to mystic thought. But these works do not fall within our period.

27. See 'Ata Malik Juwaini, *Tarikh-i-Jahan Gusha* (Gibb Memorial Series), pp. 33–35.

(*wilayats*)[28] and with clearly marked out spheres of jurisdiction set out to revitalize the spiritual life of the Muslims. The spiritual orders (*silsilahs*) were effectively organized to meet the situation and *khanqahs*, which henceforth became an integral part of the mystic discipline, were established on an extensive scale.

The earliest mystic order was the *Qadiriya Silsilah* founded by Shaikh 'Abdul Qadir Gilani[29] (1077–1166 AD), one of the most outstanding figures in the annals of Islamic mysticism. His sermons, collected in *Al-Fath-ur-Rabbani*, are, according to Professor Margoliouth, "some of the very best in Moslem literature: the spirit which they breathe is one of charity and philanthrophy."[30] It is strange that the *Qadiriya Silsilah* did not reach India during the Sultanate period. Respectful references to the saint are found in early religious literature, but his works did not reach India till the seventeenth century.

The *Silsilah-i-Khawajgan* comes next in point of time. It was founded by Khwaja Ahmad (ob. 1166), popularly known among the Turks as Ata Yasvi.[31] Ata Yasvi was followed by another great saint, Khwaja 'Abdul Khaliq Ghajdavani[32] (ob. 1179) who gave to his *silsilah* a distinct spiritual philosophy. Two centuries later there appeared Khwaja Baha-u'd-din Naqshband[33] (ob. 1388) who utilized the traditions of Ata Yasvi and the teachings of Khwaja Ghajdavani and built up the structure of the *silsilah*. His contribution towards the consolidation and expansion of the *Silsilah-i-Khawajgan* was so great that after his death the *silsilah* came to be known

---

28. "God has saints (*walis*)," writes Shaikh 'Ali Hajwiri, "whom he has distinguished by His friendship and who are the rulers of His dominion... As to the saintly officers of the Divine court who are in charge of affairs, there are three hundred, known as *Akhyar*, forty others known as *Abdal*, seven others known as *Abrar*, four more known as *Autad*, three others known as *Nuqaba* and one other known as *Qutb* or Ghauth. These saints know each other and cooperate in their work." *Kashf-al-Mahjub*, pp. 213–314.

29. For biographical details see Shattanaufi, *Bahjat-ul-Asrar* (Cairo, 1304 AH).

30. *The Encyclopaedia of Islam*, Vol. I, p. 41.

31. Literally '*Ata* means father in the Turkish language, but the term is used for eminent saints. Yasa was a town in Turkistan. For a short biographical notice of the saint see al-Kashafi, *Rashahat* (Kanpur, 1912), pp. 8–9.

32. Ghajdavan was a town at a distance of 18 miles from Bukhara. For biographical notices, see Jami, *Nafahat-ul-Uns* (Lucknow, 1915), pp. 339–41; *Rashahat*, pp. 18–27.

33. For biographical notices, see *Nafahat-ul-Uns*, pp. 345–49; *Rashahat*, pp. 53–57.

as the *Naqshbandi* order, after his name. This *silsilah*, though one of the earliest, was the last to reach India.

The other important mystic order was the *Chishtia Silsilah*. It was founded in Chisht (a village near Herat) by Khwaja Abu Ishaq Shami[34] (ob. 940 AD) but was destined to develop and flourish in India. The pre-Indian history of the *silsilah* is obscure and indefinite. Khwaja Mu'in-u'd-din Sijzi brought it to India in the twelfth century and established a Chishti mystic centre at Ajmer. Under his talented successors, Shaikh Qutb-u'd-din Bakhtiyar Kaki, Shaikh Farid u'd-din Ganj-i Shakar, and Shaikh Nizam-u'd-din Auliya the *silsilah* spread far and wide and many mystic centres were established from Ajodhan to Lakhnauti.

Another spiritual order which flourished in India simultaneously with the *Chishtia* order was the *Suhrawardia Silsilah*. It was founded by Shaikh Najib-u'd-din 'Abdul Qahir Suhrawardi[35] (ob. 1169), a native of Suhraward, a town in Jibal, the ancient Media; but was developed by his nephew, Shaikh Shihab-u'd-din Suhrawardi[36] (ob. 1234). He sent many of his disciples to India[37] but Shaikh Baha-u'd-din Zakariyya alone succeeded in firmly establishing the *silsilah* in India, particularly in Multan and Sind.

Two other *silsilahs*—the *Firdausia* and the *Shattaria*—also reached India during the Sultanate period, but they did not make any important contribution during the period under review. The *Firdausi Silsilah* was founded by Shaikh Saif-u'd-din Bakharzi,[38] an eminent saint of Bukhara. His disciple Shaikh Badr-u'd-din of Samarqand[39] introduced it in India. But the saints of this *silsilah* retired into Bihar, which was far removed from the main centres of Muslim culture during the Sultanate period. The *Shattari Silsilah*[40] was brought to India by Shah 'Abdullah (ob. 1485) during the Lodi period. It attained an ephemeral and short-lived importance during the reign of the early Timurids.

---

34. For brief biographical notices, see *Siyar-ul-Auliya*, pp. 39–40; *Nafahat-ul-Uns*, p. 296.

35. For his life, see as Subki, *Tabaqat-ul-Kubra*, Vol. IV, p. 256; see Ibn Khallikan, *Wafayat-ul-a-'yan*, Vol. I, p. 299; *Nafahat-ul-Uns*, pp. 456–58.

36. For a brief biographical account, see *Nafahat-ul-Uns*, p. 420.

37. Shaikh 'Abdul Haq, *Akhbar-ul-Akhyar*, p. 36.

38. For his life see *Tarikh-i-Guzidah*, p. 791; *Nafahat-ul-Uns*, pp. 385–86; *Habib-us-Siyar*, p. 36.

39. *Akhbar-ul-Akhyar*, p. 115.

40. For a short history of the *silsilah* see *Medieval India Quarterly*, Vol. I, part 2.

ESTABLISHMENT OF *KHANQAHS*

With the rise of these *silsilah*s, the establishment of *khanqah*s on a large scale became imperative. Though the first *khanqah* was constructed early in the second century AH by Abu Hashim Sufi,[41] these early *khanqah*s could not develop into centres of the mystic movement. They remained private in character. From the twelfth and thirteenth centuries onwards *khanqah*s become centres of mystic discipline and organization. They ceased to be simply 'places of private worship' and became the nuclei for the expanding movement of *Tasawwuf* and a forum for the discipline of the corporate life of the mystics.

The establishment of *khanqah*s was based on the conviction that a life of solitary, self-sufficient contemplation was incompatible with the highest mystic ideals because it made man egocentric, limited his sympathies, and cut him off completely from the energizing currents of social life. "In constructing *khanqah*s," writes Shaikh 'Izz-u'd-din Mahmud, the Persian translator of the famous *'Awarif-ul-Ma'arif* of Shaikh Shihab-u'd-din Suhrawardi, which was accepted by medieval Indian mystics as the best guide book for the organizers of *khanqah*s, "there are several advantages.... First it provides shelter for mystics who do not possess any house of their own...Secondly, by gathering at a place and mixing with each other, the mystics get an opportunity of regulating their life and developing uniform inward and outward ways.... Thirdly, in this way they get an opportunity of criticising and mending each other's ways."[42] In fact, when men of different temperaments and attitudes assembled in these *khanqah*s, all tensions, conflicts, and complexes in their character were resolved and their personalities were moulded in consonance with the spirit of the *silsilah*. Common penitences and sufferings drew out the noblest qualities of their souls and made them understand what Carlyle calls the 'divine significance of life'.

Shaikh Shihab-u'd-din Suhrawardi found sanction for the establishment of *khanqah*s in the Quranic verses S. XXIV, 36–37,[43] and laid down the following fundamental principles for the mystics entrusted with the task of organizing *khanqah*s:[44]

1. The people of the *khanqah*s should establish cordial relations with all men *(khalq)*.

---

41. *Nafahat-ul-Uns*, pp. 31–32.
42. *Misbah-ul-Hidayah* (Lucknow edition, 1322 AH), pp. 118–19.
43. *'Awarif-ul-Ma'arif* (Urdu trans., Lucknow, 1926), p. 123.
44. Ibid, pp. 126–27.

2. They should concern themselves with God, through prayers, meditation, etc.
3. They should abandon all efforts at earning a livelihood and should resign themselves to the will of God.
4. They should strive for the purification of their inner life.
5. They should abstain from things that produce evil effects.
6. They should learn the value of time.
7. They should completely shake off indolence and lethargy.

The *Ahl-i-Khanqah* (people of a *khanqah*) were divided into two categories: permanent residents (*muqiman*) and travellers (*musafirin*). Travellers desiring to stay in a *khanqah* were expected to arrive there before the *'asr* prayers. If they arrived late, they were advised to pass the night in some mosque and join the *khanqah* the next day. As soon as a guest arrived he was expected to offer two *rak'at* of prayer and then greet the residents of the *khanqah*. If the visitor decided to stay on after the third day, he had to undertake duties in the *khanqah* and help the inmates in their day-to-day work. The servants of the *khanqah* were instructed to show extreme hospitality to all guests and were strictly warned against ridiculing those who were ignorant of the mystic customs and conventions.[45]

The permanent residents of the *khanqah* were divided into three grades: *Ahl-i-Khidmat, Ahl-i-Suhbat,* and *Ahl-i-Khalwat,* according to their standing and the nature of duties assigned to them.[46]

Strict discipline was maintained in the *khanqah* and elaborate rules were laid down for the guidance of the inmates: how to talk to the Shaikh; how to deal with visitors; how to sit in the *khanqah*; how to walk; how and when to sleep; what dress to wear—on these and similar other topics minute instructions were given to the people of the *khanqah*.[47] The Shaikh dealt sternly with those inmates who were found guilty of the slightest irregularity.[48]

45. *Misbah-ul-Hidayah*, p. 119.
46. Ibid, pp. 120–21.
47. See Shaikh Najib u'd-din 'Abd al-Qahir Suhrawardi, *Adab-ul-Muridin*; *'Awarif-ul-Ma'arif*, Part I, chapters XIII, XIV, XV, XVIII, XX, Part II, first ten chapters: *Misbah-ul-Hidayah,* Chapters V, VI, VIII. There is hardly any aspect of *khanqah* life on which elaborate instructions are not found in these works.
48. Only one instance: Shaikh Burhan-u'd-din Gharib, a senior disciple of Shaikh Nizam-u'd-din Auliya, was in charge of the kitchen in the *khanqah* of the Shaikh. On account of pain in his leg (he was seventy at that time), he folded a blanket and sat leaning on it in front of his visitors. When the Shaikh came to know of it he was deeply annoyed. When Burhan-u'd-din, as usual, came to pay his respect to the Shaikh, the latter did not talk to him. Burhan-u'd-din kissed his

If a *khanqah* had no endowment (*waqf*) for its maintenance, the Shaikh could either instruct his disciples to earn their livelihood or permit them to beg or ask them to sit in the *khanqah* resigned to His will. If a *khanqah* had no Shaikh but was run by a group of men of equal spiritual status (*ikhwan*), the same three courses were open to them.[49]

SPIRITUAL MECHANICS

Mar'ifat (gnosis) being the *summum bonum* of a mystic's life, methods were explored through which *wasl* (union) was possible. The heart (*qalb*) was considered the only medium which could set the finite in tune with the Infinite. Every *silsilah* consequently developed its own methods for training the heart. Shah Walliullah points out that in prescribing these methods, the saints of the various schools took into consideration the temperament of the people living in a particular region.

When a person desired to be initiated into a *silsilah* he gave his hand in the hands of the Shaikh and repented for his past sins (*tauba*) and promised to lead a chaste and pure life in future. Sometimes the head of the new entrant was shaved. Sometimes a cap was placed on his head.

The following were the methods adopted in order to harness all feelings and emotions to establishing communion with Allah:

1. *Zikr-i Jahr*   reciting the names of Allah loudly, sitting in the prescribed posture at prescribed times.
2. *Zikr-i Khafi*   reciting the names of Allah silently.
3. *Pas-i Anfas*   regulating the breathing.

---

master's feet and came down to the *jama'at khanah*. He had hardly taken his seat when the personal attendant of the Shaikh conveyed to him the Shaikh's order that he was to leave the *khanqah* at once. Overwhelmed with grief, he went to the house of a disciple of the Shaikh but after two days he requested him to leave his house. A person in disfavour with the Shaikh would not be entertained by anyone else. Burhan-u'd-din went back to his own house, dejected, grief-stricken, and morose. Friends tried to console him but the shock of being expelled from the *jama'at khanah* was too severe for him. Amir Khusrau represented his case to the Shaikh but failed to secure his pardon. At last Amir Khusrau appeared before the Shaikh, wrapping his turban round his neck, as criminals do when they give themselves up to justice. The Shaikh was touched by this sight. He asked Khusrau what he wanted. Khusrau requested the Shaikh to forgive Burhan-u'd-din. The Shaikh consented and it was only then that Shaikh Burhan-u'd-din was able to re-enter the *khanqah*. See *Siyar-ul-Auliya*, pp. 278–82.

49. *Misbah-ul-Hidayah*, pp. 121–22.

4. *Maraqbah*	absorption in mystic contemplation.
5. *Chillah*	forty days during which a mystic confines himself to a lonely corner or cell and devotes himself to contemplation.

Some mystics emphasized the efficacy of audition parties (*sama'*) in the formation of a spiritual personality. Songs, they said, not only relieved the strain on a man's emotions, but also quickened his emotional response and attuned his heart to the Infinite and the Eternal. *Sama'* or *qawwali*, consequently, became one of the popular institutions of medieval mysticism and the common man, incapable of comprehending the mystic principles at a higher level, readily accepted its ceremonial aspect. If its metaphysics attracted the higher intellects, the mystic ceremonials—*sama'*, *'urs*, *langar*, etc.—drew to its fold the common man who looked upon the mystic more as a blessed miracle worker than the teacher of a higher morality.

India During the Thirteenth Century

CHAPTER I

INDIA ON THE EVE OF THE TURKISH INVASIONS

Harsha's death in 647 AD marks the end of an epoch in Indian history. He had effectively consolidated his power and had succeeded in establishing a strong centralized monarchy. As soon as he closed his eyes in death, centrifugal tendencies appeared and the empire broke into small fragments, the *Desa*s. New social and political forces altered the pattern of existing institutions and brought about a radical change in the life and conditions of the people of Hindustan. The rise of the Rajput aristocracy introduced a new and virile element in the body politic, while the decline of Buddhism and the Brahmanic revival set the tone of society.

When the Turkish military operations started, India was nothing more than a medley of principalities[1] wedded to a policy of eternal hostility and perpetual strife among themselves. "The boundaries of each state," writes Mr Bandyopadhyaya, "varied with the success or failure of a ruling prince. Consolidation of authority or the building of a stable empire was beyond the comprehension or genius of these chiefs. War for military glory continued to be the end and aim of their existence."[2]

Of the new Rajput states that dominated the political scene, the Chabamanas ruled in Sambhar and Ajmer, the Paramaras in Malwa, the Kalachuris in Chedi, the Chandellas in Bundelkhand, the Chalukyas in Gujarat, the Gahadavalas in Kannauj, the Palas in Magadha, the Suras, and later the Senas, ruled in western Bengal. Ambitious rulers of these dynasties constantly disturbed the political equilibrium of the country and strove to impose their suzerainty upon weaker princes. Political anarchy and disunity was, thus, the keynote of Indian political life when the Turks threatened to liquidate the Rajput state-system in India.

1. In the Yewur inscription of the Chalukyas of the Deccan (I.A., Vol. VIII, p. 18) the number of kingdoms is given as 59.

2. N.C. Bandyopadhyaya, *Development of Hindu Polity and Political Theories* (Calcutta, 1938), p. 161.

THE POLITICAL STRUCTURE

The Rajput king was a hereditary sovereign and exercised unlimited and autocratic authority. He claimed divine origin and traced his descent from the sun or the moon. "Despotic as the rulers were, they were bound by the Smriti-made law and could not thus add to the evils of despotic legislation."[3] A number of ministers were appointed to assist the monarch in administering the country. The titles of some of these ministers are found in the inscriptions of the period but most of the discussions about their functions and duties are based on mere speculation. It appears that their numbers, titles, and duties differed from state to state.[4] Though generally these ministers were appointed and dismissed at the pleasure of the king, in some cases they played the role of king-makers. The Kalachuri records inform us that Kokalla II was raised to the throne by *amatyamukhyas* (ministers).[5] The *dharmakaramadhikari* was in charge of religious endowments.[6] A striking feature of the Sena administration was the political influence of the queen and the *purohita*.[7]

The Rajput government was typically feudal in character. The kingdom was divided into fiefs held by the members of the ruling house, the *kulas*. This system, instead of strengthening the political fabric, divided its resources and rendered it practically impossible for the various state governments to pursue any definite and consistent policy or introduce any uniformity in administration. It is said about the *Maharajaputra Yuvaraja* Govindachandra that, without the permission of the king, he made a very large number of land grants.[8] Thus the Rajput political system and its feudal character tended more towards disunity and decentralization than towards political integration or solidarity.

The chief source of income of the Rajput rulers was, of course, the land revenue, but other taxes were also imposed. These taxes varied from state

3. Vaidya, *History of Medieval Hindu India* (Poona, 1926), Vol. II, p. 225.
4. The Bengal inscriptions refer to the following ministries: (1) Rajamatya. (2) Purohita, (3) Mahadharmadhyaksha, (4) Mahasandhivigrahika, (5) Mahasenapati, (6) Mahamudradhikarita, (7) Mahakshapatalika, (8) Mahapratihara, (9) Mahabhogika, and (10) Mahapilupati. (*Epig. Indica*, XIV, p. 159). In Gahadavala grants the following officers are mentioned: (1) Mantri, (2) Purohita, (3) Pratihara, (4) Senadhipati, (5) Bahndagarika, and (6) Akshapatalika. For the Chedi inscription of Karna and the ministers mentioned therein, see *Epig. Indica*, XI, p. 41.
5. *The Struggle for Empire*, p. 274.
6. Ibid.
7. Ibid, p. 277.
8. Ibid, p. 276.

to state. The *Arthashastra*, however, refers to the following sources of income:

> Forts; country parts; mines; buildings and gardens; forests; herds of cattle; roads; tolls; fines; weights and measures; town clerk; superintendence of coinage; superintendence of seals and passports; liquor; slaughter of animals; threads; oil; ghee; sugar; state goldsmiths; warehouse of merchandise; prostitutes; gambling; building sites; corporation of artisans and handicraftsmen; superintendence of gods; taxes collected at the gates; produce from crown lands; portion of produce payable to the government; religious taxes; *kara* (taxes paid in money); merchants; superintendence of rivers, ferries, boats and ships; towns; pasture grounds; road cess; ropes; ropes to bind thieves; all produce from mines; corals, conch shells, etc.; gardens of flowers, fruits, and vegetables; fields; forests for game, timber and elephants; herds of cows, buffalos, goats, sheep, asses, camels, horses, and mules; land and water-ways; compensation for damages; and property of men dying without heirs, etc.[9]

The state had a right to *vishti*, i.e., forced labour.[10]

For purposes of revenue administration each kingdom was divided into districts called *Bhukti* in the north, *Mandala* in Malwa, and *Rashtrakuta* in the Deccan.

THE SOCIAL STRUCTURE

(a) *The Caste System*

The principle of caste formed the basis of the Indian social system in the eleventh and twelfth centuries. Whatever the circumstances under which the system originated, it had resulted in the total annihilation of any sense of citizenship or of loyalty to the country as a whole. The demoralization that it had brought in its wake, both from the individual and the community points of view, was terrible in its proportions. Recounting its baneful effects on individual life, Dr Beni Prasad remarks: "In the exaltation of the group it [the caste system] largely sacrifices the individual values. It strikes at the root of individuality and amounts almost to a denial of personality. It refuses to admit that every individual is, in his nature, universal and that he has the right to seek his own self-expression, to

---

9. Kautilya, *Arthashastra* (Eng. trans., R. Shamasastry, Mysore, 1923), pp. 63–64.

10. Vaidya, *History of Medieval India*, Vol. II, p. 234. Kalhana writes about Sankaravarman, "Thus he introduced the well-known (system of forced) carriage of loads which is the harbinger of misery for the villages and which is of thirteen kinds." A. Stein, *Rajatarangini*, Vol. I, Book V, pp. 209–10.

determine his own ambitions and pursue his own interests. The principle of caste is the negation of the dignity of man as man."[11]

At the top of the Indian society there were four *varnas* or castes—Brahman, Kshattriya, Vaishya, and Sudra. Much, however, as these classes differed from each other, they lived together in the same towns and villages.[12]

(b) *The Brahman and His Privileged Position*

The Brahman was assigned the highest place in medieval Hindu society. He was, in the words of Manu, "the lord of (all) castes (*varna*)".[13] Everything existed for him, and Manu had declared:

> 99: A Brahmana coming into existence on earth, the lord of all created beings, for the protection of the treasury of the law.
> 100: Whatever exists in the world is the property of the Brahmana; on account of the excellence of his origin the Brahmana is, indeed, entitled to it all.[14]

Religion was the exclusive monopoly of the Brahman. He not only administered to the religious needs of the people but stood like an intermediary between God and man. Alberuni informs us that only the Brahmans and the Kshattriyas could learn the *Veda*s and, therefore, the *moksha* was meant for them alone.[15] It appears that Manu had permitted the study of the *Veda*s to the three *varna*s, though teaching them was the exclusive monopoly of the Brahman.

> 1 Let the three twice born castes (*varana*) discharging their (prescribed) duties, study (the *Veda*); but among them the Brahmana (alone) shall teach it, not the other two; that is the established rule.[16]

Apart from the pre-eminent position that they enjoyed in the social and religious life of the people, the Brahmans were exempt from the payment of all taxes.[17] Lucrative and profit-making professions were not closed to them. A Brahman could try his fortune at trading in cloth or betel nuts, but it was preferable that he did not engage in trade in person but employed a Vaishya to do it for him.

11. *The State in Ancient India*, p. 12.
12. E.C. Sachan, *Alberuni's India* (London, 1910), Vol. I, p. 101.
13. *Manu*, Chapter X, pp. 401–02.
14. *Manu*, Chapter 1, pp. 24–26.
15. *Alberuni's India*, Vol. I, p. 104. The view of the Hindu philosophers was, however, different. According to them 'liberation is common to all castes and to the whole human race, if their intention of obtaining it is perfect.'
16. *Manu*, Chapter X, p. 401.
17. *Alberuni's India*, Vol. II, p. 132.

Even amongst the Brahmans themselves the idea of theological contamination was very acute. Every Brahman was required to have his separate drinking vessels and eating utensils; if any other person used them they were broken. "I have seen," says Alberuni, "Brahmans who allowed their relatives to eat with them from the same plate but most of them disapprove of this." Hindu law had permitted the Brahmans to marry women of other castes, but Alberuni tells us: "In our time the Brahmans, although it is allowed to them, never marry any woman except of their own caste."[18]

The life of a Brahman fell into four stages—(a) *Brahmacharya* (8th to the 25th year) to be spent in the study of the *Veda* and devotion to the master. (b) *Grihastha* (25th to 50th year) to be spent in married life. (c) *Vanaprastha* (up to the 75th year) when the Brahman quits his household and dwells outside the bonds of civilization and leads a life of abstinence as in the first period. (d) *Sannayasa*, when he wears saffron garments and, remaining indifferent to worldly life, strives for *moksha*. (e) Lastly, there was the state of *Maha-atma* (the great *rishi*), which meant that he had realized *moksha*.

The third and the fourth stages of a Brahman's life were spent in itineracy. Strict limits were, however, imposed on his wanderings during the time of Alberuni. "The Brahmana is obliged," says Alberuni, "to dwell between the river Sind in the north and the river Carmavati in the south. He is not allowed to cross either of these frontiers so as to enter the country of the Turk or of the Karanata. Further, he must live between the ocean in the east and west. People say that he is not allowed to stay in a country in which the grass which he wears in his ring-finger does not grow, nor the black haired gazelles graze... If he trespasses into them he commits a sin."[19] Thus religious tradition had imposed restrictions on a Brahman's cultural and intellectual contact with the world outside and had made him deeply egocentric and insular in his attitude. An inevitable corollary of this attitude was the spirit of self-complacency and intellectual arrogance which characterized the relations of the Indians with all foreigners. "The Hindus believe," writes Alberuni, "that there is no country but theirs, no nation like theirs, no king like theirs, no science like theirs."[20] This was an unfortunate development of later days as Alberuni informs us: "Their ancestors were not so narrow-minded as the present generation."

(c) *The Kshattriyas*

The Kshattriyas came next in the scale of the social hierarchy. Though not entitled to officiate as priests, they were permitted to perform the Puranic

18. *Alberuni's India*, Vol. II, p. 156.
19. Ibid, pp. 133–34.
20. Ibid, p. 101.

rites. "Their degree is not much below that of Brahma," Alberuni informs us, "he rules the people and defends them, for he is created for this task."[21]

(d) *The Vaishyas and the Sudras*

The two twice-born castes, i.e., the Brahmans and the Kshattriyas, were the exclusive heirs to the spiritual and intellectual achievements of Hinduism. The remaining two castes—i.e. the Vaishyas and the Sudras— were assigned a lower place in the social hierarchy. "The descendants of the Vaisyas," writes R.C. Dutt, "who had an equal right with Brahmans to learn and recite the *Veda* and to sacrifice to the fire, came, after the religious and political revolutions of the ninth and tenth centuries, to be classed with and considered unworthy of religious knowledge."[22] The duty of a Vaishya was to devote himself to agriculture, cattle breeding, and business, either on his own behalf or on behalf of a Brahman. "The Sudra is a servant of the Brahman, taking care of his affairs and serving him."[23] The Sudras and the Vaishyas were deprived of all sacred knowledge. If any member of these castes dared to hear, pronounce, or recite Vedic texts, he was hauled up by Brahmans before magistrates who ordered his tongue to be cut out.[24] Since the Vedas and their *Anga*s included all the literature and sciences of the country—grammar, versification, arithmetic, etc.—the law thus effectually forced the rest of mankind to live in ignorance.

(e) *The Masses*

Below these *varna*s (castes) was the nondescript mass of humanity known as the *Antyaja*. The Antyaja were not reckoned amongst any caste, but were members of a certain craft or profession. There were eight classes or guilds of them: (1) fuller; (2) shoemaker; (3) juggler; (4) basket and shield maker; (5) sailor; (6) fisherman; (7) hunter of wild animals; and (8) weaver. They could freely intermarry with each other except the fuller, the shoe maker, and the weaver. They lived near the villages or towns of the four castes "but outside them".[25]

(f) *The Workers*

The position assigned to the workers and artisans was deplorable in certain respects. Kautilya declares: "Thus traders, artisans, musicians, beggars,

---

21. Ibid, p. 104.
22. R.C. Dutt, *Later Hindu Civilization* (Calcutta, 1909), p. 195.
23. *Alberuni's India*, Vol. II, p. 136.
24. Ibid, p. 125.
   Dr Beni Prasad thus comments on this passage: "From the mention of the Vaishya, the whole passage smacks of exaggeration, but certainly has a substratum of fact in it." *State in Ancient India* (Allahabad, 1928), p. 446.
25. *Alberuni's India*, Vol. I, p. 101.

buffoons and other idlers *who are thieves in effect*, though not in name, should be restrained from oppression on the country,"[26] and included a chapter in his work on *"Protection against artisans"*.[27]

Kautilya's regulations relating to the weavers, washermen, goldsmiths, scavengers, physicians, and musicians reveal the general attitude of the governing classes towards the workers and the artisans. During the time of Alberuni their condition was much worse than during the time of Kautilya. "If any body wants," writes Alberuni, "to quit the works and duties of his caste and adopt those of another caste, even if it would bring a certain honour to the latter, it is a sin."[28]

The lowest people were the *Hadi*, the *Doma*, the *Chandala*, and the *Badhatau*. They were assigned dirty work such as the cleaning of the villages and other services. "In fact," observes Alberuni, "they are considered like illegitimate children,"[29] and are treated as "outcasts".[30] Alberuni's statements are borne out by the code of Manu in which the position of this class is thus explained:

> The dwellings of the Chandalas and Schwapachas shall be outside the villages, they must be made *Apapatras*, and their wealth (shall be) dog and monkeys. Their dress (shall be) the garments of the dead, (they shall eat) their food from broken dishes, black iron (shall be) their ornaments and they must always wander from place to place. A man who fulfils a religious duty shall not seek intercourse with them; their transactions (shall be) among themselves, and their marriages with their equals...at night they shall not walk about in villages and in towns. By day they may go about for the purpose of their work, distinguished by marks at the king's command, and they shall carry out the corpses (of persons) who have no relatives; that is a settled rule.[31]

(g) *The Idea of Physical Contamination*

This insular social behaviour of the Indian people rendered the social structure inflexible and fragile. Whatever little semblance of corporate spirit this social system possessed was crushed by the idea of physical contamination. Alberuni, who took "pains to study that civilization and literature in a catholic spirit,"[32] has noted with disgust and amazement the working of this idea in the social life of the people. If a Hindu warrior

26. *Arthashastra*, p. 250.
27. Ibid, Book IV, Chapter 1, p. 245, et seq.
28. *Alberuni's India*, Vol. I, p. 103.
29. Ibid, p. 101.
30. Ibid, p. 102.
31. *Manu*, Chapter X, Ss 51–55.
32. Dutt, *Later Hindu Civilization*, p. 192.

was taken as prisoner by the Mussalmans, and was subsequently released, he was disowned by his caste or guild. "I have repeatedly been told," writes Alberuni, "that when Hindu slaves (in Muslim countries) escape and return to their country and religion, the Hindus order that they should fast by way of expiation; then they bury them in the dung, stale, and milk of cows for a certain number of days till they get into a state of fermentation. Then they drag them out of the dirt and give them similar dirt to eat, and more of the like. I have asked the Brahmans if this is true but they deny it and maintain that there is no expiation possible for such an individual and *that he is never allowed to return into those conditions of life in which he was carried off as a prisoner.* And how should that be possible? If a Brahman eats in the house of a Sudra for sundry days, he is expelled from his caste and can never regain it."[33] These prisoners, disowned by their own community, often embraced Islam.

THE LEGAL STRUCTURE

The legal system of the Hindus is embodied in (a) the *Dharma-Sutras* (aphorisms of law of the different schools), (b) the *Dharma-Sastras* (codes of law attributed generally to sages), and (c) commentaries and treatises by Hindu jurisprudents. Amongst these codes, the codes of Manu and Yajna-valkya are pre-eminent. The former is supposed to be the foundation of the whole orthodox system of Hindu law; the latter is the binding law of the majority of Hindus.[34] But our knowledge of the operative part of Hindu law, i.e., the law as it worked in the eleventh and twelfth centuries, is very meagre.

Alberuni says that the Hindus believed their religious law and its simple precepts to be derived from Risis. "Further, no law can be exchanged or replaced by another, for they use the laws simply as they find them."[35] A coordination of the legal maxims contained in these law books with the account of Alberuni can give us some idea of the Hindu legal structure of those days.

(a) *Family Law and the Law of Inheritance*
Manu speaks contemptuously about women and attributes all sorts of impure desires, bad conduct, and malice to them.[36] Marriage was considered a necessity and if a girl remained unmarried for some time, she became

---

33. *Alberuni's India*, Vol. II, p. 163.
34. K.P. Jayaswal, *Manu and Yajnavalkya*, p. XIX.
35. *Alberuni's India*, Vol. I, pp. 106–07.
36. *Manu*, Chapter IX, p. 330.

a *Sudra—(Vrsati)*.[37] It was laid down that a husband should never have intercourse with a wife who gave birth only to daughters.[38] Divorce was not permitted.[39] Widow marriage was forbidden,[40] while to remain a widower was prohibited.[41] The number of wives that a man could have depended upon his caste—a Brahman could take four, a Kshattriya three, a Vaishya two wives, and a Sudra one only.[42]

Intermarriages were legally allowed so long as a man did not marry a woman of a lower caste. "If twice born men wed women of their own and of other [lower castes], the seniority, honour and habitation of those [wives] must be settled according to the order of the caste (*varna*)," declares Manu.[43]

If this was not done the man was "as (despicable) as a Chandala (sprung from the) Brahman (caste)."[44] Children of a Brahman by women of the three lower castes, of a Kshattriya by a wife of the two lower castes, and of a Vaishya by a Sudra woman, were all considered as base-born (*apasada*).[45]

(b) *The Penal Law*
A society based on caste principles could not possibly avoid making discriminations on grounds of birth, sex, and status.

The two higher castes were exempt from capital punishment under all circumstances.[46] The property of a Brahman or a Kshattriya, who was found guilty of murdering a Brahman or killing a cow or of drunkenness or incest, was confiscated and he was driven out of the country. K.P. Jayaswal writes: "A privilege is claimed in the Manava code which practically places him (Brahmin) above criminal penalty in felony. He is to be (1) allowed to leave the country, (2) without a wound on him, and (3) with all his property, in proved offences of capital punishment. Neither forfeiture and fine, nor corporal punishment, is to be sentenced on him. He suffered only what Hobbes called 'a change of air' after having committed the most heinous crimes."[47]

37. Jolly, *Hindu Law and Custom*, p. 119.
38. Ibid, p. 145.
39. Ibid, p. 143; *Manu and Yajnavalkya*, p. 231.
40. *Alberuni's India*, Vol. II, p. 155.
41. *Manu and Yajnavalkya*, p. 232.
42. *Alberuni's India*, Vol. I, p. 155.
43. *Manu*, Chapter IX, pp. 342–44.
44. Ibid.
45. *Manu*, Chapter X, p. 404.
46. *Manu and Yajnavalkya*, p. 85.
47. Ibid.

These legal discriminations are best illustrated in punishments provided for slander which varied according to the status of the slanderer:

> A Kshattriya deserves a fine of 100 when he has abused a Brahman; a Vaishya 150 or 200, respectively, and a Sudra, a torture.
> When the once born man of sudra and of the mixed, Sudra-like castes attacks a twice born with terrible language, his tongue deserves to be cut [out], for he is of vile influence.
> If he mentions the personal name and caste (in opposition), an iron nail, ten inches long, shall be thrust into his mouth, red hot.
> A Brahman shall be fined 50 [for] abusing a Kshattriya; 25 [for] abusing a Vaishya, 12 [for] abusing a Sudra.[48]

In cases of theft, punishment was given as follows: In extreme cases the criminal, if a Brahman, was blinded and mutilated by the dismemberment of the left hand and right foot or of the right hand and left foot; a Kshattriya was mutilated but not blinded; and criminals of other castes were put to death.[49] The law of adultery also made discriminations on grounds of caste. The following regulations of Manu deserve to be particularly noted in this connection:

> 359: A man who is not a Brahmana ought to suffer death for adultery (*Sangra hana*): for the wives of all the four castes must always be carefully guarded.
> 374: A Shudra who has intercourse with a woman of a twice born caste (*varna*), guarded or unguarded, shall be punished in the following manner: if she was unguarded, he loses the part (offending) and all his property; if she was guarded, everything (even his life).
> 375: (For intercourse with a guarded Brahmani) a Vaishya shall forfeit all his property after imprisonment for a year; a Kshattriya shall be fined one thousand (*panas*) and shall be shaved with the urine (of an ass).
> 376: If a Vaishya or Kshattriya has connection with an unguarded Brahmani, let him fine the Vaishya five hundred (panas) and, the Kshattriya one thousand.

(c) *Legal Procedure*

So far as the law courts were concerned, it was laid down that petitions should be entertained in the order of caste.[50] Females and Chandalas were disabled from being witnesses in a law court.[51]

This gloomy picture of Indian society in the eleventh and twelfth centuries should not, however, make one oblivious of the intellectual achievements of Hinduism in the preceding ages. Long before the advent

48. *Manu and Yajnavalkya*, p. 150.
49. *Alberuni's India*, Vol. II. p. 162.
50. *Manu and Yajnavalkya*, p. 115.
51. Ibid. p. 131.

of the Turks, Hindu contributions in the sphere of mathematics, astronomy, toxicology, chemistry, medicine, astrology, parables, and politics had attracted the attention of the Arabs and a large number of Sanskrit works on these subjects had been translated into Arabic. This glorious intellectual heritage of India was, however, not open to the Indian masses in the eleventh and the twelfth centuries. The Mussalmans brought with them, besides their own sciences, many of the sciences which they had initially borrowed from the Hindus.

CHAPTER II

ADVENT OF THE TURKS

Sind was the first territorial acquisition of the Mussalmans in India, though commercial and intellectual intercourse between the Arabs and the Indians had existed long before the Arab conquest of Sind and a number of Arab colonies had sprung up on the Indian coast.[1] In 712 AD Muhammad b. Qasim overthrew the Brahman dynasty of Sind and brought India definitely within the orbit of Muslim political ambitions. But the Arab conquest of Sind, its cultural significance notwithstanding, could not develop into a nucleus for the Muslim empire of Hindustan. Geopolitically it was devoid of all 'elements of expansion', while indifferent internal government further froze its expansionist activity. Thrown exclusively on its own meagre resources, it failed to bring northern India under its aegis. The Gurjara-Pratihara Empire doggedly checked the extension of Arab political influence in India and for some time Sind had to stand on the defensive. It was with the rise of Ghaznin in the tenth century that the Turkish pressure on the north-western frontiers increased and India was faced with the danger of foreign invasions. Ghaznin was the symbol of a new imperialist movement in Central Asia aiming at the establishment of Turko-Persian hegemony over the lands of the Eastern Caliphate. Sabuktigin, a Turkish slave of Alptigin, consolidated his power around Ghaznin by conquering Lamaghan, a part of the sprawling Hindushahiyya kingdom, and Seistan on the Persian border. His son and successor, Sultan Mahmud (999–1030), continued the forward policy of his father and captured many frontier forts and strategic places which facilitated his future operations into the heart of Hindustan. During the thirty-two years of his rule, Mahmud invaded India more than seventeen times and, though he carried his successful arms up to Muttra, Kannauj, Baran, and Gwalior, he did not annex any area beyond the Ravi. In fact, India had no place in his political ambition and his Indian expeditions were only a means to the establishment of the Turko-Persian Empire. However, his campaigns laid India open to foreign invasions and exposed the wealth and

1. See *Influence of Islam on Indian Culture*, Tara Chand (Allahabad, 1946), pp. 29–31; Sulaiman Nadvi, *Arab-o-Hind kay Ta'lluqat* (Allahabad, n.d.), "Muslim Colonies in India before the Muslim Conquest" (*Islamic Culture*, Vol. VIII, p. 474. et seq; p. 600, et seq; Vol. IX, p. 144, et seq).

the weakness of the Indian ruling class. The Punjab became a part of the Ghaznavid Empire and, as such, the political frontier of Muslim power in India. During the century that followed Mahmud's exploits in Hindustan, attempts were made for the extension of Muslim cultural and political influence towards the Gangetic plains and the Rajput territories. The suggestion that the Indian rajas were taken unawares by the Ghurid armies is not correct. The Turkish danger had been increasing all through the preceding decades and the Indian states were making efforts—though individual and isolated—to combat the situation. The contemporary Muslim chronicles[2] and the Indian epigraphic evidence[3] throw considerable light on the ever-increasing concern of the Hindu states at the inroads of the Turks and the exploits of the Hindu rajas in keeping the foreign invader— invariably referred to as '*Hammira*'—at bay. So grave, in fact, was the danger that a tax, *Turushkadanda*,[4] was imposed by some of the states to meet the increasing cost of fighting the Turks.[5]

MUSLIM SETTLEMENTS BEFORE THE GHURID CONQUEST

While the extension of Turkish political influence was stoutly resisted by the Rajputs,[6] the Muslim saints and mystics peacefully penetrated the country and settled at a number of important places. These Muslim

2. *Tarikh-i-'Al-i Subuktigin*, pp. 497, 664–65; *Tabaqat-i-Nasiri*, pp. 14, 22.

3. *Indian Antiquary*, 1889, pp. 14–19; *Epigraphia Indica* I, p. 62; *Indian Antiquary*, XLL, pp. 17–18; See also *Journal of Indian History*, Vol. XV and XVI (1936–37): "References to Mohammadans in Sanskrit Inscriptions of Northern India (AC 730–1320)".

4. There has been great controversy among historians about the exact nature of this tax. V.A. Smith (*Early History of India*, 4th ed., p. 400) considers it to mean the tax levied to meet the cost of resisting the Turkish invaders. Sten Konow (*Epigraphia Indica*, IX, p. 321) says that it was a tax imposed on the resident Muslim Turks, "a Hindu Jizya." Beni Prasad (*The State in Ancient India*, p. 448) writes: "It may refer to ransom-money which had to be paid to Turuskas or western invaders and which had to be raised from the whole population. As such it would correspond to the Danish tax levied in England for a while. Or it may mean a sort of poll tax imposed on Turuskas or settlers from the north west. There is no reason to suppose that Turuskas were settled in every place of which the grants mention the *Turushkadanda*". See also Ghoshal, *Contributions to the History of the Hindu Revenue System*, p. 263.

5. *Indian Antiquary*, XIV, p. 113.

6. In an inscription of the Chauhana ruler, Chachigadeva of Nadol, dated 1162, reference is made to the defeat and destruction of a Turushka army by his ancestor, Anahilladeva (*Epigraphia Indica*, Vol. IX, pp. 62–63; *Rajputana*, Ojha,

migrants lived outside the fortified towns amongst the lower sections of the Indian population, firstly because of caste taboos, and secondly because of the facility of establishing contacts with the Indian masses. It appears that nearly half a century before the Ghurid conquest of northern India, isolated Muslim culture groups had secured a foothold in the country. Ibn-i Asir writes about Benares: "There were Mussalmans in that country since the days of Mahmud bin Sabuktigin, who continued faithful to the law of Islam and constant in prayer and good work."[7] At Bahraich was the mausoleum of Sayyid Salar Mas'ud who 'was a soldier in the army of Sultan Mahmud'.[8] The fact that his name and his grave survived through long years between the Ghaznavid invasions and the Ghurid occupation of northern India shows that there was some Muslim population to look after the grave and to preserve for posterity the tradition of Salar's martyrdom.[9] Shaikh Mu'in-u'd-din Chishti came to Ajmer before the second Battle of Tarain[10] and his deep humanism and pious way of life attracted a band of devoted followers round him. Maulana Razi-u'd-din Hasan Saghani, the famous author of *Mashariq-ul-Anwar*, was born in Bada'un[11] long before the Ghurid occupation of that town. Recent studies have shown that there existed a Muslim colony in Kannauj before the Turkish conquest.[12] In some towns of U.P. and Bihar there are Muslim shrines which are attributed by local tradition to the pre-Ghurid period. The grave of Miran Mulhim in Bada'un,[13] and of Khwaja Majd-u'd-din

---

Vol. I, p. 269). His son Kalhana also destroyed a Turushka army (*Ep. Indica*, Vol. XI, pp. 46–51). A mutilated inscription at Kiradu, near Mt Abu, dated V.S. 1235/1178 AD records the repair of an idol temple broken by a Turushka army (*E.I.*, Vol. XI, p. 72).

7. Elliot and Dowson, *History of India*, Vol. II, p. 251.

8. Barani, *Tarikh-i-Firoz Shahi*, p. 491.

All the legends and traditions about Sayyid Salar have been collected together by 'Abdur Rahman Chishti in his *Mir'at-i-Mas'udi*. See also *District Gazetteers of the United Provinces*, Vol. XLV, 1921, pp. 117–19.

9. Nasir-u'd-din Mahmud was probably the first prince of the ruling house of Delhi who lived in Bahraich and under whose regime, according to Minhaj, Bahraich attained great prosperity. (*Tabaqat-i-Nasiri*, p. 208.) But there is no reference to Salar Mas'ud in his account. Probably Muhammad bin Tughluq was the first Sultan of Delhi who visited the grave of the saint (*Barani*, p. 491).

10. *Siyar-u'l-Auliya*, p. 46.

11. *Fawa'id-u'l-Fu'ad*, p. 103.

12. R.S. Tripathi, *History of Kannauj*.

13. See Razi-u'd-din, *Kanz-ut-Tawarikh*, pp. 51–53; *Tazkirat-u'l-Wasilin*, pp. 9–11; Iltutmish and Muhammad bin Tughluq put inscriptions on his grave (*District Gazetteers of the United Provinces*, Vol. XV, p. 190).

in Bilgram,[14] the grave on the Uncha Tilla Mohalla of Mallawan in Bilgram,[15] the *dargah* of Lal Pir in Azmat Tola at Gopamau,[16] the graveyard on the Bilsi Road in Bada'un,[17] the *Ganj-i-Shahidan* of Asiwan in Unao,[18] the graves in Jaruha near Hajipur in Bihar, the grave of Imam Taqi Faqih near the western gate of the Bari-Dargah at Maner[19]—are all considered to belong to the pre-Ghurid period, and some families living in these towns claim that their ancestors settled there during this period.[20] Their claims may or may not be correct, but it is difficult to challenge the local traditions with regard to the historicity of these graves, particularly when they are corroborated by epigraphic evidence.

GHURID CONQUEST OF NORTHERN INDIA

It was in the last quarter of the twelfth century that the Ghurids turned their attention towards Hindustan. Shihab-u'd-din wrested Multan from the Carmathians in AD1175. In 1178 he marched towards Anhilvara, but long and arduous marches in the waterless Indian desert exhausted his army and he suffered a signal defeat at the hands of Mularaja II. "It was a defeat not only of his forces but also of his plans".[21] The annexation of the Ghaznavid Punjab now became an urgent strategic necessity for him. In 1179 he established himself in Peshawar and two years later he led an expedition to Lahore. He did not succeed in overthrowing Khusrau Malik but established a fortress at Sialkot. Seven years later he overthrew the Ghaznavid power in Lahore (1186). The conquest of Lahore provided him with a base of operations for launching his attacks against the Rajput kingdoms that lay across the Ravi. He was defeated in his first conflict with Prithvi Raj (1191), but he reappeared the following year and defeated his Rajput adversary at the battlefield of Tarain. Two years later the kingdom of Kannauj was attacked and its ruler, Jaychandra, was defeated at Chandawar (near Etawah). In 1202 Ikhtiyar-u'd-din Muhammad b. Bakhtiyar Khalji ravaged Bihar and established himself in Bengal. By the

---

14. Hardoi, *District Gazetteer*, Vol. XLI, p. 178.

15. Ibid, p. 130.

16. Ibid, p. 187.

17. Ibid, Bada'un, Vol. XV, p. 190.

18. Ibid, Unao, Vol. XXXVIII, p. 118.

19. See Hasan Askari's article: "Historical Significance of Islamic Mysticism in Medieval Bihar", *Historical Miscellany*, pp. 10–11.

20. See *District Gazetteer*, Hardoi, Vol. XLI, p. 225.

Tanqihul Kalam fi Tarikh-i-Bilgram, Munshi Mahmud Bilgrami (District Gazette Press, Aligarh, 1937).

21. Habibullah, *Foundation of Muslim Rule in India*, p. 53.

year 1206 when Shihab-u'd-din was assassinated at Damyak,[22] practically the whole of northern India from the Ravi in the west to Assam in the east was under Turkish domination. There were sporadic efforts by the displaced Ranas to regain their lost power and prestige, but these attempts could not crystallize into a movement of mass resistance against the foreign rule. The contemporary chronicles refer very often to 'conquest' and 'reconquest' of certain areas by the Turks—a fact which shows that, helped by geographical factors and taking advantage of the pre-occupation of the Turkish warriors, the Rajput chiefs sometimes threw off the foreign yoke but they could not retain their independence for long. Perhaps the most difficult and the most disturbing situation for the Turks arose in 1196 when the Mher tribe, who dwelt in the neighbourhood of Ajmer, entered into an alliance with the Chauhans and the Chalukyas with the intention of expelling the Turks from Rajputana. Timely help from Ghaznin, however, saved the situation from taking a critical turn. So long as the administrative institutions of the Turks did not take a definite shape, the danger of Rajput revival and resistance continued to be a serious problem for the Sultans.

CAUSES OF GHURID SUCCESS

Various reasons have been advanced to explain this phenomenal success of the Ghurid armies. Some of these theories represent only individual fads and are far from being rational explanations of the Turkish successes in India. The fact that, as regards its extent, economic resources, and political prestige, the kingdom of Ghur was smaller than most of the medieval Rajput states cannot be ignored. The Rajput was in no way inferior to the Turk in courage and spirit of sacrifice. Rajput heroism and chivalry were proverbial. The assertion that the Indians were defeated on account of their non-violent attitude towards political problems is contradicted by the history of the contemporary Rajput kingdoms. Far from being despised, war was the prevailing madness and the Rajput states were constantly quarrelling with each other. The real cause of the defeat of the Indians lay in their social system and the invidious caste distinctions which weakened their military organization and honeycombed their social structure. That patriotic fervour with which every citizen instinctively lays his hand on the sword-hilt in moments of national crises was killed by these caste distinctions. The bulk of the Indian population was apathetic towards the fortunes of the ruling

22. *Tabaqat-i-Nasiri*, p. 124. For various controversies relating to the identification of the murderer, the place, and the date of the assassination, see *Ma'arif* (Azumgarh, September, 1943), pp. 219–28; *Burhan* (Delhi, January, 1956), pp. 17–29.

dynasties. No appeal from the Rajput governing classes could possibly receive a sympathetic response from the vast mass of the Indian population because there was no unifying bond, no idea of 'social oneness', no spirit of 'common citizenship', and no 'national consciousness'. Even religion was the monopoly of a particular section and the majority of the Indian people had never had a glimpse of an Indian temple. Fighting for the preservation of the *Veda*s was completely out of the question. For it was a sealed book to them and for hearing a single verse of its sacred text exemplary punishments were often inflicted on them. Manu's regulation:

> 62: Dying, without expectation of a reward, for the sake of Brahmans and of cows or in the defence of women and children, secures beatitude to those excluded [from Aryan community, *Vahya*].[23]

could hardly make amends for the disabilities imposed upon the non-caste Hindu population of medieval Hindustan. As was natural, the call from the fortified towns fell on deaf ears and failed to evoke any patriotic sentiment in the people who lived outside the city walls under unenviable conditions. The forts consequently became a static defence and could not be linked up by any mobile striking force all around. Under a different social order these fortresses would have served as a fortified base of a very dynamic character, linking up all the striking forces to that centre. But taking things as they were, a siege very often resulted in a *jauhar* by the besieged. Whatever resistance was offered came from the privileged classes and the Rajput aristocracy. Had the Indian masses resisted the establishment of Turkish rule in India, the Ghurids would not have been able to retain even an inch of Indian territory. Commenting on the significance of the Ghurid conquest of northern India, Professor Habib remarks: "This was not a conquest, properly so called. This was a turn-over of public opinion—a sudden turn over, no doubt, but still one that was long overdue."[24]

The caste system had played havoc with the military efficiency of the Rajput states. Since fighting was the profession of a group, recruitment was confined to particular tribes or castes.[25] All others were excluded from military training. Thus the bulk of the population was either incompetent

23. *Manu*, Chapter X, pp. 417–18.

24. Introduction to the Revised Edition of Elliot and Dowson's *History of India*, Vol. II, p. 52.

25. In view of what Alberuni has said about the working of the caste system in India, it is difficult to agree with some modern writers who hold that the military profession was no monopoly of any particular caste (P.C. Chakravarty, *Art of War in Ancient India*, pp. 78–82; B.K. Majumdar, *The Military System in Ancient India*, p. 19).

or unwilling to join the defence forces. The Rajput soldier himself had to work under serious handicaps which made his position very weak on the battlefield. The idea of physical contamination must have made the division of labour practically impossible. A soldier had to fight, had to fetch water for himself, prepare food, look after his utensils, and do similar other tasks, which in the Muslim ranks were performed by non-fighting groups. Caste rigours and the idea of physical pollution made swift movement of the forces almost impossible. The Rajputs, though known for their reckless bravery on the battlefield, never realized the truth of the Napoleonic dictum that in war all is mental. Sound military planning in which all possible eventualities and emergencies—falling into the hands of the enemy, minor reversals, etc.—are taken into consideration, had little meaning for the Rajput warrior who knew how to die but not how to win a victory. If he fell into the hands of the *mlechchah* but was subsequently released, he was doomed for ever. He was disowned by his own caste. He was physically alive but socially and theologically he was dead. Naturally, therefore, where imprisonment of a few hundred or thousand warriors would have solved the problem, *jauhar*s were performed on a large scale and thousands of men and women were needlessly reduced to ashes.[26] Whatever may be said about the spirit of chivalric heroism that inspired the performance of *jauhar*, from the strictly military point of view, it was devoid of all practical wisdom. Instead of inspiring the survivors to stiffer and more sustained resistance, it made them either desperate or pessimistic. The report of every *jauhar* performed in one fort would have broken the nerves of the people living in the neighbouring forts.

METHODS OF RAJPUT WARFARE

Some reference may be made here to the Rajput methods of warfare. The Indians looked upon military art as merely an affair of personal combat at a time when the conception of the whole army as a repository of organized force had already gained ground. A careful study of the *Adab-ul-Harb wa-Shuja'at* reveals that the Turks knew how to organize and employ their army as one coordinated unit, with unity of purpose and unity

26. Only once during the long and chequered history of Muslim rule in India do we find Mussalmans seriously thinking of performing *jauhar*. When Nadir Shah invaded Delhi (1739), the Mussalmans found themselves in a very difficult situation and decided to perform *jauhar*. Shah Walliullah dissuaded them from this rash act by narrating before them the events of the tragedy of Kerbala where the descendants of the Prophet, though in a minority, fought to the last valiantly and spiritedly. *Malfuzat-i-Shah-Abdul Aziz.*

of organization. The Rajput armies mainly consisting of feudal levies—raised by different Rajput leaders, trained under different conditions, and employed on different terms—lacked unity of purpose and fought for individual glory. Fakhr-i-Mudabbir strikes a very significant note when he says: "A commander with a heterogeneous army consisting of soldiers (drawn from different sources)—hundred from here and hundred from there—cannot achieve anything. An army with so varied and so many component elements has never been able to achieve anything great."[27]

Much has been said about the destructive role of elephants in medieval Indian wars. In fact, the Rajputs did nothing wrong when they used these elephants in their battles. Mahmud of Ghaznin had used them effectively in his campaigns against the Il-khans. Balban considered a single elephant to be as effective in battle as five hundred horsemen.[28] But when the Indians gave them a pivotal place in the disposition of their armies, they made a serious mistake. This deprived their forces of that element of mobility which the Central Asian powers rightly emphasized to be the key to success. A huge and unwieldy phalanx of armies headed by elephants with gorgeous trappings was bound to be signally beaten when face to face with a swift and easy-moving cavalry which could attack the flanks and rear of the enemy. From the military point of view, it was the 'Age of the Horse' and a well-organized cavalry alone could provide that weight of accumulated force and striking power which was needed to face the Turks who had kept themselves abreast of all developments in the art of war in the Middle Ages.

The superiority of the Turks in strategy and tactics was primarily due to their well-organized cavalry.[29] "After their mobility," remarks R.C. Smail, "the second tactical characteristic of the Turks was their archery. They used the bow from the saddle, and shot without halting or dismounting. As a result they were able to combine their archery with tactical uses of their mobility... Even in retreat they were able to turn in the saddle and shoot at their pursuers."[30] The Indian armies were seriously handicapped

27. *Adab-ul-Harb wa Shuja'at* (Rotograph of MS in British Museum), ff. 147a, b. My friend and colleague Mr 'Abdul Wahid Kureishy has edited this work for the History Department of the Aligarh Muslim University.

28. *Tarikh-i-Firoz Shahi*, p. 53. For Amir Khusrau's praise of an elephant army see *Qir'an-us-Sa'dain*, pp. 45–46.

29. Ferishta says that Shihab-u'd-din invaded Lahore with twenty thousand *doaspah, sih-aspah* cavalry (Vol. I, p. 90). In his campaigns against the Indian Rajas he brought much larger cavalry units.

30. R.C. Smail, *Crusading Warfare, A Contribution to Medieval Military History*, pp. 80–81.

in this respect. Balban used to say: "I know well that no (Indian) ruler can raise his hand against the army of Delhi because the armies of the Rais and the Ranas though consisting of a lac *paik*s (footmen) and *dhanuk*s (bowmen) cannot face my army. Barely six or seven thousand horsemen of Delhi are enough to ravage and destroy them."[31] It is significant that in Sanskrit literature the Turkish Sultans of India are referred to as *Ashwapati*s, i.e., lords of horses. It was the Turk's chief title to greatness and glory, and he did not hesitate in making it known through coins which passed through every Indian hand. In the earliest coins of the Sultans the horse is seen at full charge and the rider with an upraised mace. To the Indian people the Turk was either 'the lord of the horse' or '*Hammira*', and both these legends appear on the coins.

SOCIAL CONTRAST

Besides the above, there were some other reasons which made the Indians accept the Turkish regime in India. One of the most powerful factors in that connection was the Muslim social order, which contrasted sharply with the caste-ridden social and legal structures of medieval Hindustan.

The idea of 'social oneness' which was deeply imbedded in the religious thought of the Mussalmans, was a revolutionary force. The Allah of the Mussalmans was one. Salvation was open to all. All people, high and low, assembled at the same place and prostrated alike before the unseen God—a strange phenomenon for the Hindu masses of those days. They dined together and did not believe in the idea of theological contamination. Islam completely and unreservedly rejected the idea of 'superior birth'—the bedrock on which the entire social structure of medieval Hindustan stood. "All are sons of Adam and Adam was made of earth." The idea of being born from the sun or the moon, or the head or the foot of Brahma, was meaningless in a Muslim society. Piety (*ittiqa*) was the only criterion of superiority and an ordained priesthood or a hereditary class of Brahmans was the very negation of the real spirit of Islam.

For the majority of Indian people the change from the Rajput to the Turk meant the removal of all those disabilities and discriminations under which they had long suffered. The political organization which had strengthened the fabric of the caste system yielded place to a new order in which every one acquired the same rights in the law courts. All disparities in the penal code disappeared. Trial by ordeal for the discovery and punishment of crime was definitely suppressed. The new government refused to recognize any caste distinctions or discriminations. All convictions

31. *Tarikh-i-Firoz Shahi*, p. 52.

were on the basis of evidence and grave suspicion concerning the character of the accused and his previous record. A Sudra became a freeman. There were to be no gradations in punishments and the cases were not to be considered in any caste order. All persons guilty were punished in a uniform manner on the basis of state laws. The Islamic law of evidence did not exclude any one from appearing in the witness box. The individuality of women was recognized. The civil law made no discriminations on the grounds of sex, birth, or wealth. Professor Habib's observation that "face to face with social and economic provision of the Shari'at and the Hindu Smritis as practical alternatives, the Indian city-worker preferred the Shari'at,"[32] supplies the key to an explanation of the acceptance of Ghurid rule by the Indians.

SIGNIFICANCE OF THE GHURID OCCUPATION OF NORTHERN INDIA

The success of the Ghurids in India did not mean simply the substitution of one governing class by another. It led to some very vital changes and *novae res* in various spheres of life—social, religious, political, and economic.

The Political Aspect: The establishment of Turkish rule meant the liquidation of the multi-state system in northern India and the rise of a consolidated and centralized political organization which withstood the onslaughts of even the Mongol invaders. Hindustan, which had become merely a geographical expression under the Rajputs, regained its political individuality under the Turks. It would be too much to say that feudalism—the most distinctive feature of Rajput political life—disappeared completely from India with the advent of the Turks, but it can hardly be denied that the two basic concepts of feudalism—localism in administration and legal immunity of the feudal lord—received a serious setback and centrifugal tendencies were sternly checked and controlled. The political instinct of the Turkish conquerors refused to brook any distribution or division of authority on a feudal basis. Iltutmish and Balban, the two greatest Sultans of the early Turkish period, believed in unlimited and centralized political authority.

From the eighth century onwards India had lost all contact with the outside world and the Hindu society was 'set in rigidity like a concrete structure'. One great achievement of the Turkish conquest of northern India was the ending of this isolation and the establishment of the international status of India in the then-known world. Theoretically, the

32. Introduction to the Revised Edition of Elliot and Dowson, *History of India*, Vol. II, p. 52.

Delhi Sultanate was a part of the Abbasid Caliphate and, as such, a traveller could, in the words of Arnold, "pass from the confines of China to the pillars of Hercules, from the banks of the Indus to the Cicilian Gates, from the Oxus to the shores of the Atlantic, without stepping outside the boundaries of the territory ruled over by the Caliph in Baghdad."[33]

The Religious Aspect: Similarly, as after the rise of Buddhism, Brahmanism was forced to recast its religious outlook. After the Ghurid occupation of northern India, the Hindu religious thinkers were obliged to face the changed circumstances by effecting a change in their religious outlook. Hinduism gave evidence of great dynamism when it modified its social outlook and religious behaviour according to the requirements of the time. The rigidity of the caste system was softened in the centuries that followed, and Hinduism which did not believe in making converts adopted proselytizing methods.[34] Though the Bhakti movement, which was based on the two revolutionary doctrines of a direct approach to the Ultimate Reality and the brotherhood of man, blossomed in the fourteenth century, its germination may safely be traced to the early thirteenth century. Probably never before in the annals of Hinduism had religious leadership sprung from that class of society to which saints such as Kabir, Nanak, Dadu, Dhanna, and others belonged. A comparison and contrast of the religious and social outlook of the Hindus in the twelfth and the fifteenth centuries will explain the nature and extent of the influence of Islam on Indian culture.

The Social Aspect: Though the Turkish governing class jealously guarded its interests in the political sphere, it never permitted any distinction in the social or the legal spheres.[35] The immediate and most significant effect of the Turkish occupation of northern India was the liquidation of the old system of city planning. The place of the '*caste cities*' of the Rajput period was taken by the '*cosmopolitan cities*' of the Mussalmans. The gates of the new cities were thrown open for workers, artisans and Chandalas. The city walls were constantly extended and within its fold all types of people—high and low—built their houses and lived side by side without any social stigma attaching to any one. This plan suited the Turkish bureaucrats who wanted

33. *Travels and Travellers of the Middle Ages*, p. 89.
34. See Afif's *Tarikh-i-Firoz Shahi* (pp. 380–81) for a story relating to the conversion of a Muslim woman to Hinduism.
35. Balban, in spite of his racial prejudices in the political sphere, believed that there should be no discrimination in legal matters. When Malik Baqbaq, a courtier who held the *jagir* of Bada'un and 4,000 horses, scourged his servant to death, Balban ordered that Malik be flogged likewise. *Barani*, p. 40.

all workers to be close at hand for work in their *karkhanah*s (factories), offices, and private houses. As a result, the cities grew in size and prosperity. The city boundary wall ceased to be a line of social demarcation or distinction; it became simply a wall of protection and defence and nothing more. So great was the aversion of the Muslim people to the idea of segregation that, when Aibek thought of shifting the tanners of hide (*dabbagh*) to some distant quarter of the city[36]—on purely hygienic grounds, not due to any caste consideration—the people considered it so cruel and unjust that they interpreted his sudden death as a divine punishment for this act.

The new cities that arose from Lahore to Lakhnauti were symbols of a new social order. Workers, labourers, artisans, the non-caste people, and the unprivileged classes fully benefited from the urbanization policy of the Sultans and enjoyed, for the first time, the amenities of civic life. The Rajputs and the privileged classes chafed under a sense of humiliation and defeat but the working classes joined hands with the new government and helped it in building the new cities.

The Economic Aspect: These new cities became busy centres of trade and a new impetus was given to commercial enterprise. All those political and economic barriers which had separated one state from another and had limited the merchant's world did not exist now. From Multan to Lakhnauti there was one government. The legal system was one; the tariff regulations were the same; the coinage was the same; the market was wider and there were better prospects of trade. A merchant could move from city to city without any fear of caste regulations. He could stay in any inn or mosque (within the four walls of the city) and travel under uniform conditions of taxation.[37]

Commercial relations with the outside world developed on an unprecedented scale and foreign traders and merchants began to visit the Indian towns in large numbers. 'Isami refers to the presence of Chinese traders in Delhi during the reign of Iltutmish.[38]

Under the changed social and economic conditions, forced and involuntary labour was also given up. This proved a boon for the workers. The attitude of the Muslim governments towards involuntary labour is clearly evinced by an anecdote relating to Sultan Mahmud of Ghaznin as recorded by

36. *Futuh-us-Salatin*, pp. 105–06.

37. We hear of Muslim traders from Lahore travelling to do business with the Hindus of Gujarat and making huge profits (*Fawa'id-u'l-Fu'ad*, p. 116). A Hindu merchant of Nahrwalah, Visala Abjar, carried on trade in Ghaznin. (*Jawami'-ul-Hikayat*, Vol. I, pp. 47–48).

38. *Futuh-us-Salatin*, p. 122.

Muhammad 'Awfi. The Sultan not only punished an officer in this connection but also declared forced labour to be a crime in his territory.[39]

The Military Aspect: The establishment of Turkish rule in India brought about a change in the technique of war and the composition and character of the Indian armies. Fighting ceased to be the monopoly of one group. Anyone who had the strength to bear the strain of war could join the army. In fact, it was under the Sultans of Delhi that really Indian armies—i.e., armies in which recruitment was made from all sections of the Indian population, irrespective of any consideration of caste, creed, or colour— came into existence. This Indian army was the *forte* of the Sultanate and while internally it kept down the hostile Ranas and Rawats, externally it baffled the Mongols in their attempts at sweeping over the country.

At a time when great changes had taken place in the art of warfare in Central Asian lands, India had remained wedded to its outmoded and ineffective modes of warfare, relying mainly on the elephant, the *paik*, and the fort as the chief instruments of war. The Turk ushered in the change from the *paik* (foot soldier) to the *sawaran-i-muqatala* (mounted fighting men) and thus put India militarily on a par with Central Asian powers.[40]

The idea of a strong standing army—centrally recruited, centrally paid, and centrally administered[41]—gained ground with the advent of the Turks. Levies from provincial governors and *Iqta'dars* were often requisitioned but the central army always remained the core of the military organization of the Turks. The central government recruited and utilized all the resources of the country in men and material wherever available— horses from Sind, Siwalik, and Bhatnir; elephants from Bengal;[42]

39. *Jawami'-ul-Hikayat*, Vol. I, p. 22.

40. But India could not keep herself in touch with developments in the art of war in Central Asia in subsequent centuries. If the neglect of cavalry brought disaster at the battlefield of Tarain (1191), the neglect of artillery received severe punishment at Panipat (1525).

41. The importance that the *'Ariz* and his department assumed in the administration of the Sultanate during this period was due to the emphasis laid by the Turkish Sultans on the organization of the standing army. Fakhr-i-Mudabbir describes a review by the *'Ariz*. The *'Ariz* saw the army—both cavalry and infantry—march past him. The *naqibs* stood by and the *'Ariz* scrutinized each soldier, his arms, and his horse. Every soldier had an appointed place; the *naqibs* had charts for arranging the soldiers in battle array. (*Adab-ul-Harb* MS; Compare the review of Saffarid armies, *supra*, Section Two, p. 25). For the interest displayed by Balban and his *'Ariz* in the upkeep and maintenance of the army, see *Tarikh-i-Firoz Shahi*, pp. 115–16.

42. *Tarikh-i-Firoz Shahi*, pp. 53–96.

mercenaries from the Khokar and Jat tribes of the Punjab;[43] lancers from the suburbs of Sind,[44] etc.

CHARACTER OF THE GHURID INVASIONS

The Turkish invasions were not inspired by any religious zeal or proselytizing fervour. Shihab-u'd-din's first conflict on Indian soil took place not with a Hindu raja but with a Muslim co-religionist and he faced him with the same determination and in the same spirit in which he carried his arms into the *Aryavarta*. The Ghurid successes were not followed by any retaliatory action inspired by religious zeal or fanaticism. They handled the situation in the light of expediency and entered into a series of compromises without any religious partiality or prejudice. After the conquest of Ajmer, Shihab-u'd-din did not take over the administration but entrusted it to Prithvi Raj's son on condition of vassalage. When Delhi was conquered, Khandirai's successor was allowed to rule over the territory. When the Chauhans troubled Prithvi Raj's son, Aibek decided on direct annexation but compensated the prince by placing him in charge of Ranthambhor. Fakhr-i-Mudabbir, a contemporary of the early Turkish Sultans, has discussed five types of wars.[45] Barring the religious terminology, which was inevitable in the medieval context, he seems to believe that the Turkish wars were not religious in character.

Unnecessary emphasis is sometimes laid on the destruction of temples and cities by the Turks in the twelfth and the thirteenth centuries.[46] These acts were the necessary concomitant of medieval warfare. Every invader and conqueror delighted in presenting his exploits and achievements before the people in complimentary colours. These things were not unknown to Hindus. One West Chalukyan inscription formally accuses the Chola king of having burnt Jain temples in the Belvola province. The Vaisnavas of the South level similar charges against the Cholas.[47] In fact, every age has its own code of war. In the Middle Ages the destruction of temples and houses of worship was practised by all—Indians, Turks, Mongols, and others. Every invader, like the Turkish Sultans of Delhi, delighted in magnifying his achievements. In almost the same strain in which Hasan

43. *Foundation of Muslim Rule in India*, p. 247.

44. *Qir'an-us-Sa'dain*, p. 47.

45. *Adab-ul-Harb wa-Shuja'at*, ff. 131a–132b.

46. For a modern interpretation of this type, see *The Struggle for Empire*, pp. XIV, XIX.

47. Narayan Chandra Bandyopadhyaya, *Development of Hindu Polity and Political Theories* (Calcutta, 1938), p. 178.

Nizami extols the achievements of the Ghurids, the Hindu kings of medieval India took pride in the destruction of cities and houses of worship. The burning of Vatapi by the Pallavas and the repeated sacking of Sanchi by the Chalukyas, who dominated the Deccan, may be cited as instances of this spirit. A Rashtrakuta king boasts of having reduced the great city of Kannuaj into *Kusathali*. Similarly, the Cholas assumed the title of *Madhurantaka* to signal the destruction of the city of Madura.[48] 'Vikrama Cola', writes Narayan Chandra Bandyopadhyaya, 'claimed to have burned not only the Kalinga country but also the city of Kampili as well as the whole of Rattapadi. As to the burning of the Rashtrakuta country by Rajendra Cola, we have an account in the Soartur inscription. According to that record, the Cola army numbering 9,00,000 pillaged the whole country slaughtering *ahmana*s, women and children and destroyed the modesty of women by forcibly carrying them off. Another Cola record speaks of the destruction of non-combatants while the Hoysala Visnuvardhana claims to have burned enemy towns and territories.'[49] Neither the medieval Hindus nor the medieval Turks need be condemned for what they did. They simply followed an established practice of their age.

48. Ibid, pp. 176–77.
49. Ibid.

CHAPTER III

CHARACTER OF THE EMPIRE AND THE RELIGIO-POLITICAL IDEALS OF THE SULTANS

The character of the early Turkish Empire of Delhi has often been grossly misunderstood. Sometimes a religious veneer is put on it and it is represented as a 'theocracy'; at other times it is called a 'military state', resting on sheer physical force—without roots in the soil or support from the masses. A closer study, however, reveals that it was neither the one nor the other and that all such estimates are based on a misunderstanding of the real nature of the Muslim political organizations from the time of the Prophet to the rise of the Sultanate.

As already stated,[1] all Muslim governments from the time of the Umayyads have been secular organizations. The concept of theocracy, even if the Christian or Jewish background of the term is ignored, cannot be divested of the following essential features:

(a) a government in which God is regarded as the sole sovereign;

(b) the government is devoted primarily to the achievement of religious ends;

(c) all laws are divine commands rather than human ordinances;

(d) these laws are administered by an organized priesthood or a sacerdotal order claiming divine commission; and

(e) the two societies, civil and religious, are entirely incorporated.

The *Khilafat-i-Rashida* alone might be designated as a theocracy in the light of the features mentioned above. The Sultanate did not possess these attributes. It had no sanction in *Shari'at*; nay, it was a non-legal institution. Its laws were the result of the legislative activity of the rulers and the governing classes. The administration was exclusively in the hands of the secular authorities. When Bughra Khan advised Kaiqubad to shake off his indolence and reorganize the administration, he exhorted him to appoint particularly reliable persons to look after the *Diwan-i-Wizarat*, the

1. See *supra*, Section Two.

Diwan-i-Risalat,[2] the *Diwan-i-'Arz*, and the *Diwan-i-Insha*.[3] The implication was that these departments—all of which were under secular control—constituted the pivot of the administration. In fact, it was the higher nobility and the upper class of officials, such as the *kotwal*s, *wakil-i-dar*s, *sarjandar*s, *akhurbeg*s, *dabir*s, and *mustaufi*s,[4] which influenced and formulated the policies of the Sultanate. The religious leaders played the part of second fiddle. The political authorities tried to bind them to the state chariot in order to win public support through them, but they were not allowed to determine the course of political developments. Religion was no doubt respected but it was never made the basis of the political organization and the Sultanate never strove to realize any religious ends. Even the ethico-political treatises of the period, though anxious to invest the king with divine dignity, did not hesitate in declaring the incompatibility of *dindari* with *dunyadari*, of which the Sultanate was the highest perfection.[5]

The early Turkish Empire of Hindustan was a class state in so far as its political outlook was concerned. The Turkish warriors were more anxious to consolidate and preserve their power and authority rather than attempt any propagation or exposition of the political ideals of Islam. In fact, they themselves were callow converts and had accepted the new religion at a time when decadence had set in and political rivalries and ambitions had deadened the real spirit of the faith. They were ignorant of the Islamic ideals of peace and war which had inspired the soul of the early Saracens. Their wars were not the wars of religion and their political ideals were not determined by Islam. They planned their political life on the secular basis, worked according to their secular instincts, and allowed the spirit of tribal intolerance and tribal greed—which Islam, as preached by the Prophet, had come to abolish—to continue operating in their lives. They were Muslims no doubt but were not the representatives of Islam. The chronicles of the early Muslim historians such as Sadr-u'd-din Hasan Nizami and Fakhr-i-Mudabbir often delude us into thinking that the Turkish occupation of northern India was a religious affair and that the warriors were religious heroes ready to live and die for the faith, but such a view cannot stand the test of historical scrutiny. Considered in its proper

---

2 The *Diwan-i-Risalat* did not deal with religious affairs as I.H. Qureshi states (*Administration of the Sultanate of Delhi*, Lahore, 1942, p. 85). It dealt, as the term itself suggests, with foreign and diplomatic correspondence. (Cf. Habibullah, *Foundation of Muslim Rule in India*, Lahore, 1945, pp. 223–24).

3. *Tarikh-i-Firoz Shahi*, p. 153.

4. See *Tabaqat-i-Nasiri*, p. 169; *Tarikh-i-Firoz Shahi*, pp. 37–38, 85, etc.

5. *Fatawa-i-Jahandari*, f. 159a.

historical perspective, the Turkish occupation of northern India was an inevitable result of the emigration of races from Mongolia and Central Asia. It was population pressure, rather than religious fanaticism, which had brought the Turks into Hindustan. The empire which they had so enthusiastically built up would have ended in smoke had not another wave of tribal emigration from the Turkish lands—i.e. the Mongol pressure—uprooted innumerable Muslim families and driven them pell-mell into Hindustan to supply the necessary manpower for the infant Turkish Empire of India.

The opinion that the Turkish government was military in character or that it rested exclusively on the force of Turkish arms is equally unwarranted. No political structure could be built up and no government could be carried on for decades, nay for centuries, without the active acquiescence of the people. The frequency of military operations during the period should not be construed to mean that the state was military in character. It was military only so far as all medieval empires had to be. Beyond that it was not, and could not be so. The Rajput privileged classes—Thakurs, Ranas, and Rawats—who were deprived of their pre-eminent position in the social and political life of the country—no doubt chafed under foreign domination and rebelled whenever an opportunity was available, but we do not come across a single revolt of the Hindu *masses* as such. In fact, the people in general had accepted the new government as it had guaranteed complete freedom in their peaceful pursuits. A Hindu inscription dated 1337 of the Vikrama era (1280–81 AD) describes Balban as he, "throughout whose contented realm, under his great and good government, from Gaur to Ghaznah, from the Dravida country and Rameshwaram, everywhere the Earth bears the bounty of sylvan spring." His armies "ensure the peace and security enjoyed by all." So great was the Sultan's care for his people that "Vishnu himself has retired from the care of the world and gone to sleep on the ocean of milk."[6] There may be an element of poetic exaggeration in it, but it is, nevertheless, characterized by feelings of sincere appreciation.

The circumstances under which the Sultans had to work were exacting. On one side, the displaced governing class was eager to reassert its authority and win back its lost prestige, and on the other side, the Mongols were hammering at the gates of India. A vigilant and well-organized army alone could guarantee peaceful conditions both for the individual and the society. An analysis of the military operations of the period reveals the fact that never for once were the Turkish armies called upon to deal with a hostile population. Their operations were directed either against the Mongols

6. *Epigraphia Indo-Moslemica*, 1913–14, pp. 35–45.

or against the recalcitrant Ranas and Rawats. Mr K.M. Munshi's observation that:

> the conquests so exultantly referred to by the court chronicles of the Sultanate had an Indian side of the picture. It was one of ceaseless resistance offered with relentless heroism; of men, from boys in teens to men with one foot in the grave, flinging away their lives for freedom; of warriors defying the invaders from fortresses for months, sometimes for years, in one case, with intermission, for a century; of women in thousands courting fire to save their honour; of children whose bodies were flung into the wells by their parents so that they might escape slavery; of fresh heroes springing up to take the place of the dead and to break the volume and momentum of the onrushing tide of invasion[7]

is not borne out by historical facts and may be dismissed as an attempt to misread medieval history in terms of modern national sentiments. Had this been the popular reaction to the Turkish occupation of the country, the Turkish government would have been thrown out in no time.

A scientific evaluation of the nature of any organization cannot be attempted without an analysis of (a) the atmosphere in which the organization developed, (b) the *leitmotif* of the persons who developed it, and (c) the organization itself. Studied in this light, the Sultanate appears to be essentially a secular institution which was accepted by the medieval Indian people on grounds of merit.

PERSIAN INFLUENCE ON THE TURKISH STATE

Long before his advent into India, the Turk had been Persianized in his thought and behaviour. The spirit of the Persian Renaissance, though a spent force at this time, had so captivated his imagination that he was anxious to recreate and revive as much of Persian culture and tradition as possible. From theories of kingship to names and nomenclature of institutions and officers, court etiquette and army organization, every detail of the Ilbarite political organization breathed the Persian atmosphere. The Sultanate, an anomalous but inevitable growth in Islamic polity as it was, could not turn to the Pious Caliphate for guidance or inspiration. The Sassanids had elaborated an efficient state apparatus, perhaps the most perfect in the history of Asia Minor,[8] and so the monarchical traditions of Persia could best serve the ideological and cultural needs of the Sultanate. The Sultans consequently invoked the spirit of Sassanid Persia and derived ideological vitality and cultural stamina from it.[9] They rescued the great

7. *The Struggle for Empire*, Preface.
8. Barthold, *Iran*, p. 37.
9. *Tarikh-i-Firoz Shahi*, pp. 25; 30–31; 142; 113; *Qir'an-us-Sa'dain*, p. 24.

Persian heroes such as Jamshed, Kaikhusrau, Kaiqubad, Bahram, and Afrasiyab from Sassanid oblivion and rehabilitated them in Muslim political consciousness as ideals of social conduct and political behaviour. All sorts of traditions—genuine and false—associated with these heroes were revived under the belief that kingship was not possible without emulating Persian customs and ways of life. Balban gave the popular names of Muslim families—Mahmud and Muhammad—to his sons born before his accession; but his grandsons, who were born after his accession, were named Kaiqubad, Kaikhusrau, and Kaimurs after the Persian kings. Both Iltutmish and Balban traced their pedigrees to Afrasiyab[10] and Amir Khusrau found no better compliment for Kaiqubad than:[11]

وارث اكليل كيان كيقباد

كافسر جد فر كيانيش داد

While nominating Razia as his successor, Iltutmish did not hesitate for a moment to consider the legal propriety of his action. He drew his inspiration from the Iranian traditions in which a daughter succeeding her father was not an unusual phenomenon. The fact that two daughters of Khusrau Parvez—Purandukht and Arjumanddukht—had ascended the throne one after the other in the seventh century[12] was enough to satisfy Iltutmish's conscience. He bowed down before the Iranian traditions, ignoring the interdict of the Prophet against entrusting government to women.[13]

So far as the administrative institutions of the Delhi Sultanate were concerned, most of them had evolved and developed in Persian lands and consequently the Persian stamp was very deep upon them. The slaves of the imperial household were recruited, maintained, and disciplined according to Persian traditions. The armies were modelled on the armies of medieval Persia, with the same arms, equipment, and tactics. No reader of *Adab-ul-Harb wa-Shuja'at* will be left in any doubt about the nature and extent of the Sassanid influence on the military ideals and organization of the Turks.

---

10. Addressing Nasir-u'd-din Mahmud, Imam Asir-u'd-din Muntakhab wrote:

اے چراغ دودهٔ افراسياب   ناصرالدينا شه مالک رقاب

(*Tarikh-i-Muhammadi*, Rotograph, f. 356a and 358b). See also *Tarikh-i-Firoz Shahi*, p. 37. For an account of the Afrasiyabi Maliks, see Raverty, p. 900, et seq.

11. *Qir'an-us-Sa'dain*, p. 22.

12. Malcolm, *History of Persia*, Vol. I, p. 54.

Browne, *Literary History of Persia* (Cambridge, 1928), Vol. I, p. 182.

13. Shah Walliullah, *Izalat-ul-Khifa*, p. 8; *Hujjatullah-al-Baligh*, Vol. II, p. 356. For contemporary opinion about the desirability or otherwise of acting upon the advice of women, see *Adab-ul-Harb*, p. 68a.

In their social life also the Turks adopted Persian customs, etiquette, and ceremonials. The court of the Delhi Sultan was, in certain respects, a replica of the Sassanid court.[14] The custom of *pabos* or *zaminbos*[15] was introduced and the Persian festival of *Nauroz*[16] was celebrated with great pomp and éclat. The Mongol cataclysm had dealt a severe blow to Persian culture in 'Ajam; the Turkish Sultans of India gave it the protection it needed and, when almost all its centres had fallen, Delhi rose into eminence as the last citadel of Persian traditions.

14. *Tarikh-i-Firoz Shahi*, p. 25; Amir Khusrau declares Kaiqubad's court to be superior to the courts of Kisra, Zuhak, Faridun, and Jam. *Qir'an-us-Sa'dain*, p. 25.

15. The custom of prostrating before the king was prevalent both in India and Persia. The Muslim rulers, both caliphs and sultans, adopted it very early. The Seljuqs, the Samanids, and the Ghaznavids introduced it in their courts. If it reached the Delhi court through Persian channels, Indian traditions brought it to the medieval *khanqahs*. All visitors to Shaikh Farid-u'd-din Ganj-i-Shakar and Shaikh Nizam-u'd-din Auliya showed their respect to the great saints by laying their foreheads on the ground. Amir Hasan refers to this practice again and again (*Fawa'id-ul-Fu'ad*, pp. 158–59). Shaikh Nasir-u'd-din Chiragh discontinued it on account of its illegal character and declared:

پیش مخلوق سر بر زمین نهادن روا نیست

(It is not lawful to place one's head on the ground before a creature)—*Khair-ul Majalis*, p. 157.

16. *Nauroz* (or *Naugroz* as it was called by the Sassanids) was an ancient Persian festival (Christensen, *L'Iran*, pp. 225–26). Alberuni thus describes the general pattern of the celebration of Nauroz:

"In these five days it was the custom of the Kisras [Persian kings] that the king opened the Nauruz and then proclaimed to all that he would hold a session for them, and bestow benefits upon them. On the second day the session was for men of high rank and for the members of the great families. On the third day the session was for his warriors, and for the highest *Maubadhs* [priests]. On the fourth day it was for his family, his relations and domestics, and on the fifth day it was for his children and clients. When the sixth day came and he had done justice to all of them, he celebrated Nauruz for himself and conversed only with his special friends and those who were admitted into his privacy." As cited in *Encylopaedia of Religion and Ethics*, Vol. V, p. 872.

That the festival of *Nauroz* was celebrated in India for four days is clear from the following statement of Amir Hasan Sijzi made before Shaikh Nizam-u'd-din Auliya:

پیش ازیں به چهار روز که نو روز بود بنده شعرے گفته است

Fawa'id-ul-Fu'ad, p. 127.

THEORIES AND IDEALS OF KINGSHIP

Law, tradition, and expediency—these three factors shaped the political outlook of the Sultans and conditioned their theories of kingship. Insofar as they considered themselves the 'lieutenants of the Caliph'[17] and looked for investiture from Baghdad,[18] their attitude was determined by the legal requirements of the age.[19] The traditional elements in their theory of sovereignty came from Sassanid Persia, while political circumstances accentuated or attenuated the autocratic character of their monarchical institutions.

An analysis of the processes through which the traditions of Sassanid Persia made their way into the Muslim society, an interesting sociological study no doubt, falls beyond the scope of this work. It may, however, be pointed out that the governing class had to use much ingenuity in order to make these Persian notions tolerable to Muslim society. The divinity of kings being a fundamental postulate of Sassanid polity, the court of the Sassanid Emperor was arranged like a temple where people approached him with the same servility and deference with which a devotee approaches the pedestal of an idol. When Muslim power was established in Persia, these Persian traditions were suppressed for the moment, but soon afterwards they began to reassert themselves. A Persian sect called Rawendiya (from the name of their town) surrounded the palace of Mansur (754–75 AD) and shouted: "It is the house of our Lord, he that giveth us food to eat and water to drink."[20] They demanded that the Caliph declare himself as God in human form. This demand was so glaringly opposed to the fundamentals of Muslim faith that no Muslim ruler, however indifferent towards religion, dare accept it. The Rawendis were crushed, but the hint was taken by the ruling classes that political authority could not be consolidated without introducing some divine elements into it. The power of the crown was consequently sanctified and the democratic traditions of Islam were made to yield place to the authoritarian tendencies of Iran. Ideals and traditions which were refused admittance through the front gate came surreptitiously through the back door. Kingship was declared to be the vicegerency of God (*niyabat-i-Khudawandi*)[21] and the king was placed on a divine pedestal. Many servile forms of the Sassanid court were revived and were presented as legitimate substitutes for the earlier democratic practice of

17. *Adab-ul-Harb*, ff. 9b, 10a, *Tabaqat-i-Nasiri*, p. 177; p. 206; N. Wright, pp. 15–32.
18. *Tabaqat-i-Nasiri*, p. 174; *Tarikh-i-Firoz Shahi*, p. 103.
19. Arnold, *The Caliphate*, pp. 101–02.
20. Ibn Asir, Vol. V, pp. 187–88.
21. *Tarikh-i-Firoz Shahi*, p. 34.

bay't.[22] But while all these institutions and practices were being legalized, the basic fact remained that the Sultanate itself was illegal. A school of jurists then elaborated a constitutional theory which accepted the new monarchy (Sultanate) as an unalterable reality and linked it up with the Caliphal system. Some *hadis* were also manufactured to cast a halo of legality around the person of the Sultan.[23] 'Utbi quotes the saying: *al-Sultan zill Allah fi'l arz* (The Sultan is the shadow of Allah on earth) as a genuine *hadis* at the beginning of the *Kitab-ul-Yamini*, and his commentator al-Manini says that it was transmitted by Tirmizi and others as going back to Ibn 'Umar.[24] All these attempts were dictated by the desire to facilitate the entry of Persian ideas into the body politic of Islam.

The early Turkish Sultans of Delhi drew inspiration from these reorientated traditions of Sassanid Persia. The king was proclaimed to be 'the shadow of God on earth',[25] and his heart was declared to

---

22. Ibn Khaldun, *Muqaddima* (Urdu trans., Lahore), Vol. II, p. 90.

Minhaj's use of the term *bay't-i-'am* in connection with the accession of Mu'izz-u'd-din Bahram (p. 191), 'Ala-u'd-din Mas'ud (p. 198), and Nasir-u'd-din Mahmud (p. 208) appears ridiculous when the real connotation of the term is kept in mind. What Minhaj designates as *bay't-i-'am* was really the allegiance of the nobility.

23. It may be pointed out that during the time of the Prophet the word *sultan* was never used in the sense in which it is used or understood today. It simply means *power* or *argument*. There are six passages in the Quran where *sultan* has the meaning of power, but it is always the spiritual power which Iblis exercised over men (Ss. XIV: 26; XV: 42; XVI: 101–02; XVII: 67; XXXIV: 20). In the early centuries of Islam the word came to mean governmental power. The transition in meaning from an impersonal representative of political power to a personal title is a much later development.

24. *Sharh al-Yamini* (Cairo, 1286), p. 21.

25. *Tarikh-i-Fakhr-u'd-din Mubarak Shah*, p. 13; *Taj-ul-Ma'asir*, p. 79; *Adab-ul-Harb*, f. 113a. Minhaj calls Iltutmish ظل اله فى العالمين (p. 165); Nasir-u'd-din Mahmud is called ظل اله فى العالمين and سايهٔ يزدان (p. 205). Minhaj addresses Balban also as such (p. 230). Amir Khusrau writes about Kaiqubad:

چوں تو شدى سايه يزدان پاك   سايه فشاں باش بريں مشت خاك
(*Qir'an-u's-Sa'dain*, p. 205.)

تيز نتواند بعالم ديدن اكنوں آفتاب   چوں زچترش عالم درظل يزدانى نشست
(*Diwan*, p. 30.)

افسر خورشيد بشاہى توئى   نے غلطم ظل الٰهى توئى
(*Qir'an-u's-Sa'dain*, p. 25.)

be *manzar-i-rabbani*.[26] Obedience to him was considered obedience to God,[27] while rebellion against him was condemned as a sin.[28] The Quranic verse: 'Obey God, obey the Prophet and obey those with authority,'[29] was constantly emphasized to bring home to the minds of the people the necessity of obeying the Sultan, and a *hadis* of the Prophet in which the people are exhorted to obey the orders of their ruler *'even if he be a negro or a slave or mutilated in form,'*[30] was constantly pressed forward to make obedience to political authorities a religious obligation enjoined by the Quran and the *Hadis*.

Inspired by the Sassanid traditions of distance between royalty and the *ryot*, the Turkish Sultans of Delhi also emphasized the dignified parts of kingship and looked down upon all contact with the people as derogatory to the dignity of kingly office. In adopting this attitude towards the *ryot*, the Sultans were, in fact, helped and encouraged by the nobles who considered such attitudes necessary in their own interest. Two very distinguished Turkish nobles of the period, Malik'Izz-uld-din Salari and Malik Qutb-u'd-din Hasan, persistently persuaded Iltutmish to maintain royal dignity in every sphere for "it was necessary for the Sultan to strike awe and terror into the hearts of the people" and because "one could not discharge the obligations of kingship unless he behaved with dignity".[31] But this attitude did not go unchallenged. Sayyid Nur-u'd-din Mubarak Ghaznavi boldly criticized these practices and explained their irreligious character in the presence of Iltutmish.[32] Iltutmish, however, did not discontinue them. Whatever his personal religious outlook, he refused to

26. *Tarikh-i-Firoz Shahi*, pp. 70–71; Khusrau writes about Kaiqubad:

لوح خدائيست كه محفوظ باد جبهت تو با رقم عدل و داد

Qir'an-u's-Sa'dain, p. 20.

27. *Tarikh-i-Fakhr-u'd-din Mubarak Shah*, p. 12; Fakhr-i-Mudabbir quotes the following as a Tradition of the Prophet:

من اطاعنى فقد اطاع الله ومن اطاع الامام فقد اطاعنى ومن عصانى
فقد عصى الله ومن عصى الامام فقد عصانى

28. Fakhr-i-Mudabbir (*Adab-ul-Harb*, f. 100b; f. 102a; *Tarikh-i-Fakhr-u'd-din Mubarak Shah*, p. 12) and Minhaj (*Tabaqat-i-Nasiri*, p. 183) use the phrase عاصى شدن for rebellion.

29. *Tarikh-i-Fakhr-u'd-din Mubarak Shah*, p. 12.

30. Ibid, p. 13; *Adab-ul-Harb*, f. 3b.

31. *Tarikh-i-Firoz Shahi*, p. 31.

32. Ibid, p. 41.

take any risks by ignoring the demands of political life. The reaction of the people to these servile forms of Sassanid kingship is not known. Only once during the long history of the Delhi Sultanate did a man ask a saint of Bihar about the justification for calling the Sultan 'the shadow of God on earth'.[33] Similar interrogations must have exercised the mind of at least some people, but we have no means of knowing their views. What bound the people to the Turkish Sultans and created confidence in their hearts was, in fact, their stern and implacable sense of justice which overrode all other considerations.[34] It was at this level of justice and equity—not at the level of theological speculations or personal fads and fancies—that the common man judged his ruler.

One of the most popular medieval Persian traditions was the compilation of the *wasaya* (precepts) of eminent rulers and statesmen. Some of these collections are, no doubt, apocryphal in character but they were immensely popular in the Middle Ages and were avidly read and quoted by medieval statesmen and political thinkers.[35] Of the Sultans of Delhi, the *wasaya* of Balban alone have been preserved by Zia-u'd-din Barani.[36] Balban was, in fact, an ideal ruler according to the standards of the age—firm, fair, and awe-inspiring. Endowed with rare political vision and energy, he set the confused and disorganized affairs of government in order and enhanced the dignity and prestige of the crown. "No one," rightly observes Lane-Poole, "understood better than Balban the conditions of kingship in India."[37] His *wasaya* had, therefore, a special significance for medieval governments which were faced with the problem of law and order and the consolidation of political power. His instructions to his sons—Muhammad[38] and Mahmud[39]—not only epitomize the political ideology of the Middle Ages but also bring out the inner conflicts of his own political personality in full relief.

Balban's *wasaya* to his son and heir-apparent, Prince Muhammad, comprised two parts: the first was based on what Balban had heard about the functions and duties of kingship from eminent scholars at the court of

33. *Ma'dan-ul-Ma'ani*, Vol. I, p. 25. See also *A'ijaz-i-Khusravi*, Vol. IV, p. 196.
34. *Tarikh-i-Firoz Shahi*, pp. 44–45.
35. Barani refers to many such collections of *wasaya* in his *Fatawa-i-Jahandari*.
36. Shaikh Baha-u'd-din Zakariya, a contemporary of Iltutmish and Balban, is also reported to have left a *Wasiyat Namah* for his son, Shaikh Sadar-u'd-din 'Arif (See *Siraj-ul-Hidaya, malfuz* of Sayyid Jalal-u'd-din Bukhari Makhdum-i-Jahanian, MS, f. 44a). This *Wasiyat Namah* is not available now.
37. *Medieval India under Mohammedan Rule* (London, 1926), p. 88.
38. *Tarikh-i-Firoz Shahi*, pp. 69–80.
39. Ibid, pp. 95–105.

Iltutmish. These counsels were idealistic and religious in nature. So far as acting upon them was concerned, Balban himself confessed: "How can we the slaves be competent to rule in the manner in which 'Umar bin Khattab and 'Umar b. 'Abdul Aziz ruled."[40] It was 'paternal love', he said, which induced him to mention them before him, otherwise they had no relevance to his political problems.[41] The second part of his instructions was based upon his personal political experience which extended over a period of half a century. Balban wanted his son to follow these instructions closely, strictly, and intelligently. "If we do not regularly observe these rules," he warned the Prince, "there is sure to be trouble and confusion in our territories."[42]

The first part of Balban's *wasaya* contained the following advice:

1. Do not consider the task of ruling over people an ordinary or a trifling affair. It is a serious duty which should be discharged in all seriousness and with a full sense of responsibility.

2. The heart of the king reflects the glory of God. If it does not continue catching divine radiance continuously, the king cannot fulfil or satisfy the so many and so important duties of his kingly office. The king should, therefore, strive for the purification of his heart and his soul and should always be thankful to God for His blessings. 'A thankful king is sheltered under the canopy of God's protection.'

3. If the king allows the low-born, base, irreligious, and faithless people to interfere in government affairs, he is not only guilty of being ungrateful to God but also occupies the territory of God against the orders of the Day of Creation.

4. The king must live in such a way that all his acts, words, and movements are appreciated and recognized by the Mussalmans.

5. He must follow the old kings and seek God's pleasure by doing approved and virtuous acts.

6. He must behave in such a way that his words, deeds, orders, and personal qualities and virtues may enable people to live according to the laws of *Shari'at*.

7. That king alone is a real ruler who uses his God-given glory, grandeur, army, attendants, and treasuries to extirpate infidelity, idolatry, polytheism, and vice. If he is unable to accomplish this, he must at least keep the enemies of God and His Prophet dishonoured and humbled.

40. Ibid, pp. 74–75.
41. Ibid, p. 70.
42. Ibid.

8. If the king is unable to uproot sin and immorality completely, he must at least make it impossible for sinners and immoral people to indulge in sin and vice.

9. He alone is a real king, whose friends and officers administer absolute justice and root out oppression from his dominion. His own example should incline the hearts of friends, officers, and subjects towards justice and fair play.

10. Pious, religious minded, just, and God-fearing men alone should be appointed as qazis, officials, amirdads, and muhtasibs so that the laws of Shari'at might be enforced through them. These officials should remove deceit, fraud, dissension, dishonesty, hoarding, and usury from the people.

11. The king should realize that "people follow the religion of their rulers". If the king and his officers are honest and truthful, all the people in his dominion, young and old, women and children, are drawn towards virtue, uprightness, and justice. If the king and his officers indulge in oppression and vice the people also become wicked and immoral: 'O my dear son! Jamshed, the king of kings, used to say very often that the people are obedient and subordinate to king's orders. They adopt the same things which their king likes.'

12. The king and his allies, friends, qazis, officials, and governors should know that success in this world and salvation in the next depends on purification of the inner self. So far as external decoration is concerned, the high-born and the low-born, the Mussalmans and the infidels, the skilled ones and the worthless, the learned and the illiterate, the slaves and the free born, make no difference.

Under the second category, Balban advised his son as follows:

1. Royal dignity should be maintained both in public and private. All etiquette and formalities should be meticulously followed under all circumstances.

2. You should understand that kingship is the vicegerency of God.

3. Only noble, virtuous, wise, and skilled people should be allowed to come near you. You should make huge grants in their favour so that your generosity and beneficence might earn a good name in this world and get a reward in the next. You will never be disappointed in either world if you support and patronize the noble and the virtuous people.

4. Under no circumstances should you allow the mean, the vulgar, and the faithless people, and infidels to gather around you. If any person of humble birth and low origin is already in your service, you must

be kind and generous towards him but you should not make him your favourite or confidant. God will be displeased with you if you give high posts to mean, low-born, and worthless people.

5. Do not incur the displeasure of God by indulging in luxuries.

6. Kingship and bravery are twins.

7. If a king lives in the same way as other people live and grants to people what others also can bestow, the glory of sovereignty vanishes. A king should live and behave in a way different from other people.

8. A king should be full of ambition, for kingship can never be successful without it.

9. Kingship is not possible without these things—justice, beneficence, pomp, army, treasury, confidence of the people, and a number of selected and distinguished men to assist and serve the Sultan. If there is no justice, there can be no stability in government. Army and treasury are the two great essentials of kingship. If the people begin to hate their king and lose confidence in him, dissensions and disorders appear everywhere in the kingdom. No government can be carried on successfully without assistants and allies of noble birth. Your first duty is to inquire about the birth and character of a person before taking him into your confidence. Having once elevated a man to a high position, do not search for pretexts to degrade him.

10. Whenever you chastise someone keep it in moderation; do not convert well-wishers and sincere people into opponents.

11. Sleuths and spies should not be allowed to come anywhere near the court for their closeness to the ruler terrifies the obedient and trustworthy friends, and their confidence in the king—which is the basis of good government—vanishes.

12. Whenever you think of any expedition, first consider its consequences carefully. A king should not undertake any campaign which is not expected to be fruitful for, in case of failure, the royal prestige suffers grievously. Kingship cannot stand dishonour or humiliation. You should create such conditions that no equal of yours thinks of invading your territory. Do not personally lead expeditions against the smaller fry—the low-born and the worthless people. What others can achieve, do not undertake yourself. Do not be self-willed and do not undertake any campaigns without first consulting your advisers. Unless you are convinced that a man is sincere, faithful, experienced, and far-sighted, do not make him your confidant and do not disclose state secrets to him.

13. Do not be negligent or careless in looking after your sons, brothers, helpers, allies, *muqta'is*, officials, *'amils*, army, and the people. It is

necessary for a king to be well-acquainted with the good and evil intentions of his people.

14. You should have an eye on the revenues and the expenditure of the Empire. Half of the revenue should be appropriated, the other half should be kept in the treasury to be used in times of emergency. Necessary expenses should be incurred but there should be no extravagance for 'God does not like extravagant people'. Make earnest efforts to add to your wealth and territory through means sanctioned by the *Shari'at*.

15. Keep the army, subjects, and the merchants happy and prosperous.

16. There should be perfect peace and order in the country. Things sanctioned by the *Shari'at* should be enforced; things forbidden by law should be sternly stopped.

17. Be on good terms with your people, governors, army, and the pious men.

18. Use moderation in handling the affairs of your people. Be dignified, quiet, and collected in your dealings with them. Harshness and leniency both breed disaffection and create chaos.

19. Protect your person from wicked people. Their inordinate ambition can do some harm to you. Keep sincere guards and trustworthy policemen in your court.

20. Be kind to your younger brother and do not entertain complaints against him. Treat him as your right arm and allow him to retain the territory which I have assigned to him.

Some of the instructions which Balban gave to his son Bughra Khan were mere repetitions of the advice given earlier to Prince Muhammad. The following points, however, deserve to be noted:

1. It is not advisable for any ruler of Lakhnauti to rebel against the Sultan of Delhi. He should avoid all chances of conflict with Delhi and should continue sending presents and messages to the centre regularly. If the Sultan of Delhi marches towards Lakhnauti, he should fly away to some distant land.

2. *Wilayat dari* (governorship) and *Iqlim dari* (kingship) are two different things. If a *muqta'i* commits mistakes and does not perform his duty properly, he is dismissed by the king and the matter ends there; if, on the other hand, a suzerain commits mistakes, it leads to chaos and dissensions in every direction. The people become unruly, the government loses its stability, and the army gets restive.

3. A king should use moderation in the levying of taxes, and should neither tax so heavily as to make people poor and helpless nor so

lightly as to make them disobedient and insolent. Superfluity of wealth turns the heads of the people and makes them recalcitrant and insolent.

4. A king should be very careful about two things: (a) regular payment of the salaries of his soldiers, and (b) production of enough grain to meet the needs of the people. Legislation to achieve these ends is a stupendous task which Aristotles and Buzurchimehrs alone can perform. The king should give up lethargy and luxury and should work with the advice and help of talented wazirs and advisers to achieve these ends.

5. There should be consistency and stability in royal orders. Frequent changes bring about instability in the government.

6. Special attention should be paid towards the recruitment and maintenance of the army. The king should realize that the stability and permanence of his authority depend upon the maintenance of a large army. The affairs of the army should be reported to the king every day. The *Diwan-i-'Arz* should be dignified in dealing with the old army and liberal in the recruitment of the new.

7. A king should not neglect the worship of God. The five daily prayers should be offered punctually and in congregation.

After giving these instructions Balban summed up his speech with the following note:

Mahmud! I have given you instructions according to the requirements of the time. But, if I give you instructions of religious-minded kings and say that you should use all your courage and valour in the destruction and annihilation of infidelity and *shirk*, to keep the infidels and idol-worshippers degraded and dishonoured so that you may get a place in the company of prophets and to crush and uproot the Brahmans so that infidelity vanishes, to follow the traditions of the Prophet, to regard all court etiquette as contrary to the traditions of the Prophet, and to seek the approval of Abbasid Caliphs for your government and to appoint at the capital, *'ulama, mashaikh, sayyids,* scholars well-versed in Exegesis, Traditionists, persons who know the Quran by heart, preachers, scholars, and people skilled in every art so that it may become another Egypt, to offer Friday prayers with the permission of the Caliph, all this is my business to tell you about; but it is not worthwhile to repeat the same to you as you are a victim to evil designs.... But my last instruction to you is that you should commit yourself to the protection (i.e. become the disciple) of some holy person... who has really renounced this world and who has dedicated himself completely to the devotion and worship of God. Beware! you should never attach yourself.... to a man of the world.

A careful analysis of the thought content of these *wasaya* leads to the conclusion that, notwithstanding his insistence on the regular performance of the obligatory prayers for the personal salvation of a ruler, Balban's political ideology had no reference to religion. It was political expediency, not theological sanctions, to which he turned again and again to justify his principles. Respectful references to the Prophet and his traditions, and the governments of 'Umar bin Khattab and 'Umar b. 'Abdul 'Aziz should not be construed to mean anything more than mere lip-service. His clear and unerring political vision had discerned in Jamshed and Afrasiyab, Sanjar and Muhammad Khwarazm Shah the heroes he needed to consolidate the Sultanate and enhance his dignity.

BALBAN'S COURT

No medieval Indian ruler laid greater emphasis on court decorum and etiquette than Balban who had meticulously organized every detail of court life in the light of Persian traditions. His ideals in this respect were Sultan Sanjar and Sultan Muhammad Khwarazm Shah[43] whom he tried to imitate as best as he could in the Indian environment. If the pageant of Sanjar's court had, at one time, made even the great Imam Ghazzali nervous,[44] emissaries from foreign courts, princes, and *muqaddam*s trembled and fell down on the ground in the darbar of Balban.[45] With his face bright as the sun and his beard shining like camphor,[46] Balban sat on his throne with the dignity of a Sassanid king, while *hajib*s, *salahdar*s, *jandar*s, *chaoosh*s, *naqib*s, etc. stood before him in solemn silence. Only a few trusted maliks and confidants sat behind the throne; all others kept standing in order of their ranks and positions. Every inch a king, Balban set the atmosphere of the court by his own behaviour. There was always a serious and grim look on his face and nobody ever saw him laughing or talking in a lighter mood. Storms of personal grief came in his life with

43. *Tarikh-i-Firoz Shahi*, p. 32.
44. Shibli, *Al-Ghazzali*, p. 32.
45. *Tarikh-i-Firoz Shahi*, pp. 30–31.
46. Ibid, p. 30. Fazuni Astarabadi supplies the following interesting information about his crown:

"سلطان محاسنے داشت بغایت طویل و وجه سلطان نیز طولا نی
و تاجے داشت طولانی' چنانکه ازسر تا جش تاسر محاسنش
اقلایک گز بدرازی"

Buhaira, p. 12.

unexpected fury and, though they killed the man in him, they could not disturb the routine of the Sultan. To his last moment, this stickler for court decorum scrupulously followed every detail of that exacting programme which he had set for himself.

On festive occasions his court presented a gala appearance. Embroidered carpets, brocade curtains, variegated cloth, and gold and silver vessels dazzled the vision of every spectator. The voice of the ushers went as far as two *karoh*s. "For days after these festivals," writes Barani, "people talked about the decorations at the court."[47] When the Sultan rode out in procession, Seistani soldiers accompanied him with unsheathed swords. "The shining of the sun, the glittering of the sword, and the brightness of his face all taken together made a remarkable show." The shouts of *Bismillah, Bismillah* rent the atmosphere[48] as the royal cavalcade moved on. This display of power, authority, and dignity, which was inseparably associated in his mind with his theory of kingship, made the most recalcitrant elements in the country submissive and struck awe and terror into the hearts of the people.

RACIAL JEALOUSIES

If the personnel[49] of the Turkish government in India is analysed as a whole, it will be found that ministers, high officers, provincial governors, members of the judiciary and commanders of the forces were mostly Turks. As organizers of victory the Turks took full advantage of the opportunities that political domination over a vast area brought to them. In fact, seldom has a small group of men so neatly enjoyed the revenues of a vast country as the Ghurid slave-officers whom Aibek and Iltutmish had led to victory. Fakhr-i-Mudabbir informs us that as the result of the Turkish domination over India "even a poor householder who did not possess a single slave became the owner of numerous slaves, horses and camels; a man who originally owned only one horse became a *sipah-salar* and possessed a kettle drum, standard, *naubat*, all his own".[50] It was but natural that they strove to safeguard jealously all these honours and privileges and excluded non-Turks—both Muslims and Hindus—from all effective posts in the administration. Both Iltutmish and Balban treated the Indian Mussalmans

---

47. *Tarikh-i-Firoz Shahi*, p. 32.
48. Ibid. p. 31.
49. Some of these names are supplied by Minhaj and Barani. See *Tabaqat-i-Nasiri*, pp. 177–79; 206–07; *Tarikh-i-Firoz Shahi*, p. 24.
50. *Tarikh-i-Fakhr-u'd-din Mubarak Shah*, p. 20.

with contempt and ignored even merit among the non-Turks.[51] If ever, by force of circumstances, any posts were given to the non-Turks (contemptuously called Tazik[52] by Minhaj), the Turkish bureaucracy resented it. During the reign of Sultan Rukn-u'd-din Firoz Shah, the Turkish bodyguard of the Sultan killed a number of non-Turkish officers, such as Baha-u'd-din Hasan Asha'ri, Karim-u'd-din Zahid, Ziaul Mulk, Nizam-u'd-din Sharqan, and Khwaja Rashid-u'd-din Malkani,[53] on account of racial and tribal prejudices. To some extent this racial exclusiveness was necessary in the interests of the governing class, but when carried to extremes it was bound to have its reactions. No sooner did the Turkish Sultans take up this attitude than the Indian Mussalmans began to resent the position to which they were reduced. A movement was organized under the leadership of 'Imad-u'd-din Raihan to break the monopoly of the Turks. The very fact that Nasir-u'd-din Mahmud had to dismiss Balban and entrust the administration to Raihan shows that the movement had assumed serious proportions and the ruler could not possibly shut his eyes to the rapid political changes that were taking place in the character and composition of the 'pressure groups'. But Balban's dismissal was both an insult and a challenge to the Turkish bureaucracy which was not wanting in talent at this time. Minhaj, a spokesman of the Turkish amirs, remarks: "Turks of pure lineage and Tajiks of noble birth could not tolerate 'Imad-u'd-din of the tribes of Hind to rule over them."[54] Better discipline, greater resources, and superior leadership ultimately decided in favour of the Turks. Raihan was dismissed and Balban was again put in charge of administration. Raihan's dismissal, as also his appointment, was followed by a number of dismissals and appointments. Balban jealously guarded the interests of his race. So long as he was at the helm of affairs no Indian-born Mussalman could think of any government job.[55] But Balban was

51. *Tarikh-i-Firoz Shahi*, pp. 37–39.
  Balban used to say:

اگر هزار نوع هنر باشد... پیش من ذکر کنند من بالیشان آں
کنم که عبرت جهانیان گردد

Tarikh-i-Firoz Shahi, p. 37.
  For Iltutmish's views, see Barani, pp. 38–39.
52. *Tabaqat-i-Nasiri*, p. 138.
53. *Tabaqat-i-Nasiri*, p. 138.
54. Raverty, p. 829.
55. *Tarikh-i-Firoz Shahi*, pp. 37–39.

torn by contradictions. His own policy sapped the foundations of Turkish power in India. Dynastic ambitions blinded him to the drastic political consequences that followed his policy of removing by poison and dagger[56] all the talented and gifted Turkish leaders. Thus, in the process of safeguarding his family interests he reduced the Turkish nobility to such a position that when the Hindustani elements challenged its position, it found itself utterly helpless. Within a couple of years after Balban's death, political power slipped out of the hands of the Turks and the nondescript Khaljis beat down the Turks in their race for political power. With the advent of the Khaljis the character of the Delhi Sultanate underwent a great change. The Turkish state transformed itself into an Indo-Muslim state. Racial prejudices were discarded and offices were thrown open to talent.

TWO CLASSES

Barani informs us that the early Turkish Sultans treated the low-born people contemptuously.[57] Iltutmish dismissed thirty three persons from government service on account of their low birth. When he appointed Jamal Marzuq as the *Mutassarif* of Qannauj, on the recommendation of Nizam-ul-Mulk Junaidi, 'Aziz Bahruz objected to his appointment and recited the following couplet before him:[58]

بدست دون مده خامه که گردوں را مجال افتد

سیه سنگے که در کعبه است سازد سنگ استنجا

(Do not give the pen [of office] to a low-born man for this will embolden the sky to convert the [sacred black] stone of Ka'ba into a stone for wiping urine.)

Iltutmish not only cancelled this appointment but also instituted an enquiry into the genealogy of Nizam-ul-Mulk himself. When it was found that the Wazir belonged to a weaver family, he also lost the confidence of the Sultan.[59] Thus no low-born person could be recommended for an *Iqta'* or appointed to the post of *Khwajgi, mushrafi* or *mudabbiri*.[60] Following the same traditions, Balban dismissed low-born persons from all important

56. Ibid, pp. 47–48;
   Futuh-u's-Salatin, p. 159.
57. *Tarikh-i-Firoz Shahi*, pp. 29–30.
58. Ibid. p. 38.
59. Ibid. p. 39.
60. Ibid. p. 37.

offices and sharply rebuked his courtiers for having selected Kamal Mahiyar, an Indian Mussalman, for the post of *mutasarrif* in Amroha. "As I am a descendant of Afrasiyab," he declared in his court, "I will not allow any low-born person to occupy a high place... When I happen to look at a low-born person, my blood begins to boil."[61]

Sayyid Ashraf Jahangir Samnani (ob. 1405 AD) writes in one of his letters that Balban had made very thorough enquiries about the families of all his officers and government servants. Expert genealogists had assembled in Delhi from all parts of the country to help him in redetermining the family status of these persons.[62]

Barani is our chief source of information for all these details. Since he himself had similar views about *sharif*, and *razil*, it is difficult to determine how far he has attributed his own views to Iltutmish and Balban. It should not be forgotten that Barani had singled out three persons—Mahmud of Ghaznin, Balban, and Sayyid Nur-u'd-din Mubarak Ghaznavi—to weave his own religious and political thought around them.[63] The probability cannot be ruled out that what Barani presents as contemptuous treatment of the low-born by Iltutmish and Balban was really the treatment of non-Turks which Barani twisted and misrepresented in order to suit his own theory of birth. Barani's views as given in his *Fatawa-i-Jahandari*,[64] however, deserve to be noted:

> It has been said that all men have been created equal, that they are equal in form and appearance, and that every difference that appears between men is due to the effect of their character and the consequences of their actions.[65] The merits and demerits of men have been apportioned at the beginning of time and allotted to their souls. The acts and works of men are due to Divine Commandments; whenever Almighty God instils goodness or wickedness, virtue or vice, in a man, he also grants him the power of manifesting that goodness or wickedness, virtue or vice....[66]
>
> When during the first generations the children of Adam were born and grew in numbers and the world began to be inhabited, men needed everything for

61. Ibid, p. 36–37. Sayyid Ashraf Jahangir Samnani gives his name as Muhammad Mahiyar and says that he was an expert in accounts (*'ilm-i-muhasiba-o-hindsa*) and was selected for appointment to Chanderi. *Maktubat-i-Ashrafi*, f. 67a.

62. Ibid (MS), f. 76a.

63. For details see *Fatawa-i-Jahandari*.

64. For details see Professor Habib's Introduction to and Dr Afsar Afzaluddin's translation of *Fatawa-i-Jahandari*, published in *Medieval India Quarterly*, Vol. III, Parts I and II.

65. *Fatawa-i-Jahandari*, f. 216b.

66–67. Ibid, ff. 217a, b.

the sake of their livelihood; so the Eternal Designer inspired men's hearts with the arts that were necessary for their existence. Thus some hearts were inspired with the art of letters and writing, others with horsemanship, and yet others with weaving, smith-craft, and carpentry. So all the arts, fine and coarse, from writing and horsemanship to hair-cutting and tanning, in accordance with the merits and demerits which by their basic nature had been allotted to their souls, were communicated to their minds and breasts.[67] The possessors of merit, owing to their meritorious nature, were inspired with fine capacities, while to minds involved in meanness, owing to their low natures, only capacities for the baser arts were communicated. In this way the angels inspired the minds of men with various arts, and men adopted different professions and followed them. The arts, crafts, and professions for which men have been inspired are practised well by them; and they are able properly to practise only their own specific arts: ..... This aptitude for the arts, fine and coarse, is hereditary. And as excellences have been put into those who have adopted the nobler professions, they alone are capable of virtue, kindness, generosity, valour, good deeds, good works, truthfulness, keeping of promises, protection of other classes, loyalty, clarity of vision, justice, equity, recognition of rights, gratitude for favours, and fear of God. They are, consequently, said to be noble, free-born, virtuous, religious, of high pedigree, and pure birth. These groups alone are worthy of offices and posts in the government... Owing to their actions the government of the king is strengthened and adorned.[68]

On the other hand, the low-born, who have been enrolled for practising the baser arts and the meaner professions, are capable only of immodesty, falsehood, miserliness, misappropriation, vices, wrongfulness, lies, evil-speaking, ingratitude, dirtiness, injustice, cruelty, non-recognition of rights, shamelessness, impudence, blood-shedding, rascality, jugglery, and Godlessness. So they are called low-born, bazar people, base, mean, worthless, plebian, shameless, and of dirty birth. Every act which is contaminated with meanness and based on ignominy comes elegantly from them... The promotion of the low and the low-born brings no advantage in this world, for it is impudent to act against the wisdom of creation.[69]

Teachers of every kind are to be sternly ordered not to thrust precious stones down the throats of dogs or to put collars of gold around the necks of pigs and bears—that is, to the mean, the ignoble, the worthless, to shopkeepers and the low-born they are to teach nothing more than the rules about prayer, fasting, religious charity, and the Haj pilgrimage along with some chapters of the Quran and some doctrines of the Faith, without which their religion cannot be correct and valid prayers are not possible. They are to be instructed in nothing more lest it bring honour to their mean soul. They are not to be taught reading and writing, for plenty of disorders arise owing to the skill of the low-born in knowledge[70]....

---

68. Ibid, f. 217b.
69. Ibid, f. 218a.
70. Ibid, f. 130a.

The majority of *hakims* and wise men, ancient and modern, have said on the basis of observation and experience that the great offices appertaining to the administration have not been well discharged by the low-born and the base. If a base-born man has become a ruler, he has striven so far as he could to overthrow men of good birth and to elevate the low-born and the base. The ultimate work of the low-born has never come to any good, and they have never shown loyalty in any contingency. Though owing to the flattery, agility, display of intelligence, and jugglery of the low-born and the mean, some Sultans have been captivated and have made such people their colleagues and the confidential officers of the kingdom, yet both during their lifetime and after their death, they have suffered such wounds and injuries from the low-born men they have promoted that regret for what they did will not diminish in their minds through all eternity.[71]

Further, if mean, low, base, and sordid men, bazar people, and cowards are established on the pillow of high office and succeed in their official work, then according to the principle, every group is incised towards itself, they make people of their own kind their helpers, supporters, colleagues, and assistants in their consultations as well as the work of ordering and command. They make the lowest and the meanest their partners and their intimates and delegate a part and portion of their authority to them. They do not, owing to their nature and their character, allow the nobles, the free-born, and men of merit, to come anywhere near the affairs of their government; they consider them their enemies and keep them their enemies. They detest the noble-born and strive for their degradation and overthrow with their hearts and souls. Owing to the promotion of one base and low-born man, many base and low-born men get offices and are respected and honoured. And thus owing to the consequences of the words and actions of a group of low-born men, many chasms are created in the work of government; a number of honourable and meritorious men are degraded and dishonoured.... From the splendour of the base-born only troubles and misfortunes arise.[72]

But if the king appoints the free-born (*ahrar*), the noble, and the possessors of excellent qualities as his helpers and supporters then inevitably owing to their office and command for owing to their nature and character their actions are praise-worthy the king will not be distressed and bewildered on the Day of Judgement for having to answer to many thousands and thousands of his subjects.[73]

Whence did Barani get these ideas? How far do they represent a faithful exposition of the viewpoint of the Turkish governing class? Though vital for our study, these questions cannot be answered with certainty. One

71. Ibid, f. 219b.
72. Ibid, f. 220a.
73. Ibid, f. 207a.

cannot, however, fail to discover an echo of Hindu caste regulations and Sassanid social behaviour in the political thought of Barani. Whether the Sultans believed in them or not, these views did not find acceptance among the Muslim society in general. Some of the most influential sections of Muslim society, e.g. the mystics, were fiercely opposed to such distinctions. 'Isami does not refer to such distinctions being perpetrated by Balban. Later historians, who drew their information about Balban mainly from Barani, did not give any importance to these views. Probably they dismissed them as personal fads of Barani. In fact, Muslim public opinion could hardly be made amenable to such ideas. Whatever the Sultans might have thought or done in the political sphere to safeguard their racial and dynastic interests, they could not possibly make such distinctions operative in Muslim society.

Amongst the governing class itself, we know at least of one person— Prince Muhammad—who did not believe in distinctions on the basis of birth.[74] Had he succeeded Balban, the policy of the Sultanate with reference to the low-born people would have undergone a complete change, and a more liberal attitude would have been adopted towards the non-Turkish elements, thus averting all tension between the Turkish and the non-Turkish groups, and giving a new lease of life to Turkish rule in India.

POWERS AND POSITION OF THE SULTAN

Though legal fiction had placed sovereignty in the Khalifah, in practice the Sultan was the actual sovereign and wielded immense power. Since no sanction for the Sultan or the Sultanate was available in the laws of the *Shari'at*, contemporary writers tried to justify it on grounds of *necessity* and said that, "if there were no king, men will devour each other."[75] Influenced by Greek political thought, the Muslim writers of the Middle Ages depicted the state as a living organism and the Sultan as its most vital part. Imam Ghazzali compared the Sultan to the heart,[76] and Fakhr-i-Mudabbir to the head of the human system.[77] A sixteenth-century Muslim religious leader went a step further in declaring the Sultan to be the soul and the people to be the physical frame.[78]

---

74. *Tarikh-i-Firoz Shahi*, p. 68.

75. *Adab-ul-Harb*, f. 113a; *Tarikh-i-Fakhr-u'd-din Mubarak Shah*, p. 13. Fakhr-i-Mudabbir quotes it as a saying of the Prophet.

76. *Kimiya-i-Sa'adat*, p. 8.

77. *Adab-ul-Harb*, f. 18b.

78. *Maktubat-i-Mujaddid-i-Alf-i-Sani*, Vol. II, p. 67.

The Muslim jurists assign the following functions to the Sultan:

1. to protect the faith, as defined by *ijma'*,
2. to settle disputes between his subjects,
3. to defend the territories of Islam, and to keep the roads safe for the travellers,
4. to maintain and enforce the criminal code,
5. to strengthen the frontiers of Muslim territory against possible aggressions,
6. to wage a holy war against those who act in hostility to Islam,
7. to collect the rates and taxes,
8. to apportion the shares of those who deserve an allowance from the public treasury,
9. to appoint officers to help him in his public and legal duties, and
10. to keep in touch with affairs and the conditions of the people by personal contact.[79]

Some of these are simply moral precepts which have little value outside ethical treatises. In fact, the expectations of the people from their rulers differed from group to group. The *'ulama* wanted him to champion the cause of religion;[80] the governing clique wanted him to act as the guardian of their political interests and privileges; the common man expected peace, security, and justice from him. Sometimes the expectations of one group cut across the interests of another group and under such circumstances the Sultan had to formulate his policy with great caution and care. If on one side Sayyid Nur-u'd-din Mubarak Ghaznavi and other *'ulama* of his school of thought trenchantly criticized the un-Islamic practices of the court of Iltutmish,[81] nobles such as Malik 'Izz-u'd-din Salari and Malik Qutb-u'd-din Hasan Ghuri impressed upon his mind the necessity of following more rigorously all those Persian practices which had placed royalty on a high and dignified pedestal.[82] Under such circumstances it was political expediency alone which determined the attitude of the rulers.

No ruler, however autocractic he might be, dare flout public opinion though it had no recognized ways of expressing itself. If fear of popular reactions could prevent a ruler like 'Ala-u'd-din Khalji from promulgating

79. *Suluk-ul-Muluk, Nuh Sipihr,* and *Fatawa-i-Jahandari,* as summarized by I.H. Qureshi, *Administration of the Sultanate of Delhi,* p. 47.
80. *Tarikh-i-Fakhr-u'd-din Mubarak Shah,* pp. 13–14; *Adab-ul-Harb,* ff. 19a, 29a.
81. *Tarikh-i-Firoz Shahi,* p. 41.
82. Ibid, p. 31.

a new religion,[83] his predecessors also saw to it that they did not do anything which injured public feelings on any vital matter. The way in which Razia secured the throne of Delhi[84] shows that public opinion could become a force and, though seldom expressed, it could change the course of political developments when expressed in a definite and forceful manner. At least two contemporary historians of this period—Fakhr-i-Mudabbir[85] and Sadr-u'd-din Hasan Nizami[86]—clearly appreciated the importance of *Shura* (consultation) in the Muslim polity and, though they glorified monarchy and monarchical institutions, they did not underrate the value of the democratic institution of the *Shura*. If medieval literature—political and non-political—can supply any clue to the aspirations of the people, it may be safely stated that the people could accept and tolerate any Sultan provided he guaranteed peaceful conditions and administered even-handed justice.[87] It was believed that an unjust king disturbed the equilibrium of society and created all-round chaos; while his injustice, greed, and avarice resulted in calamities such as famine, scarcity of rainfall, economic crisis, and the shedding of innocent blood.[88]

The absence of any definite law of succession had always been a problem with the Muslim states of the Middle Ages and the Sultanate of Delhi was no exception to it. When Amir Khusrau puts into the mouth of Kaiqubad the words:[89]

$$ملک بمیراث نیابد کسے   تا نزند تیغ دو دستی بسے$$

he expresses the correct position with reference to the Sultanate. The ability to wield the sceptre rather than legitimacy was the accepted principle of the period. Notwithstanding the enormous loss of life and the waste of material entailed by every war of succession, it eliminated the weaker elements and usually meant the survival of the fittest. The way in which rulers were enthroned and dethroned during the period from the death of Iltutmish to the accession of Balban may be viewed as one long process

---

83. *Ibid*, p. 266.

84. *Futuh-u's-Salatin*, p. 132.

85. *Adab-ul-Harb*, f. 68.

86. *Taj-ul-Ma'asir*, pp. 19–20.

87. See *Siyasat Namah* (p. 6) where Nizam-ul-Mulk quotes the saying

$$الملک یبقی مع الکفر و لا یبقی مع الظلم$$

and shows that government can be carried on successfully by just infidels but not by unjust believers. This view was expressed by Muslim writers on political ethics all throughout the Middle Ages.

88. *Adab-ul-Harb*, f. 29a.

89. *Qir'an-us-Sa'dain*, p. 118.

of search and re-search for a really gifted man who could equate with the circumstances. With the advent of Balban that struggle came to an end but re-started after his death and continued till 'Ala-u'd-din Khalji appeared on the stage and proved himself to be the ablest of the Khalji revolutionaries.

No Sultan could ignore the nobility and the *'ulama*; if the one controlled the administrative machinery, the other controlled the public opinion. Their influence on the Sultans and the administration is discussed in the following chapters.

PERSONAL RELIGION OF THE SULTANS

"A man's religion," says Caryle, "is the chief fact with regard to him. If you tell me what that is, you tell me to a very great extent what the man is, what the kind of thing he will do is."[90] Indeed, religion, taken in its widest sense and not merely as a body of doctrines handed down by tradition or contained in some canonical book, but regarded as that faculty of faith in man which, independent of all historical religions, enables him to apprehend the Infinite and direct his emotions and desires towards an ideal object, is a very vital factor in the life of an individual. It is all the more so in the case of rulers because they live by two morals: the moral of religion and the moral of the state. This duality in their thought becomes all the more interesting when it expresses itself in their political conduct.

Sultan Qutb-u'd-din Aibek had received his early religious training under the fostering care of a distinguished scholar and jurist of Nishapur, Qazi Fakhr-u'd-din 'Abdul 'Aziz Kufi,[91] who was known as Abu Hanifa Sani on account of his piety, scholarship, and religious devotion. The Qazi made special arrangements for the teaching of the Quran and Qutb-u'd-din so distinguished himself in the art of reciting the holy Book that he became known as *Quran Khwan*.[92] When he ascended the throne he extended his patronage to scholars, jurists, the reciters of Quran, pious men, and reformers.[93] No details about his personal religious attitude are found in contemporary records except a few general observations about his respect for the laws of the *Shari'at*[94] and his care for the religious

90. *Heroes and Hero-Worship*, p. 10.
91. *Tabaqat-i-Nasiri*, p. 138; *Tarikh-i-Fakhr-u'd-din Mubarak Shah*, p. 21.
92. *Tarikh-i-Fakhr-u'd-din Mubarak Shah*, p. 21.
93. *Taj-ul-Ma'asir* (MS), p. 466; *Tarikh-i-Fakhr-u'd-din Mubarak Shah*, p. 35.
94. For example, Hasan Nizami writes:

همت بلند بر احیاء معالم شریعت و اعلائ اعلام سنت مقصور و موقوف داشت

Taj-ul-Ma'asir, p. 4.

classes.[95] Amongst the scholars who basked in the sunshine of his royal favours, the names of Qazi Hamid-u'd-din Iftikhar 'Ali b. 'Umar al-Mahmudi,[96] Sadr-u'd-din Hasan Nizami, and Maulana Baha-u'd-din Ushi[97] may be particularly mentioned.

It is seldom that a man's disposition and character is determined by an accident. In the case of Iltutmish it was really an accident which determined his religious thought and behaviour. He was hardly ten when he fell a victim to the jealousy of his brothers, who brought him to the slave market of Bukhara and sold him to a kinsman of Sadr-i-Jahan (the Chief Ecclesiastic). The Sadr-i-Jahan's family was of honourable descent and enjoyed a religious reputation. Minhaj calls it خانواده‌ء امارت و تصدر (priestly and saintly family) and eulogizes its بزرگی و طهارت (eminence and sanctity). Here this young slave was treated as a member of the family. While in this house a very small incident took place, but it left a very deep impression on his mind. On a certain occasion one of the members of the family gave him a piece of money and ordered him to go to the bazar and buy some grapes. He went to the bazar and on the way lost the piece of money. Being of tender age, he began to cry for fear and while he was weeping, a faqir came to him and took his hand, purchased some grapes and gave them to him, saying: "When you obtain wealth and dominion, take care that you show respect to faqirs and maintain their rights!" ...This incident made such a deep impression on his young mind that we shall not be far from the truth if we trace to it the first germination of mystic love in him. Long afterwards he related this incident in his court and said:[98]

هر دولت و سلطنت که یافتم از نظر آن درویش یافتم ا

(Whatever of royalty and honour devolved upon me came through the benediction of that very saint.)

After a short stay at Bukhara, Iltutmish somehow reached Baghdad which was a great spiritual centre at this time and hundreds of eminent mystics had constructed their hospices there. The enlightening discourses and sermons of such distinguished personalities as Shaikh Shihab-u'd-din Suhrawardi,[99] Khwaja Mu'in-u'd-din Chishti,[100] Shaikh Auhad-u'd-din

---

95. *Tarikh-i-Fakhr-u'd-din Mubarak Shah*, p. 35.

96. *Lubab-ul-Albab*, Vol. I, p. 203.

97. *Lubab-ul-Albab*, Vol I, pp. 188–89.

98. *Tabaqat-i-Nasiri*, p. 167.

99. For a brief biographical notice, see *Nafahat-u'l-Uns*, pp. 307–08.

100. See *Siyar-u'l-Auliya*, pp. 45–46; *Siyar-u'l-'Arifin*, p. 4; *Akhbar-u'l-Akhyar*, pp. 22–24.

Kirmani,[101] Qazi Hamid-u'd-din Nagauri,[102] and others had filled the entire atmosphere with mystic ideas. The bank of the Tigris was studded all along with mosques and *khanqahs* and a mystic breeze blew over the entire landscape. Masjid-i-Kankari, Masjid-i-Abu-Lais Samarqandi, and Masjid-i-Junaid Baghdadi were the principal centres of mystic activity and teeming crowds flocked there.

Iltutmish also breathed this atmosphere. Two anecdotes show that he imbibed fully the pervading spirit. His master was a religious-minded man and he very often vacated his house for the mystics to hold their music parties. One night a music party was arranged in this house. Many eminent mystics, such as Qazi Hamid-u'd-din and others were invited there. The young Iltutmish kept standing throughout the night and devotedly served these *sufis* by removing the burnt wick from the candle.[103]

Another story is more significant and clearly shows Iltutmish's faith in these divines. One day he went to the *khanqah* of Shaikh Shihab-u'd-din Suhrawardi and presented a few coins to the Shaikh. The Shaikh recited the *Fatihah* and then remarked: 'I see gleams of royalty shining on the forehead of this man.' Shaikh Auhad-u'd-din Kirmani who was present there also blessed him.[104]

Shaikh Nizam-u'd-din Auliya once told his audience about Iltutmish:[105]

"او خدمت شیخ شهاب الدین سهروردی را و شیخ اوحدالدین کرمانی را
رحمة الله علیهم دریافته بود. و یکے از ینها گفته بود که بادشاه خواهی شد"ا

(He had gained access to Shaikh Shihab-u'd-din Suhrawardi and Shaikh Auhad-u'd-din Kirmani (may the blessings of God be on them). One of them had prophesied that he would be a king.)

The apocryphal *malfuz* of Shaikh Qutb-u'd-din Bakhtiyar Kaki contains the following story: "Once I (Shaikh Qutb-u'd-din Bakhtiyar Kaki) was present in the company of my *pir*, Khwaja Mu'in-u'd-din Chishti, in Baghdad. Many mystics of repute were there. It so happened that a lad of twelve passed by that way, with a bow in his hand. Incidentally these mystics glanced at him and prompt were the words that came from the lips of the Khwaja: 'This lad will be the ruler of Delhi'."[106]

101. *Nafahat-u'l-Uns*, pp. 385–87.
102. *Akhbar-u'l-Akhyar*, pp. 36–43.
103. *Futuh-u's-Salatin*, p. 119; *Tabaqat-i-Akbari*, I, p. 62; *Ferishtah*, pp. 62–66.
104. *Siyar-u'l-'Arifin*, p. 27.
105. *Fawa'id-u'l-Fu'ad*, p. 212.
106. *Fawa'id-u's-Salikin* (MS), 810b. This work is apocryphal but as it is an early fabrication it embodies the current traditions and stories about Iltutmish. That this story had a basis is clear from the *Fawa'id-u'l-Fu'ad* (p. 212).

Having passed his early years in this spiritual atmosphere of Baghdad, Iltutmish came to India as a slave of Qutb-u'd-din Aibek. He was entrusted with the *iqta'* of Gwalior and was later on appointed to the governorship of Bada'un. Bada'un was one of the earliest centres of Muslim culture. Hundreds of Muslim martyrs lie buried there.[107] Many eminent mystics who came to India subsequent to Shihab-u'd-din's invasion settled there. Distinguished saints such as Shaikh Fath ullah, Shaikh Wajih-u'd-din Khwaja 'Ali Bukhari lived and died there. A simple anecdote, mentioned in several hagiological works, shows that Iltutmish was influenced by the mystic atmosphere of this place. One day when he was going out to play *chaugan*,[108] a very aged man came forward, stretched out his hand, and begged for alms. Iltutmish did not give him anything. A few steps further he came across a stout young man and at once took out some gold pieces from his purse and delivered them to him. Later he turned to his companions and asked: "Do you know why I did not give anything to that old beggar, while I gave to this young man unasked?" His companions, who were themselves surprised at this strange standard of charity, could not make any reply to this query. Then Iltutmish himself said:

"اگر خواست من بودے پیررا دادمے' پس ہرکرا می دہد خدا می دہد می دہد' من چہ کنم"

(Had it been left to my choice, I would have preferred to give (alms) to that old beggar; but whatever is bestowed is bestowed by Him. I am helpless).

A deep mystic note underlies this sentence. Its significance can be estimated by the fact that it was often repeated by spiritual mentors before their disciples while explaining predestination and preaching "faith in Divine action".[109]

These anecdotes serve as so many clues to explain the Sultan's excessive interest in mystics and divines. With these instances in mind, many of his later actions, which otherwise would seem to be freaks of an eccentric nature, appear to mark a stage in the development of his religious thought that was nurtured at Bukhara, Baghdad, Bada'un, and Delhi—all conspicuous religious centres. It was from these places that he imbibed an esoteric spirit of religion.

Even after his accession he continued to take a keen interest in religious devotions and exercises. He offered his obligatory prayers punctually.[110]

---

107. See *Tazkirat-u'l-Wasilin* (a detailed account of the saints of Bada'un) by Razi-u'd-din, pp. 9–10.
108. *Medieval polo.*
109. *Fawa'id-u'l-Fu'ad*, p. 212;
Fawa'id-u's-Salikin (MS), f. 20a.
110. *Tabaqat-i-Akbari*, p. 30.

Special arrangements were made for congregational prayers when he went out on military expeditions.[111] Preachers and *Imams* accompanied him wherever he went and he heard their sermons regularly. While in Uch, with the royal tent pitched in front of the fort, he asked Minhaj-us-Siraj to deliver discourses in his tent.[112] Ordinarily he heard sermons thrice a week, but during the month of Ramazan daily sermons were arranged.[113] Many religious meetings were held in the palace and were attended by eminent saints and divines. After Friday prayers a special meeting was convened in which the grandees, nobles, and saints participated.[114] Balban used to say that he never saw such a brilliant assembly of scholars and divines in any other court.[115]

"The probability is," declares Minhaj, "that there was never a sovereign of such exemplary faith and of such kind-heartedness and reverence towards recluses, devotees, divines, and doctors of law and religion, ever enwrapped from the mother of creation in the swaddling bands of dominion."[116] It is mentioned in the *malfuz* of Sayyid Muhammad Gesu Daraz that Iltutmish used to visit paupers, mendicants, and destitutes *incognito*[117] at night and distribute money to them. Whenever he heard about the arrival of some saint from the Central Asian lands, he went out for miles to receive him and insisted on his stay in the palace. He warmly welcomed Shaikh Qutb-u'd-din Bakhtiyar Kaki[118] on his arrival in Delhi. He went out several miles to receive Shaikh Jalal-u'd-din Tabrizi.[119] Once Shaikh Badr u'd-din Ghaznavi went to see him in his palace. The Sultan received him at the palace door, clasped him in his arms, and led him in. In the same cordial way he received Qazi Qutb-u'd-din Kashani and conducted him to his chamber.[120] He respectfully addressed Shaikh Najib-u'd-din Nakhshabi as "Father".[121]

---

111. *Tabaqat-i-Nasiri*, p. 175; *Raverty*, p. 615; see also *Adab-u'l-Harb* for an interesting discussion on the arrangements for prayers on battlefields.

112. *Tabaqat-i-Nasiri*, p. 175.

113. Ibid.

114. *Siyar-u'l-'Arifin*, p. 112 (MS). The printed text (p. 169) does not contain this passage. The MS runs:

روز جمعه بعد نماز اکابر و اشراف و مشایخ با سلطان حلقه کرده نشستند

115. *Tarikh-i-Firoz Shahi*, p. 70.

116. *Tabaqat-i-Nasiri*, p. 167, *Tarikh-i-Haqqi* (MS), f. 7a.

117. *Jawami'-u'l-Kalim*, p. 269; see also *Fawa'id-us-Salikin*, f. 10a.

118. *Siyar-u'l-'Arifin*, p. 20.

119. Ibid.

120. *Fawa'id-u'l-Fu'ad*, p. 236.

121. *Saroor-us-Sudur* (MS).

It is said about Iltutmish that he would sit all day long in the court and attend to the business of administration, but at night he spread his prayer carpet and bent his knees before the Almighty.[122] Once, when a very severe famine broke out in Delhi, Iltutmish sent a courtier to all the saints of the capital and requested them to pray.[123]

Iltutmish's buildings also exhibit his religious sentiments. In Hauz-i-Shamsi[124] particularly, one can see the reflection of his religious feelings. It was constructed in compliance with a wish of the Holy Prophet who, it is said, appeared to him in a dream and asked him to build a tank at the very place where he stood[125] and talked to him. While this tank was being constructed, Iltutmish threw a flask of *zamzam* water into it.[126] Built under religious inspiration, the Hauz-i-Shamsi became a centre of religious activity. Many saints and recluses constructed their *hujrah*s in its vicinity and a small mosque, which still goes by the name of Auliya Masjid, was also constructed by them.[127] As it was believed that the Prophet had placed his sacred feet there, a religious sanctity hallowed the tank.[128] Shaikh Nizam-u'd-din Auliya often talked in his mystic gatherings about the عذوبت and برکت of this tank. He told his audience that once Iltutmish appeared to a man in his dream and said that it was for the construction of this tank that the Almighty had sent him to heaven.[129]

---

122. *Fawa'id-u'l-Fu'ad*, p. 213.

بعد ازاں از عقیده او حکایت فرمود که شبها بیدار بودے و هیچ کس را
بیدار نه کردے

The apocryphal *malfuz*, *Fawa'id-u's-Salikin*, develops this remark further (p. 19).

123. *Siyar-u'l-'Arifin*, p. 99 (MS); *Khair-u'l-Majalis*, p. 45.

124. See Carr Stephens, *The Archaeology and Monumental Remains of Delhi*, pp. 68–70.

125. *Siyar-ul-'Arifin*, p. 26; *Sirat-i-Firoz Shahi* (MS); *Fawa'id-u's-Salikin* (MS), p. 18; *Jawahir-i-Faridi* (MS); Ferishtah, pp. 381–82.

126. *Futuh-u's-Salatin*, pp. 115–17.

127. *Waqiat-i-Dar-u'l-Hakumat Delhi*; also Carr Stephens pp. 67–70n. The mosque is situated in an enclosure about 54 feet long and 36 feet broad; the walls are very low, scarcely three feet high in some places. In its western wall is the *masjid* which consists of an arched recess about 6 feet high. In front of the *masjid* are two slabs of sandstone which are supposed to mark the spots where Khwaja Mu'in-u'd-din and his disciple Qutb-u'd-din offered their prayers.

128. For Khusrau's praise of the tank see *Qir'an-u's-Sa'dain*, pp. 33–36.

129. *Fawa'id-u'l-Fu'ad*, p. 119.

Of all the sons and daughters of Iltutmish, Nasir-u'd-din Mahmud was the most deeply religious-minded. In him the religious aspect of Iltutmish's personality had found its fullest expression. Numerous stories about his piety and devotion have been recorded by the chroniclers. "Some of these stories," remarks Bada'uni, "resemble the narratives regarding the rightly directed Khalifahs."[130] Khusrau calls him a 'king of the angelic temperament', and lavishly praises him for his religious attributes.[131] 'Isami includes him among the favourites of God and considers him to be endowed with the attributes of saints and apostles.[132]

Nasir-u'd-din Mahmud entrusted all the affairs of government to Balban and devoted himself to the discipline of his soul.[133] He was very particular about his prayers and fasts.[134] The religious spirit had gone so deep in him that he would put on his regal robes on the occasion of a public audience only. Normally he used to wear an old ragged garment.[135] He had great regard for the ecelesiastics[136] and bestowed huge sums upon them. His respect for the Prophet was so great that he never uttered his name without proper ablutions.[137]

The Sultan devoted most of his time to making manuscript copies of the Quran.[138] These copies were sold in the bazar and the Sultan subsisted mostly on their proceeds.[139] Fazuni Astarabadi, a historian of the Mughal period, says that he had sent some of these copies even to Mecca to be sold there in the market.[140] He took special care to see that no one recognised his hand writing and paid more than its fair value.[141] Nizam-u'd-din says

---

130. *Muntakhab-u't-Tawarikh,* Vol. I, p. 90.

131. *Qir'an-u's-Sa'dain,* p. 22.

132. *Futuh-u's-Salatin,* p. 156.

133. Khusrau says:

خود او مستغرق کار الهی   با مرش بندگان درکار شاهی

Dawal Rani Khizr Khan, p. 50.

134. *Tabaqat-i-Nasiri,* p. 207.

135. *Muntakhab-u't-Tawarikh,* Vol. I, p. 89. Bada'uni himself does not seem to be certain of this. He reports this with the words: در افواه چنانست

136. *Tabaqat-i-Nasiri,* p. 207; *Tabaqat-i-Akbari,* Vol. I, pp. 72–3.

137. *Tarikh-i-Ferishtah,* Vol. I, p. ,74.

138. *Futuh-u's-Salatin,* p. 156.

139. *Tarikh-i-Firoz Shahi,* p. 26; *'Aja'ib-u'l-Asfar,* p. 56.

140. *Buhaira,* p. 12.

141. *Muntakhab-u't-Tawarikh,* I, p. 90; *Tabaqat-i-Akbari,* Vol. I, p. 77; *Tarikh-i-Ferishtah,* I, p. 74.

that he completed two copies in a year.[142] Ibn Battuta saw one of these specimens of royal calligraphy and appreciated its penmanship.[143]

Alone among the Sultans of Delhi, Nasir-u'd-din Mahmud did not take anything from the *Bait-al-Mal* for his personal expenses. He made a distinction between his privy purse and the public treasury. 'Isami says:[144]

یکے حبه از دخل هندوستاں پنے نفس خود آں شه کامراں

نکرده تصرف دراں بست سال بدے محترز دائم از بیت مال

(His wife cooked his food and acted as a maid servant.[145])

Balban, like other contemporary Turkish nobles, was fond of the good life, but when he ascended the throne he changed his ways completely[146] and adopted an almost stoic attitude. It was his sense of royal duty which acted as a great restraining force on his passions. He offered his prayers regularly and kept fasts during the month of Ramazan. He used to keep vigils frequently. Besides the five obligatory prayers, he offered *ishraq*, *chasht, awabin*, and *tahajjud*[147] prayers, and recited certain litanies (*aurad*) regularly. He did not miss his prayers or *aurad* even when on a journey.[148] Bughra Khan's remark that no scholar or saint could offer so many prayers or keep so many fasts as Balban did,[149] though a bit exaggerated, shows the extent of his interest in prayers. Even a man such as Shaikh Nizam-u'd-din Auliya could not help praising his religious devotion and his regularity in offering prayers.[150] The great Shaikh, it may be pointed out, praised only two medieval monarchs for their religious views—Iltutmish

142. *Tabaqat-i-Akbari*, Vol. I, p. 77.

143. *'Aja'ib-u'l-Asfar*, pp. 56–57;

Edward Thomas thinks that this penmanship of the Sultan had 'its influence on the execution and finish of the legends of his coinage, which display a remarkable advance upon the earlier mintage in the fineness of the lines and the improved definition of the Persian characters.' (*Chronicles*, pp. 124–25). He considers an inscription at Aligarh to represent the handwriting of the Sultan (pp. 129–30).

144. *Futuh-u's-Salatin*, p. 156; See also *Tarikh-i-Ferishtah*, Vol. I, p. 71.

145. *Muntakhab-u't-Tawarikh*, Vol. I, p. 90; *Tabaqat-i-Akbari*, Vol. I, p. 77.

146. *Tarikh-i-Firoz Shahi*, p. 46.

147. In addition to the five compulsory (*farz*) prayers, the Muslims have five recommended (or *sunnat*) prayers, *ishraq*, after sunrise, *chasht*, in the forenoon, *zawwal* after midday, *awabin* at twilight, and *tahajjud* between midnight and early dawn. All other prayers belong to a third category of *nafl* or supererogatory prayers.

148. *Tarikh-i-Firoz Shahi*, p. 46.

149. Ibid, p. 155.

150. *Fawa'id-u'l-Fu'ad*, pp. 231–32.

and Balban—both of whom had succeeded in winning the sympathies of the Muslim religious classes due to their religious devotions. Shaikh Nizam-u'd-din Auliya further narrated a story about the keenness of Balban in offering supererogatory prayers. Once he asked his *Qazi-i-Lashkar*:[151] 'What was the significance of the last night?' The Qazi replied: 'This is known to you also'. 'Yes,' said the Sultan. The Shaikh had narrated the story so far that Amir Hasan Sijzi interrupted and said: 'The night referred to must have been *shab-i-qadr*.' 'Yes,' continued the Shaikh, 'both of them (the Sultan and the *qazi*) knew each other's affairs.'[152]

Balban dealt very strictly with his sons so far as obligatory prayers were concerned. If he ever heard that Bughra or Muhammad had missed a single prayer or had remained asleep in the morning and had not offered prayers in congregation, he would not talk to them for a whole month. Whenever the defaulter appeared before him, he angrily turned his face away from him.[153] He exhorted his sons to remember the following sayings of the Prophet: 'Offering prayers in congregation is my practice, whoever gives it up is a hypocrite.' 'Whoever gives up prayers is condemned.'[154]

Balban was on the best of terms with the theologians and saints. He invited them to his meals and discussed religious problems with them.[155] Notwithstanding his high notions about the dignity of kings, he visited their houses also. He was keenly interested in religious sermons (*tazkir*) and often attended such gatherings and wept profusely.[156] Whenever he heard about the death of any saint, Sayyid, or scholar of the city, he attended his funeral and offered funeral prayers; joined, the function on the third day of his death, consoled the bereaved family, and granted stipends to his survivors.[157]

Of the *'ulama* to whom Balban showed special respect, Qazi Sharaf-u'd-din, Maulana Siraj-u'd-din Sijzi, and Maulana Najm-u'd-din Damishqi may be specially mentioned.[158] He regularly visited Maulana

---

151. Barani informs us that Balban was particularly considerate towards the *qazis* of the army (*qazian-i-lashkar*) and often accepted their recommendations. *Tarikh-i-Firoz Shahi*, p. 47.

152. *Fawa'id-u'l-Fu'ad*, pp. 231–32. The 27th night of the month of Ramadan is called *shab-i-qadr*.

153. *Tarikh-i-Firoz Shahi*, p. 155.

154. Ibid, p. 102.

155. Ibid, p. 46.

156. Ibid, p. 47.

157. Ibid, pp. 46–47.

158. Ibid, p. 46.

Burhan-u'd-din Mahmud bin 'Ali al-Khair al-Balkhi[159] after the Friday prayers. He had great faith in Shaikh Farid-u'd-din Mas'ud Ganj-i-Shakar of Ajodhan. Before ascending the throne, he went to see him and presented a dish full of coins to him, with a view to receiving the Shaikh's blessings.[160] Hagiologists have referred to his respectful relations with Shaikh 'Ali Chishti[161] and Shaikh Shams-u'd-din Panipati. He prevented the former from quitting Delhi and threatened to abdicate and accompany him to Chisht if he decided to go there.[162] A later writer[163] says that Balban had become the disciple of Shaikh 'Ali Chishti. This statement is not confirmed by earlier authorities.

Balban evinced great interest in religion so far as his personal life was concerned, but, as Barani very correctly remarks, he never cared for the laws of the *Shari'at* in dealing with those who defied his authority or who were found guilty of any political crimes.[164]

Balban's successor, Sultan Mu'izz-u'd-din Kaiqubad, plunged headlong into the pursuit of pleasure. He neglected his obligatory prayers and ignored obligatory fasts.[165]

159. Ibid, p. 46.

The Maulana was a great scholar of his age. Pupil of Maulana Razi-u'd-din Hasan Saghani, author of *Mashariq*, and Maulana Burhan-u'd-din Marghinani, the author of *Hidayah*, he was justly respected as one of the leading scholars of the day. Vide *Akhbar-u'l-Akhyar*, pp. 45–46.

160. *Siyar-u'l-Auliya*, pp. 79–80.

The Shaikh, who was endowed with remarkable intuitive intelligence, realized the purpose of Ulugh Khan's visit and recited the following quatrain:

فریدوں فرخ فرشته نبود ز عود و ز عنبر سرشته نبود

ز داد و دهش یافت آں خسروی تو داد و دهش کن فریدوں توئی

(Faridun, the blessed, was not an angel; he was not made of aggallochum or ambergris. He attained that position of kingship through his bounty and liberality. Thou shouldst bestow liberally and Faridun is thee.)

'Ali Asghar Chishti's statement (*Jawahir-i-Faridi*, MS) that Balban had given one of his daughters in marriage to Shaikh Farid is unfounded and may be rejected as a later concoction fondly circulated by uncritical minds. See also K.A. Nizami, *The Life and Times of Shaikh Farid-u'd-din Ganj-i-Shakar* (Aligarh, 1955), p. 103.

161. *Siyar-u'l-Auliya*, pp. 212–13.

162. Ibid, p. 186.

163. *Mir'at-u'l-Asrar*, by 'Abdur Rahman Chishti (MS).

164. *Tarikh-i-Firoz Shahi*, p. 47.

165. Ibid, p. 154.

RELATIONS WITH THE CALIPH

Though the Caliphate of Baghdad was fast disintegrating and had, by this time, become the phantom of a forgotten glory, it was almost an article of orthodox belief to regard the Khalifah as the final authority[166] and the legal sovereign. Khalil bin Shahin al-Zahiri says that no king of the east or the west could hold the title of Sultan unless there was a covenant between him and the Khalifah.[167] It was probably for this reason that Iltutmish celebrated with great *éclat* the grant of *manshur* (Caliphal mandate) by the Khalifah, Muntansir.[168] It cannot be said definitely whether Iltutmish had applied for this *manshur* or the Khalifah had sent it of his own accord and on his own initiative. Be it as it may, it considerably enhanced his prestige and gave him a better title against his rivals. The Khalifah's name was inscribed on the coins and pronounced from the pulpits at least four years before the receipt of this *manshur* and the formal recognition of the Delhi Sultanate.[169]

In 1258 Hulagu sacked Baghdad and put Musta'sim to death. Though the Sultans of Delhi were fully aware of the fate of Baghdad[170] at the hands of the Mongols, they continued Musta'sim's name on the coins for about forty years after this event. It was, in fact, an expression of the sentiment:

166. Taj-u'd-din Reza, a poet of this period, was mishandled by some person. He submitted a versified complaint to the Sultan in which he said:

اگر دادے نیابم این ستم را   روم زین خاك خون آشام برباد

ز آب چشم امیر المومنین را   نما یم دجله دیگر به بغداد

167. Arnold, *Caliphate*, pp. 101–02.

168. *Tabaqat-i-Nasiri*, p. 174; *Tabaqat-i-Akbari*, Vol. I, p. 60. Some of the verses of a *qasida* which Taj Reza composed on this occasion deserve to be quoted:

شادی عامست در شهر اینکه بهر شهریار   خلعت خاص امیرالمومنین آورده اند

مرکبے زین شان مبارک خلعت ممیوں' چنیں   از برائے ظل یزدان شمس دین آورده اند

169. N. Wright, p. 18.

170. It is sometimes suggested that the Sultans continued the name of the Khalifah on the coins because they were not aware of the fate of the Khilafat. This is not correct. Minhaj has given a detailed account of the irruption of the Mongols in his *Tabaqat-i-Nasiri*. Besides, the elegy which Sa'di wrote on the fall of Baghdad had reached Delhi. Large numbers of Muslim refugees had come to Delhi from Central Asian lands during the reign of Balban and were well received at the Delhi court.

'The Khalifah is dead! Long live the Khalifah!'.[171] But this devotion to the Khilafat could not blind them to the realities. Hardly two years[172] had passed since the barbarous sack of Baghdad by Hulagu when his emissaries visited Delhi and were given a royal reception. More than two lac footmen and fifty thousand horsemen lined the entire route from the town of Kilugarhi to the royal palace, while twenty rows of spectators and officials assembled there to welcome the Mongol emissaries.[173] The court chronicle would have us believe that all this was done to impress the Mongols with the glory and greatness of the Sultan but the desire to please and placate the Mongol ruler was an equally strong reason for the welcome given to them.

171. Tripathi, *Some Aspects of Muslim Administration*, p. 37.

172. Yahya Sirhindi, however, says that in the very year of the sack of Baghdad, i.e. 656/1258, embassies from Turkistan reached the Sultan who rewarded them with rich presents and valuable gifts. *Tarikh-i-Mubarak Shahi*, p. 38.

173. *Tabaqat-i-Nasiri*, pp. 317–19; *Ferishtah*, p. 73. See also the poem recited by Minhaj on this occasion, p. 319.

CHAPTER IV

THE GOVERNING CLASS

RECRUITMENT AND PROMOTIONS

Next to the Sultan, the nobles occupied a pivotal position in the political set-up of the Sultanate in the thirteenth century. It would, however, be wrong to consider them a recognized hereditary aristocracy of the Western type. At a time when the concept of a hereditary monarchy itself was in the offing, a hereditary aristocracy was completely out of the question. In fact, it was very rarely that the father's office and title were conferred on his son. Usually a noble began his career as a slave or a retainer of the Sultan and after passing through a long and graduated system attained the status of an *amir* and got an assignment in the form of an *iqta'*. This long and exacting process acted like a sieve in sifting the competent from the incompetent. Basically, the Samanid system, as described by Nizam-ul-Mulk,[1] was adopted by the Sultans of Delhi, but it could not be copied out in all its details in India since there was a constant demand for efficient and capable men to shoulder administrative responsibilities in the newly conquered regions. Moreover, in a non-Turkish land like India, the Turks considered it humiliating and derogatory to their dignity as the governing race to serve in low posts.[2] Naturally, therefore, in India a slave reached the highest rung of the ladder in a much shorter period than in other Muslim lands.

All these future administrators and *iqta'dars* started their careers in the imperial household. Usually a new entrant was assigned any one of the following services:

1. *Chashni-gir*[3]
2. *Sar-jandar*[4]

---

1. *Siyasat Namah*, pp. 74–75; See *supra*, p. 26.
2. See *Futuh-u's-Salatin* (p. 123), for the protest of the Turks against the assigning of menial work to Balban.
3. *Tabaqat-i-Nasiri*, p. 232. The *Chashni-gir* supervised the kitchen and tested the food.
4. *Tabaqat-i-Nasiri*, pp. 236–37, 252. Picked soldiers who acted as bodyguards were called *jandar* and their commander was styled as the *sar-jandar*.

3. *Amir-i-Majlis*[5]
4. *Saqi-i-Khas*[6]
5. *Sar-Abdar*[7]
6. *Tasht-dar*[8]
7. *Jam-dar*[9]
8. *Naib-Chashni-gir*[10]
9. *Sar-Jamdar*[11]
10. *Khasah-dar*[12]
11. *Saqi*[13]
12. *Naib-Sar-Jamdar*[14]
13. *Yuzban*[15]

Promotions depended exclusively on merit and personal achievements. There were slaves like Nasir-u'd-din Aitmar al-Bahai,[16] Saif-u'd-din Aibek,[17] Ikhtiyar-u'd-din Qaraqas Khan,[18] and Ikhtiyar-u'd-din

5. *Tabaqat-i-Nasiri*, p. 238. The *amir-i-majlis* was responsible for organizing the Sultan's private parties, where the Sultan met his friends. See Qureshi, *Administration of the Sultanate of Delhi*, p. 70.

6. *Tabaqat-i-Nasiri*, pp. 242, 250. The *sharab-dar* was responsible for drinks which were served by the *saqi-i-khas*. See Qureshi, *Administration of the Sultanate of Delhi*, p. 62.

7. *Tabaqat-i-Nasiri*, p. 252. It may also be read as *sharab-dar*. He was the 'head keeper of drinks'. *Administration of the Sultanate of Delhi*, p. 62.

8. *Tabaqat-i-Nasiri*, p. 254. The *tasht-dar* was the ewer-bearer who helped the Sultan in his ablutions.

9. *Tabaqat-i-Nasiri*, p. 256. The person who kept the royal wardrobe was known as the *jam-dar*.

10. *Tabaqat-i-Nasiri*, p. 261.

11. Ibid, p. 259.

12. Ibid, pp. 265, 282.
The person under whose supervision food was served was known as the *khasah-dar*.

13. Ibid, p. 268.

14. Ibid, p. 279.

15. Ibid, p. 248.
Yuzban was the keeper of the hunting leopards. Raverty, p. 745.

16. He started as *sar-jandar*, but after some time he was given the *iqta'* of Lahore. Ibid, p. 236.

17. He was first appointed as *amir-i-majlis* and later Sarsuti was assigned to him. Ibid, p. 238.

18. He was appointed as *saqi-i-khas* and later the *iqta's* of Barbahwan and Darnakwan were given to him. After some time he became *shahna-i-khalasat-i-Tabarhind*. During the reign of Iltutmish he got Multan. Ibid, p. 250.

Aitigin[19] who were given charge of *iqta*'s after serving for some time in only one of the above-mentioned posts, but there were others, like Taj-u'd-din Sanjar Kaz-Lakkhan,[20] Qamar-u'd-din Qairan Tamar Khan,[21] Ikhtiyar-u'd-din Altuniah,[22] Taj-u'd-din Sanjar,[23] Tabar Khan, Saif-u'd-din Aibek Khitai,[24] Taj-u'd-din Arsalan Khan Sanjar Khwarazmi,[25] and 'Izz-u'd-din Balban Kishlu Khan,[26] who had to serve on two posts before receiving an *iqta*' and this seems to have been the general practice. In some cases the grant of an *iqta*' was delayed due to some dereliction in the performance of duties. 'Izz-u'd-din Tughril Tughan Khan was first appointed *saqi-i-khas*, then *dawat-dar*, then *chashni-gir*, and then *amir-i-akhur* and subsequently the *iqta*' of Bada'un was assigned to him. This delay was probably due to the fact that during his term as *dawat-dar* he had lost the royal inkpot (*dawat-i-murasa-i-khas*)[27] and, as a punishment for this, he had to pass through a longer period of apprenticeship than was the normal practice during the early Turkish period. Hindu Khan was another such case. He had to go through the offices of *yuzban*, *shulah-dar*, *tasht-dar*, and *khazanah-dar* before being entrusted with the government of Uch. There was one more unusual thing about Hindu Khan. While most of the *malik*s were relieved of their duties in the imperial household after the assignment of *iqta*'s, Hindu Khan retained his office of *tasht-dar*. Minhaj writes:

---

19. His initial appointment was as *sar-jandar*. Later he was given the *iqta*' of Mansurpur and later on Bada'un was assigned to him. Subsequently, he was appointed *amir-hajib*. Ibid, p. 253.

20. He was first appointed *chashni-gir*, then *amir-akhur*, and later Multan and Gujarat were assigned to him. Ibid, p. 232.

21. He was first appointed *naib-amir-akhur*, then *amir-akhur*, and then he became the *muqta'i* of Qannauj. Ibid, pp. 247–48.

22. He was first appointed *sar-abdar*, later *sar-chatrdar*. Then he was given the *iqta*' of Baran. Ibid, p. 251.

23. He was appointed *amir-i-akhur*, then *naib amir-i-hajib*, and Janjana was assigned to him. Ibid, pp. 259–61.

24. He was appointed *sar-jamdar*, then *sar-jandar*, and then he got the *iqta*' of Samana and Kuhram. Later he was appointed *wakil-i-dar*. Ibid, p. 259.

25. He was appointed *khasah-dar*, then *chashni-gir*, and then he got the *iqta*' of Balaram. Ibid, pp. 265–68.

26. He was appointed *saqi*, then *sharab-dar*, and then the *iqta*' of Kaliwar was assigned to him. Ibid, pp. 268–73.

27. Ibid, p. 242.

هرگز تا آخیر عمر دست از طشت داری

نداشت و همچنان خدمت طشت خاص می کرد ²⁸

(He did not ever give up the office of *tasht-dar* and continued to perform the duties of personal ewer-bearer.)

Service in the imperial household was a serious discipline which did not merely qualify a man for shouldering more responsible public duties but also imbued him with the administrative ideals and principles of the Turkish Sultans. The imperial household, in fact, served as a nursery in preparing the administrative personnel of the Delhi Sultanate.

RACIAL COMPOSITIONS

Almost all the *maliks* of this period were of Turkish origin. They belonged either to the *Khita'i*,[29] *Qara-khitai*,[30] *Qipchaq*,[31] *Garji*,[32] or the *Ilbari*[33] tribes of the Turkish race. It appears that some of them were not Muslims when they were purchased or admitted to the imperial slave-household. While giving an account of the Mu'izzi and the Qutbi *maliks*, Minhaj remarks about Badr-u'd-din Sanqar Rumi:[34]

او مسلمان زاده بود و به بندگی افتاد

(He was the son of a Muslim but became a slave.)

Does it mean that other slaves were not Muslims when they found admittance into the imperial service?

Though the majority of nobles during the thirteenth century belonged to the category of slaves, the influx of Muslim refugees from Central Asian lands introduced a new element in the body politic. Since many of these immigrants belonged to distinguished ruling families and had long records of administrative experience, they were readily taken into the administration by Iltutmish. The Turkish nobility, however, resented the influence which they soon came to exercise in the administrative sphere. Iltutmish's vigilance and tact avoided a conflict between these foreign *amirs* and the *Turkan-i-Chahlgani*, but after his death many of the old refugee families

28. Ibid, p. 249.
29. Ibid, p. 238.
30. Ibid, pp. 242, 249, 252.
31. Ibid, pp. 247, 256, 258, 262.
32. Ibid, p. 259.
33. Ibid, pp. 276, 281.
34. Ibid, p. 254.

were ousted from positions of power and authority. Barani[35] writes: "As a result of the predominance of the Shamsi Turkish slaves, all those grandees and their descendants whose ancestors were *maliks*, or sons of *maliks*, or wazir or sons of wazirs, were destroyed on various pretexts during the reign of those sons of Sultan Shams-u'd-din who knew nothing about the world around them or the requirements of kingship."

Another section which had gradually worked its way to positions of authority was of the Indian-born *maliks*, such as 'Imad-u'd-din Raihan. Since their position was stronger than that of the foreigners on account of their closer links with the people, the Turkish nobility never tolerated their appointment to any post of honour or authority. While the Turkish nobility always looked for opportunities to suppress them, some of the Sultans sought to strengthen them as a counterpoise against the Turkish nobles.

Besides the three above-mentioned groups, some Mongol *amirs* and *maliks*, who had embraced Islam during the reign of Balban and had settled in India, began to aspire for positions of authority in the Sultanate. The Turkish nobility treated them also as a dangerous rival element in political life. It was at the persuasion of Nizam-u'd-din that Kaiqubad executed these Mongol nobles.[36]

These four elements—diverse in character, differing in status, training, and influence—constituted the nobility of this period. The pre-eminent position was, no doubt, that of the Turkish nobility which constituted the

---

35. Ibid, p. 27. And again he remarks:

بندگان ترك كه ايشان را چهلگانى مى گفتند بر امور ملكى مستولى
شدند و با قوت و شوكت گشتند' ملوك احرار و معارف اشراف
را پيش تخت شمسى نامور و معتبر بودند' از ميان برداشتند

(When the Turkish slaves, who were known as *Turkan-i-Chahlgani* [the Forty] dominated the administration and became strong and awe-inspiring, they removed those free-born *maliks* and dignitaries who enjoyed fame and were in the confidence of Sultan Shams-u'd-din.)

Minhaj makes no reference to the *Turkan-i-Chahlgani* as a group. Barani refers to their rivalries but does not give any details about the basis of their corporate life. It was probably the growing assertion of the Indian elements in the body politic which led the Turkish *maliks* to organize themselves into a corporate body known as the *Chahlganian*. Barani says (p. 65) that every one of them had the title of *Khan*, which signified the uppermost grade of the nobility.

36. *Tarikh-i-Firoz Shahi*, p. 133. See also *Futuh-u's-Salatin*, pp. 186–88.

real governing class, but whenever their inordinate ambition brought them into conflict with the crown, the Sultan encouraged and supported the other elements.

THE *IQTA'* SYSTEM

An important feature of the bureaucratic organization of the Delhi Sultanate was the system of granting *iqta*'s to important officers and *maliks*. Literally the word *iqta'* means a portion; technically, it was the land or revenue assigned by the ruler to an individual.[37] It may consist of:

(a) the granting of a whole province as a fief to a governor, as well as the granting of a few fields in return for tithe (*'ushr*) or taxes (*kharaj*) or rent (*kharaj-i-ujara*) or a poll tax afterwards converted into *kharaj*;

(b) the allotment of the revenue from a piece of land as salary or pension. The concept of *iqta'* was then extended and used to mean the farming of taxes and customs, duties and tolls on rivers and canals.[38]

The *iqta'* has existed since the early days of Islam as a form of reward for service to the state. It was from the time of the Buwayids that the process of its militarization began. The Buwayids gave their soldiers and *amir*s the rent of lands in guarantee of their pay, or part thereof. The Seljuqs distributed the estates as fiefs to the troops. The beneficiary retained all the revenues of the district assigned to him and the only duty that he owed to the central government was personal service in the army. If the assignment was an important one, he was bound to take with him a contingent of soldiers.

During the Seljuq period there were at least five types of *iqta*'s.[39] Of these the administrative *iqta'* was by far the most important. It was a military grant, no doubt, but carried with it some administrative duties also.

Rules about the *iqta'* and the position of the *muqta'i* (holder of the *iqta'*) have been thus described by Nizam-u'l-Mulk: "The *muqta'i*s should know that their right over the subjects is only to take the rightful amount of money or perquisite (*mal-i-haqq*) in a peaceful manner ... the life,

37. For details, see M. Sobernheim's article on *Ikta'* in the *Encyclopaedia of Islam*, Vol. II, pp. 461–63; C.H. Becker's article in *Der Islam*, V (1914); Nicola A. Ziadeh's article on 'Mamluk Syria and *Iqta*" in *Islamic Literature* (Lahore, October 1951, pp. 33–39); (Cambridge, 1929), *The Agrarian System of Moslem India*, W.H. Moreland, Appendix, pp. 216–23.

38. *The Encyclopaedia of Islam*, II, p. 461.

39. R.C. Smail, *Crusading Warfare*, pp. 64–65.

property and the family of the subject should be immune from any harm, the *muqta'i*s have no right over them; if the subject desires to make a direct appeal to the Sultan, the *muqta'i* should not prevent him. Every *muqta'i* who violates these laws should be dismissed and punished ... the *muqta'i*s and *wali*s are so many superintendents over them [the subjects] as the king is superintendent over other *muqta'i*s ... After three or four years, the *amil*s and the *muqta'i*s should be transferred so that they may not be too strong."[40]

As soon as the first phase of their military operations in northern India came to an end, the Turks found themselves confronted with a number of complicated administrative problems. Their resources, as compared with the territory they were called upon to rule, were meagre. India had till then been governed through Rajput feudal lords. This had given rise to a number of local problems which could be tackled only at a local level. The Turks lost no time in realizing that effective administration over a vast territory, with so many fissiparous tendencies working inside and the external pressure increasing on its frontiers, was not possible without evolving an effective local apparatus to help the centre in integrating its resources and consolidating its power. The *iqta'* system, as it worked in India during the thirteenth century, was a device to meet these requirements of the time.

Aibek and Iltutmish derived full advantage from this system. They used it as an instrument for liquidating the feudal order of Indian society and linking up the far-flung parts of the empire to one centre. Through it they satisfied also the cupidity of the Turkish governing class, and solved the urgent problem of the maintenance of law and order and the collection of revenues in the newly conquered territories.

These assignments had, perforce, to be of two types: big and small, though both of them were designated as *iqta'*. No details about their distinctive features are available in the contemporary records, but it appears that the smaller assignments—as were made in favour of two thousand Turkish *amir*s in the Doab[41]—carried neither any administrative duties nor any financial liabilities to the central exchequer. These small *iqta'dar*s were permitted simply to realize the revenues of some portion of land in lieu of military service. The large *iqta'*s, which were given to men of position, carried administrative responsibilities with them and the assignee was expected to maintain law and order in his territory and supply

---

40. *Siyasat Namah*, p. 37; as translated by A.B.M. Habibullah, *Foundation of Muslim Rule in India* (Lahore, 1945), p. 234.

41. *Tarikh-i-Firoz Shahi*, p. 61.

contingents to the centre in times of emergency. The revenues were collected by the *iqta'dar* and after deducting all the expenses incurred by him he remitted the surplus income (*fawazil*) to the centre.[42] It appears from later accounts that the *muqt'ai* was not given a free hand in financial matters. His accounts were regularly audited by the *Diwan-i-Wizarat*.[43]

Iltutmish's problem was solved by the distribution of *iqta*'s on a large scale. The dangers inherent in this system were eliminated by his careful and vigilant control of the administrative machinery, but during the years of anarchy that followed Iltutmish's death, the entire *iqta'* administration broke down and the *iqta'dars* adopted an attitude of defiance towards the central authority. The institution of the *iqta'*, which had been adopted in order to accelerate the process of centralization, now tended to disintegrate and decentralize the political authority. Balban could hardly tolerate this state of affairs. It was incompatible with his ideals of government. He instituted an inquiry into the terms and tenure of the *iqta*'s given to two thousand Turkish soldiers in the Doab. Many of the original grantees were dead by this time; those who survived were too old and infirm to render any military service. They retained their hold on the *iqta*'s and claimed hereditary rights over them.

The state, however, held the other view. These *iqta*'s, Balban said, were given in lieu of military service. When the grantees discontinued performing their part of the obligations, the contract, on the basis of which they held these *iqta*'s, became null and void. The occupants of the *iqta*'s argued that these lands were given to their ancestors by way of reward for the military services they had rendered to the state and carried no obligation for the future. The *iqta'dars* were probably inspired by the Seljuq traditions[44] of claiming hereditary rights over these *iqta*'s, but Balban, who looked to Sanjar for guidance in all other matters, refused to be guided by his example in the matter of the grant of *iqta*'s. Legally his attitude was correct because the generally accepted principle in this connection was:

> If the *muqta'i* remains in active service till the end of the period he naturally retains the revenue: if he dies it goes back to the state. His heirs receive a pension from other funds: if he breaks down in health his usufruct of the revenue is settled by local practice, according as his pay is continued or a pension is given from other sources on account of ill health. There is no *iqta'i* with rights for life and the right of transmitting to heirs, as the financial sovereignty of the state would thus be injured by losing the right of disposal.[45]

42. Ibid, p. 220.
43. Ibid, 'Afif, p. 414.
44. *Islamic Literature*, October, 1951, pp. 33–34.
45. *The Encyclopaedia of Islam*, Vol. II, p. 462.

Though subsequently Balban made certain concessions in favour of these *iqta'dars* at the intercession of the Kotwal of Delhi,[46] the principle of a hereditary *iqta'* was definitely rejected by him and a *khwaja* was appointed to watch and control the activities of the *iqta'dars*.

The data available about the administration of *iqta's* and the duties and functions of the *muqta'is* during the period under review is so meagre that even hypothetical observations are not possible.[47] It may, however, be definitely stated that the position of the *muqta'i* was bureaucratic, and not feudal. The Sultan had full rights over the *iqta's*. He appointed, transferred, and dismissed the *iqta'dars* at will and did not allow them to develop a particular attachment to any locality.

CONFLICT WITH THE CROWN

The Turkish bureaucracy had, no doubt, laid the foundations of the Sultanate of Delhi and had built up its administrative edifice, but it was also responsible for creating conditions which prevented the growth of those political institutions and traditions which, under more favourable circumstances, might have facilitated the evolution of a constitutional monarchy in India. The domestic history of the early Turkish Empire of Delhi centres around the nobles and their activities to control the main strings of administration. Urged on by their inordinate ambition and insatiable lust for power, they constantly urged the crown to surrender more and more of its privileges to them. Some of them, like Balban and Aitikin, did not hesitate in demanding even the insignia of royalty from the Sultans.[48] They created the office of the *naib-i-mamlikat* in order to reduce the Emperor to a mere figurehead. As was inevitable under these circumstances, the crown became a plaything in the hands of the nobles who placed kings on the throne and deposed or executed them as they pleased. Barring the eighteenth century, the conflict between the nobility and the crown in India never assumed such threatening proportions as during this period.[49] They

46. *Tarikh-i-Firoz Shahi*, pp. 61–62.

47. Most of the discussions about the distinction between the terms *iqta'dar*, *muqta'i*, and *wali* are speculative in nature because the contemporary evidence is not only meagre but also conflicting on these points.

48. *Tarikh-i-Firoz Shahi*, p. 26; *Futuh-u's-Salatin*, p. 159; *Tabaqat-i-Nasiri*, p. 253.

49. But there was a world of difference between the character and activities of the nobility during the thirteenth and the eighteenth centuries. The conflict in the eighteenth century was due to the lack of really gifted men to shoulder the burden of the administration. In the thirteenth century it was the other way round. It was not the dearth of talent but its abundance which led to constant conflict and strife.

used the crown as a bargaining counter for political concessions. Matters reached such a stage that the crown was made conditional on appointment of certain persons to key posts in the administration.[50]

TRIANGULAR TUSSLE

Broadly speaking, the Turkish bureaucracy was divided into three colleges or groups: (a) the provincial governors, (b) the army officers, and (c) the household dignitaries. Each one of them wanted to dominate the Sultan and monopolize political power and authority. A Sultan could remain on the throne so long as he prevented a conjunction of any two of these groups and played upon their mutual rivalries. But even in that case which ever group was outmanoeuvred rose in rebellion and disturbed the political atmosphere. These groups combined only when there was a common danger from the non-Turkish elements; otherwise every one pulled in his own direction and a triangular conflict became a permanent feature of Indian political life in the thirteenth century. The people of Delhi sometimes influenced the course of political developments and their support or opposition to any Sultan decided the issue. Razia came to the throne through the support of the population of Delhi, to the chagrin of the provincial governors. Later, when the household dignitaries, under the leadership of Aitikin, entered into a conspiracy with the provincial governors and sought to remove Razia from the throne, it was probably the public opinion of Delhi which damped the prospects of a palace revolution. Under these circumstances, a Sultan had to keep a vigilant watch over the activities of the provincial governors, the army officers, and the household dignitaries. When Balban consolidated his power and raised the prestige of the crown, he placed the frontier provinces under his sons, reduced the power of the dignitaries of the household, and by creating the 'king's army' he minimized all chances of revolt by the army officers. He did not allow any of his military officers to become too powerful or too influential. When Kashli Khan, his nephew, won the golden opinion of the people through his lavish distribution of wealth, Balban disapproved of his generosity and chided him on that account; but, when his own slave, Malik Amir 'Ali Sar-Jandar, treated the people with the same munificence and won the title of *Hatim Khan* he encouraged and appreciated him. The generosity of a free-born noble could produce serious political consequences, but the munificence of a slave-noble simply strengthened the master's position.

50. *Tabaqat-i-Nasiri*, p. 253.

INFLUENCE ON CONTEMPORARY POLITICS

A brief survey of the main political developments of the period is necessary in order to bring out the nature and extent of the influence of the nobility on contemporary politics.

On being asked by a noble about his successor, Shihab-u'd-din remarked: "They [my slaves] will rule my kingdom after I am dead and gone."[51] If Shihab-u'd-din had no son, he had nephews and cousins but he preferred his slaves to his kinsmen. It was as much a recognition of talent as a timely warning to the slaves to prepare themselves for the responsibility that was to devolve upon them. It, in fact, determined the character and the activities of the slaves in the years to come. Shihab-u'd-din himself did not leave anything to chance or speculation. He had three outstanding slaves—Taj-u'd-din Yildiz, Nasir-u'd-din Qubacha, and Qutb-u'd-din Aibek—and he made their relative status and position clear. He conferred a black standard on Yildiz which signified his desire to make him heir apparent at Ghaznin.[52] In order to buttress his position, Shihab-u'd-din commanded him to give his daughters in marriage to Qubacha and Aibek. Subsequently, Aibek was made the Sultan's successor in Hindustan.[53]

Shihab-u'd-din was assassinated on Sha'ban 602/March 1206.[54] It took Aibek more than three months to create conditions favourable for his accession. Probably this time was spent in persuading Sultan Ghiyas-u'd-din Mahmud, nephew of Shihab-u'd-din, to grant him the letter of manumission. But Yildiz, who had established himself in Ghaznin, was not prepared to allow Aibek an independent status. He laid claim to the Indian acquisitions of Shihab-u'd-din and prepared for a conflict with Aibek. Aibek, on his part, stoutly resisted his interference in Indian affairs and thwarted his ambitions in this direction by taking up a bold and unflinching attitude. As a counter-attack he thought of annexing Ghaznin but very soon realized the utter futility of this attempt and concentrated on his Indian possessions. On his sudden death, the Turkish *amir*s and *malik*s at Lahore elevated Aram Shah to the throne.[55] It is difficult to determine Aram's

---

51. Ibid, pp. 131–32.
52. Ibid, p. 133.
'Isami calls him the 'adopted son of the Sultan'.
Futuh-u's-Salatin. p. 99.
53. *Tarikh-i-Fakhr-u'd-din Mubarak Shah.* p. 28.
54. *Tabaqat-i-Nasiri,* p. 124.
Aibek ascended the throne on *Ziqa'd* 17, 602/June 24, 1206. *Tarikh-i-Fakhr-u'd-din Mubarak Shah,* pp. 30, 32; *Tabaqat-i-Nasiri,* p. 140.
55. Ibid, p. 141.

relationship with Aibek.[56] However, the nobles at Delhi invited Iltutmish, then governor of Bada'un, and placed him on the throne. If Aram was Aibek's son, the attitude of the nobles was an unmistakable indication of their unwillingness to accept the principle of hereditary succession.

Iltutmish's rise to the throne was due to the efforts of Sipah Salar 'Ali Isma'il, the *Amir-i-Dad* of Delhi, and the *maliks* of Delhi.[57] The protest came from the head of the bodyguards, *sar-jandar*, an important officer of the imperial household. He was joined by some other Turks and Mu'izzi *maliks*. For some days, Iltutmish refrained from taking any action against them, probably with a view to making a correct estimate of their strength and resources. He then marched against them along with eminent leaders such as 'Izz-u'd-din Bakhtiyar, Nasir-u'd-din Mardan Shah, Hizbr-u'd-din Ahmad Sur, and Iftikhar-u'd-din Muhammad 'Umar.[58] Most of the leaders of the rebellious army were put to death.[59]

This was Iltutmish's first conflict with the nobility, and, though he emerged successful, the nobles were far from being completely won over. In subsequent years they rose in rebellion several times but Iltutmish faced them with tact and determination.[60] His contact with the people and the respect he commanded in the religious circles made his position unassailable. But Iltutmish, on his part, fully recognized the position and status of the *amirs*. He is reported to have remarked that when he saw the nobles standing with folded hands in his presence, he felt like stepping down from the throne and kissing their hands and even their feet.[61]

Iltutmish's vigilance and political adroitness, however, kept the nobles tightly under his control. His death (April 30, 1236) was a signal for the nobles to start a mad race for political power. During the three decades that intervene between his death and the accession of Balban, the crown of Delhi passed through many vicissitudes. It was tossed to and fro like a shuttlecock and the nobles left no stone unturned in divesting the Sultan of all his authority and prestige. Every important noble sought to place his own protégé on the throne and control thereby the entire administrative machinery. With a view to strengthening their position, some of the *maliks*

---

56. The heading of the chapter on Aram Shah, in *Tabaqat-i-Nasiri*, has Aram Shah *bin* Sultan Qutb-u'd-din (p. 141); but further the text says that Qutb-u'd-din had only three daughters.

57. Ibid, p. 170.

58. *Taj-ul-Ma'asir* (Elliot and Dowson, Vol. II), p. 237.

59. *Tabaqat-i-Nasiri*, p. 171.

60. Ibid.

61. *Tarikh-i-Firoz Shahi*, p. 137.

even sought to establish matrimonial relations with the royal family. Balban married a daughter of Iltutmish[62] and gave one of his daughters in marriage to Nasir-u'd-din Mahmud.[63] Altuniah married Razia. All these matrimonial relations were diplomatic in character[64] and were inspired by the desire to steal a march over their opponents by establishing closer contacts with the ruling house.

Though Iltutmish had nominated Razia as his successor,[65] the nobles, particularly the provincial officers, raised Rukn-u'd-din Firoz to the throne, in complete disregard of Iltutmish's wishes. During his reign Shah Turkan, his mother, controlled the entire administration and probably relied on the support of the officers of the household and the Turkish officers of the capital. The provincial governors, such as Malik 'Izz-u'd-din Kabir Khan of Multan, Malik Saif-u'd-din Kochi of Hansi, and Malik 'Ala-u'd-din of Lahore, conspired together and broke out in rebellion.[66] Nizam-u'l-Mulk Muhammad Junaidi also deserted the Sultan and joined the governor of Bada'un.[67] This concerted action of the nobles created a difficult situation for the Sultan. When he marched out to quell these rebellions, his Turkish *amirs* and other slaves who were serving in the imperial household, killed a large number of *Tazik* (non-Turkish) officers[68] at the instigation of Malik Ikhtiyar-u'd-din Yuzbak-i-Tughral Khan and Malik 'Izz-u'd-din Balban-i-Kishlu Khan.[69]

While these troubles were brewing, Turkan Khatun's ill-treatment forced Razia to make an appeal to the people to save her from Khatun's evil machinations.[70] The army officers and the citizens of Delhi responded to Razia's pathetic appeal and placed her on the throne. The choice of Iltutmish, no doubt, stood vindicated but the provincial governors felt

---

62. *Tarikh-i-Haqqi* (MS); *Tarikh-i-Ferishtah*, Vol. I, p. 71.

63. *Tabaqat-i-Nasiri*, p. 293.

64. Matrimonial relations with the ruling house had great value for an aspirant to the throne. When the supporters of Sayyidi Maula planned a coup to place Sayyidi Maula on the throne, they arranged his marriage with a daughter of Nasir-u'd-din Mahmud. *Tarikh-i-Firoz Shahi*, p. 210.

65. *Tabaqat-i-Nasiri*, p. 184.

66. Ibid, p. 183.

67. Ibid.

68. They were: Taj-ul-Mulk Mahmud Dabir, Mushrif-i-Mamalik, Baha-ul-Mulk Husain Ash'ari, Karim-u'd-din Zahid, Zia-ul-Mulk, son of Nizam-ul-Mulk Junaidi, Nizam-u'd-din Sharqani, Khwaja Rashid-u'd-din Malkani, and Amir Fakhr-u'd-din. Ibid, p. 183.

69. Ibid.

70. Ibid, p. 184; *'Aja'ib-u'l-Asfar II*; p. 54. *Futuh-u's-Salatin*, p. 132.

humiliated for they were not consulted in this matter. They resented it and Razia proceeded to deal with them. She carefully removed all unreliable provincial officers and appointed men of her own choice to the provincial governments. Malik 'Izz-u'd-din Kabir was assigned Lahore; Hindu Khan was entrusted with the administration of Uch and Malik Aitikin was put in charge of Bada'un. Some of her appointments were severely resented, for example, when she appointed Malik Tayasai to the governorship of Awadh, the insurgents threw him into prison where he died.[71]

Fed up with the intrigues and contumacious activities of the Turkish bureaucracy, Razia tried to associate the non-Turks with the administration but this landed her in further difficulties. If Razia's career is viewed as a whole, it would appear as one long struggle to create a group of non-Turkish *amirs* and administrators as a counterpoise against the Turks who had become a source of constant embarrassment to the throne. Realizing the dangerous implications of Razia's policy, the Turkish *amirs* such as Malik 'Ala-u'd-din Jani, Malik Saif-u'd-din Kochi, Malik 'Izz-u'd-din Kabir, and Malik 'Izz-u'd-din Muhammad Salari rose against her as a body.[72] Razia handled the situation with superb tact and cleverness. She incited their mutual rivalries and thus prevented the concerted action of the recalcitrant group. When one group of such eminent nobles as Malik 'Izz-u'd-din Muhammad Salari and Malik 'Izz-u'd-din Kabir joined her, others grew panicky and fled from the field. They were pursued and many of them, including Malik Saif-u'd-din Kochi, his brother Fakhr-u'd-din, and Malik 'Ala-u'd-din Jani were imprisoned and killed.[73] For the moment the storm seemed to have subsided[74] and Razia's position was well established. But when she elevated Jamal-u'd-din Yaqut, an Abyssinian, to the office of *Amir-i-Akhur*, which had always been held by a distinguished Turkish *malik*, the Turkish nobility took it as an insult.[75] The nobles of the court formed a rebel clique under the leadership of the *Amir-i-Hajib*, Ikhtiyar-u'd-din Aitikin. But Razia's prestige with the people made a palace revolution almost impossible. The nidus consequently shifted from Delhi to the provincial towns. The provincial governors started the hostilities and the court nobility followed suit. Malik 'Izz-u'd-din Kabir rose in rebellion at Lahore while Malik Ikhtiyar-u'd-din Altuniah rebelled in Tabarhinda. Razia could have dealt with the provincial governors effectively,

71. *Tabaqat-i-Nasiri*, p. 186.
72. Ibid.
73. Ibid, p. 187.
74. Ibid.
75. Ibid, p. 153. See also p. 188.

but the simultaneous insurrection of the court nobility and the servants of the household rendered her position hopeless. Yaqut was put to death and Razia was taken prisoner. Surrounded on all sides by enemies, open and secret, and with troubles brewing in almost every direction, marriage with Altuniah seemed to her the only way to retrieve her lost position.

Though Malik 'Izz-u'd-din Muhammad Salari and Malik Qaraqash joined Razia and Altuniah,[76] the conspirators at Delhi lost no time in placing Mu'izz-u'd-din Bahram on the throne. This time the nobles bargained for the crown. Bahram was to appoint Malik Ikhtiyar-u'd-din Aitikin, the organizer of victory against Razia, as the *Naib-i-Mamlakat* and all power was to be delegated to him through a written proclamation.[77] Aitikin was an ambitious man. He assumed some of the royal prerogatives— kept an elephant and arranged for playing the *naubat* at his gate.[78] To strengthen his position further he married a divorced sister of the Sultan.[79] Had circumstances favoured, Aitikin would have turned out to be another Balban. But his ambition was greater than his ability and Bahram soon got sick of him. He commissioned two Turks[80] who stabbed Aitikin to death as soon as he came down from the upper storey of the *Qasr-i-Sufaid* after attending a *tazkir*[81] meeting arranged by the Sultan on the 8th of Muharram.[82] Muhazzab-u'd-din, the wazir, was also attacked but he escaped with two wounds and resumed his duties on his recovery.

On Aitikin's murder, Malik Badr-u'd-din Sanqar, the *Amir-i-Hajib*, assumed dictatorial powers and carried on government without consulting the Sultan.[83] He convened a secret meeting of the chiefs and sadars, such as Qazi-i-Mamalik Jalal-u'd-din Kashani, Qazi Kabir-u'd-din, Shaikh Muhammad Shami, and others at the residence of Syed Taj-u'd-din 'Ali Musavi, the *Mushrif-i-Mamalik*, with a view to deposing the Sultan.[84] This was probably the first time that a very large number of *'ulama* were directly associated with such a conspiracy, apparently with a view to mobilizing public opinion against Bahram. Sanqar invited Muhazzab-u'd-din also to this meeting but he was not prepared to be a party to the coup and so he disclosed the secret to the Sultan who took prompt action against the

76. Ibid, p. 190.
77. Ibid, p. 253.
78. Ibid.
79. Ibid, p. 192.
80. Ibid.
81. Ibid.
82. Ibid, pp. 192–93.
83. Ibid.
84. Ibid, p. 193.

conspirators.[85] Sanqar was sent away as governor to Bada'un; Qazi Kabir-u'd-din and Shaikh Muhammad Shami fled away from the capital, while Qazi Jalal-u'd-din Kashani was dismissed from his office. Thus the conspiracy was nipped in the bud and the conspirators were scattered. But dismissals and transfers could hardly mend the ways of the ambitious nobles. The Sultan hesitated to take strong action against them and nothing short of a complete purge of the subversive elements could create peaceful conditions for the royalty.

Just at this time, when the whole atmosphere seemed surcharged with guile and treachery, a Mongol army invaded India under Tayir. The nobles, who were dispatched from Delhi to check the Mongol advance, wasted their time in mutual conflicts and recriminations and shirked their duties. Muhazzab-u'd-din wrote to the Sultan: "These Turks and Amirs, a body of traitors, who are with us are not likely to become loyal. The best course for your Majesty is to dispatch an edict empowering us to kill them." The young Sultan did not understand the trick and responded to the Wazir's request by sending the desired order. The mischievous wazir showed this imperial *firman* to the Turkish *amirs* and army leaders who instantly rose against the Sultan[86] and prepared to march back to the capital to put an end to the reign of Bahram. Appeal to religious sentiments alone could pacify the excited Turkish *amirs* and so Bahram sent Shaikh-ul-Islam Sayyid Qutb-u'd-din to use his religious influence and appease the *amirs*, but the cause of the rebels appeared so strong to him that he himself joined the recalcitrant group. The *amirs* and army officers hurried to the capital and besieged the town. Fighting continued for about three months, from February to May (1242). The failure of the army leaders to occupy the town was due to the stout resistance put up by the citizens of Delhi. Minhaj-us-Siraj, who seems to have supported Bahram at this time, received injuries but was protected by his armed slaves. Ultimately the city fell and the rebels executed Bahram.[87]

Malik 'Izz-u'd-din Balban-i-Kishlu Khan who was one of the leaders of the rebellion occupied the *Daulat Khanah* and proclaimed himself as Sultan.[88] But the *maliks* and the *amirs* were not prepared to accept a

85. Ibid. pp. 193–94.

86. Minhaj says that at the instigation of Khwaja Muhazzab-u'd-din these nobles vowed to depose the Sultan:

باشارت خواجه مهذب بر اخراج و عزل سلطان بیعت کردند

Ibid. p. 196.

87. Ibid. pp. 196–97.

88. Ibid. p. 197.

comrade-in-arms as their ruler. The three surviving princes of the house of Iltutmish—Nasir-u'd-din, Jalal-u'd-din, and 'Ala-u'd-din Mas'ud—were taken out from the *Qasr-i-Sufaid* where they had been imprisoned and it was decided to place 'Ala-u'd-din Mas'ud on the throne.[89]

The failure of 'Izz-u'd-din Balban-i-Kishlu Khan to get himself recognized as the Sultan made it clear to the future aspirants to the throne that a mere coup was not enough to bring a noble to the throne. Consolidation of power behind the screen of a puppet king and the complete control over the administration should have preceded the formal assumption of regal authority. In subsequent years, the activities of the Turkish nobles were determined by this experience and 'Izz-u'd-din's impolitic action was never repeated.

'Ala-u'd-din Mas'ud appointed Malik Qutb-u'd-din Hasan Ghuri as *Naib-i-Mulk*; Muhazzab-u'd-din continued as Wazir, while the office of *Amir-i-Hajib* was entrusted to Malik Ikhtiyar-u'd-din Qaraqash. It is interesting to note that Malik 'Izz-u'd-din Balban-i-Kishlu Khan who had placed himself on the throne soon after the execution of Bahram received the extensive provinces of Nagaur, Mandor, Ajmir, and Bada'un.[90] Under more stable conditions, Kishlu Khan would have lost his head rather than receive such large assignments. These concessions, dictated by political circumstances, made the position of the crown extremely precarious.

Khwaja Muhazzab-u'd-din, who had been playing a very dangerous and mischievous role during the preceding years, again revived his activities and not only overshadowed the *Naib-i-Mulk* but also established the *naubat* and stationed an elephant at his door.[91] But Muhazzab-u'd-din was fully conscious of the fact that assumption of royal power was not possible unless the Turkish nobility was made ineffective. No sooner did he attempt to deprive the Turkish bureaucracy of its position of power and authority that the *amir*s rose up, under the leadership of Malik Taj-u'd-din Sanqar-i-Kirat Khan and Malik Nusrat Khan Sanqar, and put him to death.[92]

The reshuffle in the offices of the government necessitated by the murder of Muhazzab-u'd-din, brought Ghiyas-u'd-din Balban to the office of *Amir-i-Hajib*[93] and a new phase began in the history of the Turkish bureaucracy of Hindustan.

89. Ibid.
90. Ibid, p. 198.
91. Ibid.
92. Ibid, p. 199.
93. Ibid.

RISE OF BALBAN

Balban was an extremely ambitious and scheming person. He proceeded cautiously to consolidate his position and did not ignore the experience of his predecessors. The circumstances in which 'Ala-u'd-din Mas'ud's deposition was brought about are not known but, as Dr Habibullah remarks, "it resulted from personal ambitions and was a palace affair and that Balban, in league with Mahmud's mother, had a hand in it."[94]

During the reign of Nasir-u'd-din Mahmud, Balban took into his own hands all the strings of administration. The Sultan, who was an energetic and efficient administrator before his accession, found himself in a very embarrassing position and face to face with a domineering and ambitious *malik* like Balban, he had no alternative but to seek an escapist's pleasure in his religious devotions and prayers. Barani very correctly remarks:

He retained Sultan Nasir-u'd-din as a mere symbol while he himself ruled.[95]

To strengthen his position further, Balban gave his daughter in marriage to the Sultan on August 2, 1249. Two months later, on October 21, he was appointed *Naib-ul-Mulk* and commander of the royal forces with the title of Ulugh Khan-i-Azam.[96] The entire administration thus came under him and he controlled both the household dignitaries and the army.

Sick of this situation, Nasir-u'd-din Mahmud made a last desperate effort to shake off the tutelage of his domineering minister. He dismissed Balban on March 3, 1253 and, in order to reduce further the power of the Turkish nobility, he encouraged the non-Turkish group in the administration and appointed 'Imad-u'd-din Raihan as his *wakil-i-dar*.[97] Almost all the important offices of the state were redistributed[98] and the hegemony of the Turkish bureaucracy was sought to be broken. Raihan induced the Sultan to march against Balban and deprive him of his *iqta'*. Balban avoided a conflict by leading an expedition towards Rajputana. The Sultan confiscated the *iqta'* of Hansi and conferred it, together with the title of *Amir-i-Hajib*, on Prince Rukn-u'd-din Firoz Shah. Malik 'Izz-u'd-din Balban-i-Kishlu

94. *Foundation of Muslim Rule in India*, p. 120.
95. *Tarikh-i-Firoz Shahi*, p. 26.
96. *Tabaqat-i-Nasiri*, p. 294.
97. Ibid, p. 217.
    Balban was dismissed on March 3, 1253 and Raihan was appointed in July, which means that it took Nasir-u'd-din more than three months to find a substitute for Balban.
98. Ibid, p. 217.

Khan—that arch-conspirator of the former regimes—was appointed *Naib Amir-i-Hajib*.[99]

The Turkish *amirs* had always looked on Ulugh Khan's power with fear and jealousy, but when they found the non-Turkish elements gathering momentum, they rallied round him in order to save their racial interests.[100] All those Turkish officers who were posted in the neighbouring provinces joined the recalcitrant group and marched towards Delhi to bring about a change in the personnel of the government. Raihan was prepared for an armed struggle with Ulugh Khan but Nasir-u'd-din Mahmud, who was not confident of his position, hesitated. He responded to the compromise proposals which amounted to the virtual surrender of royal authority to Ulugh Khan and his clique. Raihan even conspired to kill the two nobles— Bat Khan-i-Aibek and 'Izz-u'd-din Balban-i-Yuzbaki—who were negotiating compromise, but he did not succeed in his attempt. The Sultan dismissed him from office and ordered him to take charge of the government of Bada'un.

A seasoned diplomat and an astute politician as Balban was, he tried to crush the power of the non-Turkish *amirs* without allowing his Turkish compatriots to grow powerful in this process. He removed through poison and dagger all those Turkish leaders whom he considered his rivals in the political field. Barani writes:

> Many of those Khans and Shamsi *maliks*, whom he considered to be his rivals or obstacles to his attaining the throne, but open execution of whom was considered to bring odium to him and reduce people's confidence in him, he secretly poisoned them with wine or with other drinks. Out of excessive love for the throne which is after all ephemeral, it never crossed his mind that for whatever reason or in whatever way he would kill the Mussalmans—by sword or by poison, openly or secretly, by starving to death or by making them die of thirst, by throwing them from heights or by drowning them in water, or by burning them in fire—he would have to answer for this shedding of blood on the Day of Judgement.[101]

It was not very long after his reinstatement that Balban demanded the insignia of royalty from the Sultan. It amounted to divesting Nasir-u'd-din Mahmud even of his titular authority. So far Balban had ruled, while Nasir-u'd-din had merely reigned, but Balban's ambition soared higher. Better qualified than Aitikin and more cautious and calculating than 'Izz-u'd-din Kishlu Khan, he did not rush at the crown. He proceeded cautiously, consolidating his power at every step.

99. Ibid, p. 299.
100. *Tarikh-i-Ferishtah*, Vol. I, p. 72.
101. *Tarikh-i-Firoz Shahi*, pp. 47–48.

'Isami has supplied interesting details about the manner in which he secured the insignia of royalty from Nasir-u'd-din. He feigned to have fallen ill and on that pretext abstained from attending the court for a few days. The Sultan sent a *hajib* to inquire about his health. He replied that he had fallen ill in his longing for the *chatr* and that he wanted a white *chatr* with a willow wand under it and a gold cup at the top in place of an eagle. The Sultan, whom circumstances had reduced to a non-entity, readily agreed to part with his *chatr* and humbly replied: "I am prepared to send you my own *chatr*; do whatever you like." The next day Balban appeared in the court with a *chatr* over his head.[102] This spectacle horrified the old nobility. Malik Qutb-u'd-din Hasan[103] could not help uttering some sarcastic remarks on this occasion. Balban was bitterly incensed and he made up his mind to get rid of the insolent *malik* who had the effrontery to laugh at him. He brought some assassins to the palace and ordered them to stand on both sides of the entrance with daggers in their hands. As soon as Qutb-u'd-din Hasan stepped into the palace gate, these assassins rushed at him and tore him to pieces. When his dying shrieks reached the ears of the Sultan, he made anxious inquiries but was calmly told by Balban:

یکے خار بودست به گلزار ملک   که هموار بودے زیاں کار ملک

بگفتیم که آن خار را بر کنند   سرش را بر ایوان شه بفگنند

(There was a thorn in the garden of the kingdom, and was a cause of injury to the kingdom. I ordered them to tear out this thorn and throw his severed head in the palace of the king.)[104]

Nasir-u'd-din was shocked to hear about the cold-blooded murder of a veteran noble; but now Balban had a full grip over the administration and it was not possible for him to utter even a single word of grief.

The methods employed by Balban to consolidate his power and enhance his prestige were, no doubt, callous and uncompromising but, when all circumstances are kept in mind, it can hardly be disputed that through

---

102. *Futuh-u's-Salatin*, p. 159.

103. 'Isami and Barani call him Hasan (*Futuh-u's-Salatin*, p. 39); but Minhaj calls him Husain (*Tabaqat-i-Nasiri*, p. 220). For his full titles, see Raverty, p. 673. Habibullah's statement that 'Mas'ud's *naib-i-mamlikat* does not appear to have survived him is incorrect in view of this account of 'Isami. There is a casual reference to the incident of Malik Qutb-u'd-din Hasan in the *Fawa'id-u'l-Fu'ad*, p. 66.

104. *Futuh-u's-Salatin*, p. 159.

these draconian measures alone could the unruly elements be forced to submit to the authority of the state. It may be said to his credit that he put an end to the conflict which had been going on between the nobility and the crown for many decades past. Later he poisoned[105] Nasir-u'd-din and himself ascended the throne.

FALL OF THE TURKISH OLIGARCHY

Balban's stern dealings with the Turkish nobles made them accept the superior authority of the crown and clipped their wings. The *Turkan-i-Chahlgani*, who had divided the revenues of the Empire amongst themselves through *iqta*'s and *wilayat*s and who used to say to one another: 'What art thou that I am not, and what wilt thou be that I shall not be', had no alternative but to change their outlook completely.[106] He resumed most of their assignments and reduced them to a position of economic dependence upon the Sultan. But Balban's attitude towards his Turkish nobles was devoid of vision. In his attempt to safeguard his own dynastic interests, he sapped the roots of Turkish power in India. He sacrificed the interests of his race at the altar of his own ambition. How fatal this policy was in the larger interests of the Turkish governing class in India became evident a few years after Balban's death. When the Khaljis entered the field as competitors for the crown, the old Turkish nobility found itself on its last legs—utterly helpless to resist the anti-Ilbarite forces. Balban had so completely depleted it of its talent that there was not a single man who could rise to the occasion and rehabilitate himself in the confidence of the people.

Kaiqubad's indulgence in wine and venery excited the latent ambitions of the nobility and it rose up again with all the ruinous violence of a suppressed force. But it had lost the vigour and vitality of the pre-Balban period. Its ambition had remained; its talent had disappeared. Nizam-u'd-din, the son-in-law of Fakhr-u'd-din, was probably the most capable man of the nobles of this period.[107] But goaded by his inordinate ambition, he

---

105. See Nizami, *Studies in Medieval Indian History* (Aligarh, 1956), article on Balban, the Regicide (pp. 48–62).

106. *Tarikh-i-Firoz Shahi*, p. 28.

107. Barani gives him a good certificate and says:

آدمی شناسے ہمچو او در عصر ہا و قرنہا پیدا نیاید و ہزار افسوس کہ آنچناں
آصف راۓ و بزر چہرے را غلبہ ہواۓ ملک و شدت طمع تخت بہ باد داد

Tarikh-i-Firoz Shahi, p. 169.

sought to extirpate the residue of Turkish talent. He sent his wife to reside in the palace in order to control the Sultan's *harem*.[108] In his anxiety to consolidate his position further, he desperately removed Turkish *maliks* and officers from all important offices. He got Kai-Khusrau murdered in the district of Rohtak[109] and deceitfully summoned all the *maliks* and *amirs* to the capital and killed four important dignitaries of the empire— Malik Bak Sariq, Malik Ghazi, Malik Karim-u'd-din, and Malik Bahrain who respectively held the offices of *Amir-i-Hajib*, *Wakil-i-dar*, *Naib-i-Barbak*, and *Amir-i-Akhur*. The *Sar-jandar* and *Mussala-dar* were exiled and fresh appointments were made to all posts, high and low. Nizam-u'd-din's policy made him unpopular with the officers who ultimately poisoned him. Kaiqubad summoned Malik Jalal-u'd-din, governor of Samana and *Sar-jandar*, and appointed him *'Ariz-i-Mamalik* and assigned the *iqta'* of Baran to him.[110] Malik Aitmar Kachchan was made *Barbak* and Malik Aitmar Surkha was given the office of *Wakil-i-dar*. Whether Kaiqubad was himself responsible for this distribution of portfolios or the political situation and the relative strength of the parties had forced it upon him, it can hardly be denied that the rival groups were now placed in such a position that a capable Sultan could effectively exploit the situation to his advantage and use these groups as a counterpoise against each other. But Kaiqubad's indolence and inefficiency led to a serious conflict between the old Turkish nobility and the Khaljis. The Khaljis rallied round Jalal-u'd-din; Aitmar Surkha was chosen by the Turks as their leader.

Kaiqubad's protracted illness made the situation still worse. His paralytic body had not yet ceased breathing when the Ilbarites raised his son, Kaimurs, to the throne and prepared a long list of the members of the Khalji group for execution. Jalal's name headed the list of the condemned persons.[111] A relation of Jalal, Ahmad Chap, who was in the service of Malik Kachchan, secretly conveyed the news to him. Jalal took instant action and, by removing his quarters to Ghiyaspur, pooled his resources and prepared himself for the coming conflict. He was joined by many non-Turkish officers who were included in the condemned list. After a brief but excited tussle,[112] the old Turkish governing class found itself completely

---

108. Ibid, p. 134.

109. 'Isami says that on receiving the intelligence of this design, Kai-Khusrau sought an alliance with the Mongol Khaqan. But he did not succeed in it. *Futuh-u's-Salatin*, pp. 196–97.

110. *Tarikh-i-Firoz Shahi*, p. 170.

111. *Tarikh-i-Firoz Shahi*, p. 172.

112. Detailed accounts of this tussle may be read in Barani's *Tarikh-i-Firoz Shahi*, and Yahya Sirhindi's *Tarikh-i-Mubarak Shahi*.

ousted from all positions of power and authority. The Khalji governing class had certain initial difficulties in getting itself recognized and winning the loyalties of the people, but very soon their superior talent succeeded in tiding over all difficulties and they established themselves firmly in the place of the Ilbarites.

PHYSICAL AND SOCIAL GIFTS OF THE NOBILITY

The *Qutbi* and the *Shamsi malik*s represented some of the best talent of the times. Their organizing capacity and experience in the art of war not only brought the Sultanate of Delhi into being but also strengthened its foundations. They displayed remarkable administrative talent in dealing with the complex and exacting problems of an empire which stretched from Multan to Lakhnauti. Whatever might have been their racial prejudices, they evinced keen interest in the welfare of the people and won the golden opinion of their subjects. Barani says about Balban that during his Khanate "every *wilayat* which was assigned to him became, as the result of his efforts, prosperous and populous."[113] Khusrau writes about Khan-i-Jahan, the *Iqta'dar* of Awadh:[114]

خان جہاں حاتم مفلس نواز گشت با قطاع اودہ سرفراز

در اودہ از بخشش او تا دو سال   ہیچ غم و نالہ نبود از منال

Sher Khan tackled the most difficult problem of the age—the increasing pressure of the Mongols on the north western frontier—with such tact, courage, and adroitness that 'the Mongols dare not come near the frontiers of India.' He was, in the words of Barani, a wall against Gog and Magog. The way in which he made the contumacious frontier tribes—*Jatwan, Khokharan, Bhattyan, Meenyan, Mundaharan*—amenable to law and order, established his reputation as an administrator *par excellence*.[115]

Barani says that Kaiqubad could not have retained his hold over the country but for the energy and resourcefulness of his two *malik*s—Nizam-u'd-din and Qiwam-u'd-din. Both of them possessed the administrative talent of Asaf and Buzurchemehr.[116]

The only outstanding *malik* of the Turkish bureaucracy who desperately resisted the establishment of Khalji power was Malik Chajju, the nephew of Sultan Balban. He rose in rebellion even after the accession of Jalal-u'd-din but was defeated.

113. *Tarikh-i-Firoz Shahi*, p. 45.
114. *Qir'an-u's-Sa'dain*, p. 221.
115. *Tarikh-i-Firoz Shahi*, p. 65.
116. Ibid, p. 169.

In personal prowess and attainments in the art of war, these nobles had established their reputations far and wide. Men such as Malik Kabir Khan Ayaz al-Mu'izzi Hazar Mardah, Muhammad Kishlu Khan, Malik 'Ala-u'd-din Kashli Khan, Malik Muhammad Bakhtiyar Khalji, and others were endowed with remarkable qualities of head and heart and their fame had crossed the Indian borders. Even Hulagu had recognized the talent of these Turkish *maliks* and had sent a dagger to Kashli Khan as a token of admiration for his military achievements.[117] Minhaj writes about Malik Taj-u'd-din Sanjar-i-Kurat Khan that he "would have two horses under saddle, one of which he would ride, the other he would lead after him and thus used to dash on, whilst the horses were galloping he would leap from this horse to that with agility, would return to this first one again so that, during a gallop he used several times to mount two horses."[118] It appears that detailed accounts of some of these *maliks* were prepared by the contemporaries[119] but these works have not survived.

The nobles drew inspiration in their social life from the imperial court and tried to emulate the Sultan in all their social and cultural activities. In certain respects their assemblies were miniature courts of the Sultan, and their generosity, which often exceeded their means,[120] sometimes, evoked the ruler's criticism.[121] It is said about Malik 'Ala-u'd-din Kashli Khan that sometimes in fits of generosity he gave everything he possessed to the objects of his favour and retained nothing except the clothes that he wore on his body.[122] Amir Khusrau once told Barani that no mother

---

117. Ibid, p. 114.

118. *Tabaqat-i-Nasiri*, p. 258; Raverty, p. 756.

119. For example, Barani informs us that volumes were written in praise of Malik Qutb-u'd-din Hasan Ghuri:

در محامد و مآثر آن ملک یگانه مجلدات پرداخته اند

Tarikh-i-Firoz Shahi, p. 113.

120. Barani informs us that they incurred heavy debts in their vain display of generosity and even mortgaged the income of their *iqta*'s. The *Multani* merchants and *Sahus* (money lenders) prospered on account of the huge amount of interest that came to them. Ibid, p. 120.

121. Ibid, p. 113.

122. Ibid, p. 114. Once he gave all the horses of his stables to Khwaja Shams Mu'in for composing a *qasida* in his praise. The *qasida* was read before Balban on the eve of the *Nauroz* celebrations and one of its verses was:

شه علاء الدین الغ قتلغ معظم باربک   پور کشلیخان معظم روئے زمین

It is surprising that Balban did not object to this sort of panegyric. See also *Wastul-Hayat*, pp. 68–69.

could give birth to another Kashli Khan so far as generosity and manly virtues were concerned.[123] Malik Amir 'Ali Sar-jandar never gave less than 100 *tankah*s to a supplicant.[124] On ceremonial occasions their lavish expenditure exceeded all limits. An ordinary Turk, Aitmar, spent one lac *jital*s on the marriage of his daughter. Shaikh Najib-u'd-din Mutawakkil, who worked as *Imam* in a mosque constructed by him, objected to this lavish expenditure. Aitmar resented this criticism and dismissed him from service.[125]

The nobles of this period led a very gay and festive life. They drank profusely and indulged in all sorts of Bacchanalian activities. Balban frequently arranged convivial parties during his Khanate and invited Khans, *malik*s, and other notables to them. Gambling, drinking,[126] and music formed a regular feature of these gatherings. *Nadim*s, *kitab-khwan*s (reciters of books), and singers were kept in regular service and were paid handsome salaries. Whatever Balban won in gambling, he distributed amongst his friends and servants.[127] During the reign of Kaiqubad, the gay life of the nobility degenerated into debauchery and licentiousness. The nobility had, in fact, its full share in creating the atmosphere which has been thus described in all its vividness by Barani:[128]

> Voluptuaries and convivialists, seekers of pleasure, purveyors of wit, and inventors of buffooneries, who had been kept in the background, lurking, unemployed, without a customer for their wares, came into request. Courtesans appeared in the shadow of every wall, and elegant forms sunned themselves on every balcony. Not a street but sent forth a master of melody, or a chanter

---

123. *Tarikh-i-Firoz Shahi*, p. 113.

124. Ibid, p. 118. Amir Khusrau composed a poem, *Asp Namah*, in his praise. He thus extols his generosity in one of his *qasida*s:

روان بلرزه درآمد که این محل نه مراست   به بحر گفتم مانی بدست خان ز کرم

گه عطا خس و خاشاك مایۀکف ماست   گه سخا در و یاقوت مایۀ کف اوست

125. *Fawa'id-u'l-Fu'ad*, pp. 78–79.

126. Balban gave up drinking after his accession. His two sons, however, continued to drink. (*Tarikh-i-Firoz Shahi*, pp. 68, 81.)

127. *Tarikh-i-Firoz Shahi*, p. 46.

128. *Tarikh-i-Firoz Shahi*, p. 129, et seq. I have quoted these passages at some length because they contain the most vivid and by far the most informative account of the life of the nobility during the thirteenth century. I have followed P. Whaeley's translation (JASB, Vol. XL, Pt. I, 1871, pp. 185–216) which, in spite of some errors, is remarkable for the translator's success in retaining the charm and vivacity of the original.

of odes. In every quarter a singer or a song-writer lifted up his head.... So the Emperor Mu'iz-u'd-din and the nobles of his realm and empire, and the children of the peers and princes of his time, and the gay, the rich, the sensualists and the epicures who lived under his rule, one and all gave themselves up to gluttony and idleness and pleasure and merriment, and the heart of high and low alike were engaged in wine and love and song and carnival.... The Emperor Mu'iz-u'd-din ceased to reside in the city. Leaving the metropolis of the red fort for Kilokhri, there, on the bank of a stream, he built a peerless palace, and laid out a park of surpassing magnificence and with his princes and chiefs and nobles and intimates and servants of the court, went thither.... All the princes and chiefs and gentlemen and men of science and officials reared booths near the palace ... and from all the quarters of the cities and of the Empire, minstrels and rhetors, and beauties, and singers and wits and buffoons and mimics came to court. The palace teemed with life, and licentiousness was the order of the day. The mosques were deserted by their worshippers and the taverns were thronged. No one cared to stay in the cloisters, but distilleries became places of note. The price of wine rose tenfold. The people were plunged in pleasure and gaiety and no thought of sadness, or anxiety, or grief, or fear, or dread, or restraint found place in a single breast. The clever, the genial, the wits, and the jesters, one and all, migrated to the town. The minstrels and courtesans invented new modes of pleasing. The purses of the vintners and distillers were gorged with gold and silver coins. Beauties and swashbucklers and itinerary panders were overwhelmed with gold and jewels. For the men of title, the men of letters there was nothing left to do but to drink wine, to make the assemblies sparkle with their wit, to vie with each other in repartee, to resign themselves to music and dice and largesse, and the zest of the passing hour, anything to prop up life against the insidious sapping of time, and give night and day their fill of pleasure and repose...the fame of his lavish gifts, and his devotion to pleasure, and his dainty, and fastidious voluptuousness bruited through the cities of the provinces and so patent to the world was his beauty-worship and libertinism, that notorious rufflers and gray sinners, in the hope of making acceptable offerings to king, had trained beautiful girls—irresistible with their bright glances and radiant wit—to sing and strike the lute, and chant canzonets, and utter pretty raillaries, and to play at drafts and chess. And every moonbright darling, bale of the city and scourge of the world, was disciplined in diverse ways, and, as her budding bosom expanded in the garden of youth, was taught to ride her horse at speed, and play at ball, and cast the javelin, and become adept in every lively and elegant accomplishment. They were instructed in diverse acts of fascination, which would make monks idolaters, and seduce the most devout to intoxication, sirens of Hindustan, slave-boys shapely as the cypress, and damsels shining as the moon, skilled in Persian and singing, pranked in gold and trinkets and embroidered dresses and brocade, soul-alluring puppets schooled in all the civilities and courtesies and fashions of the court, peerless smooth-faced boys with their ear-drops of pearl, and damsels robed like brides in their wedding glories; and the masters of minstrelsy and subtle conjurors who had in secret prepared plays in Persian and Hindi, and had embodied the praises of the Sultan in epigram and ballad and madrigal and comic song, and mimics and buffoons who, with a single jest would betray the saddest into a burst of merriment, and make the jovial hold their sides for excess of laughter, all these came from far countries to feed on the bounty of the Sultan.

It would be wrong if this atmosphere of drunken revelry—which, after all, was a temporary phase in the cultural life of the nobility—were to create the impression that the Turks were incorrigible sots and had no interest in the serious arts or humanities of the day. In fact, many of them were great patrons of art and letters and were known for their urbanity and culture. Literati, scholars, poets, and artists flocked to them in large numbers and basked in the sunshine of their favours. Some of the most distinguished poets of medieval India—for example, Amir Khusrau and Amir Hasan Sijzi—started their literary careers in the service of the nobles. Prince Muhammad's court at Multan was a great rendezvous of scholars and poets. His *nadims* recited in his presence the *Shah Namah* of Firdausi and the poetic works of Sana'i, Khaqani, and Nizami. The prince even extended an invitation to Shaikh Sa'di and offered to construct a *khanqah* for him.[129]

As in other spheres of social and political activity a noble always jealously guarded his privilege of patronizing a poet in his service. Bughra Khan was once present at a party of Malik Chajju. Being pleased with some verses of Amir Khusrau, he presented him with a dish of silver *tankahs*. Chajju was annoyed at the poet's acceptance of the gift and, though Khusrau tried to win back his favour, the Malik did not forgive him and transferred his services to Bughra Khan.

The nobles extended their patronage to the religious classes[130] as much out of conviction as out of expediency. Fakhr-u'd-din, the *Kotwal* of Delhi, had in his service twelve thousand *huffaz* who busied themselves all the time in reciting the Quran.[131] Nizam-u'd-din *Kharitah-dar* constructed a *khanqah* for Shaikh Badr-u'd-din Ghaznavi, a distinguished disciple of

129. *Tarikh-i-Firoz Shahi*, pp. 66–68.

130. For Taj-u'd-din Sanjar Kazlak Khan's respectful attitude towards Minhaj, see *Tabaqat-i-Nasiri*, p. 232. See also *Fawa'id-u'l-Fu'ad*, (pp. 67, 78) for their relations with mystics. For Prince Muhammad's respectful attitude towards Shaikh 'Usman and Shaikh Qidwa, see *Tarikh-i-Firoz Shahi*, pp. 67–68.

131. Ibid, p. 117.

Khwaja Qutb-u'd-din Bakhtiyar Kaki, and paid all its expenses.[132] 'Imad-u'l-Mulk endowed several villages for charitable purposes.[133] Such endowments considerably enhanced the popularity and prestige of a noble and endeared him to the religious classes.

Some of the nobles of this period were known for their individual fads, fancies, and interests. 'Imad-ul-Mulk, the famous *Rawat-i-'Arz* of Balban, frequently invited his staff to his house and gave robes to every one of his subordinates. This would cost him about twenty thousand *tankah*s. The whole department was provided with meals from his kitchen. He was so fond of betel leaves that fifty servants were all the time busy in distributing betel leaves in his *diwan*.[134] Malik u'l-Umara Fakhr-u'd-din, the famous *Kotwal* of Delhi, changed his clothes, bedding, etc., every day and these clothes were given as dowries to orphan girls. Whoever brought a copy of the Quran to him, he purchased it at a fabulous price.[135] Deploring the pedantic display of generosity and frivolous expenditure by the Turkish governing class, Barani says: 'If one *khan* or *malik* heard that another *khan* or *malik* entertained five hundred guests, he was ashamed if he could not arrange for entertainment of one thousand people. If one learnt that another *malik* gives two hundred *tankah*s in charity at the time of riding, he was ashamed if he could not bestow four hundred *tankah*s instead. If any *malik* bestowed fifty horses in an assembly of pleasure and clothed two hundred people, when others heard of it they grew jealous and made arrangements to bestow one hundred horses and to give robes to five hundred people.'[136]

---

132. *Fawa'id-u'l-Fu'ad*, p. 79.

133. *Tarikh-i-Firoz Shahi*, p. 117. Barani informs us that these *auqaf* functioned till the days of Firoz Tughluq and food was distributed and the Quran was recited to bless his soul.

134. Ibid.

135. Ibid.

136. Ibid, pp. 119–20.

CHAPTER V

THE *'ULAMA*

The *'ulama* constituted a very influential section of Muslim society in the Middle Ages. They were held in high esteem on account of their religious learning[1] and in many traditions of the Prophet they are referred to as his heirs and are sometimes compared to the prophets of the Israelites.[2] The attitude of medieval Muslim society towards them is very neatly expressed by a contemporary historian in the following words:

> All people know that after the apostles and prophets rank the truthful persons (*siddiqin*), martyrs (*shahidan*), and scholars (*'aliman*). The scholars are included in the category of *siddiqs* and have preference over the martyrs. The Prophet has said: "The *'ulama* are the heirs of the prophets." He further says: "On the Day of Resurrection the ink used by the scholars will be weighed against the blood shed by the martyrs and the ink of the scholars will outweigh and turn the scales.... The world exists on account of the piety of the learned.... The laws of the *Shari'at*...are enforced by them...and things illegal and not sanctioned by the *Shari'at* are suppressed by them.... The religion of God stands firm due to them..." The Prophet has said: "A single *faqih* is a greater terror for Satan than a thousand pious men." He has also said: "If there had been no Satan, the sons of Adam would not have suffered; if there had been no pious men [among them], certainly the wicked people would have been destroyed; if there had been no *'ulama*, certainly the people would have wandered about like beasts...." The Prophet has said: "The best kings and the best nobles are those who visit the doors of the *'ulama* and the worst *'ulama* are those who visit the doors of the kings and the nobles...." The *'ulama* are much superior in dignity and status to others.... After them rank the kings....[3]

1. Note particularly the following observations:

   (a) 'By acquiring knowledge a man becomes noble.' Shaikh Nizam-u'd-din Auliya in *Fawa'id-u'l-Fu'ad*, p. 44.
   (b) 'Whoever loves knowledge and scholars, his sins are not recorded.' A *hadis*, as quoted in *Fawa'id-u'l-Fu'ad*, p. 21.
   (c) 'The *'ulama* are noblest amongst the common people and the faqirs are noblest of all the noble ones.' Shaikh Farid Ganj-i-Shakar in *Siyar-u'l-Auliya*, pp. 75–76.

2. *Tarikh-i-Fakhr-u'd-din Mubarak Shah*, p. 11. See also *Al-Bukhari*, Book III: *"'Ilm"*; *Al-Tirmizi*, Book XXXIX: *"'Ilm"*.

3. *Tarikh-i-Fakhr-u'd-din Mubarak Shah*, pp. 11–12.

Indiscreet use of the terms 'clergy' and the 'clerical group' for the *'ulama* has often created the impression that they constituted a recognized hereditary class or an ordained priesthood of the Christian type. This, however, is not correct. As a matter of fact, anybody who had acquired religious knowledge up to a generally accepted and prescribed standard[4] could become an *'alim*, though his prestige and influence over the people depended on personal piety and devotion to the cause of learning. The people expected a very high standard of morality from the *'ulama* and criticized their failings and shortcomings more severely than those of the ordinary people. They believed: "When an illiterate man dies his sins also die with him, but when an *'alim* dies his sins outlive him."[5]

4. The syllabus of medieval Indian institutions—both government and private—during this period was as follows:

(a) *Tafsir* (Exegesis): (i) *Madarik-u't-Tanzil* of 'Abdullah b. Ahmad Hafiz-u'd-din Nasafi (ob. 701/1310); (ii) *Al-Kashshaf* of Abul Qasim Mahmud b. 'Umar Zamakhshari (ob. 538/1144); (iii) *Anwar u't-Tanzil wa Asrar u't-Ta'wil* of 'Abdullah b. 'Umar Baizawi (ob. 716/1316).

(b) *Hadis* (Traditions of the Prophet): (i) *Mashariq-u'l-Anwar* of Razi-u'd-din Hasan Saghani (ob. 650/1225); (ii) *Masabih-ul-Sunnah* of Abu Muhammad al-Husain al Farra Baghawi (ob. 516/1122).

(c) *Fiqh* (Islamic law): (i) *Hidayah* of Burhan-u'd-din Abul Hasan 'Ali Marghinani (ob. 593/1197).

(d) *Usul-i-Fiqh* (Principles of Islamic Law): (i) *Manar-u'l-Anwar* of Hafiz-u'd-din Abul Barakat Nasafi (ob. 701/1301); (ii) *Usul-i-Bazdawi* of 'Ali b. Muhammad Bazdawi (ob. 482/1089).

(e) *Tasawwuf* (Mysticism): (i) *'Awarif-u'l-Ma'arif* of Shaikh Shihab-u'd-din Suhrawardi (ob. 632/1234).

(f) *Adab* (Literature): *Maqamat-i-Hariri* of Abu Muhammad al-Qasim al-Hariri (ob. 516/1122).

(g) *Nahw* (Grammar): (i) *Misbah*; (ii) *Kafiyah*; (iii) *Lubub-u'l-Albab* of Qazi Nasir-u'd-din Baizawi.

(h) *Kalam* (Scholasticism): (i) *Sharh-i-Saha'if*; (ii) *Tamhid-i-Abu Shakoor Salimi.*

(i) *Mantiq* (Logic): *Sharh Shamsiya*. See also, *Al-Nadwah* (February, 1909, Vol. VI, No. 1, pp. 7–10), Maulawi 'Abdul Hai's article on syllabus.

There is no evidence of *Fusus-u'l-Hikam* being included in the syllabus during the period under review, as the writer of this article has suggested.

5. *Sarur-u's-Sudur* (MS), p. 26.

Generally, the people expected the *'ulama* to be well versed in *'ilm-i-fara'iz* (Muslim law particularly relating to inheritance, etc.) for in that way alone could they help the Muslims in organizing their lives according to the laws of the *Shari'at*.[6] Acquiring knowledge for the sake of earning money was looked down upon. An eminent contemporary mystic used to say: "Knowledge in itself is a noble thing but when it is used for earning money and the scholars go about from door to door, respect for it vanishes."[7] Participation of the *'ulama* in political matters was deemed harmful and improper. Ibn-i-Khaldun considered them utterly incompetent to tackle political problems due to their ignorance of the requirements of the time.[8]

Referring to the *muftis* and *qazis* who wasted their time and knowledge in hair-splitting theological discussions, Shaikh Farid once remarked: "The object of acquiring knowledge of the religious law is to act upon it and not to harass peoples."[9]

TWO CATEGORIES

Tradition classified the *'ulama* into two categories—the *'ulama-i-akharat* and the *'ulama-i-duniya*.[10] The basis of this division was the difference in their attitude towards worldly affairs. The *'ulama-i-akharat* led an abstemious life of pious devotion to religious learning and eschewed entanglement in materialistic pursuits and political affairs. They preferred to pass their days in penury rather than consort with kings and amass wealth. The be-all and end-all of their lives was to disseminate knowledge and strive for the moral uplift of society. The *'ulama-i-duniya*, on the other hand, were totally mundane in their outlook. They aspired to wealth and worldly prestige and did not hesitate in compromising their conscience if it served their purpose. They mixed freely with kings and the bureaucracy and gave them moral support in their actions, good or bad.[11] This type of Muslim theologians was generally designated as the *'ulama-i-su* and Muslim public opinion did not merely treat them with contemptuous indifference but held them responsible for all the vices and misfortunes of the Muslim community.[12]

6. *Sarur-u's-Sudur* (MS), p. 29.
7. *Fawa'id-u'l-Fu'ad*, p. 182.
8. Ibn-i-Khaldun, *Muqaddimah* (Urdu trans.), Vol. III, p. 216.
9. *Siyar-u'l-Auliya*, p. 85.
10. See Barani *Tarikh-i-Firoz Shahi*, (pp. 154–55), where Bughara Khan quotes Balban about the two types of the *'ulama*. The author of *Misbah-u'l-Hidayah*, however, classified the *'ulama* under three categories: *'ulama-i-rabbani*, *'ulama-i-ukhrawi*, and *'ulama-i-dunyawi* (p. 57).
11. *Tarikh-i-Firoz Shahi*, p. 154.
12. The author of *Misbah-u'l-Hidayah* says: "There is none worse than *'ulama-i-dunyavi*" (pp. 57–58). Shaikh Ahmad Sirhindi has trenchantly criticized the

THE 'ULAMA—AS STARVING TEACHERS

After completing his formal education an 'alim usually devoted himself to teaching work in some mosque[13] or under the thatched roof of his own mud house. He rejected a life of affluence and plenty and refused to be drawn into the vortex of politics. The following accounts of some of the 'ulama of the period under review will give an idea of their character, the conditions in which they lived, and their selfless devotion to the cause of learning and enlightenment.

Maulana Razi-u'd-din Hasan:[14] The famous compiler of *Mashariq-u'l-Anwar*, Maulana Razi-u'd-din Hasan was born and brought up in Bada'un. After completing his education, probably in his hometown, he came to Koil (Aligarh) and accepted the post of *Naib-i-Mushrif*.[15] One day the *Mushrif* made some inept remarks which brought a smile to the Maulana's face. The *Mushrif* got incensed and threw his inkpot at him. The Maulana escaped the ink, but the insolent behaviour of the *Mushrif* injured his sense of self-respect. He gave up his job with the remark: "We should not keep the company of the illiterates."[16]

Later on he became tutor to a son of the *wali* of Koil. His salary was only hundred *tankah*s, but he was content with it.[17] He could not, however, stick to this job for long and took to itinerary. His profound scholarship and mastery over the Traditions of the Prophet made him a respected and popular figure wherever he went. When he reached Nagaur, eminent scholars, such as Qazi Hamid-u'd-din and Qazi Kamal-u'd-din, gathered round him and requested him to give lessons in the Traditions of the

---

'ulama-i-su in his letters and has held them responsible for the degeneration of Muslim society. *Maktubat-i-Imam Rabbani*, pp. 46–47.

13. For Shaikh Nasir-u'd-din Chiragh's praise of a *danishmand* who spent his time in teaching the Quran to boys in a mosque, see *Khair-u'l-Majalis*, p. 107. See also *Fawa'id-u'l-Fu'ad* (p. 89) wherein Shaikh Nizam-u'd-din Auliya refers to a *danishmand*, Zia-u'd-din, who used to teach near the *Minarah* (Qutb Minar).

14. For biographical references, see *Fawa'id-u'l-Fu'ad*, pp. 103–04; *Mu'jam-u'l-Udaba*, Yaquti, Vol. III, p. 211; *Fawat-u'l-Wafayat*, Ibn Shakir I, p. 133; *Jawahir-u'l-Mudi'ah*, Ibn Abi'l Wafa I, p. 201.

15. For the status, position, and duties of the *Mushrif*, see *Dastur-u'l-Albab fi 'Ilm-il-Hisab* of Haji 'Abdul Hamfd Muharrir Ghaznavi (*Medieval India Quarterly*, Vol. I, Nos. 3 and 4).

16. *Fawa'id-u'l-Fu'ad*, pp. 103–04.

17. Ibid, p. 104.

Prophet. Maulana Razi-u'd-din taught his *Misbah-u'd-Duja*[18] to the scholars of Nagaur and issued certificates also. One of the residents requested him to instruct him in mysticism (*'ilm-i-tasawwuf*). The Maulana apologized and said: "I am busy here because the people of Nagaur learn the science of *Hadis* from me these days. At present I have no time to instruct you in mysticism. If you desire to learn it, you may accompany me on my itineraries in non-Muslim lands where there will be no such crowd. I shall then teach this science to you."[19]

From Nagaur the Maulana proceeded to Jalore[20] and Gujarat. Conditions in those areas were such that a Muslim could not move about freely. The Maulana changed his dress[21] and roamed about *incognito*. During this journey he instructed the above-mentioned person in mysticism. Later on he proceeded to Lahore and from there he made his way to Baghdad. His scholarship attracted the attention of the Caliph and he was soon taken into government service. In 617/1220 the Abbasid Caliph, al-Nasir (575–622/1180–1225), sent him as an ambassador to the court of Iltutmish. He again came to Delhi in the same capacity a few years later and stayed here till 637/1239.[22]

Maulana 'Ala-u'd-din Usuli:[23] A resident of Bada'un, Maulana 'Ala-u'd-din Usuli imparted free education to students who gathered round him in large numbers. Though he lived under conditions of appalling poverty, he did not accept anything from anybody. It was very rarely that he accepted any gift and, that too, to the extent of his immediate need and under extremely straitened circumstances. One day the starving scholar was

18. A collection of the Traditions of the Prophet. Its full title was: *Misbah-u'l-duja min sihah ahadis al-Mustafa*. No copies of this work are known to exist. Nawab Siddiq Hasan Khan has referred to this work in his *Ithaf'al-nubala* (Cawnpore), p. 243.

19. *Sarur-u's-Sudur* (MS), pp. 73–74.

20. Jalore was a small Chauhana principality in Rajputana. Aibek had forced it to submission, but the Rajputs re-established their hold over it (*Epigraphia Indica* IX, pp. 72–73). Iltutmish re-imposed vassalage on Udaisinha, the ruler of Jalore, but he repudiated it later. His successor, Chachigadeva, not only asserted his independence but also assumed a conquering role. Maulana Razi-u'd-din visited this place probably at a time when the tussle for its occupation was going on between the Chauhanas and the Turks.

21. *Sarur-u's-Sudur* (MS).

22. M.G. Ahmad, *The Contribution of India to Arabic Literature* (Allahabad, 1946), p. 250.

23. For brief notices, see *Fawa'id-u'l-Fu'ad*, pp. 165–66; *Khair-u'l-Majalis*, pp. 190–91; *Akhbar-u'l-Akhyar*, p. 77.

eating the remains of seeds out of which oil had been squeezed that his barber stepped in. He concealed the dregs hurriedly in his turban. A few minutes later, when the Maulana took off his turban to get his head shaved, the dregs fell on the ground. The barber was deeply touched by his poverty. He narrated the incident before some of the well-to-do persons of Bada'un and induced them to help him. A native of Bada'un sent some *ghee* and a tray full of dainties to the Maulana who not only sternly refused to accept the gift, but also summoned the barber and severely reprimanded him for disclosing his secret to the people.[24]

Only one instance will suffice to give some idea of the type of pupils that learnt at his feet. Shaikh Nizam-u'd-din Auliya—then 15 or 16 years of age, living in a small house with his widowed mother and sister, all of whom very often went hungry—came to the Maulana and began to take lessons in Muslim law. When the Maulana taught him *Hidayah*, he compared and collated his manuscript with that of his pupil. Alternately the teacher and the pupil read out and corrected the text.[25] When he had finished his lessons in Muslim law, the Maulana asked him to put on a *dastar*[26] on his head— which meant that the Maulana considered him to have completed his education. Medieval convocations, if one can use the term, were simple but solemn affairs. A *dastar* was tied round the graduate's head by some leading *'alim* before a gathering of scholars and divines and the recipient of the *dastar* was declared to have acquired the requisite amount of knowledge and read the prescribed number of books. Sometimes a certificate was also given in which the teacher mentioned the books he had taught. When Maulana 'Ala-u'd-din Usuli told his pupil to arrange for his *dastar* ceremony he was worried rather than pleased. He knew the limited means of his mother and the indigent atmosphere of his household. Worried and perplexed he went to his mother who assuaged him by promising to make the necessary arrangements. She spun and wove a sheet of cloth for his *dastar*. A small feast to which the teacher, Maulana 'Ala-u'd-din, had also contributed something, was arranged. The feast being over, the Maulana stood up and tied the *dastar* round Nizam-u'd-din's head. The young scholar, who was to distinguish himself in the academic circles of Delhi, humbly fell at the feet of his master and expressed his gratitude. 'Ali Maula, a distinguished disciple of Shaikh Jalal-u'd-din Tabrizi, was also present there. Moved by this sight, he predicted in Hindivi:

24. *Khair-u'l-Majalis*, p. 180.
25. *Fawa'id-u'l-Fu'ad*, p. 165.
26. The sash or muslin cloth wraped round the turban.

ارے مولانا! یہ بڈا ہوسی

(O Maulana! He will be a great man.)[27]

Maulana Kamal-u'd-din Zahid:[28] One of the most erudite scholars of his day, Maulana Kamal-u'd-din Zahid was known in Delhi for his piety and intimate knowledge of the Traditions of the Prophet. He gave lessons in the *Mashariq-u'l-Anwar* to his pupils. Balban called him to his court and requested him to serve as his *Imam* (leader of the congregational prayers). "Our prayer is all that is left to us," replied the Maulana regardless of the man to whom he was talking. "Does the Sultan want to take that also from us?" Balban was dumbfounded and he allowed the Maulana to go home.[29]

Maulana Zahid devoted his whole time to the instructions in the *hadis*. Amir Khurd has preserved for us the contents of a certificate which he gave to his pupil, Nizam-u'd-din Auliya. It ran:

> ...Be it known after the praise of God and His Prophet that God provided an opportunity to the great Shaikh and the Imam of the world, Nizam-u'd-din Muhammad b. Ahmad b. Ali, who is endowed with great erudition and profound learning and is the beloved of divines,....to study the entire text of *Mashariq-u'l-Anwar*—which contains a gist of the *Sahih Bukhari* and *Sahih Muslim*—with the writer of these lines ... He studied it as critically and with such diligence, effort, and perseverance as the book deserves to be read. The writer of these lines has studied this book with two great scholars: the author of *Sharh Asar al-Nayyarain fi Akhbar al-Sahihain* and Mahmud b. Abul Hasan As'ad al-Balkhi ... I have received both oral and written permission from these scholars (to teach this book). Both these scholars had studied this book with its author. I have permitted Sultan-u'l-Mashaikh to narrate the traditions of the Prophet on my authority as is laid down in the *'Ilm-i-Hadis*.... I request Sultan-ul-Mashaikh not to forget me and my descendants in his prayers.... He studied this book in a mosque of Delhi known after the name of Najm-u'd-din Abu Bakr al-Taiwasi.... May God protect this city from all calamities and misfortunes.... These words are in the handwriting of Muhammad b. Ahmad b. Muhammad al-Marikali, known as Kamal Zahid and were written on Rabi' al-Awwal 21, 679 AH.[30]

Maulana Burhan-u'd-din Nasafi:[31] He was an eminent scholar of Delhi. Whenever a student sought his permission to attend his lectures, he asked

27. *Khair-u'l-Majalis*, p. 190–91.
28. For brief notices, see *Siyar-u'l-Auliya*, p. 101; *Akhbar-u'l-Akhyar*, p. 71.
29. *Siyar-u'l-Auliya*, p. 106.
30. Ibid, pp. 104–05. See Appendix for the complete text.
31. For brief references, see *Fawa'id-u'l-Fu'ad*, p. 158; *Akhbar-u'l-Akhyar*, pp. 76–77.

him to make three solemn promises: that he would take his meals only once a day; secondly, that he would not miss a single lecture; thirdly, that he would address him only with the words *as-salam alaikum* and would not kiss his hands or touch his feet.[32]

Khwaja Shams-u'l-Mulk: He was another notable scholar of Delhi and had served for sometime as *Mustaufi*.[33] Later he gave up his job and dedicated himself to teaching work. He used to teach his pupils from a balcony. Only three of his favourite pupils—Shaikh Nizam-u'd-din Auliya, Qazi Fakhr-u'd-din Naqila, and Maulana Burhan-u'd-din—were permitted to sit by him in the balcony. Whenever any pupil absented himself or came late, the Khwaja would politely ask him: 'What wrong have I done to you that you do not come regularly?'[34]

THE 'ULAMA—AS PIOUS PREACHERS AND SCHOLARS

There were scholars who devoted themselves exclusively either to the peaceful pursuit of knowledge or to preaching. Very often they had to work under extremely indigent circumstances.[35] They disliked dabbling in politics or visiting the courts of the kings and the nobles. Their piety and scholarship, however, attracted the rulers to their doors.[36] Notwithstanding his emphasis on the dignified parts of kingship, Balban himself visited the houses of pious theologians and preachers and did not hesitate in shedding tears in public meetings addressed by eloquent *muzakkir*s.[37] His respectful attitude towards Maulana Sharaf-u'd-din Walwaji, Maulana Siraj-u'd-din

---

32. *Fawa'id-u'l-Fu'ad*, p. 158.

33. On his appointment as *Mustaufi*, Khwaja Taj Reza wrote:

صدر اکنوں به کام دل دوستان شدی   مستوفی ممالک هندوستان شدی

Fawa'id-u'l-Fu'ad, p. 68.

34. Ibid, pp. 67–68.

35. Shaikh Najib-u'd-din Mutawakkil wanted to get a copy of *Jami'-u'l-Hikayat* transcribed for himself but his means were so limited that if he had money to purchase paper, he had nothing to pay the copyist's charges. Ibid, p. 28.

36. *Tarikh-i-Firoz Shahi*, pp. 46–107. Shaikh Nizam-u'd-din Auliya once said about Shaikh Burhan-u'd-din Mahmud b. Abil Khair al-Balkhi, a contemporary scholar of Balban, that the author of the *Hidayah* had predicted about him that his academic eminence would attract kings to his door. (Ibid, p. 239; *Akhbar-u'l-Akhyar*, pp. 45–46.) This prediction proved true when Balban began to visit his house regularly after Friday prayers. (*Tarikh-i-Firoz Shahi*, p. 46.)

37. Ibid, pp. 46–47.

Sanjari, and Maulana Najm-u'd-din Damishqi has been particularly noted by Barani.[38] Among the scholars of this period, Barani has referred to two other persons who busied themselves in teaching work—Maulana Burhan-u'd-din Malkh and Maulana Burhan-u'd-din Bazaz.[39] No details are available about their life and activities.

Shaikh Nizam-u'd-din Auliya once referred to the following three *danishmand*s[40] of this period who had saintly attributes: (a) Maulana Shihab-u'd-din of Meerut, (b) Maulana Ahmad, and (c) Maulana Kaithali. Stories about their moral virtues and humanitarian qualities were frequently narrated by the Shaikh before his audience.[41] These *danishmand*s belonged to that category of scholars who spent their time in academic pursuits and did not hanker after worldly prestige or glory.

Maulana Nur Turk,[42] Maulana Nizam-u'd-din Abul Muwayyid,[43] and Shaikh Shihab-u'd-din Khatib[44] were some of those distinguished preachers of the thirteenth century who carried on their work with single-minded devotion and unspoilt by wealth and power. Maulana Nur Turk, whose eloquent sermons elicited praise from a scholar and saint of Shaikh Farid Ganj-i-Shakar's eminence, hated his contemporary theologians on account of their materialistic pursuits and criticized them publicly in his lectures. He himself led an extremely austere life; his only means of livelihood being a *dang* per day which his freed slave gave to him. Sultan Razia once sent some gold to him. He beat it with his stick and asked the royal messenger to remove it from his sight.[45]

Maulana Nizam-u'd-din Abul Muwayyid was another very gifted speaker of medieval India. Before delivering a sermon he always offered two *rak'at*s of prayer with such thrilling spiritual composure that even Shaikh Nizam-u'd-din Auliya, who had attended one of his sermons in his

---

38. Ibid, p. 46.

These scholars were distinguished in their special spheres of learning and were held in high respect in the academic circles of Delhi. Maulana Burhan-u'd-din Damishqi was a pupil of the distinguished Muslim scholar and philosopher, Maulana Fakhr-u'd-din Razi. Ibid, p. 111. See also *Firishtah*, I, p. 76.

39. *Tarikh-i-Firoz Shahi*, p. 111.

40. The word *danishmand* is used for externalist scholars ('*ulama-i-zahir*) in medieval Indian literature.

41. *Fawa'id-u'l-Fu'ad*, pp. 65–67.

42. For a brief notice, *Tabaqat-i-Nasiri*, pp. 189–90. *Fawa'id-u'l-Fu'ad*, p. 199; *Siyar-u'l-Auliya*, p. 62; *Akhbar-u'l-Akhyar*, p. 74.

43. *Fawa'id-u'l-Fu'ad*, p. 192; *Akhbar-u'l-Akhyar*, pp. 74–75.

44. *Fawa'id-u'l-Fu'ad*, p. 44.

45. Ibid, 198–99; *Akhbar-u'l-Akhyar*, p. 74.

boyhood, felt constrained to remark: "I did not see anybody offering prayers in the manner he did."[46] He then ascended the pulpit and asked Qasim, his *muqqarri* (reciter of the Quran), to recite some passages from the Holy Book. After Qasim's recitation in extremely pleasant intonation, the Maulana addressed the audience. His sermons, which sometimes comprised of a few couplets only, very often moved the audience to loud wailing and tears. One day he recited the following couplet:

نه از عشق تو ز تو حذر خواهم کرد

جان دز غم تو زیر و زبر خواهم کرد

and the gathering burst into tears. Once, when Delhi was suffering from scarcity of rains, the Maulana stood up on his pulpit and, with his eyes fixed on the sky. said: "Oh God! If Thou sendest not rain, I shall not live in any human habitation," and stepped down.[47]

It was a popular belief in those days that a preacher's power to move the heart of the people depended on his personal piety, adherence to the laws of the *Shari'at*, and punctuality in the performance of religious duties. Once the people of Lahore discovered to their great astonishment that a *khatib* who had gone on Hajj pilgrimage had lost the charm of his sermons on his return. It was later on found that he had missed his prayers during the journey.[48]

THE 'ULAMA—AS GOVERNMENT SERVANTS

"The great ambition of the *'ulama*," Shaikh Jalal-u'd-din Tabrizi once told the Qazi of Bada'un, "is to become a *mutawalli* or a teacher somewhere. If they aspire for something higher, it is to be *qazi* of some town. Their highest ambition is the office of *Sadr-i-Jahan*. Beyond that they dare not aspire for anything."[49] Ordinarily a *danishmand* alone could be appointed to the following posts:

1. *Sadr-i-Jahan* (or *Sadr-us-Sudur*) and his department
2. *Shaikh-u'l-Islam*
3. *Qazi*

46. *Fawa'id-u'l-Fu'ad*, p. 192.
47. Ibid, p. 192.
48. Ibid. p. 214. See also pp. 75–76 where a blind man refuses to listen to the sermon of a sinful person. Cf. also Shaikh Nizam-u'd-din Auliya's remark:

سخن کسے که معامله نیک ندارد' ذوق ندهد

49. *Khair-u'l-Majalis*, p. 212; *Fawa'id-u'l-Fu'ad*, p. 237.

4. *Mufti*
5. *Muhtasib*
6. *Imam*
7. *Khatib*
8. Teacher in schools maintained by the state

The *Qadi-i-Mamalik* was the highest judicial authority after the Sultan and was responsible for the working of the judicial institutions. It was usually on his recommendation that the Sultan appointed *qadi*s to different provinces and localities.[50] Usually the offices of the *Sadr-i-Jahan* and the *Qadi-i-Mamalik* were given to the same person.[51] Sometimes even the offices of *qada*, *khitabat*, *imamat*, and *hisbah* were assigned to one and the same person.[52]

Though the offices entrusted to the *'ulama* were not hereditary, some tradition seems to have developed due to which certain families came to be known as families of *qadi*s, *mufti*s, and *khatib*s. At least on one occasion during this period, some offices were given to the sons of the deceased persons. Minhaj informs us: 'In the 14th regnal year (of Nasir-u'd-din Mahmud), the *Shaikh-u'l-Islam*, the *Qadi*, the *Qarabak*, *Amir-i-Hajib*, and the *Imam* died and all the offices were conferred upon their sons.'[53]

(a) *The Shaikh-u'l-Islam*

The Shaikh-u'1-lslam[54] was in charge of the ecclesiastical affairs of the Empire. All those saints and *faqir*s who enjoyed state patronage were looked after by him. It appears from contemporary records that the *Shaikh-u'l-Islam* was both an office and an honorific title.[55] Some eminent saints were given this title though they had no specific duties or functions to perform.[56] Sometimes the title was loosely used for distinguished saints

50. *Tabaqat-i-Nasiri*, p. 175.

51. Minhaj held these two offices on three occasions. He was, however, known as *Sadar-i-Jahan*. (*Tabaqat-i-Nasiri*, p. 219). See also *Tarikh-i-Firoz Shahi*, p. 126.

52. *Tabaqat-i-Nasiri*, p. 175.

53. *Raverty*, p. 713.

54. For details about the nature of the office and its functions, see J.H. Kramer's article in the *Encyclopaedia of Islam*, Vol. IV, pp. 275–79. See also Qureshi, *Administration of the Sultanate of Delhi*, pp. 179–80.

55. For the condemnation of those who aspire to this office and pray for it, see *Fawa'id-u'l-Fu'ad*, p. 24.

56. For example, Shaikh Baha-u'd-din Zakariyya was given the title of *Shaikh-u'l-Islam* by Iltutmish (*Siyar-u'l-'Arifin*, p. 169). This title became so popular that even contemporary mystics addressed him as *Shaikh-u'l-Islam*. One day

even though it was not conferred by the Sultan.[57] Amongst those who exercised the functions of this office and formed part of the state machinery, the following names have reached us:

1. Sayyid Nur-u'd-din Mubarak Ghaznavi
2. Shaikh Jamal-u'd-din Bistami
3. Maulana Najm-u'd-din Sughra
4. Sayyid Qutb-u'd-din
5. Shaikh Rafi'-u'd-din

Sayyid Nur-u'd-din Mubarak Ghaznavi was an eminent Khalifah of Shaikh Shihab-u'd-din Suhrawardi and was held in high esteem by the people of Delhi who respectfully addressed him as *Mir-i-Delhi*.[58] Iltutmish appointed him as his *Shaikh-u'l-Islam*. In that capacity he frequently visited the court and delivered sermons in the royal presence. Barani has preserved the substance of two of his very important sermons which reveal him as a bold but narrow-minded theologian, who exhorted the Sultan to institute an Inquisition in India. Addressing the Sultan, he said:

> Whatever the kings do and deem essentials of kingship—the way in which they eat, drink wine, and dress themselves, the manner in which they sit, get up, and go out riding, the way in which they sit on their throne and compel the people to sit and perform the prostration (*sijdah*) before them, and follow with their heart and soul the customs of the *Kisras*, who were rebels against God, and the superior attitude which they take in all their dealings with the people of God—all this is opposed to [the teachings of] the Prophet; and amounts to claiming partnership in the Attributes of God. This would be a cause of their damnation in the next world.
>
> Owing to the commission of these acts, which are against the will of God and the traditions of Mustafa, the salvation of the king is not possible except by the implementation of the following four policies for the protection of the Faith:
>
> First, the kings should protect the religion of Islam with correct faith and with the intention of strengthening it. They should utilize the power,

---

Shaikh Farid Ganj-i-Shakar thought of writing a letter to Shaikh Baha-u'd-din Zakariyya. For a while he could not decide the form of address. He raised his head and looked at the sky and decided to address him as *Shaikh-u'l-Islam*. *Siyar-u'l-Auliya*, p. 82.

57. The title is used in its non-technical and general sense by Zia-u'd-din Barani for Shaikh Nizam-u'd-din Auliya (*Tarikh-i-Firoz Shahi*, p. 343) and by Amir Hasan Sijzi for Shaikh Farid (*Fawa'id-u'l-Fu'ad*, p. 5, etc.).

58. *Akhbar-u'l-Akbyar*, p. 28.

dignity, and prestige of their kingship which are opposed to the real attitude of a creature's submission to God, in establishing the supremacy of *Kalama-i-Haqq*,[59] in elevating the customs of Islam, in promulgating the commands of the *Shari'at*, and in enforcing what is ordained and in prohibiting what is forbidden. Kings will not be able to discharge their duty of protecting the Faith unless they overthrow and uproot *Kufr* and *Kafiri* (infidelity), *shirk* (setting up partners to God), and the worship of idols, all for the sake of God and inspired by a sense of honour for protecting the *din* of the Prophet of God. But if the total extirpation of idolatry is not possible owing to the firm roots of *kufr* and the large number of *kafirs* and *mushriks*, the kings should at least strive to disgrace, dishonour, and defame the *mushrik* and idol-worshipping Hindus, who are the worst enemies of God and His Prophet. The sign of the kings being protectors of religion is this: when they see a Hindu, their faces turn red [due to anger] and they wish to swallow him alive; they also desire to crush root and branch the Brahmans, who are the leaders of *Kufr* and due to whom *kufr* and *shirk* spread and the commandments of *kufr* are enforced. To maintain the honour of Islam and the prestige of the true Faith, they do not tolerate to see a single *kafir* or *mushrik* to live with self-respect or to attain to honour and live with an attitude of indifference [towards the Mussalmans] among the Mussalmans, or to pass his time in luxuries, enjoyments, and pleasures, to become the ruler of a people (*qaum*), group (*garoh*), territory (*wilayat*), or province (*iqta'*). Owing to the fear and terror of the kings of Islam, not a single enemy of God and the Prophet should be able to drink water that is sweet or stretch his legs on his bed, and go to sleep in peace.

The second policy necessary for the salvation of Muslim kings is this. The open display of sins and shameless deeds and the publication of forbidden things should be suppressed among the Muslim people, and in the cities, habitations, and towns of Islam, through the terror and power of kingship. Sinful and shameless deeds should be made more bitter than poison in the throats of the sinners by inflicting excessive punishments on them. Persons who, in spite of their claim to be Mussalmans, indulge cleverly and shrewdly in shameful works, and practise them all their lives, should be brought to such a tight corner and reduced to such distress that the world appears to them narrower than the circle of a finger ring and they are compelled to leave their sinful activities and find other means of livelihood. If prostitutes, who work for hire (*mustajira*), are not prepared to give up their sinful ways, they should practise their profession secretly and not openly and proudly. But if prostitutes practise their profession in their own disgraceful closets, and do not come out into the public, the practise of their profession should not be prohibited; for if the prostitutes are not there, many wicked people overpowered by their sex-desire will jeopardize the privacy and sanctity of family life.

59. Literally the True Word; here it means the Muslim faith.

The third principle for the protection of the Faith in which lies the salvation of kings is this. The duty of enforcing the rules of the *Shari'at* of Muhammad should be assigned to pious, God-fearing, and religious men; dishonest and godless people, who have no regard for the rights of others, as well as cheats, swindlers, worldly people, and self-seekers—should not be allowed to sit on the *masnad* of the *Shari'at* for enforcing the laws of the *Shari'at*, of giving leadership in matters appertaining to the *tariqat* (higher matters of religious discipline), or performing the duty of issuing *fatawa* in legal matters or the teaching of the religious sciences. Philosophers and believers in rationalistic philosophy should not be allowed to live in his territories, and under no circumstances should the teaching of philosophical sciences be permitted. The kings should strive to insult and disgrace heretics and believers in bad dogmas and the opponents of the Sunni creed, and none of them should be given any office in the government.

The fourth principle which is necessary for the protection of the true creed and the salvation of the kings and the enhancement in their status is the dispensation of justice. The kings will not have performed their duty in this respect unless they strive to their utmost in the enforcement of justice and are just in every matter, and, owing to the terror of the authority of the kings, oppression and cruelty are eliminated from their territories and all oppressors are overthrown....

Whenever the kings implement these four policies with firm determination and sincere faith and establish truth at the centre through the terror and prestige of their royal authority, then even if their souls are polluted by sinful desire and in the essentials of kingship they have ignored the Sunnah, their status will be among the religious people and owing to their protection of the Faith, their place on the Day of Resurrection will be among the prophets and saints. On the other hand, if a king performs a thousand *rak'ats* of prayer every day, fasts all his life, does not go near things forbidden by the *Shari'at* and spends the whole of his treasure in charity, but neither protects the Faith by using his royal power and authority for overthrowing and extirpating the enemies of God and the Prophet, nor enforces things ordained by the *Shari'at*, nor prohibits things forbidden in his realms, nor tries to enforce justice to the greatest extent, his place will be nowhere except in Hell.[60]

It is difficult to decide whether the whole of this speech was made by Sayyid Nur-u'd-din Mubarak or Barani has expressed his own sentiments

---

60. *Tarikh-i-Firoz Shahi*, pp. 41–44. No contemporary, or even later, writer has referred to this speech. Whatever its authenticity, such views (particularly with references to the non-Muslims) did not find acceptance with the Muslim society in general and did not condition the political thought or actions of the Sultans.

by putting them in the mouth of the great Suhrawardi saint. The diatribe against the teaching and learning of philosophy seems to be an interpolation of Barani, because it was a problem highlighted in the Tughluq period and did not disturb the minds of the conservative theologians during the Ilbarite regime. In his *Fatawa-i-Jahandari*, Barani has expounded all these principles as his own.[61] Did he borrow his political thought from Sayyid Nur-u'd-din or has he attributed his own views to him? A definite answer cannot be given due to want of requisite data regarding the life and activities of Sayyid Nur-u'd-din Mubarak. One incident about the saint, as recorded by Amir Hasan Sijzi on the authority of Shaikh Nizam-u'd-din Auliya, is, however, significant and shows that, notwithstanding his boldness and independence of spirit, he could not raise himself above the petty squabbles of the court. Once he quarrelled with Shaikh Nizam-u'd-din Abul Muwayyid about the order of precedence in the court of Iltutmish.[62] It may, however, be added that his religious reputation was so high that after his death Shaikh Nizam-u'd-din Abul Muwayyid went to his grave and apologized for his earlier insolence in quarrelling with him.[63]

Shaikh Jamal-u'd-din Bistami, to whom Iltutmish assigned the office of the *Shaikh-u'l-Islam* when Shaikh Qutb-u'd-din Bakhtiyar Kaki declined to accept it, was a man of genuine piety and had a very high reputation in the religious circles of Delhi. Shaikh Nizam-u'd-din Auliya once remarked about him: "He knew well the customs and etiquette of the mystics."[64] Men like him raised the dignity of the office of the *Shaikh-u'l-Islam* and rendered real service to the people. But all the *Shaikh-u'l-Islam*s of this period were not of the same calibre. It appears that some ambitious and mischievous persons had also succeeded in securing appointment to this post.

Najm-u'd-din Sughra, to whom Iltutmish entrusted the office of the *Shaikh-u'l-Islam*, was a vainglorious and unscrupulous person. If he ever found any saint or scholar coming closer to the Sultan or attracting the public eye, he resorted to mean and ignoble methods for pulling him down. He had the effrontery to cook up an obnoxious charge of adultery against Shaikh Jalal-u'd-din Tabrizi, simply with a view to disgracing him in the eyes of the Sultan. His arrogant and bureaucratic attitude brought forth condemnation from the great Chishti saint, Shaikh Mu'in-u'd-din of

---

61. *Fatawa-i-Jahandari*, ff. 9a, 9b, 121a, etc.
62. *Fawa'id-u'l-Fu'ad*, p. 193; *Siyar-u'l-'Arifin*, p. 28.
63. *Fawa'id-u'l-Fu'ad*, p. 193.
64. Ibid, p. 9.

Ajmer.[65] He was also jealous of Shaikh Qutb-u'd-din Bakhtiyar Kaki and was anxious to drive him out of the capital.[66]

Shaikh Nizam-u'd-din Auliya simply hints at Sughra's conflicts with Shaikh Tabrizi. He refrains from giving details of that scandalous episode.[67] Jamali has, however, given full details of the incident. When Shaikh Jalal-u'd-din Tabrizi reached the suburbs of Delhi, Iltutmish went out to receive him. As soon as the Shaikh came in view, he got down from his horse and ran towards him. He brought the Shaikh to his palace with great respect and asked Najm-u'd-din Sughra to make arrangements for his stay near the palace so that he might see him off and on. This made Najm-u'd-din Sughra jealous of Shaikh Tabrizi. He made arrangements for his stay in a house which was thought to be frequented by evil spirits. When the Sultan objected to this arrangement, Sughra replied that if the guest was spiritually gifted, evil spirits would do no harm to him; if he was 'imperfect' and vain, the annoyance of the evil spirits was his well-deserved punishment. Much to the surprise and distress of Sughra, the Shaikh lived in the *Bait-u'l-Jinn* unmolested by anybody. Iltutmish's faith in him increased all the more. This was unbearable for Sughra and he entered into a dirty conspiracy with Gauhar, a nautch girl of Delhi. He promised to give her five hundred gold coins if, on being summoned to some public gathering, she charged Shaikh Jalal-u'd-din Tabrizi with having committed adultery with her. Sughra even advanced half the promised amount and deposited the other half with Ahmad Sharaf, a *baqqal* of Delhi. She was presented before Iltutmish who convened a *mahzar* to make legal investigations into the matter. Eminent saints and scholars assembled in the Friday mosque. Shaikh Baha-u'd-din Zakariyya's name was suggested by Sughra for presiding over the *mahzar*. There had been some ill-feeling between Shaikh Jalal-u'd-din Tabrizi and Shaikh Baha-u'd-din Zakariyya and so Sughra was under the impression that the Shaikh's presence would strengthen his position. But he was sadly mistaken in his calculations. When Shaikh Jalal-u'd-din Tabrizi entered the mosque, Shaikh Baha-u'd-din rushed to the door, took his shoes in his hands, and respectfully

---

65. Najm-u'd-din Sughra was an old acquaintance of Shaikh Mu'in-u'd-din. When the latter visited Delhi, he went to see Sughra at his residence. Sughra was then busy supervising the construction of a platform in his house. He did not receive the Shaikh with the cordiality he expected. When the Shaikh found him so indifferent and cold, he remarked: "It appears that the office of the *Shaikh-ul-Islam* has turned your head." For details, see *Siyar-u'l-Auliya*, p. 54.

66. Ibid, pp. 54–55.

67. *Fawa'id-u'l-Fu'ad*, pp. 143–44.

conducted him to the gathering. Gauhar was summoned. She was so overawed by the presence of the Sultan and the saints and scholars that she could not play her game well. She divulged the secret and told all that Sughra had promised to her. Ahmad Sharaf was also summoned. He confirmed Gauhar's statement. Sughra was dismissed from his post then and there.[68] Though Sughra's episode was a solitary incident of its kind, it considerably damaged the reputation of the religious dignitaries of the Empire.

Sayyid Qutb-u'd-din who was the *Shaikh-u'l-Islam* during the reign of Bahram Shah, though not of the same type, was definitely of an unreliable character. He betrayed the Sultan at a very critical moment[69] and did not give any evidence of that strength of character which could properly be expected from an officer of his religious dignity.

An incident recorded in the *Fawa'id-u'l-Fu'ad* shows that some of the dependents of the *Shaikh-u'l-Islam*s of this period were looked down upon for their avarice and undignified behaviour. Kabir, grandson of some *Shaikh-u'l-Islam* of this period, was a frequent visitor to the house of Malik Nizam-u'd-din, the Kotwal of Delhi. The Kotwal got tired of his company and warned him against visiting his house. Regardless of this admonition, Kabir continued to visit his house and behaved in an utterly disgraceful manner.[70]

(b) *The Qazis*

"It was considered so necessary to have a Qazi in every town of any dimensions," writes Dr I.H. Qureshi, "that the first administrative business always included his appointment."[71] The Qazis were mainly concerned with common law or civil litigation, while the *droit administratif* was exclusively under the control of the *Diwan-i-Mazalim* and *Diwan-i-Siyasat*—departments which were neither assigned to the *'ulama* nor run according to the laws of the *Shari'at*. Medieval treatises on Muslim law and administration assign extensive powers to the Qazis, but, during the early

68. *Siyar-u'l-'Arifin*, pp. 167–69.

69. *Tabaqat-i-Nasiri*, p. 196.

Nizam-u'd-din Ahmad (*Tabaqat-i-Akbari*, Vol. I, p. 70) and Ferishtah (Vol. I, p. 70) have wrongly added the words *Bakhtiyar Ushi* with the name of Shaikh-ul-Islam Sayyid Qutb-u'd-din, thus giving the impression that the famous saint of Delhi was involved in this affair. Some modern writers have also been misled by this statement of Ferishtah. Shaikh Qutb-u'd-din Bakhtiyar Kaki had died during the reign of Iltutmish.

70. *Fawa'id-u'l-Fu'ad*, p. 125.

71. *Administration of the Sultanate of Delhi*, p. 152.

Sultanate period in India, the main function of a Qazi was to settle civil disputes. In this respect, the attitude of a section of the Muslim society towards him is very neatly expressed in a remark quoted in *Sarur-us-Sudur*: "The Qazi is for the evil-doers; what has he got to do with good people."[72]

It was probably for this reason that when Shaikh Nizam-u'd-din Auliya requested Shaikh Najib-u'd-din Mutawakkil to pray for his appointment to the post of Qazi, he replied: 'Do not be Qazi; be something else.'[73]

The following names of some of the Qazis of the period are found in medieval records, political and non-political:

1. Qazi Sa'd-u'd-din Karori[74]
2. Qazi Shu'aib of Kahtwal[75]
3. Qazi 'Abdullah of Ajodhan[76]
4. Qazi Nasir-u'd-din Kasa Lais[77]
5. Qazi Jalal-u'd-din[78]
6. Qazi Kabir-u'd-din Qazi-i-Lashkar[79]
7. Qazi Sharaf-u'd-din of Multan[80]
8. Qazi Kamal-u'd-din Jafri[81]
9. Qazi Jamal Multani[82]
10. Qazi Qutb-u'd-din Kashani[83]
11. Qazi Nasir Kashani[84]
12. Qazi Shams-u'd-din of Bahraich[85]
13. Qazi Minhaj-us-Siraj[86]
14. Qazi Fakhr-u'd-din Naqila[87]
15. Qazi Sa'd[88]
16. Qazi 'Imad-u'd-din[89]

72. *Sarur-u's-Sudur* (MS), p. 29.
73. *Fawa'id-u'l-Fu'ad*, p. 28.
74. *Tabaqat-i-Nasiri*, p. 177.
75. *Siyar-u'l-Auliya*, p. 59.
76. Ibid, p. 84.
77–79. *Tabaqat-i-Nasirt*, pp. 177, 195.
80. *Siyar-u'l-Arifin*, p. 113.
81. *Fawa'id-u'l-Fu'ad*, pp. 225, 236; *Khair-u'l-Majalis*, p. 211.
82. *Fawa'id-u'l-Fu'ad*, pp. 208–09.
83. Ibid, p. 235.
84. Ibid, p. 194.
85–86. *Tabaqat-i-Nasiri*, pp. 217–23.
87. *Fawa'id-u'l-Fu'ad*, p. 242; *Sarur-u's-Sudur* (MS).
88–89. *Faw'id-u's-Salatin*, pp. 117–19.

17. Qazi Rafi'-u'd-din Gazruni[90]
18. Qazi Shams-u'd-din Maraji[91]
19. Qazi Rukn-u'd-din of Samana[92]
20. Qazi Sadid-u'd-din[93]
21. Qazi Zahir-u'd-din[94]
22. Qazi Jalal-u'd-din Kashani[95]
23. Qazi 'Imad-u'd-din Muhammad Shaqurqani[96]
24. Qazi Muhammad Shami[97]
25. Qazi Shams-u'd-din Mehr[98]

Some of them were posted at the capital, others belonged to provincial cities and *qasbah*s. It is unfortunate that no detailed accounts of their activities are available; but the brief references and anecdotes about a few of them found in contemporary literature help us in understanding their character and the nature of their activities. It must be admitted that some of the Qazis of the centre were essentially politicians in their outlook and they could not raise themselves above that mad race for political power which had become a feature of this age. Balban's observations about his Qazis, as quoted in a mystic work, are very significant and reveal the character of some of the Qazis of the capital. "I have three Qazis," Balban is reported to have remarked, "one of them does not fear me but fears God; the other one does not fear God but fears me; the third one neither fears me nor God... Fakhr Naqila[99] fears me but does not fear God; the *Qazi-i-Lashkar* fears God but does not fear me. Minhaj neither fears me nor God."[100] It may be added that the *Qazi-i-Lashka*r who feared God, but not the Sultan, was respected most by Balban and his recommendations were always honoured by him.[101] Of another Qazi of his period, Jalal-u'd-din Kashani, Barani makes the following remarks: "He was a very venerable Qazi but he was a mischief monger."[102]

90–95. *Tarikh-i-Firoz Shahi*, p. 111.
96. *Tabaqat-i-Nasiri*, p. 198.
97. Ibid, p. 193.
98. Ibid, p. 195.
99. His name has been mentioned by Barani also (*Tarikh-i-Firoz Shahi*, p. 24). Shaikh Nizam-u'd-din Auliya once told his audience that Qazi Fakhr-u'd-din Naqila obtained the office due to the blessings of a butcher of Delhi who possessed saintly powers. *Fawa'-id-u'l-Fu'ad*, p. 242.
100. *Sarur-u's-Sudur* (MS). pp. 47–48.
101. *Tarikh-i-Firoz Shahi*, p. 47, see also *Fawa'id-ul-Fu'ad*, p. 232.
102. *Tarikh-i-Firoz Shahi*, p. 210.

Qazi Shu'aib: A native of Kabul, Qazi Shu'aib, left his homeland under the stress of Ghuzz invasions and settled at Qasur. The Qazi of Qasur received him cordially and informed the Sultan about the circumstances under which the members of this distinguished family had reached Qasur. Though Qazi Shu'aib was reluctant to accept any office, the Sultan appointed him Qazi of Kahtwal,[103] a town in the district of Multan between Maharan and Ajodhan. When Qazi Shu'aib died, his son Shaikh Jamal-u'd-din Sulaiman was appointed Qazi of Kahtwal.[104] The family, it appears, became known as 'the Qazi family'. Shaikh Farid Ganj-i-Shakar, son of Jamal-u'd-din Sulaiman, was known in his boyhood as '*qazi bachchah diwana*',[105] on account of his absorption in mystic contemplation.

Qazi 'Abdullah: He was the Qazi of Ajodhan and had, in that capacity, appointed a *khatib* for the Friday Mosque of Ajodhan. One day this *khatib* made a mistake while leading the Friday prayers. One of the disciples of Shaikh Farid pointed out the mistake and all the people present there re-offered their prayers. Qazi 'Abdullah took it as a personal insult and abused the Shaikh and his disciples on that account. The Shaikh quietly left the mosque and returned to his house with his followers.[106]

Qazi Sharaf-u'd-din: He was the Qazi of Multan during the reign of Qubachah. He joined with Shaikh Baha-u'd-din Zakariyya in writing a letter to Iltutmish, probably inviting him to attack Multan. Qubachah intercepted this letter and executed the Qazi.[107]

Qazi Kamal-u'd-din Jafri: He was the Qazi of Bada'un and was known for his piety and scholarship. He had compiled a book, *Munfiq*, probably on *Fiqh*. Shaikh Nizam-u'd-din Auliya once remarked: "Qazi Kamal-u'd-din Jafri, who was in charge of Bada'un, had many functions to perform besides his duties as Qazi, but he used to recite the Quran very extensively and very often."[108] Qazi Kamal lived with great dignity and several servants acted as *durban* at his gate.[109] In spite of his religious devotion, Qazi Kamal-u'd-din could not escape the criticism of his mystic friend, Shaikh Jalal-u'd-din Tabrizi. Once the Shaikh visited his house. He was

---

103. *Siyar-u'l-Auliya*, p. 59.
104. Ibid, p. 32.
105. *Khair-u'l-Majalis*, pp. 219–20.
106. *Siyar-u'l-Auliya*, p. 84.
107. *Fawa'id-u'l-Fu'ad*, pp. 119–20. The name of the Qazi is not mentioned by Amir Hasan but Jamali gives his name in *Siyar-u'l-'Arifin*, p. 113.
108. *Fawa'id-u'l-Fu'ad*, p. 225.
109. *Fawa'id-u'l-Fu'ad*, p. 236.

told that the Qazi was busy in his prayers. Shaikh Tabrizi smiled and asked: "Does the Qazi know how to offer prayers?"[110]

Qazi Kamal-u'd-din: In the conversations of Shaikh Hamid-u'd-din Sufi we find a reference to Qazi Kamal-u'd-din who delivered sermons on every Monday and went out for amusement (*tamashas*) the next day. Very often he used to recite the couplet:

اے مسلماناں مسمانی کنید

خانہ بفروشید و مهمانی کنید

(O Mussalmans! Behave like Mussalmans. Sell your house and entertain your guests.)

Once the price of grain went up due to scarcity and the Qazi was put to great hardship. He mounted the platform and, looking up at the sky, said: 'O God! Thou knowest well who possesses corn and who does not.' Many merchants and traders who had regrated corn and were selling it at black market rates were also present there. On returning home every one of them sent something to the Qazi so that there appeared heaps of corn in his house.[111]

It is said that Qazi Minhaj-us-Siraj was responsible for legalizing the institution of *Sama'* (mystic music) during his qaziship of Delhi.[112] Two other Qazis of the period—Qazi 'Imad and Qazi Sa'd—objected to this practice and approached Iltutmish to convene a *mahzar* to consider its legality.[113] It appears that in certain cases a Qazi could not proceed to take action on his own initiative without consulting the *'ulama* and obtaining their *fatwa*. A Qazi of Ajodhan, who did not approve of Shaikh Farid's audition parties, approached the scholars of Multan for a legal verdict against the Shaikh. "An educated man lives in a mosque, hears songs, and dances. What is your opinion about him?" The *'ulama* refrained from expressing any opinion on the basis of that meagre data. "Let us know first of all who the person is about whom you want this *fatwa*," they asked the Qazi. When they heard the name of Shaikh Farid, they replied: "You have referred to a saint against whom no *mujtahid* dare raise his finger." The Qazi then thought of putting an end to the life of the Shaikh by hiring an assassin.[114]

---

110. Ibid, pp. 236–37. See also *Khair-u'l-Majalis*, p. 211.
111. *Sarur-u's-Sudur* (MS), p. 22.
112. *Fawa'id-u'l-Fu'ad*, p. 239; *Akhbar-u'l-Akhyar*, p. 79.
113. *Futuh-u's-Salatin*, pp. 117–18.
114. *Fawa'id-u'l-Fu'ad*, p. 153; *Siyar-u'l-'Arifin*, pp. 34–35.

(c) The Khatibs and Imams

Normally, only well-read scholars were appointed as *khatibs* and *imams*[115] because Muslim public opinion did not approve of the appointment of any less qualified person to these posts. When Maulana Malik Yar, who had received no formal education, was assigned the *imamat* of the Bada'un mosque, some people objected to his appointment. Maulana 'Ala-u'd-din Usuli, the leading scholar of Bada'un, criticized the critics and, referring to his exceptional spiritual qualifications, remarked: "Even if the *imamat* of the Friday Mosque of Baghdad was entrusted to Maulana Malik Yar, it would be nothing compared to his abilities."[116]

The *khatibs* and *imams* generally led a very prosperous life. Both state munificence and public respect relieved them of all financial worries. Maulana Jamal-u'd-din, an elder disciple and *khalifah* of Shaikh Farid Ganj-i-Shakar, was employed as *khatib* when he joined his discipleship. The Shaikh asked him to give up *shughi* (government service) which was a necessary condition of his higher spiritual discipline. Maulana Jamal-u'd-din resigned his post and with it all his prosperity departed. "From the time the Khwaja has become a disciple of yours," a maidservant of Jamal-u'd-din Hansvi informed Baba Farid, "he has given up his villages, property, and the office of *khatib*. He is afflicted with starvation and sufferings." "God be praised," replied Shaikh Farid, "Jamal is happy."[117]

Guided both by religious and political considerations, the rulers appointed some scholars with rare gifts of speech as *muzakkirs* and kept them regularly in their service. We hear about *tazkir* meetings being held in the court during the months of Ramazan and Muharram. Minhaj who held the offices of *qaza*, *khitabat*, *imamat*, *ihtisab*, and all matters relating to the *Shari'at*,[118] writes about himself: "...and the writer of these, in the month of Sha'ban of the same year (629 AH) set out from Delhi and turned his face towards the threshold of sovereignty, and attained that felicity. The author, at certain stated periods, was commanded to give discourses at the private pavilion. Three times in each week discourses were fixed; and, when the month of Ramazan came round, a discourse used to be delivered

---

115. 'Awfi, who was appointed as royal *Imam* and *Khatib* by Qubachah in 617/1220, was an erudite scholar. He delivered a *khutbah* in Arabic on the occasion of *'Eid-u'l-Fitr*. *Lubab-u'l-Albab*, Vol. I, 115. Shaikh Jamal Hansvi, who had acted as *Khatib* of Hansi for some time, was also well versed in Arabic. His *Mulhamat* bears evidence of his knowledge of the Arabic language.

116. *Fawa'id-u'l-Fu'ad*, p. 166.

117. *Siyar-u'l-Auliya*, pp. 180–81.

118. *Tabaqat-i-Nasiri*, p. 175.

daily. During the whole ten days of Zi'l-Hijjah, and ten days of Muharram, discourses were delivered daily; but, during the other months, those same three stated periods were observed weekly, so that ninety-five times congregations were convened at the entrance of the sublime pavilion."[119]

Whatever might have been Balban's opinion about Minhaj as a Qazi, it cannot be gainsaid that he was one of the most gifted preachers of his age. His eloquence often moved the audience to tears. Shaikh Nizam-u'd-din Auliya, who used to attend his *tazkir* meetings every Monday, was, on one occasion, so deeply overpowered by emotions on hearing him recite verses that for a while he lost all consciousness of his whereabouts.[120] Explaining his principles of *tazkir*, Minhaj once told a pupil: "In spite of all my erudition and the esteem which I enjoy as a preacher, I do not place my foot on the pulpit without performing the following three things—first, praise of the Prophet; secondly, recitation of *Bismillah*, thirdly, recitation of the formulae *Allahu-Akbar*."[121]

We find the Sultans often asking their *khatib*s to deliver sermons before the rebels in order to pacify them. In moments of crisis, the *'ulama* were asked to inspire and encourage the people by their sermons. On the eve of a Mongol invasion, Bahram Shah convened a *tazkir* meeting in his *Qasr-i-Sufaid* and asked Qazi Minhaj to deliver discourses in his support.[122]

A very well-known *muzakkir* of this period was Maulana Husam Darwesh. Barani has praised his pungency of wit and power of speech.[123] Shaikh Hamid-u'd-din Sufi is reported to have remarked that no one in Delhi could deliver better sermons than Husam. He is referred to as *Malik-uz-Zakirin* in the *Surur-us-Sudur*.[124] During the reign of Mu'izz-u'd-din

---

119. *Raverty*, p. 619

120. *Fawa'id-u'l-Fu'ad*, p. 191; *Akhbar-u'l-Akhyar*, pp. 79–80.
Minhaj had recited the following quatrain:

لب بر لب دلبران مهوش کردن   و آهنگ سر زلف مشوش کردن

امروزخوش است لیک فردا خوش نیست   خود را چو خسی طعمۀ آتش کردن

121. *Sarur-u's-Sudur* (MS), p. 60. For Shaikh Nizam-u'd-din Auliya's compliment to Minhaj as a preacher, see *Fawa'id-u'l-Fu'ad*, p. 191.

122. *Tabaqat-i-Nasiri*, p. 195.
Referring to the extraordinary persuasive powers of Minhaj, Amir Khusrau remarks:

منهاج مذکری بود که از شعله زبان آتش در جمع زدی

I'jaz-i-Khusravi, Vol. I, p. 186.

123. *Tarikh-i-Firoz Shahi*, p. 131.

124. *Sarur-u's-Sudur* (MS), p. 90.

Kaiqubad, he felt attracted towards court life and became a *nadim* of the Sultan. Minionism demoralized him so completely that he not only became proud and self-conceited,[125] but even developed an inordinate lust for wealth. In order to win royal favour, he began to behave most oddly. One day a man presented a golden monkey to the Sultan who was then taking *tutmaj*[126] along with his courtiers and *nadim*s. He turned to them and said: "Whoever takes this *tutmaj* without touching it with his hands, will get this monkey." The moment Husam heard this, he lowered his chin into the dish. Kaiqubad was so annoyed and astonished at his avaricious conduct that he beckoned to one of his maid-servants, Huri by name, to strike a blow at his neck. Husam's face was all smeared with *tutmaj*.[127]

Another eminent contemporary of Husam Darwesh was Qazi Nizam-u'd-din. Comparing his own sermons with those of Husam he once said: "Husam-u'd-din talks about flowery (superficial) matters; I talk about weighty affairs."[128] Qazi Nizam-u'd-din was, however, very sensitive. He got irritated at Qazi Minhaj who had once discourteously left the audience while he was delivering a sermon.[129]

(d) *Teachers in Government Institutions*

Some outstanding scholars were appointed as teachers in institutions established by the Sultans. We hear of the establishment of *madrasah*s in newly-conquered territories during the early period of conquests.[130] The Mu'izzi Madrasah and the Nasiriyah Madrasah were the two most reputed centres of higher learning during the thirteenth century and eminent scholars were put in charge of these institutions. These teachers received handsome emoluments from the state and passed their days in affluent circumstances.

It appears that in certain cases the condition of having received education in the formal and traditional way was waived in view of the exceptional capabilities of a person. Maulana Zain-u'd-din had received no formal instruction but he was appointed as a teacher in the Mu'izzi Madrasah because of his extensive knowledge.[131]

Teachers were usually held in great respect. The way in which Taj-u'd-din Yildiz treated a tutor, who had killed his son while using his pedagogic rod, shows the typical attitude of the Middle Ages.[132]

125. Ibid, p. 48.
126. *Tutmaj* is a kind of dish.
127. Ibid, p. 90.
128. Ibid.
129. Ibid, p 92.
130. *Tabaqat-i-Nasiri*, p. 151.
131. *Fawa'id-u'l-Fu'ad*, p. 23.
132. *Tabaqat-i-Nasiri*, p. 133.

'ULAMA AS A POLITICAL CLIQUE

During the period under review, the 'ulama emerged as a power in politics—a position which did not materially change till the advent of Sultan 'Ala-u'd-din Khalji. This influence was, however, political in nature. They did not influence the course of political developments as interpreters of Muslim law but as politicians who had aligned themselves with one or the other of the political groups and dabbled in politics regardless of their dignity and position as religious leaders. During the long and protracted struggle between the crown and the nobility, their influence over the Muslim people was sought to be exploited by both the parties.

Sadr-u'd-din Hasan Nizami speaks again and again of the respect shown to the 'ulama by Qutb-u'd-din Aibak, but there is not a single reference to their interference in political matters. By the time Iltutmish came to the throne, they had become fully conscious of their position in Indo-Muslim society but their attitude was essentially religious. They were bold and courageous in their outlook and had sufficient independence of spirit. When Iltutmish ascended the throne a party of the 'ulama, led by Qazi Wajih-u'd-din Kashani, approached him with the intention of enquiring from him whether he had been properly manumitted. Iltutmish understood the purpose of their visit and, before they could say anything, took out the letter of manumission and placed it before them.[133] Iltutmish very tactfully handled the 'ulama and created such conditions that instead of turning into critics of his policy, they became his active supporters and helped him even in the extension of his political power.

But viewed as a whole, Iltutmish's policy towards the 'ulama did not exercise any healthy influence on their character. His respect for them excited their worldly ambition and, in course of time, they lost their independence of character and fell in line with the moods of the rulers. So much so that when Iltutmish nominated Razia as his successor, there was not a single theologian in the Delhi Empire who could protest against this nomination on grounds of the Shari'at. Shaikh 'Abdul Haq Muhaddis justly expressed his surprise at the tacit approval of Razia's accession by the theologians of the period.[134]

The influence of the 'ulama on the politics of the Delhi Sultanate became very pronounced from the time of Bahram Shah. Some of the Qazis established matrimonial relations with the ruling house.[135] Malik Badr-u'd-din Sanqar's

133. 'Aja'ib-u'l-Asfar, Vol. II, p. 52.

134. Tarikh-i-Haqqi (MS).

135. For example, Qazi Nasir-u'd-din who married a sister of Mu'izz-u'd-din Bahram. Tabaqat-i-Nasiri, p. 192.

coup was planned with the help of the *'ulama* and the *Qazi-i-Mamalik* and secret meetings were held at the residence of the Sadr-u'l-Mulk Sayyid Taj-u'd-din 'Ali Musavi.[136] The execution of the Qazi of Mahrpurar[137] was probably due to his conspiratorial activities. To counteract the designs of those rebellious groups which had succeeded in enlisting the support of the theologians, Bahram also sought to exploit the influence of the *'ulama*. He asked Minhaj-us-Siraj to deliver sermons before the people,[138] and sent the *Shaikh-u'l-Islam*, Sayyid Qutb-u'd-din, to pacify the contumacious *amirs*.[139] Minhaj once received some injuries in pleading the cause of the Sultan, but the *Shaikh-u'l-Islam* preferred to change sides rather than risk his life. Minhaj-us-Siraj, who himself belonged to this class of theologian-politicians, has refrained from giving any details about the activities of the *'ulama*, probably because the record was not very complimentary, but a few anecdotes that are found in contemporary works—both political and non-political— show that the *'ulama* had lost their religious dignity and moral prestige and were wallowing in the dirty waters of politics. No greater demoralization of the theologians associated with the court could be imagined than the way in which they condoned Kaiqubad's failure to offer his prayers and keep fasts during the month of Ramazan.[140]

136. Ibid, p. 193.
137. Ibid, p. 195.
138. Ibid.
139. Ibid, p. 196.
140. *Tarikh-i-Firoz Shahi*, p. 54.

Chapter VI

MUSLIM MYSTIC LIFE AND ORGANIZATION

Muslim mysticism reached India when it had entered the last and the most important phase of its history—the organization of *silsilah*s. Abul Fazl has referred to the work of the following fourteen orders in India:[1]

1. *Habibia*, founded by Shaikh Habib 'Ajami,[2]
2. *Taifuria*, founded by Shaikh Bayazid Taifur Bistami,[3]
3. *Karkhia*, founded by Khwaja Ma'ruf Karkhi,[4]
4. *Saqatia*, founded by Shaikh Abul Hasan Sari Saqati,[5]
5. *Junaidia*, founded by Shaikh Junaid Baghdadi,[6]
6. *Gazrunia*, founded by Shaikh Abu Ishaq b. Shahryar,[7]
7. *Tusia*, founded by Shaikh 'Ala-u'd-din Tusi,[8]
8. *Firdausia*, founded by Shaikh Najib-u'd-din Kubra,[9]
9. *Suhrawardia*, founded by Shaikh Najib-u'd-din 'Abdul Qahir Suhrawardi,[10]
10. *Zaidia*, founded by Shaikh 'Abdul Wahib b. Zaid,[11]
11. *'Iyazia*, founded by Shaikh Fuzail b. 'Ayaz,[12]
12. *Adhamia*, founded by Shaikh Ibrahim Adham,[13]
13. *Hubairia*, founded by Khwaja Hubairat al-Basri,[14] and
14. *Chishtia*, founded by Khwaja Abu Ishaq.[15]

1. *A'in-i-Akbari*, II, p. 203.

2. For a brief biographical notice, see *Tazkirat-u'l-Auliya*, pp. 60–65; *Kashf-u'l-Mahjub*, p. 88.

3. See *Tazkirat-u'l-Auliya*, pp. 125–54; *Nafahat-u'l-Uns*, pp. 59–60.

4. See *Tazkirat-u'l-Auliya*, pp. 229–32; *Nafahat-u'l-Uns*, pp. 39–40.

5. See *Tazkirat-u'l-Auliya*, pp. 232–39; *Nafahat-u'l-Uns*, pp. 55–57.

6. *Kashf-u'l-Mahjub*, p. 189; *Tazkirat-u'l-Auliya*, pp. 284–303; *Nafahat-u'l-Uns*, pp. 81–85.

7. *A'in-i-Akbari*, II, p. 204.

8. Ibid.

9. *Nafahat-u'l-Uns*, pp. 375–79; *Tarikh-i-Guzidah*, p. 789.

10. See *infra.*

11. *Siyar-u'l-Auliya*, pp. 32–33.

12. *Tazkirat-u'l-Auliya*, pp. 80–88; *Nafahat-u'l-Uns*, pp. 38–39.

13. *Kashf-u'l-Mahjub*, p. 103; *Nafahat-u'l-Uns*, pp. 42–44.

14. *Siyar-u'l-Auliya*, p. 39.

15. *Nafahat-u'l-Uns*, p. 296.

This list is so comprehensive that it includes even mystic groups and sub-branches of *silsilah*s in the category of well-organized orders. In fact, many of the *silsilah*s mentioned by Abul Fazl did not exercise any appreciable influence on the religious life and thought of the Indian people during the Sultanate period. Only two *silsilah*s—the Chishtia and the Suhrawardia—count for our period. They were introduced in India almost simultaneously with the founding of the Sultanate of Delhi. In the century that followed, they spread out in the country, built up their organizations, and established themselves in their respective zones. Within a short span of time the entire country, from Multan to Lakhnauti and from Panipat to Deogir, was studded with *khanqah*s, *jama'at khanah*s, and *zawiyah*s.[16] Early in the fourteenth century a traveller informed Shihab-u'd-din al-'Umari in Damascus: "In Delhi and its surroundings are *khanqah*s and hospices numbering two thousand."[17] These *khanqah*s, numerous and extensive as they were, soon wove themselves into the complex culture-pattern of India and helped remove that spirit of mistrust and isolation which honeycombed the relations between the various culture groups of India.

CONCEPT OF SPIRITUAL TERRITORIES

The concept of *wilayat*[18] having taken deep roots in contemporary mystic consciousness, the heads of these *silsilah*s dispatched their *khalifah*s to

16. Though broadly used in the sense of hospices, these terms differ in their connotation. The *khanqah* was a spacious building which provided separate accommodation for every visitor and inmate. The *jama'at khanah* was a large room where all disciples slept, prayed, and studied on the floor. The Chishti saints built *jama'at khanah*s; the Suhrawardis constructed *khanqah*s. Common people, unable to appreciate the distinction, used the word *khanqah* even for the Chishti *jama'at khanah*s, and now the term is used for all centres of spiritual activity without distinction. The *zawiyah*s were smaller places where mystics lived and prayed but, unlike the inmates of *khanqah*s and *jama'at khanah*s, they did not aim at establishing any vital contact with the world outside. In the seventeenth and the eighteenth centuries another type of *khanqah*s, the *daerah*s, came into existence. The primary aim of these *daerah*s was to provide place for men of one affiliation to devote their time to religious meditation. They were smaller than the *zawiyah*s.

17. *Masalik-u'l-Absar fi Mumalik-u'l-Amsar*, English translation of the portion dealing with India, by O. Spies, p. 24.

18. See *supra*, p. 57. Shaikh Sharaf-u'd-din Yahya Maneri has discussed at some length the significance of the concept of *wilayat* and the position of the *wali* in one of his letters (*Maktubat-i-Shaikh Sharaf-u'd-din Yahya*, Newal Kishore 1315 AH, p. 24, et seq). See also *Maktubat-i-Ashrafi* (Letters of Sayyid

various provinces called their *wilayat*s; and they, in their turn, appointed subordinate *khalifah*s for *qasbah*s and cities. Thus a hierarchy of saints came to be established in northern India. The chief saint at the centre stood at the apex of the whole system and controlled a network of *khanqah*s spread over the country. People reverentially referred to him as *Sultan-u'l-'Arifin, Sultan-u'l-Mashaikh, Shah-i-din, Sultan-u'l-Hind,* etc.[19] and often used political terminology to indicate his position and sphere of spiritual activity.[20] The following incident, recorded in the earliest and the most reliable authority on the mystic ideology of medieval India, the *Fawa'id-u'l-Fu'ad,* gives some idea of the exactness with which the areas of spiritual supervision and control were determined:

> A musician, 'Abdullah by name, came to Ajodhan and stayed with Shaikh Farid. After a brief sojourn, he took leave of the Shaikh and requested him to pray for his safe journey to Multan. The Shaikh replied:

ازین جا تا بدان موضع که چندیں کروه باشد'

آنجا حوضی است' تا آنجا حد من است'

سلامت خواهی رسید' از آنجا تا ملتان

در عهدهٔ شیخ بهاء الدین است

> (From this place to that *mauza*', which is at a distance of so many *karoh*s from here and where there is a tank, it is my territory. You will reach that place safely. From that place to Multan it is under the charge of Shaikh Baha-u'd-din.)[21]

Ashraf Jahangir Samnani) MS, Letter No. 73. 'Abdul Ghaffur Danapuri's *Nusah-u'l-Ibad fi Wujud-u'l-Qutb wa'l-Abdal* (Nami Press, Lucknow 1307 AH) for a detailed discussion of the subject on the basis of the early authorities.

19. *Fawa'id-u'l-Fu'ad,* p. 2; *Siyar-u'l-Auliya,* pp. 45, 48, 57.

20. *Siyar-u'l-Auliya,* p. 72; *Matla'-u'l-Anwar,* pp. 20, 23; *Shirin Khurau,* p. 12; *Majnun Laila,* p. 13; *Hasht Bihisht,* pp. 13–14. Note, for instance, the following verses about Shaikh Nizam-u'd-din Auliya:

او شه از ملک بسامان خویش

داده ولایت بغلامان خویش

کاردان ممالک ملکوت

مشرف کارخانه جبروت

21. *Fawa'id-u'l-Fu'ad,* pp. 137–38.

Medieval records abound in innumerable instances of territorial distributions of this type[22] and the seriousness with which reference is made to them by the contemporary mystic writers shows the extent of medieval faith in them. It was under the influence of these ideas that in some towns of northern India elder saints came to be known as *Shah-i-Wilayats*.[23]

Though in some other Muslim lands bitter struggles had, sometimes, taken place between saints of different affiliations for the spiritual control of certain areas,[24] such ugly situations were averted in India by the spirit of mutual trust and accommodation which characterized the relations of the Chishti and the Suhrawardi saints.[25] The Chishti supremacy in Delhi

22. Ibid. p. 133; *Tarikh-i-Firoz Shahi*, pp. 61–62. See also *Maktubat-i-Ashrafi* (MS, Letter No. 73), where he says that Hansi is the frontier between the Chishti and the Suhrawardi jurisdictions:

هانسی در اکابر چشتیه و اماثر نیک سرشتیه سهروردیه سرحد است

23. Sayyid Ashraf Jahangir Samnani writes in a letter:

"باید دانست که حق تعالیٰ تقسیم ولایت هندوستان باولیاء روزگار کرده که هر کدامی بهم خویش را محافظت نمایند از نزول بلا هائی متنوعه و حلول آفتهائی مختلفه"

(*Maktubat-i-Ashrafi*, MS, Letter No. 73). For accounts of some graves of the *Shah-i-Wilayats*, see *Tarikh-i-Amroha*, Vol. II, pp. 4–20; *Tazkirat-u'l-Wasilin*, pp. 32–36; *Ma'asir-u'l-Kiram*, p. 9.

24. See *Nafahat-u'l-Uns* (p. 299) for details of the tussle between Shaikh Maudud Chishti and Shaikh Ahmad Jam, the leader of the *Silsilah-i-Khwajgan*, for the spiritual control of Herat.

25. Two such situations arose in India also, but were amicably resolved by the saints of the two *silsilah*s. When Shaikh Qutb-u'd-din Bakhtiyar Kaki reached Multan from Baghdad, Qubachah requested him to settle there permanently. Suspecting an intrusion into his spiritual territory, Shaikh Baha-u'd-din Zakariyya went to see Qutb Sahib and conveyed to him, in a peculiar mystic manner, his desire to leave his *wilayat*. The polite way of asking a saint to leave one's spiritual territory was to place his shoes in the direction one would like him to go. Shaikh Baha-u'd-din placed the shoes of Qutb Sahib in the direction of Delhi and the latter lost no time in quitting Multan (*Siyar-u'l-Auliya*, p. 61). Jamali says that Qutb Sahib told Qubachah: 'This land has been placed under the spiritual protection of Shaikh Baha-u'd-din Zakariyya and it will remain under him.' (*Siyar-u'l-'Arifin*, p. 20). Nearly a hundred years after this, Sultan Mubarak Khalji requested Shaikh Rukn-u'd-din Multani, a grandson of Shaikh Baha-u'd-din, to set up a *khanqah* in Delhi in order to turn the public eye away from Shaikh Nizam-u'd-din Auliya, but he refused to interfere in the spiritual jurisdiction of his Chishti contemporary (*Siyar-u'l-Auliya*, p. 136).

was temporarily threatened by the activities of the Firdausi saints[26] but, very soon, the pressure of public opinion forced them to migrate to Bihar.

Eager to work out the concept of spiritual sovereignty to its full length, the medieval mystics assigned the importance of regalia to some of the articles of their daily use. The patched frock (*khirqah*), the prayer carpet (*sajjadah*), the wooden sandals (*na'lain-i-chubin*), the rosary (*tasbih*), and the rod (*'asa*) of the chief saint constituted the mystic insignia in medieval India and whomsoever a Shaikh entrusted these articles to in his last moments came to be regarded as his chief spiritual successor.[27]

THE SUHRAWARDI AND CHISHTI CENTRES OF ACTIVITY

The Suhrawardi *silsilah* flourished most vigorously in Sind and the Punjab. A few Suhrawardi saints decided to settle in Delhi and Awadh, but they were overshadowed by their Chishti neighbours. In fact, the Suhrawardi *silsilah* could not secure any permanent footing in the Gangetic plains. Multan and Uch remained throughout this period the two principal centres of its activity in India. Multan being a frontier town, all caravans from either direction stayed there and came into touch with the Suhrawardi saints and carried their fame to distant parts of the Muslim world. The Suhrawardi saints, consequently, came to be respected in the Turkish lands.[28]

The Chishtis established their centres at Ajmer, Narnaul, Suwal, Nagaur, and Mandal in Rajputana; Hansi and Ajodhan in the Punjab and in some towns of U.P. Later on the *silsilah* spread into other parts of the country and Chishti centres sprang up in Bihar, Bengal, Assam, and the Deccan. The Chishti saints succeeded in attaining an all-India status and people flocked to their hospices from every part of the country. Even Chisht, the cradle land of the *silsilah*, looked to Delhi for guidance in spiritual matters.[29]

26. Ibid, p. 147; *Khair-u'l-Majalis*, p. 202.

27. *Siyar-u'l-Auliya*, pp. 121–22; *Khair-u'l-Majalis*, p. 287. See also *A'ina-i-Sikandari*, (p. 12) where Amir Khusrau writes about his spiritual mentor:

زنعلین چوبی شده تخت گیر

یکی کرسیش گشته دیگر سریر

28. When Sultan Muhammad b. Tughluq executed Shaikh Hud, he remarked: "I know thy intention was to escape to Turkistan and tell people: 'I am a descendant of (Shaikh) Baha-u'd-din Zakariyya of Multan and the King has ill-treated me'." (Ibn Battuta, Vol. II, p. 145). This shows that Shaikh Baha-u'd-din Zakariyya was deeply respected in the Turkish lands.

29. *Siyar-u'l-Auliya*, p. 202.

Two questions may very pertinently be raised in this context: What factors determined the success or failure of a *silsilah* in a particular region and how did a saint attain all-India status in those days of limited means of communications? The success of a *silsilah* depended very largely on a Shaikh's ability to adjust and adapt himself to the mental and emotional climate of a particular region. What the mystics call *nafs-i-gira*—an intuitive intelligence that could understand, comprehend, control, and direct the mind of the people—was needed in an abundant degree to appreciate the spiritual needs and emotional requirements of the people and attract them to the mystic fold. Unless the saints of a *silsilah* identified themselves with the problems of the people—their worries, their hopes, and their aspirations—their organization floated in a vacuum and failed to strike roots into the soil. The popularity and success of the Chishti saints in India was due to their understanding of the Indian conditions and the religious attitudes and aspirations of the Indian people. They adopted many Hindu customs and ceremonials in the initial stages of the development of their *silsilah* in India. The practice of bowing before the Shaikh,[30] presenting water to visitor,[31] circulating *zanbil*,[32] shaving the head of new entrants to the mystic circle,[33] audition parties (*sama'*), and the *chillah-i-ma'kus*[34] (the inverted *chillah*) had close resemblance to Hindu and Buddhist practices and, consequently, the appeal of the Chishti *silsilah* in the non-Muslim environment—particularly when the saints who represented it led an extremely simple and pious life—was tremendous. Besides, the difference in the Suhrawardi and the Chishti attitudes towards the non-Muslims went a long way in determining the range and sphere of their influence. The Chishtis believed in the control of emotional life as a pre-requisite to the control of external behaviour. The Suhrawardis tackled the

30. *Fawa'id-u'l-Fu'ad*, pp. 158–59,
31. Ibid, p. 137.
32. *Khair-u'l-Majalis*, p. 150; *Siyar-u'l-Auliya*, p. 66.
33. *Khair-u'l-Majalis*, pp. 65–66.
34. One who wants to practise the *chillah-i-ma'kus* ties a rope to his feet and gets his body lowered into a well and offers prayers in this posture for forty nights. Some of the Chishti saints are reported to have practised this inverted *Chillah*. Shah Walliullah, however, remarks: 'We could not find any authority for it in the Traditions of the Prophet or in the sayings of the jurists.... Its legality or otherwise is known to God alone.' (*Qaul-u'l-Jamil*, p. 53) This practice was probably borrowed from the sadhus. Among the Hindus there is a class of sadhus known as the *Urdhamukhi* about whom it is said that they hang their heads downwards suspended from the bough of a tree or a suitable framework and pray. J.C. Oman, *The Mystics, Ascetics and Saints of India* (London, 1905), p. 46.

problem from the other end and emphasized the necessity of regulating actions prior to the control of emotions. This dampened the prospects of Suhrawardi expansion in a non-Muslim environment. It worked well in Muslim surroundings and served the spiritual needs of the Muslim community but when it came to non-Muslim lands, its progress stopped. The following two incidents bring out very neatly the difference in the attitudes of the two *silsilah*s and help us also in analysing the causes of their success or failure in particular areas:

(1) Sayyid Jalal-u'd-din Bukhari Makhdum-i-Jahanian (ob. 1384 AD) was on his deathbed, Nawahun, a *darogah* of Uch, called on him to enquire about his health. "May God restore your health," said Nawahun, "Your holiness is the last of the saints as the Prophet Muhammad was the last of the prophets." Sayyid Jalal-u'd-din Bukhari and his brother, Sadr-u'd-din Raju Qattal, construed it as an expression of faith in Islam and, therefore, they demanded a formal declaration of conversion from him. Nawahun firmly declined to make any such declaration. Thereupon he was charged with apostasy. He fled to the court of Firoz Shah Tughluq in search of asylum and redress. When Sayyid Jalal-u'd-din Bukhari expired, his younger brother pursued the matter further and reached Delhi in order to persuade Firoz Shah to execute Nawahun. Though some scholars of the capital did not agree with the viewpoint of Raju Qattal, the latter prevailed upon Firoz Shah in obtaining his permission for Nawahun's execution as a renegade.[35]

(2) A visitor asked Shaikh Nizam-u'd-din Auliya: "If a Hindu recites the *Kalimah* (Muslim formula of faith), and believes in the Unity of God and acknowledges the Prophethood of Muhammad; but, when a Mussalman comes, he keeps silent. What will be his ultimate end?" The Shaikh refused to pronounce any verdict on such a Hindu and remarked: "His affair is with God. He can punish him or forgive him as He likes."[36]

On another occasion a disciple of Shaikh Nizam-u'd-din Auliya brought a Hindu friend with him and introduced him saying: "He is my brother." "Has your brother any inclination towards Islam?" asked the Shaikh. "I have brought him to your feet," the man replied, "so that owing to the blessings of the Shaikh's glance, he may become a Mussalman." "You may talk to these people as much as you like," replied Shaikh Nizam-u'd-din Auliya, "but no one's heart is changed. Still if he lives in the company of a pious man, it is possible that owing to the blessing of his company, he may become a Mussalman." The Shaikh's eyes were filled with tears as he narrated a long story to show that there was lack of character among the Mussalmans themselves. When Shaikh Bayazid Bistami died, he told his Hindu visitor, people asked a Jew who lived in the neighbourhood of the saint: "Why do you not become a Mussalman?" "If Islam is what Bayazid possessed, it is

35. *Siyar-u'l-'Arifin*, pp. 159–60.
36. *Fawa'id-u'l-Fu'ad*, p. 135.

beyond me. If it is what you possess, I would feel ashamed of such Islam," replied the Jew.[37]

This difference in the attitudes of the Chishti and the Suhrawardi saints on the question of conversion was bound to react on their popularity and was a very vital factor in determining the spheres of their activity.

A saint's fame was carried from one place to another by travellers, merchants, scholars, and musicians who broke the isolation of medieval towns and established cultural and commercial contacts on a large scale. Itineracy being an integral part of mystic discipline in those days, religious-minded people enquired about saintly persons in every town they happened to visit.[38] Professional musicians who went from *khanqah* to *khanqah*, singing songs and earning money, taking pride in narrating their experiences before people and thus they increased, rather unconsciously, the circle of a saint's admirers.[39] Merchants carried with their goods the blessings of a saint and with them his name also.[40] Thus, in course of time, a saint attained all-India status. In the *khanqah*s of Shaikh Baha-u'd-din Zakariyya and Shaikh Farid-u'd-din Ganj-i-Shakar—the two most outstanding saints of all-India reputation during the thirteenth century—we find visitors from Khurasan,[41] Delhi,[42] Uch,[43] Nagaur,[44] Ajmer,[45] Buhar,[46] Lakhnauti,[47] and other places.

37. Ibid, pp. 182–83.

38. When Shaikh Jalal-u'd-din Tabrizi visited Kahtwal (near Multan), he asked people about the saints of that place and they directed him to Shaikh Farid who was at that time a boy of tender age. *Khair-u'l-Majalis*, pp. 219–20.

39. Abu Bakr, a *qawwal* of Bada'un, returned home after visiting Multan and Ajodhan. He went to a school (*maktab*) and, recounting the experiences of his journey before the schoolmaster, he praised the piety and devotion of Shaikh Baha-u'd-din Zakariyya and Shaikh Farid-u'd-din Ganj-i-Shakar. Shaikh Nizam-u'd-din Auliya, who was one of the schoolmates at that time, heard the story and developed a sudden and intense love for Shaikh Farid. *Fawa'id-u'l-Fu'ad*, p. 149; *Siyar-u'l-Auliya*, p. 100.

40. A merchant of Nagaur, who carried mustard seed to Multan and brought cotton from there to Nagaur, acted as a medium for the exchange of letters between Shaikh Baha-u'd-din Zakariyya and Shaikh Hamid-u'd-din Sufi. *Siyar-u'l-Auliya*, pp. 158–59.

41. Ibid, pp. 63–64.

42. *Fawa'id-u'l-Fu'ad*, p. 219.

43. *Siyar-u'l-Auliya*, p. 81.

44. *Fawa'id-u'l-Fu'ad*, pp. 188–89.

45. Ibid, p. 238.

46. Ibid, p. 57.

47. *Siyar-u'l-Auliya*, p. 335.

A: THE CHISHTI *SILSILAH*—ITS SAINTS AND ORGANIZATION

Founder of the Silsilah

As noted earlier, the Chishti *silsilah* was introduced in India by Shaikh Mu'in-u'd-din Sijzi[48] who reached here before the Turkish conquest of Hindustan.[49]

One trying to reconstruct an account of the life and teachings of the founder of the Chishti order in India should frankly confess the paucity of authentic records about him. The three contemporary political chroniclers—Sadr-u'd-din Hasan Nizami, Fakhr-i-Mudabbir, and Minhaj— do not refer to him at all. Of the early mystic records, the *Fawa'id-u'l-Fu'ad* and the *Khair-u'l-Majalis*, do not give any information about him. Barani makes no reference to him. 'Isami tells us only this much that Muhammad b. Tughluq had once visited his grave.[50] The two earliest mystic works that supply any information about him are the *Sarur-u's-Sudur* (conversations of Shaikh Hamid-u'd-din Sufi Suwali Nagauri, compiled by his grandson during the Tughluq period) and the *Siyar-u'l-Auliya* of Sayyid Muhammad bin Mubarak Kirmani, known as Mir Khurd,

---

48. Faulty transcription is responsible for this word being converted into *Sanjari*. The Shaikh was a native of Sijistan and was on that account called Sijzi. The following couplet of 'Isami can rhyme properly only if this word is read as *Sijzi*.

و زو در بر آں خرقه عهدی بعید   معین الدین آں پیر سجزی کشید

(*Futuh-u's-Salatin*, p. 8)

See also *Intibah fi-Salasil-i-Auliya Allah* (p. 88), for Shah Walliullah's opinion on this point.

49. Mir Khurd thus informs us on the authority of Shaikh Nizam-u'd-din Auliya (*Siyar-u'l-Auliya*, p. 46). *Sarur-u's-Sudur* refers to Shaikh Mu'in-u'd-din's visit to Delhi along with forty friends during the reign of Iltutmish. It is, however, not clear whether he had reached Delhi from beyond or had come from Ajmer. The following statement of Minhaj

ایں داعی از ثقه شنید که از معارف جبال بلاد ترلک بود لقب او

معین الدین او می گفت که من دران لشکر با سلطان غازی بودم' عدد

سوار لشکر اسلام دراں وقت صد و بست هزار برگستوان بود

(*Tabaqat-i-Nasiri*, p. 119).

has led some writers to identify Mu'in-u'd-din with the saint of Ajmer. This identification, however, does not seem to be correct.

50. *Futuh-u's-Salatin*, p. 466.

a disciple of Shaikh Nizam-u'd-din Auliya. The *Sarur-u's-Sudur* contains only a few interesting pieces of information about the saint's life, while Mir Khurd's account is of a very general nature and does not help us form any opinion about his life or work in Rajputana. The first detailed account of his life is given by Maulana Hamid b. Fazlullah popularly known as Maulana Jamali[51] (ob. 1536 AD) who had personally visited all places where Shaikh Mu'in-u'd-din is said to have passed his early years. It is, however, extremely doubtful whether Jamali could collect authentic information about the saint nearly three centuries after his death, specially when the mystic traditions were on the decline in the Persian lands. Anyway, Jamali is the only hagiologist of the early Mughal period whose account of the Shaikh deserves any credence. All later *tazkirah*,[52] with the solitary exception of *Akhbar-ul-Akhyar*,[53] have horribly confused fact with fiction and have regaled all that they found floating down the stream of time. This literature may be of value in tracing the growth of legends round the Shaikh's person; its historical value is, however, very meagre. The *malfuz* literature[54] and the *diwan* attributed to Shaikh Mu'in-u'd-din are apocryphal and it would be, therefore, unfair to the saint to

51. *Siyar-u'l-'Arifin*, pp. 4–16.

52. Of the *tazkirahs* that were produced during the Mughal period and contain an account of the great saint, the following deserve to be specially mentioned: *Gulzar-i-Abrar*, compiled by Muhammad Ghausi Shattari between 1014–22/ 1605–13. *Akhbar-u'l-Asfiya* compiled by Abdus Samad, a nephew of Abul Fazl in 1014/1605. *Mir'at u'l-Asrar* compiled by 'Ali Akbar Husaini Ardistani in 1043/1633–34. *Siyar-u'l-Aqtab* compiled by Allah Diya Chishti in 1056/1646. *Jawahir-i-Faridi* compiled by 'Ali Asghar Chishti in 1033/1623. *Ma'arij-u'l-Walayat* compiled by Ghulam Mu'in-u'd-din 'Abdullah in 1094/1682. *Munis-u'l-Arwah* compiled by Jahan Ara Begum in 1049/1640.

53. The compiler of this work, Shaikh 'Abdul Haqq Muhaddis of Delhi (ob. 1641), has carefully sifted all available evidence and has based his account of the saint on reliable authorities.

54. The following works are attributed to Khwaja Mu'in-u'd-din:

(a) *Ganj-u'l-Asrar* (MS)—said to have been compiled by the Khwaja for Sultan Iltutmish, at the instance of Khwaja 'Usman Harvani.

(b) *Anis-u'l-Arwah* (a collection of Khwaja 'Usman Harvani's conversations) said to have been compiled by the Khwaja.

(c) *Dalil-u'l-'Arifin* (a collection of the Khwaja's conversations) said to have been made by Shaikh Qutb-u'd-din Bakhtiyar Kaki.

(d) *Diwan-i-Mu'in* (really a collection of Maulana Mu'in Harvi's poetic compositions, wrongly attributed to the Khwaja.)

attempt any estimate of his life or work on the basis of this fabricated literature.[55]

Shaikh Mu'in-u'd-din was born in or about 536/1141[56] in Sijistan, an extensive province lying to the east of Persia. His father, Sayyid Ghiyas-u'd-din, a pious man of some means, died when his son was in his teens. He left as legacy an orchard and a grinding mill. Once the Shaikh was looking after the plants in his garden when a mystic, Shaikh Ibrahim Qanduzi, happened to pass by. Shaikh Mu'in-u'd-din entertained him in his garden. Hagiologists trace the germination of the mystic attitude in him to the blessings of this saint. In fact, the most powerful factor in giving a mystic touch to his personality at this early stage was the condition of Sijistan which had suffered terribly at the hands of the Qara-Khitai and the Ghuzz Turks. It drove the Shaikh's mind inwards and he realized the futility of hankering after worldly glory or seeking after worldly goods. He sold all his assets, gave the proceeds in charity, and took to itinerancy. He visited the seminaries of Samarqand and Bukhara and acquired religious learning at the feet of eminent scholars of his age. While on his way to Iraq, he passed through Harvan, a *qasbah* in the district of Naishapur. Here he met Khwaja 'Usman[57] and was so deeply impressed by his spiritual eminence that he decided to join the circle of his disciples. For twenty years he accompanied him on his arduous mystic journeys and performed all sorts of personal services for him. "I did not give myself a moment's rest from the service of my master, and carried about his night clothes during his journeys and stoppages," Shaikh Mu'in-u'd-din once told his disciples.[58] Later he undertook independent journeys and came into contact with eminent saints and scholars such as Shaikh 'Abdul Qadir Gilani,[59] Shaikh Najm-u'd-din Kubra,[60] Shaikh Najib-u'd-din 'Abdul Qahir

55. See Professor M. Habib's article, 'Chishti Mystic Records of the Sultanate Period', *Medieval India Quarterly*, Vol. I, No. 2, p. 17, et seq.

56. No earlier writer has given his date of birth. Shaikh 'Abdul Haqq informs us that he died in 633/1236 (*Akhbar-u'l-Akhyar*, p. 22). Jamali says that he attained the age of 97 years (*Siyar-u'l-'Arifin*, p. 16). Calculated on this basis, his date of birth should be *circa* 536/1141.

57. For a brief account, see *Siyar-u'l-Auliya*, pp. 44–45.

58. *Siyar-u'l-Auliya*, p. 45.

59. See *supra*, pp. 57–58.

60. Shaikh Najm-u'd-din Kubra (1145–1228 AD) was one of the most striking personalities among the Persian *sufis* of the twelfth–thirteenth centuries AD. In the long series of his disciples one finds eminent mystics such as Shaikh Majd-u'd-din Baghdadi, Shaikh Saif-u'd-din Bakharzi, and Shaikh Sa'd-u'd-din Hamavi. He was a prolific writer and left a number of valuable treatises on

Suhrawardi,[61] Shaikh Abu Sa'id Tabrizi,[62] Shaikh Malimud Ispahani,[63] Shaikh Nasir-u'd-din Astarabadi,[64] and Shaikh 'Abdul Wahid[65]—all of whom were destined to exercise great influence on contemporary religious life and thought. He visited nearly all the great centres of Muslim culture in those days—Samarqand, Bukhara, Baghdad, Naishapur, Tabriz, Aush, Ispahan, Sabzwar, Mihna, Khirqan, Astarabad, Balkh, and Ghaznin—and acquainted himself with almost every important trend in Muslim religious life in the Middle Ages. His moral and spiritual qualities attracted many people to his fold and he appointed his *khalifah*s in Sabzwar and Balkh.[66] Shaikh Auhad-u'd-din Kirmani, Shaikh Shihab-u'd-din Suhrawardi, and many other eminent mystics benefited from his company. Having thus roamed all over the Muslim lands which had not yet recovered from the terrible shocks of the Qara-Khitai and Ghuzz invasions and which were to be ravaged very soon by the Mongols, he turned towards India. After a brief stay at Lahore. where he prayed and meditated at the tomb of the pioneer mystic teacher. Shaikh 'Ali Hajweri, he proceeded to Ajmer.

Ajmer was not merely the seat of Chauhan power; it was also a religious centre where thousands of pilgrims assembled from far and near. Shaikh Mu'in-u'd-din's determination to work out the principles of Islamic mysticism at a place of such political and religious significance shows great self-confidence. Unfortunately, no details are available about the way

---

various aspects of mysticism. For his life, see *Nafahat-u'l-Uns*, pp. 375–79; *Tarikh-i-Guzidah*, p. 789; *Majalis-u'l-Ushshaq*, Bombay, p. 84; Raverty, *Tabaqat-i-Nasiri*, p. 100. Also E. Berthel's article in the *Encyclopaedia of Islam*, Vol. III, pp. 822–23.

61. See *supra*, p. 61.

62. Shaikh Yusuf Hamadani (ob. 1140 AD) was a distinguished saint and scholar of his time and a large number of students from Baghdad, Ispahan, and Samarqand visited his seminary. Khwaja 'Abdul Khaliq Ghajdawani, the famous saint of the *Silsilah-i-Khwajgan*, was his *khalifah*. For a brief account, see *Nafahat-u'l-Uns*, pp. 337–39.

63. A notable saint of Ispahan. *Siyar-u'l-'Arifin*, p. 7.

64. Shaikh Nasir-u'd-din, a distinguished saint of Astarabad, lived to the ripe old age of 107 years. Shaikh Abul Hasan Khirqani and Shaikh Abu Sa'id Abul Khair were among his friends. *Siyar-u'l-'Arifin*, p. 9.

65. Shams-u'l-'Arifin 'Abdul Wahid was an eminent saint of Ghaznin. Shaikh Nizam-u'd-din Abul Muwayyid (for whom see *Akhbar-u'l-Akhyar*, p. 45) was his disciple: *Siyar-u'l-'Arifin*, p. 12.

66. But the Khwaja's *silsilah* did not flourish in those lands. Viewed as a whole, the Chishti *silsilah* found the most congenial soil in India and it developed and flourished here more vigorously than in any other country.

he worked in the midst of a population which looked askance at every foreigner. It cannot, however, be denied that his stay in Ajmer must have been a serious trial for the principles of the Chishti *silsilah*. On his success or failure in Ajmer depended the future of the Muslim mystic movement in Hindustan. Some of his sayings, as recorded by Mir Khurd, supply the quintessence of his religious and social ideology and reveal him as a man of wide sympathies, catholic views, and deep humanism. The entire structure of his thought stood on the bedrock of the following three principles and he very neatly illustrated the working of these principles in his life:

1. Explaining his views about the Universe, the Shaikh said:[67]

چوں ما از پوست بیروں آمدیم و نگاه کردیم عاشق و معشوق
و عشق یکی دیدیم' یعنی در عالم توحید همه یکیست

(When we transcended the externals and looked around, we found the lover, the beloved, and the love (itself) to be one, i.e. in the sphere of Oneness all is one.)

This pantheistic approach brought him very close to the treasures of ancient Hindu religious thought, particularly the Upanishads, and created an atmosphere favourable for the exchange of ideas at a higher level.

2. Defining the highest form of devotion to God (*ta'at*), the Shaikh remarked that it was nothing but:

درماندگان را فریاد رسیدن' و حاجت بے چارگان
روا کردن و گرسنگان را سیر گردانیدن

(To redress the misery of those in distress; to fulfil the needs of the helpless and to feed the hungry.)

Thus, religion is not merely raised above rituals and ecclesiastical formalities but 'service of humanity' is made its very *raison d'être*.

3. Describing the qualities which endear a man to God, the Shaikh referred to the following attributes:[68]

اول سخاوتی چوں سخاوت دریا' دوم شفقتی چوں
شفقت آفتاب' سیوم تواضعی چوں تواضع زمین

(First, river-like generosity; secondly, sun-like affection; and thirdly, earth-like hospitality.)

67. *Siyar-u'l-Auliya*, p. 45.
68. *Siyar-u'l-Auliya*, p. 46.

This mystic morality saved human sympathy from running into narrow grooves and struck at the very root of parochialism, caste-ism, and religious exclusiveness.

These three principles, which reveal Shaikh Mu'in-u'd-din Chishti's attitude towards some of the basic problems of religion and morality, supplied the motive power to the Chishti organization in India during the thirteenth century. In fact, the success achieved by its saints during the period under review is inexplicable except with reference to these principles.

PRINCIPAL SAINTS OF THE CHISHTI *SILSILAH*

Two very eminent disciples of Shaikh Mu'in-u'd-din popularized the Chishti *silsilah* in northern India: Shaikh Hamid-u'd-din Sufi in Rajputana and Shaikh Qutb-u'd-din Bakhtiyar Kaki in Delhi.[69] One worked in the rural, the other in the urban, milieu.

Shaikh Hamid-u'd-din Sufi[70] (ob. 673/1276) was a posthumous child of Shaikh Muhammad al-Sufi, a descendant of Sa'id b. Zaid, one of the ten leading companions of the Prophet. He was the first Muslim child to see the light of day in Delhi after its conquest by the Mussalmans.[71] In his early years he had led a very voluptuous life,[72] but when he joined the circle of Shaikh Mu'in-u'd-din's disciples, a sudden change came upon him. He repented for his past sins and adopted the life of a mystic in all sincerity and with all its rigours. He became so thoroughly disgusted with things material and mundane that he warned his visitors against discussing worldly affairs in his mystic gatherings.[73] Impressed by his devotion to the

---

69. The *Fawa'id-u'l-Fu'ad* and the *Siyar-u'l-Auliya* refer to these two *khalifah*s only. Later *tazkirah*s have added several other names to this list.

70. For brief biographical accounts, see *Siyar-u'l-Auliya*, pp. 156–64; *Siyar-u'l-'Arifin*, pp. 13–14; *Akhbar-u'l-Akhyar*, pp. 29–36. An account of his conversations was prepared by one of his grandsons in a less-known, but very important, work, *Sarur-u's-Sudur*.

71. The *Sarur-u's-Sudur*, p. 8, quotes the following statement of the Shaikh:

اول کسی که بعد از (فتح) اسلام در دهلی زاده شد من بودم

See also, *Akhbar-u'l-Akhyar*, p. 29.

72. *Siyar-u'l-Auliya*, p. 156; *Siyar-u'l-'Arifin*, p. 13.

73. *Sarur-u's-Sudur* (MS), p. 5.

Yasin, a Turk disciple of Shaikh Hamid-u'd-din, was a man of means and possessed considerable wealth. Once, while on a journey, he lost all his property and was reduced to a state of penury. The Shaikh did not pray for the recovery of his property and said that his affection for Yasin prevented him from making such a request to God. *Sarur-u's-Sudur*, p. 7.

mystic way of life, Shaikh Mu'in-u'd-din gave him the title of *Sultan-u't-Tarikin* (King of Recluses).[74]

Far from the hurry and bustle of medieval towns, Shaikh Hamid-u'd-din lived the self-sufficient life of an Indian peasant at Suwal, a small village in Nagaur.[75] Whatever he needed—and his needs never exceeded a few maunds of grain and a few yards of rough hand-woven cloth—he himself produced and scrupulously avoided coming into contact with the government of the day. His life at Nagaur affords one of the earliest glimpses of Muslim family life in the Indian countryside. He lived in a small mud house and eked out his meagre subsistence by cultivating a single *bighah* of land.[76] The principle of the rotation of crops being unknown in those days,[77] he cultivated half of his land in one season and the other half in the next. He dressed himself like a typical Indian peasant and used two sheets of cloth to cover the upper and the lower parts of his body.[78] He kept a cow in his house and himself milked it.[79] His wife—a lady of fervent piety and strong mystic temperament—spent her time in cooking and spinning like a peasant woman.[80] Like most of the villagers amongst whom he lived, Shaikh Hamid-u'd-din was a strict vegetarian.[81] His dislike for meat eating was so great that he warned his disciples against distributing meat preparations for blessing his soul after his death.[82] The family carried on their conversations in *Hindivi*.[83]

74. *Akhbar-u'l-Akhyar*, p. 29.

75. For Nagaur, see M.A. Chaghtai's article, 'Nagaur, A Forgotten Kingdom', *Bulletin of the Deccan College Research Institute*, Poona, November 1940, pp. 166–83.

76. *Siyar-u'l-Auliya*, pp. 156–57. Jamali says that this plot measured ten *jarib* only and was situated near a river (*Siyar-u'l-'Arifin*, p. 13).

77. The principle of the rotation of crops was introduced by Sultan Muhammad b. Tughluq. Barani, *Tarikh-i-Firoz Shahi*, p. 498.

78. Amir Khurd writes about him:

یک فوطهٔ چادر درکمربستی وچادردیگر برسر وجود مبارک انداختی

Siyar-u'l-Auliya, p. 157.

79. *Sarur-u's-Sudur* (MS), p. 14.

80. Ibid, p. 9.

81. Ibid, pp. 10, 43.

82. Ibid, p. 10. The Shaikh used to say:

اگر بروح من چیزی بخواهید که بدهید باید که گوشت ندهید

83. Ibid, pp. 43, 47, 71, 104, 106, etc.

Touched by his penitence and poverty, the *muqta'* of Nagaur offered a plot of land and some cash to him. The Shaikh apologized saying that none of his elder saints had accepted a government gift. The *muqta'* then reported the matter to the Sultan who sent 500 silver *tankahs* with a *farman* conferring a village on him. When the *muqta'* presented the royal gift to him, he hastened to inform his wife just to study her reactions to the prospects of a life of material prosperity and comfort. The couple was in such a state of penury at that time that the wife had a tattered *dupatta* on her head, and the saint a grimy loincloth on his body. "O Khwaja," replied his wife, "Do you want to disgrace years of spiritual devotion and penitence by accepting this gift? Do not worry. I have spun two seers of yarn. It would suffice for preparing a loincloth for you and a *dupatta* for me." Shaikh Hamid was delighted at this reply. He informed the *muqta'* that he had decided not to accept the royal gift. Himself convinced that sainthood could not be reconciled with possession of material means, he severely criticized some of those contemporary saints who led a life of affluence and plenty. Once Shaikh Mu'in-u'd-din put a question to an audience in Delhi: "Tell me who is the Shaikh of the times these days?" To the utter surprise of all those present, Shaikh Hamid-u'd-din replied:

شیخ روزگار دریں وقت جیتل است' هرکرا
جیتل بسیار است' هموں شیخ وقت است

(These days *jital* is the Shaikh of the times. Whoever possesses the larger amount of *jital*s, is the Shaikh of the day.)

This attitude inevitably brought him into conflict with the leader of the Suhrawardi order in India, Shaikh Baha-u'd-din Zakariyya of Multan. He wrote long and acrimonious letters to him on this subject. Enraged at this blatant criticism of his father's behaviour, a son of Shaikh Baha-u'd-din Zakariyya travelled all the way from Multan to Nagaur and criticized Shaikh Hamid-u'd-din for not offering Friday prayers. Shaikh Hamid silenced his critic by raising a legal objection to the demand of offering Friday prayers in Nagaur. "Nagaur is not a town and so Friday prayers cannot be held here,"[84] declared Shaikh Hamid.

Shaikh Hamid-u'd-din was a man of affable temperament and wide human sympathies which made him a popular figure in Nagaur. His catholicity of views is best illustrated by the fact that he could discern and appreciate spiritual virtues in non-Muslims also.[85]

84. *Siyar-u'l-Auliya*, p. 158.
85. *Fawa'id-u'l-Fu'ad*, p. 70.

Shaikh Qutb-u'd-din Bakhtiyar Kaki[86] (ob. 1235 AD), the other distinguished *khalifah* of Shaikh Mu'in-u'd-din, was a native of Aush,[87] a great centre of the Hallaji mystics.[88] After finishing his education at Aush, he turned towards Baghdad where he met eminent mystics, such as Shaikh 'Abdul Qadir Gilani, Shaikh Shihab-u'd-din Suhrawardi, Qazi Hamid-u'd-din, and Shaikh Auhad-u'd-din Kirmani.[89] It was in the mosque of Abu Lais Samarqandi that he met Shaikh Mu'in-u'd-din and decided to join the circle of his disciples.

When Shaikh Mu'in-u'd-din Chishti turned towards India, Shaikh Qutb-u'd-din took to travels in other lands. He reached Delhi several years after his master's arrival at Ajmer. After a brief stay at Multan, he left for Delhi where the Turks were busy laying the foundations of Muslim political and cultural institutions. Eminent Muslim saints, divines, and scholars had flocked to this city from all sides and the enlightened and liberal patronage of Sultan Iltutmish offered them a safe haven of refuge.[90] When Shaikh Qutb-u'd-din Bakhtiyar Kaki entered the town, Iltutmish

86. For his life, see *Siyar-u'l-Auliya*, pp. 48–57; *Siyar-u'l-'Arifin*, pp. 16–31; *Akhbar-u'l-Akhyar*, pp. 24–26; *Gulzar-i-Abrar* (MS); *Mir'at-u'l-Asrar* (MS); *Siyar-u'l-Aqtab*, pp. 142–61; and *Rauzah-i-Aqtab*, pp. 3–30.

87. Aush is a town in Farghanah, south-east of Andijan. Professor Louis Massignon very kindly informed me: "I have published from the Russian translation of Sidikov, a Qaraqyrapghy text in praise of Hallaj (Mansur), in the *Revue des Études Islamiques*, 1946, pp. 77–78, proving that Osh was a centre of the Mansuri Sufis."

88. A Sufi order named after the famous Persian mystic, Abu'l Mughis al-Husan bin Mansur-al-Hallaj (244–309/858–922). The doctrines of the Hallajiya order may be thus summarized:

(a) In *Fiqh*, the five *fara'iz*, even the Hajj may be replaced by other works (*isaqata'l-wasa'it*).

(b) In *Kalam*, God's transcendence (*tanzih*) above the limits of creation (*tul arz*), the existence of an uncreated Divine spirit (*Ruh-i-Natiqah*), which becomes united with the created *Ruh* (spirit) of the ascetic (*hulul-a'l-lahut-fi'l-nasut*); the saint becomes the living and personal witness of God, whence the saying: *Ana'l-Haqq* 'I am creative Truth.'

(c) In *Tasawwuf*, perfect union with the Divine will through desire of and submission to suffering.

89. Shaikh Auhad-u'd-din Hamid al-Kirmani was an eminent disciple of Shaikh Qutb-u'd-din Albahri and had associated with the great mystic, Shaikh Muhi-u'd-din Ibn-i-'Arabi, who has referred to him in his famous work, *Futuhat-i-Makkiah*. For a brief biographical notice, see *Nafahat-u'l-Uns*, pp. 385–87.

90. *Tabaqat-i-Nasiri*, p. 166; *Futuh-u's-Salatin*, pp. 109–10.

accorded a hearty welcome to him and requested him to stay near his palace. But the Shaikh wanted to avoid identification with the centre of imperial power and conquest. He, therefore, refused to live with the Sultan. Iltutmish, however, made it a point to visit his *khanqah* outside the city twice a week.[91] Once the Shaikh thus advised the Sultan:

> O ruler of Delhi! It is incumbent on thee to be good to all poor people, mendicants, dervishes, and helpless folk. Treat all men kindly and strive for their welfare. Everyone who thus behaves towards his subjects is looked after by the Almighty and all his enemies turn into friends.[92]

Iltutmish offered the post of *Shaikh-u'l-Islam* to him, but he declined to accept it.[93] Shaikh Najm-u'd-din Sughra was then appointed to this post. A vain and self-conceited man as Sughra was, he grew jealous of Shaikh Qutb-u'd-din who was respected by the Sultan and the people alike.[94] Shaikh Mu'in-u'd-din Chishti was deeply grieved at this attitude of the *Shaikh-u'l-Islam*. He asked his disciple to quit Delhi and accompany him to Ajmer. The people of Delhi received this news with a heavy heart and when the Shaikh and his disciple set out for Ajmer, they followed them for miles. Iltutmish himself followed the two saints. Shaikh Mu'in-u'd-din was deeply touched with this spontaneous expression of love and affection for his disciple. He allowed Shaikh Qutb-u'd-din to remain in Delhi. Iltutmish kissed the feet of Shaikh Mu'in-u'd-din and brought Shaikh Qutb-u'd-din back to the capital.[95]

Though Shaikh Qutb-u'd-din Bakhtiyar did not associate himself with the ruler or the bureaucracy in building the political institutions of the Delhi Sultanate, he extended his moral support to the Sultan in the construction of public works and centres of cultural activity. Many hagiological works refer to his keen interest in the construction of the famous water reservoir, the *Hauz-i-Shamsi*.

Shaikh Qutb-u'd-din was very fond of mystic music (*sama'*). One day he was invited to an audition party held in the *khanqah* of Shaikh 'Ali Sijzi. When the singers recited the verses:

91. *Siyar-u'l-'Arifin*, p. 21.

92. *Risalah Hal Khunwadah-i-Chisht* (MS), f. 17b.

93. *Siyar-u'l-'Arifin*, p. 21. Jamali says that this offer was made after the death of Maulana Jamal-u'd-din Muhammad Bistami (p. 21), but this does not seem to be correct. It appears from the *Tabaqat-i-Nasiri* (Raverty, p. 702) that Maulana Bistam survived Iltutmish and was appointed *Shaikh-u'l-Islam* by Sultan Nasir-u'd-din Mahmud in 653 AH.

94. *Siyar-u'l-Auliya*, p. 54.

95. Ibid, pp. 54–55; *Jawami'-u'l-Kilam*, p. 208.

كشتگان خنجر تسليم را
هر زماں از غيب جانى ديگر است

(To the victims of the dagger of Submission
There comes a new life at every moment from the Unseen World),

he was suddenly overtaken by a state of ecstasy and for four days he could not get out of this emotional storm.[96] On the fifth night (*Rabi'ul-Awwal* 14, 633/November 15, 1235) he breathed his last.

Shaikh Qutb-u'd-din Bakhtiyar left two chief *khalifahs*—Shaikh Badr-u'd-din Ghaznavi[97] and Shaikh Farid-u'd-din Mas'ud Ganj-i-Shakar.[98] The former attained some popularity in Delhi but did not succeed in organizing the *silsilah* on firm foundations. The latter lived and worked mainly in Hansi and Ajodhan and it was due to his efforts that the Chishti order attained an all-India status and its branches came to be established in many important towns of India.

Shaikh Badr-u'd-din Ghaznavi was, in certain respects, a typical example of the material and moral conflicts of his age. He came to Lahore under the stress of the unfavourable conditions of his homeland and, probably, attracted by the prospects of a peaceful and prosperous life in the newly emerging Empire of Delhi. While in Lahore, he was overtaken by a feeling of homesickness. He could not decide whether he should proceed to Delhi, where he had a son-in-law, or return to Ghaznin where his parents and relatives lived. To get out of this dilemma, he consulted the Quran and was directed to go to Delhi. Later on he came to know that Ghaznin had been ransacked by the Mongols and all his relations had been killed. This tragic incident drove his mind inwards and he took to mysticism. But mysticism could not mould into unity the broken fragments of his personality and his mind remained torn by contradictions. The traditions of the *silsilah*, to which he had associated himself, demanded total rejection of all earthly ties and the severance of all contacts with the rulers and the bureaucracy. But the imperial city of Delhi had its own allurements which it was difficult to ignore. Shaikh Badr-u'd-din too could not hold fast to the traditions of his *silsilah*. He attached himself to Malik Nizam-u'd-din *Kharitahdar* who

96. *Siyar-u'l-Auliya*, p. 55; *Siyar-u'l-'Arifin*, p. 31.

97. For brief biographical accounts, see *Siyar-u'l-Auliya*, pp. 164–66; *Khair-u'l-Majalis*, pp. 187–88; *Siyar-u'l-'Arifin*, pp. 50–51; *Akhbar-u'l-Akhyar*, p. 50; *Mir'at-u'l-Asrar* (MS); *Ma'arij-u'l-Walayat* (MS).

98. For a detailed account of his life and teachings, see Nizami, *The Life and Times of Shaikh Farid-u'd-din Ganj-i-Shakar* (Aligarh, 1955).

constructed a *khanqah* for him and undertook to bear all its expenses. Not long afterwards, the *Kharitahdar* was thrown into prison on a charge of malversation. This created a financial crisis in the *khanqah* of Shaikh Badr-u'd-din and in great distress he wrote to Shaikh Farid Ganj-i-Shakar soliciting his spiritual help in the matter. Shaikh Farid expressed his disapproval of the ways of Shaikh Badr-u'd-din and charged him with deviating from the path of the Chishti saints.[99]

Shaikh Farid's criticism apart, Shaikh Badr-u'd-din commanded great respect in the mystic circles of Delhi. He was a poet[100] and preacher[101] of great eminence. But he could not make any appreciable contribution to the expansion of the *silsilah*. He was sadly mistaken in his calculations if he thought that a *khanqah* run on the basis of guaranteed payments could serve the spiritual needs of the people. Mystic records refer to only one of his disciples—Shaikh Imam-u'd-din Abdal.[102]

The most outstanding figure of the Chishti *silsilah* during the thirteenth century was, however, Shaikh Farid-u'd-din Mas'ud Ganj-i-Shakar (1175–1265). He gave to the Chishti *silsilah* the momentum of an organized spiritual movement.

Born in a Qazi family of Kahtwal (near Multan), Shaikh Farid was drawn towards mysticism very early in his life. It was in a *madrasah* attached to a mosque in Multan that he first met Shaikh Qutb-u'd-din Bakhtiyar Kaki and got himself initiated into the Chishti discipline. After completing his study of the External Sciences (*'ulum-i-zahiri*), he turned to spiritual practices and penitences. "All the Shaikhs of India," remarks Muhammad Ghausi, "are unanimous in declaring that no saint has excelled *Ganj-i-Shakar* in his devotions and penitences."[103] He was probably the first and the last Indo-Muslim saint who performed the *Chillah-i-Ma'kus*,[104] one of the most hazardous of spiritual exercises. After completing his course of mystic discipline at the feet of Shaikh Qutb-u'd-din, he settled at Hansi, an ancient

99. *Fawa'id-u'l-Fu'ad*, p. 79; *Khair-u'l-Majalis*, p. 188.

100. Amir Khurd has referred to his *diwan*. (*Siyar-u'l-Auliya*, p. 165.) It is extinct now.

101. *Fawa'id-u'l-Fu'ad*, p. 192.

102. For a brief biographical account of Shaikh Imam-u'd-din Abdal, see *Risalah Hal Khanwadah-i-Chisht* (MS), *Rauzah-i-Aqtab*, pp. 82–83.

Maulana Taj-u'd-din, the author of *Risalah Hal Khanwadah-i-Chisht*, was a spiritual descendant of Shaikh Imam-u'd-din Abdal. His spiritual mentor, Maulana 'Imad-u'd-din, was a *khalifah* of Shaikh Shihab-u'd-din 'Ashiq who was the son and successor of Shaikh Imam-u'd-din Abdal.

103. *Gulzar-i-Abrar* (MS).

104. See *supra*, note 34.

town in the Hisar district. Later on he moved to Ajodhan. It was in that neglected and out-of-the-way town that he came into the full gaze of history and spiritually starved people turned to him from every part of the country. The following two incidents, as recorded by Amir Hasan Sijzi, on the authority of Shaikh Nizam-u'd-din Auliya, give some idea of his popularity:

(i) When Shaikh Farid visited Delhi after the death of Shaikh Qutb-u'd-din Bakhtiyar Kaki, he was deluged by visitors. From early morning till late into the night he had to attend to his visitors and accept their invitations for feasts. On Fridays he had to start for congregational prayer much before the scheduled time because of the large crowds of admirers who waited for him all along the way. As he stepped out of his house, people eagerly rushed towards him, kissed his hands, and encircled him. No sooner did he manage to come out of this circle that he found himself surrounded by another group. He got rid of one circle to be enmeshed in another and this process went on until he reached the mosque, tired and wearied. One day he felt annoyed with the people who had thus surrounded him on his way to the mosque. "This is a blessing of God," a disciple told him, "Why do you get annoyed?"[105]

(ii) In the month of *Shawwal* 651/1252 Sultan Nasir-u'd-din marched towards Uch and Multan. On the way his soldiers decided to pay their respects to Shaikh Farid. When the soldiers flocked to the city all the streets and bazars of Ajodhan were blocked. It was impossible to shake hands and bless personally every one of these soldiers. A sleeve of Baba Farid's shirt was hung on a thoroughfare so that people might touch it and go. As the crowd moved, the sleeve was torn to pieces. The Shaikh himself was so painfully mobbed that he requested his disciples to encircle him in order to save his person from the eager public trying to elbow its way to him.[106]

Shaikh Farid trained and tutored a very large number of disciples who, later on, set up independent *khanqah*s and disseminated the teachings of the Chishti *silsilah*. Later mystic *tazkirah*s give legendary figures of the number of his *khalifah*s.[107] Mir Khurd, however, refers only to the following seven *khalifah*s of the Shaikh:

1. Shaikh Jamal-u'd-din Hansvi
2. Shaikh Najib-u'd-din Mutawakkil

105. *Fawa'id-u'l-Fu'ad*, pp. 145–46.
106. Ibid, p. 145
107. *Siyar-u'l-Aqtab*, p. 175. Mu'in-u'd-din 'Abdullah (*Ma'arij-u'l-Walayat* MS, Vol. I, p. 267) makes very curious statements in connection with the *khalifah*s of Shaikh Farid. He says that Shaikh Farid had 10,000 *khalifah*s on the earth, 18,000 in the sea, 400 in the air, 400 in the sky, and 400 on the *Kuh-i-Qaf*. The whole account is saturated with superstition and is incredible for our purposes.

3. Shaikh Badr-u'd-din Ishaq
4. Shaikh 'Ali Sabir
5. Shaikh 'Arif
6. Maulana Fakhr-u'd-din Safahani
7. Shaikh Nizam-u'd-din Auliya

Shaikh Jamal-u'd-din was one of the most cherished disciples of Shaikh Farid who used to say: "Jamal is our *jamal* (beauty)."[108] Shaikh Baha-u'd-din Zakariyya once offered to exchange all his disciples for him but Shaikh Farid replied that any such transaction was possible regarding *mal* (property), but not in case of *jamal* (beauty).[109] When Shaikh Jamal-u'd-din joined the discipline of Shaikh Farid he was the *khatib* of Hansi. At the instance of his Shaikh, he resigned his post and severed all ties with the government of the day. As one who had seen better days, the pangs of starvation proved too severe for him and, on one occasion, he requested Shaikh Nizam-u'd-din Auliya to inform Shaikh Farid about his miserable circumstances. Shaikh Farid, however, remarked:[110]

اورا بگوی چوں ولایت به کسی داده شود اورا واجب است استمالت

(Tell him that when a *wilayat*—spiritual territory—is assigned to anyone, it is his duty to bear its burden.)

Shaikh Jamal was a man of great learning. His two works—a Persian *diwan* and an Arabic treatise, *Mulhamat*—bear testimony to his scholarship.

Shaikh Jamal died during the lifetime of his master. His maid-servant, known as Umm-u'l-Muminin, took Maulana Burhan-u'd-din, son of Shaikh Jamal,[111] to the great Shaikh. Maulana Burhan was a boy of tender age at that time, but, regardless of this fact, the Shaikh conferred his *khilafat-namah*[112] on him and instructed him to benefit from the company of

---

108. *Siyar-u'l-Auliya*, p. 178.
109. *Gulzar-i-Abrar* (MS).
110. *Siyar-u'l-Auliya*, p. 180.
111. Shaikh Jamal had two sons. The elder one was a *majzub*, but sometimes he recovered consciousness and spoke very wisely. Once he told Shaikh Nizam-u'd-din Auliya: "Knowledge is a great veil." When asked to explain what he meant, he said: "Knowledge is distinct from truth and whatever is distinct from truth is a veil." *Siyar-u'l-Auliya*, p. 184.

For a detailed account of the descendants of Shaikh Jamal-u'd-din, see *Siraj-u'n-Nasab*, by Muhammad Siraj-u'l-Haqq (published in 1313 AH, Zia-u'l-Islam Press, Qadiyan).

112. Shaikh Farid also bestowed upon him the prayer carpet and the staff which Shaikh Jamal had left and remarked: 'You have the same authority from me as your father had.' *Siyar-u'l-Auliya*, pp. 182–83.

Shaikh Nizam-u'd-din at Delhi. The maid-servant, who was taken by surprise at this generosity of the Shaikh, submitted: '*Khwaja Burhan-u'd-din bala hai*' (Khwaja Burhan-u'd-din is a [mere] child.) Shaikh Farid promptly replied: '*Ponun ka chand bhi bala huta hai*' (The crescent moon is also small).[113]

Shaikh Burhan-u'd-din, however, did not enrol any disciples. "It is not meant for me," he used to say, "to enrol anyone as my disciple when Hazrat Nizam-u'd-din Muhammad is there."[114] Shaikh Qutb-u'd-din Munawwar,[115] a distinguished disciple and *khalifah* of Shaikh Nizam-u'd-din Auliya, was his son.

Shaikh Najib-u'd-din Mutawakkil[116] was the youngest brother of Shaikh Farid. He came to Delhi to complete his education, but, eventually, he decided to settle there permanently. "For seventy years," Shaikh Nizam-u'd-din Auliya once informed his audience, "Shaikh Najib-u'd-din lived in the city. He had neither property nor pension. He lived resigned to the will of God along with his family and passed his days happily. I have not seen anyone like him in the city."[117] Shaikh Farid had granted his Khilafat to him but we have no record of his disciples. He died a few months before Shaikh Farid and was buried outside the city, near the *Darwazah-i-Mandah*.[118]

113. Ibid, p. 183.

114. He had very great respect for Shaikh Nizam-u'd-din Auliya. Every time that he visited Delhi, Shaikh Nizam-u'd-din ordered a cot to be placed for him in his *jama'at khanah* but Shaikh Burhan-u'd-din, out of respect for the Shaikh, never slept on it. It is said that whenever he went to see the Shaikh he changed his clothes and perfumed himself. Ibid, pp. 183–84.

115. He was one of those three saints contemporary with Muhammad bin Tughluq—Shaikh Nasir-u'd-din Chiragh and Shaikh Shams-u'd-din Yahya being the other two—who kept alive the traditions of the Chishti *silsilah* at a very critical moment in its history and who refused to subordinate themselves to the dictates of the Sultan. For biographical details, see *Siyar-u'l-Auliya*, pp. 247–53. *Tarikh-i-Firoz Shahi*, '*Afif*, pp. 423–24; *Akhbar-u'l-Akhyar*, pp. 87–88; *Mir'at-u'l-Asrar* (MS), pp. 641–43; *Gulzar-i-Abrar* (MS); *Ma'arij-u'l-Walayat* (MS), Vol. I, pp. 298–303; *Matlub-u'l Talibin* (MS), f. 119a.

116. For brief biographical notices, see *Fawa'id-u'l-Fu'ad*, pp. 14–15, 28, 78–79; *Khair-u'l-Majalis*, pp. 75–76; *Siyar-u'l-'Arifin*, pp. 97–101; *Akhbar-u'l-Akhyar*, pp. 59–60; *Gulzar-i-Abrar* (MS); *Mir'at-u'l-Asrar* (MS); *Ma'arij-u'l-Walayat* (MS).

117. *Siyar-u'l-Auliya*, p. 167.

118. Ibid, p. 169.

Maulana Badr-u'd-din Ishaq,[119] another distinguished *khalifah* of Shaikh Farid, was an eminent scholar of Delhi. He used to perform the duties of personal service to the Shaikh and was in charge of the general supervision of his *jama'at khanah*. Besides, it was his duty to draft certificates of Khilafat. He did not enrol any disciple during the lifetime of his Shaikh, except the *muqta'* of Dipalpur, Malik Sharaf-u'd-din Kubra, about whom the Shaikh had instructed him to admit into his discipline.[120]

Maulana Badr-u'd-din Ishaq wrote a scholarly book on Arabic grammar—*Tasrif-i-Badari*[121]—which has not survived.

Shaikh Farid had married his daughter, Bibi Fatimah, to him. After the Shaikh's death, he shifted to the Juma' Masjid of Ajodhan and began to teach the Quran to boys of tender age. He was so deeply attached to his master that he did not long survive him. Shaikh Nizam-u'd-din Auliya, who was much indebted to him, called his family to Delhi and took a personal interest in the training and education of his sons.[122]

Shaikh 'Ala-u'd-din 'Ali b. Ahmad Sabir,[123] the founder of the Sabiri branch of the Chishti *silsilah*, is said to have been a prominent disciple of Shaikh Farid. It is most unfortunate that no early account of this great saint is available. No contemporary, or even semi-contemporary historian or *tazkirah* writer has referred to him. Literature about him becomes profuse from the time of Shah Jahan when the author of the *Siyar-u'l-Aqtab* wrote about him and the circumstances that led to the discovery of his grave in Kalyar, many years after his death.[124] The Sabiri *silsilah*, however, came into the full light of history when Shaikh Ahmad 'Abd-u'l-Haqq[125] (ob. 837/1433) established a great mystic centre at Rudauli (in the Barabanki district) and began to propagate the teachings of the *silsilah*.

---

119. For brief biographical notices, see *Fawa'id-u'l-Fu'ad*, pp. 59–74, etc.; *Siyar-u'l-Auliya*, pp. 162–78; *Khair-u'l-Majalis*, pp. 116–30, 137, 224; *Siyar-u'l-'Arifin*, pp. 42, 85, etc.; *Akhbar-u'l-Akhyar*, pp. 66–67; *Mir'at-u'l-Asrar* (MS); *Ma'arij-u'l-Walayat*, Vol. I (MS).

120. *Siyar-u'l-Auliya*, p. 175.

121. Ibid, p. 173.

122. Ibid, pp. 171–72.

123. For brief biographical notices, see *Akhbar-u'l-Akhyar*, p. 69; *Siyar-u'l-Aqtab*, pp. 177–84; *Mir'at-u'l-Asrar* (MS), Vol. I, p. 263–64.

124. *Siyar-u'l-Aqtab*, p. 183. Kalyar is near Roorkee in the Saharanpur District of Uttar Pradesh.

125. For brief biographical notices, see *Siyar-u'l-Aqtab*, pp. 215–22; *Akhbar-u'l-Akhyar*, pp. 182–84; *Mir'at-u'l-Asrar* (MS), p. 917, et seq.

Very brief and casual accounts of Shaikh 'Arif and Maulana Fakhr-u'd-din Safahani are found in the *Fawa'id-u'l-Fu'ad* and the *Siyar-u'l-Auliya*.

The most outstanding *khalifah* of Shaikh Farid was Shaikh Nizam-u'd-din Auliya.[126] It was under him that the Chishti *silsilah* reached its highest watermark.[127] For nearly half a century he lived and worked in Delhi. All sorts of men, says Barani, visited him and found spiritual solace in his company.[128] Almost all the spiritual descendants of the disciples of Shaikh Farid, as well as Shaikh Farid's own descendants, accepted him as their spiritual leader.[129]

Shaikh Nizam-u'd-din left for Ajodhan suddenly, without any previous preparation.[130] He met Shaikh Farid on a Wednesday in 655/1257.[131] The aging Shaikh discerned in him a true successor to himself, to Shaikh Qutb-u'd-din Bakhtiyar Kaki and, in fact, to all the great Chishti mystics of the past and welcomed him with the couplet:

$$ ای آتش فراقت دلها کباب کرده $$

$$ سیلاب اشتیاقت جانها خراب کرده $$

Shaikh Nizam-u'd-din excitedly struggled within himself to give expression to his own eagerness to see him, but his nerves failed him and he began to tremble. With great difficulty he told the saint:

$$ اشتیاق پابوس عظیم غالب بوده است $$

(I had a strong desire to meet you.)

"Every newcomer is nervous,"[132] remarked Shaikh Farid and admitted him into his discipline.

---

126. For his life and teachings, see *Fawa'id-u'l-Fu'ad, Siyar-u'l-Auliya, Khair-u'l-Majalis, Jawami'-u'l-Kilam*, and *Durar-i-Nizamiyah* (MS). See also *Siyar-u'l-'Arifin* (MS) 581; *Ma'arij-u'l-Walayat* (MS), Vol. I; *Gulzar-i-Abrar* (MS); *Matub-u't-Talibin* (MS); *A'in-i-Akbari*, II, pp. 208–09; *Tarikh-i-Ferishtah*, Vol. II, pp. 301–98; *Shajarat-u'l-Anwar* (MS); *Iqibas-u'l-Anwar* (MS), ff. 182a–86b; *Nafahat-u'l-Uns*, pp. 452–53.

127. *Tarikh-i-Firoz Shahi*, p. 363.

128. *A'in-i-Akbari*, Vol. II, p. 208.

129. For example, Shaikh Qutb-u'd-din Munawwar, Shaikh Kabir-u'd-din, Khwaja 'Aziz-u'd-din, Khwaja Muhammad, and Shaikh Kamal-u'd-din.

130. See *Nafahat-u'l-Uns*, p. 452; Shaikh Nizam-u'd-din spends a whole night in the Juma' Masjid of Delhi; in the morning he hears a mu'azzin recite the following verse; 'Has the time not come for the true believers that their hearts may tremble at the remembrance of the Lord.' (Quran, S. 57: 16) and decides to proceed to Ajodhan and lay his head at the feet of Shaikh Farid.

131. *Siyar-u'l-Auliya*, p. 106.

132. *Fawa'id-u'l-Fu'ad*, p. 30. *Siyar-u'l-Auliya*, p. 107.

"Should I give up my studies and devote myself exclusively to supererogatory prayers, *aurad*, and *waza'if?*," Shaikh Nizam-u'd-din asked his master after his initiation. "I never ask any one to discontinue his studies," replied Shaikh Farid, "Carry on both of them, and [finally] whichever gets the upper hand, devote yourself to that. Some knowledge is also necessary for a *dervish*."[133]

Shaikh Nizam-u'd-din visited Ajodhan three times during the lifetime of the great Shaikh.[134] During his second visit, he studied with him six chapters of the Quran, five chapters of the *'Awarif-u'l-Ma'arif*, and two other books.[135] In Jamadi I, 664/1265 Shaikh Nizam-u'd-din visited his master for the last time. The Shaikh showered many blessings on him and said: "I have given you both the worlds. Go and take the kingdom of Hindustan."[136]

On Ramadan 13, 664/1265, Shaikh Farid granted his *khilafat namah* to Shaikh Nizam-u'd-din Auliya and instructed him to devote his life to the propagation of the Chishti mystic principles. Barani has given us a detailed account of the popularity and influence of the Shaikh. He writes: "Shaikh Nizam-u'd-din had opened wide the doors of his discipleship...and admitted [all sorts of people into his discipline] nobles and plebians, rich and poor, learned and illiterate, citizens and villagers, soldiers and warriors, freemen and slaves,[137] and these people refrained from many improper things, because they considered themselves disciples of the Shaikh; if any of the disciples committed a sin, he confessed it (before the Shaikh) and vowed allegiance anew." The general public showed an inclination to religion and prayer; men and women, young and old, shop-keepers and servants, children and slaves, all came to say their prayers. Most of them who visited the Shaikh frequently, offered their *Chasht*[138] and *Ishraq* prayers regularly. Many platforms, with thatched roofs over them, were constructed on the way from the city to Ghiyaspur; wells were dug, water

133. *Siyar-u'l-Auliya*, p. 107.

134. *Fawa'id-u'l-Fu'ad*, p. 42.

135. Ibid, p. 163, *Siyar-u'l-Auliya*, p. 106.

136. Ibid, pp. 131–32.

137. For the Shaikh's explanation for admitting all sorts of people into his discipleship, see *Siyar-u'l-Auliya*, pp. 346–48, where the author gives a long extract from Zia-u'd-din Barani's *Hasrat Namah* which is no longer extant.

138. In addition to the five compulsory (*farz*) prayers—*Fajr, Zuhr, 'Asr, Maghrib,* and *'Isha*—there are five recommended (*sunnat*) prayers (i) *Ishraq,* offered after sunrise; (ii) *Chasht,* offered at forenoon; (iii) *Zawal,* offered after midday; (iv) *Awabin,* offered at twilight; and (v) *Tahajjud,* offered between midnight and early dawn.

vessels were kept, carpets were spread, and a servant and a *hafiz* was stationed at every platform so that the people going to the Shaikh might have no difficulty in saying their supererogatory prayers. Due to regard for the Shaikh's discipleship all talk of sinful acts had disappeared from the people. There were no topics of conversation among most people except inquiries about the prayers of *Chasht*, *Awabin*, and *Tahajjud*. How many genuflections (*rak'at*s) do they comprise? What *Surah* of the Quran to recite in each *rak'at*? What invocations (*du'a*) are to follow each prayer? How many *rak'at*s does the Shaikh say every night; and what part of the Quran in every *rak'at* and what *darud*s (blessing on the Prophet)? What was the custom of Shaikh Farid and Shaikh Bakhtiyar? Such were the questions which the new disciples asked from the old. They inquired about fasting and prayer and about reducing their diet. Many persons took to committing the Quran to memory. The new disciples of the Shaikh were entrusted to the old. And the older disciples had no other occupation but prayer and worship, aloofness from the world, the study of books on devotion and the lives of saints. And God forbid that they should ever talk or hear about worldly affairs or turn towards the houses of worldly men, for such things they considered to be entirely sinful and wrong. Interest in supererogatory prayers alone had developed to such an extent that at the Sultan's court many *amir*s, clerks, guards, and royal slaves had become the Shaikh's disciples. They said their *Chasht* and *Ishraq* prayers and fasted on the thirteenth, fourteenth, and fifteenth of every lunar month (*Ayyam-i-Biz*) as well as during the first ten days of *Zil Hijjah*. There was no quarter of the city in which a gathering of the pious was not held every month or after every twenty days with mystic songs that moved them to tears. Many disciples of the Shaikh finished the *tarawih*[139] prayers in their houses or in the mosques. Those with greater perseverence passed the whole night standing in their prayers throughout the month of Ramadan, on Fridays, and during the days of the Hajj. The higher disciples stood in the prayers for a third or three-fourths of the night throughout the years, while others said their morning prayers with the ablution of their *'Isha* prayer. Some of the disciples had, reached eminence in spiritual power through this education.

Owing to the influence of the Shaikh, most of the Mussalmans of this country developed an interest in mysticism, prayers, and aloofness from the world, and came to have a faith in the Shaikh. The hearts of men having become virtuous by good deeds, the very name of wine, gambling, and

---

139. The prayers of usually twenty *rak'at*s, recited at night during the month of Ramazan.

other forbidden things never came to anyone's lips. Sins and abominable vices appeared to the people as bad as unbelief. Out of regard for one another the Mussalmans refrained from open usury and regrating (*ihtikar*), while shopkeepers, from fear, gave up speaking lies, using false weights, and deceiving the ignorant. Most of the scholars and learned men, who frequented the Shaikh's company, applied themselves to books on devotion and mysticism. The books *Qut-u'l-Qulub*,[140] *Ihya-u'l 'Ulum*,[141] and its translation,[142] *'Awarif*,[143] *Kashf-u'l-Mahjub*,[144] *Shrah-i-Ta'arruf*,[145] *Risalah-i-Qushairi*,[146] *Marsad-u'l-'Ibad*,[147] *Maktubat-i-'Ain-u'l-Quzzat*,[148] and the *Lawa'ih* and *Lawama* 'of Qazi Hamid-u'd-din Nagauri[149] found many purchasers, as also did the *Fawa'id-u'l-Fu'ad* of Amir Hasan owing to the sayings of the Shaikh which it contains. People asked the booksellers about books of devotion. No handkerchief was seen without a toothbrush (*miswak*) or a comb tied to it. Owing to the great number of purchasers, the price of water and eathern vessels became high. In short, God had created the Shaikh as a peer of Shaikh Junaid[150] and Shaikh Bayazid[151] in these later days and adorned him with that divine love which cannot be understood by human wisdom. The virtues of a Shaikh—and the

140. Written by Maulana Abu Talib Macci (ob. 996 AD) published from Cairo in 2 volumes in 1310/1892.

141. Written by Imam Ghazzali (ob. 1111 AD) published from Cairo in 1311/1893.

142. That is *Kimiya-i-Sa'adat* (Newal Kishore, Lucknow, 1324/1907).

143. Written by Shaikh Shihab-u'd-din Suhrawardi (ob. 1234 AD) first published in Cairo in the margins of the *Ihya* of Imam Ghazzali.

144. Written by Shaikh 'Ali Hajweri (ob. after 1074 AD), Persian text (*Gulzar-i-Hind*, Steam Press, Lahore); English translation by R.A. Nicholson (Luzac, 1936).

145. *Kitab-i-Ta'arruf* was written by Abu Bakr Muhammad bin Ibrahim Bukhari (ob. 999 AD).

It is one of the classics on Islamic mysticism. The author of *Kashf-u'z-Zunun* quotes a saying of the mystics about this book: 'One who does not know *Ta'arruf*, does not understand mysticism.'

146. Written by Abu'l-Qasim 'Abdu'l-Karim Qushairi (ob. 1072 AD). Published from Cairo in 1346 AH/1927 AD.

147. Written by Najm-u'd-din Razi in 1123 AD.

148. 'Ain-u'l-Quzzat Hamadani (ob. 1130 AD).

149. See *infra*.

150. Abu'l-Qasim B. Muhammad b. Junaid (ob. 910 AD). See *Kashf-u'l-Mahjub* (trans.), pp. 128–30.

151. Bayazid Taifur Bistami (ob. 875 AD). See ibid, p. 106, et seq.

art of leading men (in the mystic path)—found their fulfilment and their final consummation in him.

زین فن مطلب نامی

کان ختم شد است بر نظامی

(Do not try to obtain eminence in this art, for it has come to an end with Nizami.)[152]

PERSONAL AND FAMILY LIFE OF THE CHISHTI SAINTS

Most of the Chishti saints lived under conditions of appalling poverty. They looked down upon the possession of private property as a serious impediment to the growth of one's spiritual personality. Shaikh Mu'in-u'd-din and Shaikh Qutb-u'd-din Bakhtiyar never owned houses of their own. Shaikh Farid Ganj-i-Shakar built a small *kuchcha* house[153] only when his family had considerably increased during the later years of his life. He, however, firmly turned down the offer of a disciple to rebuild this house with baked bricks. "Mas'ud will not put brick on brick," he told his disciple.[154] Shaikh Farid's younger brother, Shaikh Najib-u'd-din Mutawakkil, lived in Delhi, with his wife and two sons, in a house which consisted of a single small room. It was under a broken *chappar* (thatched roof) over this room that he entertained his visitors.[155] For many years during his early life Shaikh Nizam-u'd-din Auliya had to wander from one quarter of the city to another in search of a roof to hide his head.[156] It was towards the end of Balban's reign that he settled at Ghiyaspur and built a house for himself because without it he could not have the peace of mind necessary for fulfilling his mystic mission. Thus a small *kuchcha* house was the only exception which the Chishti mystics made to their interdict against the possession of private property. Shaikh Nasir-u'd-din Chiragh, however, did not like even this exception.[157]

Generally, starvation conditions prevailed in the houses of the Chishti saints. They subsisted mostly on *futuh* (unsolicited charity). Shaikh Hamid-u'd-din Nagauri was probably the only Chishti saint of the thirteenth century who adopted cultivation in preference to *futuh*. Shaikh Farid

---

152. *Tarikh-i-Firoz Shahi*, pp. 343–47.

153. When Shaikh Farid died, a door of this house was pulled down to provide unbaked bricks for his grave. *Fawa'id-u'l-Fu'ad*, p. 212.

154. *Siyar-u'l-Auliya*, p. 90.

155. *Khair-u'l-Majalis*, p. 75.

156. *Siyar-u'l-Auliya*, pp. 108–11.

157. *Khair-u'l-Majalis*, p. 233.

Ganj-i-Shakar was forced by his circumstances to permit his disciples to circulate *zanbil* (a bowl made from dried and hollow gourd) and collect food.[158] No Chishti saint before him had permitted such a practice. In fact, even incurring of debts for household expenses was considered unbecoming of a mystic. Shaikh Farid had once declared: "The dervishes prefer dying of starvation to incurring any debt for the satisfaction of their (baser) desires. Debt and Resignation are poles apart and cannot subsist together."[159]

When Shaikh Qutb-u'd-din Bakhtiyar settled in Delhi, his household, including his wife, children, and servants, consisted of nine souls in all.[160] When reduced to extremes, he borrowed up to 300 *dirhams* from a grocer (*baqqal*) who lived in his neighbourhood.[161] His spiritual mentor had permitted him to borrow up to 500 *dirhams*, but he instructed his grocer friend not to lend him more than 300 *dirhams*.[162] Later on the Shaikh decided to starve rather than incur any debts.[163] Following the same traditions, Shaikh Farid Ganj-i-Shakar and his brother, Najib-u'd-din Mutawakkil, quietly suffered the pangs of starvation but never borrowed anything from anybody. There were times when some *futuh* came to Shaikh Farid, but generally the atmosphere of his household remained one of starvation. In the closing years of his life, he was in extremely difficult circumstances and the door of *futuh* seemed to have been closed upon him. Almost the same was the condition of Shaikh Najib. Once some *qalandars* came to greet him on an 'Eid day. Shaikh Najib had nothing to entertain them with. Only by selling some household article might he able to buy food for his guests. He considered his wife's *daman*; it was torn and patched and could fetch no price. He considered his prayer carpet; it was no better. Failing to provide anything for the visitors, he offered cold water to them.[164] When Bibi Fatimah, a pious and saintly lady of Delhi, came to know of the starving conditions of Shaikh Najib's household, she helped the family from time to time.[165]

158. Ibid, p. 150; *Siyar-u'l-Auliya*, p. 66.

159. Ibid, p. 66; *Siyar-u'l-'Arifin*, p. 62.

160. Ibid, p. 24.

161. *Siyar-u'l-Auliya*, p. 48.

162. Ibid, pp. 48–49.

163. Jamali says that one day, during the course of their conversation, the grocer's wife told the wife of the Shaikh: "But for us you would have died of starvation." The Shaikh and his wife were deeply pained at this remark and they decided not to borrow anything in future from the grocer. *Siyar-u'l-'Arifin*, pp. 25–26.

164. *Khair-u'l-Majalis*, p. 75.

165. *Fawa'id-u'l-Fu'ad*, p. 245; *Siyar-u'l-'Arifin*, pp. 101–02.

Shaikh Nizam-u'd-din Auliya also passed his early years under the same distressing circumstances. "In the days of Ghiyas-u'd-din Balban," he used to say in his later years, "melons were sold, at the rate of two *jital* per maund, but once nearly the whole season passed away without my being able to taste a slice. On one occasion I had to go without food for a night and a day, and half the second night had passed before I got anything to eat; two *seers* of bread could be had for a *jital*, but from sheer poverty I was unable to purchase anything in the market. My mother, sister, and other persons in my house suffered along with me. Though at times visitors brought some sugar or pieces of good cloth to me, I did not sell them to purchase food and sat resigned to my fate. On one occasion we had starved for three days when a man knocked at my door with a bowl of *khichri*. I have never found anything so delicious as that plain *khichri* appeared to me then. 'We are the guests of God today,' my mother used to say when we had no food left in the house."[166]

The Chishti saints considered fasting to be 'a remarkable expedient for weakening those desires that lead never to happiness but either to disillusionment or to further desire.' They reduced their diet in order to control the calls of the flesh. A glass of *sherbet*, some dried grapes (*munaqqa*), and a piece of *juwar* (millet) bread smeared with *ghee* was all that Shaikh Farid took in twenty-four hours.[167] Similarly, Shaikh Nizam-u'd-din took only a piece of bread or half a piece with a little vegetable at the time of *iftar* (breaking the fast), and very little food at dinner. One day 'Abdur Rahim, who prepared *sahri*[168] for the Shaikh, protested: "The Shaikh eats very little at *sahri* also, it will injure his health and make him very weak." The Shaikh replied with tears in his eyes: "So many poverty-stricken people are sleeping without dinner in the corners of the mosques and before the shops. How can this food go down my throat?"[169]

Very often these saints did not possess sufficient clothes to cover their bodies.[170] Shaikh Mu'in-u'd-din wrapped himself in a patched *do-tahi* (two-plied cloth).[171] Shaikh Farid felt great spiritual pleasure in his grimy and tattered clothes.[172] When Shaikh Nizam-u'd-din Auliya reached Ajodhan, his clothes were so grimy that Bibi Rani, a pious and devoted

---

166. *Siyar-u'l-Auliya*, p. 113. *Khichri* is rice boiled with lentils.
167. *Fawa'id-u'l-Fu'ad*, p. 51. *Siyar-u'l-Auliya*, pp. 65, 386; *Akhbar-u'l-Akhyar*, p. 51.
168. The meal which is taken before the dawn to enable one to fast till sunset.
169. *Siyar-u'l-Auliya*, p. 128.
170. Ibid, pp. 62–63.
171. *Siyar-u'l-'Arifin*, p. 7.
172. *Siyar-u'l-Auliya*, p. 62; *Akhbar-u'l-Akhyar*, p. 51.

lady at the *jama'at khanah* of Shaikh Farid, gave him a *chadar* with which he covered his body and then she washed his clothes and patched them.[173]

It is said that Shaikh Qutb-u'd-din Bakhtiyar never used any bedding.[174] Shaikh Farid had a blanket (*galim*) on which he used to sit during the day. It was spread out on a loosely woven cot at bedtime, but it was so small that it did not cover the whole cot. A rug (*shuqqah*) was placed at the end of the cot. If the Shaikh covered his body with it, the end of the cot remained without any cover. The Shaikh had no pillow; instead, he put his staff (*asa'*) under his head.[175]

With the exception of Shaikh Nizam-u'd-din Auliya,[176] all the early Chishti mystics led a married life. Shaikh Mu'in-u'd-din married in his old age[177] only to realize that his spiritual powers had seriously suffered on that account. The *Sarur-u's-Sudur* says that one day he asked Shaikh Hamid-u'd-din Nagauri:

حمید ! چیست این که هرگاه مارا در جوانی که مجرد بوده ایم
حاجتی بشدی' دعا میکردیم درحال اجابت شدی' و این ساعت
که پیر شدیم و فرزندان آمدند 'هرگاه که حاجتی می شود بسیار
می باید و دعا هم کرده شود و لیکن بعد از دیرتیر با جابت می رسد
و حاجت بر می آید' این حکمت چیست؟

(Hamid! How is it that in my youth when I was a bachelor, whenever I had a need, I prayed for it and it was granted forthwith. Now that I have grown old and have begotten sons, whenever there is a need, however pressing it may be, and I pray for it, it is granted only belatedly. What is the mystery behind it?)[178]

173. *Siyar-u'l-Auliya*, p. 115.

174. Ibid, p. 49.

175. *Fawa'id-u'l-Fu'ad*, pp. 51–52; *Siyar-u'l-Auliya*, p. 65; *Akhbar-u'l-Akhyar*, p. 51.

176. His chief disciple at Delhi, Shaikh Nasir-u'd-din Chiragh, also did not marry, but his life and activities do not count for the period under review. It may, however, be pointed out here that though Shaikh Nizam-u'd-din Auliya and Shaikh Nasir-u'd-din Chiragh did not marry, they looked after their nephews and nieces with almost paternal concern and care. For Shaikh Nizam-u'd-din Auliya's views about marriage, see *Fawa'id-u'l-Fu'ad*, pp. 156, 157.

177. The *Sarur-u's-Sudur* says that he was 90 when be reached Ajmer (p. 18) and was a celibate till then. Shaikh 'Abdul Haqq says in *Akhbar-u'l-Akhyar* (p. 113) that the Prophet had asked him in a dream not to ignore his *sunnat* of leading a married life.

178. Quran, S. XIX: 25.

Shaikh Hamid replied:

"یا شیخ! شمارا بهتر روشن است از قصهٔ مریم' دراں وقت که
مجرد بود بی خواست او میوهٔ زمستانی بتابستان می رسید
ومیوهٔ تابستانی بزمستان می آمد که دلش به خدا یکتا بود' چوں
عیسیٰ علیه السلام بزاد' مریم علیهاالسلام منتظر بود که هم
چناں خواهد رسید' فرمان آمد : ٥وهُزّی الیک بجذع النخلة"

(O Shaikh! This may be clearer to you from the story of Mary. When she was
a maiden, she used to receive winter fruits in summer and summer fruits in
winter, without her asking for them, for her heart was exclusively devoted
to God. When Christ (peace be upon him) was born, Mary expected to receive
(the fruits) as usual. But she was told: '*And shake towards thyself the trunk
of the palm-tree.*')[179]

Shaikh 'Abdul Haqq says that Shaikh Mu'in-u'd-din took two wives—
Ummat-ullah and 'Asmatullah. The first was the daughter of a Hindu raja;
the second was the daughter of Sayyid Wajih-u'd-din Meshedi, uncle of
Sayyid Husain Meshedi.[180] The Shaikh had three sons—Shaikh Abu
Sa'id, Shaikh Fakhr-u'd-din, and Shaikh Husam-u'd-din—and one
daughter—Bibi Jamal—from these wives.[181] Bibi Jamal had strong mystic
leanings but his sons were not inclined towards mysticism. Nothing is
known about Abu Sa'id; Shaikh Fakhr-u'd-din took to farming at Mandal,
near Ajmer; while Husam-u'd-din disappeared mysteriously. None of them
seems to have made any contribution towards the expansion of the *silsilah*.[182]
On the contrary, once they obliged their aged father to part with the
traditions of his *silsilah*. It was due to the pressure exercised by his sons
that he came to Delhi in order to obtain a *muqarrar dasht* from the Sultan
permitting them to cultivate some fallow land near Ajmer.[183]

179. *Sarur-u's-Sudur* (MS), p. 18.
180. *Akhbar-u'l-Akhyar*, pp. 112–13.
181. Ibid, p. 113.
182. Khwaja Wahid-u'd-din, a grandson of Khwaja Mu'in-u'd-din, came to
Ajodhan and requested Shaikh Farid to enrol him among his disciples. The saint
apologetically said: "I have been as a beggar picking up crumbs from your family.
It would be against my sense of respect to extend my hand to you as a *pir*. But
Khwaja Wahid insisted and the Shaikh had no alternative but to admit him into
his discipline." *Fawa'id-u'l-Fu'ad*, p. 238.
183. *Siyar-u'l-Auliya*, p. 53.

Shaikh Qutb-u'd-din Bakhtiyar also married late in life and probably married twice. He divorced one of his wives, soon after marriage, as her presence had upset his daily programme of prayers.[184] He had two twin-born sons.[185] One of them died in infancy. The Shaikh was so deeply engrossed in his mystic contemplation that he did not know about his ailment. When he heard cries and laments rising from his house, he asked people what had happened. When he came to know that his son had expired, he said woefully: 'Had I been aware of his illness, I would have prayed to God for his recovery.'[186] Shaikh Nizam-u'd-din Auliya informs us that the surviving son of the Shaikh was not worthy of his father and did not follow his footsteps.[187]

Shaikh Farid had a number of wives and a big family. Shaikh Nasir-u'd-din Chiragh is reported to have stated on the authority of his master that Shaikh Farid-u'd-din had many wives (حرم بسیار بود).[188] The Shaikh treated them all justly and equitably so far as the marital relationship was concerned,[189] but to provide for this large family was always a problem for him, particularly in the closing years of his life when no *futuh* came to him. Very often his family had to starve. The maid-servant would come and report: "Khwaja! This son of yours has starved for two days," or "This wife of yours has starved for two days." But these reports, Shaikh Nasir-u'd-din Chiragh tells us, were like a passing wind for him.[190]

One day a wife of the Shaikh told him: "Khwaja! Today my son is about to expire from starvation." The Shaikh raised his head and said: "What has poor Mas'ud to do in this matter? If Fate has so decreed and he dies, tie a rope round his feet and throw him out and come back."[191]

Even a cursory glance at the household atmosphere of these early Chishti saints would reveal the painful fact that, with the exception of Shaikh Hamid-u'd-din Nagauri, no saint gave sufficient care to the upbringing of his children. They were always so absorbed in their mystic contemplation and so busy in attending to the problems of the people, that they knew neither about the illness of their children nor about the starving conditions of their own household. Thus deprived of that fatherly control

184. Ibid, p. 50.
185. *Fawa'id-u'l-Fu'ad*, p. 61.
186. Ibid, pp. 61–62; *Siyar-u'l-Auliya*, p. 49.
187. *Fawa'id-u'l-Fu'ad*, p. 61.
188. *Siyar-u'l-Auliya*, p. 66.
189. Ibid, p. 194.
190. *Khair-u'l-Majalis*, p. 89; *Siyar-u'l-Auliya*, pp. 66–67.
191. Ibid, p. 67; *Akhbar-u'l-Akhyar*, p. 52.

and care which alone can guarantee proper training of children, most of the sons and dependents of the Chishti saints turned out to be worldly people, unworthy of the traditions of the *silsilah*. No son of an early Chishti saint of India was mentally or spiritually in a position to keep the torch of his father burning. If the only son of Shaikh Qutb-u'd-din Bakhtiyar was "unworthy of his father,"[192] a grandson of Shaikh Farid was a drunkard[193] and a grandson of Shaikh Najib-u'd-din was a vagabond (مرد لاابالی).[194] They possessed worldly wisdom,[195] but were devoid of all spiritual integrity.[196] The way in which Shaikh Badr-u'd-din Ishaq was treated by the sons of Shaikh Farid[197] shows that they were guided more by material and mundane considerations than by any high moral or spiritual ideal. This was probably due to the indifferent family atmosphere in which they were brought up.

THE CHISHTI *KHANQAH*S

A Chishti *khanqah* usually consisted of a big hall (*jama'at khanah*) where all the inmates lived communally. The roof of this *jama'at khanah* was supported by a number of pillars and at the foot of each of these pillars a mystic could be seen with all his belongings—bedding, books, and rosary. They all slept, prayed, and studied on the ground and no discrimination, not even on the basis of seniority or piety, was permitted to prevail in the *jama'at khanah*. If food was available, all would partake of it; if not, all would suffer jointly the pangs of hunger. In the *jama'at khanah* of Shaikh Farid, the inmates had to pluck *pelu* and *delah*[198] from

---

192. *Fawa'id-u'l-Fu'ad*, p. 61.
193. Ibid, pp. 147–48.
194. *Khair-u'l-Majalis*, p. 106.
195. One very interesting instance of this worldly wisdom was the suggestion of Shaikh Farid's son, Nizam-u'd-din, to bury the Shaikh in his own house. When Shaikh Farid died, his descendants decided to bury him in a graveyard, outside the city, where the Shaikh used to spend much of his time in prayers and meditation. Nizam-u'd-din dissuaded his brothers from burying the saint outside the city. "If the Shaikh is buried outside the city walls," he told his brothers and relatives, "people would come there, pray at the tomb and depart. Who will take notice of the Shaikh's family?"—*Siyar-u'l-Auliya*, pp. 89–91.
196. See ibid, pp. 121–22, for the way in which the sons of Shaikh Farid quarrelled with Sayyid Muhammad Kirmani for mentioning Shaikh Nizam-u'd-din Auliya's name in the last moments of Shaikh Farid's life.
197. Ibid, pp. 171–72.
198. Wild fruits of thorny plants found in the Punjab and used as food.

the *kareel* trees, fetch water, collect wood from the jungle, and then a saltless dish could be prepared for them.[199] The entire household rejoiced when the efforts of these people succeeded in providing a square meal for the inmates of the *jama'at khanah*.[200] But other Chishti saints, who received large amounts of unasked for charity, provided better meals for the inmates of and visitors to their *khanqahs*. An open kitchen (*langar*), consequently, became a regular feature of *khanqah* life in medieval India.[201] The Chishtis quoted the following *hadis* in favour of their practice: "If someone visits a living man and gets nothing from him to eat; it is as if he had visited the dead."[202] A Chishti mystic would sell his wife's *chadar* or his own prayer carpet but would entertain a visitor to his *khanqah*. If nothing at all was available, he would respectfully offer a bowl of water.[203] The visitors would understand that their host was under extremely straitened circumstances, they would drink water, and take leave.

A Shaikh was always the central figure of a *khanqah*.[204] Around him revolved its entire organization and from him it derived its hue and colour. It was, therefore, necessary for a Shaikh to follow his daily programme (*zabitah*) meticulously. This programme, however, was not the same for all saints. It differed according to local conditions and the personal inclinations and preferences of a saint. Fortunately for us, the medieval records have preserved some details about the daily programme of the two Chishti saints of the period, Shaikh Farid and Shaikh Nizam-u'd-din Auliya.

199. *Fawa'id-u'l-Fu'ad*, p. 74; *Khair-u'l-Majalis*, pp. 138–50; *Siyar-u'l-Auliya*, pp. 86, 209.

200. Shaikh Nizam-u'd-din Auliya once said about the *khanqah* of his master:

در آن شب که ڈیله .... درخانۂ شیخ سیر می خوردیم مارا روزعید بودی

Khair-u'l-Majalis, p. 150.

201. The tradition of an open kitchen (*langar*) among the Indian Chishti saints was probably established by Shaikh Farid. We do not hear about any *langar* in the hospice of Khwaja Mu'in-u'd-din, while it is explicitly mentioned about Khwaja Qutb-u'd-din Bakhtiyar that کانسه وکندوری نداشت (*Siyar-u'l-Auliya*, p. 48). Shaikh Farid's *langar* did not function regularly as very often he had no *futuh* which alone could keep a *langar* going. During his earlier years, Shaikh Nizam-u'd-din Auliya also did not have a *langar*. His friends and companions very often starved. Later on, when *futuh* came to him, he established a *langar* which distributed free food to people from early morning till late into the night.

202. *Fawa'id-u'l-Fu'ad*, p. 136.

203. *Khair-u'l-Majalis*, p. 75.

204. For a detailed discussion of the relation between a Shaikh and his disciples, see *Misbah-u'l-Hidayah*, pp. 166–73.

1. Shaikh Farid's day began very early in the morning. After offering his morning (*fajr*) prayers, he remained in prostration (*sajdah*) for two hours. The doors of his room were closed when he was engaged in prayers and no one could enter it so long as he was busy in his contemplation. After the *zuhr* prayers, the Shaikh received his visitors and never retired unless he had attended to the problem of every visitor. "There can be no pleasure in devotions so long as there remains a single needy person at the door," he used to say. These interviews being over, be again busied himself in prayers and meditation. After *iftar* he would call some elder disciple and ask him about the affairs of the *jama'at khanah* and the happenings of the day.

    ام روز چه حال بود و چه گذشت[205]

2. In spite of his indifferent health,[206] Shaikh Nizam-u'd-din Auliya meticulously followed his daily programme. He fasted almost continuously. An hour before dawn, Khwaja 'Abdur Rahim knocked at the door and presented *sahri*.[207] The Shaikh then offered his morning (*fajr*) prayers in congregation and then busied himself in meditation. After sunrise, the Shaikh would sit on his prayer carpet, facing the *qiblah* and visitors would come to him in large numbers. Every visitor would bring some present—cloth, cash, or sweets— which was distributed among those present. At about mid-day, the Shaikh retired to a room adjoining the *jama'at khanah* for a short rest but even at this time he was occasionally disturbed.[208] After waking up from his mid-day rest, the Shaikh would again attend to his visitors and after the *zuhr* prayers he would retire to his room on the roof and visitors would be called there and interviews would go on, with a break for the *'asr* prayers, until sunset. At *iftar* time, he left his wooden chamber and came down to the *jama'at khanah*. A piece of bread with a little vegetable was placed before him to break his fast. He ate only part of it and distributed the rest to his audience.

---

205. *Fawa'id-u'l-Fu'ad*, p. 160.

206. *Khair-u'l-Majalis*, p. 257.

207. *Siyar-u'l-Auliya*, p. 128.

208. Once a *dervish* came to the *jama'at khanah* while the Shaikh was having his mid-day rest. Akhi Siraj sent him away. Shaikh Farid appeared to Shaikh Nizam-u'd-din Auliya in a dream and said: "If you have nothing to give to a visitor, at least treat him cordially." On waking up, the Shaikh reprimanded Akhi Siraj and gave an order that he was to be awakened from his rest if a visitor came. Ibid. p. 129.

He then offered his *maghrib* prayers in congregation and retired to his room on the upper storey where he granted interviews to visitors till the *'isha* prayers. Dinner was served upstairs. The Shaikh then came down to offer *'isha* prayers in congregation and, soon after it, returned to his room to spend some time in devotions. Then he sat down on his cot with a rosary in his hand. No disciple, except Amir Khusrau and some children and relations of the Shaikh, could remain with him at this time. When Amir Khusrau and the children had left, his personal attendant would come, place some vessels in readiness for his ablutions, and retire. The Shaikh would then get up and bolt the door. From that time onwards, he was alone, busy in meditation and prayers. The inmates of the *khanqah* saw the Shaikh's light burning throughout the silent hours of the night.[209]

Broadly speaking, the inmates of a *khanqah* had to perform two types of duties: personal service to the Shaikh and cooperative management of the *jama'at khanah*. Usually some senior disciple was given overall charge of the *khanqah* administration and it was his duty to see that every part of the machinery performed its function smoothly. In the *khanqah* of Shaikh Farid, Maulana Badr-u'd-din Ishaq performed this duty of general supervision. He kept an eye on every detail of *khanqah* life, assigned duties to the inmates, looked after the guests, and arranged for the distribution of *futuh*.

Generally, the inmates of a *jama'at khanah* rendered the following personal services to the Shaikh:

1. *Personal attendance*: One in personal attendance on the Shaikh had to be available to him at fixed hours. Maulana Badr-u'd-din Ishaq performed this service for Shaikh Farid and Iqbal and Mubashshir for Shaikh Nizam-u'd-din Auliya. How exacting this duty was may be estimated from the following incident: One day Shaikh Farid called Maulana Badr-u'd-din Ishaq who could not respond immediately as he was lost in his mystic contemplation. The Shaikh was so displeased with him on that count that when the Maulana came to him, he said: "All your previous prayers and devotions have been lost. Busy yourself in your work again."[210]

---

209. Three books—*Fawa'id-u'l-Fu'ad* of Amir Hasan, *Khair-u'l-Majalis* of Hamid Qalandar, and *Siyar-u'l-Auliya* of Amir Khurd—taken collectively shed light on almost every aspect of the Shaikh's life, character, and teachings.

210. *Siyar-u'l-Auliya*, p. 177.

2. *Ablutions*: One to whom this duty was assigned had to arrange for the five-time ablutions of the Shaikh. Khwaja Ahmad Siwistani had to perform this duty in the *khanqah* of Shaikh Farid.[211] He was sometimes asked to wash the saint's clothes also. Before washing the clothes of the Shaikh, he himself performed ablution and then touched the clothes. For some time Sayyid Nur-u'd-din Kirmani had rendered this service to Shaikh Nizam-u'd-din Auliya.[212] Later on this duty was assigned to Iqbal.[213]

3. *Personal and private affairs*: Only one Chishti saint of the period, Shaikh Farid, is reported to have appointed a disciple to look after his personal and private affairs. Amir Khurd writes about 'Isa:

در خلوت خدمت کردی و حرمی را که نوبت او بودی بخدمت
شیخ شیوخ العالم فرستادی و نوبت این مشغل نگاهداشتی تا
عدل دریں کار مرعی ماند

(He helped the Shaikh even in these private matters. He used to send the Shaikh's wives to him according to their turn. He looked after this affair so that justice might be done in marital relationships also.)[214]

4. *Food*: Since the Chishti saints very often fasted, one of the inmates was assigned the duty of presenting *sahri* and *iftar* to the saint at the fixed hours.[215]

5. *Prayer carpet*: To some one of his cherished disciples, the Shaikh entrusted the duty of carrying his *musalla* (prayer carpet) to the mosque. Khwaja Abu Bakr was assigned this duty by Shaikh Nizam-u'd-din Auliya and, consequently, he came to be known as Abu Bakr *musalladar*.[216]

Besides these services of a personal nature, the inmates had to share the responsibility of running the *jama'at khanah*. The following were usually among the duties:

---

211. *Siyar-u'l-Auliya*, p. 86.
212. Ibid, p. 108.
    The Sayyid is reported to have said:

خدمت خاص از وضو سازانیدن و کلوخ در مستراح بردن وجز
آں و الدمی فرمود که من می کردم

213. Ibid, p. 126.
214. Ibid, p. 194.
215. Ibid, pp. 108, 128.
216. Ibid, pp. 204–05.

(i)   *Provision of fuel for the kitchen*: In the *jama'at khanah* of Shaikh
      Farid every inmate had, in turn, to perform the duty of collecting
      wood in the jungle. *Khanqahs* with better resources did not approve
      of this practice.

(ii) *Kitchen*: Preparation of food and its proper distribution in the
      jama'at khanah was an important duty and was assigned to a very
      resourceful and efficient person. How sternly a Shaikh dealt with a
      person who was found guilty of any act of omission or commission
      may be estimated from the incident of Shaikh Burhan-u'd-din
      Gharib.[217]

(iii) *Khilafat Namah*: Some senior disciple, with high scholarly
      attainments, was entrusted with the most responsible job of drafting
      the *khilafat namahs*.[218]

(iv) *Ta'wiz*: Since huge crowds assembled in the *jama'at khanahs* for
      ta'wiz (amulets) and it was not possible for a Shaikh to write out
      ta'wiz personally, some senior disciple had to do this work on his
      behalf.[219]

(v)   *Guests*: Some disciple had to look after the casual visitors who came
      to the *jama'at khanah* for a brief stay.

RESIDENTS OF THE *KHANQAH*S

If any single place in medieval India could help us study the reactions of
sensitive souls to the social and economic conditions then prevailing in
the country, it was the *jama'at khanah* of the Chishti saints. Here came
people disgusted, morose, and frustrated; with their personalities torn by
inner conflicts (*tafraqa*) and their hearts bleeding at the atrocities of the
external world. The mystic teacher not only soothed their excited nerves
but also integrated their personalities to the highest point of inner harmony
(*jama'*). A statistical study of the types of persons who settled in these
*jama'at khanah*s reveals the fact that most of them belonged to one or the
other of the following categories:

1.   Externalist scholars,
2.   Government servants, or
3.   Businessmen.

The psychological reasons for this are not far to discover. The antimonies
of scholastic logic could be resolved from the mystic point only; a *khanqah*

217. See *supra*, p. 63–64.
218. *Siyar-u'l-Auliya*, pp. 118, 231.
219. *Fawa'id-u'l-Fu'ad*, p. 200.

alone possessed that spiritual serenity which a government servant, who had to work in an atmosphere of hypertension, longed for, the disturbing effects of the inordinate lust for wealth and power on the minds of men could be checked by adopting the mystic attitude of *tawakkul* (trust in God) alone. It was perfectly natural, therefore that these people turned to the dwellings of humble saints and sages in search of peace of mind. The *khanqah*'s atmosphere reacted differently on different groups. The scholar shed his intellectual arrogance and concentrated on the development and culture of his emotions, the government servant developed an aversion towards worldly power and authority and adopted the service of humanity as his ideal of life; the businessman dispensed with all his material goods and sought spiritual satisfaction in living a life of penitence and poverty. The following instances of a scholar, a government servant, and a businessman of the thirteenth century would be helpful in understanding the circumstances under which people flocked to these *khanqahs* and took up permanent residence there:

1. Maulana Badr-u'd-din Ishaq, a resident of Delhi, acquires knowledge at the feet of distinguished scholars of the capital and attains a pre-eminent position amongst the literati of the day. In the course of his studies, some doubts cloud his mind and he goes from scholar to scholar to get them removed, but in vain. At last he packs up his travelling kit and with a bundle of books starts for Bukhara to discuss his problems with scholars of that historic seat of Muslim learning. While passing through Ajodhan, a friend induces him to pay a visit to Shaikh Farid. Maulana Badr-u'd-din Ishaq meets the Shaikh and is so charmed by his personality that he abandons his journey and settles down permanently in the *jama'at khanah* of the saint.[220] Then begins the process of change in his life. All the cobwebs of doubt and intellectual perplexities are brushed aside from his mind. He loses faith in the supremacy of intellect and turns to the culture of his emotions. Uncontrolled ecstasy takes the place of intellectual excitement and perplexity. Tears constantly flow from his eyes. When he bows in *sijdah*, his tears make the prayer carpet wet.[221] One day the wife of an inmate of the *jama'at khanah* asked him: "Brother! If you refrain from weeping for a little while, I will put collyrium in your eyes." "Sister," replied the Maulana, "My tears are not under my control."[222] On one occasion, he kept on reciting a

220. *Siyar-u'l-Auliya*, p. 170.
221. Ibid, p. 172.
222. Ibid, p. 171.

verse throughout the whole day. Once the Shaikh asked him to lead the prayer. Instead of reciting the Quran, the Maulana chanted a Persian verse and fell down unconscious.[223]

It was the *khanqah* of Shaikh Farid which extricated him from the meshes of over-intellectualism and gave a new turn to his personality by developing his emotions.

2. Hamid is in the service of Malik Tughril at Lakhnauti. He has seen Tughril living in Delhi as a slave of Sultan Balban. But now, goaded by his ambition, Tughril has rebelled against his master and has proclaimed himself a king with the title of Sultan Mughis-u'd-din. Hamid is standing before him when all of a sudden a figure (*surat*) appears before him and says: 'Hamid! Why are you standing before this man?' So saying the figure disappears. Hamid is perplexed. The figure appears to him three times and repeats the same question: 'Hamid! Why do you stand before this man?' 'Why should I not stand before him? I am his servant; he is my master. He gives me my pay. Why should I not stand before him?,' replies Hamid. 'You are a scholar,' replies the figure, 'He is an ignorant man. You are a free man; he is a slave. You are a pious man; he is a sinner!'

Call it a hallucination or interpret it as the rebellion of Hamid's conscience, its appeal was so irresistible that he approached his master with the request: 'If there is anything due from me or any accounts are to be settled, please order. This, to be done. I will not serve you any longer.' 'What are you saying?' asked Tughril, 'Have you gone mad.' 'No,' submitted Hamid, 'I will not serve you. The blessing of contentment has been granted to me.'

Hamid comes to the *jama'at khanah* of Shaikh Farid and devotes himself to prayers and penitences.[224]

3. Sayyid Mahmud is a flourishing businessman of Kirman. He was born in a wealthy family with a silver spoon in his mouth. Very often he comes to Lahore in connection with his trade and meets his uncle, Sayyid Ahmad, a mint officer at Multan, whose daughter he has married. Sometimes he visits Ajodhan also and pays his respects to Shaikh Farid. One day he comes to the *jama'at khanah* and finds such spiritual solace in that tumbling hut that he decides to take up permanent residence there. He gives up all his property and prefers a

---

223. Ibid, p. 172.

For a discussion of the way in which Shaikh Farid tried to rescue him from these ecstasies and trances also, see Ibid, pp. 172–77.

224. *Fawa'id-u'l-Fu'ad*, p. 203; *Siyar-u'l-'Arifin*, pp. 54–55.

beggar's bowl to the life of affluence and plenty. He turns a deaf ear to the appeals of his father-in-law to engage in some worldly pursuit. His heart is now set on things beyond the material world. He performs all sorts of work in the *jama'at khanah*. When he plucks *pelu* and *delah* his hands get injured, but he finds spiritual pleasure in his work. His wife, Bibi Rani, also lives with him and looks after the comfort of the inmates of the *jama'at khanah* as a sister looks after her brothers.[225]

CASUAL VISITORS AND THEIR PROBLEMS

The Chishti *jama'at khanah*s remained open till midnight. All types of people—scholars, politicians, soldiers, Hindu *jogi*s, *qalandar*s—visited them. They came with different material and spiritual aims,[226] and the Shaikh's heart went out in sympathy for them. "No one in the world," Shaikh Nizam-u'd-din Auliya once told his audience, "has a sadness and sorrow like me. So many people come and tell me about their troubles and worries. And everything gets impressed upon my heart and soul."[227] It was this sympathetic response which made the Chishti saints the cynosure of public eyes. Everyone in need of sympathy and help turned to the *jama'at khanah*s. Since it was believed that a saint could heal both mental and physical ailments, many visitors asked for *ta'wiz* (amulets) which were freely distributed. If the overcrowding of visitors ever prevented a saint from paying individual attention to each one, he would earnestly implore: "Come to me one by one, so that I may attend to your problems individually."[228] The following incidents, selected from the earliest accounts, will give some idea of the nature of the problems that people brought to the saints:

1. A poet, bearing the *nom de plume* of Nasiri, came to Delhi from Transoxiana and alighted at the *khanqah* of Shaikh Qutb-u'd-din

225. *Siyar-u'l-Auliya*, p. 207, et seq.
226. "Every visitor," Shaikh Nasir-u'd-din Chiragh once told his audience, "who comes belongs to the group of worldly men or to mystics. If he is a worldly man, his heart is involved in worldly affairs. The moment he enters and my eyes fall on him, I ask him about his condition. Even if he does not say so, all that he has in his heart is revealed to me and I feel depressed and gloomy. Some people come wildly and say, 'Be quick and do this.' If I don't, they abuse me and behave insolently. A *dervish* should be patient with all." *Khair-u'l-Majalis*, pp. 105–06.
227. Ibid, p. 105.
228. *Fawa'id-u'l-Fu'ad*, p. 68.

Bakhtiyar Kaki. "I have written a *qasida* in praise of Sultan Shams-u'd-din Iltutmish," he told the Shaikh, "please pray for a generous reward for me from the Sultan." "God willing," replied the Shaikh, "you will be rewarded bountifully." Nasiri obtained an audience at the court and the Sultan gave him one thousand *tankah*s for each couplet of his *qasida* which comprised 35 couplets. Nasiri brought this amount to the Shaikh and offered half of it for distribution among the poor. The Shaikh did not accept the amount.[229]

2. A tax collector, with whom the governor of Ajodhan was extremely displeased, came to Shaikh Farid and requested him to intercede in the matter. The Shaikh sent his servant to the governor with a polite message: "Please forgive this worried tax collector for the sake of this *dervish*." The Governor turned a deaf ear to the Shaikh's request. The tax collector again came to the Shaikh, worried and perplexed. "I appealed for you to the governor," the Shaikh told him, "but he has paid no attention to my request. Maybe, you have also, in your turn, been equally indifferent to the appeals of the unfortunate." The tax collector expressed his repentance and submitted: "I promise I will not be harsh to any one in future, even if he happens to be my enemy."[230]

3. Shams, a native of Sunnam, came to the *jama'at khanah* of Shaikh Farid and recited a *qasida* in his praise. "What do you want?" asked the Shaikh as soon as he finished his *qasida*. "I have to look after an aged mother and have financial worries," submitted Shams. The Shaikh asked him to bring something for distribution among the needy and the poor. Shams presented 50 *jital*s which were distributed amongst those present. The Shaikh then prayed for his prosperity. Shams got an appointment as *dabir* in the service of Bughara Khan.[231]

4. A disciple of Shaikh Farid came to Shaikh Nizam-u'd-din Auliya and said: "I am the father of daughters. Do something for me." "Go and be patient," replied the Shaikh. "Shaikh," protested the visitor, "If you had one unmarried daughter, you would have realized my distress." "What do you want me to do?" asked the Shaikh. "Recommend me to someone." The Shaikh recommended him to a grandson of Zafar Khan.[232]

229. *Fawa'id-u'l-Fu'ad*, p. 212–13; *Siyar-u'l-'Arifin*, pp. 28–29.
230. *Fawa'id-u'l-Fu'ad*, p. 147; *Siyar-u'l-'Arifin*, pp. 38–39. See also *Khair-u'l-Majalis* (pp. 226–30) for similar incidents.
231. *Fawa'id-u'l-Fu'ad*, p. 127.
232. *Khair-u'l-Majalis*, p. 87.

5. Muhammad Shah came to Shaikh Farid, excited, worried, and trembling. "Why do you look so unhappy?" enquired the Shaikh. "My brother is ill," replied Muhammad Shah, "He may have died since I left him," "Muhammad Shah!" said Shaikh Farid "As you are at this moment, I have been like that all my life, but I have never expressed it to anyone."[233]

6. A man came to Shaikh Farid and requested him to do something to remove his misery and, poverty. The Shaikh advised him to recite the *Surah-i-Juma'* every night.[234]

TRAINING AND APPOINTMENT OF *KHALIFAH*S

Broadly speaking, a mystic teacher had to deal with two types of disciples—those who had made up their minds to consecrate their lives completely to mysticism, and those who joined his discipleship for their spiritual betterment, yet carried on their worldly pursuits. From the second type of his disciples, a Shaikh rarely expected anything more than honest dealings with their fellow men and the regular performance of obligatory religious duties. From the higher disciples, however, complete severance of all earthly ties and selfless devotion to the cause of religion was demanded.[235] The Shaikh was satisfied if a *murid* belonging to the second category regularly paid *zakat-i-shari'at* (one-fourth of what he possessed), but a higher disciple had to pay *zakat-i-haqiqat* (all that he possessed).[236] This higher class of disciples consisted of persons whom a Shaikh eventually permitted to enrol disciples and disseminate the teachings of the *silsilah*. An elaborate programme was prepared for the guidance of these disciples in their arduous mystic journey.[237] The Shaikh often overlooked minor

233. *Fawa'id-u'l-Fu'ad*, p. 232.

234. Ibid, p. 57.

235. When Shaikh Nizam-u'd-din Auliya granted a Khilafat to Khwaja Nuh he advised him thus:

بايد كه هرچه بر تو رسد' نگاه نداری' وآں را بخرج رسانی' اگر برتوچیزی
نباشد' هيچ دل خود را نگراں نداری كه خدا ترا خواهد داد و هيچ يكی را بد
نخواهی و از خدا هم يكی را بد نخواهی و جفا را بعطا بدل كنی و ديه وادرار
نستانی كه درويش قرار داد و ادرار خوار نباشد"

Siyar-u'l-Auliya, p. 204.

236. *Fawa'id-u'l-Fu'ad*, p. 103.

237. See *Adab-u'l-Muridin* of Shaikh Najib-u'd-din, 'Abdul Qahir Suhrawardi and *'Awarif-u'l-Mal'arif* of Shaikh Shihab-u'd-din Suhrawardi.

acts of omission and commission by his ordinary disciples, but he was more exacting in the case of the higher disciples and kept a vigilant eye on every aspect of their thought and activity.

The Chishti saints took considerable pains is build to up healthy and integrated personalities out of this higher class of disciples. They exhorted them to develop self-reliance and evolve the inner richness of their beings. They cultivated the emotions and tutored the intellects of their disciples. They believed that intellect, uninspired by love and uncontrolled by faith in moral and spiritual values, acts as a force of disintegration in human life. They familiarized their disciples with the higher religious thought by teaching standard mystic works to them[238] and disciplined their inner lives by a careful cultivation and control of their emotions. The Chishti saints did not believe in spinning fine ideas; they expressed in their lives the accumulated wisdom of the mystic creed and thus prepared their disciples both emotionally and intellectually for the difficult task of guiding the destinies of the *silsilah*.[239]

Permission to enrol disciples was given to eminently qualified disciples by means of a written *khilafat namah* or certificate of succession. This document was signed by the Shaikh and, in some cases, it was countersigned by some senior disciple also. The scribe of the document also had to put in his signature in order to prevent forgery by unscrupulous persons.[240] Indiscriminate grants of Khilafat, which became a feature of later-day mysticism, was strongly disapproved by the early Chishti saints. Shaikh Farid used to say: "The saints bestow their Khilafat in three ways: First is the *Rahmani* way which is the best and the stablest. There are plenty of blessings and benedictions in it. It is this: God directly puts it into the heart of a Shaikh to give his Khilafat to a particular person. The second way is that a Shaikh considers a disciple capable and (keeping his qualifications in mind) decides to grant his Khilafat to him. In it there is a possibility of a Shaikh's opinion being right or wrong. The third way

---

238. Shaikh Farid taught six chapters of the Quran, five chapters of the *'Awarif-u'l-Ma'arif*, and two other books to Shaikh Nizam-u'd-din Auliya. *Fawa'id-u'l-Fu'ad*, p. 163; *Siyar-u'l-Auliya*, p. 106.

239. Ibid, pp. 116–17.

240. One day Shaikh Farid asked Maulana Badr-u'd-din Ishaq to prepare a few copies of succession certificates for some of his disciples whom he desired to appoint his *khalifahs*. A disciple who had served the Shaikh long and devotedly but was not considered for Khilafat remarked in disgust: "If the Shaikh himself does not give me *khilafat*, I can prepare a document like this and busy myself in the work (of enrolling disciples)." The Shaikh was alarmed and he instructed Maulana Badr-u'd-din to put his name also on the document. Ibid, p. 221.

is that a Shaikh grants Khilafat to a particular person, not of his own accord, but on someone's recommendation or as a matter of grace."[241] While appointing Shaikh Nizam-u'd-din Auliya as his successor Shaikh Farid remarked:[242]

باری تعالیٰ ترا علم و عقل و عشق داده است و هر که به بدین
سه صفت موصوف باشد ازو خلافت مشایخ نیکو آید

(God Almighty has given thee knowledge, wisdom, and cosmic emotion and he alone who possesses these three qualities is qualified to discharge the duties of the Khilafat of saints.)

Maulana Fakhr-u'd-din Safabani's case is very significant in this connection. He was a prominent figure of Bilgram. He sent a messenger, Shaikh Da'ud, to Shaikh Farid with a request for the grant of a *khilafat namah*. "People pester me for the mystic cap," he said in his message. Shaikh Farid refused to accede to his request. Da'ud stayed on in the *jama'at khanah* and approached some influential disciples of the Shaikh to recommend his case. Shaikh Nizam-u'd-din Auliya and Maulana Shihab-ud-din interceded on his behalf and pleaded for the grant of the *khilafat namah* to Maulana Fakhr-u'd-din. The Shaikh, however, declined and said:[243]

این کار حق است' بآرزر نیست' هر که قابل باشد نخواسته بیابد

(This is divine work, and cannot be assigned to [everyone] who desires it. The qualified one gets it without asking for it.)

The Chishti saints did not approve of the practice of becoming the *murid* of a dead saint by wearing a cap at his grave. Once a son of Shaikh Farid went to the grave of Shaikh Qutb-u'd-din Bakhtiyar Kaki, shaved his head, and declared that he had become a disciple of the great saint. When Baba Farid came to know of it, he declared emphatically.[244]

شیخ قطب الدین خواجه و مخدوم ما است' اما این بیعت درست
نباشد' ارادت و بیعت آنست که دست شیخی گیرند

(Shaikh Qutb-u'd-din is our spiritual guide and master, but this form of initiation is not proper. Initiation and discipleship mean that one should grasp the hand of a Shaikh.)

241. Ibid, p. 345.
242. Ibid.
243. Ibid, pp. 345–46.
244. *Fawa'id-u'l-Fu'ad*, p. 78; *Siyar-u'l-Auliya*, p. 326.

Amir Khurd has briefly described the manner in which Shaikh Farid admitted people into his discipleship. He asked every new entrant to recite first of all the *Surah-i-Fatihah*,[245] the *Surah-i-Ikhlas*,[246] and a few other sacred texts. Then he told him to confirm that he owed allegiance to him, his spiritual master, the elders of his *silsilah*, and the Prophet of Islam. Later on, he asked him.[247]

باحضرت عزت عهد کردی که دست و پائی و چشم نگاهداری و برنهج شرع باشی

(Solemnly promise to God that you will control your hands, your feet, and your eyes and will follow the path of the *Shari'at*.)

When the Shaikh bestowed his *khirqah* (patched frock) on anybody he recited the sentence:[248]

و لباس التقوی ذالک خیر والعاقبة للمتقین

(This is the dress of piety and the fruits of the next world are for the pious.)

The Shaikh advised all recipients of the *khirqah*s against annoying any living being with their hands, eyes, or tongues. He exhorted them to fix their hearts on Him alone and devote their time to mystic contemplation and guard themselves against being involved in evil desires.[249]

Shaving the head (*mahluq kardan*)[250] of a new entrant to the mystic discipline was a popular practice amongst the Chishtis. It was considered to be an external expression of a disciple's determination to sacrifice his all in the way of God.

Fortunately for us, it struck the mind of Amir Khurd to copy out verbatim the text of some *khilafat namahs*[251] in his book, *Siyar-u'l-Auliya*. These documents throw valuable light on the aims and objectives of the Chishti saints in appointing *khalifah*s to various territories. The following instructions contained in these *khilafat namah*s, deserve to be particularly noted:

I: Settle in some out-of-the-way mosque in which prayers are offered in congregation.

245. Quran, S. I.
246. Quran, S. CXII.
247. *Siyar-u'l-Auliya*, p. 323.
248. Ibid.
249. Ibid.
250. For a mystic explanation of this practice, see *Fawa'id-u'l-Fu'ad*, p. 161.
251. For the text of *khilafat namah*s given by Shaikh Farid and Shaikh Nizam-u'd-din Auliya to their disciples, see the Appendix.

II: Do not attach your heart to anything worldly. Act upon the tradition of the Prophet: "Live in the world like a traveller or a wayfarer and count yourself among the dead."

III: Control the cravings of the flesh. If this struggle wears you out, pacify your passions either by religious devotions or by sleeping for a while.

IV: Abstain from idle seclusion because this makes a man's heart neglectful.

V :   To invite the people towards God is the finest work of Islam and the most necessary element of faith. God himself says: "O Muhammad! Show to the people My way and tell them about My faith and tell them that I call people towards Him and all my followers are on the path of it truth."

VI: Grant your Khilafat to one who does not deviate an inch from the Sunnah of the Prophet, devotes his time to prayers, and cuts himself off completely from all worldy connections and temptations.

VII: A *khalifah* is a deputy of the Shaikh both in religious and secular matters.

Only one instance would suffice to give some idea of the psychological methods adopted by the Chishti saints to mould the personalities of their disciples in consonance with the spirit of their *silsilah*:

Shaikh Nizam-u'd-din Auliya reached Ajodhan after having won his laurels in the highest academic circles of Delhi. He was an excellent debator and was, on that account, known as Nizam-u'd-din *mahfil shikan*. One day he met an old companion and class-fellow who was surprised to find him in grimy and tattered clothes. "Maulana Nizam-u'd-din!" he exclaimed, "What misfortune has befallen you? Had you taken to the teaching profession at Delhi, you would have become the leading scholar of the time and would have prospered." Shaikh Nizam-u'd-din did not give him any reply; he came to his master and narrated the incident before him. "What would be your answer to such a question?" asked Shaikh Farid. 'As the Shaikh directs,' replied Shaikh Nizam-u'd-din. "Tell him," Shaikh Farid replied:

نه همرهی تو مرا' راه خویش گیر' برو
ترا سعادت بادا' مرا نگوں ساری

(You are not my fellow traveller. Follow your path. Get along. May prosperity be your share in life and misfortune mine.)

The Shaikh then asked his disciple to order a tray of every variety of food from his kitchen and carry it on his head to his friend.[252]

Nothing could have been more effective in eliminating all sense of false prestige from the mind of a young disciple, fresh from the lecture rooms of Delhi, than the method adopted by the Shaikh. Thus he not only rooted out all traces of desire for the easy and comfortable life of *shughl* (government service) that might have lingered on in the heart of Shaikh Nizam-u'd-din Auliya, but also made it absolutely clear to him that the requirements of the life he had chosen for himself were entirely different from the life his friend was leading or which he wanted him to lead.

Some time later, another incident took place and brought a strong reprimand from the Shaikh. The Shaikh was teaching the *'Awarif-u'l-Ma 'arif* to his disciples. The manuscript before him contained some errors of transcription. He had, therefore, to proceed slowly, correcting every mistake and removing every inaccuracy. Interrupting the Shaikh, Shaikh Nizam-u'd-din said that Shaikh Najib-u'd-din Mutawakkil possessed a good manuscript of the book. Shaikh Farid was irritated at this remark. 'Has this *dervish* no capacity to correct a defective manuscript?' he indignantly repeated several times. Realizing that his master had disapproved his remarks, Shaikh Nizam-u'd-din fell at his feet and implored for his forgiveness. But Shaikh Farid's anger did not subside. Finding the Shaikh so deeply annoyed and displeased, Shaikh Nizam-u'd-din was overtaken by deep grief. He went into the wilderness, weeping and crying. In a mood of extreme mental torture, he even thought of committing suicide. Eventually, a son of Shaikh Farid interceded on his behalf and secured the Shaikh's pardon. The Shaikh summoned Shaikh Nizam-u'd-din and told him: "All this I have done for your perfection.... A *pir* is a dresser of brides (مشاطه)."[253]

On the face of it, Shaikh Nizam-u'd-din Auliya's remark seems quite innocent, but the Shaikh's intuitive intelligence discovered intellectual snobbishness and arrogance in it and, so he did not hesitate in adopting the most drastic method to check this tendency. In fact, it was through these methods, deeply psychological and extremely effective, that a Shaikh cleansed and purified the inner life of a disciple to the highest point of mystic excellence.

252. *Siyar-u'l-Auliya*, p. 239.
253. *Fawa'id-u'l-Fu'ad*, pp. 26–27.

B: THE SUHRAWARDI SILSILAH—ITS SAINTS
AND ORGANIZATION

The Suhrawardi Saints in India

Due to the Ghuzz and the Mongol devastation of 'Ajam, many of the disciples of Shaikh Shihab-u'd-din Suhrawardi migrated to India. "I have many disciples in India," Shaikh Shihab-u'd-din Suhrawardi is reported to have remarked.[254] Shaikh Jalal-u'd-din Tabrizi,[255] Qazi Hamid-u'd-din Nagauri,[256] Sayyid Nur-u'd-din Mubarak Ghaznavi,[257] Shaikh Baha-u'd-din Zakariyya,[258] Maulana Majd-u'd-din Haji,[259] and Shaikh Zia-u'd-din Rumi,[260] were among his celebrated *khalifah*s in India. Each one of them had a distinguished career in his own sphere, but the credit for organizing the Suhrawardi *silsilah* in India belongs exclusively to Shaikh Baha-u'd-din Zakariyya. Shaikh Jalal-u'd-din Tabrizi shot like a meteor over the Indian horizon and after short stays in Hansi, Bada'un, and Delhi disappeared in Bengal. Earlier authorities do not tell us anything about his activities after his departure from Delhi, but later writers credit him with having established a magnificent *khanqah* in Bengal and having converted a very large number of Hindus

---

254. *Akhbar-u'l-Akhyar*, p. 36.

255. Originally a disciple of Shaikh Abu Sa'id Tabrizi, he later on attached himself with Shaikh Shihab-u'd-din Suhrawardi. For brief biographical references, see *Fawa'id-u'l-Fu'ad*, pp. 33, 113, 144; *Khair-u'l-Majalis*, pp. 79–80; 191–93; 211–20; *Siyar-u'l-'Arifin*, pp. 164–71; *Akhbar-u'l-Akhyar*, pp. 43–45; *Gulzar-i-Abrar* (MS); *Ma'arij-u'l- Walayat* (MS). If any credence is put on Ibn Battuta's statement that he met the Shaikh in the mountains of Kamrau (i.e. Kamrup in West Assam) then he must have attained the age of 150 years.

256. For brief notices, see *Fawa'id-u'l-Fu'ad*, pp. 128–241, etc. *Khair-u'l-Majalis*, pp. 45, 276; *Futuh-u's-Salatin*, p. 114; *Siyar-u'l-'Arifin*, pp. 147–51; *Akhbar-u'l-'Akhyar*, pp. 36–43; *Gulzar-i-Abrar* (MS). *Ma'arij-u'l-Walayat* (MS).

257. For brief notices, see *Fawa'id-u'l-Fu'ad*, p. 193; *Tarikh-i-Firoz Shahi*, Barani, pp. 41–44; *Akhbar-u'l-Akhyar*, pp. 28–29; *Gulzar-i-Abrar* (MS); *Ma'arij-u'l-Walayat* (MS).

258. For brief notices, see *Fawa'id-u'l- Fu'ad*, pp. 5, 10, etc. Khair-u'l-Majalis. pp. 131, 137, 283; *Siyar-u'l-'Arifin*, pp. 102, 128; *Akhbar-u'l-Akhyar*, pp. 26–27; *Gulzar-i-Abrar* (MS), 18; *Ma'arij-u'l-Walayat* (MS).

259. *Akhbar-u'l-Akhyar*, p. 49.

260. Ibid. p. 72.

to Islam.[261] The devotion of a section of the Hindus to him is clearly evinced in the Sanskrit work, *Shekasubhodaya*.[262] His personal prestige and influence apart, his *khanqah* could not develop into a centre for the extension of the Suhrawardi mystic *silsilah* in Bengal. Qazi Hamid-u'd-din Nagauri was probably one of the most erudite scholars of his age[263] and his works were respected in the highest academic circles of the country but he singularly lacked in, organizing capacity. Excepting a butcher of Delhi,[264] a rope maker of Bada'un,[265] and Shaikh Ahmad of Nahrawala,[266] he did not admit anybody to his discipline.[267] The ecstatic element so predominated[268] in his life that he preferred to pass his time in mystic songs[269] and dances—much against the tradition of his elder saints—rather than attempt the arduous task of organizing a spiritual order. Sayyid

261. *Siyar-u'l-'Arifin*, p. 171. Jamali writes:

حضرت شیخ المشایخ جلال الدین تبریزی چوں در بنگاله رفت خلایق آں
دیار بر ایشاں رجوع نمود و مرید گشت و حضرت شیخ در آں مقام خانقاہ
ساخت و لنگر گردانید' و از انجا بیشتر شد و آں بندر را دیوه محل گویند۔
حضرت شیخ در آنجا بسیار کافر را مسلمان ساخت' الآں مقبره مطہرہ ایشاں
ہم دراں بت خانه است و نصف حاصل آں بندر وقف لنگر ایشاں است

262. Edited by Sukumar Sen (Calcutta).
263. *Fawa'id-u'l-Fu'ad*, p. 241.
264. His name was 'Ain-u'd-din. See *Siyar-u'l-'Arifin*, p. 151.
265. His name was Shaikh Shahi Rasan-Tab. See ibid, p. 152, *Akhbar-u'l-Akhyar*, p. 48.
266. See *Siyar-u'l-'Arifin*, pp. 150–51; *Akhbar-u'l-Akhyar*, p. 46.
267. Shaikh Nizam-u'd-din Auliya is reported to have remarked:

شیخ جلال الدین کم کسی را دست دادی وهم چنی قاضی حمیدالدین ناگوری

Fawa'id-u'l-Fu'ad, p. 33.
268. The *Sarur-u's-Sudur* (MS, p. 91) contains the following interesting information about him:

میگویند که او پیوسته چشم بسته بودی' گفتند شیخ ازچه سبب چشم
نمی کشانی' جواب داد' گفت دو چشم ندارم که این عالم رابه بینم

(It is said that he always kept his eyes closed. They asked: "Why does not the Shaikh open his eyes?" He replied: "I do not possess two eyes to be able to see this world also.")
269. *Fawa'id-u'l-Fu'ad*, p. 241; *Akhbar-u'l-Akhyar*, p. 36.

Nur-u'd-din Mubarak Ghaznavi, Maulana Majd-u'd-din Haji, and Shaikh Zia-u'd-din Rumi were too near the rulers and the bureaucracy to plan for the expansion of the *silsilah*. Shaikh Baha-u'd-din Zakariyya was a saint of different mettle. He had travelled widely in Muslim lands[270] and had studied carefully the problems of the contemporary Muslim society. Endowed with great intuitive intelligence (*nafs-i-gira*),[271] he set up his *khanqah* at Multan, a place of great political and strategic significance in those times, and succeeded in organizing his *silsilah* on an effective basis.

Life and Teachings of the Founder of the Suhrawardi Silsilah in India

Shaikh Baha-u'd-din Zakariyya[272] was born at Kot Aror (near Multan) in 578/1182–83. After completing his study of the Quran according to its seven methods of recitation, at Kot Aror, he visited the great centres of Muslim learning at Khurasan, Bukhara, Medina, and Palestine—in order to complete his study of the traditional sciences. When in Medina, he learnt the *hadis* with an eminent traditionist, Shaikh Kamal-u'd-din Yemeni, and spent several years in religious devotions at the mausoleum of the Prophet. After visiting the graves of the prophets of the Israelites in Palestine, he reached Baghdad and became a disciple of Shaikh Shihab-u'd-din Suhrawardi. At this time he was, as his master said, 'dry wood, ready to catch fire' and so, after seventeen days' instruction, he appointed him his successor and ordered him to set up a Suhrawardi *khanqah* in Multan. He lived and worked in Multan for more than half a century and his *khanqah* developed into a great centre of mystic discipline in medieval India. He died in Multan on Safar 7, 661/December 21, 1262.

Shaikh Baha-u'd-din Zakariyya was one of the most influential mystic teachers of his age. It is indeed surprising that none of his disciples thought of compiling an account of his life and teachings. The *Siraj-u'l-Hidayah* refers to a *Wasiyat Namah* of Shaikh Baha-u'd-din Zakariyya, but it is not available now. *Fawa'id-u'l-Fu'ad* is probably the earliest work which contains several very significant pieces of information about him. Later Suhrawardi writers have mainly relied on *Fawa'id-u'l-Fu'ad* in reconstructing an account of the life and teachings of the great Suhrawardi saint of Multan.

---

270. *Fawa'id-u'l-Fu'ad*, p. 5.
271. Ibid, p. 221.
272. For biographical details, see ibid, pp. 5, 10, etc.; *Khair-u'l-Majalis*,   pp. 131, 137, 283; *Siyar-u'l-Auliya*, 60, 77, etc.; *Siraj-u'l-Hidayah* (MS); *Siyar-u'l-'Arifin*, pp. 102–28; *Akhbar-u'l-Akhyar*, pp. 26–27.

Shaikh Baha-u'd-din Zakariyya held independent views on many problems of religion and politics. His mystic ideology was radically different from that of his Chishti contemporaries. He believed in living a normal, balanced life—a life in which both the body and the spirit receive equal care. He did not fast perpetually, and did not recommend a life of starvation and self-mortification to those associated with him. According to Shaikh Nizam-u'd-din Auliya, he acted on the Quranic injunction: "Eat of what is pure and act righteously".[273]

As pointed out earlier,[274] emphasis on the external forms of religion was a tradition of the Indian Suhrawardis. Shaikh Baha-u'd-din Zakariyya did not, of course, go to the length of Sayyid Sadr-u'd-din Raju Qattal, but he never spared anybody found indifferent to or ignorant of the forms of religious devotion. The way in which he expelled a *dervish*, Sulaiman by name, from Multan shows a somewhat intolerant attitude in such matters. The Shaikh had asked him to say two *rak'ats* of prayer. "I want to see how you do it," said the Shaikh. When Sulaiman rose up to offer his prayers, he did not place his feet properly; he placed them either too close or too far apart. The Shaikh got irritated and asked him to leave Multan and settle in Uch.[275]

The Shaikh did not approve of the Chishti[276] practice of bowing before a Shaikh. His followers addressed him merely with the words, '*as-salamu alaikum*' for no other form of showing respect was permitted in his *khanqah*.[277]

Unlike the Chishtis, Shaikh Baha-u'd-din believed in accumulating wealth.[278] Besides, he did not abstain from taking part in political matters or associating with the political powers. This departure from the established

273. *Fawa'id-u'l-Fu'ad*, p. 184.
274. See *supra*, p. 191–92.
275. *Fawa'id-u'l-Fu'ad*, p. 221.
276. Ibid, pp. 215; 148–59. Shaikh Nasir-u'd-din Chiragh, however, stopped this practice and emphatically declared:

پیش مخلوق سر بر زمین نهادن روا نیست

(It is not lawful to place one's head on the ground before a creature). *Khair-u'l-Majalis*, p. 157.
277. *Siyar-u'l-'Arifin*, p. 123.
278. For details, see the next chapter. See also *Jawami'-u'l-Kilam*, p. 213, where Sayyid Muhammad Gesu Daraz is reported to have remarked:

مشایخ ملتان همتی بر جمع مال دارند و مشایخ خراسان تعلقی به تجارت و
سوداگری دارند. اما خواجگان ما به هیچ از اسباب دنیاوی متعلق نشده

tradition of medieval mysticism apart, Shaikh Baha-u'd-din possessed not only great organizing capacity but also a very remarkable understanding of human nature.[279] He organized the Suhrawardi *silsilah* on firm foundations and attracted to his fold a very large number of talented disciples.

Successors of Shaikh Baha-u'd-din Zakariyya

Shaikh Baha-u'd-din Zakariyya had seven sons[280] and a very large number of disciples scattered all over Multan and Sind. His son, Shaikh Sadr-u'd-din 'Arif (ob. 1285 AD), succeeded him as his chief *khalifah* and *sajjadah-nashin* in Multan, while his disciple, Sayyid Jalal-u'd-din Surkh Bukhari (ob. 1291 AD) established a strong Suhrawardi centre at Uch. The history of the Suhrawardi *silsilah* in India mainly revolves round these two branches—the Multan branch and the Uch branch. Unlike the Chishtis, succession in the Suhrawardi order was determined on a hereditary basis. For two generations these two branches produced distinguished saints with great talent for organization but, later on the *silsilah* disintegrated because those whc had to look after its affairs were men of smaller stature and inferior mettle.

Shaikh Sadr-u'd-din 'Arif[281] worked for nearly 23 years after the death of his father from whom he differed basically in his attitude towards some of the fundamental problems of religion and politics. He hated wealth and considered it to be the source of all spiritual distractions and worldly troubles. His share in the patrimony amounted to seven lac *tankah*s, but he distributed the entire amount in charity. Unable to appreciate the reasons for this departure from the practice of his father, some people could not help interrogating him on this point. He replied that since his father had complete control over worldly desires and temptations, he could, with confidence and with justification, accrue wealth and spend it, but as he himself did not possess that strength of character, he was afraid of indulging in money matters 'lest it might lead him astray'.[282] This change

279. *Fawa'id-u'l-Fu'ad*, p. 221.

280. Their names were: Shaikh Kamal-u'd-din, Shaikh Sadr-u'd-din 'Arif, Shaikh Shams-u'd-din Muhammad, Shaikh 'Ala-u'd-din Yahya, Shaikh Mahbub, Shaikh Burhan Ahmad, and Shaikh Zia-u'd-din Hamid. Our only source for this information is the *Gulzar-i-Abrar* of Muhammad Ghausi. Barani refers to one Shaikh Qidwah as the son of Shaikh Baha-u'd-din Zakariyya. (*Tarikh-i-Firoz Shahi*, pp. 66–67).

281. For brief notices, see *Siyar-ul-'Arifin*, pp. 128–40; *Akhbar-u'l-Akhyar*, pp. 60–62; *Ma'arij-u'l-Walayat* (MS).

282. *Siyar-u'l-'Arifin*, p. 129.

in the Suhrawardi attitude was probably due to contemporary criticism. Shaikh 'Arif dispensed with the materialistic basis of his *khanqah* and preferred to be a 'debtor' rather than a 'creditor'.[283] His conversations were compiled under the title *Kunuz-u'l-Fawa'id* by his disciple Khwaja Zia-u'd-din.

Sayyid Jalal-u'd-din Surkh[284] was a native of Bukhara. He came to Multan attracted by the reputation of Shaikh Baha-u'd-din Zakariyya. The Shaikh initiated him into his discipline and instructed him to settle in Uch and propagate the Suhrawardi mystic principles. Many tribes of Uch claim that he was responsible for the conversion of their ancestors to Islam.

Sayyid Jalal-u'd-din had three sons—Sayyid Ahmad Kabir, Sayyid Baha-u'd-din, and Sayyid Muhammad. Sayyid Jalal-u'd-din Makhdum-i-Jahanian[285] (1308–83 AD) was the eldest son of Sayyid Ahmad Kabir. Under his guidance the Uch branch of the Suhrawardi order became a factor of great importance in the religious aud political life of Sind. His activities, however, do not count for our period.

Shaikh Sadr-u'd-din 'Arif (ob. 1286 AD) was followed by his son, Shaikh Rukn-u'd-din Abul Fath[286] (ob. 1335). He occupies the same position in the history of the Suhrawardi *silsilah* which Shaikh Nizam-u'd-din Auliya occupies in the history of the Chishti order. For nearly half a century he worked incessantly and with single-minded devotion to propagate the Suhrawardi mystic ideas. Zia-u'd-din Barani pays eloquent tribute to him and says that the entire population of Sind had faith in him and even a large number of the *'ulama* had joined the circle of his disciples.[287]

283. Barani, *Tarikh-i-Firoz Shahi*, pp. 66–67.

284. For brief biographical notices, see *Siyar-u'l-'Arifin*, pp. 155–56; *Akhbar-u'l-Akhyar*, p. 60.

285. For brief notices, see 'Afif, *Tarikh-i-Firoz Shahi*, pp. 514–16; *Siyar-u'l-'Arifin*, pp. 155–63; *Akhbar-i-Akhyar*, pp. 139–40; *Gulzar-i-Abrar* (MS); *Ma'arij-u'l-Walayat* (MS); *Mir'at-u'l-Asrar* (MS). For his teaching, see Yustifi, *Mahabubiyah* (I.O.-D.P. 1107a), (AH 1130/1718), D.P. 638 (AH 1268/1851); and three collections of his conversations; *Khulasat-u'l-Alfaz-i-Jami'-u'l-'Ulumi* (Rampur, MS); *Siraj-u'l-Hidayah* (MSS, Rampur and Aligarh), and *Manaqib-i-Makhdum-Jairanian* (MSS, A.S., Bengal). The *Safar Namah-i-Makhdum-i-Jahanian* (MSS in I.O., Asafiyah Lindesiana and Madras; Urdu trans., Lucknow) is a fabrication and contains incredible and fantastic stories about the saint.

286. For brief notices, see *Siyar-u'l-Auliya*, pp. 135–41; *Tutuh-u'l-Salatin*, p. 443; *Tarikh-i-Firoz Shahi*, Barani, pp. 347–48; *Rihlah*, Ibn Battuta (Urdu trans.), p. 157; *Siyar-u'l-'Arifin*, p. 140, et seq; *Akhbar-u'l-Akhyar*, pp. 62–65; *Gulzar-i-Abrar* (MS); *Ma'arij-u'l-Walayat* (MS).

287. *Tarikh-i-Firoz Shahi*, p. 347.

It is unfortunate that no Suhrawardi records about him are available. Shaikh 'Abdul Haqq Muhaddis refers to a book, the *Fatawa-i-Sufia*,[288] in which one of his disciples had given a detailed account of his life and teachings. This work is not extant.

As noted elsewhere, Shaikh Baha-u'd-din Zakariyya treated the *qalandars* with indifference. It is, however, interesting to find that some of the *qalandar* organizations of the period trace their spiritual descent from Shaikh Baha-u'd-din Zakariyya. The mystic group organized by Shaikh Ahmad Mashuq, *khalifah* of Shaikh 'Arif, closely resembled the *qalandars*. When Shaikh Rukn-u'd-din found the *qalandars* favourably disposed towards him and his *silsilah*, he adopted a very lenient and sympathetic attitude towards them.[289]

Personal and Family Life of the Suhrawardi Saints

Though no details about the family life of the Suhrawardi saints are available, it appears that they took better care of their families than their Chishti contemporaries. Shaikh Baha-u'd-din Zakariyya was very particular about the education and training of his sons. He engaged tutors for his sons and paid handsome salaries to them.[290]

A sixteenth-century Suhrawardi writer says[291] that Shaikh Sadr-u'd-din 'Arif had married a divorced wife of Prince Muhammad, the eldest son of Balban. The circumstances of this marriage are given as follows: The prince divorced his wife, whom he passionately loved, in a fit of fury. When he recovered his normal state of mind, he felt deeply pained by what he had done. Legally, he could not take her back into his *harem* unless she was married to some one else and then divorced by him. A man of genuine piety was searched to restore the broken relationship. Shaikh 'Arif, the most outstanding saint of the town, promised to marry the princess and divorce her the next day. But, after the marriage, he refused to divorce her on the ground that the princess herself was not prepared to be divorced. This incident led to bitterness between the saint and the prince. The latter even thought of taking action against the Shaikh, but a Mongol inundation cut short the thread of his life.

Khanqah Organization of the Suhrawardis

The Suhrawardi *khanqah*s of Multan were organized on a pattern basically different from that of the Chishtis. The difference arose mainly out of the

288. *Akhbar-u'l-Akhyar*, p. 62
289. Ibid. p. 65.
290. *Fawa'id-u'l-Fu'ad*, p. 223.
291. *Siyar-u'l-'Arifin*, p. 135.

fact that the Suhrawardis did not eschew politics. Shaikh Baha-u'd-din Zakariyya, the real founder of the Suhrawardi *silsilah* in India, mixed freely with the Sultans, took part in political affairs, amassed wealth, and accepted government honours. He was probably the richest saint of medieval India. Enormous *futuh* (unasked for charity) flowed into his *khanqah*.[292] Contrary to the practice of the Chishti saints, it was not disbursed immediately among the needy and the poor. He kept his wealth carefully and spent it with still greater care.[293] He had a treasury (*khazanah*) containing boxes full of gold *tankah*s. Once a box of 5000 gold *tankah*s was found missing[294] but the loss was not considered a serious one.

The abundance of his wealth[295] made the local administration of Multan look upon him in times of need[296] and excited the cupidity of robbers who resorted to blackmail[297] in order to exact money from his sons. Once the Wali of Multan borrowed some corn from him. When this corn was being removed from his granaries, pitchers full of silver *tankah*s were found hidden therein.[298] In fact, his resources compared favourably with the resources of a medieval *iqta'dar*. His grandson, Shaikh Rukn-u'd-din, accepted a *jagir* of 100 villages from Muhammad b. Tughluq.[299] The Suhrawardi *khanqah* was, in many ways, a direct contrast to the Chishti *jama'at khanah*. It was, no doubt, more magnificent, better furnished, and better organized, but not for the people. It had an aristocratic air both as to its structure and its organization, though the atmosphere of religious devotion was never wanting. A *qawwal* who visited the *khanqah* of Shaikh Baha-u'd-din Zakariyya during the reign of Sultan Nasir-u'd-din Mahmud particularly noted the fact that even the slave girls of the Shaikh were all the time busy in reciting the praises of God.[300]

Shaikh Baha-u'd-din's *khanqah* covered an extensive area and provided separate accommodation for every inmate as well as the numerous visitors

292. *Siyar-u'l-'Arifin*, p. 106.

293. Jamali informs us او بتدریج خرچ می فرمود
Siyar-u'l-'Arifin, p. 129.

294. Ibid, p. 114.

295. Ibid, p. 129. چندیں اجناس و نقود موجود بود

296. *Fawa'id-u'l-Fu'ad*, p. 223; *Siyar-u'l-'Arifin*, p. 114.

297. Mir Khurd informs us that a son of Shaikh Baha-u'd-din was kidnapped by a robber and was released on payment of a huge ransom by Shaikh Sadr-u'd-din. *Siyar-u'l-'Auliya*, p. 159.

298. *Fawa'id-u'l-Fu'ad*, p. 223; *Siyar-u'l-'Arifin*, p. 114

299. *Rihlah*, II, p. 61.

300. *Fawa'id-u'l-Fu'ad*, p. 149.

who flocked to it. In the Chishti *jama'at khanah*, on the contrary, all people, inmates as well as visitors, lived in a big hall, prayed there and slept there. Shaikh Baha-u'd-din, no doubt entertained his guests generously,[301] but he did not maintain an open table. Only those who were invited by him could take food with him.

The Suhrawardi *khanqah* had large stocks of cereals in its granaries. Its treasuries were replete with gold and silver coins. The Chishti *jama'at khanah* had no such provision. The Chishtis depended on the uncertain and irregular income through *futuh*; the Suhrawardi *khanqah*s relied on the sure and regular *jagir* revenues.[302]

Besides, the Suhrawardi *khanqah*s were not open to all and sundry. "People are of two kinds," Shaikh Baha-u'd-din used to say, "the general public and the select. I have nothing to do with the general public and no reliance can be placed upon them. As to the select, they receive spiritual blessings and benefits from me according to their capacities."

In view of this, the Suhrawardi saint did not allow *qalandars*, *jawaliqs* or others whom he did not consider fit for his spiritual training, to sojourn in his *khanqah* or waste his time. He had fixed hours for interviews. He refused to be disturbed by visitors at odd hours.

The Shaikh's spiritual greatness, his piety, and his devotion were universally acknowledged, but the contemporary mystic thought could not reconcile itself to the idea of accumulating wealth and at the same time claiming to be the guardian of the spiritual welfare of the people. This apparent contradiction they could neither understand nor condone. Shaikh Baha-u'd-din Zakariyya made every possible effort to convince his critics that it was not so much the wealth as its improper use that was detrimental to spiritual progress, but they stuck to their views and repeatedly told him:

'Two opposites cannot meet at one place' (الضدان لا يجتمعان).[303]

Medieval religious literature does not make a secret of the objections raised by contemporaries against this behaviour of the great Suhrawardi saint. Shaikh Jalal-u'd-din Tabrizi and Shaikh Hamid-u'd-din Suwali had lengthy correspondence with him on this subject.[304] Sometimes the Shaikh, when charged with a volley of questions from the other side, found himself

---

301. Ibid, p. 105.
   Shaikh Rukn-u'd-din Firdausi once visited Shaikh Sadr-u'd-din 'Arif in Multan and found his table full of dishes, daintily prepared, 'resembling the table of kings'. *Siyar-u'l-'Arifin*, p. 137.
302. *Fawa'id-u'l-Fu'ad*, 136.
303. *Siyar-u'l-Auliya*, p. 158.
304. *Fawa'id-u'l-Fuad*, pp. 99–100; *Siyar-u'l-Auliya*, p. 158.

in an embarrassing situation. Once, in a *mahzar* (a legal court) convened by Iltutmish, Shaikh Hamid-u'd-din Suwali took advantage of Shaikh Baha-u'd-din's presence in the court to put questions to him about his accumulation of wealth. The Shaikh was nonplussed. The Suhrawardi sources state that the Shaikh invoked the spiritual guidance of his mentor, Shaikh Shihab-u'd-din Suhrawardi, in order to give a suitable reply to his critics.[305]

The demand to explain this anomalous position was persistent. The replies given by the Suhrawardi saints were more rhetorical than logical and the quick-witted questioners refused to be confused by rhetoric and platitudes. Once, on being questioned about his wealth, Shaikh Baha-u'd-din replied: "Wealth is doubtless a venomous serpent. But poison does not harm one who knows the antidote." The critic retorted: "Where is the necessity of keeping a dirty venomous creature and then depending on an antidote for safety." Shaikh Baha-u'd-din replied: "Your *derveshi* has no beauty or attraction. Our *derveshi* has immense beauty. Wealth is like a black dot averting the evil effect of jealous glances."

When no convincing argument in favour of accumulating wealth, was found, they replied: "Wealth is a disease in the heart; in the hand it is a cure."[306]

Jamali, himself affiliated to the Suhrawardi *silsilah* and possessing huge wealth,[307] records these incidents in a manner which betrays his own dissatisfaction at the attitude of his elder saints.

---

305. *Siyar-u'l-'Arifin*, p. 14.
306. Ibid.
307. *Akhbar-u'l-Akhyar*, p. 222.

CHAPTER VII

MUSLIM MYSTIC IDEOLOGY AND CONTRIBUTION TO INDIAN CULTURE

"The greatest of all the spirit's tasks," remarks Albert Schweitzer, "is to produce a theory of the Universe (*Weltanschauung*). In that all the ideas, convictions and activities of an age have their roots."[1] The Muslim mystics of the Middle Ages did not merely produce a theory of the universe, they also built their lives in consonance with it.

The mystical attitude grows out of the basic metaphysical postulate adumbrated in the doctrine of *wahdat-u'l-wujud*. Briefly put, it means that whatever exists objectively as well as subjectively, outside the mind of man as well as inside it, is One; call it whatever you like—Universe, Nature, Reality, Truth, or God. Faith in this unity of the noumenal and the phenomenal world is the beginning of the mystical experience. Its highest stage is reached when, like Shaikh Muhammad b. Wasi, a mystic is constrained to confess: "I never saw anything without seeing God therein."[2]

Since a medieval mystic conceived of God as the totality of cosmic existence, cosmic emotion became the *élan vital* of his life.[3] He craved communion with Him so that the distinction between 'I' and 'Not-I' might disappear in the mystic absorption of the human soul in the Absolute. He consecrated every moment: of his life and dedicated every fibre of his being to Him and Him alone. He strove "to live for the Lord alone"[4] for that alone was life.[5] The yearning of his soul was:

1. *The Decay and Restoration of Civilization*, London, 1950, p. 81.
2. *Kashf-u'l-Mahjub*, English trans., p. 91.
3. Shaikh Nizam-u'd-din Auliya wrote in a letter to Maulana Fakhr-u'd-din Maruzi: 'The highest purpose and the supreme aim of creating mankind is the "love of God".' *Siyar-u'l-Auliya*, pp. 454–55.
4. For instances of sublimation of the two basic desires—hunger and sex—by mystics in their attempt to live for the Lord alone, see *Fawa'id-u'l-Fu'ad*, pp. 60–61; *Khair-u'l-Majalis*, pp. 178–79.
5. حیات آنست که درویش بذکر حق مشغول باشد (That alone is life which is spent by a *dervish* in meditation upon God.), *Fawa'id-u'l-Fu'ad*, p. 20.

مقصود من خسته ز کونین توئی
از بهر تو میرم ز برائی تو زیم ⁶

A single moment's engagement with the *Non-Absolute* (غیر حق) was considered tantamount to spiritual death and mystic literature is replete with stories of mystics who have appeared in sackcloth and ashes on that account.[7]

THE MYSTIC PATH

Gnosis (*ma'rifat*) or Union (*wasl*) being the *summum bonum* of a mystic's life, ways and means were explored through which one could reach his ideal. "You must know that the way to God," writes Shaikh 'Ali Hajweri, "is of three kinds: (1) *maqam*, (2) *hal*, (3) *tamkin*. *Maqam* (station) denotes anyone's 'standing' in the way of God and his fulfilment of the obligations appertaining to that 'station' and his keeping it until he comprehends its perfection so far as that lies in a man's power. It is not permissible that he should quit his 'station' without fulfilling the obligations thereof. *Hal* (state), on the other hand, is something that descends from God into a man's heart, without his being able to repel it when it comes, or to attract it when it goes, by his own effort. 'Station' denotes the way of the seeker and his progress in the field of exertion and his rank before God in proportion to his merit, the term 'state' denotes the favour and grace which God bestows upon the heart of His servant. *Tamkin* denotes the residence of spiritual adepts in the abode of perfection and in the highest grade. Those in 'station' can pass on from their 'stations', but it is impossible to pass beyond the grade of *tamkin*."[8]

The 'stations' (*maqamat*) which a mystic had to cover have been thus enumerated by Shaikh Shihab-u'd-din Suhrawardi in his *'Awarif-u'l-Ma'arif*—the guidebook of almost all the Indo-Muslim mystics of the thirteenth century:

First	Stage:	*Tauba*	(Repentance)
Second	Stage:	*Wara'*	(Abstinence)
Third	Stage:	*Zuhd*	(Piety)
Fourth	Stage:	*Faqr*	(Poverty)
Fifth	Stage:	*Sabr*	(Patience)
Sixth	Stage:	*Shukr*	(Gratitude)

6. Ibid, p. 20.
7. *Fawa'id-u'l-Fu'ad*, p. 224; *Khair-u'l-Majalis*, pp. 224–45.
8. *Kashf-u'l-Mahjub*, pp. 181, 371.

Seventh Stage:	*Khauf*	(Fear)
Eighth Stage:	*Raja*	(Hope)
Ninth Stage:	*Tawakkul*	(Contentment)
Tenth Stage:	*Riza*[9]	(Submission to the Divine Will)

Since these terms have a definite mystic connotation, it is necessary to explain them in the light of medieval mystic records.

1. Shaikh 'Ali Hajweri writes: "Etymologically *tauba* means 'return' and *tauba* really involves the turning back from what God has forbidden through fear of what He has commanded. The Apostle said: *Penitence is the act of returning.* This saying comprises three things which are involved in *tauba*, namely, (1) remorse for disobedience, (2) immediate abandonment of sin, and (3) determination not to sin again."[10] Shaikh Nizam-u'd-din Auliya used to say that *tauba* is a very comprehensive act which appertains to the present, to the past, and to the future of the repentant.[11] The most significant psychological fact about it was the assertion of the Shaikh that a repentant was equal to one who had never committed a sin.[12]

2. *Wara'* means abstaining, in word, thought, and deed, from all unnecessary and unseemly occupations, though they may be permitted by the *Shari'at*.[13] It was in view of this principle that the mystics said: "Those who are satisfied with jurisprudence (*fiqh*) and do not practise abstinence (*wara'*) become wicked."[14]

3. *Zuhd* is giving up of interest in all worldly goods and attractions. Shaikh Shihab-u'd-din Suhrawardi approvingly quotes a remark of Shaikh Junaid that *zuhd* consists in having a hand empty of provisions and a heart free of all desires.[15] Abul Mawahib Shazili considers it the seventh maxim of illumination and says: "If you do not renounce

9. *'Awarif-u'l-Ma'arif* (Urdu trans.), pp. 585–620.

10. *Kashf-u'l-Mahjub*, p. 294. See also *The Doctrine of the Sufis*, translation of the *Kitab-u'l-Ta 'arruf li-mazhabi Ahl-i-Tasawwuf* of Kalabazi by A.J. Arberry, pp. 82–83; *'Awarif-u'l-Ma'arif* (Urdu), pp. 600–02. Mir Khurd has very clearly explained the views of the Chishti mystics on *tauba* in a section of his *Siyar-u'l-Auliya*, pp. 330–33.

11. *Fawa'id-u'l-Fu'ad*, p. 139; *Siyar-u'l-Auliya*, p. 330.

12. *Fawa'id-u'l-Fu'ad*, pp. 3, 19.

13. *Misbah-u'l-Hidayah*, p. 294.

14. *Kashf-u'l-Mahjub*, p. 17.

15. *'Awarif-u'l-Ma'arif*, p. 604; *Misbah-u'l-Hidayah*, p. 294, et seq.

the petty goods of this vile world, surely you are far from the beneficence of the glorious life to come."[16]

4. *"Faqr"*, writes Shaikh 'Ali Hajweri, "is a special distinction of the poor who have renounced all things external and internal, and have turned entirely to the Causer...Poverty has a form (*tasm*) and an essence (*haqiqat*), its form is destitution and indigence, but its essence is fortune and free choice."[17]

5. *Sabr* means that whether a man is visited by a blessing or a misfortune, he should consider it from the divine source and bear it patiently.[18] Hasan Basri is reported to have said: "*Sabr* (patience) is of two sorts; firstly, patience in misfortune and affliction and secondly, patience to refrain from the things which God has commanded us to renounce and has forbidden us to pursue."[19]

6. *Shukr* means expressing gratitude to God, explicitly and implicitly, through tongue and through heart.[20]

7. *Khauf* signifies trepidation lest one's evil conduct may have unpleasant consequences in the future.[21]

8. *Raja* means looking for a desired contingency in the future.[22]

9. *Tawakkul* means trusting one's affairs to God. Shaikh 'Ali Hajweri quotes a mystic who defined *tawakkul* as "confidence in God that He will provide thy daily bread".[23] Without this faith in God, no higher spiritual attainment was possible.

10. *Riza* is "equanimity (*istiwa-yi dil*) towards Fate, whether it withholds or bestows, and spiritual steadfastness (*istiqamat*) in regarding events, whether they be the manifestation of Divine beauty (*jamal*) or of Divine majesty (*jalal*), so that it is all one to a man whether he is

16. *Illumination in Islamic Mysticism*, English translation of Abul Mawahib Shazili's *Qawanin Hikam-u'l-Ishraq*, p. 50.

17. *Kashf-u'l-Mahjub*, pp. 19–20; See also *The Doctrine of the Sufis*, pp. 86–88; *'Awarif-u'l-Ma'arif*, pp. 611–14; *Misbah-u'l-Hidayah*, pp. 296–99. Mir Khurd has discussed the Chishti viewpoint in his *Siyar-u'l-Auliya*, pp. 545–47.

18. *Misbah-u'l-Hidayah*, pp. 299–303. See also *The Doctrine of the Sufis*, pp. 84–85, *Siyar u'l-Auliya*, pp. 548–50.

19. *Kashf-u'l-Mahjub*, p. 86.

20. *'Awarif-u'l-Ma'arif*, pp. 614–17; *Misbah-u'l-Hidayah*, pp. 303–06; *The Doctrine of the Sufis*, p. 91.

21. See *'Awarif-u'l-Ma'arif*, pp. 615–17; *Misbah-u'l-Hidayah*, pp. 306–10.

22. *'Awarif-u'l-Ma'arif*, pp. 617–18; *Misbah-u'l-Hidayah*, pp. 310–13. See also *Siyar-u'l-Auliya*, (p. 550) for Shaikh Nizam-u'd-din Auliya's views on *khauf* and *raja*.

23. *Kashf-u'l-Mahjub*, p. 117. See also *Fawa'id-u'l-Fu'ad*, pp. 101–54; *Siyar-u'l-Auliya*, pp. 552–54.

consumed in the fire of wrath or illuminated by the light of mercy, because both wrath and mercy are evidences of God, and whatever proceeds from God is good in His eyes."[24]

"You must know," writes Shaikh 'Ali Hajweri, "that satisfaction (*riza*) is the end of the 'stations' (*maqamat*) and the beginning of the 'states': it is a place of which one side rests on acquisition and effort, and the other side on love and rapture: there is no 'station' above it; at this point mortifications (*mujahadat*) cease."[25]

While traversing this spiritual journey, a mystic has passed through and experienced various emotional conditions (*hal*). In mystic terminology these states are known as:

1. *Muhabbat* (love): "Man's love towards God is a quality which manifests itself in the heart of the pious believer, in the form of veneration and magnification, so that he seeks to satisfy his Beloved and becomes impatient and restless in his desire for a vision of Him, and cannot rest with any one except Him, and grows familiar with the remembrance (*zikr*) of Him, and abjures the remembrance of everything besides."[26]

2. *Shauq* (yearning or longing): It signifies "the assault of the claim of delight on account of the Beloved in the lover's heart. Its existence is the requisite of love's truth."[27] *Shauq* is of two kinds: (a) The *shauq* of the lovers of *sifat* (qualities). They long for the Beloved's grace, mercy, and kindness. (b) The *shauq* of the lovers of *zat* (essence). They long for union with the Beloved.[28]

3. *Ghairat* (jealousy): *Ghairat* means being jealous for God's service and not admitting any other thought into one's mind. It is an attribute of God Himself, Who is jealous lest His servant should commit any kind of sin.[29]

4. *Qurb* (proximity): It means a feeling of nearness to God.[30]

5. *Haya* (shame): Shame of being found wanting in sincerity.[31]

24. *Kashf-u'l-Mahjub*, p. 177.

25. *Kashf-u'l-Mahjub*, p. 182; see also *Fawa'id-u'l-Fuad*, p. 234; *Siyar-u'l-Auliya*, pp. 548–50.

26. *Kashf-u'l-Mahjub*, pp. 307–08; see also *'Awarif-u'l-Ma'arif*, p. 636, et seq; *Misbah-u'l-Hidayah*, p. 320, et seq; *Siyar-u'l-Auliya*, pp. 453–91.

27. The *'Awarif-u'l-Ma'arif*, by H. Wilberforce Clarke, p. 104.

28. *Misbah-u'l-Hidayah*, pp. 326–28.

29. Ibid, pp. 328–31.

30. Ibid, pp. 331–33.

31. Ibid, pp. 333–34.

6. *Uns-o-Haibat* (intimacy and awe): "*Uns* and *haibat* are two states of the dervishes who travel on the Way to God. When God manifests His glory to a man's heart so that His majesty (*jalal*) predominates, he feels awe (*haibat*) but when God's beauty (*jamal*) predominates, he feels intimacy (*uns*); those who feel awe are distressed, while those who feel intimacy, rejoice."[32]

7. *Qabz-o-Bast* (contraction and expansion): "*Qabz* and *bast* are two involuntary states which cannot be induced by any human act or be banished by any human exertion...*Qabz* denotes the contraction of the heart in the state of being veiled (*hijab*), and *bast* denotes the expansion of the heart in the state of revelation (*kashf*)."[33]

8. *Fana-o-Baqa* (annihilation and subsistence): "*Fana* and *baqa* are two complementary aspects of one and the same experience in which the real is seen to persist, the phenomenal to pass away—*fana* is characteristic of all that is 'other than God', *baqa*, of God alone."[34]

9. *Ittisal* (union): This is the final 'state' of mystic experience when one feels 'union' with the Reality.[35] The distinction between 'I' and 'Not-I' completely disappears and the mystic attains not merely *ma'rifat* (gnosis) but also *wasl* (union).

SERVICE OF HUMANITY

But this inward march of the human soul from one 'station' to another was futile if it did not express itself in some form of social service. "The soul of the great mystic," observes Bergson, "does not come to a halt at the (mystical) ecstasy as though that were the goal of a journey. The ecstasy may indeed be called a state of repose, but it is the repose of a locomotive standing in a station under steam pressure, with its movement continuing as a stationary throbbing while it waits for the moment to make a new leap forward...The great mystic has felt the truth flow into him from its source like a force in action...His desire is with God's help to complete the creation of the human species...The mystic's direction is the very direction of the *élan* of life."[36]

32. *Kashf-u'l-Mahjub*, p. 376. See also *Misbah-u'l-Hidayah*, pp. 334–37.

33. *Kashf-u'l-Mahjub*, p. 347. See also *Misbah-u'l-Hidayah*, p. 337, et seq.

34. *Futuhat-i-Makkiyah*, as quoted by Afifi, *Muhyi-u'd-din Ibnul Arabi*, p. 146. For detailed discussion of this mystic experience and the controversies associated with it, see, *Kashf-u'l-Mahjub*, p. 242, et seq.

35. *Misbah-u'l-Hidayah*, pp. 342–43.

36. *Les Deux Sources de la Morale et de la Religion*, pp. 246–51 as quoted by Toynbee, *Study of History* (*Vols i-vi*), pp. 212–13.

Muslim mystics of the thirteenth century looked upon 'social service' as the supreme object of all their spiritual exercises.[37] As noted earlier, when Shaikh Muʿin-uʾd-din Chishti was asked about the highest form of devotion, he replied that it was nothing but helping the poor, the distressed, and the downtrodden.[38] All the great mystic teachers of medieval India agreed with the viewpoint of the Chishti saint. They considered a life of solitary, self-sufficient contemplation to be incompatible with the highest mystic ideals. If a man became egocentric, limited his sympathies, and cut himself off completely from the energizing currents of social life, he failed to fulfil the mystic mission. "Live in society and bear the blows and buffets of the people", was the advice that one mystic teacher always gave to his disciples.[39]

"Devotion to God is of two kinds," Shaikh Nizam-uʾd-din Auliya is reported to have observed, "*lazmi* (intransitive) and *muta ʿaddi* (transitive). In the *lazmi* devotion, the benefit which accrues is confined to the devotee alone. This type of devotion includes prayers, fasting, pilgrimage to Mecca, recitation of religious formulae, turning over the beads of the rosary, etc. The *muta ʿaddi* devotion, on the contrary, brings advantage and comfort to others; it is performed by spending money on others, showing affection to people, and by other means through which a man strives to help his fellow human beings. The reward of *muta ʿaddi* devotion is endless and limitless."[40]

This *ta ʿat-i-muta ʿaddi* was the leitmotif of a mystic's efforts (*jihd*). "Nothing would bring greater reward on the Day of Judgement," a mystic teacher told his disciples, "than bringing happiness to the hearts of men."[41] This could be done by attending to the problems of the misery-stricken people, assuaging their wounds, raising their hearts, and by infusing new life and confidence in their broken spirit.

TARK-I-DUNYA

A mystic was expected to reject the world (*dunya*).[42] The question arises: What was this *dunya* and how could it be renounced? The general impression that *tark-i-dunya* meant adopting a hermit's attitude towards life and severing all earthly connections is not confirmed by contemporary mystic

37. *Sivar-uʾl-Auliya*, p. 46.
38. *Supra*, p. 185.
39. *Sivar-uʾl-Auliya*, p. 237.
40. *Fawaʾid-uʾl-Fuʾad*, pp. 13–14; *Siyar-uʾl-Auliya*, p. 411.
41. *Siyar-uʾl-Auliya*, p. 128.
42. *Fawaʾid-ul-Fuʾad*, pp. 9, 85, 130, 189, 190, 211, 224.
Siyar-uʾl-Auliya, pp. 543–45.

records. In fact, it was not the world as such which the mystics rejected but the materialistic approach towards life and its problems which they hated and despised. The more a man got involved in materialistic pursuits, the farther he drifted from his spiritual objective.

It is significant that in medieval mystic anecdotes, *dunya* is made to appear in the form of treasure, a woman, or government service. A Chishti saint told his disciples that once Christ saw the world in the form of an old woman and asked: 'How many husbands hast thou?' 'Innumerable,' replied the hag. 'Hath any of these husbands divorced thee?' asked Christ. 'No' replied the old woman, 'I have myself finished with them.'[43]

Thus lust for worldly goods and glory, *shughl* (government service) and *shahwat* (appetites) were considered to be the real barricades (حجابات) between God and man and renunciation of the world really meant rejecting these allurements. "The rejection of the world," said Shaikh Nizam-u'd-din Auliya, "does not mean that one should strip himself of his clothes or put on a loin cloth and sit idle. Instead, 'rejection of the world' means that one may put on clothes and take food. What comes to him (unasked) he should accept but not hoard it. He should not place his heart in anything. Only this is the rejection of the world."[44]

In view of these basic principles of medieval mysticism, the Chishti saints of India advised their disciples against possession of private property.[45] Keep only what is absolutely necessary,[46] such as clothes for covering the private parts of the body, and distribute the rest—was the advice which they gave to their followers. Real happiness, they said, lay not in accumulating money but in spending it.[47]

PACIFICISM AND NON-VIOLENCE

The early Indo-Muslim mystics believed in a pacific and non-violent approach towards all problems of human society. Force, they said, created more problems than it solved. It set in motion a vicious circle of wrong and retribution which disturbed the very basis of human relationship. "If a man places thorns (in your way)," said Shaikh Nizam-u'd-din Auliya, "and you do the same, it will be thorns everywhere."[48]

43. *Fawa'id-u'l-Fu'ad*, p. 21.
44. Ibid, p. 9. The famous mystic poet Rumi says:

چیست دنیا؟ از خدا غافل بودن   نی قماش و نقره و فرزند و زن

45. *Siyar-u'l-Auliya*, p. 204.
46. *Fawa'id-u'l-Fu'ad*, p. 130.
47. Ibid, p. 190; *Siyar-u'l-Auliya*, p. 404.
48. *Fawa'id-u'l-Fu'ad*, pp 86–87.

The basic ideas of the medieval Muslim mystics in this regard may be stated as follows:

1. A man should strenuously strive to develop the faculties of patience and endurance.[49] Those who get excited at the slightest provocation debase their spiritual powers. Anger should not be suppressed; it should be eliminated by forgiving the person who has committed a wrong.[50]

2. Self-criticism is the best way to minimize chances of friction in human society. The moment one begins to scrutinize his own behaviour in the face of some conflict, bitterness disappears and the enemy also cannot help being impressed by this attitude. Shaikh Nizam-u'd-din Auliya once told his audience: "If there is a strife between two persons—say, between me and some other person, its solution is this: I should, on my part, cleanse my heart of all ideas of revenge. If I succeed in doing that, the enemy's desire to do some harm to me would also be lessened."[51]

3. There are both good and bad tendencies in every man. In mystic terminology, one may say that there is *nafs* (animal soul) and there is *qalb* (human soul) in every human being. *Nafs* is the abode of mischief, strife, and animosity; *qalb* is the centre of peace, goodwill, and resignation. "If a man opposes you under the influence of his *nafs*, you should meet him with *qalb*. The *qalb* will overpower the *nafs* and the strife would end. But if a man opposes *nafs* with *nafs*, there can be no end to conflicts and strifes."[52]

4. A man's relationship with another man may be of any one of the following types: (a) He may be neither good nor bad to another. This is what happens in the non-living world (*jamadat*). (b) He may do no harm to another but only what is good. (c) A man does good to another, and if he does him harm, he remains patient and does not retaliate. According to medieval mystics the last was the ideal of the 'truthful person'.[53]

The Muslim mystics of medieval India demonstrated the working of these non-violent and pacific principles in their own lives. They tried to impress, both by precept and example, upon the minds of their followers

49. Ibid, pp. 86–237.
50. *Siyar-u'l-Auliya*, pp. 552–56.
51. Ibid, p. 555.
52. *Fawa'id-u'l-Fu'ad*, p. 124.
53. Ibid, p. 237; *Siyar-u'l-Auliya*, p. 555.

the fact that a true mystic should always strive to create love and affection in the hearts of men. "Placate your enemies," was the advice which Shaikh Farid gave to his disciples.[54] "Do not give me a knife," he once told a visitor, "Give me a needle. The knife is an instrument for cutting and the needle for sewing together."[55] Hardly a day passed in these *khanqahs* when there was not provocation from an orthodox theologian or some insolent *qalandar* or some overbearing government officer. The saints met all such situations[56] with extreme patience, sang froid, and forbearance. The mystic attitude towards all those who troubled and tortured them is very neatly epitomized in the following verses which Shaikh Nizam-u'd-din Auliya used to recite very often:

هر که مارا یار نبود' ایزد او را یار باد   و آنکه ما را رنجه دارد راحتش بسیار باد

هر که او در راه ما خاری نهد از دشمنی   هر گلی کز باغ عمرش بشگفد بیخار باد

(He who is not my friend, may God be his friend! And he who bears ill-will against me, may his joys increase. He who puts thorns in my way on account of enmity, may every flower that blossoms in the garden of his life be without thorns.)

Some saints extended the application of their non-violent principles to animals also and adopted the cult of *ahimsa*. Shaikh Hamid-u'd-din Nagauri did not like the slaughter of animals. The *Sarur-u's-Sudur* says:

نخواستند که از برائی ایشان و به سبب ایشان جانی بی جان شود

(He did not like any living being to be deprived of its life for him or on account of him.)[57]

It was his deep faith in *ahimsa* which made him a strict vegetarian. He exhorted his disciples again and again to develop vegetarian tastes.[58]

CHISHTI ATTITUDE TOWARDS THE STATE

The Muslim mystics of the early Middle Ages, particularly those belonging to the Chishti *silsilah*, cut themselves off completely from kings, politics,

54. *Fawa'id-u'l-Fu'ad*, p. 140; *Siyar-u'l-Auliya*, p. 330.
55. *Fawa'id-u'l-Fu'ad*, p. 226.
56. Ibid, pp. 125–26; 251, 48, etc. *Siyar-u'l-Auliya*, p. 84, etc. Shaikh Baha-u'd-din Zakariyya threw open the gates of his *khanqah* when some *qalandar*s began to pelt it, *Fawa'id-u'l-Fu'ad*, p. 48.
57. *Sarur-u's-Sudur*, p. 10.
58. Ibid, p. 43.

کرة از لفظ مبارك ایشان شنیده می شدکه بر سبزی خوردن عادت بایدکرد

and government service. This attitude was based on various considerations, psychological, legal, and religious.

Firstly, they believed that government service distracted a mystic from the single-minded pursuit of his ideal which was 'living for the Lord alone.'[59] Gnosis (ma'rifat) was beyond the reach of one who spent his time in shughl (government service).[60] The days when government service was a service of religion were dead and gone. Now it was the service of class interests and indulging in it, therefore, amounted to signing one's own spiritual death warrant.

Secondly, as Imam Ghazzali puts it: "In our times, the whole or almost the whole of the income of the Sultans is from prohibited sources. The permitted income is only sadaqat, fay, and ghanimah: And these have no existence in these days. Only the jiziyah remains but it is realized through such cruel means that it does not continue to be permitted."[61] Consequently, services paid from these sources of income were deemed illegal.

Thirdly, all Muslim political organizations from the fall of the Khilafat-i-Rashida were essentially secular organizations, having little to do with religion or religious ideals. The entire court life and the governmental organization breathed an atmosphere so alien to the true spirit of Islam that it was impossible to serve the state without obstructing religious advancement. Under these circumstances, as Imam Ghazzali argues, "the other alternative is that a man should keep away from kings so that he does not come face to face with them and this alone is feasible for there is safety in it. It is obligatory to have the conviction that their cruelty deserves to be condemned. One should neither desire their continuance, nor praise them, nor enquire about their affairs, nor keep contact with their associates."[62]

Fourthly, if a mystic associated himself with the governing class—which by its very nature was an exploiting class—he isolated himself from

---

59. Shaikh 'Ali Hajweri quotes the following sentence of Shibli:

الفقير لا يستغنى بشئى من دون الله

(The poor man does not rest content with anything except God). Kashf-u'l-Mahjub (English trans., p. 25).

60. Siyar-u'l-Auliya, p. 363.

61. Ihya-u'l-Ulum, Chapter IV. In this chapter the Imam very emphatically declares:

جميع ما فى ايديهم حرام

(All that is in the hands of these rulers is prohibited.)

See also Kimiya-i-Sa'adat, p. 37, et seq.

62. Ihya-u'l-'Ulum Chapter IV.

the main sphere of his activity, the masses. He ceased to be a man of the masses and became part of a bureaucratic machinery.

It was in view of these considerations that the Muslim mystics of the Middle Ages developed an attitude of contempt and indifference towards the government of the time and refused to serve under it. Imam Abu Hanifah (ob. 767 AD) turned down the request of Khalifah al-Mansur to accept the post of Qazi.[63] When Hisham b. Abdul Malik visited Medina to pay his respects to Hazrat Ta'us, the latter met him with indifference and disdain.[64] Imam Ghazzali made a vow at the mausoleum of the Prophet Ibrahim Khalilullah to abstain completely from visiting the courts of kings.[65]

Khwaja Abu Muhammad, an elder saint of the Chishti *silsilah*, declined to accept the presents of a prince with the remark:[66]

از خواجگان ما از ینها کسی قبول نه کرده است

(None of our elder saints has accepted such things.)

Khwaja Fuzail b. 'Ayaz refused to grant an interview to Harun-u'r-Rashid and when he persisted in his request, the saint upbraided him severely.[67]

Some saints adopted an extremist attitude in this matter and treated everything associated with the ruler and the state as an obnoxious symbol of materialism. Imam Hanbal refused to dine at his son's house because he had served for one year as the Qazi of Isfahan.[68] Imam Abu Islhaq Fazari (ob. 807 AD) did not permit courtiers and nobles to attend his lectures on *hadis*.[69] Shaikh Abu Sa'id Tabrizi ordered his servants to remove earth from those parts of his *khanqah* where a *hajib* from the court had placed his feet.[70] Khwaja Suhail Tastari felt deep contrition for having once visited the court of a ruler of Iraq and repented for it for full seven

---

63. *Kashf-u'l-Mahjub*, p. 93.
64. *Kimiya-i-Sa'adat*, p. 174.
65. In a letter he says:

برمشهد ابراهیم خلیل الله عهد کرد که هرگز پیش هیچ سلطان
نرود و مال هیچ سلطان نگیرد

Maktubat-i-Ghazzali, p. 7.
66. *Siyar-u'l-Auliya*, p. 41.
67. Ibid, pp. 34–35.
68. *Ihya-u'l-'Ulum*, Chapter IV.
69. *Tazkirat-u'l-Huffaz*, Vol. I, pp. 248–49.
70. *Fawa'id-u'l-Fu'ad*, p. 181.

years.[71] Khwaja Zunun Misri severely reproved a disciple who had visited
a royal court and ordered him to put off his mystic garment and burn it.[72]
The Indo-Muslim mystics of the thirteenth century followed these well-
established traditions of medieval mysticism and eschewed the society of
kings and nobles. "There are two kinds of abuses among mystics," a Chishti
saint once remarked, "*muqallid* and *jirrat. Muqallid* is a mystic who has
no master. *Jirrat* is one who asks people for money, wraps himself in a
costly cloak, puts on a mystic cap, and goes to kings and high officials."[73]

1. *Abstention from the Company of Kings*

Almost all the notable saints of the Chishti order in India scrupulously
avoided the company of kings and nobles. Khwaja Qutb-u'd-din Bakhtiyar
visited the court of Iltutmish only once and that too under circumstances,
over which he had no control. As pointed out earlier, Khwaja Mu'in-u'd-
din Chishti was forced by his sons to proceed to the court and obtain a
muqarat dasht from the Sultan. When the Khwaja reached Delhi, Qutb
Sahib requested him to remain in his house, while he himself went to the
durbar.[74] Except on this occasion, the Khwaja never visited the Sultan who
had very great regard for him. Shaikh Farid-u'd-din Ganj-i-Shakar continued
the traditions of his master. He warned his disciples against consorting
with kings and princes. "If you desire to attain the position of great saints,"
he used to tell his disciples, "do not pay any attention to the princes."[75]
The following verses composed by one of the earliest Chishti saints of India
throw considerable light on the attitude of the *silsilah* towards the rulers
and the bureaucracy:[76]

تاکی بدر امیر و سلطان رفتن   این نیست مگر بری شیطان رفتن

در خرقهٔ پشم بودن و نان جوین   خوردن به ازان که نزد ایشان رفتن

ای یار مرو بر در سلطان و وزیر   بر پای نه این نفس دنی را رنجیر

سلطان و وزیر تا شتابند بتو   این هر دو بمان و درگه یزدان گیر

It is said that Balban had great faith in Baba Farid.[77] But his respect
or devotion could not, in any way, influence the saint's outlook or policy

---

71. *Rahat-u'l-Qutub* (MS).
72. Ibid (MS).
73. *Khair-u'l-Majalis*, p. 80.
74. *Siyar-u'l-Auliya*, p. 53.
75. Ibid, p. 75.
76. *Diwan-i-Jamal-u'd-din Hansvi*, II, p. 45.
77. *Matlub-u't-Talibin* (MS).

towards the Sultan. Once a man, who was in great distress, requested him to write a letter of recommendation to Sultan Balban. It was not the Shaikh's practice to write recommendatory letters to rulers or officials but when the person insisted, he wrote to Balban:[78]

> I referred his matter first to God and then to you. If you will grant anything to him, the real Giver is God but you will get the credit for it. If you do not give him anything, the real preventer is God and you are helpless in the matter.

Sher Khan, the famous warden of the marches, was not favourably disposed towards Baba Farid. He often spoke ill about him. The saint did not curse or condemn him but recited the couplet:[79]

افسوس که از حال منت نیست خبر
انگه خبرت شود که افسوس خوری

(Alas! You have no knowledge of my condition. When you come to know, what will be the use of being sorry.)

2. *Rejection of Jagirs*

The Chishti saints not only abstained from the society of kings and nobles, they also rejected their offers of *jagirs* and endowments. They thought that the acceptance of such gifts would make them subservient to the royal wish and fetter the independence of their souls. They used to say:

شه مارا ده دهد منت نهد
رازق ما رزق بی منت دهد

(The king gives a village and holds us under an obligation; our Providence gives us our daily bread without placing any such obligation.)

When Iltutmish offered a *jagir* to Shaikh Qutb-u'd-din Bakhtiyar Kaki, he declined to accept it.[80] Shaikh Hamid-u'd-din Nagauri preferred to pass his days in poverty rather than access anything from the Sultan.[81] Baba Farid Ganj-i-Shakar's curt reply to Ulugh Khan's offer of villages was:

طالب این بسیار اند' بدیشان بدهی

(There are many who desire it; give it to them.)[82]

---

78. *Siyar-u'l-Auliya*, p. 72. For the Arabic text of this letter, see Appendix A (VI).

79. *Fawa'id-u'l-Fu'ad*, p. 221.

80. *Rahat-u'l-Qutub* (MS), f. 35(b).

81. See *supra*, p. 187.

82 and 83. *Fawa'id-u'l-Fu'ad*, p. 99.

Shaikh Nizam-u'd-din Auliya refused to accept royal grants with the remark:[83]

اگر من ازیں بابت قبول کنم مرد ماں چه گویند' شیخ در باغ می رود'

شیخ به تماشائی زرع و زمین می رود' زهی کاری که من کرده باشم

(If I accept this, the people would say: The Shaikh goes to the garden: he goes to enjoy the view of his land and cultivation. Are these acts proper for me?)

His instructions to his disciples were definite and clear on this point: "Do not accept any village or stipend or favour from kings and officials. It is not permitted to a dervish."[84]

Not to speak of *jagirs*, even presents from kings and nobles were rarely and reluctantly accepted. Khwaja Qutb-u'd-din Bakhtiyar Kaki did not accept cash in coins from Malik Ikhtiyar-u'd-din-Aibek.[85] Shaikh Nur-Turk declined to accept a bag full of gold coins sent by Razia.[86] If they ever accepted anything, they took it with one hand and distributed it with the other. Baba Farid was so particular about distributing all that he received as *futuh* that he did not tolerate even a few hours' delay in its disbursement. A seventeenth-century biographer of Shaikh Farid writes that once Balban sent a dish full of *tankah*s to the saint who accepted it after considerable reluctance and ordered Maulana Badr-u'd-din Ishaq to distribute it among the poor and the needy. The sun had already set and it was getting dark but the Shaikh would not wait for the day. His *khanqah*, he used to say, was not a storehouse for royal gifts. In obedience to his instructions, the Maulana doled out all the money. He then brought a candle to see whether anything was still left. He found just one coin and put it in his cap to hand over to a needy person the next morning. When Baba Farid went to the mosque to lead the *'isha* (night) prayer, he realized that something was disturbing his mind. Three times he began his prayer but could not finish it. In great excitement he asked Maulana Badr-u'd-din if he had distributed the royal gift. The Maulana replied that he had given away all excepting one coin. Baba Farid angrily took back that coin and threw it away, and then peacefully led the prayer. 'Ali Asghar Chishti further informs us that throughout the whole of that night Baba Farid deeply regretted having touched that coin.[87] Though not recorded by earlier authorities, this story is in conformity with the traditions of the

---

84. *Siyar-u'l-Auliya*, p. 295.
85. Ibid, p. 59.
86. *Fawa'id-u'l-Fu'ad*, p. 161.
87. *Jawahir-i-Faridi* (MS).

Chishti *silsilah*.[88] It was the practice at the *jama'at khanah* of Shaikh Nizam-u'd-din Auliya that on every Friday everything in store was given away to the poor and the house was cleared and swept.[89]

The early Chishti saints persistently told their disciples that resignation and contentment alone guaranteed human happiness. Cupidity and ambition debased a man's spiritual faculties and made him subservient to worldly powers. Only those who rose above worldly temptations developed their personalities to full moral and spiritual stature. Shaikh Nizam-u'd-din Auliya once narrated a very significant story in this connection. "There was a saint who was known as Shaikh 'Ali. One day he was sewing his *khirqah* (patched garment) with his legs stretched out when the *khalifah* arrived. He did not move from his place as he asked him to come in. The *khalifah* entered (the room) and sat down after offering the compliments. The Shaikh returned the compliment. The *hajib* who was in attendance on the *khalifah* said: 'Shaikh! Fold your legs.' The Shaikh paid no heed to it. Twice or thrice the *hajib* repeated this. When the *khalifah* and his *hajib* were about to leave, the Shaikh caught hold of their hands and said: 'I have shut my hands and therefore I need not fold my legs.'"[90]

3. *Rejection of Government Service*

Equally strong was the condemnation of government service by the Chishti saints. 'No *shughl*' was the explicit order of the Shaikh and hardly anybody who had decided to dedicate himself to spiritual work dared transgress it. The Shaikh dealt with offenders very severely. Sometimes he cancelled an offender's *khilafat namah*. At other times, he expelled him from the mystic fraternity.[91] They firmly believed that government service tainted one's spiritual qualities and rendered one incapable of any higher spiritual work. God and Mammon, they said, could not be served simultaneously. One whose hands and feet moved at royal bidding could not "have a soul of his own".[92] Shaikh Qutb-u'd-din Bakhtiyar Kaki emphatically declined to accept the distinction of *Shaikh-u'l-Islam*,[93] though he had a soft corner for Iltutmish. Another contemporary mystic, Shaikh Hasan, resorted to an

88. A saint, Khwaja Karim, did not touch a single coin after taking up *faqiri*. *Fawa'id-u'l-Fu'ad*, p. 11.

89. *Siyar-u'l-Auliya*, p. 131.

90. *Fawa'id-u'l-Fu'ad*, pp. 7–8.

91. *Siyar-u'l-Auliya*, pp. 295–96.

Shaikh Nizam-u'd-din Auliya took back the *khilafat namah* from Qazi Muhi-u'd-din Kashani the moment he found him inclined towards government service.

92. *Islamic Culture*, Vol. XX, p. 136.

93. *Siyar-u'l-'Arifin*, p. 21

interesting subterfuge in order to keep away from the administration. He turned mad in order to evade his appointment as qazi. When Khwaja Qutb-u'd-din Bakhtiyar Kaki came to know of his ailment, he remarked: "Shaikh Hasan is not mad, he is *dana* (wise)." Thereafter the saint came to be known as Shaikh Hasan *Dana*.[94]

Shaikh Nizam-u'd-din Auliya demanded from his elder disciples a definite promise to abstain from the service of kings.[95] His frequent exhortations in this respect went a long way in moulding the character of his disciples. Some years after his death, when Muhammad bin Tughluq desired to bind the saints to the state chariot, his disciples strongly opposed the policy of the Sultan. Three of his elder disciples—Shaikh Nasir-u'd-din Chiragh, Maulana Shams-u'd-din Yahya, and Shaikh Qutb-u'd-din Munawwar—withstood the threats of the Sultan with a courage and determination that elicited universal praise.

It may be pointed out in this context that these restrictions were imposed upon only those disciples who were given patents of spiritual authority (*khilafat namah*s) and were asked to lead others on the mystic path. The ordinary disciples were not so firmly warned against government service. In fact, they were permitted some sort of *shughl*. Shaikh Nasir-u'd-din Chiragh permitted services which did not interrupt a man's devotion to God. Hamid Qalandar thus records the proceedings of one of his meetings: A Mulla *danishmand* entered the *majlis* and loudly accosted the Shaikh. The Khwaja talked to the Mulla and enquired about his welfare. "Throughout the day," said the Mulla, "I remain in the *diwan* and find no leisure from the execution of orders, etc. Pray for my welfare." "One who does good to mankind," replied the Shaikh, "is not harmed by serving in the Civil Departments." Later on the Shaikh narrated a long story in the fashion of his spiritual master, Shaikh Nizam-u'd-din Auliya, and brought home to the Mulla the possibility of attending to the health of his soul even while engaged in government service. "A man may do," he told his audience, "the work he be engaged in, in government service or other worldly pursuits, but he should never give his tongue rest from reciting His Name (ذکر), whether standing, sitting or lying, he should pray to God, as enjoined by the Quran."[96] This conditional permission to join government service was given to ordinary disciples only. To the mystics of a higher order nothing of this sort was allowed.

Sometimes it is very pertinently asked: How was it that Amir Khusrau, the most cherished disciple of Shaikh Nizam-u'd-din Auliya, spent all his

94. *Rauzat-u'l-Aqtab*, p. 84.
95. *Fawa'id-ul-Fu'ad*, pp. 204–05.
96. *Khair-u'l-Majalis*, pp. 12–13; also 122.

life in courts and camps while his spiritual mentor had such dislike for government service? It may be pointed out in this connection that apart from the saint's personal regard and affection for the poet, Khusrau was not a mystic of a higher order.[97] He was not given the patent of spiritual authority (*khilafat namah*) which alone barred a disciple from government service.

Early Chishti records contain innumerable moral precepts for the general public, but hardly anything for the rulers or the bureaucracy. In fact, they were not very welcome visitors to the *khanqah*s. "Why do these people waste the time of this faqir?" Shaikh Nizam-u'd-din Auliya had once protested.[98] However, the following two observations of the Chishti saints are of great political significance:

ملک بوزیر خدا ترس ضبط کن[99]

(Entrust the country to a God-fearing *wazir*.)

حضرت رسالت صلی اللّه علیه وسلم می فرماید اگر پیر زنی در بلاد
مملکت بفاقهٔ بخسپد' روزقیامت آمناوصدقنا دامن والی خود بگیرد [100]

(The Prophet [the blessing of God be upon him] says that if any old woman goes to bed hungry in any town of a kingdom, she would hold the collar of the ruler on the Day of Judgement which is sure to come.)

Suhrawardi Attitude Towards the State

Contrary to the traditions of other mystic *silsilah*s, the Suhrawardi saints consorted with kings and put forward the following arguments in support of their attitude:

I: Visits to royal courts provided them with opportunities to help the poor people by getting their grievances redressed by the Sultan.[101] Once,

97. Once in an audition party presided over by the great Shaikh, Amir Khusrau rose up in an ecstasy of joy, common among the mystics while hearing *sama'*. The Shaikh objected to this and said, "You are connected with the world; you are not permitted to rise up." *Siyar-u'l-Auliya*, p. 506.

98. Ibid, p. 131.

99. Ibid, p. 77.

100. Ibid, p. 41.

101. Ahmad Yadgar informs us that Shaikh Sama-u'd-din had once written to Jamali:

فقرا را از صحبت پادشاهان بسی فائده دنیاست که مهم چندیں
مسکینان بوسیلهٔ آن فیصل یابد

Tarikh-i-Shahi, p. 48.

on being asked about the purpose of his visit to Delhi, Sayyid Jalal-u'd-din Bukhari said:

> I did not undertake this journey to Delhi for the sake of fame or worldly fortune. (The reason was) that the son of a teacher of mine told me: "Your teacher died leaving behind seven daughters. The Sultan of Delhi, and the dignitaries of the state have faith in you. You should go there and collect from these people something for me so that, through your kind help, I might arrange for their marriages." I have come to Delhi with this purpose; otherwise, what has a dervish got to do with the society of rich people and nobles.[102]

It is said about Shaikh Rukn-u'd-din that whenever he left his residence for the court, people gathered round him in large numbers and filled his *dolah* (palanquin) with petitions to be handed over to the Sultan with recommendations for sympathetic consideration.[103]

II: They believed that by establishing personal contact with the rulers they could bring about a change in their outlook. They did not find any valid justification for excluding the kings from their programme of spiritual upliftment. Their anxiety to guide and guard the conscience of the rulers against wayward ideas was based on their conviction that the life of the people was inseparably connected with a ruler's thought, behaviour, and convictions. Shaikh Nizam-u'd-din Auliya informs us: "Once Shaikh Shihab-u'd-din Suhrawardi came to know about a philosopher's visit to the Khalifah. On hearing this the Shaikh at once left for the court. (He said) if the Khalifah is attracted towards philosophy, the world would darken and heresy would spread."[104]

Drawing his inspiration from the Quranic verse: "Obey Allah, obey His Prophet, and obey those with authority amongst you", Shaikh Najib-u'd-din Abdul Qahir Suhrawardi exhorted his disciples to be full of reverence towards the rulers and abstain totally from finding fault with them.[105] He

---

102. *Siraj-u'l-Hidayah*, ff. 129a, b.

103. *Siyar-u'l-Auliya*, pp. 138–39.

104. *Fawa'id-u'l-Fu'ad*, p. 41.

It may be noted that the Shaikh's book *Kashf-un-Nasa'ih* is a polemical work directed against the study of Greek philosophy. "In it," writes S. Van Den Bergh, "Suhrawardi gives, on the model of the Kalam and of Ghazzali, a criticism of the hellenising philosophers but reveals a much inferior comprehension of philosophy to that of the author of the *Tahafut*." *The Encyclopaedia of Islam*, Vol. IV, p. 506.

105. *Adab-u'l-Muridin* (Urdu trans., Muslim Press, Delhi; 1319 AH), pp. 46–47.

was of the opinion that rebellion against a ruler—even if he be cruel and unjust towards his people—was not permitted.[106] Close as he was to the 'Abbasid Caliphs of Baghdad, he based his views about Khilafat on the principle of legitimacy and declared in unequivocal terms: "The Sufis do not consider any family qualified for Khilafat except the Quresh. They say that it is not permitted for anybody to quarrel with the Quresh or oppose them on the question of Khilafat."[107]

Probably no saint of the Suhrawardi *silsilah* has explained his views, *vis-à-vis* the state with such candour and clarity as Sayyid Jalal-u'd-din Bukhari. Notwithstanding his close contact with the kings and the bureaucracy, he criticized their court life and the sources of their income. But there was a contradiction in his thought which was probably due to his spiritual affiliation with both the Chishtis and the Suhrawardis who held diametrically opposite views on political matters. At one place in the *Siraj-u'l-Hidayah* he thus exalts the rulers and exhorts his disciples to obey the political authority implicitly and faithfully:

> The rulers of the world are the 'chosen' of God, the Almighty. Under no conditions is showing disrespect to them or disobeying their orders proper or permitted in the *Shari'at*. It is for this reason that God has committed to their care so many prayers and religious services e.g., Friday prayers, Eid prayers, control of the Public Treasury...Opposing their commandments, openly or secretly, is not permitted. O careless fellow! You (to whom the Sultan gives) villages, rewards, and territories, etc., why do you not help the king in [getting over] the difficulties that come in his way, and (why) do you not meet his enemies with anger? If you do not do all this, it is unlawful for you to eat or accept all these means of livelihood. Tomorrow on the Day of Judgement you shall be severely punished for this. The Prophet has said: "Whoever obeys the Sultan, obeys God and whoever obeys God attains salvation."

But on another occasion he criticized the rulers for their court etiquette and customs[108] and, in reply to a person who wanted to know whether taking meals with them was permitted or not, he declared:

106. Ibid, p. 5.
107. Ibid.
108. *Siraj-u'l-Hidayah* (MS), f. 19b (where table manners are criticized): ff. 20b–21a (where some sacrifices are declared illegal).

در فتاوی خانی مذکور است که مکروه است طعام ملوک و
سلاطین خوردن' سبب آنکه اغلب وجوهات ایشان را ام روز از مال
ظلم و تعدی است. چنانکه مال دلالت بازارها' و مال جزاری' و مال
امیر مطربی' و مال جکری غله و مال حاصل کیالان' و مال حبه
ستدن' و مال خماران و مال بگنی گران ستدن' مال ما هی فروشان'
و مال سبزی وتره فروشان' ومال لمبره یعنی اخراجات، ونسبت
وقسمت، ومال گران ستدن، و مال مصادره فروشان و مال گل
فروشان' ومال جزائی ومال مرده ستدن ومال غائبی از دیگران
ستدن' باتفاق علماء دین اسلام این احوال حرام است بغیر اختلاف'
و بر ملوک زمانه اکثر ایں وجوهات است' ازاں سبب طعام و شراب
ایشاں خوردن حرام است[109]

It is recorded in *Fatawa-i-Khani* that it is abominable to eat the food of maliks
and sultans. The reason is that most of their revenues these days are derived
from sources which are based on tyranny and oppression, e.g. the income
from: *Dalalat-i-Bazarha, Jazari, Amir Mutrabi, Jikri Ghalla, Hasil-i-
Kayyalan, Habba, Khumaran, Bagnigaran, Mahi-faroshan, Sabzi wa Tara
faroshan, Lamabra, Nisbat wa Qismat, Sabun-garan, Musadrah faroshan,
Gulfaroshan Jazai*, the property of the dead and the property placed in
another's custody.[110] All Muslim jurists are unanimously of the opinion that
all money from these sources is illegal. Since the present rulers get money
from these sources, eating and drinking with them is prohibited.[111]

109. *Siraj-u'l-Hidayah* (MS), ff. 33a–33b.

110. On the margin of the MS, it is explained as حواله و کفایه

111. Some of the taxes referred to above have been thus explained:
Dalalat-i-Bazarha: The *Futuhat-i-Firoz Shahi* refers to this tax. Dr I.H. Qureshi
considers it to be a tax on brokers. Professor Hodivala explains it as 'the
brokerage on the transactions in the market.' *Jazari* 'Afif refers to the abolition
of this tax. This tax was levied from butchers at the rate of 12 *jital*s per head
on cows for slaughter. *Mal-i-Amir-i-Mutrabi*: (Probably this is the same tax
which is referred to as *Amir-i-Tarab* in the *Futuhat*.) It was an amusement tax,
probably paid to the *Amir-i-Tarab* appointed by the state to control festive
gatherings. *Jakari-Ghalah*: It probably refers to octroi on grains and cereals.
Hasil-i-Kayalan: Tax realized from the *kayyal*s (measurer of grain, weighmen).
Mal-i-Habba: On the margin of the MS مال حبه ستدن is explained thus:

حبه بر پیشانی زدن و نزد آب آمدن

It is significant that Sayyid Jalal-u'd-din considered all Muslim rulers after the Pious Caliphs to be *malik-i 'uzuz* (i.e. rulers who had forcibly acquired and retained power).[112]

The contemporary records do not tell us anything about the arguments put forward by the Suhrawardi saints in support of their practice of hoarding wealth. Their discussions on this subject, though very frequent, were more in the nature of retorts and ripostes to the critics than a coherent and well-argued exposition of their point of view on a highly controversial issue. Shaikh Rukn-u'd-din Multani is reported to have remarked that since all sorts of people visited a saint, it was absolutely necessary for him to possess three things: (i) money, (ii) learning, and (iii) spiritual ability. With the first he could help those who thronged round him in need of money; with the second he could solve the problems of scholars; and with the third he could satisfy those who came to him for spiritual help and guidance.[113]

But these arguments carried little weight with their Chishti contemporaries who condemned all contact with the state as contamination and looked upon the good accumulation of wealth as a negation of the true spirit of *tawakkul* (trust in God).

The tradition of mixing with rulers and taking part in political affairs was established by the early Suhrawardi saints. The founder of the *silsilah*, Shaikh Najib-u'd-din 'Abdul Qahir, had intimate relations with the Caliphs of Baghdad. His presence at some of the coronation ceremonies is recorded in contemporary accounts.[114] Caliphs, Sultans, nobles, and government officers, besides a very large number of the *'ulama* and common people, visited his *ribat* and attended his lectures. The Shaikh knew how to maintain his dignity *vis-à-vis* worldly powers, and he never compromised with anybody on matters of principle. He resigned the Principalship of the

---

Mal-i-Khumaran: Tax on vintners and wine merchants. *Mal-i-Bagni-garan*: Tax on sellers of *bagni* (malt liquor). *Mal-i-Mahi faroshan*: (it has been referred to in the *Futuhat* also). Tax on the sale of fish. *Mal-i-Sabzi wa Tarra faroshan*: Tax on the sale of vegetables. *Mal-i-Sabun-garan*: Tax on soap making. For a discussion of the circumstances under which Firoz Shah Tughluq remitted these taxes, see my book *Salatin-i-Delhi kay Mazhabi Rujhanat* (Religious Trends of the Sultans of Delhi), pp. 420–23.

112. *Siraj-u'l-Hidayah* (MS), f. 16b. The saint was inspired by the following tradition of the Prophet: "The Khilafat shall remain for 30 years after me. Later it would degenerate into *Malik-i-'uzuz*." For a discussion of this *hadith*, see Shah Walliullah, *Izalat-u'l-Khifa*, p. 8, et seq.

113. *Akhbar-u'l-Akhyar*, p. 56.

114. *Tarikh-i-Kamil*, Vol. XII, p. 12.

Nizamiyah Madrasah because of the application of the law of escheat on the property of a boarder. Imam Subki informs us that so great was his prestige that if anybody sought shelter in his *ribat* he could not be forcibly taken away even by a Caliph or a Sultan.[115] When the Shaikh visited Syria, Sultan Nur-u'd-din Mahmud Zangi (1146–73 AD) accorded a hearty welcome to him and he stayed there for some time as a royal guest.[116] His sermons raised the morale of the armies recruited to fight the Christian powers at a very critical moment in the history of Islam.

Living decently and well was also a well-established tradition of the Suhrawardi *silsilah*. Shaikh Najib-u'd-din used to ride a camel with great éclat.[117] Shaikh Shihab-u'd-din, however, says that his master was not very particular about his dress and would "put on an expensive turban of ten *dinars* and of ten *dangs* (i.e. a cheap one) too."[118]

Shaikh Shihab-u'd-din followed the ways and traditions of his spiritual teacher. He preached in Baghdad under court patronage. Besides, on one occasion, he performed the onerous duties of an ambassador of Baghdad to the court of Irbal.[119] The nature and extent of his contact with the rulers may be gauged from the fact that he dedicated his works, *'Awarif-u'l-Ma'arif* and *Kashf-u'n-Nasaih-u'l-imaniya wa Kash u'l-i-ada'ih-u'l-Yunaniya*, to the Caliph al-Nasir (575–622/1180–1225). This dedication of a mystic work to a ruler was indeed unique in the annals of Muslim mysticism.[120] It is even more surprising that in his later work he has quoted some Traditions of the Prophet on the authority of al-Nasir.[121]

The Shaikh helped the 'Abbasid Caliph in critical moments. When the Khwarazm Shah invaded Baghdad, he went out to dissuade him from attacking the city. The author of the *Rauzat-u's-Safa* writes:

115. *Tabaqat-i-Kubra*, Vol. IV, p. 256.
116. Ibn Khallikan, *Wafayat-u'l-A'yan*, Vol. I, p. 299.
117. Shah Shu'aib Fridausi writes:

لباس علماء پوشیدی و بر اشتر سوار شدی و غاشیه پیش او بر
می گرفتند....... وطیلسان در برکردی

Manaqib-u'l-Asfiya (Calcutta, 1895), p. 99.
118. *'Awarif-u'l-Ma'arif* (Arabic text), Vol. II, p. 35.
119. *'Ulama-i-Salaf*, Nawab Habib-ur-Rahaman Khan Sherwani, p. 112.
120. Abul Ghalib Tamman b. Ghalib (ob. 1044 AD), wrote a book on lexicography. Mujahid b. 'Abdullah sent him one thousand coins and requested him to dedicate it to him. He refused saying: "I won't do it even if you give me the whole world." *Ibn Khallikan*, Vol. I, p. 97.
121. *The Encyclopaedia of Islam*, Vol. IV, p. 506.

شیخ بطریق سنت سلام کرد و بادشاه از غائت نخوت جواب
داد…… شیخ همچنان بریانی ایستاده به عربی خطبه بلیغ فصیح خواند و
سخنان مائل بر زبان راند¹²²

The Shaikh accosted the Padishah in the manner of the Prophet. The Padishah
replied with great haughtiness...... The Shaikh remained standing on his feet
and addressed him in eloquent Arabic and tried to dissuade him (from
proceeding further).[123]

These traditions determined the attitude of the Suhrawardi saints of
India towards the state. The early Turkish Sultans stood in need of the
support of the religious classes in order to consolidate their power and
build up an integrated and compact polity in India. When Iltutmish
ascended the throne of Delhi, he tried to employ as many religious men
as compatible with the efficiency of the administration. Since the Chishtis
were not prepared to associate themselves with the government, the Sultan
turned towards the Suhrawardis who extended their full support and
cooperation to him and accepted the posts of the *Shaikh-u'l-Islam*[124] and
the *Sadr-u'l-Wilayat*.[125]

(i) *Suhrawardi Support in Extension of Political Power*: Shaikh Baha-u'd-
din Zakariyya had set up his *khanqah* in Multan at a very critical period
of Indian history. Aibek's sudden death was followed by a mad race for
political power among the Turkish nobles and slave-officers and,
consequently, Hindustan was parcelled out into four principalities: Lakhnauti
was held by the Khalji Malik. Delhi and its contiguous territory was in the
possession of Iltutmish; Sind was governed by Nasir-u'd-din Qubacha, and
Lahore and Ghaznin were controlled by Yildiz. Iltutmish's attempt to unify
the empire brought him into conflict with the Turkish officers of Shihab-
u'd-din who challenged his claims to kingship.

Shaikh Baha-u'd-din Zakariyya, though living under Qubacha, supported
Iltutmish in extending his political prestige and authority. He joined Sharf-
u'd-din, the Qazi of Multan, in his plan to overthrow Qubacha's power and
wrote a letter to Iltutmish, probably inviting him to invade Multan. This
letter was intercepted by Qubacha who summoned the Shaikh and the Qazi
to his presence. Placing this letter before the Shaikh, Qubacha asked:

122. *Rauzat-u's-Safa*, Vol. IV, p. 118.
123. *Fawa'id-u'l-Fu'ad*, p. 212.
124. *Siyar-u'l-'Arifin*, p. 169.
125. *Akhbar-u'l-Akhyar*, p. 28.

"Have you written this letter?" "Yes," frankly confessed the Shaikh, "I have written this letter, and this is my handwriting." "Why did you write it?" asked Qubacha. "Whatever I wrote," replied the Shaikh, "was under divine guidance (*az haq*). You do whatever you can. (And for the matter of that) what is in your hands?" Qubacha was nonplussed. He ordered a meal to be served. The Shaikh did not like taking food at any body's house. Qubacha knew it but he thought that his refusal to partake of food would provide him with another excuse for punishing him. Contrary to the expectations of Qubacha, the Shaikh partook of the food from the dishes served. Qubacha's fury was cooled and he allowed the Shaikh to return home.[126] The poor Qazi, being a government servant, had to pay the usual penalty for treason; the Shaikh escaped scot-free. Medieval biographers have attributed the Shaikh's escape from punishment to his spiritual powers, but the fact is that the reasons were more political than spiritual. The Shaikh was immensely popular with the people of Multan. His execution would have incited rebellion in the newly-acquired territories of Sind and would have afforded Iltutmish a plea for marching into Multan. It was, indeed, this fear of political and popular reactions that prevented Qubacha from taking any action against the Shaikh. Popular imagination attributed to mysterious and miraculous powers what was apparently the result of political expediency.

Shaikh Nizam-u'd-din Auliya, our earliest authority for this incident, does not give any reasons for the Shaikh's ill-will towards Qubacha. He simply remarks:[127]

در انچه قباچه راج ملتان داشت و سلطان شمس الدین
در دهلی بود و میان ایشان مخاصمتی پیدا شد

(When Qubacha ruled over Multan and Sultan Shams-u'd-din was in Delhi there arose some hostility between them i.e., the Shaikh and Qubacha.)

From what Jamali has mentioned about the incident, it may be inferred that the Shaikh was definitely pro-Iltutmish in his attitude and had deliberately taken such a risk. His sympathy for Iltutmish was probably due to the latter's early contact with the Suhrawardi saints in Baghdad.

Ferishtah's remark[128] that Qubacha's failure to enforce the laws of the *Shari'at* (عدم رواج شریعت) was the cause of the estrangement is not

---

126. *Fawa'id-u'l-Fu'ad*, pp. 119–20; *Siyar-ul-'Arifin*, p. 131.
127. *Fawa'id-u'l-Fu'ad*, p. 119.
128. *Ferishtah* (II, p. 406) says:

در رواج شرع محمدی نیز نکوشیده و متعلقانش فسق و فجور آغاز کردند

supported by earlier authorities and may be dismissed as an invention of
Ferishtah's ingenious mind.

With such strong and influential supporters in Multan as Shaikh Baha-
u'd-din Zakariyya, Iltutmish could hardly allow that territory to remain in
the hands of an adversary. He marched towards Multan at the head of a
large army. Qubacha entrenched himself in the fortress of Bhakkar but was
soon forced by unfavourable circumstances to send his son 'Ala-u'd-din
Mas'ud Bahram Shah to treat with the Sultan. The young plenipotentiary
was arrested and Qubacha, disheartened by the detention of his son, tried
to escape but was drowned in the Indus (1227 AD).[129]

With Iltutmish's annexation of Multan, a long cherished desire of
Shaikh Baha-u'd-din Zakariyya was fulfilled. He now established close
personal contact with the Sultan whose religious leanings[130] always
endeared him to such people. Besides, the Shaikh accepted the honorific
title of *Shaikh-u'l-Islam*. Jamali informs us that this office continued in
the family of the Shaikh till his own time (*circa* 1535 AD).[131]

It may, however, be noted that in spite of his close contact with
Iltutmish, Shaikh Baha-u'd-din did not meddle in the struggles for
succession or the baronial conspiracies which followed the Sultan's death.
Sagacious and far-sighted as he was, he did not pursue the hazardous
career of a politician and kept himself completely out of the vortex
of politics.

(ii) *Suhrawardi Support in Dealing with the Mongol Problem*: The Mongols
constituted one of the most baffling problems of Indian politics in the
thirteenth century. Their repeated incursions into Indian territory were a
source of perennial distress to the people. The Sultans of Delhi strained
every nerve to meet the situation but sometimes they found themselves
utterly helpless in the face of these nomadic hordes that poured into the
country like ants and locusts. Shaikh Baha-u'd-din Zakariyya cooperated

---

(He did not strive to enforce the *Shari'at* and his relations started indulging
in sins and irreligious acts.) Jamali does not bring this charge against him.

He simply says that Qubacha was of a harsh nature (مزاج درشت داشت).

Siyar-u'l-'Arifin, p. 114.

129. *Tabaqat-i-Nasiri*, p. 144.

130. Vide my article 'Iltutmish, the Mystic,' *Islamic Culture*, Vol. XX, No. 2,
April 1946, pp. 165–80.

131. *Siyar-u'l-'Arifin*, p. 169.

Shaikh-u'l-Islam was both an office and a title during the Sultanate period. For
the duties of the office, see Qureshi, *Administration of the Sultanate of Delhi*,
pp. 179–80.

with the administration in dealing with the Mongol menace. In 644/1246 when the Mongols besieged Multan and the ruler of Herat made common cause with them, the Shaikh interceded for the town and saved it from destruction. Saif b. Muhammad Harawi gives the following account of this siege and the Shaikh's part in averting the crisis:

> When the year 644 AH commenced, Malik Shams-u'd-din and Sali Nuyin marched towards Hindustan. On reaching Multan, they laid siege to the city. The governor of Multan, Chengiz Khan, was among the slaves of Sultan Shams-u'd-din. On the fourteenth day Chengiz Khan sent Shaikh-u'l-Islam Qutb-i-Auliya Baha-u'l-Haq wa'd-din Zakariyya to Malik Shams-u'd-din to (intercede on his behalf and) persuade him to accept money and raise the siege. Shaikh-u'l-Islam Baha-u'l-Haq wa'd-din came to the Gate of the Blacksmiths and called on Malik Shams-u'd-din. The Malik came to the Gate escorted by ten soldiers and met the Shaikh. It was the day of '*Eid-uz-Zuha*. The Shaikh embraced the Malik and recited the couplet:

> "It is 'Eid for me now that I have seen your face. My work is accomplished as soon as I reached you."

> ...The Malik went to Sali Nuyin and reached the agreement that Chengiz Khan should send one hundred thousand *dinars* and Sali Nuyin would then effect his retreat. The next day Shaikh-u'l-Islam Baha-u'l-Haq wa'd-din came out of the city with one hundred thousand of *dinars* in cash and delivered them to Sali Nuyin. Chengiz Khan sent royal presents for Malik-i-Islam Shams-u'd-din through the Shaikh-u'l-Islam.[132]

It may be noted that *Minhaj-u's-Siraj* has not referred to this invasion of Sali Nuyin.[133]

Means of Livelihood

Muslim mystics of the Middle Ages permitted only two means of livelihood to their senior disciples: *ihya*[134] (cultivation of waste land) and *futuh*[135]

---

132. Saif b. Muhammad b. Yaqub Harawi, *Tarikh-Numa-i-Harat* (Calcutta, 1944), pp. 157–58.

133. Cf. Raverty, *Tabaqat-i-Nasiri*, p. 677 note, and p. 1201 note.

134. According to Muslim jurists wasteland if developed by a person became his property. Mawardi quotes the following *hadis*: 'The lands which come from 'Ad ('*adi al arz*) belong to God and His Prophet. Then they are given to you (i.e. the Muslims) from me.'

See also *Muhammadan Theories of Finance*, p. 503, et seq.

135. See '*Awarif-u'l-Ma'arif*, Chapter XX, pp. 180–92; *Fawa'id-u'l-Fu'ad*, pp. 40–41; *Sarur-u's-Sudur* (MS), *Siyar-u'l-Auliya*, pp. 560–61; *Ahsan-u'l-Aqwal* (MS).

(unsolicited charity). They preferred *futuh* to cultivation because it ensured greater freedom of action and minimized chances of coming into contact with the *diwan* (the revenue department). A cultivator, they said, could not be free from the control of the revenue officers and the tax-collectors. Most of the medieval mystics, therefore, lived on *futuh*, but they laid down the following conditions under which they could accept it:

1. The mystic should, first, surrender himself completely to God. He should give up faith in 'means' and look to God as his immediate as well as ultimate sustainer.
2. There should not be any desire, direct or indirect, for *futuh* in the heart of a mystic.
3. All gifts in the form of immovable property—villages, orchards, land, etc.—should be firmly rejected.
4. If there are any strings attached to a gift, it should not be accepted.
5. No regular or guaranteed payments should be accepted.
6. *Futuh* should not be amassed. It should be distributed as soon as it is received.

Strict enforcement of these rules saved *futuh* from degenerating into a parasitic institution. Since it entailed grave hardships in the initial stages, only those who were endowed with extraordinary mental and moral qualities could choose it as their means of livelihood.

Considered as a whole, the mystic attitude towards livelihood grew out of the following three basic concepts:

1. Subsistence of every living being is divinely apportioned, as the Quran says:[136]

   'And in heaven is
   Your sustenance, as (also)
   That which ye are promised.
   Then, by the Lord
   Of heaven and earth,
   This is the very Truth,
   As much as the fact
   That ye can speak,
   Intelligently to each other.'

   Shaikh Ali Hajweri approvingly quotes a mystic who used to say: "I know that my daily bread is apportioned to me, and will neither be

---

136. Quran, S. 51: 22–23.

increased nor diminished; consequently I have ceased to seek to augment it."[137]

2. Human needs, as well as desires, should be reduced to the minimum. "The more straitened one is in circumstances, the more expansive (cheerful and happy) is one's (spiritual) state, because it is unlucky for a *dervish* to have property; if he 'imprisons' anything (*dar band kunad*) for his own use, he himself is 'imprisoned' in the same proportion... Worldly wealth holds them back from the path of quietism (*riza*)."[138]

3. Fasting is one half of faith.[139] Constant fasting enables man to rise above earthly ties and conquer the animal in him.

Working out their whole philosophy of subsistence on the basis of these principles, the medieval Muslim mystics classified *rizq* into the following four categories[140] and discovered Quranic sanctions for their attitude:

1. *Rizq-i-Mazmun*, i.e., basic necessities of life like food and water. God is responsible for supplying them to every living being—man and animal. The Quran refers to *rizq-i-mazmun* when it says:

   There is no moving creature
   On earth but its sustenance
   Dependeth on God: He knoweth
   The time and place of its
   Definite abode and its
   Temporary deposit:
   All is in a clear Record.[141]

2. *Rizq-i-Maqsum*, i.e., the subsistence which has already been allotted to human beings at the time of creation and is recorded on *Lauh-i-Mahfuz*.

3. *Rizq-i-Mamluk*, i.e., private property—money, clothes, etc.

4. *Rizq-i-Mau'ud*, i.e., subsistence which God has promised to the pious people, as the Quran says:

   And He provides for him
   From (sources) he never
   Could imagine.[142]

137. *Kashf-u'l-Mahjub*, p. 13.
138. Ibid, p. 20.
139. *Fawa'id-u'l-Fu'ad*, p. 75.
140. Ibid, p. 102.
141. Quran, S. 9: 6.
142. Quran, S. 651: 3.

Trust in God (*tawakkul*) was permitted only for *rizq-i-mazmun*. Since a mystic wanted nothing more than bare subsistence—which is guaranteed by God to all His creatures—it was futile to hanker after it.[143]

It should be remembered in this context that the teaching of *tawakkul* in *rizq-i-mazmun* and *futuh* was confined to those senior disciples alone who were determined to dedicate their lives to the service of Allah and who could say:

و كلت الى المحبوب امرى كله فان شاء احيانى و ان شاء اتلفا

(I have surrendered myself to the Beloved. He may sustain me or kill me.)

To others, the advice of the Shaikh was always for *kasb* (some means of earning a livelihood). Shaikh Nasir-u'd-din Chiragh very clearly stated the Chishti viewpoint on this subject when he said: "There are two disciplines—one prescribed for the initiated and the other for the novices. For the select few the injunction was to shut their doors and pray to God; for the general run of men the instruction was to go out and earn a livelihood by dint of labour."[144] Again and again he exhorted his disciples not to eat their religion; in other words, piety is not to be exploited for worldly ends or to avoid labour. As was his habit, he narrated numerous stories to bring home to his audience the value of *kasb*.[145] In some of these stories he has illustrated his point that *kasb* (some trade or profession) and *derveshi* are not incompatible. They go hand in hand provided a man takes care of his soul and does not lose himself in the pursuit and enjoyment of wealth. Once he said that the *abdal*s earned their bread by selling

143. A mystic poet says:

بشغل جهان رنج بودن چه سود كه روزى بكوشش نيايد فزود
بدنبال روزى نبايد دويد تو بنشين كه روزى خود آيد پديد

The apocryphal *malfuz*, *Asrar-u'l-Auliya* (f. 28b), correctly records the mystic attitude when it says:

اى درويش متوكلان اين راه هرگز غم و اندوه رزق وغير او ندارد
سبب آنكه در روز ازل مقسوم شده است' خواهد رسيد

144. *Khair-u'l-Majalis*, p. 80.

145. For example, see ibid, p. 277, where the Shaikh is reported to have remarked:

لقمهٔ كسب نيكو لقمه است

(Livelihood earned through labour is good livelihood.)

grass.[146] At several places in his *malfuzat* he praises the teaching profession and commends to his disciples the vocation of trade.

The impression that these mystics discouraged the active pursuit of any vocation and thereby created a class of social parasites is based on a misunderstanding of the actual facts. Excepting those who were entrusted with higher spiritual work, all others were exhorted to earn their 'bread' with the sweat of their brow. What the mystics feared was that a man might think that subsistence was received from the man under whom he worked. This, they believed, led to the weakening of faith in the omnipotence of God. One must work for a living but must believe in God as the ultimate source of his livelihood and man as a mere agent of God. Such an attitude, they believed, led to independence of mind and fostered self-respect. Shaikh 'Ali Hajweri remarks:

> If He makes a creature the means of giving you daily bread, do not esteem that creature, but consider that the daily bread which God has caused to come to you does not belong to him but to God. If he thinks that it is his, and that he is thereby conferring a favour upon you, do not accept it. In the matter of daily bread one person does not confer upon another any favour at all, because according to the opinion of the orthodox, daily bread is food (*ghiza*), although the Mu'tazilites hold it to be property (*milk*); and God, not any created being, nourishes mankind with food.[147]

CONTRIBUTION TO INDIAN SOCIETY AND CULTURE

"From the thirteenth century," remarks Professor Gibb, "Sufism increasingly attracted the creative social and intellectual energies within the community to become the bearer or instrument of a social and cultural revolution."[148] Perhaps in no other country were the effects of this social and cultural revolution so marked and so far-reaching as in India.

The general impression that the Muslim saints came to India in the wake of the Ghurid conquering armies is incorrect and misleading. Long before Shihab-u'd-din or his Turkish slave-officers overran the country, many Muslim saints had established their mystic centres in northern India. The Hindu society was then passing through one of the most critical phases of its history. The caste system had deprived it of that dynamic energy which sustains societies in times of crises and makes them respond to new situations and new challenges. The idea of physical contamination had

146. Ibid, p. 277.
147. *Kashf-u'l-Mahjub*, p. 106.
148. 'An Interpretation of Islamic History', *Journal of World History*. Vol. I, No. 1, p. 59.

further weakened its social fabric. All amenities of civic life were denied to non-caste people who constituted the majority of the Indian population. They could not stay in the cities after sunset. They had no access to the temples and no sacred texts could be heard or recited by them. A careful analysis of the sites of the *khanqah*s of the early Indo-Muslim mystics would reveal the fact that most of them were established outside the caste cities in the midst of the lower sections of the Indian population. The unassuming ways of the mystics their broad human sympathies, and the classless atmosphere of their *khanqah*s attracted these despised sections of Indian society to its fold. Here they found a social order entirely different from their own. All discriminations and distinctions which the Hindu society had imposed upon them had no meaning here. All lived, slept, and ate together. The sacred Book was open and accessible to all. Thus demonstrating the Islamic idea of *tauhid* as a working principle in social life, the medieval *khanqah*s became the spearhead of Muslim culture.

The conquest of northern India by the Ghurids, no doubt helped the mystics to extend the sphere of their work to the cities where previously caste taboos had prevented them from establishing their hospices, but it also added to their problems by exciting the fury and odium of a section of the Indian population. Since their own attitude towards political powers was one of indifference and nonchalance, all those who looked askance at the Turkish oligarchy were naturally drawn towards them. Besides, their social outlook, which contrasted sharply with the attitude of the ruling classes, endeared them to the public. At a time when the country was resounding with the din and clatter of the arms of the Ghurids, the atmosphere of their humble dwellings acted as a corrective to the political hysteria of the period. They sat cool and collected in their *khanqah*s and taught lessons of human love and equality. The Turkish Sultans, puffed up with the Sassanid ideals of kingship, refused even to talk to low-born persons but these saints threw open their *khanqah*s to all sorts of people— rich and poor, high and low, townsfolk and villagers, men and women. The distinction between the noble (*sharif*) and the low-born (*razil*), which finds such a powerful exposition in the *Adab-u'l-Harb* of Fakhr-i-Mudabbir and the *Fatawa-i-Jahandari* of Zia Barani, was meaningless to the mystics.[149]

The governing class looked upon education as the exclusive privilege of the upper strata of society and did not like it to spread among the lower classes. The mystics, on the other hand, fought against illiteracy. In fact, it was through their persistent struggle against caste concepts and class

---

149. See *Diwan-i-Jamal-u'd-din Hansvi*, Vol. II, pp. 164–65 for the criticism and condemnation of all ideas of اصل و نسب.

distinctions that medieval Muslim mystics prevented the growth of Indo-Muslim society on the perverted ideology of the governing class and held aloft Islamic principles of equality and brotherhood. Balban might refuse to talk to low-born persons in his court, he could dismiss them if he so wished, but when he visited the cloisters and *khanqah*s of saints he must have realized that there were places in the Empire of Hindustan where his own position was not more exalted than that of any ordinary human being. Though within the political confines of the Sultanate of Delhi, the *jama'at khanah*s of the early Chishti saints of India did not form a part of the Delhi Empire. They formed a world of their own. The contamination of court life could not touch their spiritual serenity and classless atmosphere.[150]

With the settlement of the Mussalmans in India, conciliation and concord between the various culture groups was not only a moral and intellectual demand but an urgent social necessity. The conquerors had established their political supremacy by virtue of certain moral and physical qualities, but they could not continue to rule while the majority of their subjects differed from them in race, language, religion, and culture. The conservative and reactionary theologians rarely appreciated the change in the moods of the time and seldom tried to reconstruct their religious thought according to the needs of the hour. The Muslim mystics, however, rose to the occasion and released syncretic forces which liquidated social, ideological, and linguistic barriers between the various culture groups of India and helped in the development of a common cultural outlook.

A mind which failed to see any wisdom or truth in any way of life or thought except its own was the greatest obstacle to the growth of syncretic tendencies. The early Indo-Muslim mystics adopted an attitude of sympathy and understanding towards all cults and creeds. They exhorted their co-religionists:

اى كه طعنه زبت به هندو و برى
هم آموز از وى پرستش گرى

(O you who sneer at the idolatry of the Hindu,
Learn also from him how worship is done.)

150. Shaikh Hamid-u'd-din Nagauri used to say:

هيچ صفتى درآدمى زشت تر از جهل نيست' هرچه هست علم
است' هركه علم نداند گونى جمادى ست كه از وهيچ كارى نيايد

Sarur-u's-Sudur (MS), p. 75.

This broad and cosmopolitan outlook helped to break that spirit of mistrust and isolation which honeycombed relations between the various culture groups of India and paved the way for *rapprochement* at all levels, social and ideological. Amir Khusrau, who is by far the most powerful exponent of this attitude of medieval Muslim mystics, refers to Hindu customs and ceremonials[151] in a spirit which must have been instrumental in discovering the principles of essential unity between different religions. When he declares:

هست بسی جائی باقرار چوما نیست هندو ارچه که دیندار چوما

(Though Hindu is not faithful like me,
He often believes in the same thing as I do.)

he very neatly epitomizes the attitude of the early Indo-Muslim saints.

Unlike Alberuni who had studied Hindu religion at the philosophical level, the Muslim mystics desired to comprehend it at its psychological and emotional levels. They were concerned more with emotional integration than with ideological synthesis which was a very slow process and touched only a limited section of the intellectuals. Emotional integration was a more difficult venture but with surer results and on a larger scale. It is due to this basic fact that we find the early Muslim mystics more interested in Hindu religious *practices* than in Hindu religious *thought*. Historians have often complained about the paucity of material for evaluating the nature and extent of the influence of Hindu mystic ideas on the Muslim mystic thought and *vice versa*. A comparative study of the Hindu and the Muslim mystic *practices* alone can fill this gap.

---

151. Note, for instance, his attitude towards *sati*, a Hindu custom according to which a widow burnt herself on the funeral pyre of her husband:

وگر طاعتکنی بی عشق خاک ست   بعشق او بت پرستی دین پاک ست

که خود را زنده سوزد از پئی شوے   ننی کم زاں زن هندو دریں کونے

Shirin-wa-Khusrau, p. 32.

مرد ز بهر بت و یا منعم وبس   زن ز پئی مرد بسوزد بهوس

لیک چوبس کار بزرگست به بین   گرچه در اسلام روا نیست چنین

جان بدهند اهل سعادت بهوا   گر بشریعت بود این نوع روا

Nuh Sipihr, p. 195.

The eagerness of the Muslim mystics to establish closer relations with the Hindus and understand their religious life and thought facilitated the evolution of a common medium for the exchange of ideas. Since the earliest known sentences of the Hindvi language are found in the mystic records, the fact that the birthplace of the Urdu language was the *khanqah* of the medieval *sufis* can hardly be doubted.

The quintessence of mystic teachings in the thirteenth century was the Unity of Godhead and the brotherhood of man. The extent to which the Hindu mind was moved by these principles may be gauged from an analysis of the Hindu religious movements of the subsequent centuries. The fact that the religious leadership of the Bhakti movements in the fourteenth and the fifteenth centuries came from the lower strata of Hindu society—a section which had been deeply influenced by the Muslim mystics and their *khanqah* life—is too significant to be ignored. Probably never before in the long history of Hinduism had religious leaders sprung from those strata of society to which Chaitanya, Kabir, Nanak, Dhana, Dadu, and others belonged. There was hardly a saint of the Bhakti school who had not passed some of his time in a *khanqah*.

Another more significant aspect of the mystic contribution to Indian society deserves to be noted. The Urban Revolution, which had come in the wake of the establishment of Turkish power in India, had brought with it certain moral laxities and social vices, a necessary concomitant of culture growth. A cursory glance through the pages of the *Qi'ran-u's-Sa'dain* of Amir Khusrau and the *Tarikh-i-Firoz Shahi* of Zia-u'd-din Barani gives us an idea of the atmosphere that prevailed in Delhi after the death of Balban and before the advent of 'Ala-u'd-din Khalji. The *khanqahs* acted as a counterweight in maintaining the moral equilibrium of that medieval society. There is hardly any social or moral crime against which the contemporary mystics did not raise their voice—slavery, hoarding, black-marketing, profiteering, wine, and venery.[152] Barani very significantly remarks that as the result of the teachings of these mystics:

معاصی میان مردماں کم شدہ بود

(Vices among men had been reduced.)[153]

---

152. *Fawa'id-u'l-Fu'ad*, pp. 4, 40, 111–12, 116–17, etc.; *Sarur-u's-Sudur* (MS), *Jawami'u'l-'Ulum* (MS).
153. *Tarikh-i-Firoz Shahi*, p. 344.

CHAPTER VIII

MUSLIM RELIGIOUS LIFE AND THOUGHT OF THE PERIOD

A study of the Indo-Muslim religious thought requires a careful survey of the religious literature read or produced in India during the period under review. On this basis alone can the conceptual framework of the medieval mind be discovered and analyzed. But if the higher religious ideology finds its expression in the literary productions of an age, the outlook of the common man is reflected in the festivals he celebrates and the superstitions he holds dear. An attempt has, therefore, been made to study religious thought at both, higher and lower levels.

1. RELIGIOUS LITERATURE OF THE PERIOD

Due to the unsettled political, economic, and social conditions of 'Ajam during the twelfth and the thirteenth centuries, a large number of scholars, poets, traditionists, and administrators turned to India as a haven of refuge.[1] They established the traditions of Muslim scholarship in this country and raised Delhi to the status of a second Baghdad and a second Cordova. The suddenness with which many towns of northern India rushed into prominence as centres of Muslim learning is a phenomenon inexplicable except with reference to the impact of these Central Asian scholars. Their presence gave a fillip to literary activities and created such conditions that in Lahore a contemporary historian could consult one thousand books on such an abstruse subject as genealogy.[2] Hasan Nizami remarks in his characteristically

1. *Tabaqat-i-Nasiri*, p. 166; *Futuh-u's-Salatin*, p. 114–15; *Tarikh-i-Fakir-u'd-din Mubarak Shah*, p. 19; *Tarikh-i-Firoz Shahi*, p. 27; *Siyar-u'l-Auliya*, p. 59.

2. *Tarikh-i-Fakhr-u'd-din Mubarak Shah*, p. 66. Only a part of this book, named as *Bahr-u'l-Ansab*, has been published by Sir Denison Ross under the title: *Tarikh-i-Fakhr-u'd-din Mubarak Shah*. Evaluating the importance of this work in an article, Ross remarks about the author: "He speaks feelingly of the days and nights of strenuous labour which this cost him; but in the process he seems to have caught the genealogical fever and imposed upon himself the task of working out the trees of all the various famous men and dynasties of Islam. He tells us he spent twelve

hyperbolic manner that religious learning had become so widespread that in Lahore alone, out of every hundred persons ninety were scholars.[3] These scholars preserved the cultural heritage of medieval Islam.

Unfortunately, the fruits of their literary activity have not reached us. Ravages of both man and moth destroyed a substantial portion of this literary output before it could reach us.

(a) Non-extant Religious Literature

A comprehensive list of the non-extant religious literature of the period under review cannot be attempted for want of adequate information. Only works which have been referred to in contemporary or semi-contemporary literature may be noted here. Maulana Razi-u'd-din Hasan Saghani alone is reported to have produced the following works on *Hadis*:

1. *Misbah-u'd-Duja min Sihah ahadis al-Mustafa*
2. *Al-Shams al-Munirah*
3. *Zubdat al-Manasik*
4. *Kitab Darajat al-'Ilm wa'l-'Ulama*
5. *Sharh Sahih al-Bukhari*[4]

In all probability the Maulana compiled these books outside India, but contemporary records show that his works were read in India with keen interest.[5]

Another Indian scholar who died in a foreign land was Shaikh Safi-u'd-din Muhammad b. 'Abdur Rahman (644–715/1246–1315).[6] He wrote *Nihayat-u'l Wusul-'ila-'ilmil Usul* and *al-Fa'iq fi Usul-i-din*[7] on *fiqh* but these books have not survived.

Besides these works on *Hadis* and *fiqh*, some valuable contributions on mysticism have also been lost. Particular reference in this connection may be made to the works of Shaikh Hamid-u'd-din Nagauri and Qazi

---

years in collecting these materials and another year in deciding how he should arrange his tables, and in copying them out," *'Ajab Namah*, p. 409.

3. *Taj-u'l-Ma'asir* (MS).

از هر صد تن نود درو عالم   از هر ده نه مفسر قرآں

4. M.G. Ahmad, *The Contribution of India to Arabic Literature*, p. 251. It may be noted that a portion, if not the whole, of *Misbah-u'd-Duja* is incorporated in *Mashariq-u'l-Anwar*.

5. *Fawa'id-u'l-Fu'ad*, p. 103; *I'jaz-i-Khusravi*, Vol. IV, p. 284; *Sarur-u's-Sudur* (MS), pp. 55, 72, 73.

6. For a brief biographical account, see *al-Durar-u'l-Kaminah*, Vol. IV, pp. 14–15.

7. *The Contribution of India to Arabic Literature*, p. 266.

Hamid-u'd-din Nagauri. The former left a book, *Usul-u't-Tariqat*, on the principles of mysticism, besides considerable epistolary literature and poetic compositions. This book was available to Shaikh 'Abdul Haq Muhaddis (ob. 1642 AD) who has given a fairly long extract from it in his *Akhbar-u'l-Akhyar*. The *Usul-u't-Tariqat*, it appears, contained an advanced and scholarly exposition of mystic thought.[8] Qazi Hamid-u'd-din's two works *Lawa'ih* and *Tawali 'Shumusi*[9]—are not extant. It is, however, clear from medieval records that the Qazi's works were held in great respect in the higher academic circles of the country and some mystics taught his works to select disciples.[10] Khwaja Zia-u'd-din, a disciple of Shaikh Sadr-u'd-din 'Arif of Multan (ob. 1285 AD), is reported to have collected the sayings of his mystic teacher in *Kanz-u'l-Fawa'id*.[11] This work also does not seem to have survived. A seventeenth-century hagiologist says that Shaikh Farid-u'd-din Ganj-i-Shakar had prepared a summary of *'Awarif-u'l-Ma'arif*.[12] If this information is correct the work has not survived. Another important work, the *Wasiyat Namah* of Shaikh Baha-u'd-din Zakariyya,[13] which could have thrown valuable light on the religious attitudes and ideals of the great Suhrawardi saint, has also perished.

(b) *Extant Religious Literature*

The only work on exegesis which has reached us from the thirteenth-century is a fragmentary *tafsir*, *Tafsir-i-Para-i-'Amma*, by Hamid-u'd-din Nagauri.[14] It is not possible to determine who—the Qazi or the Shaikh Hamid-u'd-din Nagauri—was the author of this work. No contemporary writer makes any reference to it. The Hyderabad manuscript[15] which was copied in 1182 AH contains certain passages which give the impression of its being a later work.[16]

8. *Akhbar-u'l-Akhyar*, p. 30.

9. Barani refers to *Lawa'ih* and *Lawama'* of Qazi Hamid-u'd-din, *Tarikh-i-Firoz Shahi*, p. 341. The *Fawa'id-u'l-Fu'ad* (p. 128) contains a reference to *Lawa'ih* alone. Shaikh 'Abdul Haq writes about him:

قاضی حمیدالدین را تصانیف بسیار است، بزبان عشق و ولوله سخن می کند

Akhbar-u'l-Akhyar, p. 36.

10. *Fawa'id-u'l-Fu'ad*, 128.

11. Shaikh 'Abdul Haq has referred to this work in his *Akhbar-u'l-Akhyar* (p. 61) and has given an extract from it.

12. *Gulzar-i-Abrar* (MS).

13. *Siraj-u'l-Hidayah* (MS).

14. C.A. Storey, *Persian Literature* pp. 5–6.

15. *Catalogue of the Asafiyah Library*, Vol. I, p. 562.

16. *Misbah-u'l-'Ashiqin* (MS), a commentary on *Surat ad-Duha*, by Khwaja Baha-u'd-din b. Mahmud b. Ibrahim, grandson (*nabira*) of Qazi Hamid-u'd-din

So far as *Hadis* literature of this period is concerned, the following works of Maulana Razi-u'd-din Saghani are particularly noteworthy:

1. *Mashariq-u'l-Anwar*
2. *Risalah-fi'l-ahadis al-mawzu'ah*
3. *Durr al-Sihabah-fi-bayan mawazi' Wafayat al-Sahabah*
4. *Kitab fi-asma Shuyukh al-Bukhart*

The *Mashariq* is a collection of 2,253 sayings of the Prophet culled from the two standard works of *hadis—Sahih Bukhari* and *Sahih Muslim.*[17] Referring to Maulana Saghani's anxiety to incorporate only the genuine sayings of the Prophet in his work, Shaikh Nizam-u'd-din Auliya once said: "Whenever the Maulana came across any controversial *hadis*, he saw the Prophet in his dream and corrected the *hadis* from him."[18] Whatever personal satisfaction such a recurring phenomenon could give to the Maulana or his medieval readers, this method of testing the veracity of the Traditions of the Prophet, can hardly be considered basically sound since all *mukashatat* (revelations) or dreams have a purely personal significance. The Maulana himself was conscious of this fact. He did not, therefore, introduce this personal spiritual experience as a new principle of critical evaluation of the *Hadis* literature. He refers to such incidents just to express his personal satisfaction and faith in the correctness of certain sayings of the Prophet.

The *Mashariq* was, however, the most popular book on the Traditions of the Prophet.[19] It was introduced in the schools of Delhi by Maulana Burhan-u'd-din Mahmud b. Abi'l Khair As'ad al-Balkhi, a distinguished pupil of Saghani.[20] From that time onwards, it became a part of the syllabus of those days. Eminent scholars of Delhi who taught it to their pupils granted certificates for undergoing thorough instruction in this

---

Nagauri, refers to a work *Bahr-u'l-Marjan* from the pen of Qazi Hamid-u'd-din Nagauri. As the extracts show, the *Bahr-u'l-Marjan* must have been a work on exegesis. An Urdu translation of *Misbah-u'l-'Ashiqin* was published from Lahore (Malik Fazl-u'd-din, Kashmiri Bazar, Lahore).

17. Of these 2,253 sayings, 1,051 are common to both collections; 327 belong exclusively to *Sahih Bukhari*, while 875 are found in *Sahih Muslim* only.

18. *Fawa'id-u'l-Fu'ad*, p. 103. This statement is corroborated by internal evidence available in the *Mashariq-u'l-Anwar* (Istanbul edition, pp. 21, 75, 214).

19. For commentaries on this work by the Indian scholars, see *al-Saqafat al-Islamiya fi'l-Hind*, p. 155.

20. For a brief biographical notice see *Akhbar-u'l-Akhyar*, pp. 45–46; *supra*, p. 129.

book.[21] It was held in such high esteem in the succeeding century that Sultan Muhammad b. Tughlaq is reported to have placed it side-by-side with the Quran while taking the oath of allegiance from his officers.[22]

The *Risalah fi'l ahadis al-mawr'ah* deals with the problem of weeding out the fabricated *ahadis*. It may be 'regarded as a very early attempt to enunciate the principles of *mawzu'at*.[23] Saghani has critically drawn up a list of those persons who had tried to fabricate the Traditions of the Prophet. In this connection, he has also referred to an Indian, Ratan al-Hindi,[24] on whose authority some traditions have been quoted. The *Durr al-Sihabah* deals with the places of death of the Companions of the Prophet. Besides these works, one of the greatest contributions of Saghani towards the development of the science of *Hadis* is said to have been his edition of *Sahih Bukhari*. A. Mingana is of the opinion that the present edition of the *Sahih* which is current all over Arabia, India, Persia, and 'Iraq was prepared by Saghani.[25]

Of the surviving mystic works, the *'Ishqia*[26] of Qazi Hamid-u'd-din Nagauri and the *Mulhamat*[27] and *Diwan* of Shaikh Jamal-u'd-din Hansvi are of great significance. The *'Ishqia* is a small *risalah* dealing with the different aspects of cosmic emotion and its value in mystic experience. It is interesting so far as it goes, but the fact that interpolations and additions have been made to it by later generations[28] detracts from its value and makes it difficult to evaluate its thought content properly. The *Mulhamat* is "full of sufiistic aphorisms, sublime in ideas and sweet in expression".[29] The author possessed an almost electric aptitude for seizing upon analogies.

21. See Appendix A (i) for a certificate granted by Maulana Kamal-u'd-din Zahid to Shaikh Nizam-u'd-din Auliya.

22. Barani, *Tarikh-i-Firoz Shahi*, p. 495.

23. *India's Contribution to the Study of Hadith Literature*, p. 227.

24. Ibn Hajar al-Asqalani (*Isaba-fi-Tamyiz al-Sahaba*, ed. Biblio Indica. Calcutta. 1888) and Muhammad Ghausi Shattari (*Gulzar-i-Abrar*, MS) have given brief accounts of Baba Ratan. Ghausi refers to a work *Fazl-u'l-Khatab* from Shaikh 'Ala-u'd-din Simnani in which an attempt was made to establish the authenticity of the traditions quoted by the Baba.

25. *An Important Manuscript of the Tradition of al-Bukhari*, A. Mingana (Oxford. 1936).

26. Printed at Qaisariya Press. Delhi 1332 AH. I have an old MS of this work but its title is given as *Risalah-i-Sufiya*.

27. Printed at Yusufi Press. Alwar. 1306 AH.

28. For instance, one comes across couplets of Hafiz in this work, see pp. 38. 61, 22.

29. *The Contribution of India to Arabic Literature*. p. 85.

He has condensed and crystallized the mystic thought of the preceding generations in short and pithy sentences. He has emphasized the moral aspect of mystic discipline and has very vividly brought out the difference between the externalists and the mystics. "A *zahid* (externalist)," he remarks, "keeps his exterior clean with water; an *'arif* keeps his interior clean from passions."[30] All through this work, this difference has been very clearly delineated. The *Mulhamat* is, at its best, a work of general mystic interest and does not contain anything in particular about Indian conditions. The *Diwan* is more useful from this point of view. It throws considerable light on the contemporary religious thought and institutions.

A very important part of the religious literature of medieval India appertains to the conversations of the Chishti saints. This literature may be considered under two categories: genuine and fabricated. The *Fawa'id-u'l-Fu'ad*[31] and the *Sarur-u's-Sudur*[32] are the two most authentic records of the teachings of the early Chishti saints. The *Fawa'id-u'l-Fu'ad*, compiled by Amir Hasan Sijzi, contains an account of the conversations of Shaikh Nizam-u'd-din Auliya between 707/1307–08 and 721/1321. Chronologically, the compilation of this book belongs to the next century, but since the Shaikh had already started his mystic work during the period under review, and because it contains references to the life and teachings of the religious scholars of the earlier period, it constitutes a veritable mine of information for the religious life and thought of the thirteenth century. All through the Middle Ages, this book has been treated as the most faithful record of the teachings and tendencies of the great Chishti saints.[33] The *Sarur-u's-Sudur*, compiled by a grandson of Shaikh Hamid-u'd-din Nagauri, some time after the death of the saint on the basis of personal memoranda and notes, contains a very vivid and reliable account of the religious thought and attitudes of the period.

A small brochure, *Miftah-u't-Talibin*,[34] written during this period in the form of a *malfuz*, contains very interesting information about religious activities on the banks of the *Hauz-i-Shamsi*.

30. *Mulnamat*, p. 10.
31. Printed at Newal Kishore Press 1302 AH
32. MSS in personal collection—I have two manuscripts of this work. The earlier one seems to have been copied out by a careless scribe because several lines have been left out, making the text confusing and misleading (e.g. the remarks of Saghani, quoted *supra*, p. 163, are made to appear as the remarks of Shaikh Hamid-u'd-din). The second MS is a copy of the Habibaganj MS. It is complete and was carefully copied.
33. *Tarikh-i-Firoz Shahi*, p. 360.
34. I have a very old but incomplete MS of this work. The name of the author and the date of compilation are not given. I am not aware of the existence of any

The following *malfuzat* attributed to the Chishti saints of the thirteenth century are apocryphal.[35]

1. *Ganj-u'l-Asrar*
2. *Anis-u'l-Arwah*
3. *Dalil-u'l-'Arifin*
4. *Fawa'id-u's-Salikin*
5. *Asrar-u'l-Auliya*
6. *Rahat-u'l-Qulub*

This literature does not contain a faithful exposition of the religious thought of the persons to whom it is attributed. Nevertheless, it has a value in the wider context of the religious thought of the Middle Ages. It gives an idea of the popular assimilation and interpretation of the religious ideas of the early saints. The superstitious element in the religious thought of the Indian Mussalmans may be studied in this fabricated literature.

(c) *Religious Works Read or Referred To*

The contemporary records refer to the following religious works which, it appears, were popular in the religious circles and had, therefore, a significant share in shaping the religious outlook of the period:

(i) *Tafsir:*

1. *Kashshaf*[36] of Zamakhshari
2. *Tafsir-i-Imam Nasiri*[37]

---

other copy of this work. References to Shaikh Qutb-u'd-din Bakhtiyar Kaki, Qazi Hamid-u'd-din Nagauri, Shaikh Hasan Dana, and others show that it is an early work from the pen of a contemporary. The work is genuine and not a later-day fabrication. Leaving aside the superstitious elements, it contains information which is historically correct.

35. *Fawa'id-u'l-Fu'ad*, p. 45; *Khair-u'l-Majalis*, p. 52; *Jawami'-u'l-Kilam*, p. 134. For a critical evaluation of this fabricated literature, see Professor M. Habib's article: 'Chishti Mystic Records of the Sultanate Period' (*Medieval India Quarterly*, Vol. I, Part 2, pp. 1–43.)

36. *Fawa'id-u'l-Fu'ad*, p. 109; *Sarur-u's-Sudur* (MS), p. 44. *Dibachah Diwan Ghurrat-u'l-Kamal*, p. 24. Shaikh Hamid-u'd-din Nagauri once told his audience about a visitor from زمین بالا who had committed to memory four volumes of the *Kashshaf*.

37. *Fawa'id-u'l-Fu'ad*, p. 60. Amir Hasan Sijzi writes about Shaikh Nizam-u'd-din Auliya:

تفسیر امام ناصری پیش بود

Shaikh Hamid-u'd-din Nagauri taught it to his son and grandson. The grandson had not completed it when the Shaikh expired. *Sarur-u's-Sudur* (MS), p. 69.

3. *Tafsir-i-Shaikh 'Usman Khairabadi*[38]
4. *Tafsir-i-Maqatil*[39]
5. *Tafsir-i-Madarik*[40]
6. *Tafsir-i-Zahid*[41] of Abu Nasr Ahmad b. al-Hasan
7. *Eijaz*[42]
8. *'Umdah*[43]
9. *Tafsir-i-Haqa'iq*[44]

(ii) *Hadis:*

1. *Sahihain*[45] (i.e. *Sahih Bukhari,* and *Sahih Muslim*)
2. *Mulakhkhas*[46]
3. *Sunan-i-Abi Da'ud*[47]

(iii) *Fiqh:*

1. *Fatawa-i-Siraji,*[48] by Siraj-u'd-din Aushi
2. *Mukhtasar al-Quduri,*[49] of Abu'l Hasan Ahmad b. Muhammad al-Quduri
3. *Usul al-Bazdawi,*[50] of 'Ali b. Muhammad b. Al-Husain Bazdawi

---

38. *Fawa'id-u'l-Fu'ad,* p. 32. Shaikh 'Usman was a native of Ghaznin. For a brief notice, see *Fawa'id-u'l-Fu'ad,* pp. 32–33.
39. *Sarur-u's-Sudur* (MS), p. 29.

فرمودند که نیک تفسیرے پاکیزه است و مثل ندارد و شافعی
رحمة اللّه علیه آں را ستوده است

40. Ibid (MS), p. 41. Shaikh Hamid-u'd-din Nagauri taught this work to his grandson.
41. *Sarur-u's-Sudur* (MS), pp. 61, 68.
42. *Fawa'id-u'l-Fu'ad,* p. 109.
43. Ibid, p. 109.
44. *Sarur-u's-Sudur* (MS), p. 51.
45. *Fawa'id-u'l-Fu'ad,* p. 103.
46. Ibid, p. 105.
47. *Tabaqat-i-Nasiri,* pp. 325–26.
48. *I'jaz-i-Khusravi,* I, p. 119; II, p. 97; IV, p. 185, 284.
49. Ibid, I, p. 119; IV, pp. 189–90; *Sarur-u's-Sudur* (MS), p. 39. Shaikh Hamid-u'd-din used to say:

قدوری و منظومه را در مستظهرمی باید بود که هیچ مسئله بیرون
آں نیست که قدوری را امهات المسائل گویند

50. *I'jaz-i-Khusravi,* I, p. 119; IV, pp. 189–90.

4. *Shafi* and *Kafi* of Maulana Hafiz u'd-din[51]
5. *Nafi*[52]
6. *Nawadir-u'l-Usul*, 'Ala-u'd-din Tirmizi[53]
7. *Hiuayah*[54]
8. *Kitib-i-Fa'iq*[55]
9. *Mabsut*[56]
10. *Manzumah*[57] i.e. *Al-Manzumat fi'l Khilafiyat* by Najm-u'd-din Abu Hafs 'Umar b. Muhammad b. Ahmad al-Nasafl
11. *Muhit.*[58] There are two works of this name: one by Sarakshi (ob. 544/1140); the other by Burhan-u'd-din (ob. 616/1219).
12. *Zakhira*[59]

(iv) *Tasawwuf*:

1. *Ruh-u'l-Arwah*[60]
2. *Qut-u'l-Qulub*[61] of Maulana Abu Talib Macci (ob. 386/996)
3. *Risalah-i-Qushairi*[62] i.e. *Risalah -ila- Jama'at-i'l-Sufiya bi Buldan u'l-Islam* of Abul Qasim 'Abdul Karim b. Hawazim Qushairi (ob. 465/1072)
4. *'Awarif-u'l-Ma'arif*[63] by Shaikh Shihab-u'd-din Suhrawardi (ob. 1234)
5. *Sharh Ta'arruf*[64] i.e. Commentary on the *Kitab-Ta'arruf* of Abu Bakr Muhammad b. Ibrahim Bukhari (ob. 390/999)
6. *Mirsad-u'l-Ibad*[65] written in 1223 by Najm-u'd-din

51. *Fawa'id-u'l-Fu'ad*, p. 152.
52. *Khair-u'l-Majalis*, p. 220.
53. *Fawa'id-u'l-Fu'ad*, p. 72.
54. Ibid, pp. 165, 239; *I'jaz-i-Khusravi*, I, p. 119.
55. *Sarur-u's-Sudur* (MS), p. 40.
56. *I'jaz-i-Khusravi*, I, pp. 119; II, p. 97.
57. Ibid, I, p. 119; *Sarur-u's-Sudur* (MS), p. 39.
58. *I'jaz-i-Khusravi*, I, p. 119, 11, p. 97.
59. Ibid, p. 97.
60. *Fawa'id-u'l-Fu'ad*, p. 83. Shaikh Nizam-u'd-din Auliya remarked about this work:

نیک باراحتست' نیکو کتابی است

61. Ibid, pp. 45, 83, *Tarikh-i-Firoz Shahi*, p. 346, *Sarur-u's-Sudur* (MS), p. 92.
62. *Tarikh-i-Firoz Shahi*, p. 346.
63. *Fawa'id-u'l-Fu'ad*, pp. 26, 75, 112.
64. *Tarikh-i-Firoz Shahi*, p. 346. The *Kitab-i-Ta'arruf* has been quoted in *Sarur-u's-Sudur* (MS), p. 91.
65. *Tarikh-i-Firoz Shahi*, p. 346; *Fawa'id-u'l-Fu'ad*, p. 227.

7. *Maktubat-i-'Ain-u'l-Quddat*[66] i.e. letters of 'Ain-u'l-Quzzat Hamadani (ob. 525/1130)
8. *Suluk-u'l-Muridin*[67]
9. *Ihya-Ulum-u'd-Din*[68] of Imam Ghazzali (ob. 505/1111)
10. *Kimiya-i-Sa 'adat*[69] of Imam Ghazzali
11. *Arba'in*[70]
12. *Maqamat-i-Shaikh Abu Sa'id Abul Khair*[71]
13. *Isnad Hilya Shaikh 'Abdullah Tastri*[72]
14. *Kashf-u'l-Mahjub*[73] of Shaikh 'Ali Hajweri
15. *Akhbar-i-Nayyarain*[74]
16. *Diwan-i-Sana'*[75]
17. *Khamsa-i-Nizami*[76]

(v) *Kalam, etc.:*

1. *Maktubat-i-Fakhr-u'd-din Razi*[77] i.e. letters of Imam Fakhr-u'd-din Razi
2. *Nahj-u'l-Balaghah*[78] of Sharif al-Razi Abu'l Hasan Muhammad b. Tahir
3. *Akhbar-u's-Samar*[79]
4. *Kanz-u'l-Adab*[80]
5. *Siyar-u'l-Muluk*[81]
6. *Fazl*[82]
7. *Tamhidat*, Abu Shakoor[83]

---

66. *Tarikh-i-Firoz Shahi*, p. 346; *Fawa'id-u'l-Fu'ad*, p. 83.
67. *I'jaz-i-Khusravi*, Vol. I, p. 54.
68. *Fawa'id-u'l-Fu'ad*, pp. 72, 85.
69. *Sarur-u's-Sudur* (MS), p. 31. Shaikh Hamid-u'd-din Nagauri advised his disciples to read out one or two pages from it every day before their audience.
70. *Fawa'id-u'l-Fu'ad*, p. 103.
71. *Sarur-u's-Sudur* (MS), p. 23.
72. Ibid, p. 23.
73. *Tarikh-i-Firoz Shahi*, p. 346; *I'jaz-i-Khusravi*, I, p. 54.
74. Ibid, IV, p. 321.
75. *Tarikh-i-Firoz Shahi*, p. 67.
76. Ibid; *Sarur-u's-Sudur* (MS), p. 42.
77. Ibid, p. 27. These letters were collected after the death of Imam Razi.
78. Ibid, p. 61.
79. Ibid, p. 72.
80. Ibid, p. 61.
81. Ibid, p. 100.
82. Ibid, p. 61.
83. *Siyar-u'l-Auliya*, p. 116.

The above is a list of some of the standard works frequently referred to by different contemporary writers. To form some idea of the range and conspectus of an average writer of this period, reference may be made to the works of Sadid-u'd-din Muhammad 'Awfi. He refers to 94 works in his *Jawami'-u'l-Hikayat* and to nearly 72 authorities in his *Lubab-u'l-Albab*.

Excluding works which are apparently non-religious, the bibliography of his sources is as follows:

1. *Ihya-'Ulum-u'd-din*, Ghazzali
2. *Adyan-u'l-'Arab*
3. *Injil* (Gospel of Manes)
4. *Tarikh-i-Mashaikh-i-Khurasan*
5. *Tafsir-i-Ibn-u'l-Kalbi*, Muhammad b. as Sa'ib b. Bishr al-Kalbi
6. *Al-Taysir fi't-Tafsir*, Najm-u'd-din 'Umar al-Nasafi
7. *Jami'-u'l-Kabir*, Muhammad b. Hassan Shaibani
8. *Khalq-u'l-Insan*, Mahmud b. Ahmad called Bayan-u'l-Haq Nishapuri
9. *Rabi'-u'l-Abrar*, Zamakhshari
10. *Risalah Qushariya*
11. *Risalah al-Kindi*
12. *Rauzat-u'l-'Ulama*
13. *Zend Avesta*
14. *Sifr-u'l-Asrar*
15. *Sifr-u'l-i-Jabariya*
16. *Siyar-u's-Swalihin*
17. *Siyar-u'l-Kabir*, Muhammad b. al-Hasan Shaibani Faqih
18. *Sharf-u'n-Nabi*
19. *Sahih Bukhari*
20. *'Ayun-u'l-Akhyar*, Nasafi
21. *Ghurar wa Siyar*, Salabi
22. *Gharib-u'l-Hadis*
23. *Kitab-u'l-Maghazi*, Muhammad b. Ishaq
24. *Kanz-u'l-Akhbar*
25. *Kimiya-i-Sa'adat*
26. *Ganj-i-Khirad*, Khwaja 'Abdul Hamid
27. *Lata'if-i-Qisas-u'l-Anbiya*
28. *Musnad Akhbar-i-Nabavi*
29. *Miftah-u'l-Nijah*
30. *Asrar-u't-Tawhid fi Maqamat-i-Shaikh Abi Sa''id*
31. *Maqamat-i-Shaikh Bayazid Bistami*
32. *Malah-u'l-Nawadir*, Salabi
33. *Nasr-u'd-Durrar*, Salabi
34. *Tafsir Basa'ir-i-Yemeni*

35. *Tawilat-i Ahl-u's-Sunnah*, 'Ali Mansur Matridi
36. *Al-Tawassul-ila't-tarassul*, Baha-u'd-din Baghdadi
37. *Hanin-u'l-Mustajir*, Hamid-u'd-din Balkhi
38. *Risalah-i-Istighasa-ila-ikhwan u's-Salasa*, Hamid-u'd-din Balkhi
39. *Rauzat-u'r-Riza fi Madha Abi ar Riza*, Hamid-u'd-din Balkhi
40. *Zabur*
41. *Sama'-u'z-zahir-fi Jama'-u'z-zafir*, Zahir-u'd-din Samarqandi
42. *Fa'iq, Zamakhshari*
43. *Mani'at-u'r-Raji fi Jawahir-u't-Taji*, Hamid-u'd-din Balkhi
44. *Wasilat-u'l-'Ufat ila ikfa u'l-Kifat*, Hamid-u'd-din Balkhi
45. *Jami'-u's-Saghir*, Fakhr-u'd-din
46. *Risalah-i-Jalaliya*

II. MAIN FEATURES OF RELIGIOUS THOUGHT AND STUDIES

The above survey of the religious literature leads to the following conclusions:

1. The Indian Muslims were fully familiar with the classic contributions of Muslim scholars in the field of Quranic studies, *Hadis*, *fiqh*, and *tasawwuf*. In fact, India had become the preserver of all that was left of Muslim culture and learning in the East after the fall of Baghdad. The foundations of that academic eminence which India achieved during the Khalji period were laid during the Ilbarite regime.

2. There is little originality in the works produced in India during this period. The Indo-Muslim scholars of this period were by and large commentators, compilers, and abridgers. They have simply restated, summarized or annotated works prepared by the preceding generation of scholars. The tendency seems to have been to accept as final some standard work written outside India, and build up round it the entire structure of their ideology. This tendency which produced and perpetuated a conservative adherence to old categories of thought needs explanation.

    As Muslim thought developed from the seventh century onwards there were, in almost every subject, a number of opposed schools. But discussions gradually reconciled the ideas of these schools, or else left (as in mystic thought) two opposed schools in the field. Under medieval conditions of life—and specially the conditions of teaching—one need not be surprised to find that academic progress led to the acceptance of one standard work—or, if reconciliation of opposed ideas was not possible, to two standard works, one representing the more orthodox, and the other the less orthodox line of thought.

Broadly speaking, the religious attitude of the medieval Mussalmans had ultimately crystallized in two opposed schools—the Ash'arite and the Mu'tazalite. The Indo-Muslim intelligentsia of the thirteenth century did not accept either of these schools of thought in its entirety. But the inclination of the majority was towards the Ash'arite doctrines on which the foundations of orthodox Islam were laid. The dissolution of the social and political structures of medieval 'Ajam had thrown the best minds of the age into an attitude of defence. They thought that the survival of the Muslim society was possible only by the preservation of the old forms of life and thought. The spirit of philosophic enquiry was therefore discouraged[84] and *preservation* rather than *investigation* became the leitmotif of all scholarly undertakings.

3. Considered in order of priorities and preferences, the main interest of the Indian Muslims lay in *tasawwuf* (mysticism), *Hadis* (Traditions of the Prophet), *fiqh* (jurisprudence), and *tafsir* (exegesis). It is significant that while in almost every other country mystic tendencies had developed after the Muslim society had passed its meridian, in India mysticism gained popularity even when the Muslim society was in its early formative stages. This is why in the tangled skein of medieval Indian culture one comes across so many threads woven by the genius of Muslim mystics.

Whatever progress the study of *Hadis* made in India during the thirteenth century, it was due to the efforts of the mystics. Maulana Razi-u'd-din Hasan Saghani[85] roamed all over the country for forty years giving instructions in *Hadis* and creating interest in theological studies. Shaikh Baha-u'd-din Zakariyya went to Yemen to study *Hadis* at the feet of an eminent scholar, Maulana Kamal-u'd-din Muhammad.[86] Shaikh Nizam-u'd-din Auliya committed to memory the entire text of *Mashariq-u'l-Anwar*[87] and one of his elder disciples, Maulana Shams-u'd-din Yahya, wrote a commentary on it.[88]

---

84. *Fawa'id-u'l-Fu'ad*, pp. 50–51. See also the *Tarikh-i-Firoz Shahi* of Zia-u'd-din Barani (p. 43) for Sayyid Nur-u'd-din Mubarak Ghaznavi's diatribe against the teaching of philosophy.

85. Though technically in the category of the *'ulama*, Saghani was temperamentally a mystic and had, as shown *supra*, p. 163, instructed people in mysticism also.

86. *Siyar-u'l-'Arifin*, p. 103.

87. *Siyar-u'l-Auliya*, p. 101.

88. *Akhbar-u'l-Akhyar*, p. 96.

The inclination of the *'ulama* was more towards *fiqh* than towards *Hadis*. A careful student of Indo-Muslim religious thought cannot fail to discern in the attitude of the *'ulama* of the thirteenth century an indication of that preference for *fiqh* which characterized the religious studies of the succeeding century.

4.   The religious ideology of the period may be studied with reference to certain classics which determined the drift and direction of the Muslim mind. In *tasawwuf*, the *Ruh-u'l-Arwah* and the *'Awarif-u'l-Ma'arif* enjoyed an unrivalled place. Qazi Hamid-u'd-din Nagauri is reported to have committed to memory the entire text of *Ruh-u'l-Arwah*. His mystic perorations were mainly based on this work.[89] The *'Awarif-u'l-Ma'arif* was taught by elder mystics[90] to those disciples to whom they desired to entrust the responsibility of organizing independent *khanqah*s. The *Kashf-u'l-Mahjub* of Hajweri was also held in high esteem and Shaikh Nizam-u'd-din Auliya is reported to have remarked: "For one who has no spiritual mentor to guide him, the *Kashf-u'l-Mahjub* is enough."[91]

In *tafsir*, the *Kashshaf* of Zamakhshari and the *Tafsir* of Imam Nasiri were taken as embodying the final word. The *Kashshaf* was for the critically minded; the *Tafsir-i-Imam Nasiri* was for the orthodox. Conflicting opinions were expressed about *Kashshaf* and its author who was a renowned Mu'tazalite. Shaikh Hamid-u'd-din Nagauri was all praise for *Kashshaf*,[92] but his eminent contemporary, Shaikh Baha-u'd-din Zakariyya, did not like the works of Zamakhshari.[93] The jurists looked to *Hidayah* and *Quduri* for guidance in legal matters. The *Hidayah* formed part of the syllabus of those days. The *Sarur-u's-Sudur* refers to a *qazi* who decided all cases in the light of *Quduri*.[94]

For leading an ideal life according to the best traditions of religion and morality, people frequently studied the *Kimiya-i-Sa'adat* of Imam Ghazzali. Mystics exhorted their disciples to make this

---

89. *Fawa'id-u'l-Fu'ad*, p. 83.
90. Ibid, pp. 26–27, 75.
91. *Durrar-i-Nizamiyah* (MS).
92. See *supra*, p. 44.
93. *Fawa'id-u'l-Fu'ad*, p. 109. Shaikh Nizam-u'd-din Auliya once remarked about him:

دریغا با چندان علوم و روایات عقیده باطل داشت

94. *Sarur-u's-Sudur* (MS), p. 40.

book their constant companion and regularly recite its passages before the public.[95]

5. Within these traditionally limited forms, the standard of critical scholarship was fairly high. This is clear from the opinions expressed about various works and the assessment made of the contributions of different classical authorities. Shaikh Nizam-u'd-din Auliya was sceptical about the authenticity of traditions quoted in Imam Ghazzali's *Araba'in*. When a visitor referred to a *hadis* quoted by Imam Ghazzali, he remarked: "A *hadis* which is given in *Sahihain* (i.e. *Sahih Bukhari* and *Sahih Muslim*) is correct."[96] What the Shaikh implied by this remark was that the traditions quoted by Imam Ghazzali could not be uncritically accepted as genuine. It may be pointed out that modern scholarship has established that Imam Ghazzali was not very critical in quoting the Traditions of the Prophet.[97]

Guided by this critical spirit, the scholars never allowed any saying of any eminent saint or scholar to gain currency as a tradition of the Prophet.[98] Great care was, however, shown in the matter of outright rejection of any Tradition of the Prophet if its contents were doubtful. 'This is not given in the known and reliable works of *Hadis*,' a scholar might remark, if he could say nothing specifically against a tradition.[99]

Notwithstanding the fact that the study of *Hadis* did not make any particular advance during this period, it was not easy for any scholar to become known as a *muhaddis* unless he had committed to memory twenty thousand Traditions of the Prophet.[100]

The opinion expressed about the philosophic approach of Imam Fakhr-u'd-din Razi is based on a very sound and careful assessment of the great philosopher's work. Shaikh Hamid-u'd-din Nagauri once said: "Maulana Shams-u'd-din Halwa'i did not permit people to read the works of Maulana Fakhr-u'd-din Razi. He used to say: 'The Maulana has stated the critic's point of view in a very cogent and irrefutable manner, but his rejoinders are feeble and unconvincing.'"[101] It may be pointed out that a modern

95. Ibid.
96. *Fawa'id-u'l-Fu'ad*, p. 103.
97. Maulana Shibli, *Al-Ghazzali*, pp. 271–72.
98. *Fawa'id-u'l-Fu'ad*, p. 175.
99. Ibid, p. 109.
100. *Sarur-u's-Sudur* (MS), p. 75.

مرد را بست هزار حدیث یاد باید تا محدث شود

101. Ibid, p. 109.

scholar has expressed exactly this opinion about the *tafsir* of Imam Fakhr-u'd-din Razi.[102]

III. SOME IMPORTANT METAPHYSICAL CONCEPTS

According to Shahrastani, the problems which agitated Muslim minds in the Middle Ages related to:

1. Attributes of God,
2. Freedom of will,
3. Beliefs and actions, and
4. Reason and Revelation.[103]

A study of Indo-Muslim ideology with reference to them would, therefore, be helpful in understanding the basic categories of Muslim religious thought during the thirteenth century.

1. *Attributes of God*

The Mu'tazalites and the Ash'arites held diametrically opposite views about the Attributes of God. The Mu'tazalites denied the existence of Attributes beyond His Being. His Essence, they said, is self-contained and requires no separate Attributes. The Ash'arites, on the contrary, held that the Attributes of God have Their separate existence from His Essence and are co-eternal with Him.

The following anecdote quoted by Shaikh Nizam-u'd-din Auliya fully brings out the attitude of the Indo-Muslim scholars towards this problem:

> A mystic would be asked on the Day of Judgement: "Did you hear music in the world?" He would say: "Yes, I did." He would be further asked: "Did you ascribe to Us the Attributes expressed in (mystic) verses?" "Yes," would be his reply. "How can the casual (*hadis*) Attributes be ascribed to Our Being which is Eternal (*qadim*)?" God would remark. "O Creator!," the mystic would submit, "I did this on account of overflowing love for Thee."[104]

Qazi Hamid-u'd-din Nagauri, another great thinker of the period, thus states his point of view: God possesses Attributes, but these Attributes have no priority over His Essence. Attributes may be known only with the help of human senses, imagination, or intellect, but God is free from all these. Hence Attributes are over and above His Being.[105]

102. Abul Kalam Azad, *Tarjuman-u'l-Quran*, Vol. I, p. 13.

103. *Kitab-u'l-Milal-wa'n-Nihal*, as cited by Maulana Shibli in his *'Ilm-u'l-Kalam* (Azamgarh, 1939), p. 20.

104. *Fawa'id-u'l-Fu'ad*, p. 96.

105. *Akhbar-u'l-Akhyar*, pp. 40–41.

2. *Freedom of Will*

Whether a man has discretion in the choice of his actions or is merely a helpless pawn in the hands of destiny is a problem which exercised the minds of great religious thinkers in the Middle Ages. The Mu'tazalite scholars affirmed the absolute freedom of human beings and in that process imposed a limit on the sovereignty of God. The Ash'arites struck the other extreme and emphasized determined freedom which amounted to determinism pure and simple. An attempt to reconcile these two extreme points of view is discernible in the Indo-Muslim religious thought of the thirteenth century.

Since the problem of free will and predestination had a practical significance, it would be interesting to find out how and in what ways it was interpreted and tackled by the different strata of Muslim society. The following incidents supply a clue to the working of the medieval mind:

1. Balban is brought before Iltutmish by a Chinese slave-merchant. At the very first sight, Iltutmish discerns in him a shrewd, scheming and ambitious young man—dangerous to his family and dangerous to his throne. He declines to purchase him. After some time, Kamal-u'd-din Junaidi, the Wazir, presents Balban to the Sultan who accepts him now as a decree of fate.[106]

2. Nishapur is attacked by the Mongols. The ruler of Nishapur sends a messenger to Shaikh Farid-u'd-din 'Attar to request him to pray to God to avert the calamity. The Shaikh replies: 'The time for prayer has passed, one should be resigned to his fate now.'[107]

3. On being asked by Qubacha about the circumstances in which he had corresponded with Iltutmish, Shaikh Baha-u'd-din Zakariyya replied 'Whatever I did was at Divine instances.'[108]

4. Iltutmish's remark: 'Whatever is given, is given by God, I am helpless in this matter.'[109]

5. "Whatever a man does, good or bad," Shaikh Nizam-u'd-din Auliya told his audience, "God is the Creator of all that. Whatever happens, happens at His direction...." One day a man gave a blow on the neck of Shaikh Abu Sa'id Abu'l Khair. The Shaikh turned round to see who had struck him. The person who had struck said: "What do you

106. *Futuh-u's-Salatin*, p. 123.

به دل گفت "آن را که پروردگار   بکرد از پنے مملکت آشکار
دو صد بارش ار رد کند آدمی   به اقبال او کم در آید کمی"

107. *Fawa'id-u'l-Fu'ad*, p. 53.
108. Ibid, p. 120.
109. Ibid, pp. 211–12.

want to find out? Did you not say that whatever is done is done by God." "Certainly," replied Shaikh Abu Sa'id, "It is as I have said, but I just wanted to know who was that accursed person who was selected by Him to perform this job."[110]

The views of the medieval religious thinkers about *tawakkul*[111] (trust in God) and *rizq*[112] (subsistence) cannot be explained without reference to predestination. But these ideas could be constructive as well as destructive in individual life; they could integrate human personality and disintegrate it also. In a person with a proper attitude of mind, faith in these two principles was bound to create self-confidence and give a new orientation to his personality by developing absolute reliance on Him and relieving him of all expectations and desires from earthly powers. In a person with a different bent of mind, it could create inertia or encourage him to do things dangerous to society and government. In the anecdote quoted above, Shaikh Abu Sa'id Abu'l Khair represents the healthy, and the man who slapped him the morbid, working of these ideas.

Fully alive to the dangers inherent in such an attitude, medieval religious thinkers tried to qualify their teachings in this respect by saying that though God is Absolute, He has provided potentialities to every soul. It is the duty of every human being to actualize these potentialities within his restricted sphere. Whatever a man attains, he attains through his effort. 'Though Divine Mercy is there, one should himself strive and struggle for achieving it.'[113]

3. *Beliefs and Action*

Differences about the relative value of belief and action have led to the birth of many sects in Islam. The Karramiyans, for instance, believed that faith alone was necessary; action had no significance. A man, according to them, could persist in any action, lawful or unlawful, provided his faith was intact. Shaikh Nizam-u'd-din Auliya once explained his views on this problem in this way:[114]

The Mu'tazalites hold that the *kafir*s and all those believers who commit major sins would be condemned to eternal punishments. This is not correct. A believer who commits major sins would not be condemned to eternal punishments. The Ash'arites believe that a *kafir* who dies a repentant would be included among the believers, and a believer who dies as a *kafir* would be

110. Ibid, p. 247.
111. Ibid, pp. 54, 111; *Diwan-i-Jamal-u'd-din Hansvi*, Vol. II, pp. 43–45.
112. *Fawa'id-u'l-Fu'ad*, p. 102.
113. Ibid, p. 7.
114. Ibid, pp. 69–70.

included among the *kafirs*. Shaikh Hamid-u'd-din Nagauri used to address a Hindu as 'saint'. Imam Abu Hanifah was also asked about this matter. He said: The *kafirs* would not be condemned to Hell permanently.

These problems about faith and works, which had a merely theoretic value for the medieval writers on Muslim sects, became living problems for the Muslim religious thinkers when they were faced with a concrete problem in Indian society: Some Hindus recited the Kalima, accepted Tauhid, and developed faith in the Prophet Mohammad but (for fear of punishment and condemnation by their guilds and castes) kept their faith concealed.[115] When a contemporary Muslim saint was asked to give his opinion about this class of Hindus, he replied: "The decision of the affairs of such a Hindu rests with God. He may bless him or punish him, as He likes."[116]

4. *Reason and Revelation*

The general tendency of Muslim religious thought during the thirteenth century was to discourage the philosophic attitude. Philosophy, it was believed, could not possibly help in the integration of any social order. The attitude of Shaikh Shihab-u'd-din Suhrawardi, which was definitely hostile towards the philosophers, was approvingly quoted by medieval Indian writers.[117]

There were, however, great difficulties in determining with precision the nature and extent of the acceptability of revelation. The Prophetic revelation was considered final and legally binding but there were controversies with regard to the practical and social value of individual mystic experiences or *ilham*. The *'ulama* argued that such experiences could not possibly be made the basis of any social attitude or social discipline for individual religious and spiritual experiences or revelations were bound to differ, and in that case anarchy in social and religious spheres was inevitable.[118]

115. Ibid, p. 135.
116. Ibid, p. 135.
117. Ibid, p. 50.
118. *Sarur-u's-Sudur* (MS), p. 57.

گفته اند الهام نزد متصوفه حجت خدای ست و بعضی از سادات نیز دریں سخن با ایشان یار اند اما علماء الهام را منکر اند. میگویند اگر الهام حجت باشد' یکی گوید من از الهام ایں کار می کنم و دیگری گوید که ایں کار غلط ست که تو میکنی. پس تناقض پدید آید و در حجت تناقض روا نیست. اما هم الهام از نور دل است که بی خواست آدمی و بی اندیشه و بی تفکر حق تعالیٰ چیزی دردل پدیدمی آرد

Besides these purely metaphysical concepts, the ideas of the contemporary Muslims about some other religious problems deserve to be briefly stated.

(a) *Miracles*: Muslim religious writers have divided miracles into four types: (a) *mu'jza* or miracles of the Prophets, (b) *karamat* or miracles of the saints, (c) *mu'awnat* or miracles performed by a madman or a person without knowledge and without virtue, and (d) *istidraj* or the miracles of sinners.[119] The possibility of performing miracles was never denied but there was a tendency to look down upon any such expression of saintly power.[120] The common man was always anxious to behold some miracles of a saint but mystic teachers positively discouraged it.[121] "Performance of miracles is no achievement," declared Shaikh Nizam-u'd-din Auliya, "a Mussalman should be helpless in the path of truth."[122] On another occasion he said: "Allah has made obligatory on the saints to hide their miracles (*karamat*) just as he has made it obligatory on the Prophets to reveal their miracles (*mu'jzat*)."[123] Faith in the miracles performed by the Prophet was universal in Muslim society. Amir Khusrau refers to the performance of the miracle of splitting the moon (*shaq-u'l-qamar*) by the Prophet.[124]

(b) *Mi'raj*: There was considerable controversy on the nature of the Prophet's *mi'raj* (ascension). Was it a spiritual experience or a vision or a bodily ascension? The rationalists or the Mu'tazalites considered it to be a spiritual experience. The Muslims, in general, believed in bodily and physical *mi'raj*.[125] "What was the nature of *mi'raj*?" a disciple once asked Shaikh Nizam-u'd-din Auliya. The Shaikh replied, "From Mecca to Jerusalem it was *Asra*. From there to the first Heaven (*Falak*) it was *mi'raj*. From the first Heaven to the *Qab-i-Qausain* it was *iraj*." Apparently not satisfied with this reply, the disciple further enquired, "It is said that *mi'raj* is for the heart, for the body, and the soul. How is it possible for it to be for all the three?' The Shaikh did not want to go into details about this matter. He remarked: "One should believe in these things but he should not investigate about their character and their nature."[126]

(c) *Vision of God*: Another controversial problem was related to the vision of God. Some of the anthropomorphic suggestions in the Quran had led

119. *Fawa'id-u'l-Fu'ad*, pp. 68–69.
120. Ibid, pp. 172–73; *Sarur-u's-Sudur* (MS), p. 16.
121. Ibid.
122. *Fawa'id-u'l-Fu'ad*, p. 172.
123. Ibid, p. 117.
124. *Qir'an-u's-Sa'dain*, p. 17.
125. Ibid, p. 18. It appears that Amir Khusrau believed in bodily ascension.
126. *Fawa'id-u'l-Fu'ad*, p. 208.

people to believe in the physical vision of God. Shaikh Hamid-u'd-din rejected completely the idea of having the vision of God with the help of the intellect. Intellect, he said, created shapes and forms, but God is free from them. He approvingly cited the remark of Imam Abu Hanifah:

One who worships that which can be imagined is an unbeliever (kafir) until he returns to the worship of one that cannot be imagined.[127]

He, however, considered the vision of God to be an emotional experience with which a mystic was blessed on attaining gnosis.

(d) *Heaven and Hell*: At the popular level, heaven and hell were conceived as objective and concrete physical realities.[128] The common people interpreted the verses of the Quran literally. There were, however, people who interpreted Heaven and Hell as spiritual experiences determined by the actions of the individuals.[129]

(e) *Life after Death*: Belief in life after death is one of the cardinal principles of Muslim faith. The whole structure of Islamic religion is built upon this basic postulate, but it was interpreted differently by the different sections of Muslim society due to different levels of knowledge and understanding.

The higher religious thinkers believed in the continuity of life. They looked upon death as a bridge connecting the creature with the Creator and as an opportunity for the lover to meet his Beloved.[130] The common man interpreted life after death in a slightly different way. He thought that life in a form came to an end in this world but continued differently in the next.

IV. SOME RELIGIOUS SECTS

A. *The Hyderis*

The founder of the Hyderia sect was a Turk,[131] Shaikh Qutb-u'd-din Hyder,[132] who possessed great spiritual powers.[133] When Chengiz Khan appeared on the scene, he warned people of the impending destruction and

---

127. *Akhbar-u'l-Akhyar*, pp. 34–35.

128. *Dalil-u'l-'Arifin*, pp. 12–13 passim.

129. *Akhbar-u'l-Akhyar*, p. 35.

130. Ibid, p. 25; *'Ishqia*, p. 22.

131. The *Fawa'id-u'l-Fu'ad* has او ترك بچه بود (p. 19); but Siyar-u'l-Auliya says: سلطان المشايخ مى فرمود... كه سركيجه بود (p. 575):
(*sarkija* = vertigo). The context does not justify the word *sarkija* because the Shaikh speaks highly about his spiritual attainments in the very next sentence.

132. Ibn Battutah, *Rihlah*, Vol. I.

133. *Fawa'id-u'l-Fu'ad*, pp. 19–20.

himself retired into a cave where he shut himself off completely from society.[134] He died in 597/1200 at Zava,[135] in Eastern Khurasan, which is now known as Turbat-i-Hyderi after his name. No contemporary record gives any details about his life or teachings. Some of the practices of his followers are however, mentioned in early works. The Hyderis, it is stated, used to wear iron necklaces, rings, bracelets, etc.[136] It appears that they also carried sharp-edged instruments and razors with them.[137] A sixteenth-century mystic-writer refers to another strange practice of the Hyderis. He says that they used to pass a lead bar through their urethra and then soldered both its ends so that it appeared like a ring. This was known as *Sekh muhr*.[138] This practice was probably borrowed from the Hindu yogis, for the famous Arab traveller, Sulayman, remarks about some Indian ascetics:

ويجعل فى احليله حلقة حديد لئلا ياتى النساء

(And they put iron rings in their male organs in order to avoid intercourse with women.)[139]

Notwithstanding all these ways and means to lead a life of extreme abstinence, free from all desires of the flesh, the real spirit of the sect did not long survive. Shaikh Nizam-u'd-din Auliya sadly informed his audience in 707/1307 that while the outward form and peculiarities of the Hyderis had remained, their real spirit had disappeared.[140]

The Hyderi sect reached India very early. We first hear about a Hyderi saint in Lakhnauti. He was known as *Sultani Durwesh* on account of Tughral's faith in him. Tughral gave him three maunds of gold 'so that the rings and bracelets of the *qalandars* might be made of gold instead of iron.' When Balban marched against Tughral, he executed the *qalandar* and put his head on the gibbet.[141]

The most notable figure of this sect in Delhi was Sayyid Abu Bakr Hyderi Tusi Qalandari.[142] Contemporary records do not give any detailed life-sketch of the saint. His eminence may, however, be estimated from his contacts and the respect he enjoyed in the highest mystic circles of the

---

134. Ibid. pp. 19–20, 250; *Khair-u'l-Majalis*, p. 176.

135. For the Mongol attack on Zava, see *Tarikh-i-Jahan Gusha*, English translation by J.A. Boyle, Vol. I, p. 144, II, p. 615.

136. *Fawa'id-u'l-Fu'ad*, p. 20.

137. Barani, *Tarikh-i-Firoz Shahi*, p. 212.

138. *Siyar-u'l-'Arifin*, p. 67.

139. *Silsilat-u't-Tawarikh*, p. 51.

140. *Fawa'id-u'l-Fu'ad*, p. 20.

141. Barani, *Tarikh-i-Firoz Shahi*, pp. 91–92.

142. For brief notices, see *Siyar-u'l-'Arifin*, p. 67; *Akhbar-u'l-Akhyar*, p. 73.

country.[143] He was on the best of terms with Shaikh Jamal-u'd-din Hansvi, Shaikh Nizam-u'd-din Auliya and Maulana Husam-u'd-din Inderpati, the *Shaikh-u'l-Quzzat wa'l-Khutaba*.[144] His *khanqah*, situated as it was on the bank of the river Jumna, was a favourite resort for mystics and scholars. Whenever Shaikh Jamal-u'd-din of Hansvi came to Delhi, he stayed with him. He was on such intimate terms with him that he used to address the Hyderi saint as the *Shahbaz-i-Sufaid* (white falcon).[145] Shaikh Nizam-u'd-din Auliya also frequently attended audition parties at his *khanqah*.[146] The only saint with whom his relations were far from cordial was Shaikh Nur-u'd-din, popularly known as Malik Yar Parran.[147]

Malik Yar Parran was an eminent disciple of Shaikh Daniyal, a saint of the *silsilah-i-Ishaqia*. He used to wear purple clothes and carried purple banners with him.[148] When he reached Delhi during the reign of Balban and decided to settle in the neighbourhood of Sayyid Abu Bakr's *takia*, the latter objected to it and interpreted it as an act of intrusion in his spiritual territory. It was only when he obtained permission from the Sultan to settle in that area that Sayyid Abu Bakr allowed him to pass his days in peace.[149]

One very unfortunate incident in which Sayyid Abu Bakr Tusi and his followers were involved was the execution of Sayyidi Maula. Sayyidi Maula was a saint who came to India from the upper country (ولايت ملك بالا)[150] during the reign of Balban. While on his way to Delhi, he stayed for some time with Shaikh Farid-u'd-din Mas'ud Ganj-i-Shakar at Ajodhan.[151] When he sought the Shaikh's permission to leave

143. Note particularly the following verses composed in his praise by Shaikh Jamal-u'd-din Hansvi:

مر پای ترا سرم نثار اولی تر   یک سرچه بود بلک هزار اولی تر
در غار وطن ساز چو ابوبکر از انک   بو بکر محمدی بغار اولی تر

Diwan-i-Jamal-u'd-din Hansvi, Vol. II, pp. 42–43.

144. *Akhbar-u'l-Akhyar*, p. 73.

145. *Siyar-u'l-'Arifin*, p. 67.

146. *Akhbar-u'l-Akhyar*, p. 73.

147. For brief notices of Malik Yar Parran, see Barani, *Tarikh-i-Firoz Shahi*, p. 112; *Siyar-u'l-'Arifin*, pp. 67–68; *Gulzar-i-Abrar* (MS); *Akhbar-u'l-Akhyar*, pp. 71–72.

148. *Siyar-u'l-'Arifin*, p. 68.

149. Ibid.

150. Barani, *Tarikh-i-Firoz Shahi*, p. 208.

151. Barani's account (ibid, p. 209) gives the impression that Sayyidi Maula stayed with Shaikh Farid only incidentally, but Ferishtah (Vol. I, p. 92) writes on

for Delhi he advised him thus: "Sayyidi! You are going to Delhi and wish to keep an open door and earn fame and honour. You know well what is good for you. But keep in mind this advice of mine. Do not mix with *amirs* and *maliks*. Consider their visits to your house as calamitous. A saint who opens the door of association with *maliks* and *amirs* is doomed."[152]

Sayyidi Maula came and settled in Delhi. He could not attain any prominence during the reign of Balban but the general laxity in discipline that followed the accession of Kaiqubad gave him a chance to establish a magnificent *khanqah* and attract huge crowds of visitors. His influence reached its climax during the early years of Sultan Jalal-u'd-din's reign. Khan-i-Khanan, the eldest son of the Sultan, became one of his devotees and the Sayyidi began to treat him as his son.[153]

Sayyidi Maula's bounty and the enormous expenses he incurred in maintaining a *langar* (free kitchen) puzzled all people. Delicacies which were beyond the means of *khans* and *maliks* were served in his *khanqah* at every meal.[154] Nobody could say with confidence about the sources of his income. Whoever asked him for money, he directed him to a particular place where gold and silver coins, glittering as if fresh from the mint,[155] could be found. He never asked anybody for anything and did not even believe in the current mystic practice of accepting unsolicited charity (*futuh*). His life, consequently, became an enigma to his contemporaries who attributed all sort of things to him—magic,[156] sorcery,[157] alchemy,[158] etc.

The Sayyidi had his own eccentric ways. He did not go to the mosque to offer Friday prayers and, though he offered his obligatory prayers regularly, he did not join the congregation.[159] But he was not wanting in strenuous spiritual exercises. He did much penance and did not spend anything on his personal comfort. Clad in a blanket, he lived a simple and unostentatious life. No personal servant or slave girl looked after him. He was remarkably free from all desires of the flesh.[160]

---

the authority of *Mulhiqat-i-'Ain-u'd-din Bijapuri* that he had come to India with the specific purpose of meeting Shaikh Farid.

152. Barani, *Tarikh-i-Firoz Shahi*, p. 209.
153. Ibid. p. 210.
154. Ibid. p. 208.
155. Ibid. p. 209.
156. *Futuh-u's-Salatin*, p. 216; *Akhbar-u'l-Akhyar*, p. 73.
157. *Futuh-u's-Salatin*, p. 216.
158. *Tarikh-i-Firoz Shahi*, p. 208.
159. Ibid, p. 20.
160. Ibid.

When Sayyidi's popularity increased,[161] some intriguers and mischief-mongers gathered round him and sought to exploit the situation to their advantage. Qazi Jalal-u'd-din Kashani, who was notorious for his mischief, began to visit his *khanqah* regularly and often stayed there late into the night. His presence there converted the Sayyidi's retreat into a hot-bed of sedition and conspiracy. Many scions of the displaced families of Balban's court who nursed personal grievances against the Sultan further charged the atmosphere with intrigue and chicanery. A former *kotwal*, Brinjtan, and a wrestler of Delhi, Hatya Paik—both of whom had passed their days in luxury during the reign of Balban[162]—found in Sayyidi Maula's *khanqah* an opportunity to fan the flames against the Khalji Sultan. Soon the *khanqah* of Sayyidi Maula became the centre of anti-Khalji propaganda and Qazi Jalal, Hatya Paik, Brinjtan, and others hatched a conspiracy to kill Jalal-u'd-din Khalji and instal Sayyidi Maula on the throne.[163] Brinjtan and Hatya Paik were to kill the Sultan when the latter came out to offer prayers in the mosque. A daughter of Sultan Nasir-u'd-din was to be married to Sayyidi Maula in order to elevate his family status. Qazi Jalal was to be honoured with the title of Qazi Khan and the *iqta'* of Multan was assigned to him. Other conspirators were also assigned posts and offices.[164]

The conspiracy had almost matured when one of the conspirators divulged it to the Sultan who took prompt action and arrested all the conspirators. When questioned about their intentions, every one denied his complicity in the plot. The Sultan ordered them to pass through the ordeal of fire[165] in order to establish their guiltlessness.[166] The *'ulama*, however, declared against punishment by ordeal. "The function of fire is to burn," they said, "it will burn the truthful as well as the liar." Since there was only one witness to the conspiracy, the charges against Sayyidi Maula

---

161. According to Ferishtah, nearly ten thousand people had associated themselves with Sayyidi Maula and had joined the circle of his admirers (Vol. I, p. 93).

162. *Tarikh-i-Firoz Shahi*, p. 210. Barani informs us that they had received a lac *jitals* as salary during the reign of Balban.

163. Barani (ibid.) says: می خواهند خلیفه سازند

(I am not inclined to take the word *khalifa* in its technical sense. Here Barani only means installing him as a ruler.)

164. Ibid, pp. 210–11.

165. Trial by ordeal was practised in Hindu India. See the accounts of Sulayman. and Ibn Rusta in M.H. Nainar's *Arab Geographers' Knowledge of South India*. pp. 109–10.

166. Barani says that a fierce fire was lighted at Baharpur and the Sultan had gone there with his nobles and the *'ulama* of the city. *Tarikh-i-Firoz Shahi*, p. 211.

remained unproved and legally no action could be taken on a solitary testimony. The Sultan got exasperated. He exiled the conspirators and confiscated all their properties. The two arch-conspirators, Kotwal Brinjtan and Hatya Paik, were executed.[167]

Sayyidi Maula was then brought before the Sultan in chains and fetters. The Sultan himself began to cross-examine him but could not extract a confession from him. He then turned towards Shaikh Abu Bakr Tusi who was present there with his followers and said: 'O Dervishes! Get me justice from this Maula.' On hearing this appeal, Bahri, a reckless Hyderi, rushed forward and began to torture Sayyidi Maula with some sharp-edged instrument. Then Arkali Khan beckoned to an elephant-driver who crushed Sayyidi under the feet of an elephant.[168]

It is difficult to determine the extent of Sayyidi Maula's complicity in this conspiracy to assassinate Jalal-u'd-din. Probably he was exploited and used by elements hostile to the group then in power at the court. Yahya Sirhindi says that the charge of conspiracy against him was concocted by Malik Ulghu.[169] 'Isami holds some 'misguided mystics' (خرقه پوشان خام) responsible for his execution. He says that these people had, out of mischief, implicated Sayyidi Maula in this conspiracy. He further says that the Sultan was in Mandawar when Sayyidi Maula was arrested and all these proceedings against him had taken place without the permission of the Sultan.[170] 'Isami differs from Barani in many essential details. But when all facts and circumstances are kept in mind the conclusion cannot be avoided that rivalry between Khan-i-khanan and Arkali Khan was largely responsible for this unhappy episode. Probably the Sayyidi's secret source of income lay in the imperial palace itself.

The reaction of the credulous people of those days to the execution of Sayyidi Maula may be read in the pages of the contemporary historians. Both Barani and 'Isami say that divine wrath followed this unjust execution. "I myself remember," writes Barani, "that a black dust storm arose on the day of Sayyidi Maula's execution and the world became dark ... famine stalked the land and due to dearth of food people drowned themselves in the Jumna."[171] All this, Barani would have us believe, was due to the execution of Sayyidi Maula and was not a case of natural drought. His account, however, gives an idea of the credulous tendencies of the Middle

---

167. Ibid.
168. *Tarikh-i-Firoz Shahi*, p. 211.
169. Ibid, pp. 65–67.
170. *Futuh-u's-Salatin*, p. 216.
171. *Tarikh-i-Firoz Shahi*, p. 212.

Ages. The way in which Sayyid Abu Bakr and his disciples had played a leading role in the execution of Sayyidi Maula could not but antagonize public opinion against him and the Hyderi *qalandar*s.

B. *The Isma'ilis*

The political influence of the Isma'ilis was first established in Multan by Jalam b. Shayban in 373/983. He issued coins in the name of the Fatimid Caliph and acknowledged him as the legal sovereign. For more than a century, Multan and Mansura continued to owe allegiance to the Fatimids of Egypt. With the rise of Ghaznin, the political power of the Isma'ilis received a setback. Hamid, the Isma'ili ruler of Upper Sind, adopted a conciliatory attitude towards Subuktigin and kept him pleased with occasional presents. But his grandson, Abu Fath Da'ud, abandoned this policy of conciliation and appeasement and strained his relations with Sultan Mahmud. In 1005–06, Sultan Mahmud marched against him and forced him to recant from his heretic views. Da'ud promised to pay an annual tribute of 20,000 *dirhams*. But this treaty could not stabilize relations between Multan and Ghaznin and within five years Mahmud reappeared in Multan and murdered a very large number of Isma'ilis. Da'ud ended his life as a prisoner in the fort of Ghurak, some fifty miles from Qandhar. But Mahmud's military operations could not extirpate completely the Isma'ili influence in Sind and Mansura. A hundred and fifty years later, when Shihab-u'd-din of Ghur appeared on the Indian scene, the Isma'ili influence was a factor to be reckoned with. The Ghurid prince adopted an attitude of uncompromising sternness towards them.[172]

According to Minhaj, there were 105 forts of the Isma'ilis, 70 in Quhistan, and the rest in Alamut.[173] Shihab-u'd-din plundered Quhistan and gave a rude shock to Isma'ili power in one of its strongest centres.

The existence of an Isma'ili principality in India was a strategic danger for Shihab-u'd-din. He could not organize his Indian campaigns so long as an Isma'ili principality existed in Sind. In 571/1175 Shihab-u'd-din attacked their Indian strongholds and nearly liquidated them.[174] Referring to the results of this attack, W. Ivanow remarks: "The Isma'ilis were partly massacred, but the majority went underground living in the guise of Hindus."[175]

172. *Tarikh-i-Fakhr-u'd-din Mubarak Shah*, pp. 19–20.

173. *Tabaqat-i-Nasiri*, p. 418; *Raverty*, pp. 1205–06.

174. *Tabaqat-i-Nasiri*, p. 116.

Minhaj very jubilantly remarks: 'He delivered Multan from the hands of the Qaramatah.'

175. *Brief Survey of the Evolution of Ismailism* (Bombay, 1952), p. 20.

The extinction of the political power of the Isma'ilis in India embittered their attitude towards the Shansabanians and the Ilbarites. They retaliated by resorting to assassination and secret methods of hostile propaganda.[176] In 1206, when Shihab-u'd-din was going back to Ghaznin, after chastising the Khokars, he halted on the Indus at a place called Damyak. Here some Isma'ili fanatics[177] assassinated him while he was offering his evening prayers. This assassination made the early Sultans of Delhi inveterate enemies of Isma'ilism and other allied cults.

"About a hundred years or so later," remarks Ivanow, "a wave of Isma'ili refugees from the Mongol invasion of Persia apparently reached Sind. It is probable that their religious leaders, in the guise of dervishes, soon discovered and came in contact with the remnants of the earlier community and that by making use of their doctrine which formed a transition between Ismailism, Sufism and Hinduism, they greatly expanded their numbers."[178]

Twice during the period under review, the Isma'ilis, called *Mulahidah* by their Sunni contemporaries, sought to create disorder and lawlessness in Delhi, but Muslim public opinion was so hostile towards them that they did not succeed in their attempt to bring about a *coup d'état*. The first organized effort to achieve this objective was made during the reign of Iltutmish, probably after his investiture from the Caliph of Baghdad. They collected together in Delhi from all sides and raised a tumult in the mosque

176. On the Isma'ili 'Patterns of Assassinations and Massacre', see Marshall. G. Hodgson's scholarly study, *The Order of Assassins* (Monton and Co., 1955), pp. 110–15.

177. There is some difference of opinion among the authorities on this point. Wassaf (*Tarikh-i-Guzidah*, Vol. I, p. 52), and Nizam-u'd-din (*Tabaqat-i-Akbari*, Vol. I, p. 40) say that the Khokars had planned it. Others, like Zahabi (*Duwal-u'l-Islam*, II, p. 82). Minhaj (*Tabaqat-i-Nasiri*, p. 124), and Yahya Sirhindi (*Tarikh-i-Mubarak Shahi*, p. 12) hold the Mulahidah responsible for this assassination. Ibn-i-Asir says that when the assassins were secured, two among them were found to be circumcised (i.e. were Mussalmans). In all probability this was a joint work of the Khokars and the Mulahidah (Habibullah, *Foundation of Muslim Rule in India*, p. 79). Both of them were hostile to the Sultan and the Mulahidah who were experts in secret methods of assassination could very well join hands with the Khokars in accomplishing a common objective. Ibn-i-Asir says that after the murder some mischievous persons got it circulated that Imam Razi was aware of the Mulahidah intentions and had deliberately refrained from divulging the conspiracy. The people became furious and thought of doing harm to the Imam who sought shelter with Mu'ayyid-u'd-Mulk (Vol. 12, p. 83 as cited in Abdus Salam Nadavi, *Imam Razi*, pp. 121–23).

178. *Brief Survey of the Evolution of Ismailism*, p. 20.

with the object of capturing the city and killing the king. They were, however, suppressed by force.[179]

A second attempt to disturb the peace of the capital was made by Nur Turk during the reign of Razia. Nur Turk was a man of intensely religious temperament. He led the simple and austere life of mystics. His only means of livelihood was a *dang* per day which his freed slave gave to him.[180] So long as he lived in Delhi he did not accept anything from anybody. Razia once sent a bag of gold coins to him. He beat the bag with his stick and scornfully returned the money to the Sultan.[181] Being the man of austere and simple ways that he was, Nur Turk did not like the ways of the *'ulama* whom he found wallowing in the dirty waters of politics. He condemned them roundly for their greed of gold and glory. Minhaj was naturally chagrined at this criticism which applied to him as much as to anybody else and retaliated by painting him in lurid colours.[182] However, Minhaj's version about Nur Turk is that he was a leader of the Mulahidah.[183] He collected together his devotees from the neighbourhood of Delhi, Gujarat, Sind, and the Doab and started a campaign of criticism against the *'ulama*. He and his followers condemned the Hanafi and the Shafi'i doctrines and dubbed the Sunni *'ulama* as *Nasibi*[184] and *Murji*.[185] On 6 Rajab 634/

---

179. *Futuh-u's-Salatin*, p. 122. No other medieval historian, not even Minhaj, has referred to this rising of the Mulahidah. Since 'Isami has not referred to Nur Turk's revolt during the reign of Razia, the possibility of his confusing it with a later event cannot be ruled out.

180. *Fawa'id-u'l-Fu'ad*, p. 199.

181. Ibid; *Akhbar-u'l-Akhyar*, p. 74.

182. *Fawa'id-u'l-Fu'ad*, p. 199.

183. *Tabaqat-i-Nasiri*, pp. 189–90.

184. Amir Hasan asked Shaikh Nizam-u'd-din Auliya to explain these terms. The Shaikh replied: ناجی رافضی را گویند و مرجی طائفه را گویند که هر جا رجا کند *Fawa'id-u'l-Fu'ad*, p. 199.

185. *Murjiah* literally means procrastinators. A Muslim sect which believes that the judgement of every true believer who has been guilty of a grievous sin will be deferred till the Resurrection; for which reason they pass no sentence on him in the world, either of absolution or condemnation. They also hold that disobedience with faith hurts not, and that on the other hand, obedience with infidelty profits not As to the reason of their name there is a difference of opinion. Some think that they are so called because they postpone works to intention, and profession of the faith; others because they allow hope by asserting that disobedience with faith hurts not, etc.; others take the reason of the name to be their deferring the sentence of the sinner to the Day of Resurrection; and others their degrading of 'Ali. For details, see T.P. Hughes, *Dictionary of Islam* (London, 1935), pp. 421–22.

1237 AD, one thousand armed Mulahidah entered the Juma' Masjid from two directions and killed a number of the Mussalmans. When confusion and panic spread, some persons led by Nasir-u'd-din Balrami and Imam Nasir rushed from the city armed with weapons. They fought with the Mulahidah while the Mussalmans hurled stones at the miscreants from the mosque.[186]

This is Minhaj's account of the rising which should be taken with a grain of salt. The following facts deserve careful consideration in this context:

1. Shaikh Nizam-u'd-din Auliya very feelingly asserts that Nur Turk was purer than the rain water,[187] and, that the charges against him were maliciously cooked up by Minhaj.
2. A scholar belonging to the Mulahidah sect could not have been reverentially mentioned by scholars such as Amir Khurd and Shaikh 'Abd-u'l-Haq Muhaddis as "*Maulana Nur Turk*".[188]
3. Shaikh 'Abd-u'l-Haq could not have included him in his calendar of the Indo-Muslim saints if he had been associated with any heretic group.
4. Razia could never have thought of sending money to a member of the Mulahidah sect, for it was the declared policy of all Sunni rulers owing allegiance to the 'Abbasid Caliphate to take stern measures against the heretics.
5. If he had been one of the Mulahidah, Shaikh Farid Ganj-i-Shakar would not have gone to attend his sermon.
6. On leaving India, Nur Turk went to Mecca and settled there. No scholar of the Mulahidah would have been allowed to live like that in the sacred city of Mecca. The Nur Turk episode, therefore, is not a clear case of Mulahidah activities in Delhi. Its real nature has been obscured by the conflicts and controversies that marred the relations of Nur Turk with the Sunni *'ulama* of the day.

It is, however, certain that more than once the Isma'ilis sought to upset the peace and tranquillity of the capital and, though politically they had been liquidated long before, their secret activities continued for many decades more. The *ashab-i-ibahat* against whom Sultan 'Ala-u'd-din Khalji took severe measures, and the various heretic groups to whom Firoz Shah Tughluq refers in his *Futuhat*, were offshoots of the Isma'ili tendencies

186. *Tabaqat-i-Nasiri*, pp. 189–90.
187. *Fawa'id-u'l-Fu'ad*, p. 199.
188. *Siyar-u'l-Auliya*, p. 62; *Akhbar-u'l-Akhyar*, p. 74.

and it is difficult to believe that the inquisitional attitude of the early Turkish Sultan of Delhi succeeded in crushing this heresy root and branch.

C. *The Qalandars and the Jawaliqs*

The contemporary religious records refer to the presence of a large number of *qalandars* and *jawaliqs* in India during the thirteenth century.

Literally the word *qalandar* means a person who is free of all cares of this and the next world. In mystic terminology, however, it has a special significance. It denotes the member of a religious order called *Qalandaria*, founded by a Spanish Arab of Egypt, named Yusuf[189] or by Mufti Shaikh Jamal-u'd-din of Sawa,[190] in Persia, who, according to Ibn Battuta, settled in Damietta and ended his days there. The first *qalandar* saint who reached here was Shah Khizr, a contemporary of Shaikh Qutb-u'd-din Bakhtiyar Kaki.[191]

There is considerable difference of opinion about the place and time of the origin of this order.[192] According to Franz Babinger, the *qalanadars* "seem to have originated in Central Asia and to have been strongly influenced by Indian ideas." Maqrizi is, however, of the opinion that the first *qalandar* appeared in Damascus in 610/1213.[193]

The members of the *Qalandaria* order usually shaved their heads, eyebrows, beards, and moustaches.[194] They did not wear the traditional mystic *khirqah*, but wrapped their body with a blanket, often a coloured one, and fastened either a piece of blanket or a small sheet of cotton round the loins.[195] Those who wrapped the blanket round their body were called *jawaliq*. The *qalandars* believed in a carefree life "with utter neglect of the laws of religion or the forms of society".[196]

The *qalandars* and the *jawaliqs* always created some situation when they visited a *khanqah* or a *jama'at khanah*. They were insolently bold and refused to conform to any established tradition or convention of society. Unlike the mystics, they believed in violence and intimidation. Some

---

189. *The Encyclopaedia of Islam*, Vol. III, p. 676.

190. *Khair-u'l-Majalis*, p. 131. Shaikh Nasir-u'd-din Chiragh was eloquent in praise of Shaikh Jamal-u'd-din. 'He was a moving library. Whoever brought his difficulties to him, he resolved them instantly,' he told his audience.

191. *Akhbar-u'l-Akhyar*, p. 49.

192. *The Encyclopaedia of Islam*, Vol. III, p. 677.

193. *Al-Khitat* (Buliq, 1270 AH), Vol. II, p. 433, as cited in the *Encyclopaedia of Islam*, Vol. III, p. 677.

194. *Siyar-u'l-'Arifin*, p. 108.

195. *Khair-u'l-Majalis*, p. 131.

196. *The Encyclopaedia of Islam*, Vol. III, p. 677.

incidents recorded in medieval works show that very often their behaviour was erratic and insolent. Once Shaikh Baha-u'd-din Zakariyya did not fulfil their demands. They gathered round his *khanqah* in large numbers and began to pelt it. The Shaikh ordered the gates of his *khanqah* to be closed, but soon he realized that such an attitude could merely embolden them in their designs. "I have been ordered to sit here by Shaikh Shihab-u'd-din. I have not set up all this of my own accord. I have been put here by a *man*," he told his disciples and ordered them to throw open the gates. The *qalandar*s were deeply moved by this remark. They apologized and left the *khanqah*.[197]

Shaikh Baha-u'd-din Zakariyya had decided not to welcome *qalandar*s or *jawaliq*s to his portals.[198] But welcomed or not, they persisted in their ways. Shaikh Farid-u'd-din Ganj-i-Shakar was always ready to receive the *qalandar*s and the *jawaliq*s in his *khanqah*, but he did not escape their criticism and insolent treatment. One day a *qalandar* came to the *jama'at khanah* of Shaikh Farid at a time when the Shaikh was busy in his devotions in his room. He sat down on the Shaikh's prayer-carpet outside the *hujrah*. Maulana Badr-u'd-din Ishaq entertained him and brought food for him. Having enjoyed the food, the *qalandar* took out some hemp leaves from his leather bag and began to prepare a mixture. Some drops fell on the Shaikh's prayer-carpet. Maulana Badr-u'd-din's patience was now exhausted. He stepped forward and tried to stop the *qalandar* from polluting the Shaikh's prayer-carpet. The *qalandar* got enraged and was about to hit Maulana Ishaq with his bowl when Shaikh Farid came out from his room and caught the *qalandar*'s hand. "Forgive him for my sake," said Shaikh Farid. "The *dervish*es do not raise their hands," replied the *qalandar*, "but when they do so they do not take them down". "Throw it on that wall," said Shaikh Farid. The *qalandar* threw the pot at a wall[199] and left the *jama'at khanah*.

V. RELIGIOUS FUNCTIONS AND FESTIVALS

Our information about the religious functions and festivals of the Indian Muslims during the thirteenth century is very meagre. The contemporary records refer either to the festivals celebrated at the courts or to the ceremonies of the *khanqah*s. While the convivial element predominated over the festivals celebrated at the court, the functions at the *khanqah*s had a mystic veneer. Little is known about the popular religious festivals.

197. *Fawa'id-u'l-Fu'ad*, p. 48.
198. *Fawa'id-u'l-Fu'ad*, p. 5.
199. *Khair-u'l-Majalis*, pp. 130–31.

Orthodox Islam sanctioned only two festivals in which some element of rejoicing was present and these were the two 'Eids. Muslims of every social status celebrated them. The desire to entertain visitors on this occasion was so common that even saints who were normally proud of their poverty did not like to be absolutely destitute on 'Eid days.[200] Large-scale distribution of presents, known as 'Eidis, was a regular feature of 'Eid celebrations.[201]

The month of Ramazan was considered to be the most sacred of all months[202] and was, therefore, characterized by brisk religious activities. A change in the daily routine of life was unavoidable during this month. An elaborate and meticulous programme of religious devotions, from the small hours of the morning till late into the night, was usually followed. Even the atmosphere at the court did not remain unaffected by it. It is said that Iltutmish used to hold daily sermon meetings during the month, of Ramazan.[203] If any Sultan neglected fasting during this month, he exposed himself to criticism.[204] One was expected to devote his fasting hours to some honest work or religious devotions. Amir Khusrau has condemned those people who gambled or played chess in order to while away the exacting hours of fasting.[205] Taravi[206] prayers were regularly offered in mosques. At some places the Imam recited as much as three paras of the Quran every night.[207]

The Shab Barat[208] was celebrated in orthodox circles by offering prayers throughout the night. It appears that in India these prayers were sometimes offered in congregation also.[209] Common people celebrated the festival with large-scale illuminations. During the reign of Balban young boys used to floodlight the city on this night. There was a popular custom

---

200. Ibid, pp. 75–76.

201. Fawa'id-u'l-Fu'ad, p. 55. A saint of Lahore turns to God on an 'Eid day and says:

امروزعیداست هربنده ازخواجۀ خود عیدی بیابد مراهم عیدی بده

202. See Shaikh Jamal-u'd-din Hansvi's poem on Hilal-i-Ramadan, Diwan-i-Jamal-u'd-din, Vol. II, pp. 214–15. Also, I'jaz-i-Khusravi, IV, p. 325.

203. Tabaqat-i-Nasiri, p. 175.

204. Tarikh-i-Firoz Shahi, p. 54.

205. I'jaz-i-Khusravi, Part IV, p. 303.

206. Ibid, p. 305.

207. Ibid p. 324; Fawa'id-u'l-Fu'ad, p. 6.

208. It is celebrated on the fourteenth night of Sha'ban.

209. Fawa'id-u'l-Fu'ad, p. 88.

to send candle lamps to the mosques.[210] The use of fireworks and crackers to celebrate the *Shab Barat*, which was introduced at the popular level, was probably copied from the Christians and the Hindus.[211] In the next century, Firoz Shah Tughluq made large-scale preparations for celebrating the *Shab Barat* by using fireworks and crackers. Some eminent religious men did not approve of this practice.[212]

Special prayers were offered during the *Shab-i-Qadar*.[213] These prayers were, however, confined to religious-minded men. Of the Sultans, Balban is reported to have offered these prayers.[214] Shaikh Jamal-u'd-din Hansvi composed the following verses about the *Shab-i-Qadar*.[215]

امشب که لقای لیلةالقدر بتافت   گوئی ز سپهر طلعت بدر بتافت

تا ظلمت زلت و معاصی ببرد   چوں شمع برافروخته درصدر بتافت

The tragedy of Karbala was commemorated in India[216] by holding sermon meetings during the first ten days of the month of Muharram.[217] A book describing the incidents of the tragedy, known as *Maqtal-i-Husain*, was in great demand during this month.[218]

The *Nauroz*, a Persian festival, was regularly celebrated at the court,[219] but some contemporary religious leaders strongly objected to these celebrations. Shaikh Jamal-u'd-din Hansvi says:[220]

---

210. *I 'jaz-i-Khusravi*, Part IV, p. 324. Amir Khusrau thus describes the scene:

طفلان بهشتیکه آتش دوزخ برایشاںحرام است بازی آتش را

برخودحلال پنداشته و همه شهرازگلنارچراغ گلستان خلیل گشته.

هرکس بقدرروشنائی حال خویش چراغی چند سوئی مسجد می فرستند.

211. See Mez, *The Renaissance of Islam* (London, 1937), p. 421.

212. *Siraj-u'l-Hidayah* (MS).

213. Its precise date is not known. Generally, it is believed that it falls on the 27th night of the month of Ramadan.

214. *Fawa'id-u'l-Fu'ad*, pp. 231–32.

215. *Diwan-i-Jamal-u'd-din Hansvi*, pp. 74, 215–16. See also, Amir Khusrau, letter to Khwaja Badr-u'd-din about *Shab-i-Qadar*, *I'jaz-i-Khusravi*, Vol. IV, p. 326.

216. See *Diwan-i-Jamal-u'd-din Hansvi*, Vol. II, p. 210, for *Marsiya Amir-u'l-Muminin Husain*.

217. *Tabaqat-i-Nasiri*, pp. 175, 192.

218. *I'jaz-i-Khusravi*, Vol. IV, p. 328. Amir Khusrau refused to lend this work to a friend as his copy was in a damaged condition.

219. See *supra*, p. 44, n. 3.

220. *Diwan-i-Jamal-u'd-din Hansvi*, p. 228.

نو روز که در دین محمد نه رواست   ترسا وجہود را بدو میل و ہواست

از راہ ہوا کسی که نو روز کند   آن شخص متابع جہودوترساست

ہرنفس که گفت دیوکین نو روز کند   دل را ہدف تیر جگر دوز کند

نو روز چو موسم جہود ترسا است   مومن نبود کسی که نو روز کند

چون فضل بہار عالم افروز کند   مر باغ و چمن را طرب آموز کند

نو روز مکن اگر مسلمانی زانک   ترسا و مغ و جہود نو روز کند

چوں‌دشمن دین تست شیطان حسود   ایمن مشو از سکالش آں مردود

تا روضهٔ ایمان تو ماند خورم   نو روز مکن بسان ترسا و جہود

The following list of extra prayers, as given by Imam Ghazzali in his *Ihya-u'l-'Ulum*, has been approvingly quoted and recommended by contemporary religious teachers:

A. *Daily Prayers*: In addition to the five obligatory prayers, three other prayers were recommended—Chasht, Ishraq, Tahajjud.[221]

B. *Weekly Prayers*: Prayers offered on Saturdays and on Sundays.

C. *Monthly Prayers*: Twenty *rak'at* of prayers on the first of every lunar month.

D. *Yearly Prayers*: These were prayers offered on the occasion of the two 'Eids and the *Taravi* prayers offered during the month of Ramadan and prayers offered during the *Shab Barat*.

E. *Special Prayers*: Special prayers were recommended on the eve of solar or lunar eclipse and during days of scarcity and famine.[222]

Besides these prayers which formed part of a programme of religious devotions for the Muslim public, there were prayers for specific purposes, e.g.

(a) prayers for longevity of life,[223]
(b) prayers for seeking interviews with Khizr,[224]

221. See *supra*, p. 211, n. 138.
222. *Fawa'id-u'l-Fu'ad*, pp. 87–88.
223. Ibid, p. 23. The particular night on which these prayers were offered was known as *lailat-u'l-ragha'ib*.
224. Ibid, p. 21.

(c)   prayers known as *Namaz-i-Khwaja Uwais Qarani* for acquiring knowledge.[225]

VI. SOME SUPERSTITIONS

Some elements of superstition were very deeply rooted in the medieval mind. Even some eminent religious thinkers of the age could not rise above it. There was widespread faith in witchcraft, sorcery, and magic. It was believed that serious ailments could be created through magic. Shihab, a magician of Ajodhan, was once held responsible for a protracted illness of Shaikh Farid Ganj-i-Shakar. The saint sent some of his disciples to a graveyard where they recited a particular formula and discovered near a grave a small statue with needles pricked all over it. When this statue was taken out and its needles were removed, the Shaikh, it is said, recovered from his illness. Once Shaikh Nizam-u'd-din Auliya also fell ill and an expert magician was invited to dispel the effect of magic from him. The man moved round the house of the Shaikh, taking up dust and smelling it and, ultimately, he discovered at a place certain things which were believed to be responsible for the magical influence on the Shaikh.[226] In certain cases the government also expressed its willingness to prosecute a person against whom charges of affecting magical influences were brought.[227]

It was popularly believed that prayers at the graves of martyrs were very efficacious in averting ailments and misfortunes. When Shaikh Nizam-u'd-din Auliya's mother fell ill she sent her son to the grave of various martyr-saints to pray for her recovery.[228] Similar was the practice of Shaikh Farid Ganj-i-Shakar.[229] Otherwise too, visits to the graves of saints and religious men were considered spiritually beneficial and all sorts of people—kings, nobles, mystics, traders, villagers, and townfolk—visited them.[230] Strange superstitions came to be associated with graves. It was believed that one who prayed at the tomb of Shaikh Hamid-u'd-din had

---

225. Ibid, p. 23.

226. Ibid, p. 178; *Khair-u'l-Majalis*, pp. 116–17.

227. *Fawa'id-u'l-Fu'ad*, p. 178. When the Governor of Ajodhan came to know that Shaikh Farid's illness was due to magic and the magician's name was found out, he offered to punish the magician but the Shaikh expressed his unwillingness to accept the offer of the Governor. See also *Siyar-u'l-'Arifin*, pp. 39–40.

228. *Fawa'id-u'l-Fu'ad*, p. 59.

229. Ibid.

230. For Balban's visits to graves after Friday prayers, see Barani's *Tarikh-i-Firoz Shahi*, p. 46.

his prayers granted.[231] The dust of the grave of Shaikh Burhan-u'd-din Mahmud b. Abul Khair As'ad was given to children for their intellectual enlightenment.[232] People took away bricks from the tomb of Khwaja Mahmud Muinadoz, a disciple of Qazi Hamid-u'd-din Nagauri, and, when their prayers were granted, distributed sugar of equal weight.[233] Shaikh Nasir-u'd-din Chiragh told people that prayers at the tomb of Shaikh Muhammad Turk at Narnaul resolved all difficulties.[234] Of the seven days of the week, Wednesday was considered inauspicious. Large numbers of people visited saints and pious men every Wednesday in order to dispel its evil effects.[235] Birth of children on certain days was considered ominous. A Sayyid family of Bada'un handed a child born on a particular day when the moon was in *Burj-i-'Aqrab* (Scorpio) to a sweeper (*kannasiya*).[236]

The extent to which the credulous piety of the age tolerated religious eccentrics and maniacs may be gauged from the following incident recorded by 'Isami. An eccentric *Qazi* lived in Delhi in the upper storey of a house overlooking a thoroughfare. He was seen sitting at the window all the time and he hurled stones at whoever happened to pass by him. His slave, Yaqut, was always in attendance with two whips and some rings. Whenever the Qazi saw anybody wearing a ring, he harshly summoned him to his presence and asked him to part with it. Yaqut was then asked to whip the person. People submitted to these humiliations and tortures without murmur. When this mad Qazi rode out through the streets of Delhi, cries of 'Get aside', 'Get aside' rent the atmosphere. One day 'Ala-u'd-din, then a prince, passed by the window of the Qazi who hurriedly came down and ran after him. He took a ring from Yaqut and put it on the finger of 'Ala-u'd-din who accepted it as a happy omen of a great future.[237]

It is also said that when Sayyid Maula's execution was followed by cyclones, famine, and other calamities, it was this mad Qazi who stood up on the pulpit and fervently prayed to God to avert the distress of the people.[238]

An idea of the extent to which superstitious elements had entered the life of the medieval Indian Mussalmans may be had from a perusal of the

231. *Sarur-u's-Sudur* (MS), p. 14.
232. *Akhbar-u'l-Akhyar*, p. 46.
233. Ibid, p. 49.
234. Ibid, p. 47.
235. For Shaikh Nizam-u'd-din Auliya's disapproval of this superstition, see *Fawa'id u'l-Fu'ad*, p. 119.
236. Ibid, p. 243.
237. *Futuh-u's-Salatin*, pp. 224–26.
238. Ibid, pp. 219–20.

fabricated *malfuz* literature of this period. There is hardly any aspect of life and thought which has not been presented in superstitious colours. All fluctuations of heavenly bodies have been interpreted as indications of Divine fury and their influence on human affairs has been described as a series of punishments for human derelictions.[239]

Many superstitions had come to be associated with cities and urban life. It was believed that all cities would degenerate completely before Doomsday.

> The Abyssinians would destroy Mecca; Madina would suffer due to scarcity and people would die of starvation in large numbers. Basra, Iraq and Meshed would be destroyed on account of drunkards. Syria would be destroyed by the atrocities of its rulers.....Rum [Byzantium] would suffer on account of the homosexual habits of its people. Khurasan and Balkh would be destroyed on account of the dishonesty of traders. The Muslims would take to usury and would become carrion eaters....Khwarizm and the region around it would suffer on account of drinking and convivialism. Sistan would be subjected to storms and gales. Earthquakes would become frequent and would destroy people living in the neighbourhood. Egypt and Damascus would be destroyed on account of their misbehaviour towards women....The desolation of Sind and Hind would be due to disturbances caused by rapes and drinking...Then Imam Mehdi would appear.

If superstitions are, in the ultimate analysis, expressions of the fears, inhibitions, and dislikes of a people, the above extract may be interpreted as an indication of the disapproval by the medieval religious classes of prevailing trends in the development of urban life.

VII. SOME RELIGIOUS CONTROVERSIES

Hair-splitting theological squabbles were a feature of Muslim religious life during the Middle Ages. Apart from controversies which had a purely ideological basis, some religious practices also came in for criticism.

One of the most popular mystic practices which became a subject of great controversy during the thirteenth century was the institution of *sama'* (audition parties). Amongst the notables of Delhi, Qazi Hamid-u'd-din Nagauri and Shaikh Qutb-u'd-din Bakhtiyar Kaki were very fond of hearing *sama'*.[240] Some mystics kept musicians in their service permanently. Two eminent *qazis* of Delhi, Qazi Sa'd and Qazi 'Imad, considered this institution to be illegal. They protested against it and approached Iltutmish to stop it in the capital. The Sultan summoned a *mahzar* to discuss the legal aspect of the problem and invited Qazi Hamid-u'd-din Nagauri to participate

239. *Anis-u'l-Arwah*, pp. 6–7.
240. Ibid, pp. 7–8.

in it. When Qazi Hamid-u'd-din reached the court, Iltutmish got up to receive him and showed great respect to him. On being asked about the legality of sama', Qazi Hamid-u'd-din replied that it was permitted for the mystics but was prohibited for the externalists. He then reminded Iltutmish of an old incident: "One day," the Qazi told him, "forty sufis held a sama' gathering in Baghdad. You and I both were present there. You were a mere boy then and, without being asked to do so, you kept cutting the burnt wick of the candle. That night the mystics assigned to you the kingdom of Hindustan." When Iltutmish recollected the incident, he was obviously moved. Qazi Hamid-u'd-din noticed a change in the Sultan's attitude and asked his qawwal, Mahmud, to recite some verses. The Qazi fell into ecstasy and though fire and thorns were placed in his way he neither took any notice of them nor stopped dancing. Iltutmish took him to his khanqah and arranged for a dinner and a music party there. 'Isami has quoted this story;[241] but its authenticity cannot be established in all its details. It is probably based on legends which 'Isami found floating down the stream of time more than one hundred years after the death of the Sultan. It is, however, certain that there were frequent protests by the orthodox 'ulama against the mystic institution of sama'. But the 'ulama could not place an interdict on it. One of the most important qazis of the empire during the thirteenth century, Maulana Minhaj-u's-Siraj, the author of Tabaqat-i-Nasiri, supported the viewpoint of the mystics. It is said that it was he who gave legal sanction to the institution of sama' in India.[242]

VIII. CENTRES OF RELIGIOUS ACTIVITIES

The masjid (mosque), the madrasah (school), the maqbarah (tomb), and the khanqah (hospice) were the four main centres of religious activity in India during the thirteenth century. Shaikh Hamid-u'd-din Nagauri used to say that the purpose of constructing a khanqah,[243] a masjid, or a hujrah was to discipline the inner life of man. This is no doubt true but these places had a social significance also and occupied a pivotal place in the community life of the Mussalmans.

The mosques were not used merely for offering congregational prayers; tazkir meetings were also held there. Besides, siyyum[244] ceremonies, which usually comprised of recitation the Quran to bless the soul of the

---

241. Futuh-u's-Salatin, pp. 117–19.
242. Fawa'id-u'l-Fu'ad, p. 239.
243. Sarur-u's-Sudur (MS), pp. 59–60.
244. So called because they are held on the third day after death.

departed, were usually held in mosques. Educational institutions of different categories and standards were also attached to mosques.

The character of a mosque was determined by the locality in which it was situated. The conversion of the earliest mosque of Amroha, constructed by Kaiqubad, into Saddu's hospice[245]—where all sorts of prohibited acts including sacrificial offerings to Saddu came to be performed—was due to the impact of environmental forces. The principal mosque in the capital town was usually a great centre of learning. Mosques in *qasbah*s and villages catered to the religious needs of the Muslim population living around it. A *madrasah* attached to a village mosque confined its instructional functions to merely teaching the Quran to children. Mosques situated in out-of-the-way places were sometimes used by mystics for performing certain spiritual exercises.[246] Since there were no restrictions on sojourn in the mosques, one who had no other place to hide his head found shelter there.[247]

The *madrasah*s maintained by the state had an atmosphere of affluence and plenty but a very large number of institutions, established and maintained by individual scholars, worked under extremely difficult circumstances. These scholars probably did not charge regular fees from their pupils and subsisted on casual *futuh*. The religious activity in the *madrasah*s was primarily intellectual. Symposia and debates were a regular feature of these institutions.[248]

The *khanqah* was another great centre of religious activity during the period.[249] But no theological discussion or *manazarah* was permitted there. Books were no doubt taught but these books were either on *tafsir* or on *tasawwuf*. Emphasis was laid here on the discipline of the inner life and emotional integration in the light of religious teachings rather than intellectual advancement through casuistry.

Mausoleums also were centres of brisk activity. Ibn Battuta informs us that four hundred and sixty persons were employed at the tomb of Sultan Qutb-u'd-din Mubarak Shah to perform different religious services. "I appointed," he says, "one hundred and fifty reciters of the Quran who are known as *khatmi*, eighty students, eight repeaters called *mukarrarin*,

---

245. For an account of Saddu, see *Tarikh-i-Amroha*.

246. *Siyar-u'l-Auliya*, p. 69. Shaikh Farid performed *Chillah-i-Ma'kus* in a mosque at Uch. See also *Khair-u'l-Majalis*, p. 170.

247. *Siyar-u'l-Auliya*, p. 110.

248. It was on account of his pre-eminent debating qualities during his school-days in Delhi that Shaikh Nizam-u'd-din-Auliya became known as *bahhas* and *mahfil shikan*, *Siyar-u'l-Auliya*, p. 101.

249. See *supra*, pp. 62–63.

one professor and eighty *sufis*, and I appointed an *imam*, muezzins, pleasant-voiced readers, panegyrists and clerks who might register the absentees, as well as the ushers. All these people in this country are known as *arbab*. Further, I appointed another class of functionaries known as domestics (*hashia*), namely the valets, the cooks, the running footmen (*davadavia*), the water-bearers (*abdariya*, that is, the *saqqaun*), the sherbet dispensers, the betel-givers, the arms-bearers, the spear-bearers, the umbrella-bearers, the laver-carriers, the chamberlains and the heralds— all these numbering four hundred and sixty ... On the occasion of the great festivals—the two 'Eids, the birthday of the Prophet, the tenth of Muharram (*ashura*), the night of mid-Sha'ban and the day of Sultan Qutb-u'd-din's death—I used a hundred maunds of flour and an equal amount of meat with which I fed the poor and indigent." He further writes: "It is a custom among the Indians to provide for their dead in the same way as they do during their lifetime. They bring elephants and horses to the tomb and tie them near its gate and the tomb is highly decorated."[250]

Besides, some graveyards were chosen by mystics for performing spiritual practices which required a lonely corner. The lachrymose atmosphere of the graveyards suited their temperament and they preferred to spend as much of their time in the groves of the graveyards as possible.[251] Some tombs had memorial mosques associated with them.

Sometimes people assembled at the graves of saints or Sultans to take an oath of allegiance or a vow.[252] Some of the mystics had *dastar*s tied on their heads at the grave of an eminent mystic;[253] nobles took an oath of fealty at the grave of an eminent Sultan.[254] Ibn Battuta says about *Dar-ul-Amn*, the place where Balban was buried: "One of his (Balban's) good deeds was

---

250. *Rihlah*, pp. 141–42.
Compare the Mongol custom: "....and among that people it is the usage, when one of them dies, to prepare a palace underground about the size of a chamber or hall, in largeness proportionate to the rank and degree of the accursed one who may have departed to hell. They furnish it with a throne and covering for the ground, and they place there vessels and numerous effects together with his arms and weapons, and whatever may have been his own private property, and some of his wives, and slaves, male or female, and the person he loved most above all others. When they have placed that accursed one upon the throne, they bury his most beloved along with him in that place. In the night-time the place is covered up." *Tabaqat-i-Nasiri*, p. 407; Raverty, p. 1173.

251. *Khair-u'l-Majolis*, pp. 170–71; *Siyar-u'l-Auliya*, p. 90.

252. Ibid, p. 150–51.

253. *Siyar-u'l-Auliya*, p. 194.

254. *Tabaqat-i-Nasiri*, p. 269.

the building of a house called the house of safety (*Dar-ul-Amn*). The debtor who entered it had his debt paid by the Sultan, and whoever sought refuge in it for fear was safe. And whoever entered it after having killed somebody, the Sultan interceded on his behalf to conciliate the heirs of the deceased. And if a criminal sought shelter in it his pursuers were accorded satisfaction. It was in this house that he (Balban) was buried."[255]

Visitors from different parts of the country visited the graves of eminent saints[256] and sometimes particular festivals came to be celebrated round the graves of these saints. In Bahraich, the mausoleum of Sayyid Salar Mas'ud Ghazi became a centre of festivities.[257] A religious gathering during the days of *tashriq*,[258] known as *Khatm-i-Maulana Majd Haji*,[259] became a regular feature at the grave of Maulana Majd-din-Haji, a contemporary of Iltutmish. Most of the festivities and functions at the graves bear an obvious influence of Hindu customs.

One of the busiest centres of religious activity in Delhi was the *Hauz-i-Shamsi*. Large numbers of people visited this place. It appears from the *Miftah-u't-Talibin* that different areas of this locality were known for different reasons. One of the quarters of this locality was called *Makan-i-Khizr*[260] and it was believed that one could have an interview with Khizr if he performed certain religious practices there. Another area was known as *Maqam-i-Jinn* which was supposed to be frequented by supernatural beings. Mystics assembled on the bank of this *Hauz* and offered prayers on full-moon nights.[261] Some mystics arranged meetings on the banks of

---

255. *Rihlah*, p. 36.

256. *Fawa'id-u'l-Fu'ad*, p. 155.

257. Amir Khusrau refers to the country-wide popularity of Sayyid Salar Mas'ud's grave in the following words:

درقصبهٔ بهرائچ از مزار معطرسپه سالارشهید همه هندوستان بونے عودگرفته است

I'jaz-i-Khusravi, Vol. II, p. 155.

The institution of taking out spears, known as the spears of Balay Miyan, probably originated during the thirteenth century. It was stopped by Sikandar Lodi (*Waqi'at-i-Mushtdqi*, f. 15; *Tarikh-i-Da'udi*, p. 38).

258. Three days of *'Eid-i-Azha*.

259. *Akhbar-u'l-Akhyar*, p. 49. For some later documents about grants made for the maintenance of the tomb of Maulana Maid Haji, see *Proceedings of the Indian Historical Records Commission*, 1960, pp. 59–63.

260. See *Khair-u'l-Majalis* (p. 46) where this place has been referred to as *maqam-i-Khwaja Khizr*. There was a *maqam-i-Khizr* in Deogir also (*Siyar-u'l-Auliya*, p. 220).

261. *Miftah-u't-Talibin* (MS).

this *Hauz* to confer *khirqah*s on their disciples.[262] The old *'Eid-gah* was also situated near this *Hauz*. Shaikh Qutb-u'd-din Bakhtiyar Kaki is reported to have remarked: "Remember! Two places—the *Hauz-i-Shamsi* and the area at the back of the *Namazgah-i-Kuhna*—are unique in the capital town of Delhi on account of the sacredness associated with them."[263] But the *Hauz-i-Shamsi* was not merely a centre for religious activities alone. It represented many facets of the Muslim culture of those days.[264] Here one could find mystics lost in their contemplation; scholars busy in their debates and discussions; poets busy reciting their latest compositions, as also the pimps and prostitutes plying their abominable trade.

262. *Fawa'id-u'l-Fu'ad*, p. 174.
263. *Miftah-u't-Talibin* (MS).
264. In the fourteenth century, Ibn Battuta wrote about this tank: 'Outside Delhi is a big reservoir called after Sultan Shams-u'd-din Lalmish. The inhabitants of Delhi take their supply of drinking water from it, and it lies near the *'Eid-gah*, (*musallah*) of Delhi. It is fed by rain-water and is about two miles long and a mile broad. On its western side facing the *'Eid-gah* are built platforms of stone, one higher than another. Under each platform are stairs which help one to get down to the water. Beside each platform is a dome of stone containing seats for amusement and pleasure seekers. In the middle of the tank there is a big dome of two storeys built of sculptured stone.....Inside the dome is a mosque where one finds fakirs most of the time. These fakirs have renounced the world relying upon God.' *Rihlah*, p. 28.

Chapter IX

HINDUS UNDER THE SULTANATE

Non-Muslims in a Muslim State—Theoretical Aspect

When Muslim political influence spread to areas inhabited by people professing different faiths, the problem of determining the position of the non-believers in the Muslim political set-up assumed great significance. An Islamic State stood for the realization of certain ideals. The Muslims could be forced to live according to the laws of the *Shari'at* and help in realizing those ideals, but no such pressure could be exercised on those who did not believe in Islam. What place was then to be assigned to them within an Islamic polity?

The Muslim jurists classified the non-believers under the following three categories:

(a) those who possessed some revealed book (*ahl-i-Kitab*),
(b) those who resembled the possessors of revealed books (*mushabah ahl-i-Kitab*), and
(c) all other *kafir*s and *mushrik*s.

The jurists agreed that all non-believers falling under the first two categories were entitled to equality in status and opportunities with the Mussalmans provided they consented to pay *jiziyah.*[1] With regard to the position of the *kafir*s of the third category, there was no unanimity of opinion amongst the jurists. Imam Shafi'i restricted the application of the

1. Abdul Kalam Azad, *Jami'al-Shawahid fi Dukhul-i-Ghair Muslim fi'l-Masajid*, pp. 33–34.

About the *ahl-i-Kitab* the Quran says:

حتى يعطوا الجزية عن يدوهم صاغرون (S. IX: 29)

('Until they pay the tax in acknowledgement of superiority and they are in a state of subjection.' Trans. by Muhammad 'Ali, p. 403.)

About Zoroastrians who are included in the category of 'those resembling the possessors of revealed books' there is a *hadis* in *Sahih al-Bukhari* سنوابهم سنة اهل الكتاب cited in *Jami'al-Shawahid fi Dukhul-i-Ghair Muslim fi'l-Masajid*, p. 34.

zimmi law to the *ahl-i-Kitab* and the Zoroastrians alone. Imam Abu Hanifah and Imam Ahmad b. Hanbal extended its application to all except the infidels of Arabia. For them, it was either the sword or Islam. Imam Malik and Qazi Abu Yusuf adopted the most liberal attitude and accorded the status of *zimmis* to all non-Muslims, whether Arab or non-Arab, without any exception.

The consensus of juristic opinion was, therefore, in favour of extending the privileges of a *zimmi* to all non-believers. Once the status of a *zimmi* was accorded to a non-Muslim, the security of his life, property and religion was guaranteed.

For the first time the *jiziyah* was levied by the Prophet on the Christians of Najran in *circa* 8 AH and the privileges of the *zimmi* were thus explained in a message:

> To (the Christians of) Najran and the neighbouring territories, the security of God and the pledge of His Prophet are extended for their lives, their religion and their property—to the present as well as the absent and others besides; there shall be no interference with (the practice of) their faith or other observances; nor any change in their rights or privileges; no bishop shall be removed from his bishopric; nor any monk from his monastery, nor any priest from his priesthood, and they shall continue to enjoy everything great and small as heretofore; no image or Cross shall be destroyed; they shall not oppress or be oppressed.[2]

The Pious Caliphs—who continued the theo-centric political organization of the Prophet—followed in the footsteps of their master. In almost all the settlements which the second Caliph 'Umar made with the non-Muslims, one repeatedly comes across the words:

$$لا يغيرون عن ملة ولا يحال بينهم و بين شرايعهم^3$$

(Their religion would not be changed; nor any interference would be made in their religious affairs.)

The Caliph 'Ali is reported to have remarked that the blood of the *zimmis* was as sacred as that of the Mussalmans.[4]

Once the non-believers accepted the *jiziyah*, it became the duty of a Muslim state to protect their religion and places of worship. A Muslim general during the reign of Mu'tasim (833–42 AD) ordered a few religious

---

2. This message has been quoted in *Futuh-u'l-Buldan* and the *Kitab-u'l-Kharaj*. See also Syed Ameer Ali, *The Spirit of Islam* (London, 1931), p. 273; *Maqalat-i-Shibli* (Azamgarh, n.d.), Vol. I, pp. 188–89.

3. Tabari, p. 2633 as cited in Shibli, *Al-Faruq* (Kanpur, 1899), Vol. II, p. 155.

4. *Maqalat-i-Shibli*, Vol. I, p. 191.

men to be flogged because they had destroyed a fire temple in Sughd and had built a mosque in its place.[5] 'It is not permissible to damage a temple of long standing,'[6] was the *fatwa* (judgement) of a qazi in the reign of Sikandar Lodi. It was due to this attitude of the Mussalmans that a number of fire temples existed in 'Iraq, Fars, Kirman, Sijistan, Khurasan, Jibal and Azerbaijan in the tenth century.[7] Indeed, there was a temple in the vicinity of Baghdad.[8]

But the regulations of Islam with regard to the non-Muslims have been grossly misunderstood. This misunderstanding has arisen out of the fact that the directions of the Quran with reference to the *non-Muslims at war* (*Kafiran-i-harbi*)[9] have been taken to apply to all non-believers.

JIZIYAH—ITS HISTORICAL, LEGAL AND ACTUAL POSITION

Jiziyah is an Arabicised form of the Persian word *Gezit*,[10] which means a tax. It was known as a kind of tax long before the advent of the Prophet of Islam. Anusherwan had formulated rules about it. According to Imam Abu Ja'far Tabari, Anusherwan fixed this tax at the rate of 12, 8, 6, and 4 dirhams per capita but exempted all (a) high-born people, (b) nobles, (c) military men, (d) religious leaders, (e) scholars, (f) courtiers, and (g) persons under 20 years of age from the payment of this tax.[11] It was realized by him in lieu of exemption from military service. When the Prophet of Islam imposed this tax, after giving it the Arabic form of *jiziyah*, he followed a tradition established long before him. The second Caliph 'Umar, it is said, followed in this reference the rules laid down by Anusherwan. Apart from this, the fact should not be ignored that such taxes were not unknown to other countries in the Middle Ages. The nature of *Turushkadanda* in India, *Host Tax* in France, *Common Penny* in Germany, and *Scutage* in England, despite all the differences, was almost identical.

According to the system established by the Mussalmans, every Muslim could be forced to perform military service. No such compulsion was

5. *The Preaching of Islam*, p. 209.

6. *Tarikh-i-Da'udi*, pp. 29–30;

Ahmad Yadgar, *Tarikh-i-Shahi*, pp. 30–31.

7. Mas'udi, Vol. IV, p. 86, as cited in *The Preaching of Islam*, p. 209.

8. *Kitab-u'l-Milal wa-n Nihal*, Shahrastani, ed. Cureton, Part I, p. 198.

9. Unbelievering inhabitants of the *Dar-u'l-Harb* (enemy country). *Jihad* against the *kafirs* of the *Dar-u'l-Harb* is an obligation (*Farz ala'l-kifayah*). For *Dar-u'l-Harb*, see the *Encyclopaedia of Islam*, Vol. I, pp. 917–18.

10. *Mafatih-u'l-'Ulum*, p. 59, as cited in *Maqalat-i-Shibli*, Vol. I, p. 222.

11. *Tarikh-i-Kabir*, Tabari, Vol. II, p. 662, cited in ibid, pp. 223–24.

considered desirable or justifiable with reference to the non-Muslims. Besides, most of the wars waged by the Muslims during the early period were basically ideological conflicts and people who did not believe in that ideology could not be expected to fight for it. But apart from wars, the Muslim soldiers protected the life and property of all people—Muslims and non-Muslims—living under a Muslim government. It was in view of this later obligation that *jiziyah* was demanded from the non-believers. If at any time the Muslim government failed to protect the life or property of the non-Muslims living under it, the *jiziyah* was returned to the payers;[12] if, on the other hand, the non-Muslims undertook to perform military service, they were exempted from the payment of this tax.[13] Keeping in view the purpose of this tax, it was laid down that it would be spent on the maintenance of army and the protection of frontiers. If any amount was left over, it was utilized in constructing public works, like roads and bridges. The rate of *jiziyah* was fixed at 20, 6, 3, dirhams per head per year. Persons of less than 20 and more than 50 years of age were exempted from it; women, invalids, lunatics, mendicants and people possessing less than 200 dirhams were also exempted. The obligation to protect a *zimmi's* life or property did not cease even if he (a) subsequently refused to pay the *jiziyah*, (b) killed a Muslim, (c) committed adultery with a Muslim woman or (d) used abusive language for the Prophet of Islam. The contract came to an end only when a *zimmi* entered into any alliance or conspiracy with the non-Muslims living in *Dar-u'l-Harb*. Obviously it meant that so long as a *zimmi* did not do anything calculated to harm the safety or integrity of a Muslim state, there could be no justification for any action against him.

The connotation of *jiziyah* changed with the passage of time and, under the influence of jurists (*fuqaha*), it assumed a meaning which the Prophet and his immediate descendants had not visualized.[14] Its pre-Islamic background was forgotten while its discriminatory character was unduly emphasized. The law-books developed theories and principles quite

12. For example, Abu 'Ubaida Amin returned the entire amount received as *jiziyah* from the Syrians because the Muslims found themselves helpless to protect them. Abu Yusuf, *Kitab-u'l-Kharaj*, p. 81; *Futuh-u'l-Buldan*, p. 137, etc. as cited in *Maqalat-i-Shibli*, Vol. I, pp. 228–29.

13. For example, Caliph 'Usman exempted the Christians of Jarajma from payment of *jiziyah* on that account. Ibid, p. 229.

14. Ibid, p. 205.

Imam Nur openly declared that degradation and humiliation is wrong and is the invention of the *faqih*s of Khurasan. Tripathi, *Some Aspects of Muslim Administration*, pp. 340–41.

unrelated to the original intention of the Prophet. These later-developed principles changed *jiziyah* into a tax with which an element of humiliation also came to be associated. But the fact remained that these theories were propounded when in actual practice *jiziyah* had almost ceased to be a poll tax in its original sense.

Considered in the broad context of Islamic history, *jiziyah* has a long and chequered history[15] which should be kept in mind in order to understand its nature and scope correctly. During the time of the Prophet and his first two successors, the *jiziyah* was realized *per capita*. A very significant change took place in its nature when the third Caliph, 'Usman, realized it *per house* from the residents of Tiflis.[16] Further and more vital changes took place during the Umayyad period when the whole problem was considered from the purely monetary point of view.

Since conversion to Islam meant loss of *jiziyah* on the one hand and additional expenditure, in the form of pensions etc., on the other, the Umayyads discouraged conversions. If any one got converted in spite of this discouragement, the Umayyad government declined to exempt him from the payment of *jiziyah* and refused to enlist him as state-pensioner. Hajjaj forced most of the Mawali in the great cities of Iraq to pay all those taxes which they had been paying before their conversion to Islam. 'Umar b. 'Abdul Aziz did not approve of this policy of his predecessors. He sought to reverse it completely. When one of his officials pointed out that the revised policy of the Umayyad government would adversely affect its financial stability, 'Umar b. 'Abdul Aziz replied: "God be witness! I shall be glad to see everybody become Mussalman so that thou and I have to till the soil with our own hands to earn a living." When the Governor of Egypt complained against the fall in revenues due to increase in the number of conversions, 'Umar b. 'Abdul Aziz wrote back to him: "God

15. In all the Muslim authorities we have the most explicit statements that the Arabs did one thing in Egypt, another in Syria, another in Iraq, and another in Khurasan. The general story of the two-dinar *jiziya* in Egypt is told about no other province. In the Sawad, it is usually asserted that 'Umar measured the land, put on it the tax of *kharaj*, and on the people, the *jiziya*. In Khurasan and Transoxania, the testimony is general that different cities capitulated for a fixed tribute. There was no system of *kharaj* or *jiziya*. It is impossible to name a single Muslim jurist or historian who unmistakably asserts that there was uniformity of practice throughout the Arab Empire.

D.C. Deanett, *Conversion and the Poll Tax in Early Islam* (Harvard, 1950), p. 11.

16. *Futuh-u'l-Buidan*, p. 301, cited by Shibli, *al-Ma'mun* (London, 1889), p. 110.

sent His Prophet as a missionary and not as a tax-gatherer." The Umayyad bureaucracy in Khurasan had placed harassing conditions for those who wanted to be converted to Islam. One of the conditions being to circumcise the converts. 'Umar b. 'Abdul Aziz forbade it, saying: "Muhammad was sent to call men to the faith not to circumcise them." However, 'Umar b. 'Abdul Aziz's regulations in this respect did not survive him, and the Umayyad government returned to its old practices as soon as he closed his eyes in death.

A further change in the character of the *jiziyah* took place when quotas were fixed for the various villages. This virtually amounted to change in the levy of *jiziyah* from *per house* to *per village*. Thus, if a village with 100 non-Muslims was paying 200 dinars as *jiziyah* at a particular time, the same amount was demanded from it even when the number of taxable heads had been reduced by conversion, migration or death.

Passing through all these stages, the *jiziyah* ultimately assumed a character similar to *kharaj* and, when the distinctive character of *kharaj* as a tax realized exclusively from the non-Muslims changed, the religious connotation of *jiziyah* also disappeared. This is why we find the term *jiziyah* being used in large number of medieval works,[17] both Indian and non-Indian, as a synonym for *kharaj* or land tax. When the Muslim law books of the Middle Ages talk about *jiziyah* and lay down elaborate rules about it, emphasizing its humiliatory character, they refer to an institution which existed nowhere except in the minds of the orthodox jurists.

JIZIYAH IN INDIA

It is clear from the *Chach Namah* that Muhammad b. Qasim had levied *jiziyah* in Sind.[18] But what was the position under the Sultans of Delhi during the thirteenth century? We have practically no information about the actual state of affairs but the theoretical position has been stated by Fakhr-i-Mudabbir.[19] His views about the nature of *jiziyah*, the position of *zimmis*, and the *kharaji* and *'Ushri* lands may be thus summarized:

17. *Tarikh-i-Firoz Shahi*, p. 574; *Tarikh-i-Jahan Gusha*, Vol. II, p. 89. Barthold (*Turkestan*, p. 188, fn. 2) quotes *Mafatih-u'l-'Ulum* which identifies *kharaj* with *jiziyah*. 'Abdul Hamid Muharrir Ghaznavi has discussed *jiziyah* under the category of *Kharaj-i-Muqasima* (*Dastur-u'l-Albab fi 'Ilm-u'l-Hisab*, Photostat of MS in Rampur Library, f. 35a.). See also *Conversion and the Poll Tax in Early Islam*, p. 12.

18. *Chach Namah*, pp. 208–09.

19. *Adab-u'l-Harb wa-Shuja'at*, ff. 155b–158b.

1. If the Muslims besiege any fort or city in a *dar-u'l-harb*, their first duty is to offer Islam to the non-Muslims. If they accept it, hostilities should cease and the siege should be lifted forthwith. If they refuse to accept Islam, *jiziyah* should be demanded from them. If they consent to pay it, all conflicts should cease 'for their blood and property is like the blood and the property of the Mussalmans', and it is not proper to carry on conflict with them. If, on the contrary, they refuse to accept Islam, and also refuse to pay *jiziyah*, conflict should be continued.[20]

2. If truce is affected, it should be respected. If they visit the army of the Mussalmans, they should not be enslaved for they are like free people.

3. If any *kafir* man or woman is given shelter by any person, it is not proper for any Muslim to kill him, provided no treachery or mischief, is suspected from him.[21]

4. If any one from the *ahl-i-kharaj* embraces Islam, the same *kharaj* should be realized from him which he used to pay before his conversion. If a Mussalman purchases a land from any *zimmi*, he is expected to pay the same *kharaj*, which its former owner used to pay. *'Ushr* cannot be realized from a *kharaji* land for the Prophet of Islam has said: "*'Ushr* and *kharaj* cannot combine at one place."[22]

5. All matters concerning *jiziyah* may be decided in any one of the following ways: some men from both sides should either work out a settlement and on that basis the non-Muslims should consent to pay *jiziyah*, or the conquerors should impose it on the people. The rate of *jiziyah* should be 48 silver coins from the rich, 28 from the average and 12 from the poor. More than this should not be charged. The *jiziyah* may be taken from the *ahl-i-'Ajam* (non-Arabs), the Jews, the Christian, the Sabians, and the idol-worshippers. It should not be realized from the idol-worshippers of Arabia, heretics, children, minors, invalids, blind men, the *dervishes* who do not earn and the monks.[23]

6. The *zimmi*s should not be allowed to ride on horses in the Islamic cities (*Shahrha-i-Islam*). Their bridles, clothes and posture of sitting should be different from that of the Mussalmans.[24]

20. Ibid, f. 155b.
21. Ibid, f. 156b.
22. Ibid, f. 157b.
23. Ibid, f. 157b.
24. Ibid, f. 158a.

But this is merely a statement of the theoretical position and, that too, a mere rehash of the statements of *Hedayah*. For an assessment of the actual position, one has to bear in mind the following facts:

(a)   There is no direct or explicit reference to the imposition of *jiziyah* by the early Turkish Sultans of Delhi in the contemporary records.

(b)   The term *jiziyah* is used in contemporary works mostly as a synonym for land tax (*kharaj*).[25]

(c)   The Hindus had taken part in military expeditions during the period under review and, therefore, there was no justification for the imposition of *jiziyah* upon them.

(d)   In a country like India, there were practical difficulties in realizing *jiziyah* from individuals. An elaborate administrative machinery was required for this purpose. We are not aware of the existence of any such machinery.

(e)   Firoz Shah Tughluq says in his *Futuhat*: 'I made an announcement that whoever from amongst the *kafir*s recites the *kalimah* and embraces Islam, the *jiziyah* should not be realized from him.'[26] Does it mean that *jiziyah* continued to be realized from the people even after their conversion to Islam, or does it mean that after conversion, the outstanding amount of *jiziyah* was not permitted to be realized? Or does it mean that as a concession the land tax (of that year) was remitted?

The information available in contemporary records is tantalizing in its meagreness and it is difficult, therefore, to arrive at any definite conclusions about the nature and imposition of *jiziyah* during the thirteenth century. In all probability it was not realized as a distinct tax payable by individual non-Muslims but was merged with *kharaj* and was treated as part of the total incidence of taxation.

LEGAL STATUS OF THE HINDUS

When Muhammad b. Qasim decided to realize the *jiziyah* from the Hindus, he placed them under the category of *mushabah-ahl-i-kitab*. This position of the Hindus was accepted by all the Sultans of Delhi. Once or twice during this period, some religious fanatics demanded a change in the legal status of the Hindus, but their approach was neither approved by the rulers nor did it receive the support of the Muslim public. Such demands

25. *Fawa'id-u'l-Fu'ad*, p. 136; *Qir'an-u's-Sa'dain*, p. 35; *Tarikh-i-Firoz Shahi*, p. 574.

26. *Futuhat-i-Firoz Shahi*, p. 20.

remained 'whines of impotent fanaticism' and were never seriously considered. Barani informs us that one day some of the leading scholars of the age went to see Iltutmish and requested him to confront the Hindus with the alternative of 'death or Islam', which meant that they were not in favour of according the status of *zimmis* to the Hindus and bracketed them with the *kafirs* of Arabia with whom no such arrangement was permitted.

Iltutmish asked Nizam-u'l-Mulk Junaidi to give a reply to the *'ulama*. Referring to the impracticability of the demand, the Wazir said: "But at the moment India has newly been conquered and the Muslims are so few that they are like salt (in a large dish). If the above orders are to be applied to the Hindus, it is possible they might combine and a general confusion might ensue and the Muslims would be too few in number to suppress this general confusion. However, after a few years when in the Capital and in the regions and the small towns, the Muslims are well established and the troops are larger, it will be possible to give Hindus, the choice of 'death' or 'Islam'."[27]

No other historian has referred to this representation of the contemporary *'ulama*; even later writers who have mainly copied from Zia-u'd-din Barani's works have ignored this incident completely. Maybe they doubted the authenticity of this information or the incident was too revolting to their tolerant and realistic feelings to be recorded. That Iltutmish could not act upon the advice of the *'ulama* is too palpable to need a comment. Political realism, common sense and the true spirit of religion pointed in the other direction.

MUSLIM ATTITUDE TOWARDS THE HINDUS

For a proper study of the position of the Hindus under the Sultanate, the attitude of the different sections of Muslim society towards the Hindus and their religious institutions needs careful investigation in the light of available records.

1. *The Governing Class*
Most of the Turks who had established the Sultanate of Delhi were, no doubt, neophytes but they were singularly free from all religious bigotry or fanaticism. If there was any element of exclusive thinking in them, its source was racial, not religious. They treated the Indian Muslims and the Hindus with equal nonchalance. They were concerned more with the

---

27. *Sana-i-Muhammadi* (Rampur, MS); see also *Medieval India Quarterly*, Vol. I, Part III, pp. 100–05.

maintenance of their political power and prestige than with the religious problems or prejudices of their people. We do not come across in the contemporary records a single instance of any order of the Turkish Sultans purporting to interfere in Hindu religious practices or seeking to undermine the religious or social position of the Hindus. On the other hand, we know for certain that they never hesitated in continuing Hindu traditions if political circumstances so demanded. Shihab-u'd-din continued the figures of the goddess Lakshmi on his gold coins, a fact which "indicates the extent to which the conquerors were prepared to compromise their religious ideas with demands of the State."[28] Qutb-u'd-din Aibek allowed Rajput princes to rule over Delhi, Ajmer and Gwalior even after the conquest of those regions.[29]

The Turkish nobles did not hesitate to enter into alliances with Hindu chieftains. Minhaj writes about the rebel-malik, Qutlugh Khan:

> When he sought safety and protection in the Santur mountains, Ranah Ran-pal (Rana-pala), the Hindu, who held the chieftainship among the Hindus—and it was the usage among that people to protect those who sought shelter with them—assisted Malik Kutlugh Khan.[30]

Balban sought the co-operation of Danuj Rai, the ruler of Sonargaon against Tughral.[31]

II. 'Ulama

For the attitude of the 'ulama towards the Hindus we have no other source of information except Zia-u'd-din Barani. But he was so deeply prejudiced against Hindus that it is difficult to vouch for the truth of his statements. His personal interests had probably suffered at the hands of some Hindu landlords and this had embittered his attitude towards the Hindus in general.

In order to rationalize his attitude towards the Hindus, Barani selected a king (Sultan Mahmud of Ghaznini), a saint (Sayyid Nur-u'd-din Mubarak) and a theologian (Qazi Mughis-u'd-din) to weave his religious ideas round and used them as his mouthpiece. Like Browning he could very well say:

> ... you saw me gather men and women
> Enter each and all, and use their service,
> Speak from every mouth—the speech of power.

28. Habibullah, *Foundation of Muslim Rule in India*, (Lahore, 1945), p. 300.
29. *Taj-u'l-Ma'asir* (MS), pp. 110, 184.
30. *Tabaqat-i-Nasiri*, p. 306; Raverty, p. 839.
31. *Tarikh-i-Firoz Shahi*, p. 87.

While speaking this 'speech of power', Barani has so blurred our historical perspective that it has become impossible for us to separate his own fads and fancies from historical facts and realities. It is safer, therefore, not to accept Barani as a spokesman of the viewpoint of the entire class of *'ulama*.

As a matter of fact, the attitude of the *'ulama* was determined by what they found stated in books on *fiqh*, written outside India and without any specific reference to Indian conditions. No Indo-Muslim scholar of the thirteenth century sought to study the problem of the Indian Mussalmans and their relation with the Hindus in the light of the conditions operating in this country. Either such a study of the problem was considered unnecessary or the Muslim law was too static to take any note of the changed circumstances. Even the *Adab-u'l-Harb wa-Shuja'at* which contains some stray references to the status and position of the *zimmis* in a Muslim state does not make any reference to the Hindus. Fakhr-i-Mudabbir talks about Sabians, Christians, Jews etc. but makes absolutely no mention of the vast majority of the Hindu population in whose midst he had compiled his book. The *Fawa'id-i-Firoz Shahi*, a much later work, refers to a *Risalah* which was compiled by a great mystic and scholar, Shaikh Shams-u'd-din Yahya, about the dress of the *zimmis*.[32] This *Risalah* has not survived and it is difficult to say what attitude was taken up by the great scholar on that matter.

Of the four main schools of Muslim Law, the Hanafite school was the most liberal in its attitude towards the non-Muslims, while the Shafi'ites represented the other extreme. Probably Barani was more inclined towards the Shafi'ite creed as it vindicated his own prejudices. The fact that of all the medieval Sultans he singled out Mahmud of Ghaznin to weave his political ideology around, was probably due to the latter's Shafi'ite leanings.[33] But the majority of *'ulama* in India were Hanafites[34] and their attitude towards the Hindus was determined by the liberal approach of the Hanafite school towards other cults and creeds.

III. *Mystics*

The mystic attitude towards the Hindus and Hinduism was one of sympathetic understanding and adjustment.[35] They looked upon all religions

32. *Fawa'id-l-Firoz Shahi*, f. 116a.

33. Nazim, *The Life and Times of Sultan Mahmud of Ghaznah* (Cambridge, 1931), p. 159.

34. So far as our records go, we are aware of only two non-Hanafite *Qazis* during the Sultanate period: Maulana Farid-u'd-din Shafi'i in Awadh (*Siyar-u'l-Auliya*, p. 275), and Ibn Battuta Maliki at Delhi.

35. See *supra*, pp. 278–79.

as different roads leading to the same destination. They did not approve of any discrimination or distinction in human society which was one organism for them. They had free social intercourse with the Hindus and tried to understand their approach towards the basic problems of religion and morality.[36] It was their firm conviction that spiritual greatness could be attained by Hindus in the same way as it could be achieved by the Muslims.[37] Believers in non-violence as they were, they disliked injuring any living being, man or animal.[38] Their vegetarianism, whether due to spiritual or social considerations—was bound to increase the area of contact with the Hindus. The following observations made in *Anis-u'l-Arwah* were, it appears, due to a respect for Hindu sentiments:

> Whoever slaughters forty cows would be deemed (on the Day of Judgement) to have killed a man; and whoever slaughters a hundred goats would be likewise held guilty of massacring a man. One who slaughters an animal out of sheer pleasure is consider to have helped in the demolition of Ka'ba ... and no animal should be thrown in fire. It is as great a sin as if one committed incest with his mother.[39]

IV. *Traders and Artisans*

Relations between the Hindu and the Muslim working classes were determined by trade morality and guild-spirit which transcended all other considerations of religion and caste. The following story recorded in *Fawa'id-u'l-Fu'ad* gives some idea of the Muslim respect for the Hindu traders:

> Some merchants of Lahore went to trade in Gujarat. Gujarat was then under a Hindu Raja. When the Hindus came to purchase their articles, the merchants of Lahore demanded double the real price of all the commodities. When they finally disposed of these articles, they accepted half the price they had originally demanded. This was not the practice of the Hindus of that locality. Whatever article they sold, they demanded the correct and fixed price for it. When the Hindus found the Muslim traders behaving in this way, they asked them a question: "Wherefrom do you come?" "From Lahore", they replied. The Hindus further asked: "Is this the way in which transactions are made in your city?" "Yes," they replied. Amazed and surprised, the Hindus remarked. "Does that city continue to be prosperous?" "Yes," they said. "How can a city, where bargains are made like this, prosper," remarked the Hindus... While returning from Gujarat the Muslim traders heard that Lahore had been ravaged by the Kafirs (Mongols).[40]

36. *Fawa'id-u'l-Fu'ad,* pp. 84–85; 238, 245.
37. Ibid, p. 70.
38. *Sarur-u's-Sudur* (MS), pp. 10, 43, 52.
39. *Anis-u'l-Arwah,* pp. 21–22.
40. *Fawa'id-u'l-Fu'ad,* pp. 116–17. Probably the reference is to the invasion of Tayir in 1241.

The Multani traders were mostly Hindus. There were frequent dealings between them and the Muslims, including the Turkish nobles.[41] Indian traders were given perfect freedom to carry on their business in Ghaznin even when political relations between India and Ghaznin were strained.[42]

RELIGIOUS FREEDOM TO THE HINDUS

The hyperbolic and exaggerated narratives of Persian chronicles of the thirteenth century leave upon one's mind the impression of wholesale destruction of the Hindu houses of worship during the Turkish campaigns. For instance, Hasan Nizami speaks about the destruction of all temples in Kalinjar, a statement which is contradicted by the fact that the temples of Mahoba and Khajaraho are still intact.

The early Turkish Sultans of Delhi gave full religious liberty to their non-Muslim subjects. Even in the imperial city of Delhi they bowed before their idols, blew their conches, bathed in the river Jumna and took out their religious processions without any let or hindrance by the state.[43] In an old temple on the Bareilly-Mathura road there are records of 15 pilgrimages between the years 1241 and 1290.[44]

Archaeological evidence shows that even the construction of new temples was not checked or stopped by the Turkish Sultans. Thakur Phero's work on medieval temple architecture,[45] *Vastusara*, written during the reign of Sultan *'Ala-u'd-din Khalji*, does not make any reference to state interference in the construction of temples. There is, on the contrary, definite evidence that temples were constructed during this period. Three images of the Jaina sect, discovered in Etah, contain dated records of their installation in the year VS 1335/AD1278.[46] A fragment of a bilingual inscription, in Persian and Sanskrit, found in the Purana Qila of Delhi records the endowment of 12 *bighahs* of land to a temple dedicated to Sri Krishna.[47] Firoz Shah's protest that "the Hindus and idol-worshippers had built new temples in the city and the environs",[48] should be read against this background.

41. *Tarikh-i-Firoz Shahi*, p. 110.

42. *Jawama'-u'l-Hikavat*, Vol. I, pp. 47–48.

43. *Tarikh-i-Firoz Shahi*, pp. 216–17.

44. Cunningham, *Reports of the Archaeological Survey of India*. Vol. I, p. 206.

45. See V.S. Amarwala's article: 'A Note on Medieval Temple Architecture.' *Journal of the United Provinces Historical Society*, July 1943. pp. 112–17.

46. *Reports of the Archaeological Survey of India*, 1923. p. 92.

47. Ibid, 1909–10, p. 131.

48. *Futuhat-i-Firoz Shahi*. pp. 10–11.

CONVERSIONS

Contemporary historical works supply very little information about the conversion of non-Muslims to Islam during the thirteenth century. Stray incidents of conversions recorded in political and non-political works can hardly be of any help in understanding the processes of conversion during the early period. Tradition attributes the conversion of a large number of Hindu tribes to Islam to the missionary activities of the Muslim mystics,[49] but the genuine mystic records are silent on this point.[50] This absence of recorded evidence cannot, however, be interpreted to mean that there were no conversions. Obviously the increase in Indo-Muslim society was largely due to conversions. But it remains to be investigated how these conversions took place and what agencies worked for them. Did they take place at the individual or the tribal level? What sections of Indian society were the first to be converted? What were the attractions working for conversion? How far did these conversions represent a reaction against the caste taboos of medieval Hinduism? These and similar questions cannot be answered with certainty due to want of requisite data. After weighing all the circumstantial evidence, Professor Habib has reached the conclusion "that the acceptance of Islam by the city-workers was a decision of local professional groups, and that in making their decisions they were naturally more concerned with mundane affairs and their position in the social order than with abstract theological truths."[51] This is largely true though it underrates the role of the moral and spiritual forces released by the Muslim mystics.

Many tribes claim that their ancestors were converted to Islam by the Muslim mystics. It is difficult to controvert their claim on the basis of any negative argument. For instance, the following tribes of the Punjab claim to have been converted to Islam by Shaikh Farid-u'd-din Ganj-i-Shakar:

1. Sial
2. Sarhangwalian
3. Bahliyan
4. Adhakan
5. Jhakarwalian
6. Bakkan
7. Hakan
8. Sian

49. *The Preaching of Islam*, p. 274, et seq.

50. Professor M. Habib's article: "Shaikh Nasir-u'd-din Chiragh as a Great Historical Personality." *Islamic Culture*, April, 1946, p. 140.

51. Introduction to Elliot and Dowson's *History of India* (Vol. II, revised edition), p. 59.

9. Khokaran.
10. Dhudhiyan.
11. Tobiyan.[52]

The respect shown to the great Chishti saint of Ajodhan by generations of these tribes lends weight to their claim.

Some tribes are reported to have been converted to Islam by Shihab-u'd-din and his Turkish slave-officers. Minhaj thus refers to the conversion of a tribal chief at the hands of Muhammad b. Bakhtiyar Khalji:

> In the different parts of those mountains which lie between Tibbat and the country of Lakhnawati are three races of people, one called the Kunch, the second Mej (Meg), and the third, the Tiharu; and all have Turk countenances. They have a different idiom too, between the language of Hind and Turk. One of the chiefs of the tribes of Kunch and Mej, whom they were wont to call 'Ali, the Mej, fell into the hands of Mahammad-i-Bakhtiyar, the Khalji, and, at his hand also, the former adopted the Muhammadan faith'.[53]

Ferishtah's statement that the Khokars had embraced Islam at the hands of Shihab-u'd-din[54] lacks contemporary and even later confirmation. Amir Khusrau refers to the Khokars as a non-Muslim tribe.[55]

EMPLOYMENT OF THE HINDUS BY THE STATE

The Turkish State in India could not possibly dispense with the services of the Hindus employed in the various branches of administration, particularly at the local levels. Any such action would have completely paralysed the administrative machinery and would have created chaotic conditions in the country. Even in the case of higher officials, the Turks proceeded very cautiously and replaced them in stages. They fully realized that the indigenous institutions could be run by the Indians alone. They alone could help the new government in the collection of revenues and could act as intermediaries between the State and the peasantry. This class was, therefore, left untouched by the Turkish government. "When Qutbuddin

52. *Jawakir-i-Faridi*, Vol. II, pp. 396–98; *The Jhang Settlement Report*, Steedman, p. 244; *The Punjab Gazetter*, Vol. II, p. 207; Ibbetson, *Punjab Castes*, pp. 147–48. Lepel Griffin, *Punjab Chiefs*, p. 50, et seq.

53. *Tabaqat-i-Nasiri*, p. 152; Raverty, p. 560.

54. *Tarikh-i-Ferishtah*, Vol. I, p. 59. *The Indian Antiquary* (1907, p. 1) and the *Cambridge History of India* (Vol. III, p. 98) have accepted Ferishtah's version. But Raverty has rightly questioned its authenticity, *Notes on Afghanistan*, p. 367. See also *Foundation of Muslim Rule in India*, pp. 327–28.

55. *Tughluq Namah*, p. 128.

Aibek decided," writes Dr Tara Chand, "to stay in Hindustan he had no other choice but to retain the Hindu staff which was familiar with the Hindu administration, for without it all government including the collection of revenue would have fallen into utter chaos. The Muslims did not bring with them from beyond the Indian frontiers artisans, accountants and clerks. Their buildings were erected by Hindus who adapted their ancient rules to newer conditions, their coins were struck by Hindu goldsmiths and their accounts were kept by Hindu officers. Brahman legists advised the king on the administration of Hindu law and Brahman astronomers helped in the performance of their general functions."[56]

Apart from the spheres in which the employment of Hindus was almost indispensable, they must also have been employed in the new armies which the Sultans had to raise in order to meet the growing danger of the Mongol incursions.

ECONOMIC CONDITION OF THE HINDUS

It would be wrong to think that the economic condition of all sections of Hindu society remained unchanged after the Turkish occupation of the country. The Rajput feudal lords could not possibly continue to enjoy the privileges of a governing class when political power passed into the hands of the Turks. But the lower sections of the Rajput aristocracy did not suffer any loss of economic position. Their prosperous condition, about which Barani speaks during the Tughluq period,[57] was not an abrupt situation created in the fourteenth century. It had its roots in the policy of the Ilbarites.

Besides, the substitution of forced labour with free labour had a tremendous effect on the economic condition of the Indian masses. The fact that the Hindu moneylenders were in a position to advance money to the Muslim aristocracy[58] is too significant to be ignored.

SOCIAL RELATIONS

When two culture groups come face to face, they cannot long maintain an attitude of isolation, distrust or indifference. Social and economic forces bring them nearer each other. During the period under review, both the Hindus and the Muslims stood in danger of being destroyed at the hands of the Mongols. This common danger further accelerated the pace of syncretic forces and created a sense of unity.

56. *Influence of Islam on Indian Culture*, p. 137.
57. *Fatawa-i-Jahandari*, f. 120a–121b.
58. *Tarikh-i-Firoz Shahi*, p. 120.

The earliest references to contacts between the Hindus and the Muslims are found in the medieval records about the *khanqahs* of the Muslim saints.[59] We hear about a Hindu being introduced to Shaikh Nizam-ud-din Auliya by a Muslim as 'This Hindu is my brother'.[60] The use of a large number of Hindustani words, phrases, idioms and similies in contemporary literature[61] shows the extent to which social contacts had developed.

Some of the names given to Muslim nobles, religious men and others, are definitely Indian, e.g. Malik Chajju,[62] Malik Kachchan,[63] Faqih Mahdu,[64] Rashid Pandit,[65] Malik Haran Mar.[66]

When social contact increased, Hindu tastes and customs were also adopted by the Muslims. Barani tells us about a noble of Balban who was very fond of chewing *pan*[67] (betel leaves), a purely Indian habit.[68] Indian music found its patrons at the royal courts[69] and the *khanqahs*.[70] The Hindi poetry came to be appreciated by Muslim scholars and divines.[71] Hindu mourning practices gained currency in Muslim society.[72]

Matrimonial relationships could not have been avoided at the lower level. We have only two references about this at the higher level. Mangbarni is reported to have married a Khokar girl[73] and Shaikh Mu'in-u'd-din

59. See *supra*, p. 280.

60. *Fawa'id-u'l-Fu'ad*, p. 182.

61. *Tabaqat-i-Nasiri*, pp. 118, 148, 158, 209, 254; *Qir'an-u's-Sa'din*, pp. 32, 25, 36, 60, 70, 112, 185.

62. It is surprising that members of some renowned Turkish and Sayyid families had this name, e.g. the famous nephew of Balban (*Tarikh-i-Firoz Shahi*, p. 173) and a nephew of Amir Hasan 'Ala Sijzi (*Fawa'id-u'l-Fu'ad*, p. 15). See also *Tarikh-i-Firoz Shahi*, p. 111.

63. Ibid, p. 126.

64. *Fawa'id-u'l-Fu'ad*, p. 174.

65. *Khair-u'l-Majalis*, pp. 93, 155.

66. *Tarikh-i-Firoz Shahi*, p. 177.

67. Ibid, p. 117.

68. *Alberuni's India*, Vol. II, p. 152.

69. *Tarikh-i-Firoz Shahi*, p. 157.

70. *Siyar-u'l-Auliya*, p. 152; *Fawa'id-u'l-Fu'ad*, p. 174.

71. *I'joz-i-Khusravi*, Vol. II, pp. 177–78.

Jawami'-a'l-Kilam, p. 173; *Siyar-u'l-Auliya*, p. 200.

72. *Tarikh-i-Firoz Shahi*, pp. 109, 123.

73. *Tarikh-i-Jahan Gusha*, English trans., Vol. II, p. 414. For an account of this marriage based on tradition, see *Indian Antiquary*, 1907, p. 3. For marriages in Khokar and other families by the descendants of Shaikh Farid-Ganj-i-Shakar, see *Jawahir-i-Faridi*, p. 323, et seq.

Chishti is said to have married the daughter of a Hindu Raja of Ajmir.[74] Among the lower strata such instances must have been very frequent.

THE RURAL POPULATION

Indian villages have lived a self-sufficient life from times immemorial.[75] Political revolutions which took place in the urban areas could not disturb the rural economy or the rural pattern of life. The Indian peasant carried on his vocation without bothering about change in the composition of the governing class. Since there was no change in the class of intermediaries between the State and the peasant, the Hindu peasant had no occasion to know about the change. The new *iqta'dars* who had taken the place of the Rajput feudal lords could not possibly bring about any immediate change in the relationship between the State and the peasant. The stream of life in the rural areas flowed smoothly and uninterruptedly even after the establishment of Turkish rule. Balban realized the importance of the peasants in the general economy of the country and the State when he declared: "While he should not be allowed to develop into a rich potential rebel, ruinous exaction on him would cause a falling of in agriculture and the consequent impoverishment of the State."[76] But his regulations did not touch even the fringes of rural life.

The Turk and the Muslim refugees who came to India were urban-minded and had little interest in agriculture as a vocation. There were consequently no attempts to settle in the rural areas. But people who did not want to live in the choking atmosphere of urban society settled in rural areas. A son of Shaikh Mu'in-u'd-din took to farming in Mandal; Shaikh Hamid-u'd-din cultivated a *bigah* of land in a village near Nagaur. These Muslim cultivators adjusted themselves to the rural milieu and fitted themselves into the frame work of the rural economy. In dress, diet and living they adopted the ways of the Indian peasants.

---

74. *Akhbar-u'l-Akhyar*, pp. 112–13.
75. Mookerji, *Local Government in Ancient India*, pp. 146–78.
76. *Tarikh-i-Firoz Shahi*, p. 100.

CHAPTER X

EXTERNAL RELATIONS

"The intimate contact between India and the outer Asiatic world," remarks Sir Jadunath Sarkar, "which had been established in the early Buddhistic age, was lost when the new Hindu society was reorganized and set in rigidity like a concrete structure about the eighth century AD, with the result that India again became self-centred and isolated from the moving world beyond her natural barriers. This touch with the rest of Asia and the nearest parts of Africa was restored by the Muslim conquest at the end of the twelfth century."[1]

One of the factors responsible for this isolationist attitude of the Hindus was their sense of superiority. "According to their belief," writes Alberuni, "there is no other country on earth but theirs, no other race of man but theirs, and no created beings besides them have any knowledge or science whatsoever. Their haughtiness is such that, if you tell them of any science or scholar in Khurasan and Persia, they will think you to be both an ignoramus and a liar. If they travelled and mixed with other nations, they would soon change their mind, for their ancestors were not as narrow-minded as the present generation is."[2] This attitude was not confined to the cultural or the intellectual spheres alone. It had exercised its unhealthy influence in almost every other sphere of external relations. If the laws of Manu may be an index to the mind of the Hindu ruling classes, their attitude towards foreign powers was one of contemptuous indifference, suspicion and even hostility.[3] 'Let (the king) consider as hostile his immediate neighbour', was Manu's advice to his contemporary rulers.

The Turkish Sultans of Delhi did not believe in isolated political or cultural existence. They appreciated fully the necessity of establishing diplomatic relations with foreign powers.[4] The *Adab-u'l-Harb* of Fakhr-i-Mudabbir very neatly epitomizes the ideals and ambitions of the Turkish

---

1. *India Through the Ages*, p. 43.
2. *Alberuni's India*, p. 23.
3. *Laws of Manu* (Sacred Books of the East Series), Vol. XXV, pp. 241–49.
4. *Tarikh-i-Firoz Shahi*, pp. 30–31. Barani informs us about the visit of ambassadors from distant lands (رسولان دور دست) to the court of Balban.

oligarchy in India and lays down the following rules regarding the qualifications of ambassadors and their functions and duties in foreign courts:

When an envoy is dispatched from one sovereign to another, he should be of noble lineage, or he should come of a scholarly and pious family, or he should be high-born such that his ancestors must have earned fame and good reputation, or he should come of some pure Sayyid stock such that right from his childhood he must have been brought up before the king and must have become cultured and discriminating, having learnt court conventions, and gained celebrity in the service of the king....He should be formidable, handsome, eloquent, glib-tongued, pert, of tall stature and graceful so that he may command respect in the eyes of the people. An envoy should not be of slight appearance and of short stature, nor should he be ugly and repulsive to sight, crippled, idle-talker, disposed to laugh immoderately, refractory, rash, niggardly, parsimonious and ill-tempered, nor should he belong to such a family that any of his ancestors had been notorious for grossly immoral habits or depravity. He should be eloquent, cultured, modest, sedate, lavish, charitable, magnanimous, spendthrift, extravagant to a degree that nothing is too much in his eyes; and a number of learned divines, scholars and high-born persons should accompany him and if need be, he should be in a position to perform a task himself and make others perform it. Plenty of wealth should be sent with him so that he may not lag behind in doing some good. Again, if he spends that wealth for furthering a cause and the task is not completed or he does not rectify a mistake (for the affairs of kingdom and the king are just like river water which flows in and flows out in immeasurable quantity, i.e. the affairs of state are numerous and varied), he [who has dispatched the envoy, i.e the king] should not be slack and should send him a band of swift and ingenious messengers and experienced, nimble and intrepid horse riders and dromedaries well-acquainted with the way so that if an emergency arises, they should be able to march day and night and even in odd hours to meet that emergency. Again, the envoy should be such that when he is dispatched to the court of a king, he may be ready-witted. So long as he is not asked about anything he should not initiate it of his own accord. If he is asked about anything he should reply in a decent and befitting manner and should not cut a sorry figure. He should be calm and composed and should not laugh immoderately. If any branch of knowledge is being discussed in that court he should explain it in a proper manner and in agreeable language if he knows it; if he does not know it he should remain silent and should not begin it and should show that he knows that branch of knowledge but he should not go to the extent that he be subjected to test and may not be able to acquit himself well as a result of which he may be regarded as a jester and of mean profession....

The envoy should be such that when he commences a discourse meekly he must close it in a harsh manner, and should close it meekly if he has begun it harshly. He should be 'a tearer' and at the same time a 'sewer'; a 'maker' and a 'burner' simultaneously. He should speak with vital force and in a vigorous manner and should not speak humbly and meekly. When he is asked about the king, the territory, the retainers and the subjects he should speak in such a way as to place them in a superior position to all others. He should never behave arrogantly....his mouth is the mouth of his master. He should talk to the grandees and functionaries of that country politely and softly and in an agreeable manner so that all of them may be on friendly terms with him. If necessity demands friendship with someone, he should send him rare gifts because much love and goodwill is acquired thereby and many secrets are thus known....The presents which are sent through the envoy should be excellent even if he (that is, the king to whom those presents are sent) does not deserve them by virtue of his rank, so that the sender's degree of generosity, amicability and magnanimity may be estimated, and the assertion of his magnificence should be the primary gain which may be achieved by sending those presents which are rarely found in his [that is, the receiver's] country.[5]

Fakhr-i-Mudabbir then gives a list of articles which should be sent as presents to foreign courts:

1. The Quran.
2. Commentaries on the Quran written in good hand.
3. Cultured slaves.
4. Turkish, Rumi, Abyssinian and Indian slave-girls.
5. Gold and silver embroidered çloth.
6. Horses and camels.
7. Mules.
8. Saddles and bridles.
9. Swords.
10. Kataras (small swords).
11. Shields.
12. Double-pointed spears.
13. Arrows and bows.
14. Different types of coats-of-mail and armlets.
15. Helmets.
16. Vests worn under coats of mail.
17. Horse armour.
18. Shank covers.
19. Veils.
20. Knives, with handles made of *khatu* (bones of a Chinese bird) and *kark* (branch of a tree).

5. *Adab-u'l-Harb wa-Shuja'at*, ff. 57a–59a.
For early Islamic traditions, see *Islamic Culture*, Vol. XV, No. 2 (April, 1941), p. 201, et. seq; for Hindu traditions, see *The Laws of Manu*, pp. 225–27.

21. Sandal wood.
22. Aloe wood.
23. Ebony.
24. Tusks of elephants.
25. Ruby.
26. Turquoise.
27. Agate.
28. Jasper.
29. Arabian shells.
30. Linen and woollen clothes.
31. Mats and prayer carpets.
32. Velvet.
33. Raw silk.
34. Falcons.
35. Turkish elephants.
36. Stockings.
37. Breeches.
38. Musk.
39. Camphor.
40. Ambergis.
41. Leather table cloths.
42. Cushions.
43. Beavers.
44. Ermines.
45. Fox fur.
46. Lions, tigers and leopards, dogs, etc.
47. China vessels.
48. Morocco leather etc.[6]

Lastly, Fakhr-i-Mudabbir deals with treaties and agreements and draws attention to the following essentials in this context:

(a) All agreements should be made in writing.
(b) Both parties should vow to act upon the agreement. These vows should refer to God, His Prophet, angels, Revealed Books, prophets, divorce, manumission of slaves, Hajj, etc.
(c) All qazis, Sayyids, saints, celebrities, nobles, officers and military leaders should put their signatures on this agreement.
(d) The agreement should be read out before both the parties.

6. *Adab-u'l-Harb-wa-Shuja'at*, ff. 59a, 59b.

The way in which Fakhr-i-Mudabbir has gone into every minute detail about external contacts shows that considerable importance was attached to it in his days.

RELATIONS WITH THE MONGOLS

One of the most baffling problems of international politics which the Sultans had to tackle was the rise of the Mongols which "resembles rather some brute catacylsm of the blind forces of nature than a phenomenon of human history."[7] Wherever they went a crimson streak marked their trail and cultural centres of medieval 'Ajam were practically wiped out of existence. Minhaj read the signs of the Day of Resurrection in the irruption of the Mongols.[8]

The independent Sultanate of Delhi had come into existence almost simultaneously with the rise of Chengiz Khan. The Sultans had hardly set up their administrative institutions that the Mongol danger began to loom large on the Indian horizon. They realized fully the magnitude of the problem as well as their own limitations in dealing with it. Vigilant without being provocative and realistic without being despondent, they handled a formidable political situation with great tact.

Broadly speaking, the policy of the early Turkish Empire of Delhi towards the Mongols had three distinct phases—aloofness, appeasement and resistance. So long as Chengiz Khan was alive, Iltutmish strictly maintained an attitude of dignified aloofness and did not press his claims in Sind and Multan where the Mongols had their interests. The Mongols also respected the non-aggression pact with Iltutmish.[9] The policy of the *quriltai* changed under the influence of Ugudy and for more than two decades the Mongol pressure went on increasing on the Delhi frontier. When all efforts to check the rising tide of Mongol aggression proved to be wasted labour, the Sultanate adopted the policy of appeasement. Throughout the reign of Hulagu, the Turkish oligarchy at Delhi followed this policy and with considerable success. When Hulagu died in 1265 and Balban ascended the throne in 1266, a more vigorous policy of resistance was initiated. The Mongol tide was successfully repulsed and the frontier region was so effectively guarded that, even under a weak ruler like Kaiqubad, the Mongol invaders were pursued as far as the Salt Range.[10]

7. *Histoire des Mongols*, D' Ohsson, Vol. I, p. 387.
8. *Tabaqat-i-Nasiri*, pp. 330–31.
9. *Foundation of the Early Turkish Empire of Delhi*, p. 194.
10. *Tarikh-i-Mubarak Shahi*, p. 54.

When Chengiz Khan appeared on the Indian scene in 1221, vigorously pursuing the Khwarizmian prince, Jalal-u'd-din Mangbarni, Iltutmish found himself between the devil and the deep sea. He could neither help Chengiz nor could he protect Mangbarni. Chengiz was not the man to tolerate any hostile reaction to his movements, while Mangbarni was the scion of a ruling house which had bitterly strained relations with the Shansabanians. Besides, Mangbarni was a military leader *par excellence*[11] and, given the opportunity, could establish Khwarizmian hegemony in India. His stay in India was, therefore, as dangerous[12] to the Ilbarite interests as the presence of Chengiz. Iltutmish could neither choose one nor the other as his ally. Besides, the cis-Indus region where Chengiz had mustered his forces, was inhabited by tribes and factions hostile to the Sultanate of Delhi and had all the potentialities of turning into a dangerous zone of opposition against the Sultanate. On one side the Khokars nursed inveterate hatred towards the Sultan of Delhi and, on the other, the ruler of Multan looked upon Iltutmish as his rival. The march of events showed that a triple alliance between Mangbarni, Qubacha and the Khokars could spring up at any moment. A Khokar–Mangbarni alliance had actually come into being. It was in this complicated political situation that Iltutmish formulated his policy with reference to the Mongols.

It is said that both Mangbarni[13] and Chengiz[14] had sent their envoys to Delhi. We do not know how Iltutmish received the Mongol envoy, but the envoy of Mangbarni was put to death.[15] Iltutmish probably utilized this

---

11. Even Chengiz could not help praising him. "Such a son must a father have", he remarked when Mangbarni plunged his horse into the Indus and swam across with his royal canopy in his hand.

12. Juwaini says that Iltutmish feared "lest the Sultan might gain an ascendancy over him and involve him in ruin." *Tarikh-i-Jahan Gusha* (trans.), Vol. II, p. 414.

13. *Tarikh-i-Jahan Gusha* (Eng. trans.), Vol. II, p. 414

14. *Tabaqat-i-Nasiri*, p. 355.

15. *Tarikh-i-Jahan Gusha* (Eng. trans.), Vol. II, p. 414.

Juwaini says that Mangbarni had sent the following message to Iltutmish: "The vicissitudes of fortune have established my right to approach thy presence, and a guest of my sort arrives but rarely. If, therefore, the drinking place of friendship be purified upon either side and the cups of fraternity filled to the brim, and we bind ourselves to aid and assist one another in weal and woe then shall all our aims and objects be attained; and when our opponents realize the concord that exists between us, the teeth of their resistance will be blunted" (Vol. II, p. 413). On one side Iltutmish got the messenger killed and on the other he sent a messenger "with offerings of food worthy of such a guest, but excused himself from providing a place of abode on the ground that nowhere in that region was there a suitable climate nor any locality such as would be fit for a king" (Vol. II, p. 414).

opportunity to enter into a non-aggression pact with the Mongols according to which no enemy of the Mongols could be given asylum by the Sultan of Delhi and, in return, the territorial integrity of the Turkish Empire was to be respected by the Mongols. It is difficult to say how far this arrangement could have worked if Chengiz had decided to stay in India. Iltutmish got out of a very difficult situation when the Mongol leader decided to abandon his Indian campaign[16] and marched back through the Hindu Kush.

Mangbarni who stayed on in India for a couple of years more had to face several Mongol attacks. His military commanders advised him to settle down in India and seek the help of Delhi against the Mongols. But he decided to leave in 1224 and left Hasan Qarlugh and Uzbek Pai as his representatives in Afghanistan and Sind.

Iltutmish laid down, as in many other spheres, the basic principles on which the policy of the Sultanate was to be formulated with reference to the Mongols. It was clearly a policy of dignified aloofness from Central Asian politics and strict avoidance of provocation to the Mongols. For more than six years after the return of Chengiz, Iltutmish did not try to extend his power to the cis-Indus region, so necessary for the consolidation of his power, because it was closely linked up with Central Asian politics and the Mongols were keenly interested in its developments. A year after Chengiz's death (1227AD), Qubacha's dominions were annexed by Iltutmish.

With Iltutmish's annexation of Multan and Uch, the buffer-state between the Mongols and the Sultanate of Delhi disappeared. Iltutmish now stood in direct contact with the Mongols, without any shock-absorber in between. But internecine struggle between the sons of Chengiz gave him respite and an opportunity to consolidate his internal position. We do not hear of any major Mongol attack on India during the later years of Iltutmish's reign. But in the same year in which Iltutmish breathed his last, the Mongol power had been established in Seistan.

The Mongol attempt to establish their strongholds in India began after the death of Iltutmish. The *quriltai* assembly of the Mongol princes had no doubt decided as early as 1229 on a policy of reconquest and annexation of territories contiguous to the Delhi frontier but for many years there remained a lull on the Indian frontiers. Then the Mongol operations started in the upper Indus. In 1241 Ugudy despatched an army under the command

16. In abandoning his Indian campaign Chengiz was guided by superstition: 'He was burning shoulder-bones (of sheep) continually and examining them,' but the resulting angury never permitted his entering Hind. Raverty, pp. 1046–47.

of Tayir and occupied the city of Lahore.[17] Chengiz's non-aggresssion pact thus came to an end and the territorial integrity of the Sultanate suffered its first serious loss.

The establishment of Mongol power in Lahore made the position of Delhi extremely precarious. Open resistance was rejected as beyond the region of practical politics and a policy of appeasement was evolved. When Nuyin invaded Multan in 1246, Shaikh Baha-u'd-din Zakariyya was requested to intervene and it was through his intercession that the Mongols retired after realizing an indemnity of one lakh dinars.[18]

In 1258 Baghdad was sacked by the forces of Hulagu. Legally the Sultanate of Delhi was a part of the 'Abbasid Caliphate and, as such, it should have strongly reacted to the fall of Baghdad. But, barring rehabilitation of the refugees,[19] the Sultanate did not take any notice of the cataclysm. Two years after the incident, emissaries from the Mongol court visited India and the Sultan of Delhi, eager to win the goodwill of a powerful neighbour, accorded a royal reception to them.[20]

This gesture did not go unreciprocated and Hulagu warned his soldiers: "If the hoof of your horse enters the dominion of Sultan Nasiru'd-din, all four legs of the horse shall be cut off."[21]

When Balban ascended the throne he reversed the policy of the Sultanate towards the Mongols. He was in a better position than his predecessors to follow a vigorous defence policy. Hulagu was no more and the Mongol tribal organization and its political structure was showing signs of decay. Astute and seasoned statesman as he was, Balban carefully watched the activities of the Mongols and diverted all the resources of the Empire towards the protection of his frontiers.[22] To keep himself aware of the Mongol movements and supervise personally his defence measures, Balban went out every day up to Riwari under the pretext of military exercises and hunting excursions.[23] The appointment of Prince Muhammad as the warden of the marches was a very firm and determined step towards the elimination of Mongol influence from the cis-Indus region. Prince Muhammad very successfully carried out the policy of his father and cleared his territories of the Mongols. This provoked the Mongols and in, 1285, Timar Khan, a Chengizi noble and governor of Herat, invaded Sind

17. *Tabaqat-i-Nasiri*, p. 392, et seq.

18. See *supra*, p. 271–72.

19. *Tarikh-i-Ferishtah*, Vol. I, p. 75.

20. See *supra*, pp. 130–31.

21. *Tabaqat-i-Nasiri*, p. 322.

22. *Tarikh-i-Firoz Shahi*, p. 51.

23. Ibid, p. 54.

with an army of 20,000 men. Prince Muhammad proceeded to repel it but was killed in the encounter. Balban had to pay a heavy price for his policy of resistance but it considerably enhanced his prestige inside and outside the country.

RELATIONS WITH THE ABBASIDS

We have referred in an earlier chapter to the relations of the Delhi Sultans with the Abbasid Caliphs. The Caliphate of Baghdad disappeared during the reign of Nasir-u'd-din Mahmud. The only Sultan of Delhi who had had any opportunity of establishing contact with Baghdad was Iltutmish. He maintained diplomatic relations with Baghdad and frequently exchanged envoys. Twice during his reign, Maulana Razi-u'd-din Hasan Saghani came to Delhi as the envoy of Khalifah al-Nasir la-Din Allah (575–623/ 1179–1225) and his successors. Iltutmish did not lag behind in sending his own envoys to him. Minhaj writes about Ikhtiyar ul-Mulk Rashid-u'd-din Abu Bakr Habsh:[24]

از حضرت برسالت نصر بغداد رفته بود

which means that he was sent to Baghdad on a mission by the court of Delhi. Probably he was sent to secure *manshur* from the *khalifah*. Once the Caliph sent Qazi Jalal'Urus with an old copy of *Safinat-u'l-Khulafa* which contained some autographic inscription from Mamun-u'r-Rashid. Barani tells us that the Sultan was so pleased with this present that he wanted to give half of his kingdom to Qazi Jalal as a reward for bringing this valuable gift.[25]

COMMERCIAL RELATIONS

Under the early Turkish Sultans of Delhi commercial contacts with the outer world were developed in spite of the irruption of the Mongols. The general impression that the Mongols upset all commercial contacts and rendered all trade routes unsafe is not correct. The message which Chengiz

24. *Tabaqat-i-Nasiri*, p. 279. Raverty translates it thus: "had proceeded from the court of Delhi on a mission to Misr (Egypt) and Baghdad" (p. 796). I think the word *misr* does not indicate Egypt. It is used in its literal sense and means 'city' only.

It may be noted that Nasir la-Din Allah was himself very keen on establishing diplomatic contacts with Muslim powers. In 576/1179, a year after his accession, he had sent his envoy to Sultan Salah-u'd-din Ayyubi. *Tarikh-ul' Khulafa*, Suyuti (Matba' al-Sa'adah, Egypt).

25. *Tarikh-i-Firoz Shahi*, p. 103.

Khan sent to Sultan Muhammad Khwarizm Shah shows his anxiety to maintain and develop commercial contacts. He said:

> Let there be between us a firm treaty of friendship, amity and peace, and let traders and *karwans* on both sides come and go, and let the precious products and ordinary commodities which may be in my territory be conveyed by them into thine and those of thine, in the same manner, let them bring into mine.[26]

It was as a result of this attitude that when Tayir invaded Lahore in 1241, the merchants of that town indirectly extended co-operation and support to him. Minhaj writes:

> Most of the inhabitants of the city were merchants and traders and had undertaken journeys, during the time of the Mughals, into the upper parts, into Khurasan and Turkistan, and, by way of precaution, every one of them had obtained a pass from the Mughal, and a safe conduct, and, knowing this, in defending and fighting for the safety of the Hisar of Lahore, they used not to act in unison with Malik Kara-Kush, and would neither render assistance nor make resistance, nor encounter the enemy.[27]

It appears from medieval records that foreign merchants came to India in large numbers. Under Baha-u'd-din Tughral, Thankar (Bayana) "became so prosperous and populous that merchants from distant places like Khurasan began to visit that place".[28] Amir Khurd's grandfather, Sayyid Muhammad Kirmani. regularly traded for a long time between Kirman and Lahore.[29] 'Isami refers to the presence of Chinese traders in Delhi during the reign of Iltutmish. These merchants were allowed access to the Sultan also.[30] The two commodities which were constantly flowing into the country from foreign lands were horses and slaves. Horses were imported from Turkistan, Russia, Iraq and Bahrain.[31] When the import of horses was threatened as a result of political changes in Central Asia, Balban is reported to have boasted that he could maintain the necessary supplies even if the horses from the Mongol territory did not reach him.[32] Slaves were brought from Turkistan, Aden and Egypt.[33] Balban was

26. *Tabaqat-i-Nasiri*, Raverty, p. 960.
27. *Tabaqat-i-Nasiri*, p. 393; Raverty, p. 1133.
28. *Tabaqat-i-Nasiri*, p. 145
29. *Siyar-u'l-Auliya*, p. 208.
30. *Futuh-u's-Salatin*, p. 122.
31. *Masalik-u'l-Absar*, p. 22.
32. *Tarikh-i-Firoz Shahi*, p. 53.
33. *Tabaqat-i-Nasiri*, p. 265.

brought by Khwaja Jamal-u'd-din Qazi from Baghdad to Gujarat.[34] Malik 'Izz-u'd-din Balban Kishlu Khan was taken by the slave merchants to Mandavar where Iltutmish purchased him.[35]

INTELLECTUAL AND CULTURAL RELATIONS

Another important aspect of India's contact with the outer world was in the realm of ideas. In the early years of the foundation of the Sultanate of Delhi, Baghdad, Bukhara, Samarqand, Balkh and other Transoxianan cities were looked upon as the centres of Muslim learning. All those who desired to acquire higher education in different branches of Muslim sciences turned to these places.[36] Scholars apart, even Sultans looked to these regions for intellectual guidance.[37] Balban's son, Prince Muhammad, had correspondence with the great Persian poet, Sa'di, and had even invited him to India.[38]

When the Mongols reduced these cultural centres into shapeless ruins, many scholars and divines turned to India and settled there. Very soon the situation changed so completely that instead of Indian Muslims going to other lands for intellectual guidance, Muslims from different parts of 'Ajam began to visit India. Sayyid Husaini[39] and Fakhr-u'd-din 'Iraqi[40] came to Multan from distant lands and joined the circle of Shaikh Baha-u'd-din Zakariyya's disciples. People from Khurasan visited the *khanqah* of Shaikh Farid Ganj-i-Shakar.[41] During the reign of Balban, two saints came from Chisht—the cradle land of the Chishti *silsilah*—in order to persuade Shaikh 'Ali Chishti to return to Chisht and revitalize the *silsilah* in its homeland.[42]

---

34. *Tabaqat-i-Nasiri*, p. 281.

35. Ibid, p. 268.

36. See *Siyar-u'l-Auliya* (p. 170) for Shaikh Badr-u'd-din Ishaq's desire to go to Bukhara in order to get his difficulties solved by the *'ulama* of that place. See also *Siyar-u'l-'Arifin* (p. 103), for Shaikh Baha-u'd-din Zakariyya's education in those regions.

37. Iltutmish procured from Baghdad two very important books—*Adab-u's Salatin* and *Ma'asir-u's-Salatin*, dealing probably with Muslim political theory, for his sons. *Tarikh-i-Firoz Shahi*, p. 145.

38. Ibid, p. 68.

39. Sayyid Sadr-u'd-din Ahmad b. Najm-u'd-din popularly known as Sayyid Husaini was a native of Herat. He was a prolific writer. Of his works, *Nuzhat-u'l-Arwah, Zad-u'l-Musafirrin*, and *Kanuz-u'r-Rumuz* are well known. He lies buried in Herat. *Siyar-u'l-'Arifin*, p. 110.

40. Ibid, pp. 107–09.

41. *Siyar-u'l-Auliya*, pp. 63–64.

42. Ibid, p. 212.

Itinerancy being an essential part of mystic discipline in those days, mystics were an important medium for maintaining cultural and intellectual contacts with the world outside. The first information about the works of Shaikh Muhi-u'd-din Ibn-i-'Arabi reached India through Shaikh Fakhr-u'd-din 'Iraqi.[43]

Since many of the refugees who had come and settled in India under the pressure of Mongol invasions, had left their relatives behind, some sort of family contact continued for generations. Minhaj-u's-Siraj sent a large number of slaves and horses to his sister who was in great distress in Khurasan.[44] There must have been many other similar cases of contact between India and the outside world.

43. *Siyar-u'l-'Arifin*, p. 109.
44. *Tabaqat-i-Nasiri*, pp. 213–14.
See also *Fawa'id-u'l-Fu'ad* (p. 73) for Shaikh Badr-u'd-din Ghaznavi's desire to go home and meet his relatives.

SOME DOCUMENTS OF THE THIRTEENTH CENTURY

1. *A Fath Namah*
2. *An Ijazat Namah*
3. *A Khilafat-cum-Ijazat Namah*
4. *A Khilafat Namah*
5. *A Khutbah*
6. *A Saint's letter to the Sultan*

APPENDIX A

SOME DOCUMENTS OF THE THIRTEENTH CENTURY

1.
2.
3.
4.
5.
6.

(1) A FATH NAMAH

The following *Fath Namah* was drafted by Amir Khusrau on the occasion of Balban's Lakhnauti campaign (*I'jaz-i-Khusravi*, Vol. IV, pp. 4–13). This was the poet's first attempt at drafting a *fath namah*. He himself says:

این فتح نامه در عهد سلطان مرحوم غیاث الدین در فتح لکهنوتی بود' اول امتحانی بود که قلم انشاء خود را کردم

It appears from the *Tarikh-i-Firoz Shahi* that Malik Qiwam-u'd-din Dabir had prepared a *fath namah* on this occasion. Barani writes:

ملک قوام الدین دبیر خاص جانب دهلی فتح نامه نبشت که آن فتح نامه دستور دبیران شده است

(*Tarikh-i-Firoz Shahi*, p. 91.)

Again on p. 169 he remarks about Malik Qiwam-u'd-din:

تاچه ساحری ها که در فتح نامه لکهنوتی کرده است

This means that either more than one *fath namah* was issued on any particular occasion *or* that the *Fath Namah* prepared by Amir Khusrau was a private essay and not an official document. Since Amir Khusrau was very young at this time, it is highly improbable that he would have been asked to prepare such an important document. Malik Qiwam-u'd-din's *Fath Namah* does not seem to have survived. The present *Fath Namah*, drafted by Amir Khusrau, gives us an idea of the form and spirit of the medieval *fath namah*.

فتح نامهٔ لکهنوتی بر دست سلطان غیاث الدین بلبن شاه

حمدی که بسبب بشارات فتح و نصرت بر انصار ملت حنفی فرض گردد و ثنائی که بموجب توفیق غزا و مجاهدات بر اعوان دین هدی واجب آید' حضرت کبریای فتاح مطلق و پادشاه بحق را تعالی جده و توالی ذره که ذات فرخ صفات مارا برای تائید اوامر احمدی و تقویت شرع شرائع محمدی بمرتبهٔ جهانبانی و کشورستانی برکشیده و مقالید فتح و ضبط عالم و ازمهٔ حل و عقد طبقهٔ بنی آدم بکف کفایت و انامل اقتدار ما باز بست و ضمیر ملهم مرا در اتمام مهمات دین مختار و هدم مبانی کفرهٔ نابکار همتی واثق و رغبتی صادق بخشیده و شمشیر

معاند فرسائی مارا مصباح معابداسلام و مفتاح مغالق هفت اقلیم گردانید و رای ملک آرای مارا در ترتیب مقدمات عقل و داد و تمهید قواعد غزا و جهاد آئینهٔ تصاویر صواب و دیباجهٔ تماثیل صلاح ساخت وکسوت توفیق اسلام آرائی و نطاق توکید کفر زدای برقد اقبال وکمر اجلال ما چست و درست کرد و کتایب نصر و فیروزی و رایات فتح و بهروزی را درکنف الویهٔ منصورهٔ مامحل استظلال ارزانی داشت' تا باعتماد این سوابق نعم و استظهار این لواحق کرم درهر جهت که فوجی از جیش نصرت شعار نامزد می فرمائیم جمیع امورملک پروری و جمهور مهمات دین گستری بر حسب ارادات خاطر انور ما انتظام و التیام پزیرد و قلاع و بلاد متمردان سرکش و معاندان و متعندان گردن تاب که هیچگاه غبار نعلی از خیول اسلام برذروهٔ بقاع آن نگزشته بود و صدمهٔ نغز از اجنحهٔ جیوش سلاطین مجاهد بضیاع و بقاع آن ملحق نه گشته'.

بیشتر جهدی که از بندگان درگاه گیتی پناه در حیز وجود می آید وقلیل سعی که از فرستادگان جناب سلاطین مآب بحصول می پیوندد وکلیدآن مرادات با بشارت فتوحات مستقبل بخزانهٔ اقبال ما تسلیم می شود و بشکرانهٔ تواتر این مواهب و توالی این عوارف همت پادشاهانهٔ ما بران مقصور می باشد که عرصهٔ ملت هدی را هر روز متسع تر گردانیم و آثار بغی وضلال را هر لحظه مندرس تر و بسیط ربع مسکون را از لوث شرک و بطلان مطهر کنیم و به حلیهٔ شرع وعدل مزین و بجائی صنوف عبدهٔ اصنام صفوف عباد کرام را حسن اقامت دهیم وابنیهٔ معابد باطل را بانهدام و اندراس در خاک تزلزل افگنیم و عمارت محاریب و منابر حزب مصطفوی را بقواعد استحکام تاسیس فرما ئیم.

باقتضای این نیت صادقه که مستدعی کرم الهی و مستجلب نعم نامتناهی ست ملک ملوک الشرق اختیارالدوله والدین الغ قتلغ مبارک باربک بگلربک ادام الله مکنته' را که از بندگان پسندیدهٔ خدمت

درگاه ماست و سالها بشرف تقریب و ترحیب ما اختصاص داشته و از
آفتاب تاثیر آفتاب این دولت که برو تافته است بجمال فیروزی و کمال
عدو بندی و ترتیب لشکر کشی و تدبیر کافر کشی سر آمدهٔ روزگار و
برآمدهٔ نامدار گشته، با نواع و الوان آثار نیکو بندگی باظهار رسانیده و
بهر مهم که نامزد شده بشمشیر کامیاب و تدبیر صواب برنمطی اکتفا
کرده که در تصور فیلسوف عقل و مهندس خیال نگنجد، تا طوری که از
چشم منصور بمتابعت دهلیز همایون ما که مظله بیضه دین و ایمان
ومزله فرقهٔ بغی و طغیان است متوکلاًعلی اللّه بضبط دیارجاجنگر و
اوده که در اقصای ربع مسکون قریب شط دریای محیط است و از قدیم
الایام بسبب بعد مسافت و کثرت پیل و سوار و جمیعت پیاده بی شمار از
طوائف جهاد مصؤن و مامون مانده، نامزد فرمودیم و تواصی نمود که
در جوامع احوال و مصارف اعمال سیاق کاررانی مارا دستور پرداخت
مصالح و مقتدای کفایت مهمات سازد وطوائف غزاة را که برقضیهٔ
فضل اللّه المجاهدین علی القاعدین درجة حقوق مجاهدت و جان سپاری
بشناسد و هنگام قلع و استیصال کفره وصایاء نیت لیظهره علی الدین
کله را که باقدام و اقامت آن ماموریم و دراتمام آن ماجور، پیشوای
مناهج امور سازد.

چون بدین ارشاد صائب ضمیر قابل او را مخطی گردانیدیم،
فرمان فرمودیم که مستعد غزا و جهاد روی براه آرد آن بندهٔ مخلص
باحشمی که نامزد او بود بر سمت آن دیار دور دست نهضت نمود و کوچ
بکوچ در راه دراز بقطع شیب و فراز و مالش انجام و انجاد و شوامخ آجام
و اطواد آئین حشم گماری و ترتیب سپهداری بر نهجی رعایت نمود که نه
حوافر مراکب را مضرتی لاحق می شد و نه اخفاف مطیات را شقی ظاهر.

چون افواج لشکرهای ما داران حدود درآمدند و تزلزل در اطراف
و اکناف آن دیار اُفتاد، مالدیو رانه ساین رای جاجنگری که یکی از
زمینداران کبار آن سرحد است، با پنجاه زنجیر پیل و پنجه‌هزارسوار و دو

هزار پایک تیغ زن تازنده بعزم دست آزمائی جنود منصوره تجاسر
نمود. شیران لشکر که تشنهٔ خون آن مخاذیل بودند و آن افواج نخچیر
را بآ رزوئی تمام طلب می کردند در حال و ساعت از کمین تصویل بیرون
جستند و چون امداد آسمانی ممد حق و مبطل بطلان بود، بیک دست
برد بیشتری از ایشان را زیر تیغ آبدار گزرانیدند.

و ازانجا که اقبال نصرت آثار ما رماة قادر شست را بحسن
توصیت مرشد گردانیده بود که هنگام محاربت و مصارمت لشکرها در
تحفظ پیلان دکن باقصی الغایت کوشش نمایند، ایشان تا حد امکان
نصال کوه شگاف را کشاد مطلق نمیدادند وصیانت پیلان از کلیات
امور می پنداشتند و چون محقق کردند که در طریق مجاهدت خیرگی
خصم و قصور این جانب لازم می آید ناچار شست قادرانه را باز کشادند
و بیک سطوت چهار پیل کوه پیکر را بزخم تیر خار پشت ساختند و
مبلغی از هنود نابکار علف شمشیر گشت انهزام دران مدابر افتاد و
شست زنجیر پیل کوه پیکر در قید سلاسل بندگان درگاه آمد. مایفتح
اللّه للناس من رحمة فلاممسک لها.

بعدازان جیش نصرت شعار در سواد جهانبارکه مستقر رای و
مستودع ضرب ضلالت است، نزول کرد. سر لشکر فیروزمند، زاد اللّه
حقا و ثناء علیه از پیرا مون حصار هرگانو که در غایت حصانت و نهایت
متانت است، در استعداد حصارداری بربالای آن از مردان دلاور و
راوتان نامور و منجنیق وعراده بحد و تیر و ژوپین بیعد مرتب و مهیا
گشته بعزیمت استخلاص طوف نمود و باشارت اقبال ماکه ملقن ضمیر
منیر اوست، چشم و پیادهٔ لشکر را بارتفاع آن بارهٔ منیع اذن کرده تا
مکان را بعضی به نردبان و بعضی بحبل استوار و بعضی بحبل دیگر بر
بالا دویدند و یک بازوی حصار بقهر و غلبه ضبط کردند و خواستند که
گرد هباء منثوراً از نهاد آن قلعه مرتفعه بعیوق رسانند.

درین اثنا رای بیراحت من که بفرط درایت و وفورکیاست از

شملهٔ هنود ممتاز است، چون قاعدهٔ دست برد دلاوران لشکر منصور بر آن نوع مشاهده کرد و خود را باتمامی اسباب زمینداری در حیز تلف و زوال و معرض قمع و نکال دید تصور نمود که لَنْ تستطیع معی صبراً بنظر بصیرت هر آئینه پیش بندی گماشت و صلاح کار خویش را در استیمان و استعفاء دانست تنی چند بافور فصاحت و نهایت کاردانی بترتیب مصالح و تدبیر اصلاح شفیع طغیان و تمرد سابق بزمین بوس دهلیز سپهر رتبت ما پیش فرستاد.

بندگان درگاه چون آن معاند دین و پیشوای کفرهٔ لعین را با همه استعداد حصارداری و استبعاد از آئین مطاوعت و خراج گزاری بعجز و مسکنت معترف دیدند و بعروهٔ وثقی عفو و عواطف ما متمسک بحکم اذن و ارشادی که در حل و عقد و قبض و بسط معاهد و مامور از رای صائب و ضمیر ثاقب ما یافته اند، بتضرع و تخشع اورا باهدایاکه پیشکش کرده بود در پزیرفتند و آنهارا بنوید امن و امان مستظهر و مواعید سکونت و استقامت مستبشرباز گردانیدند. تا آن طائفه باعتماد این وثیقت واعتضاد این معاهدت با بشارت خلاص جان و صیانت ارجای ارکان جانب رای شتافتند.

رای را فرحت این حال و مسرت این نوال بر نمطی در اهتزاز آورد که پای تمکین در امن استقرار نماند. نخست بجهت تمهید مقدمات طاعت داری و تائید شرائط فرمان برداری پنجاه زنجیر پیل کوه شکوه که مداربساط کارانی و سری او بود، با خزائن و دفاین و جواهر و نفائسی که از قدیم الایام مورث و مکتسب داشت. مصرع مالیس یحصه ولویحصی الحصی. برسم خدمت در بند بندگی بندگان حضرت ما فرستاد.

دوم آن روز دست عجز برهم بسته اعتصام بحبل متین دهلیز همایون ماکرد و از حرارت آفتاب شمشیر بذیل سحاب رحمت استظلال نمود تا کرم مرحمت فرمای عاجز بخشای ما حاوی احوال و حامی اوقات

آن پناهندهٔ مستهام گشت و بندگان دولت را بر آن داشت که بر اجناس خدمتی او جائزهٔ قبول مبذول داشتند و مطالب و مآرب او را بانجاح و اسعاف اتصال دادند و بمژدهٔ جان بخشی که جسیم ترین نعمتهاست و عظیم ترین دولتها، جیب رجاء و ذیل تمناء او را گرانبار گردانیدند. تا آن منقاد و ثیق الاطاعت بفرحت این مبرت و تلذذ این مسرت که ازتلاطم امواج بلیات بساحل خلاص پیوسته بود و شجرهٔ اصالتش از ورطهٔ قلع و استیصال بقاعدهٔ اثمار اخبار استقرار یافته، گردن تعند را بطوق تعبد توشیح داد. برسوخ مطاوعت و وسوخ معاهدت حامل ذمهٔ شرع محمدی گشت. و شرائطی که برائی مستانف ایام دراطاعت اوامر و نواهی درگاه برو عرض کردند برضاء کامل و انقیاد تمام تقبل نمود.

(بیت) آری آنجا که بود ضربت تیغ. هر که گردن ننهد سر بنهد.

چون بعون وافر الهی و آثارکرم نامتناهی همگی مهمات آن حدود بر وفق ارادت اولیای دولت بکفایت پیوست، دهلیز آسمان سای مادر کنف عصمت ایزدی برسمت حضرت سپهر رتبت (لازالت محفوفة بعواطف الرحمن ومکفوفة عن طوارق الزمان) با حصول مقاصد و وصول مآرب باتفاق مراجعت توجه نمود. بتاریخ پنجم ماه شوال سنه ثمانین و ستمأیة آراسته با کوکبهٔ اقبال و مرتبهٔ اجلال بمستقر جلال وصول یافت و جیش منصور بشرف زمین بوس سدهٔ منیع ما مشرف گشت.

شعر: فالحمدلله الذی نصرالغزاة بعونه   حتی علا الاسلام اعلی من علی
برکفایت این مهم دینی و اتمام این مآرب ملکی سجدهٔ شکرحضرت عزت جل و علا که موجب ترقی درجات جهانبانی و مستجمع توظیف عطیات ربانی است، بخلوص عقیدت اقامت نمودیم و استبشار این بشارت که مهیج قلوب اهل ایمان و مکدر عیش زمرهٔ خذلان است، بر خویش واجب و لازم شناخت و باعلام این فتح بانام و اعلان این مسرت خاص و عام در اقاصی دیار و امصار ممالک مثال داد. تا سکنهٔ معمورهٔ فلان که رقم تودد و اخلاص ما بر لوح ضمائر

ایشان کالنقش علی الفض متمکن است و مآثر دعوات صالحهٔ ایشان ازین بابت ثمرهامی دهد واحسان ضعیف پرور مارا در ترفیه احوال ایشان رعایتی هرچه قوی ترمی نماید' بوصول این فتحنامه مستبشر گردند.

از نعیم طرب و شادمانی و رحیق نشاط و کامرانی حظی کامل و نصیبی شامل برگیرند و دعائی دولت قاهرهٔ ماکه حامی بیضه اسلام و مسلمانی و حارس حوزهٔ ایمانی است' فی آناء اللیل و اطراف النهار ورد وقت و حرز حال خود سازند تا بحسن عقائد آن دعا گویان غیبت که مخلصان بی ریب اند و برکات دعوات صالحهٔ ایشان درصباح و مساء عزائم غزوات که در مستقبل ایام به نیت صادقهٔ اتساع اسلام و استیصال کفرهٔ هفت اقلیم مصمم خواهد شد یا بشارت فتح و فیروزی اکتفا پزیرد بمشیة اللّه وعونه.

(2) AN IJAZAT NAMAH (SCHOOL CERTIFICATE)

No teacher in medieval India could set up an educational institution and instruct people in different religious sciences unless he had obtained an *ijazat-namah* from an authority on the subjects he intended to teach. The *ijazat namah* was the medieval form of modern certificates and diplomas.

The following certificate was granted to Shaikh Nizam-u'd-din Auliya by his teacher, Maulana Kamal-u'd-din Zahid, a renowned *muhaddis* of Delhi in 679/1280 (*Siyar-u'l-Auliya*, pp. 104–05).

This *ijazat namah* thus establishes the instructional *silsilah* of Shaikh Nizam-u'd-din Auliya with the author of *Mashariq-u'l-Anwar*.

Maulana Razi-u'd-din Hasan Saghani
|
Maulana Burhan-u'd-din Mahmud As'ad al-Balkhi
|
Maulana Kamal-u'd-din Zahid
|
Shaikh Nizam-u'd-din Auliya

بسم الله الرحمن الرحيم

الحمد لمن له الاهتداء والاعطاء و الصباح والرواح' والمدح لمن
له الآلاء والنعماء والصباح والمداح' والصلوة الفصاح على ذى الفضائل
السماء والكلمة والكلام المفتاح والمناقب العليا والاحاديث الصحاح
صلوة تدوم دوام الصباح والرواح و بعد فان الله تعالى وفق الشيخ الامام
العالم الناسك السالك نظام الدين محمد بن احمد بن على مع وفور
فضله فى العلم و بلوغ قدره ذروة الحلم مقبول المشائخ الكبار منظور
العلماء الاخيار والابرار بان قرأ هذا الاصل المستخرج من الصحيحين
على ساطر هذه السطور فى زمن الزمن الحار و درور الامطار من اوله الى
آخره قراءة بحث و اتقان و تنقيح معانيه و تنقير مبانيه و كاتب السطور
يرويه قراءة و سماعاً عن الشيخين الامامين العالمين الكاملين احد
الشيخين مولف شرح آثار النيرين فى اخبار الصحيحين والاخر صاحب
الدرسين المنيرين الامام الاجل الكامل مالك رقاب النظم والنثر برهان
الملة والدين محمود بن ابى الحسن اسعد البلخى رحمة الله عليهما رحمة

واسعة كتابة و شفاهة و هما بروبيانه عن مولفه و اجزت له ان يروى عنى
كماهوالمشروط فى هذا الباب' واللّهاعلم بالصواب' و اوصيته ان لا
ينسانى و اولادى فى دعواته فى خلوته وصح له القراءة والسماع فى
المسجد المنسوب الى نجم الدين ابى بكر التواسى رحمةاللّه عليه في
بلدة دهلى صانها اللّه عن الآفات والعاهات و هذا خط اضعف عباداللّه
واحقر خلقه محمد بن احمد بن محمد الماريكلى الملقب بكمال الزاهد
والفراغ من القراءة والسماع وكتب هذه السطور فى الثانى والعشرين من
ربيع الاول سنة ستة تسع و سبعين و ستمائة حامداللّه تعالى و مصليا على
رسوله.

(3) A KHILAFAT-CUM-IJAZAT NAMAH

The following *khilafat-cum-ijazat namah* was granted to Shaikh Nizam-u'd-din Auliya by his spiritual master Shaikh Farid-u'd-din Ganj-Shakar (*Siyar-u'l-Auliya*, pp. 117–19). It confers spiritual authority on Shaikh Nizam-u'd-din Auliya and accords permission to teach *Tamhidat* of Abu Shakoor Salimi, a book dealing with the fundamentals of faith.

بسم الله الرحمٰن الرحيم

الحمدلله الذى قدم احسانه على منته و اخر شكره على نعمته هوالاول وهوالآخر والظاهر والباطن لامؤخرلما قدم ولامقدم لما اخر ولا معلن لما ابطن ولا مخفى لما اظهر ولا يكاد نطق الاوائل والأ واخرعلى ديمومته اعتباراً او تقابلاً والصلوة على رسوله المصطفى محمد وآله واهل الود والارتضاء و بعد فان الشروع فى الاصول يوسع دعاء الشهود و يبصرلمن يكرع منهامحارق الورد على ان الطريق مخوف والعقبة وكود. و نعم الكتاب فى هذا الفن تمهيد المهتدى ابى شكور بردالله مضجعه وقد قرأ عندى الولد الرشيد الامام النقى العالم الرضى نظام الملة والدين محمد بن احمد زين الائمة والعلماء مفخرالاجلة والا تقياء اعانه الله على ابتغاء مرضاته و اناله منتهى رحمته و اعلىٰ درجاته سبقاً بعد سبق من اوله الى آخره قراءة تدبرو إتقان مستجمع رعاية سمع و دراية جنان وكماحصل الوقوف على حسن استعداده كذالک وفور تهياة اجزته ان يدرس فيه المتعلمين بشرط المجانبه عن التصحيف والغلط والتحريف وبذل الجد والاجتهاد فى التصحيح والتنقيح عن الزلل وعليه المعول والله العالم وكان ذلک يوم الاربعاء من الشهر المبارك رمضان عظمه الله بركته بالاشارة العالية ادام الله علاها وعن الخلل حماها تحررت هذه الأسطر بعون الله على يد أضعف إلى الله الغنى اسحاق بن على بن اسحاق الدهلوى بمشافهته حامداومصليا فاجزت له ايضاًبان يروى عنى جميع ما استفاده وحوى وسمع ذلک منى ودعىٰ والسلام على من اتبع الهدى واجزت له ايضاً ان يلازم الخلوة فى مسجد اقيمت فيه الجماعة ولا يخل بشرائطها التى بها حصول الزيادة و برفضها تكون

الاقدام عاتله ناصية و ذالک تجريد المقاصد من مفاسد ها و تفريد الـهمة عما تغفلها و بيان ذالک ما قال رسول اللّه صلى اللّه عليه وسلم كن فى الدنيا كانک غريب او كعابرى سبيل وعد نفسک من اصحاب القبور "الحديث" فعند ذالک صح قصده و اجتمع همته و صارت الـهمم. المختلفه همة واحدة فليد خل الخلوة مفترا نفسه معدما للخلق عالما بعجزهم تاركا للدنيا و شهواتها و اقفأ على مضارها و امنيتها ولتكن خلوته معمورة بانواع العبادات اذا سئمت نفسه عن احتمال الاعلى ينزلها الى الادنى وان حجت فلينزلها امابعمل يسير او بالنوم فان فيه احترازا عن هواجس النفس وليحترز البطالة فانها تقسى القلوب واللّه تعالى على ذالک اعانه و يحفظه عما شانه و رحمه و هو ارحم الراحمين صلى اللّه على محمد وآله وايضاً اذا استوفر حظه من الخلوة و انفتحت بها عين الحكمة واجتمعت خلواته بمنادياته و وصل اليه من لم يقدر الوصول الينا يستوفى اليه اياه فيده العزيزة نائبة عن يدنا وهو من جملة خلفائنا و التزام حكمه فى امرالدين والدنيا من جملة تعظيمنا فرحم اللّه من اكرمه وعظم من اكرمناه واهان من لم يحفظ حق من حفظنا صح ذالک كله من الفقير المسعود تم بعون اللّه و حسن توفيه و اللّه اعلم.

(4) A KHILAFAT NAMAH

No saint could set up an independent *khanqah* and enrol disciples unless he was granted a *khilafat namah* (succession certificate) from some elder saint entitled to grant such certificates.

The following *khilafat namah* was granted by Shaikh Nizam-u'd-din Auliya to his disciple Maulana Shams-u'd-din Yahya, a renowned scholar of Delhi, in 724/1323 (*Siyar-u'l-Auliya*, pp. 229, 231). It throws considerable light on the aims and objects of the medieval Muslim mystics in granting *khilafat namah* to their disciples.

بسم الله الرحمن الرحيم

الحمدلله الذى سمت همم اوليانه عن الركون الى الاكوان عارا و اعتلقت همومهم بالواحد الحنان بارا فدارت عليهم بكرة و عشيا كأس المحبة من كوثر محبوبهم داراً كلماجن عليهم الليل تشتعل قلوبهم من الشوق ناراً و تفيض اعينهم من الدمع مدرارا ويتمتعون بمناجاة الحبيب اسرارا و يطوفون بسرادقات العز افكارا لايزال منهم فى كل زمان من عليهم مكونة نضارة العرفان فيظهرفى الاقطار آثاره و يزهر فى الآفاق انواره لسانه ناطق بالحق و هو داعى الله فى الخلق ليخرجهم من الظلمات الى النور يقوبهم الى الرب الغفور. ثم. الصلوة على صاحب الشريعة الغراء والطريقة الزهراء رسول الرحمة المخصوص بخلافة ربه فى مقام البيعة و على خلفائه الراشدين الذين فازوا بكل مقام على و على آله الذين يدعون ربهم بالغداة والعشى. اما بعد فان الدعوة الى الواحد العلام من ارفع دعائم الاسلام و اوثق عروة فى الايمان على ماورد فى الخبر عنه عليه السلام والذى نفس محمد بيده لئن شئتم لاقسمن لكم ان احب عبادالله الى الله الذين يحببون الله الى عباد الله ويحببون عبادالله الى الله فى الارض با لنصيحة والامره ومامدح الله عباده الذين يقولون ربناهب لنامن ازواجنا وذرياتناقرةاعين واجعلناللمتقين اماما وقد اوجبهاالله تعالىٰ على وفقه لاتباع سيدالمرسلين و قائد الغر المحجلين بقوله عزوجل قل هذه سبيلى ادعوالى الله على بصيرة انا

ومن اتبعنى و اتباعه انما يكون برعاية اقواله والاقتداء به فى اعماله و
تنزيه السر عن كل ماسوى الله فى الوجود والانقطاع الى المعبود ثم ان
الولد الاعز التقى والعالم المرضى المتوجه الىٰ رب العالمين. شمس
الملة والدين محمد بن يحيى افاض الله الواحد انواره على اهل اليقين و
التقوى لماصح قصده الينا و لبس خرقة الارادة منا و استوفى الحظ من
صحبتنا اجزت له اذا استقام على اتباع سيد الكائنات و استغرق
الاوقات بالطاعات وراقب القلب عن هواجس النفس و اعرض عن الدنيا
و اسبابها ولم يركن الى ابنائها و اربابها و انقطع الى الله بالكلية و
اشرقت فى قلبه الانوار القدسية والاسرار الملكوتيه و انفتح باب فهم
التعريفات الالهيه ان يلبس الخرقة للمريدين و برشدهم الى مقامات
الموقنين كما اجازنى بعد مالا حظنى بنظره الخاص والبسنى خرقة
الاختصاص شيخنا الفائح فى الاقطار فوائح نفحاته الرائح فى الآفاق
لوامع كراماته السائح فى عالم القدس افكاره البائح بمحبة الرحمن اناره
قطب الورى علامة الدنيا فريد الحق والشرع والدين طيب الله ثراه و
جعل حظيرة القدس مثواه وهولبس الخرقة من ملك المشائخ سلطان
الطريقة قتيل محبة الج.... قطب الملة والدين بختيار اوشى و هو من
بدر العارفين معين الملة والدين الحسن السجزى وهومن حجة الحق على
الخلق عثمان الهارونى وهومن سديد النطق الحاجى الشريف الزندنى
وهومن ظل الله فى الخلق مودود الچشتى و هومن ملك المشائخ اهل
التمكين ناصر الملة والدين يوسف الچشتى و هومن ملجأ العباد محمد
الچشتى وهومن عمدة الابرار و قدوة الاخيار ابى احمد الچشتى و هومن
سراج الاتقياء ابى اسحاق الچشتى وهومن شمس الفقراء علودينورى و
هومن اكرم اهل الايمان هبيرة البصرى وهومن تاج الصالحين برهان
العاشقين حذيفة المرعشى و هومن سلطان السالكين برهان الواصلين
تارك المملكة والسلطنة ابراهيم بن ادهم وهومن قطب الولاية ابى
الفضل والفضائل والدراية الفضيل بن عياض وهومن قطب العالم

والشيخ المعظم عبدالواحد بن زيد و هو من رئيس التابعين امام العالمين
الحسن البصرى و هو من اميرالمومنين فى اعالى المقامات المنتهى
اليه خرقة كل طالب على بن ابى طالب كرم اللّه وجهه و قدس اللّه
اسرارهم و ابقى الى يوم القيامة انوارهم و هو من سيد المرسلين خاتم
النبيين المنوط باتباعه محبة رب العالمين محمد المصطفى صلى اللّه
عليه وسلم وعلى كل من به انتمى و اقتدى فمن لم يصل الينا و وصل
اليه فقد استخلفناه عنا فيده العزيزة نائبة عن يدنا والتزام حكمه فى
امرالدين والد نيا من تعظيمنا و عظمناه واُهان من لم يحفظ حق من
حفظناه واللّه الموفق الهادى والمستعان وعليه التكلان تحررت هذه
الاسطر بالا شارة العالية نظام الدين محمد بن احمد علاه وصانه عن كل
آفة و حماه بخط العبد الضعيف الراجى بالفضل الربانى حسين بن محمد
بن محمود العلوى الكرمانى وذلك فى اليوم العشرين من ذى الحجة
اربع عشرين وسبع مائة.

(5) A KHUTBAH

The following *Khutbah* was delivered by Muhammad 'Awfi in Multan on an 'Eid Day in 617/1220 (*Lubab-u'l-Albab*, Vol. I, pp. 115–16). The background of this *khutbah* has been explained by 'Awfi in his *tazkirah*.

ايهاالناس اعتبروا فى هذه الشهود والاحوال من تقلب الامور و
الاحوال فان اللّه تعالى جعل الغالب مغلوباً والسالب مسلوباًوالناكب
منكوبا و مواد فساد الاعداء متقطعة و رايات اوليائه مرتفعة فلما بدلوا
نعمة اللّه عليهم كفراً وأحلوا قومهم دارالبوار امطراللّه عليهم شأبيب
امطار الادبار فاقبلوا صيداً عامدين و ولوا حصيداً خامدين لم يلو عددهم
وعديدهم وجزع عليهم خواصهم وعبيدهم عبرة للنظاروتذكرة لاولى
الابصارفهذا ابن الجامجى خرج كقدح ابن مقبل و بنات الدهر محبل
فدوخ البلاد وروح العباد ولم شعث بلادالهند وصحح سقيمه و وشح
اعناق منابرها بالخطب المحبرة بالقاب الناصرين الامام وقسيمه
واعجب بهذه الدولة الغراء بان صارت فى ميدان السباق مجليا و(سائر
الدول) بعقود مطا وعتها متحليا وهذه وفود غزنة قد اقبلوا والمرد ابقلوا و
اخبروا بان اهلها قد اظهر وا شعارالطاعة واحكموانتصارالتباعة واليوم
هذه السلطان فاعتبروا ايهاالناس من صنع اللّه الكريم ذلك فضل اللّه
يوتيه من يشاء واللّه ذوالفضل العظيم.

(6) A SAINT'S LETTER TO THE SULTAN

The following letter was written by Shaikh Farid-u'd-din Ganj-i-Shakar to Sultan Ghiyas-u'd-din Balban.

رفعت قصته الى اللّه ثم اليك فان اعطيته شيًا فالمعطى هواللّه وانت المشكوروان لم تعطه شيا فالمالغ هواللّه وانت المعذور۔

(*Siyar-u'l-Auliya*, p. 72.)

GENEALOGICAL AND OTHER TABLES

I. Genealogical Tree of the Early Turkish Sultans of Delhi

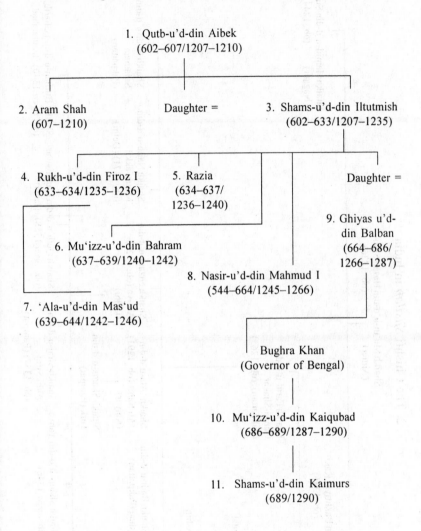

1. Qutb-u'd-din Aibek
(602–607/1207–1210)

2. Aram Shah
(607–1210)

Daughter =

3. Shams-u'd-din Iltutmish
(602–633/1207–1235)

4. Rukh-u'd-din Firoz I
(633–634/1235–1236)

5. Razia
(634–637/
1236–1240)

Daughter =

9. Ghiyas u'd-
din Balban
(664–686/
1266–1287)

6. Mu'izz-u'd-din Bahram
(637–639/1240–1242)

8. Nasir-u'd-din Mahmud I
(544–664/1245–1266)

7. 'Ala-u'd-din Mas'ud
(639–644/1242–1246)

Bughra Khan
(Governor of Bengal)

10. Mu'izz-u'd-din Kaiqubad
(686–689/1287–1290)

11. Shams-u'd-din Kaimurs
(689/1290)

2. The Chishti *Silsilah* in India

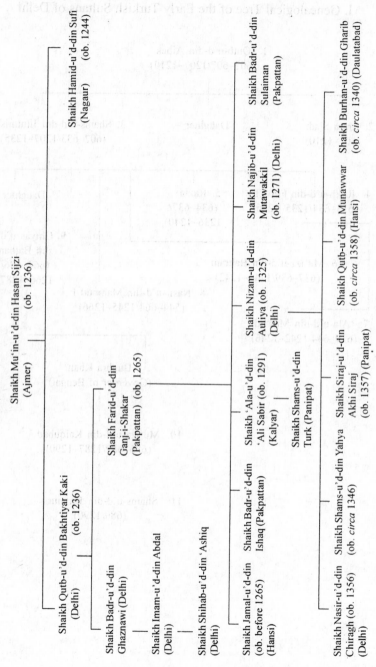

3. The Suhrawardi *Silsilah* in India

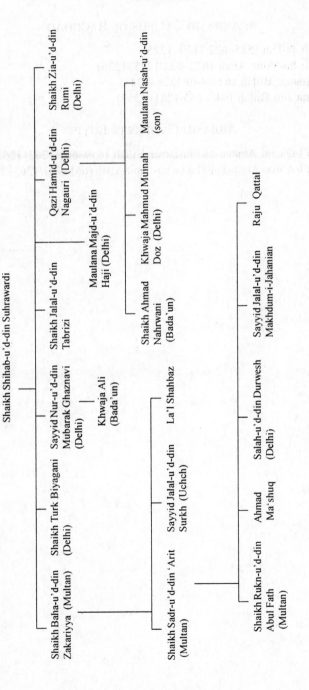

Shaikh Shihab-u'd-din Suhrawardi

Shaikh Baha-u'd-din Zakariyya (Multan)

Shaikh Turk Biyagani (Delhi)

Sayyid Nur-u'd-din Mubarak Ghaznavi (Delhi)

Shaikh Jalal-u'd-din Tabrizi

Qazi Hamid-u'd-din Nagauri (Delhi)

Shaikh Zia-u'd-din Rumi (Delhi)

Khwaja Ali (Bada'un)

Maulana Majd-u'd-din Haji (Delhi)

Maulana Nasah-u'd-din (son)

Shaikh Ahmad Nahrwani (Bada'un)

Khwaja Mahmud Muinah Doz (Delhi)

Shaikh Sadr-u'd-din 'Arif (Multan)

Sayyid Jalal-u'd-din Surkh (Uchch)

La'l Shahbaz

Shaikh Rukn-u'd-din Abul Fath (Multan)

Ahmad Ma'shuq

Salah-u'd-din Durwesh (Delhi)

Sayyid Jalal-u'd-din Makhdum-i-Jahanian

Raju Qattal

4. ABBASID CALIPHS OF BAGHDAD

1. Nasir la-Din (575–622/1179–1225)
2. Zahir-ba-'Amr Allah (622–623/1225–1226)
3. Mustansir Billah (623–640/1226–1243)
4. Musta'sim Billah (640–655/1241–1257)

ABBASID CALIPHS IN EGYPT

1. Abu'l-Qasim Ahmad al-Mustansir Billah (659–661/1262–1263)
2. Abu'l-Abbas Ahmad al-Hakim ba-'Amr Allah (661–701/1263–1301)

APPENDIX C

(1) EVALUATION OF SOURCE MATERIAL

I had not originally intended to incorporate a separate note in the form of an Appendix evaluating the source-material, as comments bearing on the value of the sources used here have already appeared at different places in the body of this work. But, with the publication of Dr Peter Hardy's scholarly study of the *Historians of Medieval India*, it has become necessary to do just that.

The contemporary source-material used in preparation of the present work falls broadly under two categories:

(a) Political chronicles, and
(b) Non-political literature, comprising general religious works, mystic treatises, *malfuzat*, poetic compositions, *tazkirahs* of poets, saints, etc.

While a modern writer cannot possibly ignore in the preparation of his work the apparatus of historical criticism provided by recent developments in the science of historiography, it would be anachronistic to determine the value of the historical literature of the Middle Ages in the light of modern theories and principles of criticism. The literature of every country and, in fact, of every age, has its roots in the attitudes and traditions of the people who produced it and can be scrutinized only in the light of their own conceptual framework. Any indiscriminate application of later date principles of historical criticism to the literature of the Middle Ages is bound to obstruct a clear appraisal of the medieval ideas and institutions.

1. In the history of Muslim historiography one comes across two very distinct traditions of history-writing—the Arab and the Persian. Until the eleventh century the Arab method of writing history was generally in vogue in almost all Muslim countries and all scholarly works were written in Arabic. The Arab historians had a very wide concept of history and included in it almost everything relating to human society and institutions. They did not confine their histories to the camp or the court alone but tried to write the *history of an age* in which social and cultural events were given equal, nay even greater, importance than mere political details. So, instead of arranging historical events according to successive reigns of various kings, they classified them year by year—a practice which in Europe is not earlier than 1597 AD Tabari (ob. 923 AD), Miskawayh (ob. 1030 AD) and later Arab historians like, Ibn-i-Asir (ob. 1234), Abul Fida (ob. 1331) and Zahabi (ob. 1348 AD) have followed this method in their historical compositions. The spirit of the Persian Renaissance however, brought about a change in Muslim historiography. When

the Arabic language was no longer used, the Arab method of writing history was also dispensed with. The ancient spirit of Persia was invoked to forge a new path and the *history of the age* was converted into the *history of the kings*. Towards the beginning of the thirteenth century historical works were written in Persian in all countries from India to Asia Minor under the influence of Persian culture. It was seldom that one came across a historian who, like Hassan Nizami Nishapuri, still longed to write in Arabic. The general trend was to plan all historical works on the Persian model and survey the social landscape from the foot of the royal throne, and treat the biography of a sovereign as the history of the times.

2. The historical literature of medieval India is largely the product of chroniclers who were brought up in these Persian traditions. They were either associated with the imperial courts or were anxious to win royal favour through their compositions. In this respect also, the histories of medieval India mark a complete departure from the Arab traditions. "Th Arab historians," observes Margolionuth, "were very rarely official historians whose duty it is to record what the government wants to record. Tabari and others mention cases wherein literary works were ordered by Caliphs, such as the collection of ancient lays ordered by al-Mahdi, and the manuals of the four orthodox systems ordered by al-Oadii. They do not seem to mention a case of a historical work ordered by a Caliph" (*Lectures on Arab Historians*, p. 13).

3. Apart from the fact that a Persian historian's historical conspectus was limited to the court, he had to write under one very serious handicap. His selection of material and criticism of events was determined by the wishes, both explicit and implicit, of his royal patron. Conscious of the fact that "one of the indispensable conditions of history writing, and one which is absolutely obligatory in the interest of piety, is that when the historian writes of the excellences, the good deeds, the justice and equity of the ruler or of a great man, he must also not conceal his vices and evil deeds," they suggested the following remedy to an official historian: "If a historian considers it expedient he should speak openly, but if not, he should speak by insinuations, in hints, and in covert and learned allusions" *Tarikh-i-Firoz Shahi*, pp. 15–16). It is difficult to say how far this subterfuge worked successfully, but it is certain that the problem was so serious that it exercised the mind of many a medieval chronicler. Mir Khwand (ob. 1498 AD) almost repeats Zia-u'd-din Barani when he writes: "The official historian should, by hints, insinuations,

overpraise, and such other devices as may come to hand, never fail to express his true opinion, which, while remaining undetected by his illiterate patron, is sure to be understood by the intelligent and the wise." This being the common attitude of the political chroniclers of medieval India an Persia, it becomes extremely difficult to determine where a historian is sincere in his observations and where he is merely 'playing a part'. Quotations or references picked up at random from medieval chronicles can hardly be of any use unless the author's psychology is fully analyzed and his preferences and prejudices are clearly understood. A modern writer has, therefore, to put different questions to his historical data in order to separate 'facts' from 'fiction' and distinguish between 'facts' and 'interpretation'. What is a writer's source of information? Is he merely recording hearsay or had he any direct or indirect contact with the events he has recorded? To which social, religious or political 'group' did he belong? What was his personal attitude towards the different problems of religion and politics? What was his purpose in compiling his work? While thus 'screening' a political chronicle, the historical sense of a modern historian may not be satisfied with the 'interpretations' of a medieval chronicler, but, if he succeeds in eliciting answers to these questions and it is established that a 'fact' has been correctly recorded, he can proceed to interpret it in his own way. For instance, both Barani and 'Isami independently write that the execution of Sayyidi Maula was followed by a black dust storm, drought and famine. Now, so far as these occurences are concerned, the mere fact that two historians have independently recorded them is enough to establish their truth. But a modern writer can refuse to accept any causal relationship between the execution of Sayyidi Maula and these calamities and can dismiss these 'interpretations' as expressions of their credulous bent of mind.

4. It would be unjust to the medieval Persian chroniclers to think that they recorded facts and incidents without making necessary investigations in their own ways. The Arab writers of the Middle Ages had evolved elaborate principles of historical criticism in the form of *usul-i-isnad* whereby a narrative can be traced to the original eye witness who narrated it. The extent to which the Arab historian utilized these principles may be estimated from Ibn Asakir's (ob. 1175 AD) *History of Damascus* wherein he quotes different chains of authorities for the same or nearly the same matter. The Persian historians did not apply these principles to their historical writings with the same meticulous care with which the Arab historians had

applied them but, since these principles had become part of Muslim theological studies and were applied with uncompromising sternness to the most sacred branch of Muslim religious literature i.e. the *ahadis*—they became part of the academic discipline of the medieval Muslim scholars and consciously or unconsciously determined their treatment of all historical subjects. The relationship which the medieval historians established between *hadis* and history is clear from the following observations of Zia-u'd-din Barani: "Secondly, the science of *Hadis*—all the words and deeds of the Prophet and the most precious form of knowledge after Quranic Commentary, the discovery and confirmation of narrations, and of events recorded in Tradition, the warlike activities of the Holy Prophet, the establishment of a chronology, the abrogation of Traditions—all these are connected with history and it is on this account that the science of history is entirely bound up with the science of Tradition. The great Imams of tradition have said that history and Tradition are twins and if the traditionist is not an historian he will not be informed, of the activities of the Holy Prophet...." (*Tarikh-i-Firoz Shahi*, pp. 10–11.) This tie-up of history with the science of *Hadis* led to the application to history of all those principles of criticism which the *muhaddisin* had evolved and which, according to Hitti, meet the most essential requirements of modern historiography. 'Isami says that while recording the events of the reigns of the various Sultans,

همه با تواريخ کردم رجوع

چو ديدم موافق اصول فروع

5. The best corrective to the impressions created by the political chronicles of the period is the *malfuz* literature of medieval India. If the political chroniclers concentrated on the courts and the camps, most of the mystics of the period disliked even a reference to the rulers of the age and kept themselves at a distance from the centres of political power and authority. The political chronicles and the *malfuzat* breathe two different atmospheres and seem to belong to two different worlds. It is for a modern historian to establish a liaison between the two and present on this basis a synthetic picture of the medieval society and institutions. In the present work an attempt has been made to make a fairly extensive and critical use of both these sources.

POLITICAL CHRONICLES

The three most outstanding historians of the thirteenth century are Sadr-u'd-din Hasan Nizami, Fakhr-i-Mudabbir and Minhaj-u's-Siraj. All of them wrote for the rulers and with a view to win royal favour but their approach and treatment of the subject is far from identical. Minhaj's effort seems to have been to justify all actions of the Turkish governing class. In almost all the conflicts and tensions of the period which he has described, he has been on the right side of the Turkish oligarchy. He is truthful in so far as the actual details of incidents he has recorded are concerned, but in his analysis of causes and circumstances he has been carried away by his prejudices. His evaluation of the characters and activities of 'Imad-u'd-din Raihan and Nur Turk is coloured and prejudiced for the simple reason that both represented forces which were arrayed against his collaborators in the religious and the political spheres. 'Imad-u'd-din Raihan wanted to break the Turkish monopoly of power and Minhaj's interests were clearly linked up with the interests of the Turkish oligarchy; Nur Turk was critical of the materialistic pursuits and mundane ambitions of the 'ulama and Minhaj was actually wallowing in it. Minhaj's account of all men and movements where such tensions are involved should be read with a grain of salt.

Hasan Nizami's approach towards history was more literary than historical. He strained after a pedantic display of eloquence and rhetorics and reduced history to epigrams and enigmas. His endless metaphors and allegories and allusions fall like whips upon a reader's nerves, and tire him out at last. But this style was largely due to the circumstances in which he had to prepare his work. He left Nishapur with the intention of seeking his fortune in India. While on his way to Delhi from Ghazni where he had stayed for some time and had enjoyed the company of eminent saints and scholars (شفای روح و غذای دل), some bandits deprived him of all his belongings, and in a state of utter destitution he reached Delhi. Soon afterwards he fell ill. Destitution combined with illness reduced him to a state of abject misery. Somehow he attracted the eye of the *Sadr*, Sharaf-ul-Mulk. This must have mitigated to some extent his poverty but his talent was far from being duly recognized. This is why he so often talks about "unfavourable circumstances" and laments the lack of opportunities for the "recognition of talent". However, he was in a mood of utter frustration and complete disillusionment when a royal announcement was made inviting scholars to prepare an account of the conquests of Shihab-u'd-din. This was an ideal opportunity to make a public display of his literary talent and earn fame and fortune. He set out to prepare a history of the Turkish conquests so that در انواع بلاغت و اقسام فصاحت چشم عالميان خيره ماند. This purely personal motive apart, he does not seem to have had any particular party affiliations or prejudices like Minhaj. His failings were the failings of an unrecognized genius. When the husk of verbiage is removed from his narrative, he comes out as a truthful narrator without any axe to grind. At places his information is definitely more revealing than the information supplied by his eminent contemporary, Minhaj-u's-Siraj. For instance, Minhaj sends the Rai of Ajmer "to hell" soon after his capture but Hasan Nizami tells us that his life was spared after his capture and that he was put to death subsequently on account of his hostile activities. Again, according to Minhaj, the Rai of Delhi was slain in the battle, but Hasan Nizami tells us that the Sultan spared his life when he consented to pay tribute. With regard to the capture of the fort of Ranthambbor by Iltutmish, Minhaj says that "more than seventy kings had appeared at the foot of the forts, and not one of them had been able to reduce it" (p. 172); Hasan Nizami on the other hand tells us that Ranthambbor was in possession of the Mussalmans in the time of Qutb-u'd-din Aibek.

Since Hasan Nizami was writing in compliance with a royal proclamation, he could not help following the traditional style of the medieval *fath namah*s. His account of the destruction of temples is exaggerated because this exaggeration alone could produce the effect he was straining after and which, of course, was the purpose of this compilation. Fakhr-i-Mudabbir refers to the destruction of temples at Benares alone (p. 24), but Hasan Nizami speaks about wholesale demolition of temples at Ajmer, Meerut, Delhi, Kol and Kalinjar. Archaeological evidence militates against some of his exaggerated statements. If the number of Hindus killed in different campaigns, as given by Hasan Nizami, is put together, it would appear that the entire population of India was destroyed as a result of the Turkish campaigns! Such statements, if taken literally, can only blur our historical perspective.

Fakhr-i-Mudabbir's family was closely associated with the later Ghaznavid rulers. His great grandfather, Abul Farah, was the treasurer of Sultan Ibrahim Shah of Ghaznin (1059–99), and held twenty-one different offices from time to time. Unfortunately, Fakhr-i-Mudabbir does not say anything about his own early life. It appears that most of his life was spent at Lahore where he compiled his *Bahr-u'l-Ansab*. He seems more inclined towards the Ghaznavids than towards the Ghurids and probably his work was also intended to be presented to the Ghaznavids but change of political circumstances obliged him to dedicate it to Iltutmish, The *Adab-u'l-Harb* abounds in a large number of stories relating to the Ghaznavids but contains little information about the early Turkish Sultans of Delhi. It is strange that this solitary work on the art of warfare written early in the thirteenth century completely ignores any detailed analysis of the Turkish campaigns in India. A careful study of his works reveals that he belonged to the school of traditional theologians but was deeply influenced by the spirit of the Persian Renaissance. He quotes verses from the Quran and the sayings of the Prophet very frequently, but the respect for Sassanid traditions ultimately determines his conclusions. His style shows maturity of thought and expression. It is neither matter-of-fact and simple like Minhaj's, nor ornate and embellished like that of Hasan Nizami. Taken as a whole, Minhaj's approach was more that of a government servant and politician; Fakhr-i-Mudabbir represented the approach of a traditional theologian; Hasan Nizami had a litterateur's point of view.

So far as the sources of information of these three chroniclers are concerned, Minhaj alone seems to have had detailed personal knowledge of the contemporary events he has recorded in his *Tabaqat-i-Nasiri*. Since he had been closely associated with the Ghurid ruling house, his knowledge of the Ghurid family, its traditions and achievements, was definitely more comprehensive and minute than that of any other contemporary. Hasan Nizami had come to Delhi when the first phase of conquest was over and the Sultanate of Delhi had definitely come into being. He cannot, therefore, be expected to be more detailed in his account of the Turkish campaigns than Minhaj. Besides, Minhaj had a better sense of history than Fakhr-i-Mudabbir or Hasan Nizami. His anxiety to give chronological details and arrange his data in chronological order is an indication of his disciplined mind. The other two historians are parsimonious with dates. While utilizing these three sources, Minhaj's party affiliations, Fakhr-i-Mudabbir's emphasis on traditional values in religion and politics, and Hasan Nizami's literary exuberance, have been kept in mind.

Amongst the later historians who have supplied valuable information about the thirteenth century, 'Isami and Barani deserve to be particularly noted. Both of them belonged to families which had a long record of association with the Sultans of Delhi. 'Isami's grandfather, 'Izz-u'd-din 'Isami, under whose fostering care he was brought up, was a *sipah salar* in Balban's army. He lived to the ripe old age of 90 and died during the reign of Sultan Muhammad bin Tughluq when the latter forced the citizens of Delhi to migrate to Daulatabad. 'Izz-u'd-din's father, Zahir-ul-Mulk, was the *wakil-i-dar* of Sultan Nasir-u'd-din Mahmud. Fakhr-ul-Mulk 'Isami, a Wazir of Iltutmish, was the father of Zahir-ul-Mulk. It is true that no contemporary historian refers to any of the ancestors of 'Isami but this is not enough to reject 'Isami's account of his ancestors as spurious. One might suspect that this noble lineage was concocted by 'Isami in order to establish his position in the Bahmanid kingdom, but the fact cannot be ignored that the Muslim contemporaries of 'Isami in the Deccan were originally the residents of Delhi and a concocted genealogy could little serve his purpose. However, 'Isami's account of the early Turkish Sultans of Delhi is based on reports transmitted to him by his ancestors who were associated in one capacity or the other with the Ilbarite administration. Likewise Zia-u'd-din Barani was also the member of a family having a long record of association with the Sultans of Delhi. His father Mu'ayyid ul-Mulk was *naib* to Arkali Khan, second son of Jalal-u'd-din Khalji. His paternal uncle, 'Ala ul-Mulk, was the Kotwal of Delhi under 'Ala-u'd-din Khalji. His maternal grandfather, Sipah Salar Husam-u'd-din, was appointed *shahna* of Lakhnauti by Balban. Barani himself had been a *nadim* of Muhammad b. Tughluq for more than seventeen years. Thus both 'Isami and Barani were in a position to know many details about the life and activities of the Ilbarite Sultan.

So far as their sources of information are concerned, 'Isami does not mention any authority for the account of the individual Sultans or the various incidents recorded about them. He simply remarks that he had taken great pains to ascertain the truth of the various incidents recorded by him. But Barani cites his father, grandfather and his teachers as his authorities for his account of the reigns of Balban and Kaiqubad (pp. 25, 127). He picks up the thread from the point where Minhaj leaves off. But 'Isami begins his narrative from Sultan Mahmud of Ghazni. This is a departure from the contemporary conventions. Probably he was very much impressed by the legendary stories which were circulating in India in his day about Sultan Mahmud. 'Isami does not seem to have made any thorough use of either the *Tabaqat-i-Nasiri* or the *Taj-u'l-Ma'asir* for his account of the early Turkish Sultans of Delhi. However, so far as the earlier portion of the book which deals with the Ilbarites is concerned, we find the following details which remain unconfirmed from other sources:

1. It was, according to 'Isami, Shihab-u'd-din's *third*, not *second*, conflict with Prithvi Raj in which he defeated his Chauhan adversary.
2. Shihab-u'd-din Ghuri is made to participate in the Anhilwara campaign, though Minhaj says that Qutb-u'd-din alone had gone there.
3. According to 'Isami, Qutb-u'd-din Aibek had gone to Ghaznin because there were some doubts about his loyalty and fidelity in the mind of Shihab-u'd-din.
4. 'Isami refers to a conflict between two *'alims*,—Qazi Sa'd and Qazi 'Imad,—and Qazi Hamid-u'd-din Nagauri on the question of mystic songs. No earlier authority refers to it.
5. 'Isami refers to an attack of the Mulahida on Delhi during the reign of Iltutmish.
6. 'Isami's presentation of Razia's character is damaging and unconfirmed by any earlier evidence.

7. According to 'Isami, Razia fought Sultan Mu'izz u'd-din *twice* after her marriage with Altuniah.

8. 'Isami says that Sultan Nasir-u'd-din Mahmud was the *grandson* and not the *son* of Iltutmish.

9. 'Isami gives the story about a bet between the sons of Sultan Nasir-u'd-din Mahmud and a son of Balban and traces from it a change in the attitude of Balban towards Nasir-u'd-din.

10. 'Isami says that Tughril rebelled in the eighth regnal year of Balban but Barani says that the rebellion took place in the fourteenth year of Balban's reign.

Barani is, in fact, infinitely more interesting than 'Isami. But he can hardly be properly understood if his own individual fads and prejudices are ignored and his terminology is not closely followed. He was a rank reactionary in politics and a die-hard conservative in religion. He scanned and scrutinized every man and movement in the light of his own ideals and standards. Besides, he was fond of character-portrayal through conversation. Taking these conversations literally and basing conclusions upon them is, therefore, dangerous because the possibility of their being mere *ex post facto* deductions cannot be completely ruled out. Barani is out and out a subjective writer but his subjectivism is not, in the least, deceptive. One can easily discern and detect the elements of subjectivism in his narrative. He is sincere in so far as he does not try to assume an air of objectivity and does not introduce his subjective attitudes surreptitiously. To understand his work, one should understand *him* first. His terminology is also the result of his subjective attitudes. His reference to the Turks in connection with the rise of the Khaljis has no racial connotation; his use of the term Hindu with reference to the regulations of 'Ala-u'd-din Khalji has no communal implications and his phrases, like یکی به ده in connection with Muhammad bin Tughluq's enhancement of taxation in the Doab, are not to be interpreted mathematically. These terms are closely linked up with his subjective exposition of particular situations. But for Barani, Balban would not have been known to us so well and as intimately as he is known today. Through animated conversations and lively character-sketches he has succeeded in giving us a full-size pen-portrait of Balban. His account of Kaiqubad's revelries and the atmosphere of drunken revelry prevailing in Delhi during his regime is living and breathing. Barani approached his subject with the feeling of an artist. His aim was not to prepare a directory of events or a chronicle of incidents but to present some portraits from an angle that appealed most to his aesthetic sense. While recording his impressions, he has not been able to adhere to historical accuracy at some places. To some extent this was due to senility and the failing health in which he was obliged to compile his work.

WORKS ON POLITICAL THEORY

The *Adab-u'l-Harb wa'sh-shuja'ah* of Fakhr-i-Mudabbir and the *Fatawa-i-Jahandari* of Zia-u'd-din Barani are extremely valuable for a study of medieval political thought. Both these books are soaked in the spirit of Persian ideology and throw considerable light on the political and religious trends of the period. But Fakhr-i-Mudabbir's is a synthetic study, with a straightforward point of view; Baraini's work is a typical illustration of the contradictions in Muslim thought and institutions. Barani has presented in the boldest relief the incompatibility of the laws of the *Shari'at* with the actual requirements of the time. It is interesting to note that the need for fresh interpretation (*ijtihad*) was realized by one who was out and out a *muqallid* in his thought and behaviour. There were, however, certain similarities in the political thought of Fakhr-i-Mudabbir and Zia-u'd-din Barani. Both stood for discrimination on grounds of birth; both discouraged appointment of low-born persons to government offices; both disliked the spread of education amongst the lower sections of society.

LITERARY WORKS

Amongst the literary works of the period, Amir Khusrau's historical *masnavi, Qir'an-u's-Sa'dain*, occupies a pre-eminent position. Its real value does not lie so much in the details that it supplies about the historic meeting of Kaiqubad with his father, Bughra Khan, and the fine artistic sensibility with which the psychological situations have been depicted, but in the fullness with which the social life and cultural atmosphere of the period, have been described. If it is correct that no study of men or institutions can be considered complete without an understanding of the spirit of the age, the *Qir'anu's-Sa'dain* should be given a high place in the historical literature of medieval India. It gives a clear idea of the different aspects of the urban revolution initiated by the Turks. With this background in mind, it becomes easier to evaluate the significance of many of the social and economic measures of 'Ala-u'd-din Khalji. Since Khusrau had, even at that early age, seen Indian life from Multan to Lakhnauti, one finds a largeness in his perspective which is not available in any other account. The *Dibacha Ghurrat u'l-Kamal* supplies interesting autobiographical details about the poet and throws interesting light on some of the cultural and literary trends of the period.

Sadid-u'd-din Muhammad 'Awfi's *Jawami'-u'l-Hikayat* and *Lubab-u'l-Albab* contain much useful information. The *Jawami'-u'l-Hikayat* is, no doubt, a collection of anecdotes and stories covering almost every period of Muslim history and even pre-Islamic Persia, but some of the stories dealing directly with the period under review are of great significance. It would be unjustifiable to make generalizations on the basis of these stray stories, for a story-teller is often not very particular about the historical accuracy of his anecdotes but it helps us to understand the medieval atmosphere and contains much which is of great historical value.

The *Lubab-u'l-Albab* gives valuable information about some of the most outstanding literary figures of the Ghaznavid and the Ghurid periods. Mirza Muhammad Qazwini has rightly protested against 'Awfi's omission of almost all dates and biographical particulars which must have been, in many cases, within his knowledge. However, some of the extracts from contemporary works which he has given, are of great value since those works are no longer extant. For instance, 'Awfi quotes the following verses of his grandfather Qazi Sharaf u'd-din Abu Tahir Yahya b. Tahir b. 'Usman about the change in the character of his contemporaries:

پیدا شدن میان مسلمانی اندرون
ترکی و رومیانه و هندی خصالها
با قول بایزید و دم شبلی وجنید
پیدا شدن ز خلق یزیدی فعالها

(*Lubab*, Vol. I, p. 179.)

Note also the following verses of Fakhr-u'd-din Khattat Harwai about a Turk *Jandar*:

آن ترک چو یافت منصب جانداری   یک لخط نمی شکیبد از دلداری
گفتم دل من نگه نمی داری گفت   جانداران راچه کار با دلداری

(*Lubab*, Vol. I, p. 248.)

Such bits of information have a value of their own in illumining many a generally neglected aspect of contemporary life.

'Awfi had travelled widely in search of knowledge through Khurasan, Transoxiana and parts of India, visiting Samarqand, Khwarazm, Merv, Harat, Nishapur, Sistan, Ghazna, Farah, Lahore, Delhi, etc., and making the acquaintance of princes, nobles, scholars and saints of the age. A careful study of his works gives us a very good idea of the literary and cultural climate of the period.

RELIGIOUS LITERATURE

The contemporary works on *tafsir*, *Hadis*, and *fiqh* contain almost nothing which can be considered of any historical value. One cannot even get a sense of the 'mental' and 'emotional' climate in which these works were compiled. But some vague idea of the drift and direction of the Muslim mind at this time may be gathered from these works. The popularity of *Mashariq* and *Misbah-u'd-Duja* is indicative of the religious interests of the contemporary Mussalmans.

The mystic literature has, however, greater historical value than any other type of non-political literature produced in India during the medieval period. Broadly speaking, this literature is of two types—(a) *malfuzat*,—both genuine and fake, and (b) general works on mystic subjects.

Malfuz writing is one of the most important literary inventions of medieval India. Works of similar nature were, no doubt, compiled in other Muslim lands also, but the credit of giving this art a definite shape goes to Amir Hasan Sijzi, the compiler of *Fawa'id-u'l-Fu'ad*. The historical value of this type of mystic literature cannot be over-emphasized. Through these records of conversations we can have a glimpse of the medieval society, in all its fullness, if not in all its perfection—the moods and tensions of the common man, the inner yearnings of his soul, the religious thought at its higher and lower levels, the popular customs and manners, and, above all, the problems of the people. There is no other type of literature through which we can feel the pulse of the medieval public.

Besides, this literature acts as a corrective to the wrong impressions created by the contemporary political chronicles. Apart from their mystic approach towards various problems of human life, their estimate of men and movements is not coloured by any prejudices. For instance, Nur Turk's estimate in *Fawa'id-u'l-Fu'ad* and Balban's remarks about Minhaj-u's-Siraj as quoted in *Sarur-u's-Sudur* help us to understand the significance of some of the most important events of the period. Shaikh Nizam-u'd-din Auliya's remarks about the religious interests and attitudes of Iltutmish and Balban are revealing and illuminate an aspect of these Sultans' lives which has not been so clearly depicted by any contemporary writer. Besides extremely valuable biographical details about leaders of ideas and religion, we get in this literature interesting information about the religion, ideas, institutions, superstitions, and attitudes of the period. How did the common man live and think? What were his reactions to different situations of medieval life?—If any literature of medieval India give us any idea about these problems, it is certainly the mystic literature of the period. Political chronicles tell us about Tughril in detail but it is only in the *malfuz* literature that we meet his servant, Hamid, and get an opportunity to know his attitude towards the governing class. We know about the lavish expenditure of the governing class on marriage ceremonies from many contemporary sources, but it is in the *malfuz* literature that we come to know about the distressing problems of a poor father with several daughters of marriageable age. Details about the economic regulations of Sultan 'Ala-u'd-din Khaiji are, of course, given in *Tarikh-i-Firoz Shahi*, but it is from the *Khair-u'l-Majalis* that we know that, as a result of these measures, even a mendicant could afford to get two blankets (*lihaf*) prepared for himself. Stories about the measures of poor relief by the *amir*s of Balbah are, no doubt, recorded by Barani, but it is in the *malfuzat* literature that one comes across stories of a widow of Delhi supporting a starving neighbouring family or a *patwa* offering a helping hand to a starving saint. This information is of infinite value in understanding and appreciating medieval life in all its fullness.

Of the early collections of mystic conversations, the following three have been particularly used in this work:

1. *Fawa'id-ul-Fu'ad*
2. *Sarur-u's-Sudur*
3. *Khair-u'l-Majalis*

The *Fawa'id-u'l-Fu'ad* contains conversations of Shaikh Nizam-u'd-din Auliya from Sha'ban 3, 707/1307 to Sha'ban 20, 722 AH But since the Shaikh had reached Delhi during the reign of Sultan Balban and ideologically belongs more to the thirteenth than to the fourteenth century, the book has a value in understanding the thought and tendencies of the period under review.

The way in which this book was compiled has been described by the compiler himself. On Sha'ban 3, 707, Amir Hasan Sijzi decided to write down whatever he heard from his master, Shaikh Nizam-u'd-din Auliya. He went on noting down whatever he heard or saw about his Shaikh till at last on Shawwal 28, 708 he disclosed to his Shaikh that he was compiling a *malfuz*. The Shaikh went through his jottings and approved them. As the work proceeded he revised it and filled up the lacunae (*bayaz*). This work was completed on Sha'ban 20, 722 AH, in five thin volumes and soon afterwards it became a popular study in the mystic circles and attained the position of a *dastur-u'l-'amal* for the mystics. There is hardly any Indo-Muslim mystic work of the Middle Ages in which the *Fawa'id-u'l-Fu'ad* has not been approvingly quoted. It gives us an insight into the life and principles of the Chishti saints besides illuminating many aspects of popular life during the early Middle Ages.

The *Sarur-u's-Sudur* is a collection of the sayings of Shaikh Hamid-u'd-din Nagauri and his son Shaikh Farid-u'd-din Mahmud. It was compiled by a grandson of Shaikh Hamid-u'd-din after the exodus to Deogir demanded by Sultan Muhammad bin Tughluq. Apart from the valuable information it supplies about the life and thought of a Chishti saint in a far-off village of Rajputana during the thirteenth century, it contains illuminating references to some notable figures of that century—Iltutmish, Minhaj-u's-Siraj, Fakhr Naqila, Husam Darvesh, and others. It tells us a lot about the literary atmosphere and the standard of Muslim scholarship reached in medieval India. The arrangement of the book is, however, arbitrary. There is no chronological order in the narrative. Some dates are given, but after 1327 AD we are taken to an earlier date and again to later dates. The earliest reference to the *Sarur-u's-Sudur* is found in the *Akhbar-u'l-Akhyar* of Shaikh 'Abdui Haq Muhaddis Dehlavi. The compiler's main source of information was his grandfather, Shaikh Hamid-u'd-din Nagauri, a distinguished disciple of Shaikh Mu'in-u'd-din Chishti of Ajmer and a notable scholar of his time. He lived to a ripe old age and came into contact with some of the eminent religious figures of the age.

The *Khair-u'l-Majalis* contains the conversations of Shaikh Nasir-u'd-din Chiragh Dehlavi (ob. 1356 AD), compiled by his disciple, Maulana Hamid Qalandar. Problems relating to the authenticity of this work and its historical value have been discussed by the writer of these lines in his Introduction to the edition of *Khair-u'l-Majalis*. Like the *Fawa'id-u'l-Fu'ad*, this *malfuz* was also carefully revised by the Shaikh whose conversations it contains. The compiler says:

از ابتدامجلس تاانتهی هیچ حرفی نیست که منظوروملحوظ خواجه نشده

It is an important source of information for the lives and activities of the early Indo-Muslim saints e.g.—Shaikh Qutb-u'd-din Bakhtiyar Kaki, Shaikh Farid-u'd-din Ganj-i-Shakar, Shaikh Jalal-u'd-din Tabrizi, Shaikh Baha-u'd-din Zakariyya and Malik Yar Parran. But for this *malfuz*, many aspects of mystic life and activity in medieval India would have remained totally obscure. The importance of these accounts may be estimated from the fact that almost all hagiographers of medieval India have drawn their material from this book. Of the political chroniclers of the period, Shams-i-Siraj 'Afif is the first to refer to *Khair-u'l-Majalis*.

The *Siyar-u'l-Auliya* of Amir Khurd is a mine of information for the religious and cultural life of the Sultanate period. The Kirmani family to which Mir Khurd belonged was closely associated with the Chishti saints. Mir Khurd's grandfather, Sayyid Muhammad Mahmud Kirmani, was a devoted disciple of Shaikh Farid Ganj-i-Shakar. Mir Khurd himself had joined the discipline of Shaikh Nizam-u'd-din Auliya at a very early age. After the saint's death he kept close personal contact with some of the distinguished disciples of his master. When Muhammad bin Tughluq forced the *'ulama* and the *masha'ikh* of Delhi to migrate to the Deccan, Mir Khurd readily complied with the royal order and left for Daulatabad. When the Sultan's Deccan project failed and the administration collapsed, he came back to Delhi, frustrated and heart-broken. The thought that he had forsaken the principles of his master in leaving Delhi, pricked his conscience like a thorn. To atone for this 'sin', he sat down to write a history of the Chishti *silsilah*. He was well-equipped for this job. He had received good education in Arabic and Persian and was well-versed in the religious literature of the Middle Ages. His family had an unbroken tradition of association with the Chishti saints. Over and above all this, he was fortunate in having access to a very large number of notes, jottings and personal memoranda of Shaikh Nizam-u'd-din Auliya which had fortunately escaped the ravages of time. Thus personal knowledge combined with deep erudition has raised the value of his work, which contains the earliest and by far the most reliable account of the Chishti saints. It is a noteworthy fact that where he had no authentic details about any saint, he confined his account to the meagre data available to him and did not try to fill in the gaps by incorporating unauthenticated facts which were floating down the stream of time. Where he had two slightly varying accounts about any incidents, he has mentioned his authorities and has left it to the reader to accept or reject any version (p. 530). Further, Mir Khurd's personal contacts with distinguished figures of the period, like Amir Khusrau, Amir Hasan, Zia-u'd-din Barani, Shaikh Nasir-u'd-din Chiragh and others, helped him immensely in obtaining reliable information about the life and activities of the saints of the earlier period. But for *Siyar-u'l-Auliya*, a detailed account of the *khanqah*-life during the thirteenth century would have been impossible.

Besides the *malfuz* collections referred to above, several other semi-contemporary collections of mystic conversations have been carefully utilized in the preparation of this work. Particular reference in this connection may be made to the following:

1. *Siraj-u'l-Hidayah*. Conversations of Sayyid Jalal-u'd-din Bukhari, popularly known as Makhdum-i-Jahanian, compiled by Makhdumzada 'Abdullah.
2. *Madin-u'l-Ma'ani*. Conversations of Shaikh Sharaf-u'd-din Yahya Maneri, compiled by Maulana Zain Badr 'Arabi.
3. *Ahsan-u'l-Aqwal*. Conversations of Shaikh Burhan-u'd-din Gharib, compiled by Maulana Hammad.

4. *Jawami'-u'l-Kalim*. Conversations of Sayyid Muhammad Gesu Daraz, compiled by Sayyid Muhammad Husaini.

Critical examination of these works on the basis of internal evidence—atmosphere, thought-content, references etc.—establishes their authentic character. They reveal the working of the mystic institutions in Sind, Bihar and the Deccan. It may, however, be noted that, since these works were compiled when, as a result of the exodus of Muslim population demanded by Muhammad bin Tughluq, the traditions of the saints of the thirteenth century were fast declining, the element of glorification and idealization of the earlier mystics characterizes this literature.

In addition to the genuine *malfuz* literature discussed above, there are the following fabricated collections of *malfuzat*:

1. *Anis-u's-Arwah*
2. *Dalil-u'l-'Arifin*
3. *Fawa'id-u's-Salikin*
4. *Asrar-u'l-Auliya*
5. *Rahat-u'l-Qulub*

Both internal and external evidence has now established beyond doubt the apocryphal character of this literature. (See Professor Habib's article in *Medieval India Quarterly*, Vol. I, Part II, pp. 15–42; Nizami, *The Life and Times of Shaikh Farid Ganj-i-Shakar*, Appendix B). In almost all these works there are horrible chronological blunders which no contemporary, however indifferent to chronology, could possibly commit. Persons born years after the death of the saints to whom these conversations are attributed have been introduced in the mystic gatherings and crude mystic ideas which were, in the words of Shaikh Nasir-u'd-din Chiragh, 'unworthy of the great Chishti saints', have been put into their mouths. Besides, the discussions in these *malfuzat* lack spontaneity of treatment and warmth of human company. In the genuine *malfuz* literature one comes across a huge variety of discussions, but in these apocryphal collections, every *majlis* is in the form of a sermon on a topic. It is clear from the *Fawa'id-ul-Fu'ad* and the *Khair-u'l-Majalis* that this literature came into existence very early but in all responsible academic and mystic circles there were protests against it. It would be unwarranted to use this literature in preparation of an account of the ideology of the Chishti saints, but it gives us a good idea of the popular assimilation and understanding of the contemporary mystic thought. The superstitious atmosphere which pervades all these conversations presents an interesting aspect of popular life. Very sparing use of this literature has been made and that too in order to study the religious thought at its lower level.

Of the general mystic works of this period, the *'Ishqia* of Qazi Hamid-u'd-din Nagauri and the *Mulhamat* and the *Diwan* of Shaikh Jamal-u'd-din Hansvi deserve special consideration. Otherwise a very important work, the *'Ishqia* has lost much of its reliability on account of the very large number of interpolations that one comes across in it. But most of these interpolations are in the form of verses which seem to have been introduced in the text by some early scribe and then continued in subsequent copies. The thought-content of this *risalah* is, however, indicative of the intellectual eminence and deep erudition of the author. More important than *'Ishqia* is the collection of the poetical compositions of Shaikh Jamal-u'd-din Hansvi. As well as poems on purely mystic subjects, there are verses on many topics of general cultural significance. The attitude of the religious classes towards some popular customs, cultural practices, important religious and political figures of the period, political institutions etc., is not so clearly available in any other contemporary work as in the *Diwan* of Shaikh Jamal-u'd-din. Its value as a source of information for the history of the early thirteenth century has not been properly recognized so far. This is probably the earliest poetical work from the pen of a thirteenth century Muslim mystic of India and clearly records the attitude of the contemporary mystics towards different problems of religion and politics.

The above is a brief survey of the contemporary and semi-contemporary literature on which this study is based. Later works, both political and non-political, have been used only to the extent that corroborative or confirmatory evidence is available from other sources. In the case of hagiological literature, later works have been used just to trace the growth of legends.

Apart from this literature, archaeological and numismatic evidence has also been carefully considered. A list of works on which this study is based is given in the following pages.

(2) A SELECT BIBLIOGRAPHY

(i) *Texts on Religion, Law, and Administration*

al-Ahkam-u's-Sultaniyah
> Abul Hasan 'Ali al-Baghdadi al-Mawardi
> Text: Cairo, 1298 AH; Urdu translation: Hyderabad, 1931 ·

Arthashastra
> Kautilya
> English translation by R. Shamasastry (Mysore, 1923)

al-Farq bain al-Firaq
> Abu Mansur 'Abdul Qahir Baghdadi
> Text edited by Muhammad Badr (Cairo, 1323 AH)
> English translation by A.S. Halkin, *Moslem Schisms and Sects*
> (Tel Aviv, 1935)

al-Fath-u'r-Rabbani
> Sixty-two Sermons of Shaikh 'Abdul Qadir Gilani (Cairo, 1302 AH)

Fusus-u'l-Hikam
> Muhi-u'd-din Ibn al-'Arabi
> (Cairo, 1309–1321 AH)

Futuhat-i-Makkiya
> Muhi-u'd-din Ibn al-'Arabi (Bulaq, 1274 AH; Cairo, 1329 AH)

Hujjat-ullah al-Balighah
> Shah Walliullah of Delhi (Lahore, 1323 AH)

Ihya' 'Ulum-u'd-din
> Abik Hamid Muhammad b. Muhammad al-Ghazzali (Cairo,
> 1311 AH)

Insaf fi Biyan-i-Sabab-u'l-Ikhtilaf
> Shah Walliullah of Delhi (Delhi, 1308 AH)

Izalat-u'l-Khifa-'an-al-Khulafa
> Shah Walliullah of Delhi (Bareilly, 1286 AH)

Jami'
> Abu 'Isa Muhammad Tirmizi. 2 volumes. (Cairo, 1292 AH)

Jami'al-Bayan fi Tafsir al-Quran
> Abu Ja'far Muhammad b Jarir Tabari. 30 volumes. (Bulaq, 1323–
> 1329 AH)

al-Jami' al-Sahih
    Muhammad b. Isma'il Bukhari
    Edited by L. Krehl (Leyden 1862–68); Vol. IV edited by T.W.
    Junyboll (Leyden, 1907–1908)

al-Kashshaf an Haqa'iq al-Tanzil
    Abul Qasim Mahmud b. 'Umar Zamakhshari
    Edited by W. Nassau Lees, Khadim Husain and 'Abdul Hai.
    (Calcutta, 1856)

Kimiya-i-Sa'adat
    Abu Hamid Muhammad b. Muhammad al-Ghazzali (Lahore, 1907)

Kitab-u'l-Milal wa-n-Nihal
    Muhammad b. 'Abdul Karim Shahrastani
    Edited by Cureton, *Book of Religious and Philosophical Sects*,
    2 volumes. (London, 1842–46)

Kitab-u'l-Sunan
    Abu Da'ud Sulaiman.
    2 volumes (Cairo, 1292 AH)

Manu Dharmshatra
    English translation by:
    (i) G. Buhler, *The Laws of Manu*.
    (Sacred Books of the East Series; Oxford, 1886)
    (ii) A.C. Burnell and Edward W. Hopkins
    (Trubner's Oriental Series; London, 1884)

Marsad-u'l-'Ibad min al Mab'da-ila al-ma'ad
    Najm-u'd-din Razi

Mashariq-u'l-Anwar
    Razi-u'd-din Hasan Saghani (Istanbul)

Muqaddamah
    Ibn-i-Khaldun
    Urdu translation: Maulvi 'Abdur Rahaman (Lahore, 1904)
    English translation: by Franz Rosenthal

Nasihat-u'l-Muluk
    Imam Ghazzali
    Text: edited by Agha Jalai Humi'i. (Tehran, 1317 AH)

Nusah-u'l-'Ibad-fi-Wujud-u'l-Qutb Wa'l-Abdal
    'Abdul Ghaffur Danapuri. (Lucknow, 1307 AH)

Qabris Namah
'Unsur-u'l-Ma'ali Kaika'us b. Sikandar b. Qabus text: edited by Sa'id Naficy. (Tehran, 1933)

Qaul-u'l-Jamil
Shah Walliullah of Delhi. (Kanpur, 1291 AH)

Qut-u'l-Qulub
Abu Talib Macci. 14 volumes (Cairo, 1310 AH)

Risalah-i-Qushairi
Abul Qasim 'Abdul Karim Qushairi. (Cairo, 1359 AH)

al-Sahih
Abul Hasan Muslim Nishapuri. 5 volumes. (Cairo, 1283 AH)

Siyasat Namah
Nizam-u'l-Mulk Tusi. (Tehran)

(ii) *Early Political Authorities*

Adab-u'l-Harb wa'sh-Shuja 'ah
Fakhr-i-Mudabbir. Rotograph of MS in British Museum (Add. 1653)

Adab-u'l-Muluk via Kifayat-u'l-Muluk
Fakhr-i-Mudabbir. Rotograph of MS in India Office (I.O. 647)

Chach Namah
'Ali b. Hamid b. 'Abi Bakr al-Kufi
Text: edited by 'Umar b. Muhammad Daudpota. (Delhi, 1939)
English translation by Mirza Kalichbeg Faridunbeg. (Karachi, 1900)

Dastur-ul-Albab fi'ilm-i'l-Hisab
Haji 'Abdul Hamid Muharrir Ghaznavi
Rotograph of MS in Rampur Library

Fatawa-i-Jahandari
Zia-u'd-din Barani
Text: Rotograph of MS in India Office Library (I.O. 1149)
English translation with Notes and Introduction by Professor Habib and Dr Afsar Afzal-u'd-din, *The Political Theory of the Delhi Sultanate.* (Aligarh, 1960)

Futuh al-Buldan
Ahmad b. Yahya Baladhuri
Text: edited by de Goeje. (Leyden, 1866)
English translation; Part I by P.K. Hitti *The Origins of The Islamic*

State (New York, 1916)
Part II by F.C. Murgotten (New York, 1924)

Futuh-u's-Salatin
'Isami
Editions: (i) M.M. Husain (Agra, 1938)
(ii) M. Usha (Madras, 1948)

Futuhat-i-Firoz Shahi
Firoz Shah Tughluq. (Aligarh, 1943)

al-Kamil fi al-Tarikh
'Izz-u'd-din Ibn al-Asir
Text: Egypt, 1290 AH
Urdu Translation: Hyderabad, 1927

Khaza 'in-u'l-Futuh
Amir Khusrau
Editions: (i) S. Mo'in-u'l-Haq (Aligarh, 1927)
(ii) M. Wahid Mirza (Calcutta, 1953)
English translation: by Professor M. Habib, *The Campaigns of 'Ala-u'd-din Khalji.* (Madras, 1931)

Kitab-u'l-Hind
Abu Raihan Albiruni
Text: edited by E.C. Sachau (London, 1887)
English translation by E.C. Sachau *Albiruni's India.* (London, 1910)

Masalik-u'l-Absar fi mumalik-i'l-Amsar
Ibn Fazl-ullah al-'Umari
English translation of the chapter dealing with India, by O. Spies (Aligarh)

Nuh Sipihr
Amir Khusrau
Edited by M. Wahid Mirza. (Calcutta, 1948)

Qir'an-u's-Sa'dain
Amir Khusrau
Editions: (i) Maulvi Qudrat-ullah (Hussani Press, 1261, AH)
(ii) Maulvi Mohd. Isma'il (Aligarh, 1918)

Rauzat-u's-Safa fi Sirat al-ambiya wa'l-muluk wa'l-Khu'afa
Muhammad b. Khwand Shah *alias* Mirkhwand
Persian text: Lucknow, 1270–74 AH

Partially translated into English by E. Rehatsek (Oriental Translation Fund, New Series, London 1891–93)

Rihlah
Ibn Battuta
Arabic text: Cairo, 1928
Urdu translation Vol. II: by K.B. Maulvi Muhammad Husain (Delhi, 1345 AH)
English translation Vol. II: *The Rehla of Ibn Battuta*, by A. Mahdi Husain (Baroda, 1953)
Abridged English translation: H.A.R. Gibb (Broadway Travellers Series; London, 1929)

Sirat-i-Firoz Shahi
Anonymous
(Photostat of MS in Bankipur Public Library)

Tabaqat-i-Nasiri
Minhaj-u's-Sirai Jurjani
Persian text: edited by Nassau Lees, Khadim Husain and 'Abdul Hayy. (*Bib. Indica*, 1864)
English translation by H.G. Raverty (*Bib. Indica*, 1897)

Taj-u'l-Ma'asir
Sadr-u'd-din Hasan Nizami
(Professor M. Habib's MS)

Tarikh-i-A'l-i-Subuktigin
Abul Fazl Baihaqi
Editions: (i) by W.H. Moreley (*B. Indica*, Calcutta, 1861–62)
(ii) Vol. I by Dr Ghazi (Tehran)
Vol. II by Agha Sa'id Naficy (Tehran, 1327 AH)

Tarikh-i-Fakhr-u'd-din Mubarak Shah
A portion of Fakhr-i-Mudabbir's *Bahr-ul-Ansab*, edited by Denison Ross. (London, 1927)

Tarikh-i-Firoz Shahi
Zia-u'd-din Barani
Edited by Sir Sayyid Ahmad Khan. (*Bib. Indica*, Calcutta, 1862)

Tarikh-i-Firoz Shahi
Shams-i-Siraj 'Afif
Text: edited by Maulvi Wilayat Husain. (*Bib. Indica*, Calcutta, 1890)

Tarikh-i-Guzidah
> Hamd-ullah Mustawfi
> Text: edited by E.G. Browne (Gibb Memorial Series; Leyden and London, 1910)
> Abridged English translation by E.G. Browne: (Gibb Memorial Series. Leyden and London, 1913)

Tarikh-i-Jahan Gusha
> 'Ala-u'd-din 'Ata Malik Juwaini
> Persian text: vols. I and II edited by Mirza 'Abdul Wahhab Qazwini (*Gibb Memorial Series*, 1911–1912)
> Vol. III, Facsimile with an Introduction by Dension Ross (London, 1931)
> English translation by J. Boyle: *The History of the World Conqueror*. 2 volumes. (Manchester University Press, 1958)

Tarikh Nama-i-Harat
> Saif b. Muhammad b. Ya'qub Haravi
> Text: edited by M. Zubair Ahmad. (Calcutta, 1944)

Tarikh al-Rusul wa'l-Muluk
> Abu Ja'far b. Jarir Tabari
> Text: edited by de Goeje. 15 volumes. (Leyden, 1879–1901)
> Urdu Translation: Hyderabad,

Tarikh-i-Yamini
> Abu Nasr Muhammad b. Muhammad al Jabbar al-'Utbi
> Arabic text: edited and annotated by Ahmad Manini (Cairo, 1286 AH)
> Persian translation by Abu Sharaf Nasih b. Zafar b. Sa'd (Tehran, 1272 AH)
> English translation by Rev. James Reynolds. (Oriental Translation Fund; London, 1858)

Tughluq Namah
> Amir Khusrau
> Text: edited by Sayyid Hashmi Faridabadi. (Aurangabad, 1933)

Zain-u'l-Akhbar
> Abu Sa'id 'Abdul Hai b. 'Abdul Haq b. Mahmud Gardizi
> Text: edited by Mohd. Nazim

(iii) *Early Religious, Literary and Other Works*

Adab-u'l-Muridin
>Shaikh Zia-u'd-din Abu Najib 'Abd al-Qahir Suhrawardi
>Urdu translation: published by Ghulam Ahmad Biryan (Muslim
>Press, Delhi, 1319 AH)

Afzal-u'l-Fawa'id
>Alleged conversations of Shaikh Nizam-u'd-din Auliya Compiled by
>Amir Khusrau.
>(Rizvi Press, Delhi, 1305 AH)

Ahsan-u'l-Aqwal
>Conversations of Shaikh Burhan-u'd-din Gharib, compiled by Hamad
>bin 'Ammad Kashani in 738 AH/1337 AD (MS.)
>(MS. Personal collection)

A'ina-i-Sikandari
>Amir Khusrau
>Text: edited by Maulana Sa'id Ahmad Faruqi. (Aligarh, 1917)

Anis-u'l-Arwah
>Alleged conversations of Shaikh 'Usman Harvani. Compiled by
>Shaikh Mu'in-u'd-din Chishti. (Qadiri Press, Lucknow)

Asrar-u'l-Auliya
>Alleged conversations of Shaikh Farid-u'd-din Ganj-i-Shakar.
>Compiled by Shaikh Badr-u'd-din Ishaq (Newal Kishore Press,
>Lucknow)

Asrar-ut-Tauhid fi Maqamat-i-Abi Sa'id
>Muhammad b. Munawwar
>Text: edited by Ahmad Bahmanyar (Tehran, 1934)

'Awarif-u'l-Ma'arif
>Shaikh Shihab-u'd-din Abi Hafs 'Umar Suhrawardi
>Arabic text: Cairo
>Urdu Translation: by Maulvi Abul Hasan. (Newal Kishore Press,
>Lucknow, 1926)

Bahjat-u'l-Asrar wa-ma'din-u'l-Anwar
>Nur-u'd-din Shattanaufi (Cairo, 1304 AH)

Dalil-u'l-'Arifin
>Alleged conversations of Shaikh Mu'in-u'd-din Chishti. Compiled
>by Shaikh Qutb-u'd-din Bakhtiyar Kaki. (Qadiri Press, Lucknow)

Dawal Rani Khizr Khan
 Amir Khusrau
 Text: edited by Rashid Ahmad Salim: (Aligarh, 1917)

Dibachah Diwan Ghurrat-u'l-Kamal
 Amir Khusrau
 (Published by Maulvi Sayyid Yasin 'Ali, Delhi)

Diwan-i-Amir Khusrau
 Amir Khusrau
 (i) Published by Maulvi Sayyid Yasin 'Ali, Delhi
 (ii) Newal Kishore Press, Lucknow, 1288 AH

Diwan-i-Hasan Dehlavi
 Edited by Mas'ud 'Ali Mahvi. (Ibrahimiah Machine Press, Hyderabad, 1352 AH)

Diwan-i-Jamal-u'd-din Hansvi
 Poetical compositions of Shaikh Jamal-u'd-din Hansvi. (Chashmah-i-Faiz Press, Delhi, 1889)

Diwan-i-Mu'in
 Poetical compositions of Shaikh Mu'in-u'd-din Chishti. (Newal Kishore Press, 1868)

Durar-i-Nizamiyah
 Conversations of Shaikh Nizam-u'd-din Auliya. Compiled by 'Ali b. Mahmud Jandar. (MS. Buhar, 183)

al-Durar-u'l-Kaminah
 Ibn Hajar 'Asqalani
 (Da'irat-ul-Ma'arif, Hyderabad,   1348 AH)

Fatawa-i-Firoz Shahi
 (MS in Aligarh Muslim University Library)

Fawa'id-u'l-Fu'ad
 Conversations of Shaikh Nizam-u'd-din Auliya. Compiled by Amir Hasan 'Ala Sijzi. (Newal Kishore Press, Lucknow, 1302 AH)

Fawa'id-u's-Salakin
 Alleged conversations of Shaikh Qutb-u'd-din Bakhtiyar Kaki. Compiled by Shaikh Farid-u'd-din Ganj-i-Shakar.
 (Newal Kishore Press, Lucknow)

Futu-u'l-Ghaib
 Shaikh 'Abdul Qadir Gilani. (Cairo, 1304 AH)

Ganj-u'l-Asrar
    Ascribed to Shaikh Mu'in-u'd-din Chishti of Ajmer
    (MS in Personal Collection)

Hasht Bihisht
    Amir Khusrau
    Text: edited by Maulana Sulaiman Ashraf. (Aligarh, 1918 AD)

I'jaz-i-Khusravi
    Amir Khusrau. (Lucknow, 1876)

Jawami'-u'l-Hikayat wa lawami'-u'r-Riwayat
    Sadid-u'd-din Muhamniad 'Awfi.
    Introduction by Muhammad Nizam-u'd-din (London, 1929)
    Urdu Translation in 2 Volumes by Akhtar Sherani, (Delhi, 1943)

Jawami'u'l-Kalim
    Conversations of Sayyid Muhammad Gisu Daraz. Compiled by
    Sayyid Muhammad Akbar Husaini, (Intizami Press, Hyderabad)

Kashf al-Mahjub
    Shaikh 'Ali b. 'Usman al-Jullabi al-Hujwiri
    Persian text: Gulzar-i-Hind Steam Press, Lahore
    English translation by R.A. Nicholson. (London, 1939)

Khair-u'l-Majalis
    Conversation of Shaikh Nasir-u'd-din Chiragh of Delhi. Compiled
    by Hamid Qalandar
    Text: edited by K.A. Nizami (Aligarh)

Kitab-u'l-Ta'arruf li-mazahib-i-ahl-i-Tasawwuf
    English translation: by A.J. Arberry *The Doctrine of the Sufis*

Lubab-u'l-Albab
    Muhammad 'Awfi
    Edited by E.G. Browne and Mirza Muhammad b. 'Abdul Wahhab
    Qazwini. (London, 1903–1906)

Ma'dan-u'l-Ma'ani
    Conversations of Shaikh Sharf-u'd-din Yahya Maneri. Compiled by
    Maulana Zain Badr 'Arabi.
    (Ashraf-u'l-Akhbar Press, Bihar 1301 AH)

Majnun Laila
    Amir Khusrau
    Text: edited by Maulana Habibur Rahman Khan Sherwani. (Aligarh,
    1335 AH)

Maktubat-i-Shaikh Sharf-u'd-din Yahya
     Editions: (i) Newal Kishore Press, 1808
     (ii) 'Alavi Press, 1287 AH

Miftah-u't-Talibin
     An account of the conversations of Shaikh Qutb-u'd-din
     Bakhtiyar Kaki
     (MS. Personal Collection)

Misbah-u'l-Hiddyah-wa-Miftah-u'l-Kifayah
     'Izz-u'd-din Mahmud b. 'Ali Kashani
     Editions: (i) Newal Kishore Press, Lucknow, 1322 AH
     (ii) Agha Jalal Huma'i. (Tehran)

Maktubat-i-Rashidi
     Letters of Khwaja Rashid-u'd-din Fazl-ullah
     Text: edited by Khan Bahadur Mohammad Shafi'. (Punjab
     Educational Press, Lahore 1947)

Mulhamat
     Shaikh Jamal-u'd-din Hansvi (Yusufi Press, Alwar, 1306 AH)

Qawanin Hakam-u'l-Ishraq
     Abu Mawahib Shazili
     English translation: *Illumination in Islamic Mysticism*

Risalah Hal Khanwadah-i-Chisht
     Maulana Taj-u'd-din, a descendant of Maulana Shihab-u'd-din Imam
     (MS. in Personal Collection)

Sana-i-Muhammadi
     Zia-u'd-din Barani
     (MS in Rampur Library)

Sarur-u's-Sudur
     Malfuzat of Shaikh Hamid-u'd-din Nagauri
     (MS in Personal Collection)

Shirin Khusrau
     Amir Khusrau
     Text: edited by Haji 'Ali Ahmad Khan. (Aligarh, 1927 AD)

Siraj-u'l-Hidayah
     Conversations of Sayyid Jalal-u'd-din Bukhari Makhdum-i-Jahanian.
     Compiled by Mahdumzada 'Abdullah.
     MSS (i) Personal Collection

(ii) Jawahar Museum, Islamic College, Etawah, (MS catalogued as *Malfuzat-i-Qutb-i-'Alam.*)

Siyar-u'l-Auliya
Sayyid Muhammad b. Mubarak Kirmani, known as Amir (or Mir) Khurd. (Delhi, 1302 AH)

Tazkirat-u'l-Auliya
Shaikh Faird-u'd-din 'Attar
Text: edited by R.A. Nicholson (London and Leiden)
Urdu Translation: by 'Allama 'Abdur Rahman Shauq (Lahore)

Wast-u'l-Hayat
Amir Khusrau
Text: edited by Fazal Ahmad Hafiz. (Aligarh, 1920)

(iv) *Later Political Authorities*

A'in-i-Akbari
Abul Fazl 'Allami
Persian Text: edited by Sir Sayyid Ahmad Khan (Delhi, 1272 AH)
English translation: by H. Blochmann and Jarrett. (*Bib. Indica*, Calcutta, 1868–1894)

Buhaira
Fazuni Astarabadi.
(Press of Mirza Aman-ullah, Iran, 1328 AH)

Habib-u's-Siyar fi akhbar afrad-ul-hashar
Ghiyas-u'd-din b. Humam-u'd-din *alias* Khwandmir. (Bombay, 1857)

Muntakhab-u't-Tawarikh
'Abdul Qadir Bada'uni
Text: edited by W. N. Lees, Maulvi Kabir-u'd-din Ahmad and Maulvi Ahamd 'Ali. (*Bibliotheca Indica*, 1869)

Tabaqat-i-Akbari
Nizam-u'd-din Ahmad Bakhshi
Text: edited by B. De and Maulvi Hidayat Husain (*Bib. Indica*, Calcutta)

Tarikh-i-Du'udi
'Abdullah
Text: edited by S.A. Rashid (Aligarh)

Tarikh-i-Ferishtah or Gulshan-i-Ibrahimi
Abul Qasim Hindu Shah Ferishtah. (Newal Kishore Press, 1865)

Tarikh-i-Haqqi or Zikr-u'l-Muluk
> Shaikh 'Abdul Haqq Muhaddis Dihlavi. (MS in Muslim University Library)

Tarikh-i-Mu'barak Shahi
> Yahya b. Ahmad Sirhindi
> Persian Text: edited by M. Hidayat Husain. (*Bib. Indica*, Calcutta, 1931)
> English translation by K.K. Basu
> (Gaekwad's Oriental Series; Baroda, 1932)

Tarikh-i-Muhammadi
> Muhammad Bihamid Khani
> Rotograph of MS in British Museum

Tarikh-i-Shahi
> Ahmad Yadgar
> Text: edited by Muhammad Hidayat Husain. (Bib. Indica, 1939)

Waqi'at-i-Mushtaqi
> Rizq-ullah Mushtaqi
> Rotograph of MS. in British Museum (Ad. 11633)

(v) *Later Religious, Literary and Other Works*

Akhbar-u'l-Akhyar
> Shaikh 'Abdul Haqq Muhaddis Dihlavi
> (Delhi, 1309 AH)

Akhbar-u'l-Asfiya
> 'Abd-u's-Samad b. Afzal Muhammad
> (MS)

*An*war *u'l-'Arifin*
> Hafiz Muhammad Husain Moradabadi. (Newal Kishore Press, Lucknow, 1876 AD)

Gulzar-i-Abrar
> Muhammad Ghausi Shattari
> Persian text: MS in Personal Collection
> Urdu translation: by Maulvi Fazl Ahmad *Azkar-u'l-Abrar*. (Agra, 1326 AH)

Iqtibas-u'l-Anwar
> Muhammad Akram Baraswi. (Lahore, 1895)

Jawahir-i-Faridi
    'Ali Asghar Chishti
    Persian text: Lahore, 1301 AH
    MS: Personal Collection
    Urdu translation: Karimi Press, Lahore

Khazinat-u'l-Asfiya
    Hafiz Ghulam Sarwar. (Samar-i-Hind Press, Lucknow, 1872 AH)

Lata'if-i-Ashrafi
    Maulana Nizam-u'd-din Yemeni. (Nusrat-u'l-Mataba, Delhi, 1295 AH)

Ma'arij-u'l- Walayat
    Ghulam Mu'in-u'd-din 'Abdu-llah, known as Khalifah Khweshgi Chishti
    2 Volumes, MS in Personal Collection

Ma'asir-u'l-Kiram
    Ghulam 'Ali Azad Bilgrami. (Agra, 1910)

Maktubat-i-Ashrafi
    Letters of Sayyid Ashraf Jahangir Samnani. (MS in Muslim University Library)

Maktubat-i-Imam-i-Rabbani
    Letters of Shaikh Ahmad Sirhindi. (Newal Kishore Press, 1877)

Malfuzat-i-Shah 'Abdul 'Aziz
    Edited by Qadi Bashir-u'd-din. (Muitaba'i Press, Meerut 1314 AH)

Matlub-u't-Talibin
    Sayyid Muhammad Bulaq Chishti (MS. in Personal Collection)

Majalis-u'l-'Ushshaq
    Sultan Husain Mirza. (Newal Kishore Press, 1897)

Majma'-u'l-Auliya
    Mir 'Ali Akbar Ardistani
    (MS)

Mir'at-i-Mas'udi
    'Abdur Rahman Chishti
    (MS in Personal Collection)

Mir'at-u'l-Asrar
    'Abdur Rahman Chishti
    (MS in Personal Collection)

Misbah-u'l-'Ashiqin
> Khwaja Baha-u'd-din b. Mahmud b. Ibrahim *nabira* of Qazi
> Hamid-u'd-din Nagauri
> Text: MS in Personal Collection
> Urdu translation: Lahore

Munis-u'l-Arwah
> Jahan Ara Begum
> (MS in Personal Collection)
> Urdu Translation by Muhammad Fazal Haq, *Anis-u'l-Ishbah.*
> (Nami Press, Lucknow 1898 AD)

Nafahat-u'l-Uns
> Maulana 'Abdur Rahman Jami'.
> (Bombay, 1284 AH)

Rashhat 'ain-al-Hayat
> 'Ali b. Husain al-Wa'iz al-Kashafi. (Kanpur, 1912)

Rauza-i-Aqtab
> Sayyid Muhammad Bulaq Chishti.
> (Muhibb-i-Hind Press, Delhi)

Shekasubhadaya
> Edited by Sukumar Sen. (Calcutta)

Shijrat-u'l-Anwar
> Maulana Rahim Bakhsh Fakhri
> (MS in Personal Collection)

Siyar-u'l-Aqtab
> Allah Diya Chishti. (Newal Kishore Press, 1913)

Siyar-u'l-'Arifin
> Maulana Fazl-ullah known as Darwesh Jamali. (Rizvi Press, Delhi,
> 1311 AH)
> MS Personal Collection
> Urdu translation by Ghulam Ahmad. (Moradabad, 1319 AH)

(vi) *Modern Works on Religion*

Afifi, A.E., *The Mystical Philosophy of Muhyiu'd-din-Ibn-ul 'Arabi*
    (Cambridge, 1939).
Ameer Ali, Syed, *The Spirit of Islam* (Macmillan, London, 1931).
Arberry, A.J., *Sufism* (London, 1956).
Azad, Maulana Abul Kalam, *Tarjuman-u'l-Quran* (2nd revised edition,
    Lahore).

Azad, Maulana Abul Kalam, *Jami'al-Shawahid fi Dukhul-i-Ghair Muslim fi'l Masajid* (Azamgarh).

Bell, Richard, *The Origin of Islam in its Christian Atmosphere* (London, 1926).

Bismil, Razi-u'd-din, *Tazkirat-u'l-Wasilin* (An account of the saints of Bada'un), (Lahore, 1318 AH).

Bousquet, G.H. and J. Schacht (eds.) *Selected Works of G. Snouck Hurgronje* (Leyden, 1957).

Dennett, Daniel C., *Conversion and the Poll Tax in Early Islam* (Harvard University Press, 1950).

Faruqi, Burhan Ahmad, *The Mujaddid's Conception of Tawhid* (Lahore, 1940).

Gibb, H.A.R., *Mohammedanism* (Home University Library, London, 1951).

Gibb, H.A.R., *Modern Trends in Islam* (Chicago, 1946).

Grunebaum, G. von, *Medieval Islam* (Chicago, 1946).

Grunebaum, G. von, *Islam* (London, 1955).

Hodgson, Marshall G.S., *The Order of Assassins* (Mouton and Co., 1955).

Hurgronje, G. Snouck, *Mohammedanism* (Lectures on its origin, its religious and political growth and its present state), (London, 1916).

Iqbal, Dr Muhammad, *The Reconstruction of Religious Thought in Islam* (Lahore, 1944).

Iqbal, Dr Muhammad, *The Development of Metaphysics in Persia*.

Ishaq, Muhammad, *India's Contribution to the Study of Hadith Literature* (Dacca University Bulletin No. XXII, Dacca, 1955).

Ivanow, W., *Brief Survey of the Evolution of Ismailism* (Bombay, 1952).

Lammens, H., *Islam, Beliefs and Institutions* (London, 1929).

Lewis, Bernard, *The Origin of Ismailism* (Cambridge, 1940).

MacDonald, D.B., *Development of Muslim Theology, Jurisprudence and Constitutional Theory* (London, 1903).

Mingana, A., *An Important Manuscript of the Tradition of al-Bukhari* (Oxford, 1936).

Nizami, K.A., *The Life and Times of Shaikh Farid-u'd-din Ganj-i-Shakar*, (Aligarh, 1955).

Oman, J.C., *The Mystics, Ascetics and Saints of India* (London, 1905).

Schacht, J., *The Origins of Muhammadan Jurisprudence*, (Oxford, 1950).

Shibli, Maulana, *Sirat-u'n-Nabi* (Urdu) Vol. I, Part 2 (Azamgarh, 1369 AH).

Shibli, Maulana, *'Ilm-u'l-Kalam* (Azamgarh, 1939).

Smith, A.L., *Church and State in the Middle Ages* (Oxford, 1913).

Tritton, *Muslim Theology*.

Watt, W.M., *Muhammad at Madina* (Oxford, 1956).

Watt, W.M., *Free Will and Predestination in Early Islam* (London, 1948).

(vii) *Modern Works on Politics, Law and Administration*

Aghnides, Nicholas P., *Mohammadon Theories of Finance* (New York, 1916).

Amos, Sheldon, *The History and Principles of the Civil Law of Rome.*

Arnold, T.W., *The Caliphate* (Oxford, 1914).

Azad, Abul Kalam, *Mas'ala-i-Khilafat-aur-Jazirah-i-'Arab* (Al-Balagh Press, Calcutta, 1920).

Bandyopadhyaya, Narayan Chandra, *Development of Hindu Polity and Political Theories* (Calcutta, 1938).

Chakravarty, P.C., *Art of War in Ancient India.*

Ghoshal, U.N., *Contributions to the History System* (Calcutta, 1929).

Ghoshal, U.N., *The Agrarian System in Ancient India* (Calcutta, 1930).

Hasan, Amir, *Caliphate and Kingship in Medieval Persia.*

Jayaswal, K.P., *Hindu Polity* (Calcutta, 1924).

Jayaswal, K.P., *Manu and Yajnavalkya: A Comparison and a Contrast* (Calcutta, 1930).

Jolly, *Hindu Law and Custom.*

Kremer, Von, *Politics in Islam.* Translated and enlarged by S. Khuda Baksh (2nd edition, Lahore, 1948).

Lane-Poole, Stanley, *Medieval India under Mohammedan Rule* (London, 1926).

Leage, R.W., *Roman Private Law.*

Lokkegard, Frede, *Islamic Taxation in the Classic Period* (Copenhagen, 1950).

Majumdar, B.K., *The Military System of Ancient India* (Calcutta, 1955).

Mookerji, R.K., *Local Government in Ancient India* (Oxford, 1920).

Moreland, W.H., *The Agrarian System of Moslem India* (Cambridge, 1929).

Prasad, Beni, *The State in Ancient India* (Allahabad, 1928).

Prasad, Beni, *The Theory of Government in Ancient India* (Calcutta, 1925).

Qureshi, I.H., *Administration of the Sultanate of Delhi* (Lahore, 1942).

Qutb, Sayed, *Al-'Adalah al-Ijtima'iyah fi al-Islam.* Translated into English by John B. Hardie: *Social Justice in Islam* (Washington, 1953).

Tripathi, R.P., *Some Aspects of Muslim Administration* (Allahabad, 1936).

(viii) *Modern Works on Social, Economic and Cultural Subjects*

'Abdul Hai, Maulana Syed, *al-Saqafat al-Islamiya fil-Hind* (Damascus, 1958).

Ahmad, M.G., Zubaid, *The Contribution of India to Arabic Literature* (Allahabad, 1946).

'Ajab Namah, A volume of Oriental Studies presented to E.G. Browne, edited by T.W. Arnold and R.A. Nicholson (Cambridge, 1922).

Baksh, S. Khuda, *Essays: Indian and Islamic* (London, 1912).

Bismil, Razi-u'd-din, *Tazkirat-u'l-Wasilin* (Lucknow, 1318 AH).

Browne, E.G., *A Literary History of Persia*, 4 Volumes (Cambridge, 1928).

Christensen, A., *L'Iran sous Les Sasanides*. Urdu translation by Dr Muhammad Iqbal: *Iran-dar-ahd-i-Sassanian* (Delhi, 1941).

Habib, Muhammad, *Life and Works of Hazrat Amir Khusrau of Delhi* (Aligarh, 1927).

Dutt, R.C., *Later Hindu Civilization* (Calcutta, 1909).

Grunebaum, G.E. von, *Muhammadan Festivals* (New York).

Law, N.N., *Promotion of Learning in India during Muhammadan Rule by Muhammadans* (London, 1916).

Le Bon, Gustave, *La Civilization des Arabes*. Urdu translation by Sayyid 'Ali Bilgrami *Tamaddun-i-'Arab* (Agra, 1898).

Levy, R., *The Social Structure of Islam* (Cambridge, 1957).

Mahrahravi, Sa'id Ahmad, *Hayat-i-Khusrau* (Lahore, 1909).

Mez, Adam, *The Renaissance of Islam* (London, 1937).

Mirza, Muhammad Wahid, *Life and Works of Amir Khusrau* (Calcutta, 1935).

Mubarakpuri, al-Qazi Abul Ma'ali Athar, *Rijal al-Sind wa'l Hind illa al-Qarn al-Saba* (Arabic) (Bombay, 1958).

Nainar, Muahad Husain, *Arab Geographers' Knowledge of South India*.

Rostovtzeff, M., *The Social and Economic History of the Roman Empire*.

Schweitzer, Albert, *The Decay and Restoration of Civilization* (London, 1950).

Shibli, Maulana, *Maqalat-i-Shibli* (Azamgarh).

Sulaiman Nadvi, Maulana *'Arab-o-Hind kay Ta'lluqat* (Hindustani Academy, Allahabad).

Tara Chand, *Influence of Islam on Indian Culture* (Allahabad, 1946).

Yusuf Husain, *Glimpses of Medieval India Culture* (2nd edition, Bombay, 1959).

(ix) *Histories by Modern Writers*

Ameer Ali, Syed, *A Short History of the Saracens* (London, 1927).

'Aziz Ahmad, *Political History and Institutions of the Early Turkish Empire of Delhi* (Lahore, 1949).

Barthold, W., *Iran*. Translated into English by G.K. Nariman (Bombay).

Barthold, W., *Four studies on the History of Central Asia*. Translated into English by V. and T. Minorsky, Vol. I (Leyden, 1956).

Barthold, W., *Turkistan down to the Mongol Invasion*. Translated into English by H.A.R. Gibb (London, 1928).

Bismil, Razi-u'd-din, *Kanz-u't-Tawarikh* (History of Bada'un), (Nizami Press, Bada'un, 1907).

Bury, J.B., *History of the Later Roman Empire*, Vol. II (London, 1923).

(The) *Cambridge Medieval History*, Vol. II.

(The) *Cambridge History of India*, Vol. III.

Elliot and Dowson, *History of India as told by its own Historians*, Vol. II (Revised edition by Professor Habib, S.A. Rashid and K.A. Nizami, Aligarh, 1952).

Habibullah, A.B.M., *The Foundation of Muslim Rule in India* (Lahore, 1945).

(The) *History and Culture of the Indian People*, Vol. V: *The Struggle for Empire* (Bharatiya Vidya Bhawan).

Hitti, P.K., *History of the Arabs* (London, 1951).

Hodivala, S.H., *Studies in Indo-Muslim History* (Bombay, 1939).

Khan, Ghulam Mustafa, *A History of Bahram Shah of Ghaznin* (Lahore, 1955).

Malcolm, *History of Persia*.

Nicholson, R., *Literary History of the Arabs*.

Nazim, Muhammad, *The Life and Times of Sultan Mahmud of Ghazna* (Cambridge, 1931).

Nizami, K.A., *Studies in Medieval Indian History* (Aligarh, 1956).

Ray, H.C., *The Dynastic History of Northern India* (Calcutta, 1931).

Sarkar, J.N., *India Through the Ages* (Calcutta, 1950).

Sherwani, Habibur Rahman Khan, *'Ulama-i-Salaf* (Urdu). (Aligarh).

Sherwani, Harun Khan, *The Bahmanis of the Deccan* (Hyderabad, 1953).

Shibli, Maulana, *al-Mamun* (Urdu), (Lucknow, 1889 AD).

Shibli, Maulana, *al-Faruq* (Urdu), (Kanpur, 1899).

Shibli, Maulana, *Sirat al-Nu'man* (Agra, 1892 AD).

Smail, R.C., *Crusading Warfare, Contribution to Medieval Military History*.

Sykes, Sir Percy, *A History of Persia* (London, 1930).

Tod, James, *Annals and Antiquities of Rajasthan*, edited by W. Crook (London, 1920).

Tripathi, R.S., *History of Kannauj* (Benares, 1937).
Vaidya, C.V., *History of Medieval Hindu India* (Poona, 1926).

(ix) *Works on Geography and Archaeology*

(The) *Archaeology and Monumental Remains of Delhi*, Carr Stephens.
Asar-u's-Sanadid, Sir Syed Ahmad Khan (Lucknow, 1900).
Hudud al-'Alam, edited and translated by V. Minorsky (Gibb Memorial
    Series, Oxford, 1937).
Lands of the Eastern Caliphate, Le Strange (Cambridge, 1930).
Waqi'at-i-Dar-u'l Hakumat Delhi, Maulvi Bashir-u'd-din (Agra, 1919).

(x) *Books of Reference*

(*Journals, Encyclopaedia, Gazetteers, and Numismatical Works*)
Asiatic Researches.
Bulletin of the Deccan College Research Institute.
The Chronicles of the Pathan Kings of Delhi, Edward Thomas (London,
    1871).
The Coinage and Metrology of the Sultans of Delhi, H. Nelson Wright
    (Delhi, 1936).
A *Dictionary of Islam*, T.P. Hughes (London, 1935).
Encyclopaedia of Religion and Ethics. Edited by James Hastings
    (Edinburgh, 1914).
Encyclopaedia of Islam.
Epigraphia Indo-Moslemica.
Indian Antiquary.
Indian Historical Quarterly.
Islamic Culture.
Islamic Literature.
Journal of Indian History.
Journal of the Asiatic Society of Bengal
Journal of the U.P. Historical Society.
Journal of the Pakistan Historical Society.
Journal of World History.
Ma'arif, Azamgarh.
Medieval India Quarterly.
al-Nadwah.
Oriental College Magazine, Lahore.
Journal of Royal Asiatic Society of Great Britain and Ireland.
Persian Literature, C.A. Storey.
Proceedings of the Indian History Congress.
Reports of the Archaeological Survey of India.
Reports of the Indian Historical Records Commission.

INDEX